EDINBURGH LEVENTIS STUDIES 6

EDINBURGH LEVENTIS STUDIES 6

GREEK NOTIONS OF THE PAST IN THE ARCHAIC AND CLASSICAL ERAS

History without Historians

Edited by
John Marincola,
Lloyd Llewellyn-Jones and
Calum Maciver

EDINBURGH
University Press

© editorial matter and selection, John Marincola, Lloyd Llewellyn-Jones and
Calum Maciver, 2012
© in the individual contributions is retained by the authors, 2012

Edinburgh University Press Ltd
22 George Square, Edinburgh EH8 9LF

www.euppublishing.com

Typeset in 11/13pt Times NRMT
by Servis Filmsetting Ltd, Stockport, Cheshire, and
printed and bound in Great Britain by
CPI Group (UK) Ltd, Croydon CR0 4YY

A CIP record for this book is available from the British Library

ISBN 978 0 7486 4396 7 (hardback)
ISBN 978 0 7486 4397 4 (webready PDF)
ISBN 978 0 7486 5466 6 (epub)
ISBN 978 0 7486 5465 9 (Amazon ebook)

CONTENTS

PREFACE

This volume brings together revised versions of papers originally presented at the Sixth A. G. Leventis conference, 'History without Historians: Greeks and their Past in the Archaic and Classical Era', which was held at the University of Edinburgh, 5–7 November 2009. The conference was an attempt to get at the issue of what we would know about Greek conceptions of the past if we lacked the historiographical texts of Herodotus, Thucydides and others.

J.M. would like to thank the Classics Department at the University of Edinburgh for the honour of naming him the A. G. Leventis Chair in Greek Studies in 2009. The hospitality shown by the department and the School of History, Classics and Archaeology during his stay was extraordinary, and he thanks in particular Sandra Bingham, Glenys Davies, Elaine Hutchison, Gavin Kelly, Lloyd Llewellyn-Jones, Wendy and Keith Rutter, and – last but assuredly not least – his nonpareil assistant, Kate Collingridge. At a later stage he benefited (as always) from the sage advice of Christopher Pelling. He also thanks his research assistant, Anastasia Belinskaya, for her help in compiling the Index Locorum.

We are grateful to the Department for its care in putting on the conference and in making it such a wonderful occasion. We also offer thanks to Fiona Sewell, our excellent copy-editor, and especially to Carol Macdonald, our editor, who encouraged and supported the project from the beginning and patiently awaited the final version.

Tallahassee, Edinburgh, Leeds

J.M.
L.L-J.
C.M.

ILLUSTRATIONS

NOTES ON CONTRIBUTORS

Deborah Boedeker is Professor Emerita of Classics at Brown University. From 1992 to 2000 she directed Harvard's Center for Hellenic Studies in Washington, DC, jointly with Kurt Raaflaub. Her publications focus on early Greek poetry, tragedy, historiography and religion; she is especially interested in how these areas interact with each other in the development of a shared past.

Ewen Bowie was Praelector in Classics at Corpus Christi College, Oxford, from 1965 to 2007, and successively University Lecturer, Reader and Professor of Classical Languages and Literature in the University of Oxford. He is now an Emeritus Fellow of Corpus Christi College. He has published articles on early Greek elegiac, iambic and lyric poetry; on Aristophanes; on Hellenistic poetry; and on many aspects of Greek literature and culture from the first century BCE to the third century CE, including Plutarch and the Greek novels. He has recently edited (jointly with Jaś Elsner) a collection of papers on Philostratus (2009) and (jointly with Lucia Athanassaki) a collection of papers entitled *Archaic and Classical Choral Song* (2011) and is currently completing a commentary on Longus, *Daphnis and Chloe*, for Cambridge University Press.

Bruno Currie is Monro Fellow and Tutor in Classics at Oriel College, Oxford, and Lecturer at Oxford University. He is the author of *Pindar and the Cult of Heroes* (2005), and of various articles on Greek epic and lyric poetry.

Lin Foxhall is Professor of Greek Archaeology and History at the University of Leicester, and has held posts at St Hilda's College, Oxford, and University College London. She has worked in Methana, the southern Argolid, Sparta and Metaponto. She currently co-directs a field project in Bova Marina, southern Calabria, Italy. She has written extensively on agriculture, land use and gender in classical antiquity and has published *Olive Cultivation in Ancient Greece: Seeking the Ancient Economy* (2007) and *Studying Gender in Classical Antiquity* (2012).

Simon Goldhill is Professor of Greek at the University of Cambridge. He is also a fellow of King's College, Cambridge, Director of the Cambridge Centre for Research in Arts, Social Sciences and the Humanities, and a fellow of the American Academy of Arts and Sciences. He has published broadly on Greek literature, especially on Greek tragedy, and on Victorian culture. His most recent books are *Victorian Culture and Classical Antiquity: Art, Opera, Fiction and the Proclamation of Modernity* (2011) and *Sophocles and the Language of Tragedy* (2012).

Jonas Grethlein is Professor of Classics at Heidelberg University. His recent publications include *The Greeks and their Past: Poetry, Oratory and History in the Fifth Century BCE* (2010) and, co-edited with C. Krebs, *Time and Narrative in Ancient Historiography: The 'Plupast' from Herodotus to Appian* (2012).

Jeffrey Henderson is the William Goodwin Aurelio Professor of Greek Language and Literature, and former Dean of the College and Graduate School of Arts and Sciences, at Boston University. Since 1998 he has been the general editor of the Loeb Classical Library. His many publications include *The Maculate Muse: Obscene Language in Attic Comedy* (2nd edn, 1991), an edition of Aristophanes' *Lysistrata* (1987), and the five-volume Loeb edition of Aristophanes (1998–2007). He was elected to the American Academy of Arts and Sciences in 2011.

Jon Hesk is Senior Lecturer in Greek at the University of St Andrews. He is author of *Deception and Democracy in Classical Athens* (2000) and *Sophocles: Ajax* (2003). He has also published a number of essays and articles on Homer, Greek drama and Attic oratory.

Emily Kearns is a Senior Research Fellow at St Hilda's College, Oxford. She has written on various aspects of Greek religion and literature, and her most recent publication is *Ancient Greek Religion: A Sourcebook* (2010).

S. D. Lambert is an Attic epigraphist and historian. He is editor of *IG* II^3 1, fascicule 2 (2012), author of *Inscribed Athenian Laws and*

Decrees 352/1–322/1 BC: Epigraphical Papers (2012) and editor of *Sociable Man: Essays on Ancient Greek Social Behaviour in Honour of Nick Fisher* (2011). He has also published a series of books and articles on Attic associations and more recently on Athenian priesthoods, all of which deploy inscriptions extensively. He is Reader in Ancient History, Cardiff University.

Lloyd Llewellyn-Jones is Senior Lecturer in Ancient History in the School of History, Classics and Archaeology at the University of Edinburgh. He specialises in Achaemenid Persia and Greek socio-cultural history, and in the reception of antiquity in popular culture. He is the author of *Aphrodite's Tortoise: The Veiled Woman of Ancient Greece* (2003), *Ctesias' History of Persia: Tales of the Orient* (2010), *King and Court in Ancient Persia* (2012) and the forthcoming *Designs on the Past: How Hollywood Created the Ancient World*. His latest project focuses on dress and the body in Achaemenid culture. He is also the general editor of *Edinburgh Studies in Ancient Persia* for Edinburgh University Press.

Calum Maciver (PhD Edinburgh 2009) is a lecturer in Greek at the University of Leeds. He is the author of *Quintus Smyrnaeus' Posthomerica: Engaging Homer in Late Antiquity* (2012).

John Marincola is Leon Golden Professor of Classics at Florida State University in Tallahassee. His main interests are in Greek and Roman historiography and rhetoric. His books include *Authority and Tradition in Ancient Historiography* (1997), *Greek Historians* (2001) and, in collaboration with M. A. Flower, an edition of Book IX of Herodotus' *Histories* (2003). He is currently at work on a book on Hellenistic historiography.

Kathryn A. Morgan is Professor of Classics at the University of California, Los Angeles. She is the author of *Myth and Philosophy from the Presocratics to Plato* (2000) and editor of *Popular Tyranny: Sovereignty and its Discontents in Classical Athens* (2003), and has written numerous articles on Platonic narrative and cultural ideology. She is currently completing a book on the construction of monarchy in Pindar's odes for Hieron of Syracuse.

Maria Pavlou is an Adjunct Lecturer at the Open University of Cyprus. Her research lies mainly in archaic lyric poetry, narratology and the representation of time and space in literature. She has published on Apollonius Rhodius, Thucydides and especially

Pindar. She is currently revising her PhD thesis, 'Time in Pindar', for publication.

Christopher Pelling is Regius Professor of Greek at Oxford University. His books include commentaries on Plutarch's *Antony* (1988) and *Caesar* (2011), *Plutarch and History* (2002) and *Literary Texts and the Greek Historian* (2000); he has also edited volumes on *Characterization and Individuality in Greek Literature* (1990) and *Greek Tragedy and the Historian* (1997), and co-edited collections on *Ethics and Rhetoric* (with D. C. Innes and H. M. Hine, 1995) and *Ancient Historiography and its Contexts* (with C. S. Kraus and J. Marincola, 2010). He is now working on a book on *How the Greek Historians Explained History,* to be published by the University of Texas Press.

Allen Romano is Assistant Professor of Classics at Florida State University. His main research interests lie in Greek poetry and drama, especially tragedy and Hellenistic poetry, in myth and in digital humanities. He has recently completed a monograph-length study of aetiological myths and Attic tragedy.

Suzanne Saïd is Emerita Professor at Columbia University. She has published extensively on Greek literature (especially Homer, tragedy, historiography and the novel) and mythology. Her latest book is *Homer and the Odyssey* (2011).

Ruth Scodel, educated at Berkeley and Harvard, is D. R. Shackleton Bailey Collegiate Professor of Greek and Latin at the University of Michigan. Her books include *Credible Impossibilities: Conventions and Strategies of Verisimilitude in Homer and Greek Tragedy* (1999), *Listening to Homer* (2002), *Epic Facework: Self-Presentation and Social Interaction in Homer* (2008), (with Anja Bettenworth) *Whither Quo Vadis? Sienkiewicz's Novel in Film and Television* and *An Introduction to Greek Tragedy* (2010). She was Leventis Professor at Edinburgh in 2011.

H. A. Shapiro is the W. H. Collins Vickers Professor of Archaeology and Professor of Classics, Johns Hopkins University (Baltimore). He is the author of *Art and Cult under the Tyrants in Athens* (1989) and *Myth into Art: Poet and Painter in Classical Greece* (1994), and editor of *The Cambridge Companion to Archaic Greece* (2007).

Julia L. Shear is a Senior Associate Member at the American School of Classical Studies at Athens. Formerly a post-doctoral researcher at the Faculty of Classics, University of Cambridge, and King's College, Cambridge, and Lecturer in Classics at the University of Glasgow, she is the author of *Polis and Revolution: Responding to Oligarchy in Classical Athens* (2011), as well as articles on Athenian religion, society and culture. She is currently working on a monograph on the Panathenaia and Athenian identities.

1

INTRODUCTION: A PAST WITHOUT HISTORIANS

John Marincola

I

The year 2009 marked an important anniversary, for it was exactly one hundred years earlier that Felix Jacoby, one of the greatest of twentieth-century classical scholars, published his fundamental article on the development and growth of the various forms of Greek historiography.[1] The article, astonishing in its comprehensiveness and in the clarity of its conception and vision, had a two-fold purpose: first to explain how Jacoby saw the relationship between the various types of Greek historical writing; and, second and more pragmatically, as Jacoby's explanation and justification for the arrangement of the collection of the fragments of the Greek historians that he was just beginning. This enterprise saw the publication of the first volume in 1923, and the final volume some thirty-five years later in 1958. By that time, exile and war had taken its toll on Jacoby, and the collection was left unfinished at his death, with about 60 per cent of the material collected and an even smaller percentage commented upon. Even so, the work measured out at fifteen volumes, some of enormous size and importance, and the collection, now itself a fragment, stands as one of the great monuments of twentieth-century scholarship.

Anyone who has tried to use Jacoby's collection – and very often 'tried' is the key word – knows that the work is organised not on alphabetical, chronological or regional principles. Jacoby had considered

---

1 F. Jacoby, 'Über die Entwicklung der griechischen Historiographie und den Plan einer neuen Sammlung der griechischen Historikerfragmente', *Klio* 9 (1909), pp. 80–123; repr. in Jacoby, *Abhandlungen zur griechischen Geschichtsschreibung*, ed. H. Bloch (Leiden: Brill, 1956), pp. 16–72. For the reception of this article and Jacoby's other work, see A. L. Chávez Reino, 'Felix Jacoby aux prises avec ses critiques: lettres, comptes rendus et scholia Jacobiana', in F. Grebible and V. Krings (eds), *S'écrire et écrire sur l'antiquité* (Grenoble: Editions Jérôme Millon, 2008), pp. 281–300.

these but rejected them, deciding instead that the most useful edition would be one in which the fragmentary authors were arranged according to their place in and within the historical development of Greek historiography ('die entwicklungsgeschichtliche Prinzip') – that is, as Jacoby himself understood that development. As I have elsewhere critiqued this arrangement and its consequences for our understanding of Graeco-Roman historiography,[2] I shall here merely summarise my main points.

Jacoby divided the historical writing of the Greeks into five sub-genres, arranged according to the order in which he believed that they developed: mythography or genealogy; ethnography; chronography; contemporary history (*Zeitgeschichte*); and local history or horography. The third, contemporary history, was the most important, of course, but it could be seen to have predecessors in those who had previously tried to bring order to the complex genealogies of Greek myth and those who had studied the customs of non-Greeks – Hecataeus, for example, who had done both. In this discussion of the development of Greek historiography and even more in his Pauly–Wissowa article of 1913, Jacoby assigned a role of particular importance in the development of Greek historiography to Herodotus, who, Jacoby believed, had begun as a geographer in Hecataeus' footsteps, had progressed thence to become an ethnographer, and, finally, under the influence especially of Athens and Pericles, came to compose an actual war narrative.[3] For Jacoby, therefore, Herodotus' individual 'progress' represented the development of an entire genre and, we might even say, an entire people's historical consciousness.

This model, long influential, has come under fire recently on several fronts. First, the model has an unrealistic tidiness;[4] second, its teleology is also problematic, since it suggests that history was all along trying to become the genre it ultimately became with Thucydides;[5] third, Jacoby's notions of 'genre' suggest that he sees it as fixed and

2 J. Marincola, 'Genre, convention and innovation in Greco-Roman historiography', in C. S. Kraus (ed.), *The Limits of Historiography: Genre and Narrative in Ancient Historical Texts* (Leiden: Brill, 1999), pp. 281–324, esp. pp. 283–301.

3 F. Jacoby, 'Herodotos', *RE Suppl.* II (1913), pp. 205–520.

4 R. Fowler, 'Herodotos and his contemporaries', *JHS* 116 (1996), pp. 62–87, at p. 68.

5 Sally Humphreys has pointed out that Jacoby's lack of sympathy with historians after Thucydides is a product of the nineteenth-century belief in evolutionism, of the assumption of 'progress' from myth to science, and of his own age's imprisonment 'in a contradictory amalgam of romanticism and positivism': see S. Humphreys, 'Fragments, fetishes, and philosophies: towards a history of Greek historiography after Thucydides', in G. Most (ed.), *Collecting Fragments/ Fragmente sammeln* (*Aporemata: Kritische Studien zur Philologiegeschichte* 1; Göttingen: Vandenhoeck & Ruprecht, 1997), pp. 207–24, at pp. 207–8, 211.

prescriptive, whereas innovation and boundary-crossing are consistently present;[6] and finally, it has been pointed out that it is inherently unlikely that the historical consciousness of an entire people can be laid at the door of one individual writer, no matter how gifted, insightful or brilliant he was.[7]

II

Jacoby's schema stands in stark contrast to the one ancient testimonium we have of the origins of Greek historiography, which is contained in Dionysius of Halicarnassus' *On Thucydides*. This work, written in the late first century BCE or just possibly early in the first century CE, is one of the few 'theoretical' works on historiography to survive from antiquity. Modern scholars generally find it a disappointing performance, mainly because Dionysius deals mostly with issues of style and arrangement, and his criticisms of Thucydides do not strike us as particularly forceful or even, at times, germane. However that may be, we find at the beginning of this work a very different suggestion of how Greek historiography developed (*Thuc.* 5):

> Before beginning my account of Thucydides I wish to say a few things both about the writers who preceded him and about his contemporaries, so that the plan of his work, in which he surpassed his predecessors, as well as his overall ability will become apparent. The old writers (ἀρχαῖοι συγγραφεῖς), then, were many and came from many places; among those living before the Peloponnesian War were Eugaion of Samos, Deiochos of Proconnesus, Eudemos of Paros, Demokles of Phygela, Hecataeus of Miletus, the Argive Acusilaus, the Lampsacene Charon, the Chalcedonian < . . . and the Athenian> Amelesagoras; born a little before the Peloponnesian War and living down to the time of Thucydides were Hellanicus of Lesbos, Damastes of Sigeion, Xenomedes of Keos, Xanthus the Lydian and many others.
>
> These writers had a similar plan in respect of subject matter, and did not differ greatly from one another in ability. Some wrote about Greece, others about barbarians, not joining their inquiries together into a continuous whole, but separating them

---

6 Marincola, 'Genre, convention, and innovation', pp. 281–324.
7 Good remarks on this in N. Luraghi, 'Introduction', in Luraghi (ed.), *The Historian's Craft in the Age of Herodotus* (Oxford: Oxford University Press, 2001), pp. 1–15.

by nations and cities and bringing them out individually, with one and the same object in view, that of bringing to the attention of the public traditions preserved among the local people by nations and by cities <or> written records preserved in sacred or profane archives (ὅσαι διεσῴζοντο παρὰ τοῖς ἐπιχωρίοις μνῆμαι κατὰ ἔθνη τε καὶ κατὰ πόλεις ἢ εἴτ' ἐν ἱεροῖς εἴτ' ἐν βεβήλοις ἀποκείμεναι γραφαί), just as they received them, without adding or subtracting anything. Among these sources were to be found occasional myths, believed from time immemorial, and dramatic tales of upset fortunes, which seem quite foolish to people of our day. The style which they all employed was for the most part the same (at any rate among those who used the same dialect): clear, ordinary, unaffected, concise, suited to the subject and displaying none of the apparatus of professional skill; nonetheless a certain grace and charm attends their works, some more than others, and this has ensured their preservation. But Herodotus of Halicarnassus, who was born a little before the Persian Wars and lived down to the time of the Peloponnesian War, both raised the choice of subject to a more ambitious and impressive level . . . and added to his style those virtues which had been omitted by writers before him.

It is clear from this passage that Dionysius saw a great deal of historical activity before Herodotus, and there is also the suggestion that these works served in some sense as the basis for Herodotus' own work. That view, at least in antiquity, was not unique, since the fourth-century historian Ephorus stated that Xanthus was older than Herodotus and that his work gave Herodotus his ἀφορμαί, either his starting point or his source material.[8] Interestingly enough, what this seems to mean, among other things, is that the ancients saw no contradiction in believing that there were historians before Herodotus and that Herodotus was nonetheless the 'father of history'. Jacoby, by contrast, argued that 'there was no Herodotus before Herodotus', and he rejected Dionysius' picture of the development of Greek historiography, especially its suggestion that there could have been a

8 Ephorus, *FGrHist* 70 F 180: 'Ephorus the historian makes mention of him [Xanthus] as being older than Herodotus and giving Herodotus his starting point (*or* source material).' (Ἔφορος ὁ συγγραφεὺς μνημονεύει αὐτοῦ ὡς παλαιοτέρου ὄντος καὶ Ἡροδότωι τὰς ἀφορμὰς δεδωκότος.) On the meaning of ἀφορμαί see G. Parmeggiani, 'I frammenti di Eforo nei *Deipnosophistai* di Ateneo', in D. Lenfant (ed.), *Athénée et les fragments d'historiens* (Paris: De Boccard, 2007), pp. 117–37, at pp. 127–8; Parmeggiani, *Eforo di Cuma: Studi di storiografia greca* (Bologna: Pàtron, 2011), pp. 648–9.

local historiography before Herodotus. Jacoby's argument that local history was the last of all the genres of history to develop is based both on the dates he assigned to the figures named by Dionysius in this passage (whom he dated, not always with good evidence, much later than did Dionysius) and on the absence in Herodotus' work both of magistrate dates (which Jacoby saw as characteristic of local history) and more generally of explicit references to local sources by Herodotus: if these had existed, the argument goes, Herodotus would surely have used them.

I have argued elsewhere that I see Herodotus adopting a stance towards his material that is very similar to that taken by Homer. Andrew Ford has pointed out that although Homer's heroes are presented as having existed a long time before the poet and his audience, Homer nonetheless portrays himself as an 'immediate' narrator of events, recognising no intermediaries in the handing on of the tradition.[9] Herodotus, it is true, recognises previous treatments of some of the material he narrates, especially where he engages in polemic with predecessors. On the other hand, it must be admitted that despite this feature, Herodotus in most of his narrative has, like Homer, 'erased' any predecessors and for the most part presents himself as wrestling *directly* with the sources themselves – that is to say, for most of his work he portrays himself implicitly as the first to write up these events.[10] Now it may well be that for much of his work Herodotus *was* the first and had no predecessors; but it is important to realise that this impression of priority might be the effect that Herodotus, imitating Homer, desired to create in the minds of his audience: a directly mediated account in the sense that the narrator, as he attempts to construct the history of the past, is engaged not with other chroniclers but with the *logoi* themselves.[11]

To return to Dionysius: another argument raised against the reliability of this schema is that it is clearly based on style and perhaps goes back to Theophrastus, who in a lost work *On Style* (Περὶ Λέξεως)

---

9 A. Ford, *Homer: The Poetry of the Past* (Ithaca, NY, and London: Cornell University Press, 1992), esp. pp. 90–130.

10 In Book II, for example, Herodotus mentions the island of Chemmis and states that it is said 'by the Egyptians' to float and move about, a claim that Herodotus then strongly ridicules (2.156). We happen to know from a later source that it was Hecataeus who stated that the island moved (*FGrHist* 1 F 305), yet Herodotus does not mention Hecataeus here, and instead ascribes the belief to the Egyptians. As it is not likely that he did not know Hecataeus' work, it must be the case that Herodotus has deliberately suppressed mention of his predecessor.

11 J. Marincola, 'Herodotus and the poetry of the past', in Marincola and C. J. Dewald (eds), *The Cambridge Companion to Herodotus* (Cambridge: Cambridge University Press, 2006), pp. 13–28.

dealt with the development of Greek historiography. The thinking goes that because these historians wrote in a simple, clear style it was assumed by later critics that they must have been early. Yet not all of Dionysius' arguments in this passage are in fact based on style. Moreover, where we can check the accuracy of his dating by comparing it with other sources, Dionysius comes out pretty well. Both Robert Fowler and David Toye have pointed out that Dionysius' placing of these historians agrees with what other ancient sources say, and Fowler adds that although Dionysius may have stretched a date here or there to accommodate an author's place in the history of style, such a move does not invalidate the entire passage.[12]

Some scholars have sought to reclaim some of Dionysius' observations as valuable and as perhaps reflecting the actual state of affairs in early Greek historical writing. The most thorough treatment known to me is an article, now some forty years old, by Sandra Gozzoli.[13] She begins by examining the passage of Dionysius and demonstrating that the early authors mentioned by Dionysius were known to him not from some pre-existing list or treatment – Theophrastus again! – but rather from his own reading and independent evaluation. She then tries to see whether there might be anything in Dionysius' remark that these early authors brought to the attention of the public 'written records preserved in sacred or profane archives'. There was no difficulty, of course, in establishing that such records and archives existed in the ancient Near East, as we have evidence for such amongst the Sumerians, Babylonians, Hittites and Egyptians. But the task becomes rather more difficult closer to home. Gozzoli displays a great deal of care and caution, but she does at least suggest, from literary and epigraphical evidence, that the notion of early records (perhaps quite bare and having only the most minor 'historical' notation) kept in archives and temples may have been known to the Greeks from early times, and that such record-keeping may owe something to the knowledge of ancient Near Eastern cultures. If we were to imagine that the Greeks did something of this sort, then we would be placing the historical impulse very far before the time of Herodotus himself – whose achievement might then have to be seen precisely in that role of 'collector' or 'synthesiser' that Dionysius gave him.

The main issue, it seems to me, is what exactly Dionysius might mean by μνῆμαι and γραφαί. As to the first, there seems little difficulty

12 Fowler, 'Herodotos and his critics'; D. L. Toye, 'Dionysius of Halicarnassus on the first Greek historians', *AJP* 116 (1995), pp. 279–302.
13 S. Gozzoli, 'Una teoria antica sull'origine della storiografia greca', *SCO* 19–20 (1970–1), pp. 158–211.

in assuming that Dionysius meant oral tradition, stories or accounts that were handed down and known by individuals, families or communities. But what did he mean by the second? We do not have very much evidence for early times that the Greeks maintained the kinds of archives that the kingdoms of the ancient Near East did. Toye suggests that they might be 'epics and oracles ascribed to mythical bards', but he seems hesitant to think that these were written down. Yet it is difficult to imagine that Dionysius could use the term γραφαί without thinking of written material. I wonder whether the γραφαί referred to here might be in fact collections of oracles or the like: Herodotus mentions that the Spartan king Cleomenes brought to Sparta oracles that had been left in the temple on the Athenian Acropolis by the Peisistratids when they fled Attica (5.90). These same Peisistratids figure later at the court of Persia, bringing with them the Athenian diviner (*chresmologos*) Onomacritus, who had been caught by Lasos of Hermione interpolating into the writings of Musaeus an oracle stating that the islands off Lemnos would vanish into the sea (Hdt. 7.6). Both passages suggest written texts, and in the one case they are housed within a temple.[14]

Another way around the issue of the priority of local historiography has been attempted by Leone Porciani,[15] who, like Jacoby, dismisses the testimony of Dionysius as worthless, noting that Dionysius is alone among ancient writers in positing the existence of archives, and that in fact he is contradicted by Josephus in the *Against Apion* (1.6–13), who contrasts the paucity of Greek written records with the abundance of them in other Near Eastern societies. Porciani suggests that a local historiography may nevertheless have existed before Herodotus, although he believes that its form was oral, and that some of its nature can be glimpsed in the *epitaphios*, the funeral oration, where the deeds of the city are rehearsed on occasions of public remembrance. Porciani believes that individual aristocratic funeral orations were replaced in the isonomic city by a single *epitaphios* designed to highlight the past deeds of the entire state. Thus for Porciani there is local *tradition* before Herodotus (and obviously a tradition that Herodotus could exploit), but still no *written* local history.

It is certainly not the case that all modern scholars have followed

---

14 I should also add – though I will not make anything of it here – that such collections, if they existed in the Greek world, would provide a link with certain practices of the ancient Near East, where the Mesopotamians, among others, kept collections of omens. One might think here of the importance that oracles play as a structuring device in Herodotus' history.

15 L. Porciani, *Prime forme della storiografia greca: Prospettiva locale e generale nella narrazione storica* (*Historia Einzelschriften* 152; Stuttgart: Steiner, 2001).

Jacoby's basic outline, and other ideas about the development of Greek historiography have been put forward. French scholars in particular have engaged with the concept of ἱστορίη and what that might entail. They have also been much more open to introducing a whole range of texts from the philosophers, medical writers, tragedians and orators in their search for what is distinctive about ἱστορίη. In some cases, such as in the work of François Chatelet and André Sauge, the main goal is to discover not history in the sense of the genre of history but rather the activity of ἱστορίη, as it might appear in any number of writers and genres, including tragedy, the medical writers and philosophy.[16] Both in their books and in Catherine Darbo-Peschanski's recent and comprehensive treatment of Greek historiographical beginnings, the notion of ἱστορίη as research based on autopsy has been greatly de-emphasised.[17]

I must not fail to mention here one of the most interesting forays into the origins of Greek historical thought, that made by Santo Mazzarino in his *Il pensiero storico classico*.[18] At the outset, Mazzarino sets himself the goal of discovering the origins of Greek historical thought, and he finds it in an unusual place, namely, Orphism. Now this term he understands in an extended sense to mean not just the actual practitioners of Orphic religion, but all those influenced by its world-view. (I should add that Mazzarino throughout his work draws a close correspondence between economic life and intellectual life: so, for example, in the case of Orphism's criticism of established religion, he sees at work a new class of men who made their wealth largely through trade and who then took on the aristocracy both politically and intellectually.) Mazzarino is aware that his choice of Orphism may seem paradoxical since Orphism is often portrayed as hostile to rationalism, but in Orphism, he argues, we see the first manifestation

16 F. Chatelet, *La naissance de l'histoire: La formation de la pensée historienne en Grèce* (Paris: Éditions de Minuit, 1962); A. Saugé, *De l'epopée à l'histoire: Fondement de la notion de l'histoire* (Frankfurt: Peter Lang, 1992).
17 C. Darbo-Peschanski, *L'historia: Commencements grecs* (Paris: Gallimard, 2007).
18 S. Mazzarino, *Il pensiero storico classico*, 3 vols (Bari: Laterza, 1966–8). This astonishing work treats the entire classical historiographical tradition from its origins to the late empire. Its influence, however, at least so far as I can tell, has been rather limited and much dependent on the country involved: perhaps not surprisingly, it is very well known and often cited in Italy; it is rather less well known or cited in French scholarship; and in German and Anglo-American scholarship it seems to be largely ignored. It is indeed an unusual book in many ways, and its reputation was perhaps not helped by rather negative reviews by Edouard Will (*RH* 237 (1967), pp. 433–5, *RH* 246 (1971), p. 87) and, at much greater length, by Arnaldo Momigliano (*RSI* 79 (1967), pp. 206–19, repr. in Momigliano, *Quarto contributo alla storia degli studi classici e del mondo antico* (Rome: Edizioni di storia e letteratura, 1969), pp. 59–76).

of the Greek critical spirit: here for the first time traditional Greek religious beliefs were questioned. So when we look, for example, at Herodotus' criticisms of religion in Book II, we need to realise that this type of intellectual activity had begun centuries before. Even if we look earlier to Hecataeus and the famous opening of his *Genealogies* – 'I write what follows as it seems to me to be true; for the stories of the Greeks are many, and, as is manifest to me, ridiculous'[19] – and we ask, 'When, for the first time, did the criticism of myth begin to be exercised?', Mazzarino's answer to this is at least a century before.

A figure of cardinal importance for Mazzarino is Epimenides of Crete. Epimenides is famous, of course, for his role at Athens in the aftermath of the Cylon affair. Cylon, an Olympic victor, tried c. 632 BCE to seize control of the Acropolis during a festival, and when this failed, he and his followers took refuge at Athena's temple. Although it was promised that they would not be harmed, they were nonetheless cut down by the magistrates, led by Megacles of the Alcmaeonid clan. When pollution ensued, Epimenides was called to Athens and he purified the city. Mazzarino emphasises that the characteristic aspect of Epimenides' purification was that in his effort to rid the city of its ills, he made an inquiry into the past, and examined Athens' faults in earlier times, in this case the sacrilege of the Alcmaeonids. Mazzarino identifies this as a specifically historical activity, and concludes that this is what Aristotle meant when in the *Rhetoric* he says that 'Epimenides gave his oracles not about the future, but on things in the past which were obscure.' Mazzarino also connects this, by the way, with activity in the ancient near east, since in the Hittite world, he argues, plagues similarly gave rise to notions of the need for purification, and the demand for purification in turn led to an enquiry into the past in order to discover the cause of the plague. He adds that as Crete was an important place of cultural exchange between the Greeks and the Near East, it is not surprising to find there the figure of Epimenides.

Having begun in this way, Mazzarino then goes on to look everywhere for signs of historical consciousness and historical thought, including the visual arts. In fact, his very first example of historical thought is the early fifth-century vase portraying Croesus on his pyre, and he notes as well the statues of Harmodius and Aristogeiton made at Athens shortly after their assassination attempt in 514. He looks to early poetry, specifically that of Mimnermus and Callinus, and of

---

19 Hecataeus, *FGrHist* 1 F 1a: Ἑκαταῖος Μιλήσιος ὧδε μυθεῖται· τάδε γράφω, ὥς μοι δοκεῖ ἀληθέα εἶναι· οἱ γὰρ Ἑλλήνων λόγοι πολλοί τε καὶ γελοῖοι, ὡς ἐμοὶ φαίνονται, εἰσίν.

course he examines Aeschylus' *Persians* where he sees the tragedian transforming a contemporary event by making of it an image of myth. Only after some hundred and twenty pages do we finally come to Herodotus and his history.

Now even though one must take issue with quite a lot of what Mazzarino says, he nevertheless is to be praised for looking everywhere and at different manifestations of the Greek historical spirit. He also deserves credit for his on-going engagement with influence of the ancient near east on the Greeks' historical thought, an influence that I have mentioned off and on. Such an interest may not sound particularly surprising in light of recent scholarship, but it is noteworthy that when, not long ago, Greek studies were very much concerned with the 'orientalising revolution' and were focusing on 'the east face of Helicon', the one area, so far as I can see, left out of consideration altogether was historiography.[20] Now this may have been simply the result of the interests of those scholars studying the influence of the ancient Near East on Greek culture, who were far more focussed on religion, epic, myth and the like, or it may be that the development of Greek historiography was seen as occurring later, after the strong wave of Near East influence. But I wonder as well whether it might much more be a strongly ingrained cultural prejudice about the nature of western historiography. We need not go so far perhaps as Jack Goody in his recent book arguing that the west has stolen its ideas of history from the east;[21] yet at the same time, one can hardly avoid the notion that classical scholars see a fundamental gap between, on the one hand, history as practised in the societies of Assyria, Persia, and Egypt, which magnified the achievements of kings and closely allied itself with state religion, and, on the other hand, the 'secular', 'democratic' and 'rational' historiography developed by the Greeks and bequeathed to the west. And there is certainly the sense in scholarship that when Greek historiography is 'influenced' by the east, the result is always bad, and produces someone such as Ctesias, with his emphasis on dissolute kings, harem politics and – God help us – women in charge.

Let me come back one last time to Herodotus' 'development' as imagined by Jacoby. I mentioned above that this seems to put too much responsibility on the shoulders of Herodotus, but it also has

---

20 W. Burkert, *Die orientalisierende Epoche in der griechischen Religion und Literatur* (Heidelberg: C. Winter, 1984); Eng. tr. by W. Burkert and M. E. Pinder, *The Orientalizing Revolution: Near Eastern Influence on Greek Culture in the Early Archaic Age* (Cambridge, MA: Harvard University Press, 1992); M. L. West, *The East Face of Helicon* (Oxford: Oxford University Press, 1997).

21 J. Goody, *The Theft of History* (Cambridge: Cambridge University Press, 2006).

the effect of isolating Herodotus from the background and interests of the age in which he lived. An important corrective to this was provided by Nino Luraghi's volume, *The Historian's Craft in the Age of Herodotus*, published in 2001 and reflecting the proceedings of a conference held in 1997.[22] Many of the contributors in this volume were explicitly reacting to the splendid isolation of Jacoby's Herodotus, and they sought throughout to show Herodotus in the context of other inquirers into the past, as part of a larger group interested in collecting, sorting and analysing the past – in the editor's words, the essays focused on aspects which make Herodotus 'a typical product of his time'. It is an excellent volume with many strong contributions throughout, and should put to rest for good the idea that Herodotus is to be envisioned as a lone pilgrim on the road to historical method.

Yet at the same time, I think that there is a need for still more. I wonder whether the search for the origins of Greek historical thought can ever yield anything more than impressions and suggestions. Jacoby's arrangement, whatever its faults, did at least give us both a fixed point for the origin of Greek historical thought (the proem of Hecataeus' *Genealogies*) and a fixed point for the origin of Greek historiography (Herodotus' *Histories*). But with an issue such as historical consciousness and historical thought, any beginning that we can imagine is likely to be a messy and complex affair.

Nor does a focus on historians or those engaged in what we might clearly identify as 'historical activity' necessarily help, since the Greeks did not always maintain the kinds of generic boundaries that one might expect. Here in particular the work of the French scholars mentioned above is of great value in reminding us that history and historical thought were hardly the preserve of historians, and much of what we might consider 'historical' activity was practised by any number of writers with different interests and emphases in a variety of forms.

III

And so I come, at last, to the theme of this volume. It is a truism often repeated that the academic discipline of history over the last generation or so has undergone a revolution – maybe multiple revolutions. On the one hand, there has been the attack (or attacks) on the subject matter of traditional history, particularly what was seen as its narrow concern with political and military events. One of the results of this has been the development of new types of history and of

22 Above, n. 7.

new and non-traditional interests shown by historians. On the other hand, there has been an ongoing debate about the epistemic claims of history, about what history really teaches or can claim to teach, and what kind of knowledge it can actually impart. As a result, the practice of history itself has ceased to be considered a self-evident activity with a clear and obvious methodology, and inquiries into the past are now seen as complexly conditioned by a whole host of factors on the individual, social and even disciplinary level.

Add to this that although historians have hardly abandoned their desire to know what actually happened and why, they have at the same time expanded their interests by looking more carefully at the structures and means with which individuals and societies deal with their pasts. The interest here is less in what actually happened and more in what people believed to have happened and how such beliefs affected their identity and the social environment – in short, how history was meaningful to them in their actual lives. Jan Assmann has coined the term 'hot memory' (*heisse Erinnerung*) for the type of history that creates an identity for a group or community: he equates it with myth and identifies it as 'a story that one tells to orient oneself vis-à-vis oneself and the world, a truth of a higher order that is not merely right but also makes normative demands and possesses formative power'.[23] Hans-Joachim Gehrke has coined the term 'intentional history' for those stories and sagas that were embraced by communities and were of considerable and at times decisive significance for real life and political behaviour – even though the modern historian would hardly characterise these as history.[24]

Gehrke also emphasises the ubiquitous nature of the past: he writes, 'one always had a story, even when one, according to our criteria, did not know one's past at all. To put it differently, one knew one's past very well. It was that which everywhere impinged upon one's eyes and ears in the world of portraits and statues, in the milieu of poems and songs.'[25] Now you will notice that I have made a transition from speaking of history to speaking of the past, and that is not accidental. For it seems to me that an interest in how the Greeks saw their past rather than in how certain figures perceived history strictly speaking will enable us to construct a larger canvas, one that more

---

23 J. Assmann, *Das kulturelle Gedächtnis: Schrift, Erinnerung und politische Identität in frühen Hochkulturen* (Munich: Beck, 1992).

24 H.-J. Gehrke, 'Mythos, Geschichte, Politik – antik und modern', *Saeculum* 45 (1994), pp. 239–64; Eng. tr. by M. Beck in J. Marincola (ed.), *Greek and Roman Historiography* (*Oxford Readings in Classical Studies*; Oxford: Oxford University Press, 2011), pp. 40–71.

25 Gehrke, *Saeculum* 45 (1994), p. 251 = English translation, p. 55.

fairly represents the vast variety of engagement with the past that is everywhere visible in Greek culture.

In making this examination, we shall, naturally, have recourse to texts, though again we will want the greatest variety of media. To state only the most obvious, it is almost certainly the case that the vast majority of Greeks did not get their sense of the past from Herodotus and Thucydides or any of the other historians. They understood it within the life of their city-state, in their rituals and celebrations, in the physical landscape around them, and in the man-made spaces of the polis, including the theatres and the law-courts. If the past was everywhere present for the Greeks, then we ought to be able to find it no matter where we look.

So in a sense this volume might represent a thought experiment: if the histories of the Greeks of the archaic and classical ages had not survived, what would we know or be able to infer about their relationship to the past? I hope that some answers to this question appear in the contributions that follow; imagining, if only for a short time, a world without historians can be an occasion for engagement and excitement.

2

HOMER AND HEROIC HISTORY

Jonas Grethlein

'Homer is to be taken seriously.'[1] Inspired by new excavations in Hisarlık, Joachim Latacz has recently renewed the argument for the value of the *Iliad* as a source for a war that a Greek alliance had waged against Troy around 1200 BCE. While this thesis was granted plenty of attention in the mass media, Latacz did not meet with much approval from his peers, who reacted just as sceptically as more than a hundred years ago Wilamowitz had responded to attempts at identifying details of the *Iliad*'s topography in Hisarlık in the wake of Schliemann's excavations: 'One does not rant about it, but one does not take it seriously either.'[2] In antiquity, on the other hand, the Trojan War and the return of Odysseus were considered historical events. Of course, beginning with Xenophanes, Hecataeus and Pindar, Homer was criticised for exaggerations, but not even Thucydides, hailed as the father of critical historiography, cast doubt on the historicity of the Trojan War. In the *Archaeology*, he even considers the numbers given for the ship crews in the *Catalogue of Ships* to calculate the size of the expedition to Troy (1.10.2–5). Not only were Achilles, Helen and Odysseus deemed historical, but the epic presentation of the past was crucial for historical thinking in ancient Greece. The Homeric heroes figured prominently in art, politics and education.[3] Epic also left a strong imprint on other commemorative genres such as tragedy, epinician

---

1 J. Latacz, *Troia und Homer: Der Weg zur Lösung eines alten Rätsels*, 5th edition (Munich: Koehler und Amelang Verlag, 2005), p. 342 ('Homer ist ernstzunehmen').

2 U. von Wilamowitz-Moellendorff, *Über die Ionische Wanderung* (Berlin: Königliche Akademie der Wissenschaften, 1906), p. 60: 'Darüber ereifert man sich nicht, man nimmt es aber auch nicht ernst.' For critical assessments of Latacz's views, see the contributions in C. Ulf (ed.), *Der neue Streit um Troja: Eine Bilanz* (Munich: C. H. Beck, 2003).

3 On the reception of Homer, see, e.g., R. Lamberton and J. J. Keaney (eds), *Homer's Ancient Readers: The Hermeneutics of Greek Epic's Earliest Exegetes* (Princeton: Princeton University Press, 1992); E. Pallantza, *Der Troische Krieg*

poetry and historiography. Given the reign of teleological models for the 'grip of the past' on the Greeks, it bears pointing out that the establishment of historiography did not eliminate memory in epic.

The *Iliad* and *Odyssey* not only present canonical accounts of what Greeks took for their archaic past. Embedded in the narratives of the Trojan War and Odysseus' *nostos*, we also find a previous past. Both the narrator and the characters frequently refer to what we could call the 'epic plupast', the past that preceded the main action of the song.[4] The 'epic plupast' can be read as a *mise en abyme*, that is to say the embedded past of the heroes figures as a mirror to the heroic past presented in epic poetry.[5] In the first two sections of this chapter, I will use an examination of the 'epic plupast' as a way of approaching the epic presentation of the past. The first will explore the relation between past and present, the second will be concerned with the mediality of memory. Then, in a third section, I will directly discuss the view of history underlying the epic, in particular the issue of theodicy. Finally, I will look beyond Homer to historiography and argue that even where Greek historians define themselves against epic they share common ground with it.

I PAST AND PRESENT

When Aeneas encounters Achilles on the Trojan plain, he boasts about his genealogy, which he traces back over six generations to Dardanus (*Il.* 20.213–41). The temporal reach of this analepsis is exceptional; in most cases the embedded past stretches back only one or two generations. This limited extent of the 'epic plupast' ties in nicely with the anthropological observation that in oral societies memory only includes the most recent generations, which are directly linked to the mythical origin.[6] It is striking, however, that in Homer the very recent past is already separated from the present by a gap. At the beginning of the *Iliad*, Nestor invokes his age in order to lend authority to his voice in the conflict between Achilles and Agamemnon (1.259–64):

---

in der nachhomerischen Literatur bis zum 5. Jh. v. Chr. (Stuttgart: Franz Steiner, 2005).

4 Cf. W. Kullmann, 'Vergangenheit und Zukunft in der *Ilias*', *Poetica* 2.1 (1968), pp. 12–37; J. Grethlein, *Das Geschichtsbild der Ilias: Eine Untersuchung aus phänomenologischer und narratologischer Perspektive* (Göttingen: Vandenhoeck & Ruprecht, 2006), pp. 42–153.

5 The term *'mise en abyme'* was coined in 1893 by A. Gide, *Journal 1889–1939* (Paris: Gallimard, 1948) and the concept was developed further by L. Dällenbach, *Le récit spéculaire: Contribution à l'étude de la mise en abyme* (Paris: Seuil, 1977).

6 E.g. J. Vansina, *Oral Tradition as History* (London: James Currey, 1985).

ἀλλὰ πίθεσθ'· ἄμφω δὲ νεωτέρω ἐστὸν ἐμεῖο.
ἤδη γάρ ποτ' ἐγὼ καὶ ἀρείοσιν ἠέ περ ὑμῖν
ἀνδράσιν ὡμίλησα, καὶ οὔ ποτέ μ' οἵ γ' ἀθέριζον.
οὐ γάρ πω τοίους ἴδον ἀνέρας, οὐδὲ ἴδωμαι,
οἷον Πειρίθοόν τε Δρύαντά τε ποιμένα λαῶν
Καινέα τ' Ἐξάδιόν τε καὶ ἀντίθεον Πολύφημον.

Yet be persuaded. Both of you are younger than I am.
Yes, and in my time I have dealt with better men than
you are, and never once did they disregard me. Never
yet have I seen nor shall see again such men as these were,
men like Peirithoös, and Dryas, shepherd of the people,
Kaineus and Exadios, godlike Polyphemos.

and (1.271–2):

καὶ μαχόμην κατ' ἔμ' αὐτὸν ἐγώ· κείνοισι δ' ἂν οὔ τις
τῶν οἳ νῦν βροτοί εἰσιν ἐπιχθόνιοι μαχέοιτο.

And I fought single-handed, yet against such men no one
of the mortals now alive upon earth could do battle.

The heroes mentioned form part of the generation previous to the
Greeks fighting at Troy, but they seem to belong to a different world.
This tendency to distance the recent past also comes to the fore in
Phoenix's speech in the embassy scene. Introducing the exemplum of
Meleager, Phoenix remarks (9.527–8):

μέμνημαι τόδε ἔργον ἐγὼ πάλαι, οὔ τι νέον γε,
ὡς ἦν, ἐν δ' ὑμῖν ἐρέω πάντεσσι φίλοισιν.

For I remember this action of old, it is not a new thing,
and how it went; you are all my friends, I will tell it among you.

Phoenix presents his story as belonging to an age long gone, but
according to the epic genealogy Meleager is only one generation older
than the heroes of the Trojan War.

The distancing of the 'epic plupast' mirrors the distance of the epic
past which is not linked to the present of the performance. There are
only vague references to 'later men' or to a deluge which will erase all
traces of the walls built by the Greeks (*Il.* 12.3–33), but otherwise the
epic past unfolds as a time *sui generis*. The Homeric heroes are larger
than life just as the heroes of the 'epic plupast' tower over Ajax and his

peers. The spear of Peleus is so heavy that only Achilles can wield it (*Il.* 16.140–4; 19.387–91) and Nestor's cup can only be lifted by Nestor himself, relic of a previous generation of heroes (*Il.* 11.632–7). In the same vein, Diomedes, Ajax, Hector and Aeneas throw stones that 'men as they are today' could not even move (*Il.* 5.302–4; 12.381–3; 12.445–9; 20.285–7).

The gap between epic past and present of performance ought not to be mistaken for the difference which we feel separates our time from the past. Since around 1800 CE western historical thinking has centred on an awareness of the autonomy of epochs which is nicely captured in the opening words of *The Go-Between*: 'The past is a foreign country.'[7] The ideas of progress and development created an awareness of the differences between ages. The epics, on the other hand, do not envisage a development which leads from the heroic age to the present. As the references to 'men as they are today' reveal, the difference between epic past and the present is rather quantitative than qualitative.

Some features which are often taken as bearing an awareness of specific features of Mycenaean culture can be explained more satisfyingly along other lines.[8] Scholars have, for example, seen in the bronze weapons used by Homeric heroes an awareness that iron came into wider use only after the breakdown of the Mycenaean culture. However, if the bronze weapons in the epic are owed to such a historical consciousness, the Homeric references to iron, notably for agricultural tools, are hard to explain.[9] Particularly challenging is the club of Areithous, which dates from a time even before Nestor's, but is nonetheless made of iron (*Il.* 7.141).[10] Thus, the use of bronze weapons does not attest a consistent awareness of specific differences between epochs, but seems rather owed to the shininess of bronze which is apt to express the glamour of heroic combat.

Despite the distancing, the 'epic plupast' is strongly linked to the epic past. Demodocus and Phemius sing of the past in order to delight the heroes, but the passages quoted so far suggest that often present interests prompt the heroes to turn to their past. The 'epic plupast' is in the firm grip of the epic past. There are three major modes in which

---

7 See, e.g., D. Lowenthal, *The Past is a Foreign Country* (Cambridge: Cambridge University Press, 1985).

8 See also J. Grethlein, 'From imperishable glory to history: The *Iliad* and the Trojan War', in D. Konstan and K. Raaflaub (eds), *Epic and History* (Malden, MA, and Oxford: Wiley-Blackwell, 2010), pp. 128–9.

9 Iron is mentioned as precious material in 6.48 = 10.379 = 11.133; 7.473; 23.261, 850. For iron tools, see 4.485; 18.34; 23.30, 834. On the use of metals in the *Iliad*, see D. H. E. Gray, 'Metal-working in Homer', *JHS* 74 (1954), pp. 1–15.

10 See also the arrows in 4.123 which are made of iron.

the heroes link their past to the present. First, there can be a causal link. Odysseus, for example, tells his hosts of his travels in order to explain how he has come to them. While causal links between past and present seem to be limited to the heroes' own experiences, two other modes are used to reach back further while still tying the past to the present.[11] In tradition, the past is linked to the present by the idea of continuity. This is most obvious in genealogies like the one already mentioned: Aeneas unfolds the history of his family after Achilles has slighted him. He invokes the glory of his ancestors, their wealth and close contact with the gods, in order to buttress his own position and to demonstrate that he and his opponent are on a par.[12] Tradition can also be adduced as a standard to which heroes have to live up – noblesse oblige. For example, Athena as well as Agamemnon reminds Diomedes of the model of his father (Il. 4.372–5; 5.801–11). Hector invokes his and his father's fame when he rejects Andromache's request to stay at home (Il. 6.444–6). In the same scene, he projects this family tradition into the future and prays that his son will be a mighty ruler of Troy (Il. 6.476–81).

The third and arguably most prominent mode which links the 'epic plupast' to the epic past is the exemplum.[13] While tradition establishes a continuum that reaches from the past to the present, exempla directly juxtapose a past event with the present. The heroes frequently evoke parallels from the past, as does Phoenix when he tries to persuade Achilles to join the ranks of the Greeks again by telling the story of Meleager (Il. 9.524–99): Meleager too had been caught by anger and had withdrawn from the defence of his polis. He rejected the gifts he was offered, returned to battle only at the last minute and thereby gambled away his gifts. While Phoenix argues ex negativo – Achilles ought to abandon his anger while he is still offered gifts – exempla in Homer tend to be positive because of the superiority of previous generations. The gap allows conclusions to be drawn a maiore ad minus. The prominence of exempla also underscores my argument that in Homer the past is not perceived to be qualitatively different from the present. Whereas our focus on historical developments and specific features of epochs undermines the historia magistra vitae topos,[14]

11 Cf. Grethlein, Geschichtsbild, pp. 42–84.
12 For a detailed interpretation of Aeneas' genealogy, see Grethlein, Geschichtsbild, pp. 65–70. See also P. M. Smith, 'Aineiadai as patrons of Iliad XX and the Homeric Hymn to Aphrodite', HSPh 85 (1981), pp. 17–58.
13 On exempla in the Iliad, see M. Alden, Homer Beside Himself: Para-Narratives in the Iliad (Oxford: Oxford University Press, 2000); Grethlein, Geschichtsbild, pp. 43–63.
14 Cf. R. Koselleck, Futures Past: On the Semantics of Historical Time, tr. K. Tribe (Cambridge, MA: MIT Press, 1985), pp. 21–38.

in Homer the quantitative difference provides exempla with special authority.

The three modes in which the Homeric heroes link their past to the present also apply to the Greeks' reception of the epic past. I have already mentioned that the heroic world is presented as a time *sui generis*, but the Greeks linked it to their present by causality, through tradition and in exempla. Herodotus, for instance, mentions the abduction of Helen as an element in the chain of rapes which, according to Persian wise men, led to the Persian Wars (1.4). Aristocrats were prone to trace back their ancestry to Homeric heroes, as did Miltiades, who held Philaus, the son of Ajax, to be the founder of his family,[15] and Andocides, who claimed to be descended from Odysseus and Hermes.[16] Not only individuals but also communities invoked their epic heritage to strengthen their positions in the here and now. Aristotle and Plutarch, for instance, report that the Athenians drew on the *Iliad* to back up their claims to Salamis.[17]

Finally, the Homeric epics provided the Greeks with a treasure chest of exempla. The exemplary use of the epic past could serve not only legitimising functions, as when Alexander stylises himself as Achilles *redivivus*,[18] but also a better understanding of the present. The frequent comparisons of the Persian Wars with the capture of Troy are owed to the need for a template for recent experiences as well as to the desire for glorification.[19] However, the significance of the heroic past could be challenged in political controversies. In Thucydides, the Athenians start their speech at a meeting in Sparta with a reflection on how to present their claims most effectively (1.73.2): 'Now as for the remote past (τὰ . . . πάνυ παλαιά), what need is there to speak of events for which the audience would have the evidence of hearsay accounts rather than their personal experience?' While the reason for the rejection of myths is reminiscent of Thucydides' own

15 Hellanicus *FGrHist* 323a F 24.
16 Pherecydes *FGrHist* 3 F 2.
17 Aristot. *Rhet.* 1375b29f.; Plut. *Sol.* 10.
18 Cf. L. Edmunds, 'The religiosity of Alexander', *GRBS* 12 (1971), pp. 363–91, at pp. 368–81, who points out the religious background and argues that the Achilles *imitatio* was not merely propaganda; A. Stewart, *Faces of Power: Alexander's Image and Hellenistic Politics* (Berkeley: University of California Press, 1993), pp. 78–86; E. D. Carney, *Women and Monarchy in Macedonia* (Norman: University of Oklahoma Press, 2000), pp. 274–85.
19 On the comparison of the Persian with the Trojan Wars, cf. D. Boedeker, 'Presenting the past in fifth-century Athens', in Boedeker and K. Raaflaub (eds), *Democracy, Empire, and the Arts in Fifth-Century Athens* (Cambridge, MA: Harvard University Press, 1998), pp. 185–202; T. Hölscher, 'Images and political identity: The case of Athens', in Boedeker and Raaflaub, *Democracy, Empire, and the Arts*, pp. 153–83.

methodological reflections,[20] the explicit privileging of history over myth is amply paralleled in our corpus of fourth-century oratory. Isocrates, for example, considers possible exempla for successfully mastering difficult situations (6.42):

> Now if I were to recount the wars of old which they fought against the Amazons or the Thracians or the Peloponnesians who under the leadership of Eurystheus invaded Attica, no doubt I should be thought to speak on matters ancient and remote from the present situation; but in their war against the Persians, who does not know from what hardships they arose to great good fortune?

While the bigger-than-life frame gave myths special authority for questions of identity and moral conduct, it seems to have undermined their value in more pragmatic interactions.[21]

The 'epic plupast', it can be summed up, mirrors essential features of the epic past. The world of the heroes is separated from the present by a gap just as the 'epic plupast' is distanced from the Homeric world. At the same time, its superiority provides it with particular weight. The epic was used to endow tradition with authority and provided exempla which legitimised claims or permitted a better understanding of the present.

II MEDIA OF MEMORY

Besides shedding light on the relation between epic past and present of performance, the 'heroic plupast' also illustrates the mediality of epic memory. The *quaestio Homerica* is still highly controversial, with continental scholars tending towards a unitarian approach and many Anglo-American classicists favouring oralist models, but nobody will seriously deny that the *Iliad* and *Odyssey* rest on oral traditions and that in the archaic and classical ages the epics circulated in the form of performances. Poetic performances embedded in the Homeric narratives have therefore been fruitfully examined as cases of *mise en*

---

20 Cf. S. Hornblower, *A Commentary on Thucydides: I–III* (Oxford: Oxford University Press, 1991–2008): ad 1.73.2. See also T. Rood, 'Thucydides' Persian Wars', in C. S. Kraus (ed.), *The Limits of Historiography: Genre and Narrative in Ancient Historical Texts* (Leiden: Brill, 1999), pp. 141–68, at p. 145, for interesting thoughts on the passage.

21 Cf. J. Grethlein, *The Greeks and Their Past: Poetry, Oratory and History in the Fifth Century BCE* (Cambridge: Cambridge University Press, 2010), pp. 142–4.

abyme.[22] The *Odyssey* in particular contains such implicit reflections: in Ithaca, the bard Phemios sings of the return of the Achaeans (*Od.* 1.325–7), and the Phaeacian singer Demodocus presents the quarrel between Odysseus and Achilles (*Od.* 8.72–82), Ares' affair with Aphrodite (*Od.* 8.266–366) and the ruse of the wooden horse (*Od.* 8.499–520). In addition, Odysseus, whose narrative of his adventures fills Books 9–13, is compared to a singer by Alcinous and Eumaius (*Od.* 11.367–9; 17.518–21).[23]

It is generally assumed that the Homeric epics were performed at such festivals as the Panathenaia.[24] At the same time, the songs embedded in the *Odyssey* suggest banquets as a further occasion for epic performances. Needless to say, such ἀναθήματα δαιτός (*Od.* 1.152; 21.430)[25] cannot have embraced the entire text of our *Iliad* and *Odyssey*, but the recital of such episodes as the *Doloneia* or the *toxou thesis* seems possible.[26] It is also tempting to find encapsulated in the reaction of the heroes to the rhapsodic recitals a reflection on the reception of the epics.[27] As the patronymic of Phemius, Terpiades (*Od.* 22.330), indicates, bardic performances are supposed to bring the audience pleasure (e.g. *Od.* 8.367–9).[28] However, when Phemius sings of the return of the Greeks from Troy, Penelope asks him to 'leave off singing this sad / song, which always afflicts the dear heart deep inside me' (*Od.* 1.340–1). In the same way, the songs of his quarrel with Achilles and the wooden horse cause Odysseus so much pain that he breaks into tears (*Od.* 8.33–6, 521–31). Both are too much involved in the sorrows sung of and thereby prove Aristotle's later observation

22 Cf. C. W. Macleod, 'Homer on poetry and the poetry of Homer', in Macleod, *Collected Essays* (Oxford: Oxford University Press, 1983), pp. 1–15; G. Nagy, 'Early Greek views of poets and poetry', in G. A. Kennedy (ed.), *The Cambridge History of Literary Criticism I* (Cambridge: Cambridge University Press, 1989), pp. 1–77; A. Ford, *Homer: The Poetry of the Past* (Ithaca, NY: Cornell University Press, 1992); C. Segal, *Singers, Heroes, and Gods in the Odyssey* (Ithaca, NY: Cornell University Press, 1994). J. M. Foley (ed.), *A Companion to Ancient Epic* (Malden, MA: Blackwell, 2005), p. 199, on the other hand, argues that we ought to be rather careful with conclusions drawn from songs within the epics about the epics themselves.

23 See also the comparison of Odysseus' bow with a lyre in 21.405–9.

24 Cf. the discussion by G. S. Kirk, *The Songs of Homer* (Cambridge: Cambridge University Press, 1962), pp. 274–81. See also G. Nagy, *Poetry as Performance: Homer and Beyond* (Cambridge: Cambridge University Press, 1996); D. B. Collins, 'Improvisation in rhapsodic performance', *Helios* 28 (2001), pp. 11–27.

25 On the two passages, see Segal, *Singers, Heroes and Gods*, p. 117.

26 Cf. B. Heiden, 'The three movements of the *Iliad*', *GRBS* 37.1 (1996), pp. 5–22 on possible divisions of the *Iliad* for performances.

27 Cf. Macleod, 'Homer on poetry', pp. 1–15; Segal, *Singers, Heroes and Gods*, pp. 113–41.

28 *Terpein* signifies the effect of poetry in *Il.* 1.474; 9.189; *Od.* 1.347; 422; 8.91; 368; 429; 542; 12.188; 17.385, 606; 18.304.

that a certain degree of distance is necessary for the poetic arousal of pity and indulgence.[29] If one is also willing to take Odysseus' Cretan stories into account, then the *Odyssey* contains a reflection not only on its performance and reception, but also on the poetics of epic, particularly the delicate balance between fictional and factual elements, as for example Simon Goldhill has shown.[30]

In this section, I would like to highlight another aspect which has received less attention: the 'epic plupast' is preserved not only in song and narrative, but also in material objects, or, to be more precise, in many cases it is relics which trigger stories about the past.[31] Mostly through gift-exchange, but also through inheritance and theft,[32] material objects change their owners and thereby accumulate stories, as illustrated by the example of Odysseus' bow, which prompts the narrator to a lengthy flashback (*Od.* 21.11–41): Odysseus received the bow from Iphitus, whom he met in the house of Ortilochus. Their guest-friendship was cut short when Iphitus was received and killed by another guest-friend, Heracles, who was keen on his horses. The digression on the bow illustrates the subtle narrative use which the Homeric narrator makes of the 'biography of goods':[33] as a gift from a guest-friend, the bow will serve Odysseus well in his punishment of the suitors who have breached the laws of hospitality.[34] Furthermore, the story of Iphitus and Heracles refracts the topic of hospitality.[35] The commemorative function of gift-exchange comes to the fore when Alcinous gives a cup to Odysseus 'so that all his days he may remember me / as he makes libation at home to Zeus and the other immortals' (*Od.* 8.432–3).

---

29 Aristot. *Rhet.* 1383a8–12; 1386a24–6. For a more complex interpretation of Odysseus' reaction to the last song of Demodocus, see R. B. Rutherford, 'The philosophy of the *Odyssey*', *JHS* 106 (1986), pp. 145–62, at pp. 155–6, who argues that Odysseus identifies with the Trojan victims just as at the end of the *Iliad* Achilles takes on the perspective of Priam.

30 S. Goldhill, *The Poet's Voice: Essays on Poetics and Greek Literature* (Cambridge: Cambridge University Press, 1991), pp. 36–56.

31 Cf. J. Grethlein, 'Memory and material objects in the *Iliad* and the *Odyssey*', *JHS* 128 (2008), pp. 27–51.

32 Meriones' helmet combines these three forms of exchange: Autolycus stole it from Amyntor and passed it on to Amphidamas, who presented it as a gift to Molus, from whom Meriones inherited it (*Il.* 10.261–70).

33 The concept of the 'biography of goods' was put forward by W. H. R. Rivers, 'The genealogical method of anthropological inquiry', *Sociological Review* 3 (1910), pp. 1–12. For more recent approaches, see the survey in *World Archaeology* 31 (1999).

34 This aligns the bow with the wine which Odysseus receives from Maron as a guest-gift (9.196–211) and uses to punish the Cyclops for a less than friendly reception.

35 Cf. Grethlein, 'Memory and material objects', pp. 42–3.

Not only circulating commodities but also monuments evoke the memory of the past. This is most obvious for tombs, such as the tomb of Ilus which is used for assemblies (*Il.* 10.414–16) and thereby inscribes the memory of Priam's grandfather into everyday reality. Hector reflects on, and inverts, the commemorative function of tombs when he speculates about the tomb of his future opponent which will spread his fame (*Il.* 7.87–91):[36]

καί ποτέ τις εἴπῃσι καὶ ὀψιγόνων ἀνθρώπων,
νηῒ πολυκλήϊδι πλέων ἐπὶ οἴνοπα πόντον·
'ἀνδρὸς μὲν τόδε σῆμα πάλαι κατατεθνηῶτος,
ὅν ποτ' ἀριστεύοντα κατέκτανε φαίδιμος Ἕκτωρ.'
ὣς ποτέ τις ἐρέει, τὸ δ' ἐμὸν κλέος οὔ ποτ' ὀλεῖται.

And some day one of the men to come will say, as he sees it,
one who in his benched ship sails on the wine-blue water:
'This is the mound of a man who died long ago in battle,
who was one of the bravest, and glorious Hector killed him.'
So will he speak some day, and my glory will not be forgotten.

There are also buildings which have not been erected for commemorative purposes, but nonetheless carry stories about the past. The walls of Troy are a particularly interesting case in point: one wall bears the memory of Poseidon's and Apollo's servitude to Laomedon (*Il.* 7.451–3; cf. *Il.* 21.441–7). Another wall testifies to their revenge: Laomedon did not pay the gods for their service, and Poseidon sent a sea-monster to him. In order to rid the city of this plague, Heracles erected a wall (*Il.* 20.144–8). When he did not receive the promised reward of Laomedon's partly divine horses, he sacked the city in revenge.[37] During their siege, the Greeks are building yet another wall which will attest to the Trojan War. Taken together, the walls serve as an 'archaeological history' of Troy.

This embedded 'archaeology of the past' illustrates the relation between epic and relics. Many scholars are still under the spell of the idea that the Homeric epics have preserved knowledge of historical events in the Mycenaean age. However, comparisons of the epics with archaeological evidence have demonstrated that, by and large, the heroic world mirrors and refracts the reality of the early archaic age just as comparative evidence about oral traditions undermines

36 Cf. Grethlein, 'Memory and material objects', p. 30.
37 For glimpses of the story in the *Iliad*, see 5.638–42; 14.250–6; 15.25–30.

the thesis of a stable tradition through the Dark Ages.[38] Most of the
Mycenaean elements in Homer, such as the boar-tusk helmet and
Nestor's cup, are material objects. They do not prove a continuous
epic tradition from the Mycenaean to the archaic ages, but were probably inspired by relics still visible in the archaic age.[39] The reuse of
Mycenaean gems and the intensification of hero cult in archaic Greece
attest to a strong interest in old objects.[40] I would even argue that
Mycenaean ruins and finds such as weapons were a major source of
inspiration for the rise of Greek epic.[41] The relevance of ruins and old
objects for the construction of a heroic world in Greek epic is mirrored
by the strong material side of the 'epic plupast'.

Let me push this interpretation further by suggesting that the
Homeric epic uses the 'archaeology of the past' to throw into relief its
own commemorative function.[42] The wall built by the Greeks at Troy
is so great that Poseidon is afraid that it will outshine his wall. At the
same time, the wall of the Greeks will be damaged during combat (*Il.*
12.256–62; 14.55–6; 15.361–6) and, as the narrator remarks in a long
prolepsis, will eventually be annihilated by a deluge (12.3–33). The
instability of memory preserved by material objects comes to the fore
also in other passages. For example, before the chariot race Nestor
shows his son Antilochus a sign which will help him to steer his course
(*Il.* 23.326–33). Not even 'Mr Memory' is able to tell whether the
stump with two white stones leaned against it is the 'grave-mark of
someone who died long ago' or 'was set as a racing goal by men who
lived before our time' (*Il.* 23.331–3).[43] Monuments such as walls and
tombs are unreliable and limited as bearers of memory and thereby
highlight the claim of epic to establish 'imperishable fame' in the
medium of song.

---

38 Cf. I. Morris, 'The use and abuse of Homer', *Classical Antiquity* 5 (1986), pp.
    81–138; J. P. Crielaard, 'How the west was won', in C. Gillis, C. Risberg and
    B. Sjöberg (eds), *Trade and Production in Premonetary Greece* (Jonsered: Paul
    Åström, 1995), pp. 125–7.
39 Cf. Grethlein, 'From imperishable glory to history', pp. 128–9.
40 On the reuse of gems, see J. Boardman, *Greek Gems and Finger Rings* (London:
    Thames and Hudson, 1970), p. 107; J. Boardman, *The Archaeology of Nostalgia:
    How the Greeks Re-Created their Mythical Past* (London: Thames and Hudson,
    2003), pp. 81–2. On hero cult, see, e.g., C. Antonaccio, *An Archaeology of
    Ancestors: Tomb Cult and Hero Cult in Early Greece* (Lanham, MD: Rowman
    & Littlefield, 1995); R. Hägg (ed.), *Ancient Greek Hero Cult* (Athens: Svenska
    Institutet i Athen, 1999); D. Boehringer, *Heroenkulte in Griechenland von der
    geometrischen bis zur klassischen Zeit* (Berlin: Klio, Akademie, 2001).
41 Cf. D. Hertel, *Die Mauern von Troia: Mythos und Geschichte im antiken Ilion*
    (Munich: Beck, 2003); Grethlein, 'Imperishable glory to history'.
42 Cf. Grethlein, 'Memory and material objects', p. 35.
43 See Grethlein, 'Memory and material objects', pp. 31–2.

III THEODICY

In the first two sections of this chapter, I have used the 'epic plupast' to explore the relation between past and present and the mediality of memory in Homer. I would now like to approach directly the epic presentation of the past and examine how Homer envisages human life in time. In mentioning heroic suffering and divine agency, the proems of *Iliad* and *Odyssey* highlight two important aspects of their narratives and raise the question of theodicy. Are the sorrows of Achilles & Co. embedded in a system of divine justice? According to the traditional view, the *Odyssey* presents a more advanced conception than the *Iliad*:[44] whereas the gods appear as arbitrary and amoral in the earlier poem, the later one features gods concerned about righteous conduct and is therefore a step towards the cosmic order we find in Hesiod. Such evolutionary models of divine justice in Greek literature, however, have been forcefully challenged by Hugh Lloyd-Jones.[45] More recently, William Allan has made a case that the *Iliad* and *Odyssey* share a common belief about human and divine justice which also underlies the hexameter corpus of Hesiod, the Epic Cycle and the Homeric Hymns.[46] Allan assembles on the one hand passages from the *Iliad* which testify to a divine concern with moral issues; on the other, he shows that in the *Odyssey* the gods have not lost their unpredictable and troubling side.

There are indeed passages in the *Iliad* which view the fall of Troy as punishment for Paris' crime. A particularly interesting case in point, not discussed by Allan, is a prayer of Menelaus in *Il.* 3.351–4:

Ζεῦ ἄνα, δὸς τείσασθαι, ὅ με πρότερος κάκ' ἔοργεν,
δῖον Ἀλέξανδρον, καὶ ἐμῇς ὑπὸ χερσὶ δάμασσον,

---

44 See, e.g., F. Jacoby, 'Die geistige Physiognomie der *Odyssee*', *Antike* 9 (1933), pp. 159–94; K. Reinhardt, 'Tradition und Geist im homerischen Epos', in C. Becker (ed.), *Tradition und Geist: Gesammelte Essays zur Dichtung* (Göttingen: Vandenhoeck & Ruprecht, 1960), pp. 5–15, at p. 6; K. Rüter, *Odysseeinterpretationen: Untersuchungen zum ersten Buch und zur Phaiakis* (Göttingen: Vandenhoeck & Ruprecht, 1969), p. 70; Rutherford, 'Philosophy of the *Odyssey*', pp. 147–8; most recently, E. A. Schmidt, 'Die Gerechtigkeit des Gottes als Axiom frühgriechischer Weltdeutung: Zum Recht in der frühgriechischen Dichtung von Homer bis Solon', in B. Greiner, B. Thums and W. Graf Vitzthum (eds), *Recht und Literatur: Interdisziplinäre Bezüge* (Heidelberg: Universitätsverlag Winter, 2010), pp. 29–74, at pp. 44–53.
45 H. Lloyd-Jones, *The Justice of Zeus* (Berkeley: University of California Press, 1971).
46 W. Allan, 'Divine justice and cosmic order in early Greek epic', *JHS* 126 (2006), pp. 1–35. For a nuanced account of divine justice in the *Iliad* and *Odyssey*, see also B. Fenik, *Studies in the Odyssey* (Wiesbaden: F. Steiner, 1974), pp. 209–27; on the *Odyssey*, J. S. Clay, *The Wrath of Athena: Gods and Men in the Odyssey* (Princeton: Princeton University Press, 1983), pp. 213–39.

ὄφρα τις ἐρρίγησι καὶ ὀψιγόνων ἀνθρώπων
ξεινοδόκον κακὰ ῥέξαι, ὅ κεν φιλότητα παράσχηι.

Zeus, lord, grant me to punish the man who first did me injury,
brilliant Alexandrus, and beat him down under my hands'
    strength
that any one of the men to come may shudder to think of
doing evil to a kindly host, who has given him friendship.

The reference to 'men to come' gives the passage a meta-poetic touch
and suggests reading the *Iliad* as testimony to the workings of divine
retribution.

At the same time, the programmatic statement of Zeus at the beginning of the *Odyssey*, while foregrounding the idea of divine punishment, does not exclude the gods also sending sorrows to humans who
have committed no crimes (*Od.* 1.32–4):[47]

ὢ πόποι, οἷον δή νυ θεοὺς βροτοὶ αἰτιόωνται.
ἐξ ἡμέων γάρ φασι κάκ᾽ ἔμμεναι· οἱ δὲ καὶ αὐτοὶ
σφῇσιν ἀτασθαλίῃσιν ὑπὲρ μόρον ἄλγε᾽ ἔχουσιν.

Oh for shame, how the mortals put the blame upon us
gods, for they say evils come from us, but it is they, rather,
who by their own recklessness win sorrow beyond what is given.

There are entire episodes in the *Odyssey* which are hard to explain for
advocates of a new moral order: the Phaeacians who receive Odysseus
in accordance with the laws of hospitality definitely do not deserve
Poseidon transforming their escort into stone.[48] The same god's
revenge for the blinding of Polyphemus seems barely justified given
that Odysseus was about to serve as the Cyclops' breakfast.[49] The
destruction of Odysseus' companions after their sojourn on Thrinacia
is at least ambiguous. They refrain from touching the cattle of Helios
for a long time and lay hands on them only when, forced to stay by
adverse winds, they start starving.[50]

While agreeing with Allan that the moral universes of the *Iliad* and
Odyssey are both not only more multifaceted than the traditional

---

47 See Fenik, *Studies*, p. 211; Allan, 'Divine justice', p. 16.
48 E.g. Rutherford, 'Philosophy of the *Odyssey*', p. 148.
49 E.g. Fenik, *Studies*, pp. 210–11.
50 Cf. Fenik, *Studies*, pp. 213–15; Clay, *Wrath of Athena*, pp. 218–19. Segal, *Singers,
    Heroes and Gods*, pp. 215–18, on the other hand, emphasises the guilt of the
    companions.

juxtaposition has it, but also share basic patterns of belief, I think his reading ignores crucial aspects of the *Iliad* and thereby plays down weighty differences from the *Odyssey*. These differences are due not to another view of the divine, let alone to progress in theology, but to the story and discourse of the epics. To start with the level of the story, whilst the *Iliad* centres on the mortality of its hero, Achilles, and paradoxically foregrounds his death by only adumbrating it,[51] the *Odyssey* deals with the survival of its hero. Odysseus is subjected to the most dire experiences, from being tossed around by the sea to watching Polyphemus eat his companions, and further trials await him after the end of the poem,[52] but nonetheless he returns, is reunited with his family and recaptures his regal position on Ithaca.

In addition to this point, which is well known and has led to the juxtaposition of the two Homeric epics as tragic and comic,[53] the narrative form of presentation also contributes to the difference between them. There are passages in the *Iliad* which suggest taking the fall of Troy as punishment for the abduction of Helen (see above), but this falls short of explaining the pains inflicted upon the Greeks. More importantly, the narrative of the *Iliad* highlights not so much the moral aspect of suffering as the force of contingency. The *condicio heroica* is presented as an exacerbated version of the *condicio humana*. Not only do the heroes frequently reflect on their fragility, most prominently Glaucus in the simile of the leaves (*Il.* 6.146–9) and Achilles in the parable of the jars (*Il.* 24.524–33), but also the narrative presentation of combat underscores how little control the heroes have over their lives. The merciless rule of chance on the battlefield comes to the fore in the topos of the 'missing hit'.[54] A hero aims at an opponent, whom he misses, but hits another, who becomes an unintended victim (*Il.* 8.300–8):

ἦ ῥα, καὶ ἄλλον ὀϊστὸν ἀπὸ νευρῆφιν ἴαλλεν
Ἕκτορος ἀντικρύ, βαλέειν δέ ἑ ἵετο θυμός·

---

51 On the central place of death in the *Iliad*, see W. Marg, 'Kampf und Tod in der Ilias', *WJb* 2 (1976), pp. 7–19; S. L. Schein, 'On Achilles' speech to Odysseus, *Iliad* 9.308–429', *Eranos* 78 (1980), pp. 125–31.
52 Cf. 23.264–84. Cf. A. Bergren, 'Odyssean temporality: Many (re)turns', in C. Rubino and C. Shelmerdine (eds), *Approaches to Homer* (Austin: University of Texas Press, 1983), pp. 38–73.
53 For a recent version of this juxtaposition, see N. J. Lowe, *The Classical Plot and the Invention of Western Narrative* (Cambridge: Cambridge University Press, 2000), pp. 103–56.
54 Cf. M. Lossau, 'Ersatztötungen: Bauelemente in der *Ilias*', *WS* 104 (1991), pp. 5–21; M. Stoevesandt, *Feinde – Gegner – Opfer: Zur Darstellung der Troianer in den Kampfszenen der Ilias* (Basel: Schwabe, 2004), pp. 161–6; Grethlein, *Geschichtsbild*, p. 160.

καὶ τοῦ μέν ῥ' ἀφάμαρθ', ὃ δ' ἀμύμονα Γοργυθίωνα
υἱὸν ἐὺν Πριάμοιο κατὰ στῆθος βάλεν ἰῶι,
τόν ῥ' ἐξ Αἰσύμηθεν ὀπυιομένη τέκε μήτηρ
καλὴ Καστιάνειρα δέμας εἰκυῖα θεῆισιν·
μήκων δ' ὣς ἑτέρωσε κάρη βάλεν, ἥ τ' ἐνὶ κήπωι
καρπῶι βριθομένη νοτίηισί τε εἰαρινῆισιν·
ὣς ἑτέρωσ' ἤμυσε κάρη πήληκι βαρυνθέν.

He spoke, and let fly another shaft from the bowstring,
straight for Hector, and all his heart was straining to hit him;
but missed his man, and struck down instead a strong son of
    Priam,
Gorgythion the blameless, hit in the chest by an arrow;
Gorgythion whose mother was lovely Castianeira,
Priam's bride from Aisyme, with the form of a goddess.
He bent drooping his head to one side, as a garden poppy
bends beneath the weight of its yield and the rains of
    springtime;
so his head bent slack to one side beneath the helm's weight.

While the 'missing hit' calls attention to the fragility of human life, the
flashback to the birth of Gorgythion and the flower simile underscore
the rupture of death.

There are many similar obituaries in the *Iliad* which add pathos to
the battle scenes.[55] Particularly tragic is the obituary which throws
into relief the *mors immatura* of Iphidamas (11.241–7):

ὣς ὃ μὲν αὖθι πεσὼν κοιμήσατο χάλκεον ὕπνον,
οἰκτρός, ἀπὸ μνηστῆς ἀλόχου ἀστοῖσιν ἀρήγων
κουριδίης, ἧς οὔ τι χάριν ἴδε· πολλὰ δ' ἔδωκεν·
πρῶθ' ἑκατὸν βοῦς δῶκεν, ἔπειτα δὲ χείλι' ὑπέστη,
αἶγας ὁμοῦ καὶ ὄϊς, τά οἱ ἄσπετα ποιμαίνοντο.
δὴ τότε γ' Ἀτρεΐδης Ἀγαμέμνων ἐξενάριξεν,
βῆ δὲ φέρων ἀν' ὅμιλον Ἀχαιῶν τεύχεα καλά.

So Iphidamas fell there and went into the brazen slumber,
unhappy, who came to help his own people, and left his young
    wife

---

55 Cf. J. Griffin, 'Homeric pathos and objectivity', *CQ* 26 (1976), pp. 161–87;
Stoevesandt, *Feinde*, pp. 126–59; C. Tsagalis, *Epic Grief: Personal Laments in
Homer's Iliad* (Berlin: de Gruyter, 2004), pp. 179–92; Grethlein, *Geschichtsbild*,
pp. 155–9.

a bride, and had known no delight from her yet, and given much
    for her.
First he had given a hundred oxen, then promised a thousand
head of goats and sheep, which were herded for him in
    abundance.
Now Agamemnon, son of Atreus, stripped him and went back
to the throng of the Achaeans bearing the splendid armour.

The flashback to the recent wedding underscores the *mors immatura*.
Marriage as the institution for procreation strongly contrasts with
death, the end of his life. Instead of receiving his due after giving such
a rich dowry, Iphidamas becomes himself object of another exchange
when Agamemnon takes his armour.

Although not all of the 240 deaths in the *Iliad* are presented with
the same elaboration, Griffin's study of 'Homeric pathos and objectivity' impressively demonstrates the variety of comments by which the
Homeric narrator throws into relief the horrors of death.[56] It is therefore most striking that there is not a single obituary in the *Odyssey*.[57]
The *Odyssey* does not lack deaths, but while the companions of
Odysseus tend to remain anonymous,[58] the dying suitors obviously do
not deserve such narrative highlighting. Whereas the *Iliad*, in accordance with its focus on the mortality of its hero, uses the fate of small
heroes to ponder on the rupture of death, the *Odyssey* does not elaborate on the death of Odysseus' companions and depicts the killing of
the suitors primarily as a punishment.

Other than analepses, the narrator of the *Iliad* also uses prolepses
to underscore human fragility, as the presentation of the major heroes
illustrates.[59] Time and again, narratorial foreshadowing or divine
predictions reveal the vanity of the heroes' aspirations, which will be
thwarted by an unexpected death. For example, as early as Book 11,
when Achilles sends Patroclus to Nestor, a sombre comment by the
narrator alerts us to his impending death (*Il.* 11.602–4):

---

56 Griffin, 'Homeric pathos'. R. Garland, 'The causation of deaths in the *Iliad*',
    BICS 28 (1981), pp. 43–60, at pp. 52–3, counts 240 dead warriors, S. E. Bassett,
    The Poetry of Homer (Berkeley: University of California Press, 1938), p. 256 n. 37,
    notes the killing of 318 heroes of whom 243 are named. According to Stoevesandt,
    Feinde, p. 127, about every fourth victim, be he Trojan or Greek, is given an
    obituary.
57 J. Griffin, *Homer on Life and Death* (Oxford: Clarendon Press, 1980), p. 139.
58 See, for example, Clay, *Wrath of Athena*, p. 35, who states that the reference to
    the companions in the *Odyssey*'s proem is noteworthy given their minor role in the
    action.
59 Cf. Grethlein, *Geschichtsbild*, pp. 208–39.

αἶψα δ' ἑταῖρον ἑὸν Πατροκλῆα προσέειπεν,
φθεγξάμενος παρὰ νηός· ὃ δὲ κλισίηθεν ἀκούσας
ἔκμολεν ἶσος Ἄρηϊ· κακοῦ δ' ἄρα οἱ πέλεν ἀρχή.

At once he spoke to his own companion in arms, Patroclus,
calling from the ship, and he heard it from inside the shelter, and
    came out
like the war god, and this was the beginning of his evil.

Later, Patroclus, full of confidence that he will rout the Trojans, asks
Achilles for his armour (*Il.* 16.46–7):

ὣς φάτο λισσόμενος, μέγα νήπιος· ἦ γὰρ ἔμελλεν
οἷ αὐτῶι θάνατόν τε κακὸν καὶ κῆρα λιτέσθαι.

So he spoke supplicating in his great innocence; this was
his own death and evil destruction he was entreating.

The contrast between Patroclus' zeal and the impending of his death is
borne out again in *Il.* 16.684–7:

Πάτροκλος δ' ἵπποισι καὶ Αὐτομέδοντι κελεύσας
Τρῶας καὶ Λυκίους μετεκίαθε, καὶ μέγ' ἀάσθη,
νήπιος· εἰ δὲ ἔπος Πηληϊάδαο φύλαξεν,
ἦ τ' ἂν ὑπέκφυγε κῆρα κακὴν μέλανος θανάτοιο.

But Patroclus, with a shout to Automedon and his horses,
went after Trojans and Lycians in a huge blind fury.
Besotted: had he only kept the command of Peleiades
he might have got clear away from the evil spirit of black death.

Patroclus is killed by Hector, who earlier had predicted the fall of Troy
and his own death (*Il.* 6.859–61), but is now victim of the same illu-
sions as Patroclus.[60] When Hector strips his opponent of his armour,
boasting about his strength, Zeus envisions his death and comments
on his ignorance (*Il.* 17.201–3):

ἆ δείλ', οὐδέ τί τοι θάνατος καταθύμιός ἐστιν,
ὃς δή τοι σχεδὸν εἶσι· σὺ δ' ἄμβροτα τεύχεα δύνεις
ἀνδρὸς ἀριστῆος, τόν τε τρομέουσι καὶ ἄλλοι.

60 Patroclus and Hector are compared with one another by R. Rutherford, 'Tragic
form and feeling in the *Iliad*', *JHS* 102 (1982), pp. 145–60, at p. 157.

Ah, poor wretch! There is no thought of death in your mind
   now,
and yet death stands close beside you as you put on the
   immortal armour
of a surpassing man. There are others who tremble before him.

In one of the most touching scenes of the *Iliad*, the narrator uses
Hector's death to home in on the limits of human knowledge (*Il.*
22.442–6):

κέκλετο δ' ἀμφιπόλοισιν ἐϋπλοκάμοις κατὰ δῶμα
ἀμφὶ πυρὶ στῆσαι τρίποδα μέγαν, ὄφρα πέλοιτο
Ἕκτορι θερμὰ λοετρὰ μάχης ἒκ νοστήσαντι.
νηπίη, οὐδ' ἐνόησεν, ὅ μιν μάλα τῆλε λοετρῶν
χέρσ' ὕπ' Ἀχιλλῆος δάμασε γλαυκῶπις Ἀθήνη.

She called out through the house to her lovely-haired
   handmaidens
to set a great cauldron over the fire, so that there would be
hot water for Hector's bath as he came back out of the fighting;
poor innocent, nor knew how, far from waters for bathing,
Pallas Athena had cut him down at the hands of Achilles.

Andromache's ignorance is not due to the opaqueness of the future,
but to spatial distance. While she is taking care of a warm welcome
for Hector, Achilles has started mutilating his corpse. The tragic irony
is deepened by a play with the ritual of the bath: the death of Hector
transforms the bath for the returning warrior into the cleaning of his
corpse, which again will be deferred until the last book of the *Iliad*.[61]
   The last hero in the chain of deaths which structures the final third of
the *Iliad*, Achilles, is distinct from the others in that he is aware of his
own mortality, even knows that his own death is to follow soon upon
Hector's (*Il.* 18.95–6), and nonetheless rushes to avenge Patroclus.
When Hera lends a voice to the divine horse Xanthus, which then
prophesies Achilles' death to him, the hero replies (*Il.* 19.420–3):

Ξάνθε, τί μοι θάνατον μαντεύεαι; οὐδέ τί σε χρή.
εὖ νύ τοι οἶδα καὶ αὐτός, ὅ μοι μόρος ἐνθάδ' ὀλέσθαι,
νόσφι φίλου πατρὸς καὶ μητέρος· ἀλλὰ καὶ ἔμπης
οὐ λήξω, πρὶν Τρῶας ἅδην ἐλάσαι πολέμοιο.

61 Cf. J. Grethlein, 'The poetics of the bath in the *Iliad*', *HSCPh* 103 (2006),
   pp. 25–49.

Xanthus, why do you prophesy my death? This is not for you.
I myself know well it is destined for me to die here
far from my beloved father and mother. But for all that
I will not stop till the Trojans have had enough of my fighting.

Achilles' awareness and acceptance of his own death prefigure *avant la lettre* the attitude of 'anticipatory resoluteness' ('vorlaufende Entschlossenheit') which Heidegger privileges as an 'authentic' ('eigentlich') mode of *Dasein*.[62] The *Iliad*'s emphasis on human fragility culminates in its hero, for whom contingency has been transformed into necessity.

The *Odyssey* also features prolepses which contrast the characters' expectations with their future experiences. However, the emphasis on human fragility is far less dramatic because of the focus on the fate of Odysseus, who is not going to die. Moreover, Odysseus is provided with rough sketches of his future by Teiresias (*Od.* 11.100–37), Circe (*Od.* 12.37–110) and Athena (*Od.* 13.393–415). Part of the adventures are narrated by Odysseus himself (Books 9–12), who occasionally comments on wrong expectations he has harboured (e.g. 9.224ff.), but in general emphasises his foresight.[63] The *Odyssey*, it can be noted, does not capitalise on tragic irony to the same extent as the *Iliad*.

To sum up: the *Iliad* and *Odyssey* share the same templates for viewing human life in time, notably a general feeling of insecurity and the belief that crimes provoke divine punishment. However, story and discourse make the two epics different from one another. The idea of divine retribution is not alien to the *Iliad*, but through such devices as 'missing hits', obituaries and prolepses contrasting expectations with experiences, the poem highlights human fragility. The *Odyssey*, on the other hand, does not fail to mark the insecurity of human life, but it concentrates on the successful return of Odysseus and the punishment he inflicts on the suitors.

IV BEYOND HOMER

Let me finally go beyond Homer and briefly look to historiography. In taking up the three points that I have examined – the relation between past and present, the mediality of memory and theodicy – it is not my aim to explore fully the differences or the Homeric influence on the historians. Instead, I would like to illustrate the claim that epic

---

62 M. Heidegger, *Being and Time*, tr. J. Macquarrie and E. Robinson, 8th edn (Oxford: Oxford University Press, 1988; 1st pub. 1962), p. 351 (p. 304).
63 Cf. Rutherford, 'Tragic form and feeling', p. 150.

and Greek historiography share some common ground.[64] Without denying the crucial differences, I will argue that even the attempts of the historians to set themselves off against Homer reveal an idea of history that also underlies the *Iliad* and *Odyssey*. Needless to say, I can offer here no more than spotlights.

We have first seen that the epics focus on a distant past which is not linked to the present, but is highly apt to provide exempla because of its superiority. On the other hand, at least the canonical historians privilege the more recent past. To mention only the two founding fathers of Greek historiography, Herodotus gives an account of the Persian Wars and Thucydides makes a case for concentrating on contemporary history. In his *Archaeology*, Thucydides even challenges the superiority of the heroic age and takes pains to demonstrate that the Peloponnesian War is by far the greatest military event in Greek history. Nonetheless, he draws heavily on the exemplary view of history which is so prominent in Homer.[65] Thucydides' account will, he hopes, permit the readers to understand future events better (1.22.4; cf. 3.82.2). The past will not simply repeat itself, but may be similar. Due to the stability of human nature, the insights won by his rigorous method will prove valuable for later generations and make his account a κτῆμα ἐς ἀεί. The notion of a 'possession forever' evokes and transforms the epic notion of 'imperishable glory' (κλέος ἄφθιτον).[66] Whereas the epic defines its own eternity via its objects, Thucydides claims eternity in relation to his readers. Fame has been replaced with usefulness, but the underlying exemplary view of the past is the same.

In a second step, I have dealt with the mediality of epic, arguing for a very high degree of implicit reflection on oral poetry. Herodotus' *Histories* still bear the traces of epideictic performances and it seems that local historians also presented their works orally,[67] but the medium of writing is as crucial to the history of historiography as

64 On the epic influence on Greek historiography, see, e.g., H. Strasburger, *Homer und die Geschichtsschreibung* (Heidelberg: C. Winter, 1972); J. Marincola, *Greek Historians* (Greece & Rome New Surveys in the Classics 31; Oxford: Oxford University Press, 2001), pp. 9–10.

65 On the intricacies of the exemplary view of the past in Thucydides and also Herodotus, see J. Grethlein, '"Historia magistra vitae" in Herodotus and Thucydides? The exemplary use of the past and ancient and modern temporalities', in A. Lianeri (ed.), *The Western Time of Ancient History: Historiographical Encounters with the Greek and Roman Pasts* (Cambridge: Cambridge University Press, 2011), pp. 247–63.

66 Cf. G. Crane, *The Blinded Eye: Thucydides and the New Written Word* (Lanham, MD: Rowman & Littlefield, 1996), pp. 211–15.

67 On the ancient tradition of oral presentations by Herodotus, see S. Flory, 'Who read Herodotus' *Histories*?', *AJPh* 101 (1980), pp. 12–28, at pp. 14–15; on oral

oral composition and tradition are to Homer. That being said, the meta-historical reflection on material bearers of memory in Homer prefigures the attempts by historians to highlight their own accounts by comparing them implicitly with material records, in particular with inscriptions.[68] Herodotus, for example, announces as the goal of his *Histories* that 'what was done by men does not fade away with time (τῷ χρόνῳ ἐξίτηλα γένηται), that great and marvellous achievements, shown forth by Greeks and barbarians, do not lose their fame (ἀκλεᾶ γένηται)' (proem). ἐξίτηλος is a technical term for the fading of colours in inscriptions. Thus, Herodotus not only takes up the idea of epic fame (ἀκλεᾶ), but also presents his account as more durable than inscriptions set in stone. Both epic and historiography underscore their claims by referring to material bearers of memory which are inferior to their own commemorative acts.

My last point was theodicy. We have seen that there is a tension between the idea of divine retribution and the general insecurity of human happiness. Herodotus' *logos* of Helen (2.112–20) illustrates that even where the father of historiography challenges Homer he draws on a similar idea of history. Herodotus rejects the *Iliad*'s account and argues that Helen never went to Troy, but was left in Egypt. After discussing the evidence for this account, particularly the reports of Egyptian priests, he ponders on why, despite the absence of Helen, the Trojan War took place, and finally comes up with a religious explanation (2.120.5):

ἀλλ' οὐ γὰρ εἶχον Ἑλένην ἀποδοῦναι οὐδὲ λέγουσι αὐτοῖσι τὴν ἀληθείην ἐπίστευον οἱ Ἕλληνες, ὡς μὲν ἐγὼ γνώμην ἀποφαίνομαι, τοῦ δαιμονίου παρασκευάζοντος ὅκως πανωλεθρίῃ ἀπολόμενοι καταφανὲς τοῦτο τοῖσι ἀνθρώποισι ποιήσωσι, ὡς τῶν μεγάλων ἀδικημάτων μεγάλαι εἰσὶ καὶ αἱ τιμωρίαι παρὰ τῶν θεῶν.

But they [i.e. the Trojans] did not have Helen to give back and the Greeks did not believe that they spoke the truth. To declare my

(footnote 67 *continued*)
features of the *Histories*, see M. Lang, *Herodotean Narrative and Discourse* (Martin Classical Lectures; Cambridge, MA: Harvard University Press, 1984). See also R. Thomas, *Herodotus in Context: Ethnography, Science and the Art of Persuasion* (Cambridge: Cambridge University Press, 2000), who contextualises Herodotus in an epideictic milieu. On oral presentations of local historians, see K. Clarke, *Making Time for the Past: Local History and the Polis* (Oxford: Oxford University Press, 2011).
68 See J. Moles, '*Anathema kai ktema*: The inscriptional inheritance of ancient historiography', *Histos* 3 (1999), pp. 27–69.

own opinion, this was because the *daimonion* arranged things so that, in their complete annihilation, they should make this clear to mankind that for severe crimes the punishment at the gods' hands is severe.

The phrase πανωλεθρίῃ ἀπολόμενοι evokes the epic, which was indeed *the* medium from which 'mankind' learnt about the Trojan War.[69] Herodotus' implicit reference to Homer presupposes the same moralist interpretation of the *Iliad* that is suggested by the prayer of Menelaus quoted above. The idea of divine retribution figures prominently in the *Histories*, for example when Herodotus mentions the death of Pheretime, who had the leaders of Barca impaled and the breasts of their women cut off (4.205): 'For, while still alive, she became infested with worms, as excessive cases of vengeance make the gods hostile towards men' (ὡς ἄρα ἀνθρώποισι αἱ λίην ἰσχυραὶ τιμωρίαι πρὸς θεῶν ἐπίφθονοι γίνονται). However, Herodotus does not provide us with a clean-cut moralist philosophy of history, but the notion of divine retribution competes with other concepts.[70] The disconcerting idea of divine envy of human success, visible for example in the *logos* of Polycrates (3.39–60, 120–5), is reminiscent of the fickleness of the gods in epic.[71] The epic tension between the ideas of divine justice and the insecurity of human life is expressed in Herodotus' reflection on Cambyses' late confusion and frenzy against his relatives: 'Cambyses committed these mad acts against his closest relatives, either because of Apis or for another reason, as generally many evils afflict humans' (3.33).[72]

Of course, Herodotus shies away from attributing divine interventions to individual gods, but nonetheless the uneasy combination of the idea of divine justice with the gods' arbitrariness aligns the *Histories* with the *Iliad* and *Odyssey*. Similar attempts to get to grips with human fragility can be seen in tragedy and various poetic genres, ranging from elegy to epinician.[73] Even Thucydides, who does not explain historical events by referring to the gods, emphasises the role

---

69 Cf. Grethlein, *Greeks and Their Past*, p. 157.
70 Cf. Grethlein, *Greeks and Their Past*, pp. 187–202.
71 Polycrates' Egyptian friend Amasis points out 'that the gods are jealous of success' (3.40.2), which seems to be confirmed when Herodotus later states in his narratorial voice that Polycrates died in a manner 'worthy neither of himself nor of his ambitions' (3.125.2).
72 The maltreatment of the Apis bull is recounted in 3.29. Cf. W. H. Friedrich, 'Der Tod des Tyrannen: Die poetische Gerechtigkeit der alten Geschichtsschreiber – und Herodot', *A&A* 18 (1973), pp. 97–129, at pp. 116–20.
73 Cf. Grethlein, *Greeks and Their Past*.

of chance in history.[74] As different as all these genres are, their views of history bear striking similarities. This need not be due to the influence of Homer, but is rather the expression of a common gravitational field. While modern historical thinking focuses on developments, ancient Greeks strongly felt exposed to forces beyond their control. The idea of divine justice as well as the construction of regularities and continuities in exempla and tradition, all of which have been challenged in the modern age, can be seen as an attempt to create some stability in a world full of insecurity.

74 See, e.g., F. M. Cornford, *Thucydides Mythistoricus* (London: Edward Arnold, 1907); H.-P. Stahl, *Thucydides: Man's Place in History* (Swansea: Classical Press of Wales, 2003).

3

HESIOD ON HUMAN HISTORY

Bruno Currie

The focus of this chapter is one passage of barely one hundred lines. This concentration of focus is justified, I hope, by the complexity of the passage in question and by its undoubted relevance to our topic.[1] Hesiod's 'myth of the races' (*WD* 106–201; henceforth 'MoR') has been evaluated repeatedly by scholars as a proto-historical account, sometimes in conjunction with the myth of Prometheus and Pandora which precedes it (*WD* 48–105). Notable discussions include those of T. G. Rosenmeyer, D. J. Stewart and C. J. Rowe.[2]

What kind of account is provided in these hundred lines? The lead-in (lines 106–8) furnishes tantalising suggestions. It is billed as a λόγος, not μῦθος (cf. *Od.* 11.368) or αἶνος (cf. *WD* 202).[3] Further,

---

1 The *Catalogue of Women* would have a place in a discussion of 'Hesiod on human history' which pretended to greater inclusivity; and it would raise quite different questions from those considered here.
2 T. G. Rosenmeyer, 'Hesiod and historiography', *Hermes* 85 (1957), pp. 257–85; D. J. Stewart, 'Hesiod and history', *Bucknell Review* 18 (1970), pp. 37–52; C. J. Rowe, 'Archaic thought in Hesiod', *JHS* 103 (1983), pp. 124–35. The following quotations may be illustrative. Rosenmeyer, 'Hesiod and historiography', p. 260: 'On the scores of systematisation, of secularisation, of the revolt against epic untruthfulness or epic narrowness, and of the skilful collection of recognised data under the aegis of a moral theme, Hesiod's Five Ages ought to be ranked as an early piece of Greek historical writing . . . It is the objective of this paper to plead Hesiod's case, if not as a historian, at least as a forerunner of the historical perspective.' Rowe, 'Archaic thought', p. 126 n. 27: 'The ultimate question will be how Hesiod works in contexts which appear to raise issues likely to interest the scientist or the historian; in particular, contexts which are apparently concerned with explanation'; p. 134: 'if we assume that Hesiod is in competition with an Anaximander or a Herodotus (or a Thucydides), then he comes off badly; but though there is some overlapping, as for example in Hesiod's description of the birth of the world, he is really playing a different game, under different rules.' Cf. also P. Smith, 'History and the individual in Hesiod's myth of five races', *CW* 74 (1980), pp. 145–63, at pp. 150–1.
3 M.-C. Leclerc, 'Le mythe des races: Une fiction aux sentiers qui bifurquent', *Kernos* 6 (1993), pp. 207–24, at p. 220; C. Calame, 'Succession des âges et pragmatique poétique de la justice: Le récit hésiodique des cinq espèces humaines',

it is ἕτερον λόγον, a different account from the preceding account of Prometheus and Pandora. But it purports to be a different account of the same state of affairs: 'another account of how gods and mortal men are born of the same origin'.[4] Rosenmeyer took ἐκκορυφώσω in 106 to indicate that this was a distinctively historical sketch.[5] C. Calame on the other hand has pointed to ἐπισταμένως in 107 as an indication that Hesiod is operating as a poet.[6]

THE UNDERLYING CONCEPTION, THE MEANING OF ΓΕΝΟΣ, AND THE METALLIC SCHEME

Our first task must be to try to ascertain the underlying conception of Hesiod's scheme and the precise meaning of γένος, which occurs nine times in the passage (with a single occurrence of γενεή).[7] We may proceed deductively (identify the most promising construction of what Hesiod might be trying to say and map this onto the language used) or inductively (identify the most plausible meanings of the language used and work up to a construction of what Hesiod is trying to say). Clearly we must proceed in both ways, but it will be helpful to begin

---

(footnote 3 *continued*)
Kernos 17 (2004), pp. 67–102, at p. 67: 'ces vers ne représentent pas un "mythe", mais un *lógos*; il s'agit donc d'un simple récit.' Not that these function reliably as technical terms; cf. R. G. A. Buxton, *Imaginary Greece: The Contexts of Mythology* (Cambridge: Cambridge University Press, 1994), pp. 12–13, on the interchangeability of *mythos* and *logos* in the archaic period.

4 For Leclerc, 'Mythe des races', p. 224, this verse (*WD* 108) 'donne la clé de l'histoire'. Cf. Calame, 'Succession des âges', p. 72.

5 Rosenmeyer, 'Hesiod and historiography', p. 269: 'Hesiod does not wish to go into detail; like Thucydides in his archaeology, he realizes that he cannot supply as full a picture as he wishes.' Criticized by Rowe, 'Archaic thought', pp. 132–3; L. Bertelli, 'Hecataeus: From genealogy to historiography', in N. Luraghi (ed.), *The Historian's Craft in the Age of Herodotus* (Oxford: Oxford University Press, 2001), pp. 67–94, at p. 82. The inference from the narrative's sketchiness to its historical intent is weak; for mythological 'sketches', cf. Hygin. *Fab.*, and of course Hesiod (and 'Hesiod') himself in several passages of *Th.* (and *Cat.*).

6 Calame, 'Succession des âges', p. 72 on ἐπιστάμενος: 'Le *lógos* proféré est bien celui d'un sage, par référence au savoir du poète homérique ou mieux encore par allusion au savoir faire du poète élégiaque' (referring to *Od.* 11.368, *Theogn.* 769–72, Solon fr.13.51–5 West; add Archil. fr. 1.2 West); cf. M. L. West, *Hesiod: Works and Days* (Oxford: Clarendon Press, 1978), p. 178; M. Griffith, 'Contest and contradiction in early Greek poetry', in Griffith and D. Mastronarde (eds), *The Cabinet of the Muses: Essays on Classical and Comparative Literature in Honor of Thomas G. Rosenmeyer* (Atlanta: Scholars Press, 1990), pp. 185–207, at p. 196. It seems εὖ καὶ ἐπισταμένως was used especially of a skilled *craftsman* (and hence of a craftsman of *words*?): *Od.* 17.341 = 21.44, 23.197, cf. 5.245, *Il.* 10.265.

7 *WD* 109 = 143 = 180 γένος μερόπων ἀνθρώπων, 121, 127, 140, 156, 159, 176. Cf. *WD* 160 γενεή.

by critiquing some constructions which would make Hesiod's thinking quite straightforwardly historical.

First, Hesiod's γένη are not 'ages', like the *yugas* of the *Mahābhārata* (3.148, 187), despite the Latin rendering *saecula* and the common English rendering 'golden (silver, etc.) *age*'.[8] The γένη should not be glossed as 'epochs', as they are by Rosenmeyer, who wished to see Hesiod as the originator of 'a historical imagination which sees the past, and time in general, not as a steady flow toward the present . . . but rather as a succession of epochs'. According to Rosenmeyer, Hesiod's conception is a fits-and-starts view of history, which he compares with Tacitus' reference to *intervalla ac spiramenta temporum* (*Agricola* 44).[9] Hesiod's γένη are, however, not synonymous with 'periods of history' (as we may speak for scholarly convenience of 'archaic-classical-Hellenistic' or 'republican-imperial' as periods of Greek or Roman history); they are actual human 'races'. While these do occupy discrete historical periods (they have 'a spatio-temporal extension'),[10] that cannot be said to be the essence of Hesiod's conception.

Second, Hesiod's γένη are not 'civilisations'. We should contrast the analogous passage from the Old Testament book of Daniel (2:31–45), where the vision in Nebuchadnezzar's dream of a statue made of gold, silver, bronze, iron and clay intimates successive historical 'kingdoms': to wit (probably), the Babylonian (under Nebuchadnezzar himself), the Persian (under Cyrus the Great), the Greek (under Alexander the Great) and Greek again (under the Seleucids).[11] Homeric epic too seems to have a conception of history as defined by the rise and fall of great civilisations, if the end of the age of heroes is synchronous with the ruin of Mycenae, Sparta and Argos (*Il.* 4.51–3) and Troy itself (*Il.* 12.15–33, cf. 24.543–6). We, too, readily conceptualise history as a sequence of empires (e.g. Assyrian, Persian, Greek, Roman, etc.). But this is not Hesiod's conception either, for there is no prospect of correlating Hesiod's γένη with any civilisations known to him.

---

8 H. C. Baldry, 'Who invented the golden age?', *CQ* n.s. 2 (1952), pp. 83–92, at p. 88; Rosenmeyer, 'Hesiod and historiography', p. 265 and n. 3; B. Gatz, *Weltalter, goldene Zeit und sinnverwandte Vorstellungen* (Hildesheim: Olms, 1967), pp. 205–6. J. Fontenrose, 'Work, justice, and Hesiod's five ages', *CP* 69 (1974), pp. 1–16, at p. 1 n.1, with reservations retains 'ages', finding 'races' 'misleading and inaccurate'; cf. L. Koenen, 'Greece, the Near East, and Egypt: Cyclic destruction in Hesiod and the Catalogue of Women', *TAPA* 124 (1994), pp. 1–34, at p. 2 n. 3; Calame, 'Succession des âges', pp. 68, 71.
9 Rosenmeyer, 'Hesiod and historiography', p. 267.
10 Calame, 'Succession des âges', p. 68.
11 Calame, 'Succession des âges', p. 95.

Third, Hesiod's scheme does not simply resolve itself into human generations. When the heroes of the *Iliad* talk about the past they typically speak of a former generation, superior to the present (e.g. *Il.* 1.250–2, 260–72: the Lapiths; 4.405: the Argive Seven; 5.636–7: Herakles; etc.).[12] This resembles Hesiod's conception in so far as his successive γένη too are worse than their predecessors, but that is about as far as the resemblance goes; his γένη are not 'generations'.[13] Some scholars, including G. W. Most and C. Calame, have argued for taking γενεή at *WD* 160 as 'generation', where the heroes are referred to as προτέρη γενεὴ κατ' ἀπείρονα γαῖαν.[14] On this view the heroes and the men of the present belong to the same γένος, namely the iron race, of which the heroes are early representatives, an earlier generation (γενεή) within that race.[15] This would bring Hesiod's account into line with other Greek thinking, which traced the ancestors of certain historical Greeks back to the heroic period.[16] But the attempt to make the heroes just an earlier generation within the race of iron seems to founder on *WD* 176: '*now* the kind/breed is made of iron' (νῦν γὰρ δὴ γένος ἐστὶ σιδήρεον). That emphatic 'now' indicates that it is only the 'fifth men' (*WD* 174) who are made of iron: by implication, the preceding fourth men (the heroes)

---

12 E.g. G. W. Most, 'Hesiod's myth of the five (or three or four) races', *PCPS* 43 (1997), pp. 104–27, at pp. 121–2.

13 Except in an obsolete sense recognized by *OED*: 'Family, breed, race; class, kind, or "set" of persons.' Cf. Stewart, 'Hesiod and history', p. 44 n. 17: 'The word *genos* is better translated "generation" – though not *one* of ours only – or "race" than as "age".' M. Schmidt, 'γένος', in B. Snell et al. (eds), *Lexikon des frühgriechischen Epos* (Göttingen: Vandenhoeck & Ruprecht, 1955–2010), vol. ii, pp. 130–2, at p. 131, gives γένος throughout MoR (*WD* 109, 121, 127, 140, 143, 156, 159, 173d, 176, 180) and at *Il.* 12.23 the translation 'Generation der Menschenheitsgesch[ichte]' (s.v. γένος 5a), and similarly of γενεή at *WD* 160 (p. 127, s.v. γενεή 5b).

14 Most, 'Hesiod's myth', pp. 112–13; cf. Calame, 'Succession des ages', p. 81 and n. 26.

15 Fontenrose, 'Work, justice', p. 10: 'In effect, [the heroic *genos*] is not a separate age, but the first part of the fourth and final age of iron'; J. Rudhardt, 'Le mythe hésiodique des races et celui de Prométhée: Recherches des structures et des significations', in Rudhardt, *Du mythe, de la religion grecque et de la compréhension d'autrui = Revue Européenne des Sciences Sociales* 19 (Geneva: Droz, 1981), pp. 246–81, at p. 249: 'l'introduction des héros dans le mythe des âges métalliques n'en altère pas le schéma autant qu'il le paraît à première vue; conformement à la donnée traditionelle le récit hésiodique connaît quatre races créées par les dieux; son originalité consiste seulement à distinguer deux phases dans l'histoire de la quatrième'; Most, 'Hesiod's myth', p. 113: 'there is good reason to believe that Hesiod wanted to suggest not so much that that the heroes belonged to a γένος different from that of the iron men as rather that both belonged to the same γένος – call it iron'.

16 M. L. West, *The Hesiodic Catalogue of Women* (Oxford: Clarendon Press, 1985), p. 9.

were not.[17] Hesiod's is evidently an account of five human races, not four with the fourth subdivided into two. At *WD* 160 γενεή is better understood as a synonym of γένος[18] in the sense of 'kind', 'breed', 'race'.[19] The relationship between the γένη is not expressed in terms of generations, despite the undoubted importance of generational-genealogical thinking in both Greece and the Near East (cf. e.g. Hdt. 2.121ff. on the Egyptian priests on their kings: 341 γενεαί were counted, Hdt. 2.142.1; see further below).[20]

The meaning that we must accept for γένος (and γενεή) in MoR is 'race', 'breed' or similar.[21] A convenient approximation is offered by the word's English cognates, 'kin' and 'kind', as in 'mankind', 'humankind' or 'natural kind'.[22] The phrase γένος μερόπων ἀνθρώπων[23] means 'the breed or kind of men', i.e. 'mankind'. We also find 'the kind of mules' (ἡμιόνων γένος: *Il.* 2.852), 'the kind of oxen' (βοῶν γένος: *Od.* 20.212, *HHerm* 309), 'the kind of gods' (*Th.* 21 = 105 ἀθανάτων ἱερὸν γένος, μακάρων γένος *Th.* 33, θεῶν γένος *Th.* 44), 'the kind of men and [the kind] of giants' (ἀνθρώπων τε γένος κρατέρων τε γιγάντων: *Th.* 50),

---

17 According to Most, 'Hesiod's myth', p. 113 n. 41, 'this particular race could already previously have been called by the name of iron, but only now has it demonstrated . . . that it deserves the name'. But there is little to support a 'use of δή to strengthen the claim that a name is appropriate' (ibid.). On the other hand, the emphatic temporal use of νῦν γὰρ δή is well attested (cf. Xenophanes fr. 1.1 West νῦν γὰρ δὴ ζάπεδον καθαρὸν κτλ.), and for the antithesis between *WD* 176 νῦν γὰρ δή and 109 πρώτιστα, cf. Calame, 'Succession des âges', pp. 83–4 'Le point axial de ce temps présent, en contraste avec le *prótista* du vers 109, est signifié par le connecteur *nûn gàr dé*, "car maintenant précisément", situé en position forte au vers 176', cf. 99. Cf. R. Gagné, 'Invisible kin: *Works and Days* 280–285', *Hermes* 138 (2010), pp. 1–21 at p. 10.
18 *Pace* Most, 'Hesiod's myth', pp. 111–12.
19 The notion of the heroes as a separate race (γένος or γενεή) from contemporary men recurs at *Il.* 12.23 ἡμιθέων γένος ἀνδρῶν. Cf. R. Scodel, 'The Achaean wall and the myth of destruction', *HSCP* 86 (1982), pp. 35–50, at p. 35: 'The phrase ἡμιθέων γένος ἀνδρῶν evokes the Hesiodic depiction of the heroes as a separate race, for γένος in such a context can mean nothing else.' Similarly Herodotus' 'the so-called human race' (τῆς . . . ἀνθρωπηίης λεγομένης γενεῆς, 3.122), in an implied contrast to a heroic γενεή. For the antithesis in Pindar: ἥρωες versus ἄνδρες, cf. *P.* 8.27–8, *O.* 6.24–5.
20 On 'genealogical thinking' in Greece, see R. L. Fowler, 'Genealogical thinking, Hesiod's Catalogue and the creation of the Hellenes', *PCPS* 44 (1998), pp. 1–19.
21 See Schmidt, 'γένος'; R. D. Woodard, 'Hesiod and Greek myth', in Woodard (ed.), *The Cambridge Companion to Greek Mythology* (Cambridge: Cambridge University Press, 2007), pp. 83–165, at pp. 141–2. Compare the use of φῦλον: one φῦλον of men and another of gods, *Il.* 5.441–2; cf. *WD* 90 φῦλ' ἀνθρώπων, 199 ἀθανάτων . . . φῦλον.
22 *OED* s.v. 'kind' 10; cf. s.v. 'kin' 5.
23 Three times in MoR (*WD* 109, 143, 180), otherwise at *Cat.* fr. 204.98 M-W and *HDem* 310, both times in the context of the destruction of mankind. Cf. *Th.* 50.

'the kind of satyrs' (γένος . . . σατύρων: Hes. fr. 10(a).18 M-W), 'the kind of women' (γένος . . . γυναικῶν: *Th*. 590), 'the kind of iron/bronze' (γένος πολιοῦ ἀδάμαντος: *Th*. 161).

Hesiod may be doing something more idiosyncratic than is often recognised in multiplying the 'kind*s*' of man and in implying the possibility of an indefinite article, '*a* mankind', which may be as much of a solecism in Greek as in English. This is a history not of one humankind, but a story of five humankinds. This conception of five humankinds is probably as unconventional as Hesiod's more explicitly revisionist doctrine of the two Strifes at the beginning of the poem: 'there is not, after all,[24] a single kind of Strifes (οὐκ ἄρα μοῦνον ἔην Ἐρίδων γένος), but there are two over the earth' (*WD* 11–12). It can hardly be historical thinking that inspires a story of this sort. There is a crucial difference between this conception and a conception of ages (epochs), civilisations or generations.

Technically the relation of these 'humankinds' to one another ought to be no closer than that of *Homo sapiens* to Neanderthal, or even less close, for there is no chronological overlap. MoR presents these as discrete successive races, the one race being destroyed *in nihil*, the next being created thereafter *ex nihilo*. Genealogical continuity between successive kinds thus seems excluded, although it is controversial whether continuity between the heroes and the iron race is nevertheless presupposed.[25] The creation of genealogical ties between the heroes and Greeks of the historical period has indeed been seen as a necessary first step for the creation of a historical attitude towards the heroic age.[26]

---

24 οὐκ ἄρα . . . ἔην: J. D. Denniston, *The Greek Particles*, 2nd edn (Oxford: Oxford University Press, 1950), pp. 36–7; West, *Hesiod: Works and Days*, p. 143; Rowe, 'Archaic thought', p. 133; W. J. Verdenius, *A Commentary on Hesiod Works and Days, vv. 1–382* (Leiden: Brill, 1985), p. 15 and n. 57.

25 Genealogical continuity is assumed by Fontenrose, 'Work, justice', p. 2; Rudhardt, 'Le mythe hésiodique', p. 248 and n. 11, cf. pp. 257–8 n. 66; Leclerc, 'Le mythe des races', p. 219; Most, 'Hesiod's myth', p. 113; C. Sourvinou-Inwood, 'The Hesiodic myth of the five races and the tolerance of plurality in Greek mythology', in O. Palagia (ed.), *Greek Offerings: Essays on Greek Art in Honour of John Boardman* (Oxford: Oxbow, 1997), pp. 1–21, at pp. 8, 11–12. Differently, K. Matthiessen, 'Form und Funktion des Weltaltermythos bei Hesiod', in G. W. Bowersock, W. Burkert and M. C. J. Putnam (eds), *Arktouros: Hellenic Studies Presented to B. M. W. Knox on the Occasion of his 65th Birthday* (Berlin: de Gruyter, 1979), pp. 25–32, at p. 31: 'Wenn nun Hesiod in seiner Erzählung das Geschlecht der Heroen vom gegenwärtigen eisernen Geschlecht als ein vergangenes abhebt, dann betont er die Diskontinuität zwischen den adligen Herren seiner Gegenwart und ihren angeblichen heroischen Vorfahren. Diese deutlich antiaristokratische Auffassung entspricht der auch sonst vom Selbstbewußtsein des Bauernstandes geprägten Denkweise Hesiods.'

26 F. Graf, *Greek Mythology: An Introduction*, tr. T. Marier (Baltimore and London: Johns Hopkins University Press, 1993), pp. 129–30 '[The practice of

Yet for all that genealogical continuity between successive kinds seems to be excluded in MoR, the narrative still somehow wishes, and needs, to be considered a narrative of a *continuous* human history.[27] Verse 108 invites us to understand Hesiod's narrative as '[a story of] how gods and mortal men were born of the same origin'. This only seems to work if the other races are seen as being in a linear descent from the golden race, who 'lived as gods'.[28] Moreover, there seems to be an intriguing *thematic* or *ethical* progression between successive races; ethically the one race seems to pick up where the last left off. To begin with, the men of the golden race have everything they want apparently without being spoilt by it.[29] The men of the silver race are apparently heirs to this externally favoured existence,[30] but they are internally less able to deal with it. To have all one wants without any effort resembles the condition of a spoilt child.[31] Appropriately, therefore, the silver race live as pampered children for one hundred years (130–1), and it seems to follow that when they reach maturity a refusal to share leads to *hubris* towards one another (134–5) and impiety towards the gods (135–7).[32] The men of the bronze race inherit this propensity to *hubris* (146) and

linking historically real genealogies with those of the heroic age] marked a highly significant conceptual development . . . The age of the heroes enters into a datable relation to the present age . . . With the elaboration of a chronology, the Greeks had a rational way of including the heroic age in their past, which they understood as a quantifiable time continuum.' Cf. Smith, 'History and the individual', p. 150. However, this step appears to have been taken already by the time of Homer (cf. *Il.* 20.300–8; A. Faulkner, *The Homeric Hymn to Aphrodite: Introduction, Text, and Commentary* (Oxford: Oxford University Press), pp. 5–6) and Hesiod (cf. *Th.* 1011–16; N. J. Richardson, Review of P. Dräger, *Untersuchungen zu den Frauenkatalogen Hesiods*, *CR* 50 (2000), pp. 263–4, at p. 263), even though they have a clear sense of the distinctness of the 'race of heroes' (*Il.* 12.23; *WD* 160).

27 We may compare and contrast, for the continuity of mankind through heaven-sent destruction, the Mesopotamian flood myth (cf. *Atrahasis*) and the Greek Deukalion myth; cf. Plat. *Tim.* 22a–23a, *Laws* 677a–c.

28 Cf. B. G. F. Currie, 'Heroes and holy men in early Greece: Hesiod's *theios aner*', in A. Coppola (ed.), *Eroi, eroismi, eroizzazzioni* (Padua: SARGON, 2007), pp. 163–203, at pp. 178–81.

29 Contrast Virg. *Geo.* 1.121–4.

30 Cf. Rudhardt, 'Le mythe hésiodique', p. 253: 'La race d'argent est moins bonne [*sc.* que la race d'or] mais son infériorité ne réside pas dans les conditions extérieurs auxquelles elle se trouve soumise. Hésiode ne dit pas que ces conditions aient changé: la terre continue de fournir aux hommes ce qui leur est nécessaire et rien ne leur impose l'obligation de travailler.'

31 For a comparison of the condition of the golden race with childhood, cf. Smith, 'History and the individual', pp. 156–7.

32 Compare and contrast Fontenrose, 'Work, justice', p. 7, on the silver race; J. S. Clay, *Hesiod's Cosmos* (Cambridge: Cambridge University Press, 2003), p. 88; Stewart, 'Hesiod and history', p. 46: '[The silver and bronze races] are destroyed for and *by* their *hubris* towards one another.' Calame, 'Succession des âges', p. 76, describes the silver race as 'un âge adulte abrégé par la démesure, la violence et l'impiété qui conduit ces hommes à une rapide disparition'. The short life of the

are addicted to the works of war (146), in which they kill one another
(152–3).[33] The heroes in the following race are killed in wars (161–5),
one of which was fought apparently between two brothers over their
patrimony (163 μαρναμένους μήλων ἕνεκ᾽ Οἰδιπόδαο, with echoes of
Perses and Hesiod in Polyneikes and Eteokles, if indeed it is their
dispute which is meant),[34] and the other was fought over Helen, that
is, over a guest's abduction of his host's wife. The men of iron race are
to be destroyed when familial and social relations break down, so that
guest is at odds with host (183 οὐδὲ ξεῖνος ξεινοδόκῳ, sc. ὁμοίιος) and
brother is not as before a dear one (184 οὐδὲ κασίγνητος φίλος ἔσσεται).
'Not . . . as before' (ὡς τὸ πάρος περ, 184); but as we have seen this did
not go unproblematically for the race of heroes either. The negative
traits of each race appear to be passed on to its successor.[35] There is
then an ethical evolution, even if a genetic or genealogical evolution
seems ruled out.

We have not yet considered the association with a metal that is
found with four of the five 'mankinds', which is plainly fundamental
to any understanding of Hesiod's conception. The association with a
metal can be seen as literal or metaphorical or both.[36]

(footnote 32 *continued*)
men of the silver race after reaching maturity may reasonably be seen as caused
by acts of violence (*WD* 134–5), rather than just genetics (Sourvinou-Inwood,
'Myth of the five races', p. 5: 'their biological cycle', cf. 2 'the "proper" proportion
between childhood and maturity was reversed'; Most, 'Hesiod's myth', p. 109:
'biological lore'; cf. Rudhardt, 'Le mythe hésiodique', pp. 250, 253). The role of
Zeus in their destruction (*WD* 138) can be seen as double motivation (cf. *WD* 239,
245).

33 On the thematic transition from silver race to bronze race, cf. Calame, 'Succession
des âges', p. 78: 'Même s'il est dit "en rien semblable à la famille d'argent" (vers
144), le *génos* de bronze partage avec les hommes précédents des traits assez
nombreux pour s'inscrire dans leur suite non seulement du point de vue temporel,
mais également du point de vue sémantique. Comme les hommes d'argent, les
hommes tout de bronze vêtus font preuve d'une folie et d'une démesure qui les
engage à retourner leur violence contre eux-mêmes.'

34 So West, *Hesiod: Works and Days*, p. 192; differently, Verdenius, *Commentary*,
p. 101.

35 An anticipation of the degenerate ethos of the iron race is seen in the race
of heroes by Rudhardt, 'Le mythe hésiodique', p. 257: 'C'est donc l'immoralité
qui caractérise la race de fer et produit sa dégénérescence. Elle se trouvait sans
doute en germe dans la race des héros dont certains représentants s'adonnèrent
à l'injustice et à la démesure, même si elle n'était pas alors si générale'; p. 258 (on
the heroes): 'Les uns plus justes, les autres plus enclins à l'*hybris*, leurs actions se
combinent, produisent des conséquences et l'humanité évolue. A partir de la race
des héros que leurs qualités apparentent aux dieux, cette évolution produit la race
de fer qui lui est inférieure'; cf. p. 261.

36 Cf. Baldry, 'Who invented the golden age?', p. 86: 'How far were the words
literally meant, and how far was their use metaphorical or symbolic? For Hesiod
the question probably did not exist. His "bronze race" and "iron race" are so

Taking the metallic association literally would permit one to see MoR as a history of mankind through technological, and specifically metallurgical, innovations. We might compare Lucretius' account of early man, whose weapons progressed from hands, nails and teeth to stones and branches to fire to bronze and finally iron.[37] Real historical thinking can be in play here; a similar conception, after all, under-lies the modern archaeological-historical categories of 'Stone Age', 'Bronze Age' and 'Iron Age'. Such was the view of J. G. Griffiths: '[WD 150–1] makes [Hesiod's] idea clear. The "bronze race" lived until the discovery of a new metal, that is iron. Apart from these lines, it is true, there is no mention of the use of metals . . . But there can be little doubt that this is the underlying idea. If the poet had chosen the metals merely as symbols of increasing degeneration, he would not have referred so clearly to the use of two of them.' For Griffiths, MoR was 'an amalgam of history and myth, where myth undoubtedly predominates but where history lies behind the sequence of metals'.[38] On this view MoR would preserve a historical memory of people first widely using gold, then silver, then bronze, then iron.[39]

This is not the place to pursue the questions whether there really was any such historical memory in Hesiod's time or whether there ever had been such a historical reality to be remembered; a more urgent question is whether such a historical interpretation is sup-ported by Hesiod's language. The most natural understanding of 109 and 128 is, surely, 'the gods made a race of men out of gold (silver)', with the adjectives as predicative complements of ποίησαν denoting the substance out of which these first two humankinds were fash-ioned.[40] The bronze race deviates from this (WD 143–51), but the deviation is signalled by two additions: this race was made 'from ash trees' (WD 145), i.e. was not fashioned from the metal in question; and this race used bronze for everything under the sun (WD 150–1). That is, the bronze race, for whom the association with a metal is

called because they use these metals . . . , but he does not explain – and presumably did not ask himself – in what sense the first race was χρυσέον.'
37 Lucr. 5.1281–96. Cf. Lucr. 5.1241–2. J. G. Griffiths, 'Archaeology and Hesiod's five ages', JHI 17 (1956), pp. 109–19, at p. 114.
38 Griffiths, 'Archaeology and Hesiod's five ages', quotations from pp. 112 and 119. H. C. Baldry, 'Hesiod's five ages', JHI 17 (1956), pp. 553–4, esp. p. 553, is a reply to Griffiths, 'Archaeology and Hesiod's five ages' (and Griffiths, 'Did Hesiod invent the golden age?', JHI 19 (1958), pp. 91–3 is a reply to Baldry, 'Hesiod's five ages').
39 Griffiths also suggests that historical memory lies behind the metallic myths of the Near East: Griffiths, 'Archaeology and Hesiod's five ages', pp. 115–19.
40 With the idea that humankind might be 'made of' gold or silver, compare womankind (Pandora) as made of earth and water (WD 61), men being made from ash trees (WD 145: bronze race), men made from stones in the Deukalion myth (cf. 'Hes.' Cat. fr. 234 M-W, Pind. O.9.42–6).

literal, represents a clear departure from the scheme that has obtained thus far in the narrative.

Taken metaphorically, on the other hand, the association of the races with a metal would be a way of expressing the differing ethos of these various 'human kinds'. We might compare Semonides fr. 7 West, on womankind: 'god first made the mind of woman in different ways: one [he made] from a shaggy-haired sow' – and the others he made from a vixen, a bitch, the earth, the sea, an ass, a weasel, a monkey and a bee. Not so dissimilar (but with reversed sexism) is the English nursery rhyme: 'What are little boys made of? / Frogs and snails / And puppy-dogs' tails / . . . What are little girls made of? / Sugar and spice / And all things nice.' Again this is not very historical, or very scientific, thinking. R. G. A. Buxton is right to observe that in MoR 'metals are used to make statements about the moral world'[41] and to recognise that this constitutes a difference between 'traditional' and 'scientific' – we might add 'historical' – categories of thought.[42] B. M. W. Knox has also knocked on the head the kind of historical interpretation argued for by Griffiths: 'There is not much use pretending that Hesiod is thinking in modern terms of the Bronze and Iron ages; for one thing his own age used bronze as well as iron and so, clearly, did the Homeric heroes of the fourth age. And the gold and silver ages have to be passed over in silence.'[43]

It must be right that the basic conception underlying Hesiod's metallic scheme is the metaphorical one. But there is no reason why the scheme should be monovalent: no reason why the metals should not start off being used symbolically with the gold and silver races, but then also acquire a literal dimension with the bronze and iron races. A quasi-historical notion seems to be grafted on with these two races; there seems little point otherwise in insisting that the bronze race used bronze because 'black iron did not exist' (WD 151). One of the ways in which Homeric epic seems keen to distinguish the world of the heroes from the contemporary world is their inhabitants' differential uses of bronze and iron, and this seems to be a way of capturing genuine historical difference between the Mycenaean and the archaic worlds.[44] The tradition (probably Near Eastern: see below) that gave Hesiod the

41 Cf. already 'Socrates' at Plat. *Crat.* 398a4–6: 'I think that [Hesiod] spoke of the golden race not as created from gold, but as noble and fine.'
42 Buxton, *Imaginary Greece*, pp. 202–4, at pp. 203 and 204.
43 B. M. W. Knox, 'Work and justice in archaic Greece', in Knox, *Essays: Ancient and Modern* (Baltimore: Johns Hopkins University Press, 1989), p. 12.
44 Cf. Most, 'Hesiod's myth', pp. 122–3. Differently, West, *Hesiod: Works and Days*, pp. 188–9: 'probably due more to the conservatism of the formulaic language . . . than to deliberate avoidance of anachronism'.

(metaphorical) metallic scheme gold–silver–bronze–iron is evidently distinct from the Greek epic tradition, which implicitly contrasted the bygone heroes as predominantly (literal) users of bronze with contemporary men as predominantly (literal) users of iron; but Hesiod found a neat way of combining the two traditions.[45] Thanks to this combination his account wins a genuine historical dimension. But the historical thinking in question is the product of the heroic epic tradition, and cannot be considered an original intellectual contribution of Hesiod.

REFINEMENTS AND QUALIFICATIONS TO THE SCHEME

The sequence gold–silver–bronze–iron implies a clear devaluation. But there is, several scholars have recognised, no straight linear deterioriation in Hesiod's scheme.[46] The descent in value of the metals is disrupted by the heroes, who are explicitly said to be superior to the preceding bronze race (*WD* 158).[47] The breakdown of any linear decline with the race of heroes should not be seen as a flaw in the narrative.[48] The fact that there is a possibility of halting, even reversing, the decline is a vital aspect of MoR. I would see significance in the facts, first, that it is the race of heroes which breaks the decline; second, that this race is an ambivalent race, being divided into two contrasting groups (166 τοὺς μέν, 167 τοῖς δέ); and third, that this race is the race immediately preceding the present race. The heroes are our immediate

45 Cf. A. Heubeck, 'Mythologische Vorstellungen des Alten Orients im archaischen Griechentum', *Gymnasium* 68 (1955), pp. 508–25, at p. 510.
46 Rosenmeyer, 'Hesiod and historiography', pp. 270–1, esp. p. 271: 'even if we disregard the heroic age, the other four γένη do not, contrary to the popular assumption, present us with a steady decline'; Fontenrose, 'Work, justice', p. 8; Sourvinou-Inwood, 'Myth of the five races', p. 3 and 17 nn. 22–3, 9, 15: 'this myth is not structured by strict linear logic but by a more complex multivocal schema'; Most, 'Hesiod's myth', p. 108, cf. p. 120.
47 It is sometimes argued that, before the heroes, the decline is broken by the bronze race, who are said just to be 'nothing like' the silver race (*WD* 144), but not 'worse' than them: cf. Fontenrose, 'Work, justice', p. 8; Rudhardt, 'Le mythe hésiodique', p. 254; C. W. Querbach, 'Hesiod's myth of the four races', *CJ* 81 (1985), pp. 1–12, at p. 3; Sourvinou-Inwood, 'Myth of the five races', p. 3; Most, 'Hesiod's myth', p. 108. But *WD* 144 probably intends inferiority, not just difference. The silver race had similarly been said to be unlike the golden race ('like the golden race in neither body nor mind', *WD* 129) and is explicitly said to be 'much worse' than the golden race (*WD* 127). *WD* 144 is probably an abbreviated form of the same statement.
48 Cf. M. Heath, 'Hesiod's didactic poetry', *CQ* 35 (1985), pp. 245–63, at p. 248 n. 10; Most, 'Hesiod's myth', p. 120. Differently, West, *Hesiod: Works and Days*, p. 174: 'the Heroes have been inserted . . . into a system of four metallic races'; J. Griffin, 'Greek myth and Hesiod', in J. Boardman, J. Griffin and O. Murray (eds), *The Oxford History of the Classical World* (Oxford: Oxford University Press, 1986), pp. 78–98, at p. 96.

predecessors on the earth and are our most pressing moral exemplars; our race, like theirs, is ambivalent and has a chance of stemming the decline.[49] The 'fortunate' heroes, those hailed ὄλβιοι ἥρωες in *WD* 172, stem the decline by dint of recapturing, after their death, the conditions enjoyed by the golden race (170 echoes 112; 172–3 echoes 117; the interpolated 173a echoes 111). The notion that decline is not inevitable, that alternative fates are possible, is an important idea that emerges also from other parts of the poem, especially the so-called 'diptych of the Just and the Unjust City' (*WD* 225–47).

The diptych illustrates in a way MoR had not prepared us for the ambivalence of the present (iron) race. Verbal and thematic echoes reveal this passage to be in a continuing dialectic with MoR. The conditions enjoyed by the citizens of the Just City evoke those enjoyed both by the men of the golden race and, posthumously, by the 'fortunate' heroes on the isles of the blessed (231 echoes 115; 236 echoes 116–17; 237 echoes both 117 and 172–3).[50] The plight of the citizens of the Unjust City evokes that of the heroes in their more negative aspects: annihilation in warfare or on the sea (*WD* 246–7, cf. 161–5). A similar passage that illustrates the ambivalence of the present race is *WD* 280–5, which we may for convenience call the 'syncrisis of the just man and the unjust man'. This passage describes Zeus

49 Cf. Koenen, 'Greece, the Near East and Egypt', p. 8: 'the paradigm of the heroic age exemplifies the possibility of reversal, for, at that time, humankind was better and more just than in the previous ages (δικαιότερον καὶ ἄρειον, 158). The deterioration in the other series of ages is underscored by the descending value of the metals – gold, silver, bronze, and iron . . . Because the age of heroes reverses this deterioration and is not named after a metal, it is not fully integrated into the rest of the series and signals the possibility of a return to the better.' Most, 'Hesiod's myth', p. 119: 'the heroes hold out to us paradigms of good and bad behaviour in which our own possibilities for success or failure are spelled out in a grander and more intelligible form. They share our biological constitution and our moral chances in a way that the golden, silver, and bronze men did not . . . We may see in them models of moral choice which we can choose to emulate or to avoid.' Rudhardt, 'Le mythe hésiodique', p. 256: 'A la différence de toutes les races antérieures, la race héroïque et la race de fer sont formées d'individus différenciés, appelés chacun d'un nom propre, et qui n'ont pas tous de pareilles qualités et de pareils défauts'; cf. p. 258. Currie, 'Heroes and holy men', pp. 169–71.

50 Fontenrose, 'Work, justice', p. 15: 'The truth is that men through justice and work can improve their condition. The righteous city has much of the happiness and abundance of the golden age'; J.-P. Vernant, 'Hesiod's myth of the races: An essay in structural analysis', in Vernant, *Myth and Thought Among the Greeks*, tr. of *Mythe et pensée chez les Grecs* (London and Boston: Routledge and Kegan Paul, 1983), pp. 3–32, at pp. 10 and 28 n. 39; Knox, 'Work and justice', pp. 15–16; Querbach, 'Hesiod's myth', p. 6; P. Rousseau, 'Instruire Persès: Notes sur l'ouverture des *Travaux* d'Hésiode', in F. Blaise, P. Judet de La Combe and P. Rousseau (eds), *Le métier du mythe: Lecture d'Hésiode* (Lille: Presses Universitaires du Septentrion, 1996), pp. 93–167, at p. 156 n. 163; Calame, 'Succession des âges', p. 89. Currie, 'Heroes and holy men', p. 170.

giving prosperity and a flourishing progeny to the just man, while the progeny of the unjust man is blighted.[51]

Another passage of *WD* which importantly continues the dialectic with MoR is the 'nautilia' (618–94, esp. 632–62). Here, in the context of his sea-passage from Aulis to Chalcis, the narrator mentions the 'Achaeans' who once sailed from Greece to Troy (*WD* 651–3). These Achaeans are, of course, identical with the heroes of MoR whom war 'brought in their ships over the great expanse of sea to Troy for the sake of fair-haired Helen' (*WD* 164–5). The Amphidamas for whose funeral games the narrator crossed from Aulis to Euboea was, according to Plutarch (*Sept. sap. conv.* 153F), a casualty of the Lelantine War, a contemporary conflict which, if any, might be seen as a latter-day Trojan War (compare the remarks of Archilochus, fr. 3 West, and Thucydides, 1.15.3); the epithet δαΐφρονος (*WD* 654) may hint at his warrior status. Amphidamas' funeral games with their lavish prizes (*WD* 655–6) evoke a heroic model, most obviously Patroklos' funeral games in the twenty-third book of the *Iliad*. Perhaps Amphidamas was even heroised, as other casualties of the Lelantine War may have been.[52] But if Amphidamas is honourably approximated to the heroes, the narrator in this passage is, no less honourably, *contrasted* with the Achaeans. They sailed from Greece to Troy ('over a great expanse of sea') and were killed in war; he sailed (a voyage of some hundred yards) from Aulis to Euboea to triumph in a singing contest. There is, further, a strong contrast between the narrator and his own father. The latter sailed frequently (πλωΐζεσκ') for want of a good livelihood, and was given poverty by Zeus (*WD* 634, 638). By contrast the narrator has never sailed but once, when he was enriched with a tripod which he promptly reinvested in the economy of the sacred by dedicating it to the Muses, through whom he knows the mind of Zeus (*WD* 650–1, 661). The narrator – 'Hesiod'[53] – leads a life of self-sufficiency, exemption from sea-faring, and good relations with the gods. His life thus quietly evokes that of the men of the golden race. His life seems more straightforwardly positive in ethical terms than the largely positive but also somewhat ambivalent lives of the heroes and Amphidamas.

The preceding tells us something about Hesiod's view of human history. A first and important point to be made concerns Hesiod's way of discoursing about the past (rather than just his view of the

---

51 Cf. Gagné, 'Invisible kin', p. 11.
52 B. G. F. Currie, *Pindar and the Cult of Heroes* (Oxford: Oxford University Press, 2005), p. 106.
53 It is *WD* 658–9, referencing *Th.* 22–34, where the narrator names himself as 'Hesiod', that justifies the identification of the narrator of *WD* as Hesiod.

past). MoR delivers not the definitive word, but a version of the 'truth', exaggerated for rhetorical effect, that is subject to qualification in other, later, parts of the poem. Hesiod's procedure here resembles that of Virgil, perhaps especially in his most Hesiodic work, the *Georgics* (though Virgil's tendency is to qualify an optimistic passage with pessimistic touches scattered throughout the poem, rather than to temper an initial pessimistic account with subsequent optimistic refinements).[54]

Second, reading MoR alongside the diptych and the nautilia shows MoR to have a crucial synchronic as well as a diachronic dimension. This important point has been emphasised by various scholars, notably J.-P. Vernant and J. Fontenrose.[55] The γένη, 'humankinds', represent not just past realities, but present possibilities. One could characterise MoR as a retrojection onto the past of possibilities in the present. 'History' under this guise appears not as an investigation into what the past was really like, but a reification (presentation as historical reality) of ethical alternatives available to us in our contemporary lives. This 'history' is a fictional construct whose purpose is to illuminate the present from an ethical standpoint. Not that this is *all* MoR is. There seems to be also, for instance, an irreducible diachronic-historical component, in the bronze–iron races, as I argued above. And there seems also to be a significant attempt to correlate the account with independently known mythical and cultic data (as we shall see below; only the bronze race, who depart the earth 'nameless', *WD* 154 νώνυμνοι, do not leave behind them palpable traces of their presence in the world).[56] But the synchronic reading is an important part of MoR, and it finds a resonance in Hesiod's ancient

---

54 E.g. D. O. Ross, *Virgil's Elements: Physics and Poetry in the Georgics* (Princeton: Princeton University Press, 1987), pp. 109–28; J. J. O'Hara, *Inconsistency in Roman Epic: Studies in Catullus, Lucretius, Vergil, Ovid and Lucan* (Cambridge: Cambridge University Press, 2007), pp. 83–4.

55 Cf. Fontenrose, 'Work, justice', p. 15: 'The myth is a paradigm, an exemplum of his argument, a synchronic scheme presented as history . . . There are silver, bronze, and iron men among his contemporaries – and there are some golden men too, though now they live under Zeus and have to work for their bread'; Matthiessen, 'Form und Funktion des Weltaltermythos bei Hesiod', p. 28; Rowe, 'Archaic thought', p. 134; Currie, 'Heroes and holy men', p. 169. MoR is analysed rather differently as synchronic not diachronic (as structural not genetic) by Vernant, 'Hesiod's myth of the races', esp. pp. 5–6; cf. V. Goldschmidt, 'Théologia', *REG* 63 (1950), pp. 20–42, at pp. 33–9.

56 Cf. Matthiessen, 'Form und Funktion', p. 27; Rudhardt, 'Le mythe hésiodique', p. 256; Querbach, 'Hesiod's myth', p. 3; Leclerc, 'Le mythe des races', p. 210; Sourvinou-Inwood, 'Myth of the five races', p. 8; Calame, 'Succession des âges', p. 79 and n. 22.

reception.[57] The poem as a whole shows us how to 'read' MoR, with at least two shifts of perspective. First, as we have already noted, what starts off as a diachronic account gets reinterpreted as a synchronic account. Second, there is a progressive narrowing of focus, whereby what was presented to begin with, in MoR, as a fate befalling a whole γένος indiscriminately (but with a distinction made for the heroes: *WD* 166–8) gets successively redefined: first, in the diptych, as the fate befalling one whole city-state (*WD* 240 ξύμπασα πόλις) but not another; second, in the 'syncrisis' and nautilia sections, as the fate befalling one individual but not another.[58] The progressive narrowing of focus means that the 'lesson' of 'history' is devolved onto us with increasing immediacy:[59] the conditions of our life are largely of our own making.[60] Even now the life of the golden race may be, to an extent, recoverable.[61]

57 Plat. *Crat.* 398a8–b1; Orph. fr. 216 Bernabé (Proclus in Plat. *Resp.* 2.74.26 Kroll); Isodorus *apud* Suda *s.v.* Σαραπίων. People of the present after their death likened to the golden race: Plat. *Rep.* 468e4–469a3; Heracl. 22 B63 D–K (C. H. Kahn, *The Art and Thought of Heraclitus* (Cambridge: Cambridge University Press, 1979), pp. 254–6, 261; T. M. Robinson, *Heraclitus: Fragments* (Toronto: University of Toronto Press, 1987), pp. 125–6). See Currie, 'Heroes and holy men', pp. 171 and n. 38, 191 n. 157.

58 In the 'syncrisis' the individuals are left indefinite (τὶς, ὃς δέ κε), but named in the nautilia (the narrator 'Hesiod' versus his father and Amphidamas).

59 Cf. Gagné, 'Invisible kin', p. 13: 'The degressive sequence Race–City–Family is clear.'

60 Fontenrose, 'Work, justice', pp. 15–16: 'when rulers and citizens are just, Zeus and the gods prosper their cities, and they come near to the happy existence of the golden men and of the heroes in the Blessed Isles (225–37). In Hesiod's age, as distinct from the iron age of myth, men can live this happier life, if they follow the ordinance of work and the way of justice.' Rudhardt, 'Le mythe hésiodique', p. 261: 'les hommes sont aujourd'hui responsables de leur propre destin. Le malheur qui les accable résulte de leurs propres fautes.' Leclerc, 'Le mythe des races', p. 220: 'Suspendus entre l'âge antérieur, qui offre un modèle de justice et une promesse de récompense, et l'âge postérieur, qui en est l'inverse exact, les auditeurs d'Hésiode doivent choisir. La curieuse expression "plût au ciel que je fusse ou mort plus tôt ou né plus tard" [*WD* 174–5] pourrait témoigner, plutôt que d'une conception cyclique du temps, de la confiance d'Hésiode dans un avenir qui, "hommes et dieux ayant même origine" [cf. *WD* 108], reste ouvert à des évolutions positives'; ibid.: 'Il y a ce qui nous échappe: l'état dans lequel nous a mis l'évolution du monde voulue par les dieux; il y a ce qui nous revient: la manière dont nous disposons de cet état est de notre responsabilité.' Cf. Sourvinou-Inwood, 'Myth of the five races', pp. 10–11, 16 (downward movement and an upward movement). Cf. G. W. Most, *Hesiod: Theogony, Works and Days, Testimonia* (Loeb Classical Library; Cambridge, MA: Harvard University Press, 2006), p. xli. Currie, 'Heroes and holy men', p. 169.

61 N. Brout, 'La mauve ou l'asphodèle ou Comment manger pour s'élever au-dessus de la condition humaine', *DHA* 29/2 (2003), pp. 97–108; Currie, 'Heroes and holy men', pp. 165–85.

CONFRONTATION OF MoR WITH THE MYTH OF
PROMETHEUS AND PANDORA

A key question in evaluating MoR as a proto-historical account is
what claim to truth it makes. This question is raised in particular by
the *Wahrheitsanspruch* at the beginning of each Hesiodic poem (*WD*
10, *Th.* 26–8).[62] Rosenmeyer surely exaggerates Hesiod's commitment to truth when he writes of 'Hesiod's striking insistence on the
importance of his own person and on the veracity of his account; an
insistence which is equalled by Hecataeus later on . . . Hesiod, in his
emphasis on the truth, sets himself apart from the lies, the illusory
beauty and polish of the epic poetry . . . Truth is the chief objective
of Hesiod's enterprise.'[63] Others, for instance Leclerc, have seen it as
a consciously *fictional* discourse.[64] It is reasonable to be suspicious
of attempts to hive off MoR from other parts of the narrative of the
Erga, such as the myth of Prometheus and Pandora and the fable of
the hawk and the nightingale, and claim a quite special veridical status
for MoR.[65]

The relationship between MoR and the myth of Prometheus and
Pandora (*WD* 48–105; henceforth PromPand) is particularly important for the question of what kind of narrative about the past each is.
For if the two narratives straightforwardly conflict, it would appear
that Hesiod cannot be in the business of uncovering historical truth.[66]
The two narratives are often seen as simply incompatible.[67] But
equally it is hard not to be struck by the thematic links that can be

---

62 *Th.* 26–8 is considered in the context of the development towards historiography
    by Bertelli, 'Hecataeus', p. 81.
63 Rosenmeyer, 'Hesiod and historiography', p. 261.
64 Cf. Leclerc, 'Le mythe des races', pp. 220, 221 (MoR has the 'statut de récit
    fictif assumé comme tel par le poète'). Cf. West, *Hesiod: Works and Days*, p. 177:
    'Hesiod presents the story not as absolute truth but as something that people tell,
    worth serious attention.'
65 Rosenmeyer, 'Hesiod and historiography', p. 269: 'whereas the Pandora story
    is myth, the Five Ages is history' (Stewart, 'Hesiod and history', on the other
    hand, regards the myth of Prometheus and Pandora as a step towards historical
    analysis). Criticized, Rowe, 'Archaic thought', pp. 132–3.
66 Rowe, 'Archaic thought', p. 133: 'the charge of inconsistency goes deeper: if
    Hesiod's purpose is to explain, he must choose between the explanations offered.
    In so far as he does not, he is neither Fränkel's philosopher nor Rosenmeyer's
    historian.' Sourvinou-Inwood, 'Myth of the five races', p. 14: 'if the audience saw
    the two myths as contradicting each other, they would have perceived them as
    mutually falsifying'. Smith, 'History and the individual', p. 151.
67 Fontenrose, 'Work, justice', p. 2; West, *Hesiod: Works and Days*, p. 172; S.
    A. Nelson, *God and the Land: The Metaphysics of Farming in Hesiod and Vergil*
    (New York and Oxford: Oxford University Press, 1998), pp. 68 and 190 n. 42.

discovered between them.[68] The following six links deserve attention. (1) In PromPand during Zeus' reign a 'separation' (or 'settlement') occurred between gods and men (*Th*. 535), implying that previously they existed on a more equal footing; in MoR during Kronos' reign men lived 'as gods' (*WD* 111–12). (2) In PromPand Prometheus swindled Zeus at a *sacrifice* (*Th*. 538–41); in MoR the silver race was unwilling to *sacrifice* to the gods (*WD* 135–6). (3) In PromPand *Zeus grew angry* at Prometheus' deception (*WD* 47); in MoR *Zeus grew angry* at the silver race (*WD* 138). (4) In PromPand *Zeus hid* fire from men (*WD* 50, cf. 47, 42);[69] in MoR *Zeus hid* the silver race (*WD* 138). (5) At the end of PromPand, countless 'banes' (λυγρά, substantive) are dispersed among men by Pandora's action, and only the personified Elpis remains in the jar (*WD* 94–104); at the end of MoR, personified Zelos accompanies all men while personified Aidos and Nemesis abandon men, and 'baneful pains' (λυγρά, adjective) are left for men (*WD* 195–201). (6) In PromPand the ambivalence of woman (*WD* 57, but cf. 702–5) and of Elpis (*WD* 96–9)[70] is matched in MoR by the ambivalence of the heroes (*WD* 166–8) and of the iron race (*WD* 179);[71] in each case terms initially presumed to be wholly negative turn out to be at least potentially or partially positive. Undoubtedly, it is possible to add to or subtract from this list of correspondences; but in general their weight renders problematic the view stated baldly by M. L. West that Hesiod 'presents [the Myth of Ages] simply as ἕτερος λόγος and does not attempt to reconcile it with the Prometheus-Pandora myth, with which it is in fact incompatible'.[72] Perhaps we should be struck as much by the congruence between these accounts as by their incongruity, or more so (see further below).[73]

---

68 Cf. Rudhardt, 'Le mythe hésiodique', pp. 273–7.
69 Rudhardt, 'Le mythe hésiodique', p. 273 and n. 96 on the equivalence between πῦρ and βίος.
70 E.g. Buxton, *Imaginary Greece*, pp. 212–13.
71 I take it that *WD* 179 ἀλλ' ἔμπης καὶ τοῖσι μεμείξεται ἐσθλὰ κακοῖσι means 'for these men too [*sc.* the men of the iron race] good things will be mixed with bad'. The verse invites us to compare the iron with the golden race, of whom it was said 'they had all good things', 'with many good things' (115–16 ἐσθλὰ δὲ πάντα / τοῖσιν ἔην, 119 σὺν ἐσθλοῖσιν πολέεσσιν). Differently, Woodard, 'Hesiod and Greek myth', pp. 137–47, who argues that at *WD* 179 and at Theogn. 192 σὺν γὰρ μίσγεται ἐσθλὰ κακοῖσι the nouns γένεα, γένεσσι should be understood with the respective adjectives.
72 West, *Hesiod: Works and Days*, p. 172. Cf. Buxton, *Imaginary Greece*, p. 178: 'there is no way in which the two stories can be exactly integrated with one another'.
73 Rudhardt, 'Le mythe hésiodique', p. 262: 'Même si le poète n'établit point entre eux de relations systematiques, ces mythes ne sont donc pas contradictoire à ses yeux; leurs significations se complètent pour fonder l'enseignement qu'il donne à Persès'. Cf. Querbach, 'Hesiod's myth', p. 9 and n. 24.

Attempts to explain the juxtaposition of contradictory accounts of the past in PromPand and MoR may take us down various avenues.

One approach is to see each of the two accounts as having truth-values, and incompatible ones; if one is true, the other is false (though both could of course be false). It is because the truth-value of each is *unclear* that Hesiod has determined to give us both: either one *could* be true. The juxtaposition of PromPand and MoR thus invites comparison with Herodotus' inclusion of alternative and mutually exclusive *logoi*: Hesiod feels in such a case bound to λέγειν τὰ λεγόμενα but not committed to any view regarding their truth or falsity (cf. Hdt. 7.152.3). This is the approach of Rosenmeyer to the collocation of PromPand and MoR.[74] Hesiod would then operate as a historian, though not so much for his view of the past as for his respect for others' views of the past. A historian may properly be interested in people's beliefs as historical data in their own right.[75] But it is hard to accept that Hesiod 'decided not to select', but just report, what had been said by others on human history.[76] We have seen that both Hesiodic accounts resonate with the thematic interests of *WD*. Both PromPand and MoR are thus redolent of authorial selection, manipulation, interpretation. And in fact just the same can be said of Herodotus' inclusion in his narrative of 'uncriticised variants'. Here too we have in all likelihood not a decision not to select, not abstention from interpretation, but rather a decision to include at least one version that the historian knows must be false precisely for its thematic contribution to the wider narrative.[77]

74 Rosenmeyer, 'Hesiod and historiography', p. 268: 'Hesiod . . . tries to account for the social and moral situation of his own world. To do this, he collects a certain class of data and arranges them to fit the aetiological and moral purposes of his design. The data with which he is concerned are what Herodotus calls τὰ λεγόμενα. In trying to arrange the λεγόμενα, he finds he has more material than was needed for his objective, and what is more, some of his material is contradictory. His task then is twofold; first, he must reconcile conflicting τὰ λεγόμενα, and second, he must decide which of them to select, or whether to select at all. Herodotus, in similar moments of quandary, often decided not to select . . . Over against the proud rationalism of Hecataeus, ever ready to select, remodel, or reject, Herodotus introduces the patient resignation of the empiricist who knows that the truth is neither simple nor one-sided . . . Some of that same spirit may be seen in Hesiod.'
75 D. Lateiner, *The Historical Method of Herodotus* (Toronto, Buffalo and London: University of Toronto Press, 1989), p. 77: 'The historian finds cultural meaning and historical significance even in fictions.'
76 Quotation from Rosenmeyer, 'Hesiod and historiography', p. 268 (see above for full context).
77 S. Flory, *The Archaic Smile of Herodotus* (Detroit: Wayne State University Press, 1987), p. 63: 'At times [Herodotus] even says explicitly that he feels obligated to give all possible versions . . . Many readers of Herodotus have believed that such passages amount to a pledge by the author to give us, to the best of his ability, *all* the evidence: every version of every story and every fact he ever heard . . . We cannot, I believe, accept such statements uncritically'; p. 67: 'What influences

A second approach is to deny PromPand and MoR truth-values in that sense. Though disguised as an account of the past, each is really concerned to convey ever-present moral truths. *Prima facie* descriptive and past-tense narratives, they are in fact protreptics to piety and justice in the present and future. This in essence is the approach of Rowe and Buxton, of whom the latter compares the conflict between PromPand and MoR with the situation presented by conflicting proverbs ('many hands make light work', but 'too many cooks spoil the broth').[78] If Hesiod's interests are unlike those of a historian or scientist, if he does not purport to describe and explain the real world as they do, then his attitude to inconsistency can be unlike theirs. This is not the place to discuss whether proverbs as a system do or do not tolerate contradiction.[79] One disconcerting consequence of this view

Herodotus to include some false versions and not others? Despite the commonly held view that he is unable to resist any really good story, Herodotus' false versions of events almost always contain identifiable themes that are significant in the *Histories* as a whole'; p. 68: 'two versions of a story exist, neither is contradicted by material evidence, but both contain themes that interest Herodotus. In this case Herodotus tells both versions without discrimination or disclaimer.'

78 Rowe, 'Archaic thought', p. 134: '[Hesiod] proceeds as he does in the case of the myths of Prometheus and Pandora and the Five Races, and elsewhere, not because of a lack of capacity on his part, or of the "primitiveness" of his habits of thought, but rather because of the nature of his fundamental preoccupations: it is that in the end the business of explanation, in the sense of looking for causes, matters rather less to him than reflection of a different sort, and especially of a moralising sort'; cf. Rowe, *Essential Hesiod* (Bristol: Bristol Classical Press, 1978), p. 7: 'It is typical of Hesiod's methods of composition generally . . . that he works in *sections* . . . What is particularly interesting is that even adjoining sections are often developed independently of each other, so that they say things which seem either incompatible, or at least difficult to reconcile . . . [This habit of Hesiod's of composing in what are almost watertight, self-contained units] has something to do with the absence from Hesiod of a clear distinction between what is *factual* and what is *non-factual*. Questions of compatibility worry us because of our obsession with the idea that there is, ideally, only a single proper way of describing what is the case or was the case; and Hesiod does not share this obsession.' Buxton, *Imaginary Greece*, pp. 178–9: 'What concerns us here is . . . the fact that immediately after the Prometheus/Pandora explanation of why things are so rough nowadays comes a story which is explicitly said by Hesiod to be a *different* one . . . The point to note is that there is no way in which the two stories can be exactly integrated with one another . . . To accuse Hesiod of inconsistency, of being unable to sustain a logical argument, would be wholly to misunderstand him. He *signals* the fact that the two stories are different. The contrast between past and present is there in each case, but is worked out in different ways, first with an emphasis on guile and concealment, then through a set of variations on the opposition between fair dealing and aggressive violence. The compatibility of alternatives is basic to Greek mythology. We come back to the question of belief, and of proverbs. "Look at it this way; or if you like, look at it *this* way"'; cf. pp. 163–4.

79 Cf. T. J. Morgan, *Popular Morality in the Early Roman Empire* (Cambridge: Cambridge University Press, 2007), p. 15, taking a different view from Buxton, *Imaginary Greece*, pp. 163–4.

is that it risks leaving too little difference between MoR and the fable (*WD* 202–12), a moralising narrative with no pretensions to describe the real world (as MoR, in places, apparently does have). Can we be happy to accord MoR *just* the status of a parable?[80] We may also hesitate in an early Greek context to contrast a description of the real world that leads to scientific (historical or physical) explanations of the world's processes with an account that purports (at least) to be of the real world but leads to the formulation of moral truths. The difficulty here is that the physical and historical investigations of Anaximander and Herodotus themselves ultimately serve to demonstrate the operation in the physical and human worlds of *dikē* and *tisis*: two distinctly moral, and very Hesiodic, concepts.[81] An overriding concern with moral principles that underlie the working of the world does not clearly distinguish Hesiod from the early Greek scientist or historian.[82]

A third approach is to take the ensemble 'PromPand+MoR' as self-refuting in so far as some of its parts contradict one another, but as self-validating in so far as other of its parts agree. In this way the juxtaposition of the two accounts can reveal the truth as much as the fiction. It is the coincidence in the 'substrate' of PromPand and MoR that will indicate what should count as 'true'.[83] Guided by Hesiod's two contiguous accounts we (Hesiod's audience) may construct our own narrative of human history approximately as follows: mankind has had a very long history; men were once much closer to the gods; life for man was once much better than it is now; while there has been a succession of cultural and technological developments, there has also been in tandem with these an ethical deterioration and an increasing alienation of man from the gods; yet in the past that deterioration and alienation could be arrested, and so (and here comes the 'lesson' of history) it can be arrested again in the present and the future. Such a procedure of including mutually self-refuting accounts that are also

---

80 Cf. Smith, 'History and the individual', pp. 151–2.
81 Anaxim. 12 B1 D–K (cf. Heracl. 22 B94 D–K); Hdt. 3.126.1, 4.205, 6.84.3, 8.105, etc.. Cf. Lateiner, *Historical Method*, pp. 203–4 '[In Anaximander] the physical universe is expressed in moral or judicial terms by an Ionian "scientist"; history is similarly conceived by the Ionian historian.'
82 Cf. Rowe, 'Archaic thought', p. 134 (cited above, n. 2), for the contrast between Hesiod on the one hand and Anaximander and Herodotus on the other.
83 Cf. in general G. S. Kirk, 'On defining myths', in E. N. Lee, A. P. D. Mourelatos and R. M. Rorty (eds), *Exegesis and Argument: Studies in Greek Philosophy Presented to Gregory Vlastos* (Assen: Van Gorcum, 1973), pp. 61–9, at p. 66 on the ὑποκείμενον ('substrate') of a myth, the 'narrative structure' that persists through retelling. This is comparable with the 'deep structure' discerned by structuralist-formalist critics of myth (cf. E. Csapo, *Theories of Mythology* (Malden, MA: Blackwell, 2005), pp. 190–201).

self-validating should not be assumed to be intrinsically unhistorical. Herodotus can be held to have done something very similar: to have included unreconciled, incompatible alternatives in his narrative in order that their agreement on certain key points might highlight what is meant to stand as historical fact.[84] This approach to PromPand and MoR presupposes that it is possible, indeed necessary, to separate an untrue 'casing' from a true 'core' within each of PromPand and MoR.[85] Then Hesiod would implicitly have assumed something like what the fifth-century mythographers assumed in their rationalisation of myth, for example Hecataeus (frr. 26–7 Fowler) or Herodotus himself (2.55–7).[86] The shared assumption is that there is an underlying truth to a mythical account that can be freed by a critical mind from the distortions worked on it by successive story-tellers' embellishments. The difference is that the mythographer does the thinking for us and sets out prosaically what he thinks the truth is; Hesiod with a poet's indirectness requires us to do the thinking for ourselves. This approach to the problem of PromPand and MoR, unlike the last, takes Hesiod to be *implying* a discourse with truth-values: there *are* facts about the world implied in this narrative, but Hesiod leaves us to dig and sift them ourselves. Or *is* this indirectness in fact distinctively a poet's *modus operandi*, rather than a historian's? Herodotus once

84 Flory, *Archaic Smile*, p. 70: 'Often Herodotus tells a story in two or more variants without any comment about their relative truth or falsity. Is he reluctant or for some reason unable to make a judgment? Yet these variant versions rarely present clearly opposed points of view or important contradictions but actually confirm a single point of view he wishes to establish'; p. 70: 'Herodotus gives two versions of how [Cambyses' wife] angers her husband . . . [3.32]. Both versions, and that is their purpose, make a similar point about Cambyses' violent and impetuous character . . . This fact Herodotus does not question. The effect of his alternative stories about Cambyses is not to introduce a note of caution or uncertainty about what actually happened, but just the opposite. He emphasizes Cambyses' stupidity and cruelty even more intensely through two stories with a similar point.'
85 Somewhat in this vein Leclerc, 'Le mythe des races', pp. 223–4, distinguishes between 'coffrage' and 'l'essentiel' of MoR. Cf. Stewart, 'Hesiod and history', p. 44: 'Obviously Hesiod is not interested in the literal details of the two stories but in their general agreement on "ideological" matters.' This route is rejected by Rowe, 'Archaic thought', p. 132: 'They [*sc.* PromPand and MoR] follow the same broad pattern, in the shape of the idea of man's fall from an original and better state. But this cannot by itself be the common truth Hesiod is trying to convey, since if it were, we should have to treat the myths as such simply as *fictional elaborations* of a basic theme; and this they cannot be, unless the Prometheus episode in the *Theogony* is fiction too – and that will take the rest of the *Theogony* with it. But how can the *Theogony* be fiction? It bears all the marks of serious theology.'
86 The methods of Hesiod and Hecataeus are contrasted rather than compared by Bertelli, 'Hecataeus', pp. 82–3; V. Pirenne-Delforge, 'Under which conditions did the Greeks "believe" in their myths? The religious criteria of adherence', in U. Dill and C. Walde (eds), *Antike Mythen: Medien, Transformationen und Konstruktionen* (Berlin and New York: de Gruyter, 2009), pp. 38–54, at p. 48.

again can be argued to do something very similar, to work his readers similarly hard.[87]

Probably none of these approaches to the problem of PromPand and MoR can fully satisfy. Yet it is a merit of the third is that it takes seriously the presence of striking and extensive correspondences between PromPand and MoR. Two things in all this are worth emphasising. First, Hesiod surely juxtaposes PromPand and MoR with some understanding of his own as to how they cohere, but that understanding remains entirely implicit: we can do no more than impute an understanding to him. And second, the size of the gap that we perceive between Hesiod and Herodotus depends on how we choose to nuance our conception not just of Hesiod's but also of Herodotus' historiographical method.

CONFRONTATION OF MoR WITH A NEAR EASTERN MYTH OF RACES

Let us leave for a moment the question of the relationship and compatibility of MoR and PromPand and consider a parallel question: the relationship and compatibility of MoR and the putative Near Eastern myth that is often claimed as Hesiod's 'source'.[88] It must first be admitted that Near Eastern origins of MoR are not universally acknowledged. MoR has variously been seen as Hesiod's own extrapolation from the Greek epic tradition, an Indo-European inheritance, and simply an instance of a very ancient and widespread theme.[89] The

---

87 Lateiner, *Historical Method*, p. 164: 'Explicit, authorial evaluation and analysis are subordinated to the presentation of additional stories with similar issues'; p. 167: 'Patterns . . . occur and recur in order to guide the reader through the maze of historical data and to lead him to an interpretation lurking in the text, the intellectual result of a vast and obscure sorting process on the author's part.' E. Baragwanath, *Motivation and Narrative in Herodotus* (Oxford: Oxford University Press, 2008), p. 33: 'Herodotus' narrative technique appears to *require* attentive and perceptive readers, who may sense the subtleties and complexities of his account, and even develop them'; p. 126 'readers frequently suspect that the alternatives are not mutually exclusive, but rather that each of the two has played some part in precipitating the outcome, even though the narrative presents them as alternatives.'
88 So esp. West, *Hesiod: Works and Days*, pp. 176–7; West, *The East Face of Helicon: West Asiatic Elements in Greek Poetry and Myth* (Oxford: Oxford University Press, 1997), pp. 312–19.
89 An extrapolation from native Greek epic tradition: Most, 'Hesiod's myth', pp. 120–3. An Indo-European inheritance: Woodard, 'Hesiod and Greek myth', pp. 124–48 (attaching much weight to a questionable interpretation of *WD* 179; see above). An ancient and widespread motif: I. C. Rutherford, 'Hesiod and the literary traditions of the Near East', in F. Montanari, A. Rengakos and C. Tsagalis (eds), *Brill's Companion to Hesiod* (Leiden and Boston: Brill, 2009), pp. 9–35, at pp. 20–2 (differently, Gatz, *Weltalter, goldene Zeit*, p. 11; cf. Woodard, 'Hesiod and Greek myth', p. 127, text to n. 160).

extant Indo-European parallels for MoR from Sanskrit (*Mahābhārata* 3.148, 3.187) and Pahlavi texts (*Vahman Yašt*; *Dēnkard*) are arguably more impressive than the extant parallels in texts from the Near East (e.g. Old Testament, Daniel 2:32–6, 39–41).[90] Nevertheless Near Eastern influence perhaps remains the most reasonable assumption.[91] Near Eastern influence is generally granted for the succession myth of the *Theogony*[92] and it seems the conception of *Works and Days* as a whole must be allowed a Near Eastern pedigree.[93] Moreover, Hesiod's handling of the MoR narrative, and of the succession myth, suggests to me 'horizontal' rather than 'vertical' transmission and a relatively recent import rather than an ancient inheritance.[94] That question cannot be settled here, if indeed anywhere. Suffice it to say that the assumption of Near Eastern inspiration for MoR is viable enough, though unproven, for its consequences to be worth exploring.

Greek thinking about human (pre)history must always have received a jolt when confronted with Near Eastern traditions.[95] Greek heroic genealogies do not extend back more than a few generations before the Trojan War, at which point human ancestors peter out and divine ancestors take over.[96] By contrast, Herodotus heard Egyptian priests indicate kings going back 341 generations, i.e. 11,340 years, before the reign of the early seventh-century 'Sethos' (Hdt. 2.142.1). The situation in Sumer was even more extreme. 'Sometime early in the second millennium BC, let us say *ca.* 1800, a scribe in the temple of Isin compiled a list of all the kings who had ruled over Sumer. Supporting

---

90 Woodard, 'Hesiod and Greek myth', pp. 115–18.
91 For reasons reiterated by M. L. West, *Indo-European Poetry and Myth* (Oxford: Oxford University Press, 2007), p. 23. Differently, Woodard, 'Hesiod and Greek myth', p. 124.
92 West, *East Face of Helicon*, pp. 276–86; Woodard, 'Hesiod and Greek myth', pp. 92–104; Rutherford, 'Hesiod and the literary traditions', pp. 22–35. Differently, R. Mondi, 'Greek mythic thought in the light of the Near East', in L. Edmunds (ed.), *Approaches to Greek Myth* (Baltimore and London: Johns Hopkins University Press, 1990), pp. 141–98, at pp. 151–7.
93 West, *East Face of Helicon*, pp. 306–33; Rutherford, 'Hesiod and the literary traditions', pp. 17–19; Woodard, 'Hesiod and Greek myth', p. 108.
94 M. L. West, 'The rise of the Greek epic', *JHS* 108 (1988), pp. 151–72, at p. 170, would see in the *Iliad*'s reception of Near Eastern motifs 'a freshness and vividness . . . which suggests that it is comparatively modern material'; and I would see the same in these two Hesiodic narratives. On 'vertical' and 'horizontal transmission', cf. West, *Indo-European Poetry and Myth*, pp. 19–24.
95 A. Dihle, *Hellas und der Orient: Phasen wechselzeitiger Rezeption* (Berlin and New York: de Gruyter, 2009), pp. 12–13, mentions 'das Alter der "barbarischen" Überlieferung' as one of three things that especially amazed the Greeks about the civilisations of the Near East (the other two being the Egyptians' monumental buildings and the importance of religion in their daily life); cf. p. 58.
96 Cf. West, *Hesiodic Catalogue of Women*, pp. 173–82; J. Hall, *Ethnic Identity in Greek Antiquity* (Cambridge: Cambridge University Press, 1997), pp. 79–85.

himself upon archives of hoary antiquity, this priest began his story 273,444 years, three months, and three and a half days before his own time.'[97] Greek narratives of the classical period themselves highlighted the problem. When Hecataeus traced his own genealogy back sixteen generations to a divine ancestor for the benefit of priests of Amun in Egyptian Thebes, the priests reciprocated with their own account of 345 preceding human generations (Hdt. 2.143.4).[98] When Solon asked the most experienced of the Egyptian priests about 'ancient history' (τὰ παλαιά) he discovered that he, like all the other Greeks, was clueless: he told them the myths of Phoroneus and Niobe, Deukalion and Pyrrha and rehearsed the generations starting from them, only to get from an elderly Egyptian priest the rejoinder, 'You Greeks are always children . . . You are all young in your souls'; for their own historical records went back 8,000 years (Plat. *Tim.* 22a–b, 23e). The huge disparity in chronological perspectives presented a major challenge for any Greek who wished to opine on the past and who was acquainted with Near Eastern traditions. It is plausible that Hesiod in MoR was exercised by the problem of chronological disparity arising from the confrontation of Greek with Near Eastern traditions, and that Hesiod's way of dealing with that problem resembles that of the 'Father of History' in a well-known passage.

Herodotus in his second book describes becoming acquainted in Egypt, Tyre and Thasos with a god whom he had no hesitation in identifying with the Greek Herakles but whom he found persistently assigned a date of birth far earlier than the Greek Herakles, by a margin of up to 16 millennia (2.43–4)![99] In the face of this cross-cultural data Herodotus makes two noteworthy assumptions: first, that a Greek, an Egyptian and a Phoenician divine figure are to be identified with each other;[100] second, that the truth of the matter is recoverable ('the current inquiries show clearly that Herakles is an ancient god', 2.44.5). Herodotus does not, here, take the relativist route, à la Xenophanes ('for the Greeks Herakles is so-and-so, for

---

97 J. M. Sasson, 'Some literary motifs in the composition of the Gilgamesh epic', *Studies in Philology* 69 (1972), pp. 259–79, at p. 259. For the Sumerian king list, see T. Jacobsen, *The Sumerian King List* (*Assyriological Studies* 11; Chicago: University of Chicago Press, 1939).

98 See I. S. Moyer, 'Herodotus and an Egyptian mirage: The genealogies of the Theban priests', *JHS* 122 (2002), pp. 70–90.

99 Cf. P. Veyne, *Did the Greeks Believe in Their Myths? An Essay on the Constitutive Imagination*, tr. P. Wissing (Chicago and London: University of Chicago Press, 1988), pp. 32–3; Moyer, 'Herodotus', pp. 85–6. Cf. Hdt. 2.145–6.

100 On the identification of non-Greek with Greek deities, cf. T. Harrison, *Divinity and History: The Religion of Herodotus* (Oxford: Oxford University Press, 2000), pp. 208–22.

the Egyptians so-and-so, for the Phoenicians so-and-so; the truth is not to be found in any of these'), although he is evidently acquainted with that route (cf. 3.38.1–4).[101] Here the assumption is rather that both Greek and eastern traditions are truth-bearing and that conflict between them must be resolved. Herodotus' solution involves a multiplication of categories: the positing of two Herakleses, one an Olympian god and son of Zeus, the other a hero and son of Amphitryon, of which the former, much the elder, can be identified with the Near Eastern Herakles.[102] And this solution finds confirmation for Herodotus in existing Greek cult practice, for there are Greeks who (properly, in his eyes) observed distinct forms of worship for the Olympian and the heroic Herakles (2.44.5).

A comparable procedure can be imputed to Hesiod in MoR. Here too there was an issue of chronological discrepancy. Greek epic tradition knew of only one race prior to the present race, the heroes or 'demigods' (earlier and later generations may be distinguished within the heroic race, and there may be 'earlier men', *Il.* 21.405, 23.332, 23.790; but there is no antecedent *race*: see above). By contrast the metallic scheme of the Near East (if Near Eastern it is) knows several races prior to the present race.[103] Hesiod, like Herodotus, seems willing to identify figures of Near Eastern tradition with figures of Greek tradition: he imaginatively associates the last two metallic races from the Near Eastern sequence gold–silver–bronze–iron with the users of bronze and of iron familiar to Greek conceptions through epic. Like Herodotus', Hesiod's solution involves a multiplication of existing categories: four earlier races of man instead of the traditional one. Finally, Hesiod's innovative analysis is justified, like Herodotus', by an appeal to the realities of Greek cult practice. Greek popular religion recognised a plethora of indeterminate divine beings of lesser status than the gods; Hesiod now recognises these as specific races of bygone men. The golden and silver races have a continuing presence in seventh-century cultic reality as respectively 'deities above the earth' (*daimones . . . epichthonioi*) and 'blessed mortals below the earth' (*hypochthonioi makares thnetoi*). The use of καλέονται (*WD* 141, 159) makes it clear that these are meant to correspond to categories of

---

101 Cf. S. Scullion, 'Herodotus and Greek religion', in C. Dewald and J. Marincola (eds), *The Cambridge Companion to Herodotus* (Cambridge: Cambridge University Press, 2006), pp. 192–208, at pp. 198–204.

102 On this expedient of postulating homonymies, cf. Veyne, *Did the Greeks?*, pp. 75 and 147 n. 154.

103 Koenen, 'Greece, the Near East and Egypt', pp. 24–5, disputes that the metallic scheme is Near Eastern.

deity recognizable to contemporaries (which is not to say that modern scholars can agree who made up these two groups).[104]

This construction of Hesiod's procedure in MoR attributes a notable common methodology to Hesiod and Herodotus. (1) There is the cognizance of alternative and discrepant accounts in Greece and the Near East as a result of wide data-gathering through Herodotean *historiē* and Hesiodic *polymathiē* (cf. Heracl. fr. 22 B40 D–K). (2) There is the identification of these accounts as competing accounts of the same situation and thus a need to resolve the conflict. (3) The resolution involves a multiplication of terms, so that identification of Greek with Near Eastern terms becomes possible while conflict is avoided. (4) The solution is justified by an appeal to the 'evidence' of tradition (cult and myth) to support the new terms introduced. (5) The traditional Greek chronology is radically revised and becomes vastly more extended.

This is of course a speculative account of how and why Hesiod may have approximated a Greek tradition of human history to a putative Near Eastern story of human history. It will be clear, however, how such an account parallels our thinking about how and why Hesiod may have approximated the narratives of PromPand and MoR. In each case we see a concern to establish coherence between alternative versions of the past. This concern for coherence *could* be interpreted as a concern for historical truth, but it is far from clear that it *must* or *should* be. The difficulty is that coherence is not just a criterion of truth but can also be a more purely aesthetic quality. When archaic Greek poets offered a new version of a traditional tale they typically took pains to make the new version cohere in certain key details with the old.[105] But it would be rash to assume they must have done so because of a conviction of the *historical truth* of the details retained.[106] This

---

104 Cf. Clay, *Hesiod's Cosmos*, pp. 89–90; Sourvinou-Inwood, 'Myth of the five races', pp. 6–9; Currie, 'Heroes and holy men', p. 168 n. 27.

105 See, famously, Pind. *O.* 1.26b–27, with J. G. Howie, 'The revision of myth in Pindar *Olympian* 1: The death and revival of Pelops (25–27; 36–66)', *PLLS* 4 (1983), pp. 277–313, at p. 288: 'The audience can . . . simultaneously see the roots of both the traditional myth and the revised version in these lines'; E. Krummen, *Pyrsos Hymnon: Festliche Gegenwart und mythisch-traditionelle Tradition als Voraussetzung einer Pindarinterpretation* (Berlin and New York: de Gruyter, 1990), p. 176: 'Pindar behält offensichtlich Struktur und Material des alten Mythos . . . vollständig, wie sie uberliefert sind, bei, gibt ihnen aber als ganzes eine neue Erklärung.' See Currie, *Pindar and the Cult of Heroes*, pp. 50–2; Currie, 'L'*Ode* 11 di Bacchilide: il mito delle Pretidi nella lirica corale, nella poesia epica e nella mitografia', in E. Cingano (ed.), *Tra panellenismo e tradizioni locali: Generi poetici e storiografia* (Alexandria: Edizioni dell'Orso, 2010), pp. 211–53, at pp. 222–3, for further examples and references.

106 The assumption is often made, e.g. W. Kullmann, 'Oral poetry theory and neo-analysis in Homeric research', *GRBS* 25 (1984), pp. 307–23, at p. 313: 'mythological characters were taken to be historical persons', 'respect for tradition is

mode of innovation in which the new was thoroughly integrated with the old is at once more satisfying and calls for more ingenuity than invention *ab initio*; such a mode of innovation seems to have become something like a 'rule of the game' for Greek poets.[107] It is obvious that there is an issue here of poetic virtuosity as well as any simple concern for historicity. There is without doubt a self-conscious display of poetic virtuosity in Hesiod's fitting of Greek traditions of human history to Near Eastern traditions of human history within MoR and in his fitting of MoR to PromPand (that poetic virtuosity is proclaimed in εὖ καὶ ἐπισταμένως, *WD* 107!). The question is whether the coherence for which Hesiod strives pertains solely to a closed poetic system or is meant further to argue a faithful fit with reality. Consider for a moment the uses made of etymology and aetiology, devices which may serve to connect a novel account with independently existing features of language or of the world. The mythographers and Herodotus employ etymology to confirm the veracity of an account; but Hesiod's etymologies (e.g. Pandora, *WD* 81–2; Aphrodite, *Th.* 195–8; etc.) must frequently be regarded as 'merely heuristic or playful'.[108] The same might be said of aetiologies. When Hesiod identifies *daimones* as the posthumous spirits of the golden race (*WD* 121–6) or the Delphic stone as the one swallowed by Kronos (*Th.* 498–500), these need not be more seriously meant than, say, the identification of a rock formation at Sipylos as the petrified Niobe (*Il.* 24.614–17). It is thus unclear whether the similarities in method observed between Hesiod and Herodotus are profound or superficial, whether they go beyond the merely formal to encompass the ends of the works in question. There is no mistaking that Herodotus is interested not only in how Greek beliefs about Herakles fit non-Greek beliefs but in how these mutually accommodated beliefs fit the real world ('my inquiries *show clearly* [δηλοῖ σαφέως] that Herakles *is* [ἐόντα] an ancient god', 2.44.5). Precisely because there is no such clarity with Hesiod, it is hard to

---

combined with poetic invention'; P. Burian, 'Myth into *mythos*: The shaping of tragic plot', in P. E. Easterling (ed.), *The Cambridge Companion to Greek Tragedy* (Cambridge: Cambridge University Press, 1997), pp. 178–208, at p. 185: 'myth is subject to interpretation and revision, but not to complete overturn, because it is also history'; A. Kelly, *Sophocles: Oedipus at Colonus* (London: Duckworth, 2009), p. 36 'Greek poets could not move in utterly new directions . . . for the new to be believable, it had to accommodate itself to the old, to grant to the audience that the stories they knew were not very far from the truth.'

107 On the tragic poets, cf. Burian, 'Myth into *mythos*', pp. 183–6. A notable exception to this 'rule of the game' is Agathon's *Anthos/Antheus* (Aristot. *Poet.* 1451b21–2), where the tragic *mythos* was invented *ab initio*.

108 Griffith, 'Contest and contradiction', p. 195. Etymology in the mythographers: R. L. Fowler, 'Herodotus and his contemporaries', *JHS* 116 (1996), pp. 62–87, at pp. 72–3.

demonstrate Hesiod the historian who deals in truth as opposed to Hesiod the poet who deals in traditional tales.[109]

CONCLUSION

By way of conclusion it may be helpful to reiterate the ambiguities and indeterminacies inherent in MoR's view of the past. First, this is a history of discrete 'mankind*s*'; but it is also somehow a history of a unified mankind. Second, it is an account of discrete races, but not entirely discrete races (one race bleeds into the other; ethical attitudes, moral behaviours, seem to be passed on, almost like genes). Third, the scheme is premised on a decline, but this turns out not to be a complete or irreversible decline. Fourth, the identification with metals is symbolic, but it also becomes literal. Fifth, it starts out as a diachronic account, but it is also (no less importantly) synchronic.[110] Sixth, the account appears to be simply descriptive, but it is also normative and prescriptive (there is an implicit, but fundamental, ethical dimension to the account). Seventh, the account of the past is different from PromPand, but not entirely different; it can be approximated to PromPand, but not completely. Last, Hesiod is arguably interested in accommodating Greek with non-Greek traditions about the past and in making a wide range of data cohere (in this very like Herodotus); but that does not necessarily equate to a concern for historical truth.

It is obvious that MoR is a remarkably fluid form of discourse that defies reductive analysis. A great many different, and contradictory, views of the past can be discerned in these hundred lines. It does not seem absurd to see MoR as some kind of potential precursor to a historical account. But there is too much that remains implicit in Hesiod's methodology, and too much that requires scholarly construction, to make us confident about seeing it so. The comparisons that can be drawn between Hesiod's method and Herodotus' are striking both for their quantity and quality, but these do not clinch the issue: MoR remains tantalisingly poised between poetic fiction and history.

---

109 For this distinction in the possible objects of a poet's discourse, cf. Aristot. *Poet.* 1460b10.
110 Cf. R. G. A. Buxton, 'Introduction', in Buxton (ed.), *From Myth to Reason? Studies in the Development of Greek Thought* (Oxford: Oxford University Press, 1999), pp. 1–21, at pp. 9–10: 'the myth of the Races stresses that things now are . . . *not* as they once were: iron is not gold. And yet . . . the sequence of Races exhibits, albeit in different blends, the same, recurring traits: aggressive violence, and righteousness'; cf. p. 9, on 'the past in the present' in Hesiod.

4

HELEN AND 'I' IN EARLY GREEK LYRIC

Deborah Boedeker

Early Greek lyric invokes the shared histories of speaker and audience
– both local and panhellenic, long-ago (or 'mythical') and recent – in
many modes of discourse, including narratives, exempla and exhor-
tations.[1] This chapter will focus on four sixth-century texts – from
Stesichorus, Alcaeus, Sappho and Ibycus – that rely on Helen, that
most enigmatic figure in the most familiar of shared Greek pasts, to
help define the speaker's persona. These works are no strangers to
critical analysis; indeed, several recent studies have fruitfully examined the treatment of Helen in some of them (among others), concerning themselves largely with the important areas of ethics and/or
gender.[2] My interest is in how the poetic 'I' in each fragment uses this
figure not primarily to construct a narrative about the past, but as a
way to show, by analogy or contrast, the kind of attitude or intention the speaker is adopting in the poetic performance.[3] Each lyric
'I' in a different way uses the 'historical' Helen (malleable though

---

1 For recent general studies of poetry and history see J. Marincola, 'Herodotus
  and the poetry of the past', in C. Dewald and J. Marincola (eds), *The Cambridge
  Companion to Herodotus* (Cambridge: Cambridge University Press, 2006), pp.
  13–28; D. Boedeker, 'Early Greek poetry as/and history', in A. Feldherr and G.
  Hardy (eds), *The Oxford History of Historical Writing*, vol. 1 (Oxford: Oxford
  University Press, 2011), pp. 122–47.
2 For example, C. P. Segal, 'Beauty, desire, and absence: Helen in Sappho, Alcaeus,
  and Ibycus', in Segal, *Aglaia: The Poetry of Alcman, Sappho, Pindar, Bacchylides,
  and Corinna* (Lanham, MD: Rowman & Littlefield, 1998), pp. 63–83, on Sappho,
  Alcaeus and Ibycus; N. Worman, 'The body as Argument: Helen in four Greek
  texts', *Classical Antiquity* 16 (1997), pp. 151–203, on Sappho together with
  Iliad 3, Gorgias' *Encomium of Helen* and Euripides' *Troades*; and R. Blondell,
  'Refractions of Homer's Helen in archaic lyric', *American Journal of Philology*
  131 (2010), pp. 349–91, on the Iliadic Helen compared with Helen in the Sappho,
  Alcaeus and Ibycus fragments.
3 I assume that the performance context is, at least to a degree, constructed rather
  than biographical; likewise, in using an author's name, I refer to the persona of
  the speaker in that work – also to some degree a construction – rather than to a
  historical human being.

she is) as a kind of fulcrum to help position himself or herself in the contemporary situation.

STESICHORUS FR. 192 *PMG*

I begin with Stesichorus' tantalising 'Palinode', which provides a particularly striking instance of the singer's relationship to Helen:[4]

Οὐκ ἔστ' ἔτυμος λόγος οὗτος,
οὐδ' ἔβας ἐν νηυσὶν εὐσέλμοις,
οὐδ' ἵκεο πέργαμα Τροίας·

This story is not true,
you did not go on the well-benched ships
and you did not arrive at the citadel of Troy.

The short fragment is quoted by Plato's Socrates (*Phaedrus* 243ab), when he decides that he must 'purify himself' from the abusive speech (κακηγορία) he has just delivered to Phaedrus about Eros, who after all is a god. The philosopher declares that there is 'an ancient purification for those who have gone wrong concerning mythology' (τοῖς ἁμαρτάνουσι περὶ μυθολογίαν καθαρμὸς ἀρχαῖος), a cure known not to Homer but to Stesichorus; clearly he is referring to traditions that each singer was blind. Homer never understood what caused his loss of sight, says Socrates, but Stesichorus did. He also knew the remedy: he revised the slanderous tale (κακηγορία) that Helen went with Paris to Troy, and immediately his vision was restored. Accordingly, Socrates will now compose his own palinode to Eros.

The evidence for Stesichorus' Helen poem(s) is far from clear, but with most scholars I believe that the Palinode was part of a longer work that acknowledged the familiar story in which Helen went to Troy with Paris.[5] Adrian Kelly suggests that the same poem also described the poet's personal encounter with Helen, perhaps in a

---

4 In the vast literature on the Palinode I have found especially useful the following studies: K. Bassi, 'Helen and the discourse of denial in Stesichorus' Palinode', *Arethusa* 26 (1993), pp. 51–75; E. Pallantza, *Der Troische Krieg in der nachhomerischen Literatur bis zum 5. Jahrhundert v. Chr.* (Stuttgart: Steiner, 2005), esp. pp. 98–123; A. J. Beecroft, 'This is not a true story: Stesichorus's Palinode and the revenge of the epichoric', *Transactions of the American Philological Association* 136 (2006), pp. 47–70; A. Kelly, 'Stesikhoros and Helen', *Museum Helveticum* 64 (2007), pp.1–21.

5 E.g. W. Allan (ed.), *Euripides: Helen* (Cambridge: Cambridge University Press, 2008), pp. 18–22; Bassi, 'Helen and the discourse of denial'; Kelly, 'Stesikhoros and Helen'. E. Cingano, 'Quante testimonianze sulle palinodie di Stesicoro?',

dream. Such a meeting of poet and divinity would be reminiscent of Hesiod's commissioning by the Muses (*Theogony* 30–1) and is attested in other texts as well (e.g. Sappho and Aphrodite, Sappho fr. 1).[6]

Whether or not it related a direct encounter with Helen, the poem very likely alluded to Stesichorus' losing and regaining his sight.[7] Not only is this tale of narrative offence, punishment and atonement the whole point of the *Phaedrus* citation, but it is regularly connected with the Palinode in other ancient sources as well.[8] Being struck blind for telling the 'wrong' version (from Helen's perspective) leads the speaker to renounce the familiar panhellenic account that Helen went to Troy with Paris and thereby became a cause of the Trojan War.[9] Most strikingly, he addresses his recantation to Helen herself: 'You did not go . . . you did not arrive.'[10] No longer just a character in the *logos*, she becomes present in the performance situation.

Kelly contends that Stesichorus' reason for this remarkable recantation is to win authority for his version of events, in competition with his predecessors: he has learned what happened from Helen herself.[11] This authority would be undercut, however, if Stesichorus appeared to revise his story in order to appease an angered immortal, and thereby cure his blindness. Dreams may be deceptive (if Kelly's suggestion is correct that Helen appeared to the poet in a dream), and in

---

Quaderni Urbinati di Cultura Classica 41 (1982), pp. 21–33, offers the strongest arguments for the existence of more than one Palinode.

6 Kelly, 'Stesikhoros and Helen', cites parallels from epic and lyric, noting that many mortals come into direct contact with gods in Homeric epic. Another parallel to the Palinode would be Pheidippides' meeting with Pan on his way to Sparta, when the god chides the Athenians for not recognising his helpfulness to them; he later receives proper recognition in cult (Herodotus 6.105).

7 *Pace* Bassi, 'Helen and the discourse of denial', pp. 54–5 n. 6.

8 E.g. Isocrates, *Encomium of Helen* 10.64. On the basis of the Isocrates passage, D. Sider, 'The blinding of Stesichorus', *Hermes* 117 (1989), pp. 423–31, suggests that the singer's blinding and sudden recovery of sight might have been mimed in performance.

9 This non-Homeric version of Helen's role, perhaps even including the *eidolon* that went to Troy in her stead, may already have been transmitted in the Hesiodic corpus (see F 358 M–W), based on a paraphrase of Lycophron, *Alexandra* 822.

10 This point receives relatively little emphasis from commentators, with the exception of Kelly, 'Stesikhoros and Helen', pp. 3–6, who mentions it in connection with his thesis that the 'Palinode' was part of a single poem that began with the standard version of the Helen story, and then restarted (in the manner of some Homeric Hymns) with an address to the divine figure whose story has just been told. See D. Boedeker, 'Paths to heroization at Plataea', in Boedeker and D. Sider (eds), *The New Simonides: Contexts of Praise and Desire* (Oxford: Oxford University Press, 2001), pp. 148–63, esp. pp. 155–61, for an analogous argument that Achilles is directly addressed as an immortal in Simonides fr. el. 11.19–20 W².

11 Kelly, 'Stesikhoros and Helen', p. 3 and *passim*.

any case gods readily take offence when their honour is impugned.[12] In other words, was the poet blinded because he got his 'history' wrong, or rather because his version annoyed one of its (immortal) subjects?[13] If we follow this line of thought, the Palinode could be read as an admission of a mortal's unheroic 'adaptability', along the lines of Archilochus' dropping his shield but saving his life (Archilochus fr. 5 W).

In the *Phaedrus* story that frames the fragment, Socrates' ironic fear of being harmed by Eros certainly allows that he understood Stesichorus' Palinode in this way; the philosopher declares that he will be smarter (σοφώτερος) than either Homer or Stesichorus, by offering the god a recantation even before anything bad happens to him (*Phaedrus* 243b). Stesichorus' readiness to change the familiar story (λόγος οὗτος[14]) in reaction to its negative consequences for himself may thus present him as an unreliable 'historian', however skilled he is in dealing with angry immortals.

Alexander Beecroft offers a more charitable reading. Building on the arguments of Claude Calame and Bruce Lincoln about types of poetic and mythological 'truth', Beecroft expands on the widely held thesis that the mortal Helen of Homeric epic is pitted here against an epichoric divine Helen, and is found wanting. 'When Stesichorus performs the Panhellenic version of the *logos* of Helen . . . it is ritually ineffective – which is demonstrated concretely through the blinding of the poet.'[15] I agree that the story of a Helen who followed Paris to Troy might be deemed inappropriate (and even 'untrue') in the context of a cult of Helen such as existed at Sparta, Athens and other places.[16] A blameworthy portrait could offend the goddess – or from a more mundane perspective, as often suggested, Stesichorus may

---

12 E.g. the dream sent to Agamemnon in *Iliad* 2.1–282; cf. the dream that forces Xerxes to invade Greece.

13 Bassi, 'Helen and the discourse of denial', argues perceptively that it is impossible for Stesichorus to recast entirely Helen's dangerously unstable, female nature.

14 On the deictic significance of λόγος οὗτος '*this* story' in the fragment see Beecroft, 'This is not a true story', pp. 49–52.

15 Beecroft, 'This is not a true story', p. 66. See further Beecroft's stimulating analysis of ἔτυμος in the Stesichorus passage (pp. 55–66).

16 On cults of Helen see Herodotus 6.61–2; M. L. West, *Immortal Helen: An Inaugural Lecture Delivered on 30 April 1975* (London: Bedford College, 1975); L. L. Clader, *Helen: The Evolution from Divine to Heroic in Greek Epic Tradition*, *Mnemosyne* Suppl. 42 (Leiden: Brill, 1976), pp. 63–80, J. Larson, *Greek Heroine Cults* (Madison: University of Wisconsin Press, 1995), pp. 65–70, 79–81; and D. Lyons, *Gender and Immortality: Heroines in Ancient Greek Myth and Cult* (Princeton: Princeton University Press, 1997), pp. 44–7. See Pallantza, *Der Troische Krieg*, pp. 112–18, for a critical overview of the relationship between literary and religious-historical approaches to the Palinode.

be distancing himself from the panhellenic story here because the local audience would react (or did react) negatively to a portrayal of Helen in keeping with the familiar epic tradition. The Palinode thus points to the complex nature of certain figures in the panhellenic tradition – mortal in epic, but immortal in local cults – and hence to the multiplicity of stories about them.

Whatever exactly was conveyed in the missing parts of Stesichorus' song, the extant fragment showcases a remarkable engagement of the speaker with his subject/addressee Helen, as an active divine power with an ego and power of her own (again, like Socrates' Eros in the *Phaedrus*). While it highlights Stesichorus' respect for the goddess, the Palinode also exposes a lack of reliability in songs about events and characters in the shared past: circumstances may prompt the singer to change his tune, as Stesichorus does here, in full view of the audience. As Ann Bergren concluded long ago, such ambiguity is a distinctive characteristic in portrayals of Helen.[17]

ALCAEUS FR. 42 V[18]

ὡς λόγος κάκων ἀ[
Περράμω<ι> καὶ παῖσ[ι
ἐκ σέθεν πίκρον, π[
   Ἴλιον ἴραν.

οὐ τεαύταν Αἰακίδαι[ς
πάντας ἐς γάμον μάκ[αρας καλέσσαις
ἄγετ' ἐκ Νή[ρ] ηος ἔλων [μελάθρων
   πάρθενον ἄβραν

ἐς δόμον Χέρρωνος· ἔλ[υσε δ'
ζῶμα παρθένω· φιλο[
Πήλεος καὶ Νηρεΐδων ἀρίστ[ας.
   ἐς δ' ἐνίαυτον

παῖδα γέννατ' αἰμιθέων [
ὄλβιον ξάνθαν ἐλάτη[ρα πώλων,
οἰ δ' ἀπώλοντ' ἀμφ' Ἐ[λέναι
   καὶ πόλις αὔτων.

17 A. Bergren, 'Language and the female in early Greek thought', *Arethusa* 16 (1983), pp. 69–95, esp. pp. 80–2; similarly Bassi, 'Helen and the discourse of denial', pp. 61–2, and Blondell, 'Refractions of Homer's Helen', pp. 390–1.
18 I use Voigt's text of the fragment with my own translation.

As the story goes . . . to Priam and his children a bitter . . . from you . . . holy Ilium. Not such a woman did Aeacus' son wed, inviting all the blessed ones to the marriage, bringing her, a maiden pure, from the chambers of Nereus to the house of Cheiron. He loosened the maiden's girdle . . . the love . . . of Peleus and the best of the Nereids. And in a year she bore a son . . . of demigods, a prosperous driver of tawny mares, but they [i.e. the Trojans] perished for Helen, and their city too.

At the start of his introductory essay on 'The "I" in personal archaic lyric', Simon Slings cites Hermann Fränkel on the 'judgemental' lyric I: 'Das *urteilende* Ich in der archaischen Lyrik ist immer repräsentiv gemeint'.[19] Although there is no first person pronoun or verb in Alcaeus fr. 42, in this poem the judgements applied to Helen and Thetis appear to be 'representative'. The speaker is performing for a like-minded audience; he has no controversial argument to make, as Stesichorus does very differently in the Palinode, or Sappho in fr. 16 (discussed below). Although the fragment does not vividly conjure up a performance context as do some of Alcaeus' songs (e.g. the great house all hung with armour in fr. 140), fr. 42 would surely be at home in a sympotic context, performed in the company of Alcaeus' *hetairoi*.[20]

The extant fragment begins 'as the story goes' (ὡς λόγος), and refers to the tradition that Troy was destroyed because of the marriage of Paris and Helen. As is clear from the Stesichorean Palinode, in early Greek poetry a *logos* may or may not accord with 'historical' reality; the speaker does not take responsibility for the tale's veracity.[21] In the

19 H. Fränkel, *Dichtung und Philosophie des frühen Griechentums: Eine geschichte der griechischen Epik, Lyrik und Prosa bis zur Mitte des fünften Jahrhunderts*, 2nd edn (Munich: Beck, 1962), p. 169 n. 50; quoted in S. R. Slings, 'The "I" in personal archaic lyric: An introduction', in Slings (ed.), *The Poet's 'I' in Archaic Greek Lyric* (Amsterdam: VU University Press, 1990), pp. 1–30, esp. p. 1. Slings goes on to argue for a more varied 'I' in early lyric, especially in Archilochus, which would allow for a more autobiographical as well as a collective perspective.

20 So Blondell, 'Refractions of Homer's Helen', pp. 353–4. See the pioneering work of W. Rösler, *Dichter und Gruppe: Eine Untersuchung zu den Bedingungen und zur historischen Funktion früher griechischer Lyrik am Beispiel Alkaios* (Munich: W. Fink, 1980), for the argument that Alcaeus composed exclusively for his political/social circle at Mytilene. In my opinion, as that of most critics, Rösler's views are overly restrictive, but his work demonstrates that much of Alcaeus' corpus deals with contemporary concerns from the perspective of a self-conscious *hetairia*.

21 A number of similar phrases in tragedy refer to things the speaker does not know for sure, but which accord with the reality portrayed or discovered in the course of the drama; cf. Aesch. *Supplices* 230, Eur. *IT* 532–4, Eur. *Helen* 18–19, Eur. *Phoen.* 396. See again Beecroft, 'This is not a true story'.

Alcaeus fragment, however, nothing speaks against the panhellenic *logos*;[22] rather, the song's final stanza confirms that the Trojans 'perished [fighting] about Helen' (lines 15–16). The audience is expected to know and accept this version of the tale, to understand the baneful effects on Priam's Troy of the marriage of Helen and Paris, and to pity those who lost their lives and their city fighting over her. They would also agree with the speaker's evaluation of the marriages (and women) contrasted here: whereas Helen's union with Paris produced only destruction for the city of Troy, Peleus married a chaste and comely bride, who became the mother of great Achilles.

As critics have noted, the speaker stops far short of telling the whole *logos*. He does not mention that Thetis' great son Achilles was among those who perished at Troy, and that he himself killed many of Priam's sons.[23] Moreover, his audience may well know the story, attested in the *Cypria*,[24] that the wedding of Peleus and Thetis marked a beginning of the Trojan War: Eris provoked a dispute about which goddess was most beautiful, which led to the Judgement of Paris. Possible narrative connections between the two marriages in this song are many, but the poet elides them, in part by using the unusual trope of direct address to help him focus attention where he wants it.

Very differently from the Stesichorus Palinode, but also with striking effect, Alcaeus addresses one of his characters in the second person: 'from you (ἐκ σέθεν) [came?] a bitter [end?] to Priam and his children' (lines 1–4). Here again, he appears to be speaking with and for his audience as together they consider the sufferings of Priam's family and acknowledge the one responsible for them. And quite unlike the tradition that accompanies Stesichorus' Palinode, there is no reference here to a reaction from the character addressed; the 'you' is a figure within the historical narrative, not an immanent immortal.

This addressee is usually taken to be Helen, according to Page's widely accepted supplement in line 3: π[οτ', Ὤλεν', ἦλθεν 'once, O Helen, [a bitter end] came'. The second person (σέθεν), however, may instead refer to Paris, as Elena Pallantza has lucidly argued.[25] For the

22 Blondell, 'Refractions of Homer's Helen', pp. 353–4, proposes that this distancing allows the sympotic audience to contemplate Helen without having to confront her erotic beauty.

23 E.g. G. Liberman, *Alcée: Fragments* (Paris: Belles Lettres, 1999), 1.36; Blondell, 'Refractions of Homer's Helen', pp. 356–9.

24 Proclus, *Chrestomathia* 1.

25 Pallantza, *Der Troische Krieg*, pp. 28–34, accepts Wilamowitz's supplement παῖσ[τέλος φίλοισιν at line 2. The main problem with her reading, as I see it, is to reconcile οὐ τεαύταν (line 5), meaning that Peleus' bride was 'not such a one' (as Helen), if Helen has not yet been mentioned in the poem. Pallantza, however, builds a strong case on structural and stylistic grounds that there was at least a

speaker to focus on Paris' misdeed more than Helen's would accord
with the emphasis in another Alcaeus fragment that also deals with the
fateful pair, in which the host-betraying Trojan prince is blamed far
more than the woman for whom the war was fought (fr. 283.3–6 V):[26]

κ' Ἀλένας ἐν στήθ[ε]σιν [ἐ]πτ[όαισε
θῦμον Ἀργείας Τροΐω<ι> δ' [ἐ]π' ἄνδ[ρι
ἐκμάνεισα ξ[ε.]ναπάτα<ι> 'πι π[όντον
    ἔσπετο νᾶϊ

and . . . [Eros? Aphrodite? Paris?] caused the heart in Argive
Helen's breast to flutter . . . driven mad by the Trojan man, host-
deceiver . . . she followed [him] to sea in his ship.

A third Alcaeus fragment also presents a moralising view of the
Trojan War that may shed light on the speaker's perspective in fr. 42.
Fr. 298 V deals with the rape of Cassandra by Locrian Ajax, and the
'historical' tale clearly holds a lesson for the Mytilenean present. The
first extant stanza offers advice pertinent to the contemporary situation of singer and audience: it is best to shame and kill those who do
unjust things. To illustrate his point, the speaker turns to the past,
saying that the Achaeans should have killed Ajax for his impious
behaviour (Alc. fr. 298.1–5):[27]

Δρά]σαντας αἰσχύν[...]τα τὰ μήνδικα
...]ην δὲ περβάλοντ' [ἀν]άγκα
ἄυ]χενι λα[β]ολίωι π.[..]αν

ἦ μάν κ'] Ἀχαίοισ' ἦς πόλυ βέλτερον
αἰ τὸν θεοβλ]άβεντα κατέκτανον

disgracing those who did unjust deeds, and it is necessary to cast
a [noose] on their neck and [kill] them by stoning. Truly it would
have been much better for the Achaeans if they had killed the
sacrilegious man.

(footnote 25 *continued*)
stanza before the start of the extant fragment, in which Helen could have been
mentioned.
26 A focus on Paris would also align the speaker with the Homeric tradition.
As Blondell, 'Refractions of Homer's Helen', pp. 349–50, emphasises, no Homeric
male blames Helen for the war. As if pre-empting any reproach, she blames herself
– to Priam (*Il.* 3. 173–80), to Hector (*Il.* 6.344–58) and in the *Odyssey* to Menelaus
and Telemachus (4.145).
27 For this citation I use Campbell's text and translation, slightly modified.

This is followed by a brutal account of Ajax' rape of the maiden as she clasped the statue of Athena. His impious deed turned the goddess against the conquering Achaeans because they did not take it upon themselves to punish the evil-doer. The shipwrecks they suffered as a result of her wrath (lines 24–45?) stand as a warning to the speaker and his contemporary audience about how they should treat those guilty of shameful deeds in their own society. Although the papyrus is extremely fragmentary at this point, one of those evil-doers is called by his patronymic: 'son of Hyrrhas' (line 47): Pittacus, arch-nemesis of Alcaeus' *hetairia*.[28]

In fr. 42 as well, particularly if Paris is the 'you' blamed for the destruction of Troy, the speaker may be drawing an analogy to the political world he shares with his fellow symposiasts. Paris' treachery, his illicit marriage to Helen, caused the destruction of his own family and city. Whether or not this applies specifically to Pittacus or some other enemy of Alcaeus' group,[29] the results of evil deeds in the past are clear, and the speaker refers to a familiar *logos* to show the consequences of actions that break the bonds of trust and propriety.

SAPPHO FR. 16 V[30]

ο]ἰ μὲν ἰππήων στρότον οἰ δὲ πέσδων
οἰ δὲ νάων φαῖσ' ἐπ[ὶ] γᾶν μέλαι[ν]αν
ἔ]μμεναι κάλλιστον, ἔγω δὲ κῆν' ὄτ-
    τω τις ἔραται·

πά]γχυ δ' εὔμαρες σύνετον πόησαι
π]άντι τ[ο]ῦτ', ἀ γὰρ πόλυ περσκέθοισα
κάλλος [ἀνθ]ρώπων Ἐλένα [τὸ]ν ἄνδρα
    τὸν .[αρ]ιστον

καλλ[ίποι]σ' ἔβα 'ς Τροΐαν πλέοι[σα
κωὐδ[ὲ πα]ῖδος οὐδὲ φίλων το[κ]ήων
πά[μπαν] ἐμνάσθ<η>, ἀλλὰ παράγαγ' αὔταν
    [   ]σαν

28 See G. O. Hutchinson, *Greek Lyric Poetry: A Commentary on Selected Larger Pieces* (Oxford: Oxford University Press, 2001), pp. 215–27; the seminal work of Rösler, *Dichter und Gruppe*, on Alcaeus' use of mythical/historical allegory for political purposes; and the careful analysis of this fragment by Pallantza, *Der Troische Krieg*, pp. 47–56.

29 Pallantza, *Der Troische Krieg*, pp. 33–4 also discusses the likelihood that fr. 42 responds poetically to a contemporary situation in Mytilene.

30 The text is Voigt's; the translation is Campbell's, slightly modified.

[   ]αμπτον γὰρ [
[   ]...κούφωςτ[   ]οη.[.]ν
..]με νῦν Ἀνακτορί[ας ὀ]νέμναι-
   σ' οὐ] παρεοίσας,

τᾶ]ς <κ>ε βολλοίμαν ἔρατόν τε βᾶμα
κἀμάρυχμα λάμπρον ἴδην προσώπω
ἢ τὰ Λύδων ἄρματα κἀν ὄπλοισι
[πεσδομ]άχεντας.

[   ].μεν οὐ δύνατον γένεσθαι
[   ].ν ἄνθρωπ[..(.) π]εδέχην δ' ἄρασθαι

Some say a host of cavalry, others of infantry, and others of ships, is the most beautiful thing on the black earth, but I say it is whatever a person desires. It is completely easy to make this understood by everyone, for she who far surpassed humankind in beauty, Helen, left her most excellent husband and went sailing to Troy, and she recalled not at all her child or dear parents, but . . . led her astray . . . lightly . . . this calls to my mind Anaktoria who is not here. I would rather see her desirable footstep and the bright sparkle of her face than the Lydians' chariots and their infantry in armour . . . not possible to happen . . . humankind. . . pray to share in . . .

In this much-admired masterpiece, the speaker uses the story of Helen and Paris overtly to illustrate her proposal that the *kalliston*, 'finest', 'most beautiful' or 'best', derives its value from the *eros* 'desire' that one feels for it. This approach to the Helen question is quite different from the comparison of two marriages in Alcaeus fr. 42, which looks to consequences rather than motivation. It is no wonder that critics often compare these two works, both of them in Sapphic strophes, almost as if they were in dialogue with each other.[31]

Unlike the relationship between speaker and audience that informs the Alcaeus fragment, the speaker here does not assume that her audience already shares her view that everyone considers fairest whatever it is that they desire.[32] She needs to explain, and does so by recalling

31 E.g. G. W. Most, 'Sappho Fr. 16.6–7 L-P', *Classical Quarterly* 31 (1981), pp. 11–17; W. H. Race, 'Sappho, *Fr.* 16 L-P. and Alkaios, *Fr.* 42 L-P.: Romantic and classical strains in Lesbian lyric', *Classical Journal* 85 (1989), pp. 16–33; Segal, 'Beauty, desire, and absence'; Blondell, 'Refractions of Homer's Helen'.
32 A. Bierl, 'Ich aber (sage), das Schönste ist, was einer liebt! Eine pragmatische Deutung von Sappho Fr. 16 LP/V', *Quaderni Urbinati di Cultura Classica* n.s. 74

a famous example from the past. As Glenn Most has nicely shown, Sappho recruits a figure with whom she can support her case through authority if not through logical argument: who better than the super-latively beautiful Helen to prove how the *kalliston* is determined by desire?[33] Led astray (line 11), presumably by Eros or Aphrodite, Helen left her excellent husband to follow Paris to Troy. In doing so, she forgot those who were nearest to her, her parents and child. Her action exemplifies the primacy of what one desires.

In the rhetoric of the poem, Helen is neither condemned nor praised.[34] Her story plays an epistemological function, an extreme and clear illustration of the speaker's self-declared understanding of human values, by referring to a well-known situation in the shared past. We noted that in Alcaeus fr. 42 the speaker passes over those parts of the *logos* that might undercut his moral point by suggesting that in fact *both* marriages contributed to the destruction at Troy. Sappho even more boldly elides a great part of the familiar story. She does not mention the great war that was the consequence of Helen's decision (if it can be called that) to follow Paris to Troy. Nonetheless, the enormity of that war surely adds to the impact of the example she selects: even with so much at stake, Helen found 'best' that which she desired (or was made to desire).

Sappho brings to life Helen's point of view, making her a true subject, as many commentators have discussed. At the same time she uses this figure as an analogue, a parallel to her own subjectivity – and, she declares, to everyone's. Helen's past action thus illuminates the speaker's present assertion.

This original yet straightforward use of the past takes another turn, however, when the 'I' says that Helen's story brings to her mind the absent Anaktoria, whose lively beauty she herself values most highly.[35] Helen's story thus turns out to provide more than an explan-atory example, for it triggers thoughts of the speaker's own situation, which involves separation from that which is *kalliston* for her. This revelation suggests that yearning for the beautiful girl colours even the speaker's self-assured priamel.[36]

(2003), pp. 91–124, argues that the speaker, in the role of *thiasos* leader, models for her youthful audience the values they should cultivate.

33 Most, 'Sappho Fr. 16.6–7 L-P', pp. 13–15.

34 Allan, *Euripides: Helen*, p. 13, argues on the contrary that Sappho condemns Helen by mentioning everyone she left behind – husband, daughter, parents – when she was led astray by Aphrodite.

35 Segal, 'Beauty, desire, and absence', p. 77, notes Helen's 'forgetting' and Sappho's 'remembering'.

36 H. C. Fredricksmeyer, 'A diachronic reading of Sappho fr. 16 LP', *Transactions of the American Philological Association* 131 (2001), pp. 75–86, argues for a

Sappho's sweet-bitter situation, her vivid memory of and longing for absent Anaktoria, in turn leads to further reflection on the sentiments of characters in the Helen story. Might Helen too have remembered, once they were gone, the value of what she once 'entirely forgot' (fr. 16.11) – her daughter, her dear parents, her *panariston* husband (fr. 16.7–8)? Certainly the Homeric Helen voices those sentiments (*Iliad* 3.173–5).[37] The speaker's own yearning for the desirable one who is absent also recalls Menelaus, whose departed wife 'far surpassed mankind in beauty' (fr. 16.6–7). This would foreshadow Aeschylus' Menelaus in a choral song of the *Agamemnon*, ranging desolately through his palace, beset with piercing memories of Helen's beauty (*Ag.* 407).[38]

From the perspective of how a lyric 'I' relates to the past, what fascinates most in this fragment is the dynamic interaction established between the speaker and her 'historical' subject. Helen's famous action, part of the common past of singer and audience, is called upon to explain the speaker's professed value system. In turn the performance situation (Anaktoria is gone but vividly remembered) casts light back onto the actions and feelings of both Helen and Menelaus. The present illuminates the past as much as the past does the present.

IBYCUS S151 *PMGF*[39]

...]αι Δαρδανίδα Πριάμοιο μέ-
γ᾽ ἄσ]τυ περικλεὲς ὄλβιον ἠνάρον
Ἄργ]οθεν ὀρνυμένοι
Ζη]νὸς μεγάλοιο βουλαῖς

ξα]νθᾶς Ἑλένας περὶ εἴδει   (5)
δῆ]ριν πολύυμνον ἔχ[ο]ντες
πό]λεμον κατὰ [δ]ακρ[υό]εντα,
Πέρ]γαμον δ᾽ ἀνέ[β]α ταλαπείριο[ν ἄ]τα
χρυ]σοέθειραν δ[ι]ὰ Κύπριδα·

(footnote 36 *continued*)
    'diachronic' reading of fr. 16, in which the audience's response changes as the poem progresses. This is a fruitful and reasonable approach and I follow here its principles, but I disagree with Fredricksmeyer that the response moves from a positive to a negative ethical reading of Helen.
37 On the resemblances between these two passages see Race, 'Sappho, *Fr.* 16 L-P', pp. 24–5, and Worman, 'The body as argument', p. 171.
38 This analogy is eloquently drawn by Worman, 'The body as argument', p. 168.
39 For this fragment I use Davies' text and Campbell's translation, slightly modified.

νῦ]ν δέ μοι οὔτε ξειναπάτ[α]ν Π[άρι]ν   (10)
..] ἐπιθύμιον οὔτε τανί[σφ]υρ[ον
ὑμ]νῆν Κασσάνδραν
Πρι]άμοιό τε παίδας ἄλλου[ς

Τρο]ίας θ' ὑψιπύλοιο ἁλώσι[μο]ν
ἆμ]αρ ἀνώνυμον, οὐδεπ[(15)
ἡρ]ώων ἀρετὰν
ὑπ]εράφανον οὕς τε κοίλα[ι

νᾶες] πολυγόμφοι ἐλεύσα[ν
Τροί]αι κακόν, ἥρωας ἐσθ[λούς·
τῶν] μὲν κρείων Ἀγαμέ[μνων   (20)
ἆρχε Πλεισθ[ενί]δας βασιλ[εὺ]ς ἀγὸς ἀνδρῶν
Ἀτρέος ἐσ[θλοῦ π]άις ἔκγ[ο]νος.

καὶ τὰ μὲ[ν ἂν] Μοίσαι σεσοφι[σ]μέναι
εὖ Ἑλικωνίδ[ες] ἐμβαίεν †λόγω[ι,
θνατ[ὸ]ς† δ' οὔ κ[ε]ν ἀνὴρ   (25)
διερὸς τὰ ἔκαστα εἴποι,

ναῶν ὄ[σσος ἀρι]θμὸς ἀπ' Αὐλίδος
Αἰγαῖον διὰ [πό]ντον ἀπ' Ἄργεος
ἠλύθο[ν ἐς Τροία[ν
ἱπποτρόφο[ν, ἐν δ]ὲ φῶτες   (30)

χ]αλκάσπ[ιδες, υἶ]ες Ἀχα[ι]ῶν·
τ]ῶν μὲν πρ[οφ]ερέστατος α[ἴ]χμαι
....]. πόδ[ας ὠ]κὺς Ἀχιλλεὺς
καὶ μέ]γας Τ[ελαμ]ώνιος ἄλκι[μος Αἴας
.....]...[.....]λο[.].υρος·   (35)

.... κάλλι]στος ἀπ' Ἄργεος
.... Κυάνι]ππ[ο]ς ἐς Ἴλιον
[   ]
[   ].·[.]...

..............]α χρυσόστροφ[ος   (40)
Ὕλλις ἐγήνατο, τῶι δ' [ἄ]ρα Τρωίλον
ὥσει χρυσὸν ὀρει-
χάλκωι τρὶς ἄπεφθο[ν] ἤδη

Τρῶες Δ[α]ναοί τ' ἐρό[ε]σσαν
μορφὰν μάλ' ἔισκον ὄμοιον.   (45)

τοῖς μὲν πέδα κάλλεος αἰὲν
καὶ σύ, Πολύκρατες, κλέος ἄφθιτον ἑξεῖς
ὡς κὰτ ἀοιδὰν καὶ ἐμὸν κλέος.

. . . they destroyed Dardanian Priam's great city, famous and prosperous, setting off from Argos by the plans of great Zeus, enduring much-sung strife over the beauty of blonde Helen in tearful war; and ruin mounted long-suffering Pergamon because of the golden-haired Cyprian.

But now I do not long to hymn Paris the host-deceiver or slender-ankled Cassandra and Priam's other children, or the unspeakable day when high-gated Troy was captured, and I will not recount the overweening valour of the heroes whom hollow, many-bolted [ships] brought as an evil for Troy, fine heroes. Lord Agamemnon led them, Pleisthenid king, leader of men, fine son born of Atreus.

Indeed the learned Muses of Helicon might embark on these things in story, but no mortal man alive could tell the details, what number of ships came from Aulis across the Aegean sea from Argos to horse-rearing Troy, with bronze-shielded men on them, sons of the Achaeans. The best of them with the spear [came] swift-footed Achilles and great, mighty Telamonian Ajax . . . fire . . .

The fairest from Argos came Cyanippus to Ilium [descendant of Adrastus, and Zeuxippus, whom the Naiad] gold-belted Hyllis bore [to Phoebus]; to him Trojans and Danaans compared Troilus, as thrice-refined gold to orichalc, very similar in his lovely appearance.

In company with them you too, Polycrates, will have unfading fame for beauty, as my fame too for song.

As transmitted in a second-century BCE papyrus (*P. Oxy.* 1790), this song originally consisted of at least four triads in a heavily dactylic metre. We do not have the beginning of the poem; a four-line strophe (and possibly one or more triads before that[40]) is missing at the top of

---

40 Hutchinson, *Greek Lyric Poetry*, p. 237, argues that the song must have begun with a reference to the performance context in which Polycrates is being celebrated. This would follow the marked tendency of early lyric to return to the opening deictic situation after a mythological parallel, as shown by L. Edmunds, 'Tithonus in the new Sappho and the narrated mythical exemplum', in E. Greene and M. Skinner (eds), *The New Sappho on Old Age* (Hellenic Studies 38; Cambridge, MA: Harvard University Press), pp. 58–70; it would also resemble the typical structure of Pindaric and Bacchylidean epinicians (also largely triadic), for which Ibycus – as Hutchinson notes – may be seen as a predecessor.

the papyrus, but the fragment's final line (48) is followed by a coronis, so we can be confident that the song was intended to end there. The structure of the extant work is remarkable: forty-five extant verses dealing with the Trojan War – over half of them on subjects the speaker says he will not or cannot address – followed by three lines in praise of Polycrates, presumably the famous tyrant of Samos.[41]

Ibycus' poem does not dispute the panhellenic tradition that Helen went to Troy, but no blame is cast on her. Argives and Trojans fought over her beauty (eidos) because of the 'plans of great Zeus' (line 4), and the Greeks destroyed Troy 'because of the golden-haired Cyprian' (8–9).[42] Paris is called a 'deceiver of his host' (xeinapatan, 10) but Helen is wholly passive; her beauty is the reason for epic struggle, sorrow and fame.[43]

It is significant to note which aspects of the Trojan saga the speaker says he has no desire to sing. Glorious though they may be in song, the events are all sorrowful and wearisome: the siege of Troy, the treacherous Paris, Cassandra and the other children of Priam, the disastrous fall of a great city, caused by the aretê of heroes led by magnificent Agamemnon (10–22). Moreover, how could any singer rehearse all this? The learned (σεσοφι[σ]μέναι) Muses might be able to venture into such a story (23–4), Ibycus says, but no mortal man could tell the details (lines 25–6).[44]

This general statement on the limits of poetic accuracy about so vast a topic subtly casts doubt on the 'historical' accuracy and authority of Homer. Moreover, as G. O. Hutchinson points out, the declaration of human limitation is followed by a clear reference to the Iliadic Catalogue of Ships (lines 27–31), which the epic bard presents as a tour de force and something he could not do without help from the Muses

---

41 L. Woodbury, 'Ibycus and Polycrates', Phoenix 39 (1985), pp. 193–220, esp. p. 206, argues that this must be an erotic ode praising a young (still beardless) Polycrates, before he has become famous, but this is not necessarily the case. In a few Pindaric odes, for example, athletes in men's (not boys') events could be praised for their beauty: Epharmostos of Opus, a wrestler, was kalos when he won at Marathon (Ol. 9.94), although it is possible that he was a boy at the time; the pancratist Aristokleides of Aegina is kalos and does deeds that match his appearance (N. 3.19).

42 Segal, 'Beauty, desire, and absence', p. 72: 'Even her renowned beauty is only part of a larger scheme.'

43 Blondell, 'Refractions of Homer's Helen', p. 364, remarks that Helen 'is simply objectified – as she is by men in the Iliad – as the prize of male struggle'.

44 Blondell, 'Refractions of Homer's Helen', pp. 366–7, argues that Ibycus is more likely to be claiming here his (Muse-given?) ability to create epic verse. I agree that the speaker is flaunting his skill at composing Homeric-sounding verse to outdo even Homer, and that he does not intend to disparage his ability to bestow everlasting praise on Polycrates. I would emphasise, however, that in doing so Ibycus differentiates himself from, and undercuts, Homer's vaunted authority.

(*Il.* 2.484–93).[45] The lyric 'I' here coyly disclaims his desire or ability to recount the grievous details and noble heroes of the epic past, while demonstrating his ability to speak of them in a style that could well be called hyper-Homeric.[46] This includes three lines of honorific epithets for the magnificent leader Agamemnon son of Atreus (20–2),[47] as well as such familiar tags as 'sons of the Achaeans' (31) and even 'swift-footed Achilles' (33).

A certain disparagement of Homeric heroism can even be heard when the *arête* of the 'noble heroes' is called *hyperaphanon* (16–17). The term, attested only twice in early epic, is used of unusually violent fighters: the three Hundred-Handers, ὑπερήφανα τέκνα 'overweening children' of Gaia and Ouranos (*Theogony* 148–50), and the overweening (ὑπερηφανέοντες), hubristic Epeans who once plotted against the kingdom of Neleus (*Iliad* 11.692–5).

Bypassing (through praeteritio) an account of the grievous war that brought fame and destruction to those fighting over Helen's beauty, the speaker turns instead to the beauty of three young warriors; two of them are not even mentioned by Homer, while the third receives half a line.[48] It turns out that the war that was fought for Helen's beauty (Helen's *eidos*, line 5), with its disastrous consequences for Troy, also served as a display ground for masculine comeliness.[49]

Unlike the *eidos* of Helen, the beauty of Argive Cyanippus, Zeuxippus the son of Hyllis and Apollo,[50] and Trojan Troilus – although it must have been observed on the battlefield[51] – causes no

---

45 My discussion of meta-poetics in this fragment has been enriched by Hutchinson, *Greek Lyric Poetry*, pp. 235–56, esp. pp. 236, 249–50 and 254–5.

46 See also Blondell, 'Refractions of Homer's Helen', p. 367.

47 B. C. MacLachlan, 'Personal poetry', in D. E. Gerber (ed.), *A Companion to the Greek Lyric Poets* (Leiden: Brill, 1997), pp. 133–220, esp. p. 194 (citing Willein), however, notes that his epithet ἀγὸς ἀνδρῶν 'leader of men' (line 21) with a simple change of accent would become ἄγος ἀνδρῶν 'accursed of men'.

48 Priam describes Troilus as ἱππιοχάρμην 'chariot-fighter (?)', as he lists his brave sons who were killed by Achilles (*Iliad* 24.257); the death of Troilus was also mentioned in the *Cypria* (Procl., *Chrest.* 1). See Woodbury, 'Ibycus and Polycrates', p. 204; E. Krummen, 'Alcman, Stesichorus and Ibycus', in F. Budelmann (ed.), *The Cambridge Companion to Greek Lyric* (Cambridge: Cambridge University Press, 2009), pp. 184–203, esp. pp. 201–2.

49 Cf. Blondell, 'Refractions of Homer's Helen', pp. 369–70: 'Helen's beauty, the cause of heroic but "tearful" warfare, is displaced in favor of an appreciation of male beauty that transcends hostilities, uniting Greeks and Trojans in harmonious admiration.'

50 On the identity of these two Greeks and the restoration of this passage see J. P. Barron, 'Ibycus: To Polycrates', *Bulletin of the Institute of Classical Studies* 16 (1969), pp. 119–49, at pp. 130–1.

51 As Blondell, 'Refractions of Homer's Helen', p. 372 observes from a different perspective.

strife. On the contrary, the speaker goes out of his way to say that both sides agreed on their relative beauty, using a rather elaborate analogy: the Trojan Troilus was to the Greek Zeuxippus as triple-purified gold is to orichalc.[52]

Just as we hear nothing of Helen's motives or actions, we hear nothing of deeds performed by the three young warriors. It is not for *arête* as warriors that they earn everlasting *kleos*, but rather for outstanding loveliness of form; it is this quality that the speaker (in implied contrast to Homer) chooses to sing. This leads, of course, to the praise of the contemporary honorand, Polycrates, to whom the speaker promises *kleos aphthiton* for his beauty like that of the beautiful heroes of Troy (lines 46–8).[53] At the same time, he predicts similar *kleos* for himself, because of his (beautiful) song.[54]

The famous Helen, it turns out, is a foil for the speaker. She serves as his entrée into the relationship of beauty to praise-poetry. Throughout the poem beauty is the spark of fame, but the relationship between the two develops in unexpected ways. At first we learn that Helen's beauty provided those who went to Troy with an occasion for fame; then attention shifts to the most beautiful of those who fought there, whether Greek or Trojan. Their appearance gives rise only to praise from those who see them, friend and foe alike. Unending fame for beauty will also come to Polycrates, the singer promises – just as he himself will have *kleos* for his song, a song that self-consciously differentiates itself from Homeric narrative.

CONCLUSION

In these texts, the lyric 'I' conjures up a past that raises questions, including intentionally or not questions about versions and segments of the Helen story that are not mentioned, or not accepted, in the current song. The familiar yet ambiguous Helen is a historical figure implicitly shared with the audience, and serves as a point

52 On the comparison of the two metals, and men, see Woodbury, 'Ibycus and Polycrates', pp. 201–3.
53 MacLachlan, 'Personal poetry', pp. 193–4, points out the inherent dangers in beauty, with the mention of Helen, Aphrodite and Cassandra, and suggests that this may look ahead, as if prophetically, to the troubles that will come about because of beautiful Polycrates. But Ibycus avoids any hint of dangers coming from masculine beauty, a topic he certainly could have opened up in connection with the guest-deceiver Paris.
54 I am persuaded by the arguments of Woodbury, 'Ibycus and Polycrates', pp. 203–5, and Hutchinson, *Greek Lyric Poetry*, pp. 253–5, to follow Wilamowitz in removing the stop attested at the end of line 46; thus the speaker promises 'immortal fame for beauty' to Polycrates as well as Zeuxippus and Troilus.

of contact, a baseline from which to define the speaker's intent in each song.[55]

To summarise very briefly: Stesichorus changes his tune, we are told, when Helen blinds him for slandering her. In any case, his Palinode questions the authority of the Trojan *logos*, and suggests tensions between panhellenic and local versions of a story: is Helen a historical mortal or an immortal goddess? Alcaeus in turn uses Helen's marriage to Paris to comment on human justice and the dire consequences of illicit behaviour: contemporaries should learn from history not to tolerate evil-doers who threaten the community's welfare. The speaker in Sappho fr. 16 explains her contention that *eros* determines what is most highly valued by pointing to Helen's relative valuation of Paris and Menelaus. Vice versa, she casts light on the long-past inner world of Helen and Menelaus through her own experiences of beauty and absence in the present. Ibycus claims that he will not, or cannot, rehearse the disastrous and glorious tale of Troy, a fight for Helen's beauty, and turns instead to other beauties at Troy, young warriors whose fame will be matched by the beautiful Polycrates.

Such interactions with the past are not entirely different from what early Greek prose historians do;[56] history is inescapably written from the present situation of the historian and his audience, and is often used to shed light on current issues.[57] But among many other generic distinctions, we have seen that the lyric 'I' allows itself more freedom to comment on analogies between past and present than does the historiographical (or indeed the epic) narrator, and may even be found to ironise itself in so doing. Nor does the speaker in lyric affect to efface himself or herself in telling of the past, but plays a prominent role in shaping it in view of the performance situation. The lyric 'I' thus conjures up the 'historical' Helen not only to help explain, blame or praise events in the past but also to illuminate, and perhaps to justify, the context of the present song.

---

55 I do not mean to imply that the performance situation is not to some degree constructed, let alone invariable in reperformances of the song.

56 See again Marincola, 'Herodotus and the poetry of the past', and Boedeker, 'Early Greek poetry as/and history', for extended discussion.

57 See K. Raaflaub, 'Ulterior motives in ancient historiography: What exactly, and why?', in L. Foxhall, H.-J. Gehrke and N. Luraghi (eds), *Intentional History: Spinning Time in Ancient Greece* (Stuttgart: Steiner, 2010), pp. 198–210, for an overview of the question of ancient historians' motives.

5

STESICHORUS AND IBYCUS: PLAIN TALES FROM THE WESTERN FRONT

Ewen Bowie

The conceptions and perceptions of their past found in both individuals and communities are very frequently related to place.[1] That this was so in many places in the Greek world of the Roman empire is clear from (e.g.) Plutarch's life of Theseus, which is replete with references to archaic and classical Athenian topography, and on a much larger scale Pausanias' *Guide to Hellas*. This sort of writing did not even yet exist, far less survive, for mainland Greece of the archaic period, though the evocative power of place names is extensively exploited in the Homeric poems, and by such references as that of the Spartan elegiac poet Tyrtaeus to Ithome,[2] or by an unknown elegiac poet from Laconia to Taygetus and Platanistous.[3] There can be little doubt that in Greek communities throughout mainland Greece, the islands and Asia Minor, oral traditions about the pasts of these communities would often be attached to places or monuments. For example, the monument to 'The Seven', now known to have existed in Argos, probably as early as the sixth century, would have been a catalyst for

---

1 See above all P. Nora, *Les lieux de mémoire* I–III (Paris: Gallimard, 1984–92). For the Scottish ambience of the conference on which this volume is based one could adduce the associations of the Agricolan two-legion camp at Inchtuthill and the associated fortification of Cleaven Dyke; Macbeth's fortress on the top of Dunsinan(e); the Cistercian Abbey at Coupar Angus; Bannockburn; Mary Queen of Scots and the palace of Holyrood; Greyfriars Bobby.

2 ἡμετέρωι βασιλῆϊ, θεοῖσι φίλωι Θεοπόμπωι, | ὃν διὰ Μεσσήνην εἵλομεν εὐρύχορον,| Μεσσήνην ἀγαθὸν μὲν ἀροῦν, ἀγαθὸν δὲ φυτεύειν·| ἀμφ' αὐτὴν δ' ἐμάχοντ' ἐννέα καὶ δέκ' ἔτη | νωλεμέως αἰεὶ ταλασίφρονα θυμὸν ἔχοντες | αἰχμηταὶ πατέρων ἡμετέρων πατέρες·| εἰκοστῶι δ' οἱ μὲν κατὰ πίονα ἔργα λιπόντες | φεῦγον Ἰθωμαίων ἐκ μεγάλων ὀρέων, Tyrtaeus fr. 5 West.

3 πῖν' οἶνον, τὸν ἐμοὶ κορυφῆς ἄπο Τηϋγέτοιο | ἄμπελοι ἤνεγκαν, τὰς ἐφύτευσ' ὁ γέρων | οὔρεος ἐν βήσσησι θεοῖσι φίλος Θεότιμος, | ἐκ Πλατανιστοῦντος ψυχρὸν ὕδωρ ἐπάγων.| τοῦ πίνων ἀπὸ μὲν χαλεπὰς σκεδάσεις μελεδῶνας,| θωρηχθεὶς δ' ἔσεαι πολλὸν ἐλαφρότερος, *Theognidea* 879–84; cf. E. L. Bowie, 'Wandering poets, archaic style' in R. L. Hunter and I. C. Rutherford (eds), *Wandering Poets* (Cambridge: Cambridge University Press, 2009), pp. 105–36, at p. 117.

stories about the expedition against Thebes by Argive warriors of the heroic age.[4]

It is a corollary that when sections of communities went to settle on new and often very distant sites some local traditions concerning their metropolis would be likely to fade and even perish, while others relating to the process and location of resettlement would grow up. Within a few generations the storied past of an ἀποικία might acquire a quite different profile from that of its metropolis. Such has certainly been my experience in both the United States and Australia; Lewis and Clark are heroised in St Louis and in Washington State, Ned Kelly has pride of place in art galleries in Canberra.

I had hoped, therefore, in setting out to comb, not for the first time, the surviving fragments of some archaic Greek poets, that something would emerge that chimed with this pattern. I must admit at this point that I found much less than I hoped. This in itself perhaps invites an explanation, which I shall attempt when concluding.

I was encouraged in my exploration, however, by the case of early narrative elegy. As I have discussed more than once,[5] several early elegiac poets seem to have narrated at some length both the early and the more recent history of their cities: some – Mimnermus, Xenophanes, Ion of Chios – touched on migration eastwards from mainland Greece to the islands and Asia Minor; another, Semonides of Amorgos, on westward movement back from the eastern Aegean, Samos, to the western Aegean, Amorgos. Tyrtaeus' *Eunomia* presented a different sort of colonisation, that of conquered Messenia by expansionist Sparta.[6] Might something similar be discovered for the

---

4 For the early (? sixth century BCE) commemoration of the Seven at Argos cf. A. Pariente, 'Le monument argien des "Sept contre Thèbes"', in M. Piérart (ed.), *Polydipsion Argos: Argos de la fin des palais mycéniens à la construction de l'état classique* (*BCH Supplément* 22; Paris: de Boccard, 1992), pp. 195–225. Note also the later Argive statues of the Seven at Delphi, Pausanias 10.10.3; on Argos' sixth-century presentation of its role in the Trojan War see E. L. Bowie, 'Sacadas of Argos', in A. Moreno and R. Thomas (eds), *Epitedeumata: Essays in Honour of Oswyn Murray* (forthcoming).

5 E. L. Bowie, 'Early Greek elegy, symposium and public festival', *JHS* 106 (1986), pp. 13–35; E. L. Bowie, 'Ancestors of Herodotus in early Greek elegiac and iambic poetry', in N. Luraghi (ed.), *The Historian's Craft in the Age of Herodotus* (Oxford: Oxford University Press, 2001), pp. 45–66; E. L. Bowie, 'Historical narrative in archaic and early classical Greek elegy', in D. Konstan and K. A. Raaflaub (eds), *Epic and History* (Malden, MA, and Oxford: Wiley-Blackwell, 2010), pp. 145–66.

6 My reconstruction of the form of such early elegiac narratives has recently been challenged by J. Grethlein, *The Greeks and Their Past: Poetry, Oratory and History in the Fifth Century BCE* (New York and Cambridge: Cambridge University Press, 2010), but whatever the form of the poems, it is indisputable that their content included some narrative of 'colonisation'.

west? Here we have no such elegiac poetry – the possible reason for this is something I shall discuss elsewhere – and for traces of proto-historical narrative we must turn to melic poetry. There my two test cases are Stesichorus of Himera and Ibycus of Rhegion.

STESICHORUS

I start with Stesichorus, a melic poet composing long poems, seemingly for public performance, and in my view performance by a χορός, around 570 BCE.[7] The first performances of these choral works were probably in his own city, Himera, the Greek settlement that lay furthest west on the north coast of Sicily, or in other Greek cities of Sicily or South Italy, though one papyrus fragment variously ascribed to Stesichorus (by Lobel and West) and Ibycus (by Page and Davies) has been argued to be designed for performance in a Spartan context.[8] To whichever of these two poets that fragment is ascribed, it does not alter the general picture. Stesichorus' narrative material is overwhelmingly drawn from the same range of Greek mythology that circulated in the cities of old Greece and that was in many cases developed to enhance the past of one of these cities. The Trojan War provides Stesichorus with his largest group of poems. The Argonauts, Thebes, the Calydonian boar are likewise traditional themes. Perhaps the *Geryoneis*, the melic epyllion in which Heracles steals the cattle of the three-headed Geryon, resident of the Hesperid island Erytheia in the ocean beyond Tartessus/Cadiz, had especial interest for an audience living in Himera on a trade route from the eastern and central Mediterranean to Spain. But there is no hint in the poem's surviving fragments (admittedly only a small proportion of what was originally probably more than 1,800 lines) that its poet brought Sicily into his story:[9] contrast the Cacus story in Vergil's *Aeneid* Book 8.

---

7 My arguments are very briefly stated in E. L. Bowie, 'Performing and re-performing Helen: Stesichorus' Palinode', in A. M. González de Tobia (ed.), *Mito y performance: De Grecia a la modernidad* (La Plata: Centro de Estudios de Lenguas Clásicas, 2010), pp. 385–408. Among other scholars who still accept the traditional classification of Stesichorus' melic poetry as entirely or predominantly for choral first performance is E. Cingano, 'L'opera di Ibico e Stesicoro nella classificazione degli antichi e dei moderni', *A.I.O.N.* 12 (1990), pp. 189–224.

8 *P.Oxy.* 2735 fr. 1 = SLG and Davies Ibycus S166, Campbell Ibycus 282A.

9 For a good study of the presentation of Geryon in the poem of Stesichorus see M. Lazzeri, *Studi sulla Gerioneide di Stesicoro* (Naples: Arte tipografica, 2008). I have not been persuaded by the arguments of C. Franzen, 'Sympathizing with the monster: Making sense of colonization in Stesichorus' *Geryoneis*', *QUCC* 121 (2009), pp. 55–72, that Stesichorus' sympathetic representation of the western monster Geryon was intended to appeal to indigenous elements in his Sicilian audiences, but that there will have been some such elements seems likely. For

During the song-dance performance of this poem and the others that handled traditional Greek myth, neither performers nor audiences in Sicily – unlike, for example, those of Alcman's first *Partheneion* – were confronted with elements of *their* community's past, at least as far as we can tell. But of course we have to work with very small samples of what there once was. Admittedly Stesichorus was notorious in Hellenistic scholarship for his innovation in mythical detail:[10] but there is no sign that this tweaking was done to accommodate his stories to the perspectives of a west Greek audience. Indeed it might rather be argued that he chooses some central, traditional Greek myths in order to emphasise the Greekness that the settlers in Sicily and South Italy shared with their metropoleis in mainland Greece and the islands.

One group of Stesichorus' poems constitutes an exception. Three poems attributed to him in antiquity had as their themes unhappy love-stories that have no relation to the main body of Greek mythology. All three have been declared spurious, initially by H. J. Rose,[11] followed by Page and Davies in their editions (1962 and 1991). But their ascription to Stesichorus has been convincingly defended by Luigi Lehnus.[12] The poems are as follows.

(1) The *Calyce* (fr. 277 *PMGF*, quoted by Athenaeus 14.619D). This poem is about a girl, Calyce, who prayed to Aphrodite to be able to marry a young man, Euathlus, and who threw herself off the Leucadian rock when he turned her down. The Leucadian rock, in the Ionian sea, gives the story a western but still mainland Greek setting. Athenaeus cites the fourth book of Aristoxenus περὶ μουσικῆς for its content, and for its sung performance by women: ᾖδόν, φησι, αἱ ἀρχαῖαι γυναῖκες Καλύκην τινα ᾠδήν.[13]

(2) The *Rhadine* (fr. 278 *PMGF*, quoted by Strabo 8.3.20) concerns a girl who was sent off to be bride to a tyrant of Corinth and

(footnote 9 *continued*)
the complexity of the cultural situation in Sicily see A. Willi, *Sikelismos: Sprache, Literatur und Gesellschaft im griechischen Sizilien 8.–5. Jh. v. Chr.* (Basel: Schwabe, 2008).

10 See *P. Oxy.* 2506 (= Stesichorus fr. 193 *PMGF* = Chamaeleon fr. 29 Wehrli) citing Chamaeleon for the form of the Palinode, but registering other innovations of content too.

11 H. J. Rose, 'Stesichoros and the Rhadine-fragment', *CQ* 26 (1932), pp. 88–92.

12 L. Lehnus, 'Note Stesicoree: I poemetti "minori"', *SCO* 24 (1975), pp. 191–6.

13 Aristoxenus' use of the word γυναῖκες suggests that the poem was not a *partheneion* but for singing by a group of married women, but perhaps the term should not be pressed. We might also wonder whether the unhelpful adjective ἀρχαῖαι conceals an ethnic: Ἀκραγαντῖναι? Ἀμβρακιωτικαί?

was pursued to Corinth by a cousin who had fallen in love with her. The tyrant killed them both and sent their bodies back on a chariot, but later repented and buried them. Strabo cites the first two lines, specifying helpfully that they are the poem's ἀρχή:

ἄγε Μοῦσα λίγει᾽ ἄρξον ἀοιδᾶς †ἐρατῶν ὕμνους†
Σαμίων περὶ παίδων ἐραταῖ φθεγγομένα λύραι

Strabo goes on to associate the story with a place called Samos in Elis, noting that it was the west wind, Zephyros, that had carried Rhadine's ship, and hence she was not on a voyage from Aegean Samos. Pausanias, however, notes a tomb of Rhadine and her lover Leontichus precisely on the island of Samos, on the road leading to the temple of Hera.[14] Perhaps Stesichorus took an East Aegean story and relocated it nearer Sicily. But it still has little to do with the past of Himera. It may just be relevant, however, that the bad guy in the story is a tyrant of Corinth. It had been colonists from Corinth who founded Syracuse; and when Himera was founded by Ionian Zancle (c. 648 BCE) the settlers were joined by some exiles from Syracuse.[15] Some citizens of Himera might have had access to oral traditions about a tomb of Rhadine and Leontichus at Corinth.

(3) The *Daphnis*. I offer both the text and a translation of Aelian, *Varia Historia* 10.18:

Δάφνιν τὸν βουκόλον λέγουσιν οἱ μὲν ἐρώμενον Ἑρμοῦ, ἄλλοι δὲ υἱόν· τὸ δὲ ὄνομα ἐκ τοῦ συμβάντος σχεῖν. γενέσθαι μὲν αὐτὸν ἐκ Νύμφης, τεχθέντα δὲ ἐκτεθῆναι ἐν δάφνῃ. τὰς δ᾽ ὑπ᾽ αὐτοῦ βουκολουμένας βοῦς φασιν ἀδελφὰς γεγονέναι τῶν Ἡλίου, ὧν Ὅμηρος ἐν Ὀδυσσείᾳ μέμνηται. βουκολῶν δὲ κατὰ τὴν Σικελίαν ὁ Δάφνις, ἠράσθη αὐτοῦ νύμφη μία, καὶ ὡμίλησε καλῷ ὄντι καὶ νέῳ καὶ πρῶτον ὑπηνήτῃ, ἔνθα τοῦ χρόνου ἡ χαριεστάτη ἐστὶν ἥβη τῶν καλῶν μειρακίων, ὥς πού φησι καὶ Ὅμηρος. συνθήκας δὲ ἐποίησε μηδεμιᾷ ἄλλῃ πλησιάσαι αὐτόν, καὶ ἐπηπείλησεν ὅτι πεπρωμένον ἐστὶν αὐτὸν στερηθῆναι τῆς ὄψεως, ἐὰν παραβῇ· καὶ εἶχον ὑπὲρ τούτων ῥήτραν πρὸς ἀλλήλους. χρόνῳ δὲ ὕστερον βασιλέως θυγατρὸς ἐρασθείσης αὐτοῦ οἰνωθεὶς ἔλυσε τὴν ὁμολογίαν καὶ ἐπλησίασε τῇ κόρῃ. ἐκ δὲ τούτου τὰ βουκολικὰ μέλη πρῶτον ᾔσθη, καὶ εἶχεν ὑπόθεσιν τὸ πάθος τὸ κατὰ τοὺς ὀφθαλμοὺς αὐτοῦ. καὶ Στησίχορόν γε τὸν Ἱμεραῖον τῆς τοιαύτης μελοποιίας ὑπάρξασθαι.

---

14 Paus. 7.5.13.
15 Thuc. 6.5.

Daphnis the cow-herd is said by some to have been the *eromenos*
of Hermes, and by others to have been his son, and to have got his
name from the circumstances of his birth – he was the child of a
nymph, and on his birth he was exposed in a laurel bush (*daphne*).
And they say that the cattle tended by him were sisters of those of
the Sun, which Homer mentions in the *Odyssey*. While Daphnis
was tending his cattle in Sicily, a nymph fell in love with him and
had intercourse with him, since he was handsome and young and
growing his first beard, at which point the prime of beautiful
young boys is at its most attractive, as indeed Homer also says.
She made a compact with him that he would not have sex with
any other woman, and threatened that it was fated that he would
be deprived of his sight if he broke the agreement. And they had
a contract with each other about this. But later a princess fell in
love with him, got him drunk, so that he broke the agreement
and had sex with her. And it was on the basis of this that bucolic
[cattle-tending] songs were first sung and had as their theme what
happened to his sight. And (they say?) Stesichorus of Himera
initiated this sort of sung poetry.

Here we are firmly on Sicilian territory. The story of Daphnis was
picked up several times by the Syracusan poet Theocritus in his
bucolic hexameter poems. In his most extended treatment, *Idyll*
1.64–9, Theocritus seems to locate the story on the slopes of Etna:
Daphnis' woes, ἄλγεα, are sung by a shepherd, Thyrsis of Etna, and
Thyrsis complains that, when Daphnis was dying, the nymphs who
might have saved him were not by the rivers of eastern Sicily, the
Anapus and the Acis:

> Θύρσις ὅδ' ὡξ Αἴτνας, καὶ Θύρσιδος ἀδέα φωνά.
> πᾷ ποκ' ἄρ' ἦσθ', ὅκα Δάφνις ἐτάκετο, πᾷ ποκα, Νύμφαι;
> ἦ κατὰ Πηνειῶ καλὰ τέμπεα, ἢ κατὰ Πίνδω;
> οὐ γὰρ δὴ ποταμοῖο μέγαν ῥόον εἴχετ' Ἀνάπω,
> οὐδ' Αἴτνας σκοπιάν, οὐδ' Ἄκιδος ἱερὸν ὕδωρ.
>   ἄρχετε βουκολικᾶς, Μοῖσαι φίλαι, ἄρχετ' ἀοιδᾶς

This is Thyrsis from Etna, and sweet is Thyrsis' voice.
'Wherever were you, tell me, when Daphnis was wasting,
     wherever, nymphs?
Were you in the fair glens of the Peneus, or were you in those of
     Pindus?
For you were not dwelling in the mighty stream of the river
     Anapus,

nor on Etna's peak, nor in the sacred water of the Acis.
Begin the cowherd's . . . begin, dear Muses, the song.

In Theocritus *Idyll* 7.72–5, however, the Daphnis story is set near
Himera:

ὁ δὲ Τίτυρος ἐγγύθεν ᾀσεῖ
ὥς ποκα τᾶς Ξενέας ἠράσσατο Δάφνις ὁ βούτας,
χὠς ὄρος ἀμφεπονεῖτο καὶ ὡς δρύες αὐτὸν ἐθρήνευν
Ἱμέρα αἵτε φύοντι παρ' ὄχθαισιν ποταμοῖο

And Tityrus will sing nearby
how once Xenea kindled the desire of Daphnis the cowherd,
and how the mountain voiced distress all around, and how oaks
    lamented him,
oaks which grow by the banks of the river Himeras.

We cannot tell whether Theocritus knew the Daphnis story in two
versions, one linked to Himera and the other to Etna, or only in one
Himeran version that he consciously relocated in *Idyll* 1, just as he
seems consciously (if enigmatically) to have changed the nature of
Daphnis' fatal affliction. That the Syracusan poet relocated an Etna
version in Himera is the least likely explanation; so *Idyll* 7 offers some
support for the hypothesis that a story about Daphnis was linked to
Himera before Theocritus.

A version related to Himera is also attested by Servius, giving
Cefalù as the location of Daphnis' sad end: *ab irata nympha* (in this
version called Nomia) *amatrice luminibus orbatus est deinde <in>
lapidem versus. nam apud Cephaloeditanum oppidum saxum dicitur
esse, quod formam hominis ostendit* ('he was deprived of his sight by
the nymph who loved him, and whom he angered, and then turned
to stone. For in the town of Cephalù there is said to be a rock which
has the shape of a man').[16] One can compare a version ascribed to
unnamed writers by the scholiast on Theocritus who distinguishes the
version of a (probably) third-century tragedian Sositheus, apparently
from Syracuse, who calls the nymph Thaleia and has Daphnis pining
to death, from a variant according to which Daphnis, blinded, wan-
dered over a cliff to his death: οἱ δὲ λοιποί φασι τυφλωθῆναι αὐτὸν καὶ
ἀλώμενον κατακρημνισθῆναι.[17] But there was also a version locating

16 Servius on Verg. *Ecl.* 8.68.
17 Σ Theoc. 8.93, citing Sositheus *TrGrF*, p. 821 N².

the tale of Daphnis in the Heraean hills of central Sicily, told by Diodorus of Sicilian Agyrrhium.[18]

Admittedly there remains some ground for doubting whether Stesichorus told the Daphnis story at all. The version in Aelian is almost identical with that of Parthenius, ἐρωτικὰ παθήματα 29, which the manchette attributes to the Sicilian historian Timaeus.[19] Lightfoot justly observes that the last sentence of the Aelian passage, usually taken to mean the story was sung by Stesichorus, says simply that he initiated 'singing like this', and that 'this' arguably refers to 'bucolic songs'. Neither she nor Nigel Wilson in his Loeb Aelian, *Varia Historia*, raises the problem of the last sentence having an infinitive, ὑπάρξασθαι, as its only visible verb.[20] I remain uncertain as to what 'this sort of sung poetry' refers, but I retain a shred of credence in a Stesichorean Daphnis because of the Himeran connections attested by Theoc. 7.72–5 and Servius. This is partly because there is also other evidence that Himera figured in at least some context in Stesichorus' poetry. Vibius Sequester says of the river Himeras that gave its name to the city: *hoc flumen in duas partes findi ait Stesichorus, unam in Tyrrhenum mare, aliam in Libycum decurrere* ('Stesichorus says that this river splits into two parts, and that one flows into the Tyrrhenian sea, the other into the Libyan').[21]

That the Daphnis story was told by Stesichorus in some relation to Himera seems, then, very probable. Whether he presented it as a part of Himera's *past* we cannot be sure. The ποκα of Theocritus 7.73 is not there in Aelian's *faux-naïf* version of the story, and even if it were it would not be unambiguously diagnostic – though compare the use of ποτε in Stesichorus fr. 223 *PMGF*, concerning Tyndareus' fateful omission of Aphrodite in a sacrifice. If the tale of Daphnis has any bearing on Himera's construction of its identity, it may be more to do with issues arising from the relations of the settlers with earlier inhabitants of the quite small Himeran plain, or with current inhabitants of its hilly back-country, than with the past of the immigrants themselves.

IBYCUS

The remains of Ibycus of Rhegion are only a little more illuminating, but that little is a large little. Most, if not all, of Ibycus' handling of

---

18 D.S. 4.84.
19 Timaeus *FGrHist* 566 F83.
20 J. L. Lightfoot, *Parthenius of Nicaea* (Oxford: Clarendon Press, 1999), pp. 526–30.
21 Vibius Sequester, *De fluminibus fontibus etc.*, p. 15 Gelsonino; cf. Himerius, *Or.* 27.27: τὴν Ἰμέραν . . . λόγοις κοσμεῖ Στησίχορος.

myth seems not to have been in long, self-standing treatments like those of Stesichorus but in comparisons or *praeteritiones* in praise-poems, of which that for Polycrates is the best and most famous example.[22] Here on Samos, as in the fragment of a poem argued to be designed for a Spartan context,[23] the range of myth is 'standard': in the Polycrates poem, Troy; in the other, Castor and Polydeuces, Heracles, Iolaus, Peleus and (perhaps the single whiff of the West) Geryon.[24] As I have argued elsewhere, the emphasis that Ajax and Achilles were the greatest warriors at Troy (S151.32–4) may be an endorsement of a claim by Ibycus' host Polycrates, son of Aeaces, to have an Aeacid past going back to Aeacus and his grandsons.[25] Oedipus and Ino also figure in some erotic poems known from a papyrus commentary.[26]

The Polycrates poem reminds us that some of Ibycus's poems were first composed for audiences in the Aegean. It is only rarely possible to judge when a poem belongs there, and when back in his native Rhegion or other cities of the western Greeks. But a papyrus commentary on Ibycus and other lyric poets has provided some tantalising detail. S220 Davies = 282B Campbell begins as follows:

```
[        ν]ύμφα· οἶον χωρ[
[        ].ε ταῖς νύ[μ]φαις .[
[        ].αι Κρονίου πτυχαὶ φα[
[        Κ]ρόνιον ἐν Λεοντίνοις [..].[
[        πυ]κνῶς ἔρχεσθαι τὸν              (5)
[        ]τ. ποτὲ μὲν κυνηγε-
[        ] ἐπιδείξαντα τοῖς
[        ]χωρα[ ] καὶ τα
[        ].ν χαλεπὸν
[        ε]ὔκολόν φησιν              (10)
[        ].α..ι πλεῖον
[        ].αι δυσα-
[        ].[ ]ς αὖχα γλυ-
[κερὰ    ]σα ἰδίως ἀν-
[        ]τις ἐλπὶς του              (15)
         γ]λυκερὰ αὐ-
```

22 S151 SLG and *PMGF*, = 282(a) Campbell, to which G. O. Hutchinson, *Greek Lyric Poetry: A Commentary on Selected Larger Pieces* (Oxford: Oxford University Press, 2001), is an excellent introduction.
23 *P.Oxy.* 2735 fr. 1 = Ibycus S166–S219 SLG and *PMGF*, Ibycus 282A Campbell.
24 S176.18 *SLG* and *PMGF* = 282A viii 18 Campbell.
25 Bowie, 'Wandering poets'.
26 S222 *SLG* and *PMGF* = 282B (iii) Campbell.

χ]εῖ καυχ[ᾶται .... ἐ]λπίς· ἢ οὕτως· γλυ-
κερὰ γίν[εται ἡ καύχη]σις ἐὰν ἐπιτύ-
χηι· ἇιπερ[   ]ν ποδῶν· ὥσ-
περ καὶ ο.[πόδ]ας ἐν τῆι ἀθλ[ή-   (20)
σει ἐπαν[   ]βηι γεγεν[
ὁ γὰρ νικ[   ]κ.[.].[
πονουδι[
ἀναγινω[σκ-
νας ἀδηλ[(25)
τεύων α.[πο-
λὺν γενέσ[θαι
σιν αὐτ.[
ἵν' οὕτως δεκα[
θος γίνεται οπ[ἐ-   (30)
πιτύχηι.

There is not space in this chapter to explore all the many problems of this fragment.[27] The papyrus commentator seems to be sure that the 'glens of Kronios' (Κρονίου πτυχαί) are in the territory of Leontini, which of course extends towards the undulating slopes of Etna These could simply be a backdrop for hunting (6, ποτὲ μὲν κυνηγε-) by a young *laudandus* from Ibycus' contemporary world, and the poem could be, as Barron suggested, a proto-epinician. But the presence of a nymph might give us pause. The poem was composed for performance in sixth-century Sicily, but the nymph suggests mythical time. A phrase a little later in the commentary has been thought by some to describe the eagle that carried off Ganymede,[28] a story we know that Ibycus told in a poem addressed to a Gorgias.[29] The commentator here is discussing a poem to Callias,[30] but cross-refers to another phrase of Ibycus (S223(a) col. ii 6–7 Davies = 282B (iv) fr.5, col. ii 6–7 Campbell):

            Ἴ]βυκος ἑτέρω
]αν.[   ].ο χθονὸς ἐς
..].[..]αν βαθ[ὺν ἀ]έρα τάμνων

27 In the papyrus text (http://163.1.169.40/gsdl/collect/POxy/index/assoc/HASH0
   13e/bd7befec.dir/POxy.v0032.n2637.a.01.hires.jpg), note how S220 is immediately
   followed by a lemma headed Καλλίας, presumably an *eromenos.*
28 S223(a) 6–7 *SLG* and *PMGF* = 282B (iv) Campbell.
29 Fr. 289 (a) *PMGF* = scholiast on Apollonius Rhodius 3.114–17.
30 For the name see the papyrus, S221 *PMGF* = 282B (ii) fr.1(a) 32–42
   Campbell.

If the reference of βαθ[ὺν ἀ]έρα τάμνων to Ganymede's eagle is correct, then it is likely that the phrase comes from that poem to Gorgias. As I have already suggested elsewhere,[31] the name Gorgias is unusual enough for an ancestor of the later fifth-century Gorgias to have some claim to be its bearer in this poem of Ibycus. The family of that Gorgias came from Leontini. Might the first surviving part of the commentary, asserting Leontini as the location of the 'glens of Zeus', be a commentary on Ibycus' poem to Gorgias? If so, it may have been discussing a variant of the abduction of Ganymede, relocated on the slopes of Etna to offer a paradigm for Ibycus' fantasies about abducting the (presumably) ephebic Gorgias.[32]

Whether any of this speculation, if correct, would give us an Ibycus singing of Leontini's past is an unanswerable question. The *mythos* could have been so told that it validated the idea that Greek youths and Greek gods could have been found in eastern Sicily in the period of the Trojan War, a notion that would chime with traditions of Greeks and Trojans reaching the west in the war's aftermath. For the possible appearance of such traditions in Stesichorus and Ibycus, we might compare the scene on the admittedly much later *Tabula Iliaca* labelled Μισῆνος. Αἰνήας ἀπαίρων εἰς τὴν Ἑσπερίαν.[33]

One other fragment of Ibycus attested by the same papyrus refers to Chalcidians, a colony and oaths (S227 *PMGF* = 282B (viii) fr. 7 Campbell):[34]

```
                    ].συ.[
        [ ] Χαλκιδέων[
        [ ]ς προηγη[
        [    ] ἀποικίασ.[
        [    ]ορκια πο[                          (5)
        [    ]νως κυμ[
        [    ἐ]πὶ τοῖς ὄμμ[ασι
        [    κ]ορύσσεται δε[
        [    κορθ]ύεται με[τ]εω[ρίζεται
        [    ]ος ὁ πόθος.[                        (10)
        [    ] φησὶν ο.[
        [    ]ερω[..].[
```

31 Bowie, 'Wandering poets'.
32 It is also possible, but in my view less likely, that the presence of a nymph indicates that here Ibycus is offering a Leontini version of the Daphnis story: the Acis is very much a Leontini river.
33 Cf. C. M. Bowra, *Greek Lyric Poetry* (Oxford: Clarendon Press, 1935, revised 1961), pp. 104–6; N. M. Horsfall, 'Stesichorus at Bovillae', *JHS* 99 (1979), pp. 26–48.
34 S227 *PMGF* = 282B (viii) fr. 7 Campbell.

Like the other poems that are commented upon in the papyrus this
too seem to involve desire (cf. line 10, πόθος): but it is hard not to take
the first five lines as referring to the foundation of some Chalcidian
colony, with Ibycus' Rhegium the prime candidate. So thought
Mosino in 1975.[35] To me he seems likely to be right in his suggestion
that this part of this poem is about Rhegium's colonisation.

Here at last, then, we have a tiny scrap of evidence of melic poetry
by one of the two great western poets, Stesichorus and Ibycus, that
touches on themes that seem to have been treated in the Aegean by
several elegiac poets – Mimnermus, Xenophanes, Ion of Chios – and
by Archilochus in trochaic tetrameters as well as in elegy.[36] What I
have found has been so little as to constitute a negative result.

Why has this result been negative?

Genre is, I suppose, the most important factor. Ibycus' love poems
bring in mythical or historical figures as paradigms or comparandi,
and no extended account of foundation or early settlement would be
appropriate. Stesichorus' poems require a different sort of explanation. They are perhaps of the same sort of length as Mimnermus'
Smyrneis, and very probably performed for the same sort of civic
audience. But they are, I suggest, aiming consciously to be panhellenic
in a way that Ionian elegy of the seventh century did not. As Burkert
argued, Stesichorus saw himself in competition with performers of
Homeric hexameter poetry. His poems could be performed anywhere,
and perhaps they were. They were certainly known to Aeschylus
in Attica around 458 BCE and to audiences of Aristophanes' Peace
around 421 BCE.[37] From my point of view, today, it is a great pity that
he was not more parochial, like Alcman or Corinna: if he had been he
would have been rather more help in reconstructing how early sixth-
century Himera perceived its past.

---

35 F. Mosino, 'La fondazione di Reggio in un frammento di Ibico?', Calabria
   Turismo 25/6 (1975), pp. 23ff.
36 For an attractive argument that Archilochus' Telephus poem appealed to a
   mixed population of Parian settlers on Thasos and an earlier population involved
   in a cult of a Phoenician Heracles, see C. Nobili, 'Tra epos ed elegia: Il nuovo
   Archiloco', Maia 61 (2009), pp. 229–49.
37 For knowledge of Stesichorus in Athens in the fifth century see now C. Carey,
   'Alcman from Laconia to Alexandria', in L. Athanassaki and E. L. Bowie (eds),
   Archaic and Classical Choral Song (Berlin: de Gruyter, 2011), pp. 437–60, at pp.
   457, 459.

6

PINDAR AND THE RECONSTRUCTION OF THE PAST

Maria Pavlou

The past holds a central and prominent position in Pindar's poetry as a whole. Even his *Epinicians*, whose overarching concern is the praise of contemporary victors, are rich repositories of local traditions and myths with a wider geographic and cultural scope. The Pindaric past covers a vast period which spans from the very beginnings and formation of the world up to the Persian Wars and contemporary reality. Nonetheless, the great majority of Pindar's stories concern *illud tempus*,[1] that is, the remote mythical past. This said, it should be noted that Pindar makes no great distinction between what we would nowadays call *spatium mythicum* and *spatium historicum*. He never disputes the historicity of the mythical period, but endows mythical data and historical events with equal validity.[2] A telling example of his outlook is the recital of ancient Theban stories which opens *Isthmian* 7 and which functions as 'an epitome of Theban history', as Young aptly called it.[3] Here Pindar begins with a reference to Demeter and

Thanks go to John Marincola for his invitation to the Leventis Conference, and to the audience there for their suggestions and remarks; also to the J. F. Costopoulos Foundation for its generous financial support, which enabled me to conduct the research for this chapter. Last but not least I thank my PhD supervisor, Robert Fowler, for many stimulating discussions on the notion of time in Pindar.

1 The phrase was first used by M. Eliade, *The Myth of the Eternal Return*, tr. W. R. Trask (New York: Pantheon Books, 1954), in order to indicate the sacred time of origins when the world was first created.

2 On the Greek view of myth and history see among others C. Brillante, 'History and the historical interpretation of myth', in L. Edmunds (ed.), *Approaches to Greek Myth* (Baltimore: Johns Hopkins University Press, 1990), pp. 91–140, at pp. 93ff; T. Harrison, *Divinity and History: The Religion of Herodotus* (Oxford: Clarendon Press, 2000), pp. 197–207.

3 D. C. Young, *Pindar Isthmian 7: Myth and Exempla* (Leiden: Brill, 1971), pp. 16–18. On the cluster of myths that opens *Isthm.* 7 see, among others, R. Sevieri, 'Cantare la città: Tempo mitico e spazio urbano nell' *Istmica* 7 di Pindaro per Strepsiade di Tebe', in P. A. Bernardini (ed.), *Presenza e funzione della città di Tebe nella cultura greca: Atti del Convegno Internationale,*

Dionysos and their relationship to Thebes, progresses to Theban heroes, and finally comes down to his own time through a reference to the Theban Aegeidai, thus linking myth and history in a continuum. What should be stressed at the outset is that Pindar's mythical detours are not generated by his desire to report the past *per se*, but rather serve as a kind of eulogistic device. Being an encomiast, Pindar's aim is to praise, extol and glorify contemporary victors. Accordingly, his narration of the past is always triggered by the current occasion and seeks to interpret forms and institutions of the present; in other words, the reconstruction of the past in Pindar is first and foremost prescriptive and explanatory.[4] Furthermore, this is the reason why most of the stories he narrates refer to the birth of heroes, the colonisation of cities, the establishment of hero cults, rituals and athletic games, and other inventions.[5] Whereas some of these accounts had a panhellenic appeal (e.g. the myth of Heracles), Pindar's self-exhortation in *Nem.* 3.31 to 'search at home' (οἴκοθεν μάτευε) underpins the whole epinician corpus; as a result, most of his material is derived from local lore and is associated, in one way or another, with the victors' family and/ or their home towns.

In what follows, I will attempt to examine a few aspects of this intricate and fascinating Pindaric epinician past.[6] My discussion will be divided into two parts. In the first part I will focus on the temporal perspective of Pindar's narratives and the relationship he tries to establish between past and present. I will then research Pindar's sources: more particularly, I will concentrate on the way in which he acquires his information about the past, with particular emphasis on his comments and views on the transmission of the past and the reliability of tradition.

(footnote 3 *continued*)
Urbino 7–9 Luglio 1997 (Pisa and Rome: Istituti editoriali e poligrafici internazionali, 2000), pp. 179–92; P. Agócs, 'Memory and forgetting in Pindar's Seventh Isthmian', in L. Doležalová (ed.), *Strategies of Remembrance: From Pindar to Hölderin* (Cambridge: Cambridge Scholars, 2009), pp. 33–91.

4 G. Huxley, *Pindar's Vision of the Past* (Belfast: Author, 1975), p. 43.
5 Birth of heroes: Iamos (*Ol.* 6.35–45); Aristaios (*Pyth.* 9.59–65); Asklepios (*Pyth.* 3.38–46). Foundation/colonisation of cities: *Pyth.* 4, 9 (Kyrene); *Ol.* 7 (Rhodes). Institution of athletic games: *Ol.* 10 (Olympic games); *Nem.* 9 (Nemean games). Cults of heroes: *Ol.* 1; on allusions to hero cults in Pindar see B. Currie, *Pindar and the Cult of Heroes* (Oxford: Oxford University Press, 2005).
6 Even though scholars tend to examine Pindar's epinician and cult poems together, the way in which Pindar treats time and establishes the relationship between past and present in these two poetic genres differs considerably. On this see M. Pavlou, 'Past and present in Pindar's religious poetry', in A. P. M. H. Lardinois, J. H. Blok and M. G. M. van der Poel (eds), *Sacred Words: Orality, Literacy and Religion* (*Orality and Literacy in the Ancient World* 8; Leiden: Brill, 2011), pp. 59–78.

1 LOCATING THE PAST IN THE TIMELINE

One striking thing about Pindar is his disregard for placing events in a temporal framework. For instance, he never specifies the interval that separates the moment of the narration and the moment of the story. The transition from the present to the past is usually made through the indefinite conjunctions τότε, ὅτε and especially ποτε, followed by a relative pronoun.[7] Despite the vagueness of the above conjunctions, Pindar shows no particular interest in providing a somewhat more specific location of events in the sphere of the past. As a result, events are always presented as 'floating' in a kind of 'ageless past'.[8] Even in the case of recent historical events, where a more precise chronology could be easily provided, Pindar prefers to locate these events by employing the indefinite ποτε in lieu of a more specific temporal term. In *Pyth.* 3, for example, the victory of Hieron's horse Pherenikos, which occurred just a few years before the composition of the ode, is said to have taken place 'once upon a time' (ἕλεν . . . ποτέ, 74).[9]

A similar stance is adopted in relation to the various temporal levels within a particular mythical story. Not only does Pindar radically alter the order and chronological sequence of events, but he also refrains from designating their extent and duration. In fact, in many cases the transition from one temporal level of a story to the other is achieved through the repetition of the indefinite ποτε. In *Ol.* 7, for instance, in line 30 ποτε refers to the period of the colonisation of Rhodes by Tlepolemos; at line 34 it refers to an earlier period, when Athena was

---

7 See e.g. τότε (*Nem.* 9.11); ὅτε (*Ol.* 7.55); ποτε (*Ol.* 3.13, *Ol.* 9.9; *Pyth.* 1.16, 9.5; *Nem.* 8.18, 9.13; *Isthm.* 1.13). The transition to the past can also be achieved through the use of the temporal adjectives παλαιός (*Pyth.* 9.105) and ἀρχαῖος (*Nem.* 1.34).

8 G. Genette, *Narrative Discourse*, tr. J. E. Lewin (Oxford: Blackwell, 1980), p. 220.

9 See also *Isthm.* 8.65; *Nem.* 6.36, 42; *Nem.* 9.52; *Nem.* 10.25. D. C. Young, 'Pindar *Pythian* 2 and 3: Inscriptional ποτε and the "poetic epistle"', *HSCP* 87 (1983), pp. 31–42, at p. 36, suggests that in these instances ποτε has a future point of view, not a present one; in other words, it does not indicate distance in time from the moment of the narration, but rather reflects the viewpoint of later audiences on the victory. He calls this ποτε 'inscriptional' as it is often used in inscriptions in the same sense. Even though I agree with Young's observation, in my view it is also significant to consider the impact that this 'inscriptional' ποτε would have upon the current audience; through the use of ποτε recent events are put on a par with the mythical events of the past and are 'traditionalised', so to speak. In this way the temporal distance between past and present seems to collapse and the audience is invited to experience time as a unity. Another thing that should be stressed is that only a few instances of ποτε in Pindar pertain to the 'inscriptional' ποτε. Whenever ποτε refers to the distant mythical past, its vagueness suggests a significant remove in time; see C. Carey, 'Prosopographica Pindarica', *CQ* 39 (1989), pp. 1–9, at p. 8.

born; and at line 71 it refers to an even earlier period, when Helios united with Rhodes. The effect is more poignant in *Pyth.* 4, where ποτε occurs eight times, each time referring to a different temporal level. Occasionally ποτε is accompanied by spatial adverbs (πρόσθε ποτέ, *Ol.* 10.31, and ὄπιθεν οὐ πολλόν, *Ol.* 10.35–6), which contribute nothing, however, to the more precise dating of events. Furthermore, the chronological terms used in a handful of cases are also quite vague and indefinite. In *Pyth.* 11 we are told that Agamemnon returned from Troy χρονίῳ, while in *Ol.* 1.46 Ganymede's transfer to Olympos is said to have taken place δευτέρῳ χρόνῳ. In *Pyth.* 2.58 the locution ἑκὰς ἐών most probably gives in spatialised terms the temporal distance that separates Pindar from Archilochus, once again without specifying the interval.[10] This overall lack of temporal perspective, in conjunction with Pindar's tendency to resort to anachronies by distorting and altering the chronological sequence of events, creates difficulties; and it sometimes leads to hermeneutic *aporia*s. A salient example is *Ol.* 3, where the unspecified lapse of time between Herakles' two journeys to the Istrian Land has caused debate and led a number of scholars to conflate the two journeys into one.[11]

The only instance where Pindar offers a more precise (in terms of chronology) narrative is *Pyth.* 4, a poem that celebrates the chariot victory of the king of Kyrene, Arkesilas IV. Here, not only does Pindar designate the temporal interval that separates the story, as he narrates from the performative now, but he also defines the intervals between the different stages of the story. We learn, for instance, that a lapse of twenty years intercedes between Jason's birth and his arrival at Iolkos (εἴκοσι δ' ἐκτελέσαις ἐνιαυτούς, 104), and that there is an interval of five days between his meeting with Pelias and the beginning of the Argonautic expedition (131–3). We are also informed that the Argonauts were carrying the *Argo* across land for twelve days (δώδεκα ἁμέρας, 25–6). What merits particular attention, however, is the use of genealogical chronology, the only instance throughout the *Epinicians* where Pindar resorts to the use of generations in order to reckon time. As he declares, eight

10 See W. J. Slater, *Lexicon to Pindar* (Berlin: de Gruyter, 1969), s.v. ἑκάς; C. G. Brown, 'Pindar on Archilochus and the gluttony of blame (*Pyth.* 2.52–5)', *JHS* 126 (2006), pp. 36–46. It should be noted that many scholars maintain that the adverb ἑκάς here designates moral distance; see, among others, A. M. Miller, 'Pindar, Archilochus and Hieron in *Pyth.* 2.52–56', *TAPA* 111 (1981), pp. 135–43, at pp. 140–1.
11 The bibliography on this poem is vast; see the informative article by A. Köhnken, 'Mythical chronology and thematic coherence in Pindar's Third Olympian Ode', *HSCP* 87 (1983), pp. 49–63, who also provides relevant bibliography.

generations separate Arkesilas from Battos, progenitor of his clan
and founder of Kyrene (παισὶ τούτοις ὄγδοον θάλλει μέρος Ἀρκεσίλας,
65); twenty-seven generations separate Battos from the Argonauts
(ἑβδόμᾳ καὶ σὺν δεκάτᾳ γενεᾷ, 10); and there are three generations
separating Kretheas from Jason. Pindar also adds that, if the clod of
earth given by Triton to the Argonaut Euphamos (from whose race
came Arkesilas' ancestors) had not been washed away prematurely,
the colonisation of Kyrene would have taken place thirteen generations earlier and would have coincided with the Danaans' forced
migration from the Peloponnese (47–9).[12]

The temporal perspective adopted in *Pyth.* 4 is noticeable, not only
because it is at odds with Pindar's overall practice, but also because
of its particularly detailed chronological specificity. Even though
Pindar was a fervent advocate of inborn excellence and laid much
emphasis upon lineage, this is the only instance where he designates
the full length of a victor's genealogy. Not only this, but he also
attempts to locate the various events of the story by means of generations. He even goes so far as to designate the temporal point at which
the colonisation of Kyrene *could* have taken place! Undoubtedly,
Arkesilas must have provided Pindar with the details of his genealogical lineage.[13] The crucial question concerns the chronology of the
other events. Given that the reconciliation between the journey of
the Argonauts and the Battiads (the clan of king Arkesilas) was most
probably Pindar's invention, what was his criterion for locating the
various events of his account in the timeline? Considering that the
first systematic attempts to map the past appear later, with Herodotus
and Hellanicus, shall we assume that the designation of the intervals
between the events in *Pyth.* 4 is arbitrary and circumstantial? Would
it be far-fetched to propose that Pindar's genealogical construction was based on a certain kind of genealogical chronology that
was in use during the fifth century? Could we suppose the existence
of a genealogical framework with some fixed landmarks indicating

12 The 'Danaans' were forced to leave the Peloponnese because of the Dorians'
   invasion of Greece. Note that Pindar employs the term 'Danaans' to indicate the
   generation that lived in Greece before the Dorian invasion; see B. K. Braswell,
   A Commentary on the Fourth Pythian Ode of Pindar (Berlin and New York: de
   Gruyter, 1988), *ad Pyth.* 4.48.
13 See M. Giangiulio, 'Constructing the past: Colonial traditions and the writing
   of history. The case of Cyrene', in N. Luraghi (ed.), *The Historian's Craft in the
   Age of Herodotus* (Oxford: Oxford University Press, 2001), pp. 116–37, at p. 124,
   who, based on the affinities between the Pindaric and Herodotean version of the
   Battiad genealogy, argues for the existence of an earlier written version. See also
   R. Thomas, *Oral Tradition and Written Record in Classical Athens* (Cambridge:
   Cambridge University Press, 1989), p. 172 n. 39.

significant events, such as the Trojan War and the Dorian invasion?[14] Of course, such a genealogical framework would presuppose the use of an 'average' genealogy for its construction. Pindar's much younger contemporary Herodotus informs us of the Egyptian standard of three generations per century (each generation equalling 33.3 years); and it seems that he himself used this standard for at least some of his own calculations in the *Histories*.[15] Considering the geographical proximity of Kyrene and Egypt, could we assume that Pindar used a similar standard for his own genealogical reckoning in *Pyth.* 4? Even though, *prima facie,* this suggestion may seem merely conjecture, if we attempt to convert the genealogies of *Pyth.* 4 into years by using an 'average' genealogy, the results are indeed striking and thought-provoking. Twenty-five generations equal approximately 800 years, eight generations equal 233 years and four generations make 100 years.[16] Given that the ode was performed around 462 BCE, this places the Argonautic expedition as far back as 1300 BCE, the colonisation of Kyrene by Battos as 700 BCE and the Danaans' migration from the Peloponnese as 1200 BCE. We know that the colonisation of Kyrene took place around 650 BCE, while in antiquity the conjectural date of the Trojan War, which was considered to have taken place one or two generations after the Argonautic expedition, was the thirteenth or early twelfth century.[17] Furthermore, we also know that the Dorian invasion of Greece must have taken place between 1200 and 1100 BCE. Certainly, this correspondence might be sheer coincidence. It is, however, striking and, if nothing else, it does invite us to think more

14 Some had credited the construction of a kind of 'genealogical backbone' to Hekataios, even though this thesis does not find many advocates nowadays. See the discussion by L. Bertelli, 'Hecataeus: From genealogy to historiography', in Luraghi, *Historian's Craft*, pp. 67–94, at pp. 89–94, who also provides relevant bibliography.

15 In 2.142–3 Herodotus reports that, according to the Egyptian priests, Egyptian human history has a depth of 341 generations. He then converts these generations into 11,340 years by using the Egyptian standard of three generations per century. Herodotus uses genealogical chronology around sixteen times in the *Histories*; yet there is no consensus on whether he used the Egyptian standard for all his calculations. See A. Mosshammer, *The Chronicle of Eusebius and Greek Chronographic Tradition* (Lewisburg, PA: Bucknell University Press, 1979), pp. 105–11; J. Cobet, 'The organization of time in the *Histories*', in E. Bakker, I. J. F. de Jong and H. van Wees (eds), *Brill's Companion to Herodotus* (Leiden: Brill, 2002), pp. 387–412.

16 For the calculations it is important to keep in mind that ancient arithmetic was inclusive; therefore one needs to multiply the Egyptian standard by twenty-four, seven and three generations respectively.

17 Herodotus dates the Trojan War to the thirteenth century BCE (Hdt. 2.145.4). See also Eratosthenes of Kyrene (*FGrHist* 241 F 1a), who dates the Trojan War to 1183 BCE, 407 years before the first Olympiad of 776 BCE. Timaios of Tauromenium (*FGrHist* 566 F 125) places the Trojan War at the same period.

carefully about the forms of chronological reckoning that were in use before Herodotus and his contemporaries.[18]

Pindar's disregard for a temporal perspective in his narratives about the past was interpreted by Herman Fränkel and his followers as an indication of his archaic mentality and his inability to perceive the past as an extended continuum.[19] Yet Pindar's stance does not testify to his 'primitivism'; rather, it is premised by the etiquette of the epinician genre. As the example of *Pyth.* 4 makes clear, Pindar was perfectly capable of adopting a temporal perspective in his narratives if he wished. However, chronology and the dating of the past were not the point. Pindar's primary concern was not to map the past by resorting to genealogical time-reckoning or synchronisations, but rather to draw analogies between past and present, and to stress the continuity between these two temporal units.[20]

2 PAST AND PRESENT

Pindar does not refer to the past and present as 'past' and 'present'; he does, however, designate these two temporal entities by using different vocabulary and terminology. When he refers to the past and his ancestors or predecessors in general, he usually employs the temporal adverbs πάλαι and πρότερον, and terms such as οἱ παλαιότεροι, οἱ παλαίγονοι and οἱ πρότεροι. Things associated with the past are normally defined by the adjective παλαιός, its derivatives and compounds, as well as by the adjective ἀρχαῖος. Whereas both παλαιός and ἀρχαῖος have primary reference to time and appear to share virtually the same semantic range, they are not interchangeable.[21] Ἀρχαῖος is employed when Pindar wants to stress the 'oldness' of something; therefore it is not used in relation to the past in general but merely to the remote/ mythical past. In contrast, παλαιός can designate the whole spectrum of the past. As far as the present is concerned, Pindar normally refers to it by using the adverb νῦν, while things related to the present are

---

18 Whatever the case is, if my conjecture is valid, then some sort of chronological reckoning seems to have been in use even before Herodotus.

19 See, among others, H. Fränkel, 'Die Zeitauffassung in der griechischen Literatur', *Beilagenheft zur Zeitschrift für Aesthetik und allgemeine Kunstwissenschaft* 25 (1931); P. Vivante, 'On myth and action in Pindar', *Arethusa* 4 (1971), pp. 119–36; Vivante, 'On time in Pindar', *Arethusa* 5 (1972), pp. 107–31.

20 Like Pindar, Bacchylides shows no particular interest in the chronology of the events he narrates. The only exception is *Ep.* 11; but see R. Garner, 'Countless deeds of valour: Bacchylides 11', *CQ* 42 (1992), pp. 523–5.

21 Contrast I. Rumpel, *Lexicon Pindaricum* (Leipzig: B. G. Teubner, 1883), and Slater, *Lexicon to Pindar*, both of whom translate παλαιός and ἀρχαῖος in a similar way without paying attention to this semantic nuance.

often designated with the comparative and superlative form of the adjective νέος.[22]

Leaving terminology aside, let's move on and discuss briefly the relationship that Pindar registers between past and present. In Homer the past is absolute and superior to the present ('chrono-tope of historical inversion').[23] In *Il.* 12.445–9 we hear that people of old could lift stones that not even two people in the present can lift, while the stories of Nestor leave it to be inferred that the past of the past had been even greater and superior.[24] In the Hesiodic myth of ages the past also stands for a golden age, with the present being merely its degenerated form. In Pindar the relationship between past and present is seen from a new perspective and is given a different spin; Pindar collapses the qualitative distance between these two temporal entities, and the present is now seen as continuing, repeat-ing and renewing forms of the past. Reference to cities named after their heroic founders, expressions in the form of 'even now', mythi-cal genealogies which come down to the present,[25] the setting up of explicit parallels between present-day victors and mythical heroes: all these serve to bridge the temporal gap between past and present. Pindar's faith in the permanence and transcendent nature of certain values, especially his belief in the notion of inner excellence (*phya*) and the unfailing prosperity and *eudaimonia* of aristocratic families, also serve as a hinge between 'then' and 'now'.[26] In some cases the continu-ity between past and present is also mapped spatially: in *Ol.* 6.71–3, for instance, the Iamids are depicted travelling along a conspicuous road, while in *Nem.* 2.6–7 the victor walks on the path inscribed by his fathers (πατρίαν . . . καθ' ὁδόν).

22 *Ol.* 1.90; *Pyth.* 1.17, 6.43; *Ol.* 9.49; *Pyth.* 8.33.
23 According to M. Bakhtin, *The Dialogic Imagination*, tr. C. Emerson and M. Holquist (Austin: University of Texas Press, 1981), pp. 147–8, 'historical inversion' occurs when an Edenic past is measured against an inferior present. Bakhtin has wrongly applied this chronotope to all high genres of antiquity, including those of Pindar (15–18). In Homer there is a vague connection between the past and the present achieved through the heroes' claims that their κλέος will remain ἄφθιτον among future generations (e.g., *Il.* 3.351ff, 6.352ff, 7.87ff; *Od.* 1.302).
24 See e.g. *Il.*1.261–7 and 2.707.
25 R. Fowler, *Early Greek Mythography. Vol. I: Text and Introduction* (Oxford: Oxford University Press, 2000), p. xxviii. There are only a few examples where early historiographers continue their genealogies down into the historical period. See e.g. the Philaid genealogy (*FGrHist* 3 F 2) and the genealogy of Hippokrates (*FGrHist* 3 F 59).
26 Even though Pindar admits that interruptions of a family's 'prosperity' are likely to occur, he stresses that such periods of 'fallow' last only for a short period of time.

But the past in Pindar is often portrayed as being immanent in the present in a more direct and forceful way. It is portrayed as still living in the present, and as having a share in it. On many occasions Pindar invokes mythical heroes as if they were still alive,[27] while in *Pyth.* 8 he even claims that the Argive *mantis* Amphiaros (or according to others, his son Alkman) prophesied to him as he travelled to Delphi. Finally, the deceased are also claimed to have a share in the present. As Pindar says in *Ol.* 8.78–80: 'And for those who have died there is also some share in ritual observances, nor does the dust bury the cherished glory of kinsmen.'[28]

Undoubtedly, the similarity that Pindar establishes between past and present conjures up cyclic ideas of time, where the past is seen as the subject of periodic re-establishment and the present receives its value and *raison d' être* through association with it. In light of this, it is not surprising that Pindar is often cited as the Greek exemplum *par excellence* of the cyclical view. As Toohey remarks vis-à-vis Pindar's victory odes: 'Pindar's epinicians perhaps provide the earliest and most striking example of a conception of mythology that relies on a cyclical, non-linear concept of time.'[29] Because of this Pindar has been repeatedly criticised for lacking historical consciousness and evolutionary reason, and for holding a strongly deterministic view of the world.

Yet a more careful look at the *Epinicians* reveals that these (still dominant) allegations about Pindar's 'archaic mentality' and his narrow and parochial outlook should be reconsidered, in so far as the cyclical view of history that the poems evoke is merely one side of the coin. In the victory songs recurrence is seen as an incremental rather than a merely cumulative process; the present may be very similar to the past, but at the same time it is also new and takes us a step forward. Besides, it is not irrelevant that Pindar portrays time (*chronos*) as a force which rushes forward, is irreversible, and brings destruction and forgetfulness. Even though Pindar often explicitly defines events and actions as predetermined, and ascribes the causality of events to external factors such as time, the Gods, Fate, Necessity and Fortune, his figures are not presented as mere playthings at the mercy of these transcendental forces, but as being partly responsible for their actions and deeds. Even when an event is fated, this does not perforce eliminate an agent's free

---

27 See *Ol.* 1.36; *Nem.* 4.46–53; *Isthm.* 6.19. On the invocation to Pelops in *Ol.* 1 see L. Athanassaki, 'Deixis performance and poetics in Pindar's First Olympian Ode', *Arethusa* 37 (2004), pp. 317–41.

28 See also *Pyth.* 5.96–103; *Ol.* 14.20–4.

29 P. Toohey, *Melancholy, Love, and Time: Boundaries of the Self in Ancient Literature* (Ann Arbor: University of Michigan Press, 2004), p. 205.

will or constrain his choices, as he can also respond and adapt to these. In fact, on some occasions the gods are forced to intervene in order to ensure that a fated event will be actualised. So, in *Pyth.* 4 the Pythia must remind Battos of Medea's prophecy regarding the colonisation of Kyrene, and in *Pyth.* 5 Apollo must intervene and protect Battos from the lions so that 'he might not fail to fulfil his oracles' (60–2). This semi-openness of time is also manifested in the 'counterfactuals', that is, in those cases where Pindar refers to possibilities that existed at a given point in the past but were not actualised.[30] Mention should also be made here of the notion of *kairos*, which plays a central and prominent role in Pindar. In a world where everything is determined *a priori*, *kairos* would have no place and would have lost its meaning, in so far as it is based on human action and decision, and permits man to control and harness contingency.[31] What is more, Pindar keeps emphasising that, just like heroes who through their actions altered, destroyed, created anew and left concrete traces in the material world within which they lived, present-day victors will leave their own individual trail in space and time. Accordingly, in the victory songs man is visualised as having a share in the development and change of events, and as being not merely part but also creator of history.[32]

The linear dimension of time which crops up in the *Epinicians* is significant, for it puts the dynamics between past and present in a new perspective. Despite its similarities with the past, the Pindaric epinician present is not entirely in its grip, but retains its own particularity. Far from passively repeating forms of the past, the present is portrayed as actively continuing and increasing the glory of the past.[33] In fact, I would even dare to say that it is allocated an almost equally significant place next to it. Whereas it is true that the exemplary nature and para-

30 See *Pyth.* 4.42–57; *Nem.* 10.83–8; *Nem.* 7.24–7; *Isthm.* 8.32–6.
31 Unlike *chronos*, *kairos* clearly depends on human action and decision and, as E. Csapo and M. Miller, 'Democracy, empire, and art: Toward a politics of time and narrative' in D. Boedeker and K. Raaflaub (eds), *Democracy, Empire and the Arts in Fifth-Century Athens* (Cambridge, MA: Harvard University Press, 1998), pp. 87–126, at p. 103 observe, 'permits one to triumph over contingency'.
32 Something similar occurs in Homer, where events are described as caused either by the god's will or by human action. On ancient causality, see A. Lesky, 'Divine and human causation in Homeric epic', in D. L. Cairns (ed.), *Oxford Readings in Homer's Iliad* (Oxford: Oxford University Press, 2001), pp. 170–202; R. Gaskin, 'Do Homeric heroes make real decisions?', in Cairns, *Oxford Readings in Homer's Iliad*, pp. 147–69; cf. R. V. Munson, '*Ananke* in Herodotus', *JHS* 121 (2001), pp. 30–50, esp. pp. 31–3.
33 *Nem.* 5.8: Αἰακίδας ἐγέραιρεν ματρόπολίν τε; *Nem.* 3.12–17: χαρίεντα δ' ἕξει πόνον / χώρας ἄγαλμα, Μυρμιδόνες ἵνα πρότεροι / ᾤκησαν, ὧν παλαίφατον ἀγοράν / οὐκ ἐλεγχέεσσιν Ἀριστοκλείδας τεάν / ἐμίανε κατ' αἶσαν ἐν περισθενεῖ μαλαχθείς / παγκρατίου στόλῳ.

digmatic value of the Pindaric past rely on a sense of its superiority, this past is never 'walled off' or cast as superior to the present, as is the case in Homer and Hesiod. How else could we explain Pindar's claim in *Pyth.* 2 that no king of old was greater than Hieron in the present, or his assertion in *Ol.* 13 that the victor 'has attained what no mortal man ever did previously'?[34] What does the opening of *Isthm.* 2, where Pindar compares contemporary and old poetry, indicate if not change and a step forward? Taking into account all the above, one could say that in the *Epinicians* past and present share not a one-way but a reciprocal relationship: the present does not just passively find itself being glorified with the glamour of the past, but contributes to empower and increase this glamour through its own lustre and light.

3 THE PINDARIC MUSE

Let's now move on to the second part of the chapter, where we will examine the way in which Pindar acquires his information about the past. Homer typically ascribes his knowledge of the past to the transcendent vision of the Muse. As Andrew Ford remarks, in Homeric poetry the transmission of any information about the past comes 'vertically', directly from the Muses, and not 'horizontally', through poetic and historical influence.[35] In Pindar the Muse still occupies a significant and prominent place. Yet the activities she patronises are quite distinctive and differ from the ones that characterise her epic counterpart. A closer look at Pindar's invocations to his Muse reveals that *his* are not requests for information about what is distant and gone, but rather appeals to her to join the performance and assist with the creation of the song.[36] To be more precise, Pindar raises a question regarding the past five times throughout the epinician corpus: in *Ol.* 13, *Isthm.* 4, *Pyth.* 4, *Ol.* 10 and *Pyth.* 11. Notably, with the exception of *Pyth.* 4, the Muse is not explicitly addressed in any of these questions.[37] What is more, whereas these requests are modelled on the

---

34 A similar statement is also to be found in Simonides 23 (Diels), where a present-day athlete is said to be braver than ancient heroes such as Polydeukes and Herakles.
35 A. Ford, *Homer: The Poetry of the Past* (Ithaca, NY, and London: Cornell University Press, 1992), p. 95; see also E. L. Bowie, 'Lies, fiction and slander in early Greek poetry', in C. Gill and T. P. Wiseman (eds), *Lies and Fiction in the Ancient World* (Exeter: Exeter University Press, 1993), pp. 1–37, at p. 10.
36 See e.g. *Ol.* 3.4–6. In addition to the Muse other divinities are also invoked to help with the orchestration of the song; see *Ol.* 14; *Ol.* 2; *Isthm.* 7.
37 Examples of implicit invocations to the Muse occur in Homer as well (e.g. *Il.* 5.703; 8.273); see W. W. Minton, 'Invocation and catalogue in Hesiod and Homer', *TAPA* 93 (1962), pp. 188–212, at pp. 208–9; I. J. F. de Jong, *Narrators*

Homeric ones in terms of style, content and diction, either the questions raised are rhetorical, and therefore remain unanswered, or the answer is provided from a source other than the Muse.[38] In *Ol.* 10, for example, Pindar asks for the first victors at Olympia and then provides a catalogue listing their names accompanied by their home-land and the event in which they excelled. The catalogue's lack of elaboration and aesthetic value, however, seems to suggest that Pindar had probably derived his information from an authoritative source, most likely a victory list kept at the site of the games.[39]

In the light of the above, it would not be far fetched to say that the Pindaric Muse is associated more with the skilful composition of song and the commemoration of the present than with the remembering of the past, as is commonly believed.[40] The new attributes that Pindar ascribes to the Muse are indicative of her new role and transformation: far from standing still and issuing information about the past, the Pindaric Muse ploughs (ἀρόσαι, *Nem.* 10.26), welds gold with ivory (κολλᾷ χρυσὸν ἔν τε λευκὸν ἐλέφανθ᾽ ἁμᾶ, *Nem.* 7.78), tends weapons (καρτερώτατον βέλος ἀλκᾷ τρέφει, *Ol.* 1.112) and swells hymns (αὔξῃς οὖρον ὕμνων, *Pyth.* 4.3), while in *Isthm.*1 she is even attributed with wings (πτερύγεσσιν ἀερθέντ᾽ ἀγλααῖς / Πιερίδων, 64–5). In other words, she creates, alters, transforms and is highly energetic and active, features which arguably distinguish her from the static epic Muse. The only instances where Pindar associates the Muse with mere song are *Pyth.* 3.89–91 and *Nem.* 5.5.22–3, where he recounts the weddings of Peleus and Kadmos, at which the Muses were present, and *Isthm.* 8.57–8, where the Muses are depicted mourning over Achilles' dead body. Interestingly, however, the Muses that feature in these examples are the epic, not the epinician, ones.

4 TRADITION

The new role that Pindar assigns to his Muse leads naturally to the question: if the Muse ceases to be the main source of information about the past, from where or whom does Pindar acquire his

(footnote 37 *continued*)
and *Focalizers: The Presentation of the Story in the Iliad* (Amsterdam: Grüner, 1987), pp. 45–50.

38 In *Ol.* 13 and *Pyth.* 11 the questions remain unanswered, while in *Isthm.* 5 the answer is presented as widely known. An answer to the question raised is provided only in *Pyth.* 4.

39 G. Norwood, *Pindar* (Berkeley: University of California Press, 1945), p. 114.

40 This feature is not peculiar to Pindar but seems to apply to the lyric Muse in general; see M. Finkelberg, *The Birth of Literary Fiction in Ancient Greece* (Oxford: Clarendon Press, 1998), p. 163 n. 6.

information? As will become clear in what follows, this role is now taken over by tradition.[41] Pindar very often resorts to tradition and leaves it to be inferred that his knowledge of the past is based on nothing more immediate than verbal narratives. Attributions to tradition are normally introduced with the verbs φασί and λέγεται (both in the singular and in the plural), and locutions such as λόγος ἐστι, φάτις ἐστι, λεγόμενόν ἐστι.[42] Even though Pindar occasionally refers and credits *gnomai* to specific poets, such as Homer and Hesiod,[43] most often his attributions to tradition remain anonymous. Even when it can be surmised with some certainty that he draws on a specific poetic work, Pindar chooses to camouflage the name of his poetic predecessor with a φασί statement. In *Pyth.* 6.21–3, for instance, he says that his *laudandus* Xenokrates upholds the precept which 'they say (φαντί) that Philyra's son once gave to the mighty son of Peleus in the mountains'. From the scholia[44] we learn that the precept which follows is drawn from *The Precepts of Cheiron*, a work attributed to Hesiod.[45] Yet Pindar omits any reference to him and chooses instead to attribute his narrative to the unspecified φαντί (21).[46] Some Pindarists have attempted to narrow down such appeals, arguing that all references to the πρότεροι should be understood as allusions to literary predecessors and not to tradition in general. Despite this being both a possible and a plausible reading, there is nothing in these passages which favours this over a more general interpretation; in fact, one could even suggest that Pindar deliberately leaves such attributions quite vague so that he can have his cake and eat it too. On the one hand, by attributing a narrative to tradition in general he presents it as the canonical account, not merely as a version entertained by a particular poet. On the other hand, by leaving it to be inferred that he derives his accounts from earlier poets, Pindar stresses his knowledge of the previous poetic

---

41 R. Scodel, 'Poetic authority and oral tradition in Hesiod and Pindar', in J. Watson (ed.), *Speaking Volumes: Orality and Literacy in the Greek and Roman World* (Leiden: Brill, 2001), pp. 109–38, at p. 123ff, was the first who drew attention to and discussed the significant role that tradition plays in Pindar. See also H. Mackie, *Graceful Errors: Pindar and the Performance of Praise* (Ann Arbor: University of Michigan Press, 2003).

42 See e.g. *Ol.* 7.54; *Nem.* 7.84; *Pyth.* 6.21. Such statements are rare in other lyric poets; see e.g., Alc. 42.1, 339.1; Sapph. fr. 166; Sim. 579.1.

43 See e.g. Homer: *Pyth.* 4.277–8; Hesiod: *Isthm.* 6.66–7. See also *Pyth.* 9.94–6. where a *gnome* is attributed to Nereus.

44 Schol. *ad Pyth.* 6.22 (Drachmann II, 197).

45 Hes. fr. 283 (M-W).

46 Bacchylides is normally declared to be more receptive of tradition because he acknowledges his literary predecessors by name; see D. Fearn, *Bacchylides: Politics, Performance, Poetic Tradition* (Oxford: Oxford University Press, 2007), p. 20. Yet his attributions to tradition are by far fewer.

tradition and establishes himself in a line of transmission, thus elevat-
ing his status *qua* poet. Besides, we should bear in mind that, unlike
Homer, who clearly values poetic over other oral discourses,[47] Pindar
never draws a sharp line between the two but rather classifies everything under the heading of 'tradition'.[48]

Now, how are we to explain Pindar's tendency to ground his narratives on tradition, and what purpose do these φασί statements serve?
Mackie has recently argued that Pindar's appeals to tradition serve
to indicate 'that mythic narrative is not the official or the primary
province of an epinician poet'.[49] Certainly, this is a plausible interpretation. Yet the sheer fact that Pindar does not ascribe information to
tradition passively but engages with it actively and, at times, even critically renders Mackie's remark problematic. Rather, I would propose
that by presenting his accounts as socially acceptable and believed,
Pindar seeks to legitimise and confer authority on his discourse.[50]

The ability of such φασί statements to authorise an account has significant implications, especially when local and less well-known stories
favoured by the victor's clan or home town are concerned. Exemplary
in this respect is *Ol.* 6, an ode that celebrates Hagesias, a member
of the family of the Iamids. Here the mythical narrative focuses on
the story of the seer Iamos, son of Evadne and Apollo, and progenitor of the clan of the Iamids. The family had an Arkadian origin, as
the mother of Iamos was from Arkadia. In Pindar's epoch the most
famous Iamid was Teisamenos of Elis, who happened to be granted
Spartan citizenship. In order to insert this new Spartan element into
the ancestry, Pindar presents Pitana (the homonymous heroine of a
Spartan city) as the mother of Evadne and grandmother of Iamos.[51]
This new component of the story is introduced by a φασί statement.
Thus, Pindar manages to present the recent insertion into the Iamid
genealogy as already traditional and socially authoritative.[52] By
introducing local or ancestral myths with an inherently limited scope
with a φασί statement, Pindar suggests that they are well known and
widespread stories shared not only by the victor's family and fellow
citizens, but also by all Greeks. In this way Pindar confirms the truth-

---

47 See e.g. the celebrated passage in *Il.* 2.485–6 where tradition is juxtaposed
    with the superior eyewitness knowledge of the Muses.
48 Scodel, 'Poetic authority and oral tradition', p. 125. It should be noted, however,
    that Pindar acknowledges the epistemic difference between seeing and knowing;
    see *Nem.* 4.91–2: ἄλλοισι δ' ἄλικες ἄλλοι· τὰ δ' αὐτὸς ἀντιτύχῃ, / ἔλπεταί τις ἕκαστος
    ἐξοχώτατα φάσθαι.
49 Mackie, *Graceful Errors*, p. 71.
50 Scodel, 'Poetic authority and oral tradition', p. 124.
51 See Huxley, *Pindar's Vision of the Past*, pp. 29–30.
52 Something similar occurs in *Ol.* 9 for Epharmostos of Opous.

fulness of such lesser-known myths, and at the same time contributes to their establishment as canonical accounts. There is, however, another equally significant implication: by presenting these myths as 'canonical', Pindar manages to safeguard their dominance and authority not only in the present but also in the future, as the present tense of the verbs φασί and λέγεται guarantees that these accounts will be 'current', alive and dominant in the reports of men forever. In every future reperformance the version embraced and voiced by Pindar in the present will be the one shared by all.

In spite of his appeals to tradition, Pindar also frequently adopts a polemical stance towards earlier authorities, censuring their unreliability and treachery. Whereas time (*chronos*) is irreversible and the past an unchanging reality,[53] stories about the past vary (πολλὰ γὰρ πολλᾷ λέλεκται, *Nem.* 7.20) and often provide distorted reflections of reality. Accordingly, Pindar often repudiates traditional stories that he considers have been incorrectly handed down. The best example is *Ol.* 1.36, where he openly declares that his account will force the established story of Pelops to be considered from a new perspective (υἱὲ Ταντάλου, σὲ δ᾿ ἀντία προτέρων φθέγξομαι, *Ol.* 1.36).[54] In a similar vein is *Ol.* 7.21, where Pindar once again declares that he will 'correct' (διορθῶσαι)[55] the standing tradition about the beginnings of Rhodes and tease out what really happened. It is impossible to say whether this new version was Pindar's own invention or a story with local scope. At any rate, the Rhodians were so pleased with their new 'straightened out' past that they inscribed the ode on the temple of Athena at Lindos in golden letters.[56]

To be sure, Pindar was not the first to criticise tradition openly. Apart from Homer and Hesiod, whose criticisms are always veiled, and a few scattered examples among the lyric poets, the most celebrated reproaches of tradition are credited to Herakleitos[57] and the elegiac poet Xenophanes.[58] What distinguishes Pindar from his

53 τῶν δὲ πεπραγμένων / ἐν δίκᾳ τε καὶ παρὰ δίκαν ἀποίητον οὐδ᾿ ἄν / Χρόνος ὁ πάντων πατὴρ / δύναιτο θέμεν ἔργων τέλος (*Ol.* 2.15–17).

54 See, among others, J. G. Howie, 'The revision of myth in Pindar *Olympian* 1', *PLLS* 4 (1983), pp. 277–313.

55 On the meaning of διορθῶσαι see W. J. Verdenius, *Pindar's Seventh Olympian Ode: A Commentary* (Amsterdam: North-Holland, 1972), *ad* 21.

56 See schol. *ad Ol.* 7 (Drachmann I, 195).

57 In fr. 42 D–K Herakleitos argues that both Homer and Archilochos deserve to be expelled from the contests and be flogged, because their narratives abound in lies: see also frr. 56 and 57 D–K.

58 Xenophanes fr. 11. A. Gostoli, 'La critica dei miti tradizionali alla corte di Ierone di Siracusa: Senofane e Pindaro', *QUCC* 62 (1999), pp. 15–24, at p. 16, points out that such criticisms of tradition must have been common in the literary-philosophical circles of the fifth and sixth centuries. See also K. Freeman, *The*

predecessors and peers is that apart from engaging critically with tradition, he also explicitly discusses the three factors which he believes contribute to the wrong transmission of the past and the formation of 'false stories': envy (φθόνος),[59] the limitations of mortal knowledge and – last but not least – poetry.[60]

Considering how highly he values tradition, Pindar's critical stance towards it seems contradictory. Why does he decry tradition's unreliability and deceptive character and, most importantly, why does he draw attention to poetry's contribution to the falsification of the past? Pindar's moral judgements of the myths he narrates have been interpreted by many scholars as an indication of his prudery and tendency to moralise tradition in order to reveal the real truth.[61] Even though this is a possible explanation, we must not forget that Pindar's aim and primary concern are to provide not an accurate but a 'usable' account of the past, an account that would meet the expectations of his *laudandus* and audience.[62] This is not to say that his claims about the truthfulness of his poetry are merely a pretence, but rather that the ultimate yardstick against which he chooses what to remember and what to forget is not truthfulness but 'appropriateness'.[63] This is starkly articulated in the 'hush passages' where Pindar refuses to recount certain unflattering aspects of the past which could be offensive to the gods or certain heroes.[64] It is important to remember that in

---

(footnote 58 *continued*)
Pre-Socratic Philosophers: A Companion to Diels, Fragmente der Vorsokratiker (Oxford: Oxford University Press, 1953), p. 94, who argues for a possible encounter between Xenophanes and Pindar at the court of Hieron in Syracuse.

59 Even though *phthonos* is a generic *topos*, it is significant that Pindar explicitly associates it not only with the distortion of the present, but also with the distortion of the past. See P. Bulman, *Phthonos in Pindar* (Berkeley and Oxford: University of California Press, 1992).

60 See e.g. *Nem.* 7.20–3: ἐγὼ δὲ πλέον' ἔλπομαι / λόγον Ὀδυσσέος ἢ πάθαν διὰ τὸν ἁδυεπῆ γενέσθ' Ὅμηρον· / ἐπεὶ ψεύδεσί οἱ ποτανᾷ <τε> μαχανᾷ / σεμνὸν ἔπεστί τι· σοφία δὲ κλέπτει παράγοισα μύθοις. See also *Ol.* 1.28–9.

61 Cf. C. M. Bowra, *Pindar* (Oxford: Clarendon Press, 1964), pp. 285–7; Howie, 'Revision of myth', esp. p. 299; C. Carey, 'Pindar and the victory ode', in L. Ayres (ed.), *The Passionate Intellect: Essays on the Transformation of Classical Tradition Presented to Professor I. G. Kidd* (New Brunswick, NJ, and London: Rutgers University Press, 1995), pp. 97–8. See also D. Loscalzo, 'Pindaro tra μῦθος e λόγος', in M. Cannatà Fera and G. B. d' Alessio (eds), *I Lirici Greci* (Messina: Dipartimento di Scienze dell'Antichità dell'Università degli Studi di Messina, 2001), pp. 165–85, at p. 185: 'Pindaro, in particolare, cerca nuove prospettive di interpretazione delle varianti del mito e in questo senso la sua poesia si profila come ermeneutica e quindi ha un valore attivamente etico.'

62 L. Pratt, *Lying and Poetry from Homer to Pindar* (Ann Arbor: University of Michigan Press, 1993), esp. pp. 11–53 and 115–29.

63 Pratt, *Lying and Poetry*, p. 123.

64 *Ol.* 9.35–41; *Nem.* 5.14–18. See Norwood, *Pindar*, p. 80.

these cases Pindar does not dispute the facts and truthfulness of these events, but merely treats them as parts of the past that should be forgotten and remain unspoken. Besides, as he emphatically declares in *Nem.* 5.16–18, 'for not every exact truth / is better for showing its face, / and silence is often the wisest thing for a man to observe'.

In order to appreciate Pindar's stance better, it would be instructive to examine it in conjunction with the conventions of the epinician genre and, most importantly, the way in which he seeks to portray his encomiastic persona. It is true that despite the new role assigned to his epinician Muse, in most scholarly discussions Pindar is still referred to as a 'vatic poet' and a 'proclaimer of the Muses'. This is not fortuitous, in so far as Pindar often styles himself as *mantis* (*Dithyramb* 75.13 and *Parthenion* 1.5–6), *prophatas* (*Paean* 6.6), herald of wise verses (*Dithyramb* 2.24), attendant of the gods (*Paean* 5.45) and 'priest of the Muses' (fr. 150 and 52f.6). However, what we tend to overlook is that all these references occur in the fragments (cult poetry), not in the victory songs. This cannot and should not be taken as an insignificant detail.

In a nutshell, in the *Epinicians* Pindar is not the priestly figure of the fragments, whose role is that of the mediator between gods and men, but instead assumes a more active and energetic role: that of the *maître du temps*. He is the one who through his song can rewrite the past and secure for the present a place in the future by erecting for it a poetic *monumentum aere perennius*.[65] Through his song Pindar ensures that the victors' good reputation will not be distorted by φθόνος and πάρφασις, and that the right *kleos* will be propagated in the future.[66] Even if someone tries to distort the truth and corrupt the victors' name with false stories, Pindar's poetry will serve as the safety valve for the true account; due to his high status as a poet and the authority of his poetry, Pindar's versions will be perceived by future generations as 'a mirror' of *their* past, as he nicely puts it in *Nem.* 7.14–16.[67] Paradoxically Pindar must both honour tradition and at the same time criticise and challenge it if he is both to be part of tradition and to have a special place within it. Only if he presents himself as unique within tradition can he confirm that *his* versions and no one else's will determine the shape of the present in the future and the judgements

---

65 On the distinct ways in which Pindar pitches his epinician and religious persona see Pavlou, 'Past and present'.

66 See G. M. Kirkwood, 'Blame and envy in the Pindaric epinicion', in D. Gerber (ed.), *Greek Poetry and Philosophy: Studies in Honour of Leonard Woodbury* (Chico, CA: Scholars Press, 1984), pp. 169–83.

67 ἔργοις δὲ καλοῖς ἔσοπτρον ἴσαμεν ἐνὶ σὺν τρόπῳ, / εἰ Μναμοσύνας ἕκατι λιπαράμπυκος / εὕρηται ἄποινα μόχθων κλυταῖς ἐπέων ἀοιδαῖς.

of posterity. This also seems to explain why even when he openly acknowledges his dependence on tradition, he is at pains to underline the distinctive character of his poetry.[68] But whereas Pindar's stance towards tradition and the past is premised by his role as a panegyrist, we should not forget that he did not live in a vacuum. The recurrent comments on the fluidity and unreliability of tradition, on his selective 'remembering' and on the malleability of the past seem to reflect a broader contemporary and lively discussion about the *Vergangenheit* and its transmission. Besides, it can scarcely be a coincidence that Herodotus and the first historiographers lived during roughly the same period.

---

68 Indeed, many of his accounts which are introduced with a φασί-statement are preceded by remarks or images which denote innovation. In *Ol.* 9.47–9, for example, Pindar proclaims that he will rehearse the story of the foundation of Opous with novelty; yet the account that follows is introduced with the verb λέγοντι (49). See also *Nem.* 7.77–9, 84.

7

DEBATING THE PAST IN EURIPIDES' *TROADES* AND *ORESTES* AND IN SOPHOCLES' *ELECTRA*

Ruth Scodel

This chapter will examine three passages from tragic *agones* that reflect on the problem of finding out what actually happened in the past. Tragedies present variant versions of events that supposedly happened, so when disagreement about facts is articulated within the world of the play itself, it is hard not to take it as a threat to the usual suspension of concern about the literal truth of any one presentation. Most tragic *agones* are not about facts, but about the evaluation of the facts, and there is at least basic agreement about what is relevant. In many other debates (in Euripides' *Hippolytus*, for example), one speaker is simply wrong. But some passages raise the question of whether what actually happened can be extracted from narratives that are usually self-serving or partisan or biased in other ways. Implicit in these passages are fundamental hermeneutic problems. All three at least approach a situation we would more readily associate with Hellenistic poetry; they raise the possibility that different characters actually belong to slightly different versions of the story. When different versions of a story seem to be active in one play, even in a context that recalls the everyday difficulty of deciding on the truth in a law-court, it becomes hard to avoid profounder questions of historical truth: the question becomes not which speaker is lying, but what historical truth is and how it could be known. Euripides and Sophocles sometimes seem to be reflecting on the difficulty of ascertaining historical truth, on its methodological problems.

In *Orestes*, the disagreement between Tyndareus and Orestes is not exactly about fact, but it is not exactly about how agreed facts should be evaluated, either. Tyndareus' tirade against Orestes (491–539) presents the famous anachronism problem.[1] As Porter has shown in detail, Tyndareus follows contemporary Athenian styles of forensic

---

1 P. E. Easterling, 'Anachronism in Greek tragedy', *JHS* 105 (1985), pp. 1–10, at p. 9.

argument in his claim that Orestes ignored *nomos* (law or custom) in killing his mother:[2]

ὅστις τὸ μὲν δίκαιον οὐκ ἐσκέψατο
οὐδ' ἦλθεν ἐπὶ τὸν κοινὸν Ἑλλήνων νόμον . . .
χρῆν αὐτὸν ἐπιθεῖναι μὲν αἵματος δίκην
ὁσίαν διώκοντ', ἐκβαλεῖν τε δωμάτων
μητέρα· τὸ σῶφρόν τ' ἔλαβ' ἂν ἀντὶ συμφορᾶς
καὶ τοῦ νόμου τ' ἂν εἴχετ' εὐσεβής τ' ἂν ἦν. (494–5, 500–3)

Who did not consider what was just, and did not have recourse to the common law of the Greeks . . . He should have imposed the pious penalty for bloodshed by prosecuting, and thrown his mother out of his house. Then he would have got [credit for] *sophrosyne* instead of a calamity, he would be keeping inside the law, and he would be reverent.

Tyndareus' language is difficult and ambiguous when he directly addresses what Orestes should have done. West takes ὁσίαν as a noun rather than an adjective, and translates the phrase as 'while aiming for religious correctness'.[3] Still, even if we think that ὁσίαν is the adjective, and even if διώκοντ' *could* mean only 'drive away', in such a context it surely implies a prosecution (Biehl takes it as the noun, but still treats διώκοντ' as a judicial term).[4]

Tyndareus' argument, then, resembles the claims, common in Athenian forensic speeches, that the opponent despises and threatens to overturn the city's laws. However, it is different from these because the audience cannot be certain that there is a clearly applicable *nomos* in Orestes' situation, although Tyndareus' argument makes no sense without such a *nomos*. He later states that the ancestors created the applicable rules:

2 J. Porter, *Studies in Euripides' Orestes* (*Mnemosyne* Supp. 128; Leiden: Brill, 1994), pp. 99–172, esp. pp. 110–13.
3 C. W. Willink (ed.), *Orestes* (Oxford: Clarendon Press, 1986), p. 169 (on 500–1), points out that Orestes did impose a blood-penalty, so the adjective is essential. M. L. West (ed.), *Euripides: Orestes.* (Warminster: Aris & Phillips, 1987), p. 217 (on 501), thinks that the participle is redundant if we take ὁσίαν with δίκην, but I do not understand why. See M. Lloyd, *The Agon in Euripides* (Oxford: Clarendon Press, 1992), pp. 115–17, on the ambiguity of Tyndareus' language.
4 W. Biehl (ed.), *Euripides Orestes* (Berlin: Akademie, 1965), p. 57 (on 501): 'Eine gerechte, innerhalb der Grenzen des religös Erlaubten verlaufende Anklage führend.' V. Di Benedetto (ed.), *Euripidis Orestes* (Florence: La Nuova Italia, 1965), p. 105 (on 501): 'intendando una legittima azione legale'.

καλῶς ἔθεντο ταῦτα πατέρες οἱ πάλαι·
ἐς ὀμμάτων μὲν ὄψιν οὐκ εἴων περᾶν
οὐδ᾽ εἰς ἀπάντημ᾽ ὅστις αἷμ᾽ ἔχων κυροῖ,
φυγαῖσι δ᾽ ὁσιοῦν, ἀνταποκτείνειν δὲ μή. (512–15)

Our fathers of long ago regulated these issues well: they did not
allow anyone who had blood-taint to go where he would be seen
or addressed, but to purify by exile, but not to kill in return.

However, he does not support exile in this case, but urges Menelaus to
allow Orestes to be stoned by the citizens (536). So he has two distinct
claims: that exile is the traditional penalty for homicide, and that civic
procedures must preclude private vengeance. In any case, by giving
no subjects to the infinitives that explain how the ancestors forbade
contact with a polluted killer, he makes the subjects general and so
implies a communal behaviour.

The difficulties that most commentators see in this speech are not
the ones that concern me. For example, even if the *Oresteia* had
established a tradition that no legal procedure for homicide existed
until Athena created the Areopagus, Euripides was entirely within his
poetic rights to invent a court at Argos – and it would not be unusual
for him to disturb mythological tradition (indeed, he had already
introduced unplacated Erinyes in *Iphigenia in Tauris*). Indeed, Homer
and Hesiod presuppose the existence of legal institutions. Achilles'
shield, for all the difficulties of its trial scene, shows a procedure in
the aftermath of a homicide. So when Euripides makes the Argive
assembly debate the fate of Electra and Orestes, he could be seen
as correcting the implications of Aeschylus' version. In *Choephori*,
Orestes leaves Argos very quickly after the matricide, so that the
question of how the city would have reacted is easily ignored. Also,
the play emphasises the illegitimacy of Aegisthus' rule and defines
his killing as a tyrannicide, and in *Eumenides* Orestes, once acquitted, speaks as ruler of Argos without hesitation. So the action
avoids any messy problems about how Argos would have or should
have responded. Still, the grandeur with which Athena endows the
Areopagus implies that the heroic world has had no procedure other
than blood-vengeance for handling homicide. *Eumenides* elides the
differences between ordinary killings and murder within the family,
for which legal institutions dependent on relatives to prosecute were
not satisfactory. For murders committed by tyrants, no institutions
could ever provide a satisfactory solution.

So Euripides, by having Orestes and Electra tried by the assembly,
creates an Argos in which a legal procedure exists without denying that

the Areopagus was the first real homicide court. The constitutional situation at Argos is vague: the assembly functions as if it were sovereign. Scholars disagree about whether the audience should believe that Menelaus is scheming to obtain rule, but Orestes certainly says that he is (1058–9).[5] When Apollo tells Menelaus at 1660–1 to let Orestes hold power in Argos and himself to go rule Sparta, he evokes the stereotype that Spartans were unlikely to be contented with Sparta.[6] In any case, Orestes will rule in Argos; it is not a democracy. Euripides may be assuming that even in the heroic world, the assembly would have full sovereignty during an interregnum, as the Ithacan assembly in the *Odyssey* apparently would if it could achieve any unity for action. Antinous, for example, is concerned that if Telemachus reports to the assembly how the suitors tried to murder him, the people will drive the suitors out (*Od.* 16.381–2).

So the difficulty is not anachronism as such. We should see the assembly, though deliberately contemporary in tone, as almost the opposite of an anachronism. It is more like a historical thought experiment: if Orestes had not fled immediately after the matricide, what would the Argives have done? The assembly debate is not so much a false intrusion of democracy into the heroic past as an attempt at creating a plausible scenario based on the assumption that human (that is, political) nature is always the same, as Thucydides believes (1.22, 3.84.2). Euripides works with an old, Homeric institution, the assembly; he has the model of Achilles' shield for some kind of legal procedure for homicide in the remote past; he considers the likelihood that the assembly could assert itself in the absence of a ruler; and he examines the way politics work. The Argive assembly is more imagined history than anachronism, and if the assembly is possible, Tyndareus' argument is not inherently anachronistic either.

Nor is the problem with Tyndareus' speech that, in practice, Orestes *had* to kill Aegisthus, who held tyrannical power, and that he would have found it very difficult to expel his mother or initiate proceedings against her. Simply driving her out of the house before some legal process would not be a wise plan – we may remember her call for an axe at *Choephori* 889; she would not have gone quietly. It is far from certain that Orestes could control even the household with Clytemnestra alive and present, and in the world of the play, Aegisthus had his own faction. These may be reasons for the audience not to be

5 R. P. Winnington-Ingram, 'Euripides: *Poiêtês Sophos*', *Arethusa* 2.2 (1969), pp. 127–42, at p. 134, accepts Orestes' interpretation of Menelaus; Willink, *Orestes*, pp. 191–2 (on 682–716), criticises this as an 'illegitimate back-inference'.
6 Biehl, *Orestes*, p. 182 (on 1661), compares *Andr.* 582, fr. 723 Kannicht (*Telephus*), Sophocles *Aj.* 1102.

convinced by him to abandon sympathy for Orestes. Tyndareus' argument may well seem unfair in not recognising the extraordinary difficulties of Orestes' situation. But that does not make the argument strange. A speaker in an *agon* can ignore practicalities of that kind, and it is open to the opposing speaker to introduce them in refutation.

Orestes, however, does not introduce the practical difficulties in following Tyndareus' belated legalistic advice.[7] Tyndareus' argument is truly strange because Orestes' utterly fails to respond to it. Orestes argues entirely as if he were in the world of *Choephori*. He argues, for example, that while he now suffers from his mother's Erinyes, he would have been pursued by his father's if he had failed to avenge him (580–4). His argument recasts Apollo's complaint in *Eumenides* that the Furies did not pursue Clytemnestra, to which they reply that she had not spilled *kindred* blood. He speaks as if the only alternatives he had were to do nothing against Clytemnestra or to kill her. Orestes uses several lines to claim that he obeyed the command of Apollo (591–9), and he accuses Tyndareus of calling the god ἀνόσιον, but he does not say that Apollo told him to kill his mother rather than to try to exile her. His argument could have been just the same had Tyndareus never raised the possibility that Orestes could have acted to avenge his father without killing his mother. Precisely because a refutation speech in tragedy normally proceeds point for point, this is a striking oddity, and it is strange whether or not we think that Tyndareus' language implies a judicial procedure.

The Argive assembly does not consider any such possibility either. The speakers disagree about whether Orestes was right to kill his mother and about how he should be punished if he was wrong, but nobody says that he had any choice between matricide and inaction. Talthybius, who praises Agamemnon but says that Orestes created a bad precedent (νόμους, 891), seems to be trying to define some middle ground in the debate, but does not specify what Orestes ought to have done. Tyndareus' argument falls into the play as a foreign element that is utterly irrelevant to everyone else. *That* is the most significant problem. It feels out of place because no place is made for it. So what purpose does it serve? The main dramatic functions of Tyndareus are to intimidate Menelaus and to show on a small scale the pattern of Orestes' behaviour: when he is received sympathetically, he acknowledges how guilty he feels;

---

7 D. J. Conacher, *Euripidean Drama: Myth, Theme and Structure* (Toronto: University of Toronto Press, 1967), p. 219, argues (in my view unconvincingly) that Orestes' failure to respond proves that the argument should be taken seriously.

when he is attacked, he defends himself and counterattacks.[8] But nothing requires that Tyndareus make an argument that dangles in air. The development of the play as a whole would not be different if Tyndareus simply criticised the matricide.

This isolation of Tyndareus' argument is an invitation to interpret it at a different level. It is as if he were trying to contest the fictional world in which he has been placed. Although different characters judge the matricide very differently and consider very different precedents it could establish, nobody other than Tyndareus thinks that it could be evaluated by being compared to an alternative but effective action. Yet Tyndareus stresses that his alternative is the ancient *nomos* of the ancestors – which, from the perspective of Euripides' audience, would make it profoundly ancient. Tyndareus seems to want Orestes to have followed a procedure nobody else ever considers, but he is an old man, and a Spartan – not a character from whom we would expect new ideas – who sees that procedure as belonging to hoary antiquity. *Orestes* was produced in 408, exactly at the time Draco's homicide law was reinscribed (409/8) in the context of the revision and republication of Athenian law that followed the restoration of the democracy after the oligarchy. The surviving section concerns unpremeditated homicide. Scholars have extensively discussed the nature of the full law and whether Tyndareus' speech reflects the old law. Holzhausen plausibly suggests that Tyndareus does not mean that a court could not have imposed the death penalty, but is referring only to the limits of self-help.[9]

This debate, however, does not consider the wider context of both the play and the reinscription of the laws. Whether Tyndareus' argument refers to the substance of the old Athenian law may be less important than that he refers to ancient laws mentioned by nobody else. The reinscription of those old laws still in force surely indicates both the restored democracy's concern to demonstrate its historical continuity with the past, and the democrats' concern that claims about old laws would be problematic without an authoritative display of exactly what was valid. The infamous chapter 4 of the *Ath. Pol.*, the 'Constitution of Draco', was probably forged around the time of

---

8 I thus see Orestes as somewhat more consistent than many interpreters do. A good discussion of the inconsistencies of character as survival strategy is M. O'Brien, 'Character in the *agon* of the *Orestes*', in S. Boldrini (ed.), *Filologia e forme letterarie: Studi offerti a Francesco Della Corte* (Urbino: Università degli studi di Urbino, 1987), pp. 183–99.

9 J. Holzhausen, *Euripides Politikos. Recht und Rache in 'Orestes' und 'Bakchen'* (Beiträge zur Altertumskunde 185; Munich and Leipzig: Saur, 2003), pp. 52–67, has a full discussion.

the oligarchic revolution.[10] Certainly democrats and oligarchs both claimed ancestral support. According to *Ath. Pol.* 29.3, Clitophon proposed that the *probouloi* examine the laws of Clisthenes, on the grounds that his constitution was not popular but close to Solon's.[11] Thucydides 8.97.6 makes democrats in the fleet at Samos speak of πατρίους νόμους that the new government has (wrongly) dissolved. The expression 'ancestral laws' was evidently, as Mogens Hansen has pointed out, a 'hurrah-word'; it indicated approval of the laws.[12]

In this political climate, it is not perhaps so strange that everyone else ignores what Tyndareus describes as ancient and ancestral rules. Someone may assert that the ancestors established a law long ago, but that does not mean that he is right, or that, even if the law is ancient, it has been in consistent use and had not been superseded. So having one character seem to live in a different past from the others is not pointless, since contemporary Athenians profoundly disagreed about what their past was.

We cannot know, however, exactly how this rough similarity between Tyndareus' speech and contemporary political discourse would have impressed the contemporary audience. The play takes place far in the past, soon after the Trojan War, and Tyndareus refers to 'the fathers, long ago'. Draco would be recent in comparison to Tyndareus, let alone to his ancestors. Maybe Tyndareus is simply modelled on an elderly Athenian oligarchic type: that he is old, Spartan and unyielding would cue the audience to see Tyndareus' ancestors as the oligarchic Draco rather than the Draco the restored democracy could claim.[13] In that case, the difference between Tyndareus' long-ago ancestors and the long-ago ancestors of the audience was erased: he could be heard as if he were arguing in late fifth-century Athens, so that the historical argument was completely ahistorical in its framing. However, it would also be possible to see the speech as a deliberate transfer of a contemporary kind of argument about the

---

10 P. J. Rhodes, *A Commentary on the Aristotelian Athenaion Politeia* (Oxford: Clarendon Press, 1981), pp. 53–6, 84–7.

11 M. H. Hansen, *The Athenian Democracy in the Age of Demosthenes: Structure, Principles and Ideology* (Oxford: Blackwell, 1991), pp. 162–3.

12 M. H. Hansen, 'Solonian democracy in fourth-century Athens', *ClMed* 40 (1989), pp. 71–99, at pp. 75–7.

13 Views of Tyndareus have differed widely. At one extreme, A. P. Burnett, *Catastrophe Survived: Euripides' Plays of Mixed Reversal* (Oxford: Clarendon Press, 1971), p. 106, sees him as 'a sensible old aristocrat, the Argive equivalent of a good Athenian dicast'. M. Heath, *The Poetics of Greek Tragedy* (London: Duckworth, 1987), pp. 58–60, points to the effect on audience sympathy of the contrast between Orestes' respectful demeanour and Tyndareus' harshness. Discussion and bibliography in Porter, *Studies in Euripides' Orestes*, pp. 101–3.

past to a remote past, and so as a commentary on the futility of such arguments. From this perspective, the isolation of Tyndareus would implicitly support the decision to reinscribe laws that were still valid in contrast to attempts to re-establish an imagined earlier constitution as a whole.

Troades presents very different problems. The central issue for the *agon* is whether Helen came voluntarily to Troy. Helen treats the Judgement of Paris as a serious event and argues that Aphrodite was committed to her abduction, so that she was subject to superior force. Hecuba rejects Helen's interpretation of the Judgement of Paris as a serious dispute and sees Aphrodite as a metaphor for Helen's attraction to Paris. This leads to her curious argument that Helen cannot have been taken by force, since she did not cry for help (998–1001) – but Helen has not argued that she was forced in that sense. The Gorgianic defence of Helen is surely in play here in a complex way: Hecuba, though she rationalises the story by treating Aphrodite as metaphorical, rejects Gorgianic claims about the power of desire, while Helen, whose version is traditionally mythological, speaks with a sophistic edge.[14] In the end, the entire debate is irrelevant to the outcome. Helen will survive because Menelaus succumbs to her erotically and so proves himself no stronger in resisting desire than Helen.

While this is the main debate in the *agon*, there are points that do not belong to the grand design but raise slightly different questions. Helen and Hecuba disagree about what happened after Paris was killed. Although this issue is relevant to the main argument, since if Helen tried to leave Troy it is more credible that she followed Paris only under divine influence, the disagreement also indicates another, subordinate problem in the debate. Helen claims that she then tried to escape by letting herself down from the walls with a rope, but was compelled to marry Deiphobus (955–60). She calls on the guards as witnesses – but of course they are all dead. Hecuba's first counterargument, though, is very odd:

> Where, then, were you caught fixing knots, or sharpening a sword, as a noble woman would do in longing for her previous husband? (1012–14)

The first alternative could describe preparations for the escape from the walls, but once the second appears it is clear that Hecuba is saying that if Helen had really regretted going with Paris she would have

14 R. Scodel, *The Trojan Trilogy of Euripides* (Göttingen: Vandenhoeck & Ruprecht, 1979), pp. 90–104.

killed herself. She then quotes herself as offering to help Helen escape (1015–19).

Ὦ θύγατερ, ἔξελθ'· οἱ δ' ἐμοὶ παῖδες γάμους
ἄλλους γαμοῦσι, σὲ δ' ἐπὶ ναῦς Ἀχαιικὰς
πέμψω συνεκκλέψασα· καὶ παῦσον μάχης
Ἕλληνας ἡμᾶς τ'.

My daughter, leave. My sons will make other marriages, but I will help you slip away and convey you to the Greek ships. And make the Greek and ourselves cease from battle.

Helen is presumably lying about her attempts to escape from Troy, but Hecuba's reply is strange and unreliable. Is the audience supposed to take Helen's failure to commit suicide as proof that she did not regret her actions? Hecuba quotes herself as speaking to Helen with maternal affection, when everything else she says gives the impression that she has loathed Helen all along. (Even if Helen had wanted to escape, she would not have been likely to trust Hecuba.) Hecuba sees Helen as drawn to Paris not just by his good looks, but by the prospect of extraordinary luxury (991–7), and not wanting to leave because she enjoyed barbarian subservience (1020–2); she uses forms of ὑβρίζειν twice. In Hecuba's account, Helen is a stereotypical Spartan, whose longing for Persian extravagance and opportunities for lording it over others becomes manifest once she leaves home (cf. Thuc. 1.77 and especially 1.130 on Pausanias' luxurious and oppressive behaviour).

This section of the debate echoes the stories Helen and Menelaus tell at *Odyssey* 4.235–89, where the issue is, again, whether Helen returned her loyalties to Menelaus after the death of Paris. The question is thus traditionally unresolved. In Homer, Helen narrates how she helped the disguised Odysseus when he came to spy in Troy; Menelaus then tells how she tried to induce the men hidden in the wooden horse to betray themselves by imitating the voices of their wives. These opposing stories are told only after Helen has drugged the wine, and the problem of whether the two tales could be reconciled is not addressed. It does not need to be, not only because the participants are immunised against any real consequences of what is said, but also because the stories are in any case directed mainly at confusing Telemachus and the external audience about the extent to which Penelope should or will be trusted. But while Menelaus simply tells a story that requires a Helen who assists the Trojans, Hecuba's speech in Euripides is very different: she has a full and completely negative interpretation of Helen's character, and judges all her actions accordingly. In Hecuba's view, Helen desires sexual satisfaction, luxury and opportunities to behave hubristically to others, and everything she does is solely and exclusively motivated by self-interested calculation of how these desires can be satisfied. The passage is an exceptionally rich instance of tragic theory of mind in operation. Whether one believes Helen's claim that she tried to escape or Hecuba's insistence that she did not cannot be a matter of weighing the external evidence. It is a matter of ἦθος.

Hecuba, furthermore, is self-interested. Helen has begun her speech by blaming Hecuba for giving birth to Paris and not killing him (919–22) – the first play in Euripides' production of this year was *Alexandros*, which dramatised a murder attempt on Paris when he came to Troy after surviving exposure. So there is some obvious unfairness in Helen's accusation – Paris seems unkillable – but she is right that the war cannot be blamed entirely on her. Her accusation, though, gives a particular edge to Hecuba's response. Everything Hecuba says could be true, but it is also, we can assume, driven by her need to displace the responsibility of the Trojans themselves. In this light, her account of how she offered to help Helen flee is also self-justifying. So we are left in a typical Herodotean situation. We have two accounts. One may seem more credible than the other, but both come from self-interested reporters, and because the reporting situation is agonistic, there is no space for a nuanced approach.[15] In any case, there is still a blunt question of fact. Either Helen tried to escape Troy or she did not. The interpretation will inevitably precede the judgement of fact instead of deriving from it: we will believe Helen or Hecuba depending mostly on whether we accept Hecuba's understanding of Helen's character. While the speeches are relatively balanced intellectually, Hecuba is sympathetic, while Helen certainly is not, so probably most members of the audience will be inclined to Hecuba's side.[16] Still, the scene could prompt reflection on the underlying problem, which is the danger of actor-observer bias or fundamental attribution error (also called 'correspondence bias').

Hecuba assumes that Helen has fixed characteristics that determine everything she does. Despite cultural variation, people generally

15 Lloyd, *Agon in Euripides*, pp. 105–10.
16 M. Dubischar, *Die Agonszenen bei Euripides: Untersuchungen zu ausgewählten Dramen* (Stuttgart: Metzler, 2001), pp. 342–57. On the difficulty of judging between the arguments, see N. T. Croally, *Euripidean Polemic: The Trojan Women and the Function of Tragedy* (Cambridge: Cambridge University Press, 1994), pp. 151–3; A. M. van Erp Taalman Kip, 'Truth in tragedy: When are we entitled to doubt a character's words?', *AJP* 117 (1996), pp. 517–36, at pp. 533–4.

overemphasise the role of individual character in the behaviour of others while placing far more weight on situational factors in explaining their own actions. Behaviour is generally less consistent than people assume when making judgements about others. For a historian, this fundamental attribution error is a constant danger in making historical assessments, especially because the process of understanding why historical figures acted as they did is inevitably a hermeneutic circle: character is inferred from actions, and then that inferred character is used not only to explain other actions, but to decide what a particular person did when other evidence is insufficient. Euripides obviously did not have the benefit of the vast research conducted on fundamental attribution error since 1967.[17] But the problem is basic and universal – and one could base a credible reading of the *Orestes*, especially, as a critique of standard Greek assumptions about consistency of character.

In Sophocles' *Electra*, Clytemnestra argues that she killed Agamemnon justly, in vengeance for the sacrifice of Iphigenia. She offers arguments about why Agamemnon's action cannot be excused. For example, he may have acted on behalf of the Greeks, or of Menelaus, but they had no right to kill her daughter (535–41). Menelaus had two children of his own, who were more obvious candidates for the sacrifice. Electra responds by claiming (on the authority of hearsay, 566) that Artemis demanded the sacrifice of Agamemnon because he had hunted a stag in her grove and boasted in a way that offended her. Artemis then demanded the sacrifice of Agamemnon's daughter as 'equal weight' (ἀντίσταθμος) for the deer (570–1). This detail gives Artemis two slightly different motives: the boast, which goes back to the *Cypria* (p. 32, 55–7 Davies), and the killing of the sacred deer itself, which alone explains why the sacrifice is a fitting punishment (the two are combined in Dictys, *FGrHist* 49 F 5). Electra says that without the sacrifice the army was unable either to go to Troy or to disband, so with great reluctance (575) Agamemnon performed it.

This latter claim is a little odd, since the traditional story has the expedition held back by winds, and Aulis is not an island. If Electra's version is to make sense, it requires a prophetic or oracular intervention that would warn Agamemnon against trying to avoid the sacrifice by abandoning the expedition. Parker, followed by Finglass, sees Electra's assertion as unproblematic, comparing Lichas' knowledge

17 E. E. Jones and V. A. Harris, 'The attribution of attitudes', *Journal of Experimental Social Psychology* 3 (1967), pp. 1–24.

of why Zeus required Heracles to serve Omphale at *Trach.* 274–79.[18] However, that passage is also not entirely straightforward, and tragic convention allows Lichas, as a messenger, to drift toward omniscience, a licence Electra cannot share.[19] In any case, I do not think the parallel means that we must assume that Electra reliably knows of a prophecy that fully guarantees her account. Although, of course, a prophecy of Calchas is prominent in the tradition, we cannot simply fill in what is missing from that tradition, because there is no reason to think that in any earlier version Artemis forbade Agamemnon to abandon the war. In both Aeschylus' *Agamemnon* and Euripides' *Iphigeneia at Aulis*, going home is a real choice. If Electra cited such a prophecy, we would have to accept her version, but here there are unclear boundaries dividing what Calchas said, what Electra has heard, and how Electra has understood what she heard.

It is just as likely that the spectator would guess that she has inferred that Agamemnon could not have abandoned the expedition, because she is subjectively certain that her father would not have sacrificed her sister if he had any choice at all. Still, Electra is the sympathetic character here, and the audience must be inclined to take her side. She must be telling the truth as she understands it, which means it is what she has heard, and therefore what has been reported. She proposes asking Artemis for the cause, before saying that such an inquiry would not be *themis* (563–5). Certainly, we should not treat it as Winnington-Ingram does: 'Electra's account . . . is the story she would like to believe; and we can hardly suppose that Sophocles wishes us to take it too seriously as an explanation of events.'[20] This reading of these lines is tendentious, governed by a larger interpretation of the play as condemning the matricide. Yet Electra's story, with its essential but unreported prophecy, is not entirely transparent, and her version should not be treated unambiguously as Sophocles' version.[21] Since Electra is constructing her story from hearsay, we can see her as an

---

18 R. Parker, 'Through a glass darkly: Sophocles and the divine', in J. Griffin (ed.), *Sophocles Revisited: Essays Presented to Sir Hugh Lloyd-Jones* (Oxford: Oxford University Press, 1999), pp. 11–30, at p. 17; P. Finglass, *Sophocles: Electra* (Cambridge: Cambridge University Press, 2007), pp. 267–8 (on 566–76).

19 J. Barrett, *Staged Narrative: Poetics and the Messenger in Greek Tragedy* (Berkeley: University of California Press, 2002), *passim*, esp. p. 96.

20 R. P. Winnington-Ingram, *Sophocles: An Interpretation* (Cambridge: Cambridge University Press, 1980), p. 220, following J. H. Kells (ed.), *Sophocles: Electra* (Cambridge: Cambridge University Press, 1973), on 566–633. So also M. Ringer, *Electra and the Empty Urn: Metatheater and Role Playing in Sophocles* (Chapel Hill: University of North Carolina Press, 1998), pp. 159–60.

21 As J. R. March, *Sophocles: Electra* (Warminster: Aris & Phillips, 2001), pp. 176–7, does, esp. on 564.

amateur historian. She is trying to combine and make sense of all she has heard, and using her experience of her mother as further evidence.

So how are we to understand these speeches? One possibility is that Clytemnestra is simply lying. In Electra's account, Agamemnon could certainly be blamed for the transgression that caused Artemis' anger, but he had no choice about the sacrifice. Clytemnestra's claim that she killed him in vengeance is then a further lie, and she killed him for her relationship with Aegisthus, using the sacrifice as a self-serving pretext.[22] This is what Electra says at 561–2. In any case, if Agamemnon was at fault, her arguments about Menelaus' children are a sham. The other alternatives are more complicated, but also more interesting: Clytemnestra is speaking in partial good faith (only partial, since she certainly has not acted solely for the motive she offers). If she knows Electra's version, she does not believe it. She could be arguing from within the story of Aeschylus' *Agamemnon*, where Artemis' anger does not have a direct and obvious motivation. She could also accept the story that Agamemnon angered Artemis by killing the stag (while deliberately ignoring it in her speech), but not believe that he had no choice in sacrificing his daughter. There is no way to tell from the text whether she was actually present at Aulis.

What we may have here, then, is again something very much like a Herodotean 'he said/she said'. The disputants accept accounts of the past that justify their present beliefs, just as Herodotean figures present versions of the past that make their own nations appear guiltless. Clytemnestra implicitly denies that any prophecy or other authoritative source required that the sacrifice be Agamemnon's child. The question of why the victim should be Agamemnon's child is raised elsewhere in tragedy, and in Euripides' *Iphigeneia at Aulis*, Agamemnon at least implies that Calchas' prophecy requires Iphigenia, both in the prologue (90) and in response to Clytemnestra (1262). Clytemnestra introduces a degree of choice that the tradition does not. Once Aeschylus' *Agamemnon* had told the story of the sacrifice without any particular motive for Artemis to punish Agamemnon, the question had to arise. Electra's version, on the other hand, gives Agamemnon no effective choice at all. One version has an Agamemnon implausibly unconstrained, while the other creates so much constraint that he really has no dilemma. These interpretations of the past correspond to problems of interpretations of the present: Electra tells the chorus that her endless laments are entirely forced on her (256–7), at least in so far as she is εὐγενής, and she tells her mother

---

22 L. MacLeod, *Dolos and Dike in Sophokles' Elektra* (Leiden: Brill, 2001), pp. 84–7; van Erp Taalman Kip, 'Truth in tragedy', p. 519.

that her abuse of her mother is also completely involuntary (619–21). On the other hand, she certainly does not see Clytemnestra's behaviour as in any way forced on *her*, and she generally refuses to accept limits imposed by others on her own freedom of action.

Electra's account leaves no moral ambiguities. If her version is correct, Agamemnon, apart from the folly of his boast, is guiltless, while Clytemnestra was not actually motivated by Iphigenia's sacrifice at all – it is entirely an excuse. Clytemnestra, on the other side, (repellently) does not acknowledge any moral complexity in her own actions; she says that she is 'not distressed by what was done' (549–50), while she insists that Electra's behaviour in speaking ill of her is blameworthy (523–4) and indeed regards it as *hubris*. In fact, she regards Electra's constant references to the murder of Agamemnon as an excuse (πρόσχημα, 525), although she does not say what she believes Electra's real motives are.

This *agon*, like the one in *Troades*, probes beyond the basic preference of any group for the story that makes it look better. People in antagonistic situations produce versions that dismiss the pressures and situational constraints of others while making themselves and those they support victims of circumstances. Tragic characters expect more consistency than reality typically presents. This is a danger for the historian who must interpret their accounts, and these tragedies put the spectator into the situation of such a historian. In *Orestes*, Tyndareus refers to an ancestral and panhellenic norm that nobody else recognises, so that an appeal to the past does not settle the controversies of the present. Instead, present controversies seem to be projected into the past, in potentially infinite regress.

8

EURIPIDEAN EXPLAINERS

Allen Romano

There is wide consensus that tragic aetiologies (or *'aitia'*)[1] connect the mythic, remote, past of the dramatic world to the real, experienced, present world of practice. Euripidean aetiologies, for example, 'function as references to the more stable present and help the audience bridge the gap between mythical time and contemporary life'.[2] They are 'one way of bringing myth into the present' and 'link the heroic and mythical world of the play to that of the fifth-century audience'.[3] Tragic aetiology is 'a strategy by which the Athenians define their

---

1 I define aetiology broadly as that class of communication which, by narration or implication, uses legendary or mythic stories to explain the origins of things. The labels 'aetiology' or *'aitia'* do not reflect or reproduce fifth-century concepts. Herodotus refers to a given origin story not as an αἴτιον, but as a λόγος (or ἱερός λόγος), as for example at 2.156.3 (λόγον δὲ τόνδε ἐπιλέγοντες) or where he refuses to elaborate sacred λόγοι (2.47.2, 2.48.3, 2.51.4, 2.62.2, 2.81.2). When he speaks of causality in such stories, he uses a simple and unmarked construction such as διά followed by the accusative. By contrast, he uses the term αἴτιον elsewhere of natural causes, usually ones that he finds particularly amazing (and thus in need of explanation). So, for example, at *Histories* 3.12, he wonders at the strong bones of Egyptians and the equally weak skulls of Persians and recounts the reason he is told to explain this difference, a reason rooted in the particular habits of each group. Cf. 2.25–6, 3.108, 7.125 and the unmarked use of the term αἴτιον at 1.91, 4.43, 8.128, 8.129, 9.8, 9.93. In philosophy and medicine, the terminology of cause has a particular prestige, but is also not obviously akin to the phenomenon of aetiological stories we find in pre-Hellenistic literature. Telling is the fact that Plato in the *Phaedo* (99a), in Socrates' criticism of Anaxagoras' account of cause, speaks of people using the term αἴτιον in a wrong sense, thus explicitly problematising the term for the first time in extant literature: ἀλλ᾽ αἴτια μὲν τὰ τοιαῦτα καλεῖν λίαν ἄτοπαν. So too, despite Aristotle's overdeveloped theoretical edifice of causality, in *Metaphysics* Δ 5 he lists a number of different definitions and examples of αἴτια, none of which could easily refer to the sorts of mythic explanations which modern critics label *'aitia'*.
2 D. J. Mastronarde, *The Art of Euripides: Dramatic Technique and Social Context* (Cambridge: Cambridge University Press, 2010), p. 158.
3 R. Parker, *Polytheism and Society at Athens* (Oxford: Oxford University Press, 2005), pp. 142–3, and W. Allan, *Euripides: Helen* (Cambridge: Cambridge University Press, 2008), p. 340, on the end of Euripides' *Helen*.

relations to the panhellenic past and hence to the rest of Greece', and 'the aitiological poet is the civic poet, whose audience is the citizen body'.[4] Such assessments focus strikingly on one dimension of communication. Aetiology is, in these familiar formulations, first and foremost an exchange between playwright and audience and one whose specific permutations through the mouths of a diverse range of speakers directed towards specific auditors on stage for specific goals would seem to matter little to the overarching authorial end of connecting past and present. This is problematic. Emphasis on the playwright who explains the origins of things, who knows or does not know details of cult, place and etymology, and whose skill is put on display in expressing such knowledge squeezes tragic aetiology into the idealised and idolised shape of a Herodotean *logos*, lopping off features which are not meaningless excess and paying insufficient attention to contemporary non-historiographic modes of talking about foundations and origins. Euripides is not a historian and Euripidean aetiology is not foreshadowing of historiographic narrative explanation.

Despite the ever-widening appropriation of the label 'aetiology' in analyses of tragedy,[5] we would do well to heed the advice of G. S. Kirk, who recognised, some forty years ago, that the story of

4 B. Kowalzig, 'The aetiology of empire? Hero cult and Athenian tragedy', in J. Davidson, F. Muecke and P. Wilson (eds), *Greek Drama III: Essays in Honour of Kevin Lee* (London: Insitute of Classical Studies, 2006), pp. 79–98, at p. 81, and Parker, *Polytheism and Society*, p. 143.

5 Recent work finds in aetiology a general hermeneutic for tragedy as a genre, described well by Easterling as 'the play's implicit references to its contemporary theatrical, ritual, and political functions', in P. E. Easterling, 'Theatrical furies: Thoughts on *Eumenides*', in M. Revermann and P. Wilson (eds), *Performance, Iconography, Reception: Studies in Honour of Oliver Taplin* (Oxford: Oxford University Press, 2008), pp. 219–36, at p. 221. F. I. Zeitlin, 'The dynamics of misogyny: Myth and mythmaking in the *Oresteia*', *Arethusa* 11 (1978), pp. 149–84, posits an aetiology of patriarchy in *Eumenides*. Richard Seaford's work has provocatively expanded the scope of tragic aetiologies from isolated instances within specific plays to more general relevance: R. Seaford, *Reciprocity and Ritual: Homer and Tragedy in the Developing City-State* (Oxford: Oxford University Press, 1994), esp. pp. 123–39 and 385: 'tragedy, in concluding with the foundation of cult involving the collective and regular renewal of the kind of liminality perverted in the drama by interfamilial violence, itself encapsulates that historical transformation of cult which issued in the genesis of tragedy'. Most recently, Claude Calame argues that satyr plays have a 'quasi-aetiological function with regard to the cult given in honour of the city god [Dionysus] by participants in the Great Dionysia', in C. Calame, 'Aetiological performance and consecration in the sanctuary of Dionysos', in O. Taplin and R. Wyles (eds), *The Pronomos Vase and Its Context* (Oxford: Oxford University Press, 2010), pp. 65–78, at p. 66. P. Wilson and O. Taplin, 'The "aetiology" of tragedy in the *Oresteia*', *PCPhS* 39 (1993), pp. 169–80, suggest that the *Oresteia* dramatises the aetiology of the tragic genre itself. M. Revermann, 'Aeschylus' *Eumenides*, chronotopes, and the "aetiological mode"', in Revermann and Wilson, *Performance, Iconography, Reception*, pp.

aetiological myths and legends is, in practice, always one of multi-plicity more than of singular function.[6] Discourse about origins can take the form of narrative or prophecy or be implied through the juxtaposition of story and context, as is demonstrated by examples in the tragic corpus. Most familiar in tragedy are the predictions of cult often (but not always) found at the end of Euripidean plays and deliv-ered often (but not always) by divinities. Though pronouncements by deities (or divinised ex-mortals like the Dioscuri or Heracles) are relatively explicit in their prediction of future practice, there is great variation across the tragic corpus.[7] So, for example, at the begin-nings and endings of plays we regularly find references to the origins of peoples, names and cities, and elsewhere there are references to the origins of civilisation and of the universe.[8] There are rarer cases of aetiological narrative delivered retrospectively, including Orestes'

237–61, at p. 252, highlights some of these predecessors to argue that the *Oresteia* is similarly about 'the meta-level' and what he terms 'the aetiological mode'.

6 G. S. Kirk, 'Aetiology, ritual, charter: Three equivocal terms in the study of myths', *YClS* 22 (1972), pp. 83–102 (esp. p. 84: 'these explanatory modes tend to be functionally distinct, so that the application of the one generic label of "aetiology" – and most critics are content with that – is inadequate and misleading'), prefigured in Kirk, *Myth: Its Meaning and Functions in Ancient and Other Cultures* (Berkeley: University of California Press, 1970), pp. 13–31, and echoed in Kirk, *The Nature of Greek Myths* (Woodstock: Overlook Press, 1975), pp. 53–68.

7 In addition to the nine cases of divine appearance at the end of extant plays (*Hippolytus, Andromache, Supplices, Electra, Iphigenia among the Taurians, Ion, Helen, Orestes, Bacchae*), all of which contain aetiological information of some sort, Athena's appearance at the end of *Erechtheus* and Hermes' at the end of *Antiope* both survive in substantial papyrus fragments and contain aetiological information. Dionysus' appearance at the end of *Hypsipyle* is marked in the margin of the papyrus, but the speech does not survive. Other cases of the *deus ex machina* (and aetiology), though frequently inferred by modern scholars, are inferences of varying likelihood from later plot summaries. At the end of *Medea*, Medea boasts to Jason that she will bury her children at Corinth and they will receive cult worship, but we should not interpret this case as a variety of divine intervention scenes. The play predates the earliest securely attested *deus ex machina* scene (*Hippolytus* of 428) and Medea's arrival on the chariot of the Sun differs greatly in tone and emphasis from the appearance of a god, particularly in foregrounding Jason's inability to touch either Medea or their children. The non-Euripidean *Rhesus* ended with the Muse predicting, among other things, the future cult for Rhesus.

8 Both Euripides' *Ion* and the fragmentary *Archelaus* begin with extensive genealogies. Etymology is common as, for example, in *Antiope* fr. 181 and 182, *Archelaus* fr. 228.7–8, *Erechtheus* fr. 370, *Hec.* 1270, *Hel.* 1670–5, *Hipp.* 29–33, *Ion* 661–2 and 1577–81, *Or.* 1643–7, *Phrixos* fr. 819, *Telephus* fr. 393, *Tro.* 13–14. See further the list of *figura etymologica* in J. D. Smereka, *Studia Euripidea* (Leopoldi: Sumptibus Societatis Litterarum, 1936), pp. 172–6. City foundation is predicted at *El.* 1273–5 and mentioned at *Archelaus* fr. 228.6. *Alexandros* fr. 61b gives the origin of human kinds. On the origins of the universe, Aeschylus fr. 44, Euripides, *Melanippe the Wise* fr. 484, *Chrysippus* fr. 839 (cf. *Hippolytus Veiled*, fr. 429).

report of the foundation of the Athenian Choes in *Iphigenia among the Taurians* (958–60), and aetiology often features in choral songs (for example, *Hecuba* 802 on the origin of the olive at Athens from Athena).[9] Scholars have long claimed a type of aetiological resonance for plays like Sophocles' *Ajax*, where the future cult of Ajax is only hinted at but seems crucial for understanding the play, or Euripides' *Bacchae*, where aspects of Dionysus' cult resonate through the play.[10] This is a diverse body of stories and presentations. Folklorists like Barre Toelken remind us that the very assumption of a category of aetiological myth often conditions us, as cultural interlopers, to misunderstand what tellers of such tales find salient.[11] Paradoxically, in order to understand what Euripides is doing with his particular expressions of aetiology, it can be helpful first to de-emphasise the extra-dramatic category of 'aetiology' and focus instead on varieties of origin talk in their specific contexts. We must, similarly, decentre Euripides in favour of the characters who are the immediate mouthpieces of aetiological information within any given play. In what follows, I argue against familiar descriptions of Euripidean aetiology as bridge between past and present in order to show how Euripides exploits, with great variety and inventiveness, fifth-century discourse about foundations and, further, how Euripidean explainers all speak

---

9 Mastronarde, *Art of Euripides*, p. 122. See especially his discussion on pp. 123–4 and 165.

10 R. C. S. Jebb, *Sophocles: The Plays and Fragments* (Cambridge: The Cambridge University Press, 1893), pp. xxx–xxxii; J. C. Kamerbeek, *The Plays of Sophocles: Commentaries* (Leiden: Brill, 1953), pp. 14–15; P. H. Burian, 'Supplication and hero cult in Sophocles' *Ajax*', *GRBS* 13 (1972), pp. 151–6; P. E. Easterling, 'Tragedy and ritual: Cry "woe, woe", but may the good prevail!', *Métis* 3 (1988), pp. 87–109; A. Henrichs, 'The tomb of Aias and the prospect of hero cult in Sophokles', *ClAnt* 12/2 (1993), pp. 165–80; J. R. March, 'Sophocles' *Ajax*: The death and burial of a hero', *BICS* 38 (1991–3), pp. 1–36; Kowalzig, 'Aetiology of empire?'. Cf. J. P. Poe, *Genre and Meaning in Sophocles' Ajax* (Frankfurt: Athenäum, 1987), pp. 9–18, and A. F. Garvie, *Sophocles, Ajax* (Warminster: Aris & Phillips, 1998), pp. 5–6. On the connections of the Salaminian chorus, Ajax and Athens, see Seaford, *Reciprocity and Ritual*, pp. 398–9. For *Bacchae*, see especially R. Seaford, *Euripides, Bacchae* (Warminster: Aris & Phillips, 1996), and Seaford, *Reciprocity and Ritual*.

11 B. Toelken, 'The "pretty languages" of Yellowman: Genre, mode, and texture in Navaho Coyote narratives', in D. Ben-Amos (ed.), *Folklore Genres* (Austin: University of Texas Press, 1976), pp. 145–70, at pp. 146–7, describing an aetiological tale for the origin of snow recounted by a Navaho elder: 'I found by questioning him that he did not in fact consider it an aetiological story and did not in any way believe that that was the way snow originated; rather, if the story was "about" anything, it was about moral values, about the deportment of a young protagonist whose actions showed a properly reciprocal relationship between himself and nature. In short, by seeing the story in terms of any categories I had been taught to recognize, I had missed the point.'

with idiosyncratic and distinct perspectives on past, present and future. Consequently, Euripidean aetiology does not function primarily as an act of communication about the past between playwright and audience, nor does it make salient any sort of message connecting one temporal domain to another; rather, the range of functions for tragic aetiology is highly variable and, to the extent that we can generalise about Euripides' motives, a tool for filling in a fuller picture of the past as enacted on stage and making vividly alive the minds of those inhabiting that past.

For a modern reader primed to see the past as something that can be recorded and therefore known, but the future as a thing inherently unknown and, to non-believers in divination, unknowable, the gulf between predictions of foundation and narrative recounting of foundation seems wide; but in an ancient idiom where the past, and particularly the poetic access to the past, regularly requires appeal to divine knowledge or employing divinely given gifts, the line between vision of the future and vision of the past is far finer. It is not necessarily to ancient chroniclers or historiographers that we should look for fifth-century discourse about foundations and origins against which to contextualise aetiology generally, and especially Euripidean aetiology of the prophetic form which has received the bulk of scholarly attention. We have clues as to one important context for cult prediction in scenes that have frequently been misunderstood as mortal variations on divine patterns. For example, in *Hecuba*, Polymester speaks with Hecuba and Agamemnon and predicts Hecuba's metamorphosis into a dog, her death and the naming of the headlands near the site of her drowning, etymologising the promontory Cynossema as κυνὸς . . . σῆμα ('bitches' grave'). It is misleading to lump these details together with Euripidean aetiologies in other closing scenes as if this is the slightly unusual offspring of the normative divine ending found elsewhere; aligning this case too closely with the function of gods who deliver aetiological predictions misses the specific tenor of the scene.[12] Polymestor is trying to pain his interlocutors, as he makes clear towards the end (1283, ἀλγεῖς ἀκούων; 'Does it hurt to listen?', to Agamemnon). When his predictions of Hecuba's own death do not have much effect on her (Hecuba even mocks him at 1272, 'You going to give a name about my form [as a dog]?'), Polymestor turns to the death

12 *Contra* J. Gregory, *Euripides, Hecuba: Introduction, Text, and Commentary* (Atlanta: Scholars Press, 1999), pp. xxxv–xxxvi. See also K. Matthiessen, *Euripides 'Hekabe': Edition und Kommentar* (Berlin: de Gruyter, 2010), p. 416, and J. Mossman, *Wild Justice: A Study of Euripides' Hecuba* (Oxford: Oxford University Press, 1995), pp. 200–1.

of her daughter Cassandra. Though Hecuba rejects this prediction (1276), it ensnares Agamemnon. Polymestor predicts, accurately, Agamemnon's future death at the hands of Clytemnestra and it is only then, with Agamemnon's growing anger, that Polymestor is silenced by gagging and his removal from the stage. Presumption that the normative aetiological speaker is either the divine speaker or, more perniciously, the playwright obscures the specific and much more salient context for explanation structuring this scene.

Polymestor locates his authority in the prophecies he heard from Thracian Dionysus (1267). To Polymestor's claims of divine authority for his predictions, Hecuba responds with derision. She mocks him that the oracles did not foretell Polymestor's own current misfortune, himself captured and his son brutally murdered by a ragtag group of women. This derision can be situated against the complex ambivalence towards divinatory professionals in Athens. In Michael Flower's recent, vivid characterisation, seers 'combined the role of confidant and personal adviser with that of psychic, fortune-teller, and homeopathic healer'.[13] Despite frequent fifth-century rhetoric discrediting their activities, seers were authoritative and very stable sources of knowledge about religious matters – matters which, in the ancient world, always bled across social, political and medical spheres. Thus when Plato in the *Republic* mocks prophets as beggars out for a quick buck, we also get a snapshot of how potent they were as sources of authoritative knowledge about both past and present:

and begging priests (ἀγύρται) and seers (μάντεις) go to rich men's doors and persuade them that they possess the power from the gods that through sacrifices and incantations, if any wrong has been done to him or his ancestors, they can cure with pleasurable festivities and, if a man wishes to harm an enemy, it's only a small fee to harm just and unjust alike, since they can, through certain enchantments (ἐπαγωγαῖς) and spells (καταδέσμοις), persuade the gods to serve them.[14]

That seers might claim to be able to mould even the gods to their needs is probably exaggeration, but indicates the popular conception

---

13 M. A. Flower, *The Seer in Ancient Greece* (Berkeley: University of California Press, 2008), p. 22. Distinguishing the activities of *manteis, chresmologoi* and others who would claim to divine is a notorious problem. See further Flower's discussions at pp. 58–71. I echo his terminology here. On the diverse roles and manifestations of seer-craft, see also the essays in S. I. Johnston and P. T. Struck, *Mantikê: Studies in Ancient Divination* (Leiden: Brill, 2005).
14 364b–c with Flower, *Seer in Ancient Greece*, pp. 27–9.

of their utility. Though the portrait is negative, it attests both the wide competence claimed by seers (or their imitators and rivals in divinatory craft) and a few of their working methods. Box-office seers came from elite families, may have advised the leading generals, and could demand high fees for their services.[15] As Plato continues, mashing practices of *chresmologoi* and *manteis* in order to bring disrepute upon the whole divinatory apparatus, such prophets

> make not only ordinary men but cities believe that there really are resolutions (λύσεις) and purifications (καθαρμοί) for injustices through sacrifice and pleasant games (παιδιᾶς ἡδονῶν) for the living, and that there are also special observances for the dead, which they call rites (τελετάς), that release us from ills in that place, while horrors await those who do not sacrifice.[16]

Part of the divinatory process is recommending the proper corrective procedures, a process which could involve performing old or new rituals. So, for example, at *Bacchae* 255–7, Pentheus charges Tiresias with trying to profit from introducing a new cult: 'You want to introduce this new divinity (δαίμον') to mankind and read his bird signs and entrails to make money.' Seers were essential to the decision-making of battle, as is expressed strikingly by the way that legendary seers like Tiresias could claim to have won a war (*Phoenissae* 854–7, of Athens against Eleusis) or in the way the Spartans, according to Herodotus (9.33.3), would find it important to bribe the seer Tisamenus to be their leader in war.[17] As Radermacher observed (echoed more recently by Dillery), the period from the beginning of the Peloponnesian War to the Sicilian expedition is rich in diviners.[18] They were both crucial (at least until widespread outrage at the failure to help stave off the Sicilian disaster of 414), but also an object of derision. They were outsiders, but in with the leaders of the city. They were self-interested, such that they could be mocked as only pursuing their own profit, but also had a vital role in the polis, particularly for crucial decisions in wartime. Further, if we take seriously the notion that behind Aristophanes' staging of an oracular contest in *Peace* (1043ff.) was a real practice of presenting

---

15 Flower, *Seer in Ancient Greece*, pp. 37–50.
16 364e–365a.
17 Flower, *Seer in Ancient Greece*, pp. 94–7, and J. Dillery, 'Chresmologues and *manteis*: Independent diviners and the problem of authority', in Johnston and Struck, *Mantikê*, pp. 167–231.
18 L. Radermacher, 'Euripides und die Mantik', *Rheinisches Museum* 53 (1898), pp. 497–510, at pp. 504–9, and Dillery, 'Chresmologues and *manteis*', p. 184.

oracles, as Dillery suggests,[19] the interchange at the end of *Hecuba*
resonates strikingly with the contemporary Athenian landscape of
divination. Euripides stages an oracular contest where Polymestor's
true predictions are ignored and eventually silenced. These are human
institutions of oracle-giving and a human context for evaluating and
suspecting prophetic explanations, whatever the epistemic basis in
divine sources. The relevant analogy for the aetiology in this moment
is not knowledge like that of the god, but rather scenarios of human
explanation and prediction. The analogy supplies information which
is left unstated in the scene, allowing the audience to see in sharp
relief the characters involved: the old woman from a defeated people,
Hecuba, for whom her own impending death is not all that much of
a threat; Agamemnon, blind to his future; and Polymestor, barbarian and outsider (much like the independent *chresmologoi* at Athens),
who happens to be right in everything that he predicts. The scenario
of oracular contestation makes Polymestor's villainy stand out, as he
is not playing the part of beneficial seer, but rather is only interested in
his own need to abuse his captors.

Similar is Eurystheus in *Heraclidae*. At the end of the play he claims
the authority of the oracles of Apollo to predict the benefit he will
bring to Athens (1028). Eurystheus is predicting, of course, his own
death and its beneficent effects rather than death and destruction to
come for others. Eurystheus is the paradigm of heroism, seeking to
die a noble death when, as he has explained, death on the battlefield
has been denied.[20] The relevant scenario here is not that of gods at the
end of other Euripidean plays, but rather the contemporary marketplace of explanation and prophecy.[21] Even more so than in the case
of *Hecuba*'s Polymestor, the structural analogy of Eurystheus with
independent, often foreign *manteis* is marked. Eurystheus is here a
foreigner and exile at Athens who claims to be a boon to the city,
and a benefit in wartime. He even claims to think that the oracles
were useless. It was not that he was not told what would happen
to him; rather, he thought that Hera was stronger than oracles and
would protect him (1038–40). Though we cannot know for certain

19 Dillery, 'Chresmologues and *manteis*', pp. 194 and 210–12, interprets the
    'wooden walls' episode of Themistocles as oracular competition.
20 This is a heroic paradigm rather than a divine one and his concerns are not unlike
    those of heroes of epic. See G. Nagy, *The Best of the Achaeans: Concepts of the
    Hero in Archaic Greek Poetry*, revised edn (Baltimore: Johns Hopkins University
    Press, 1999), pp. 118–19 and 222–42.
21 *Contra* J. Wilkins, *Euripides: Heraclidae* (Oxford: Oxford University Press,
    1993), p. 188: 'the speech of Eurystheus stands in the place of an *ex machina*
    speech, and his report of the oracle covering his heroization and the Spartan
    invasion is equivalent to the *aition* expected at the end of a Euripides play'.

whether the audience had detailed (rather than general) knowledge of Eurystheus' fate in Attica, recognising that the scene presents him as a source whose claims are open to questioning may solve a long-standing problem in reconciling our non-Euripidean evidence for the cult with what Eurystheus says in the play. Though we have no independent evidence for this specific cult at Pallene, according to Strabo (8.6.19), Eurystheus' body was buried nearby (at Gargettos), though his head elsewhere.[22] If this were the analogue of divine intervention, then we might expect, as most scholars have, that Eurystheus predicts a truth about his future heroisation which the audience registers as relevant to their locale. But it is quite important that Eurystheus' role as explainer be not entirely secure. Is he the interpreter of oracles that he claims to be? His report of the oracle here conceals bluster that is not entirely accurate. He predicts his cult in approximately its correct place but does not know that in fact it will be only his headless body that will lie there. Such a slip would be in keeping with his character, a man who ignored the oracle he was given and ends up dead despite his forewarning.[23]

The messy marketplace of seers and their competing, contingent explanations about past and future foregrounds the way prediction always involved differences in perspective, selection and aim. That human figures activate analogies with the practices of seers is not surprising, but I would go further and suggest that divine speakers, through the act of prediction, likewise cannot be thought of by ancient audiences uncoloured by analogous mortal practices. To understand the actions of any figure on stage, audiences must attribute intentions, desires and bias in ways that draw on a wealth of human interactions surrounding foundations. Recent research in the cognitive sciences show that individuals make immediate and automatic inferences about potential future behaviours of any other individual by, in part, creating a working model of another person's mind.[24] Audiences

---

22 See R. Seaford, 'Aitiologies of cult in Euripides: A response to Scott Scullion', in J. R. C. Cousland and J. R. Hume (eds), *The Play of Texts and Fragments: Essays in Honour of Martin Cropp* (Leiden: Brill, 2009), pp. 221–34, at pp. 225–8; Wilkins, *Euripides: Heraclidae*, p. 189; and S. Scullion, 'Tradition and invention in Euripidean aitiology', *ICS* 25 (2000), pp. 217–33.

23 Socrates in Xen. *Symp.* 4.5 notes that seers cannot foresee what will happen to themselves.

24 For the application of theory of mind to the study of literature see, with further references, L. Zunshine, *Introduction to Cognitive Cultural Studies* (Baltimore: Johns Hopkins University Press, 2010), and, for drama, B. A. McConachie, *Engaging Audiences: A Cognitive Approach to Spectating in the Theatre* (New York: Palgrave Macmillan, 2008), and McConachie and F. E. Hart, *Performance and Cognition: Theatre Studies and the Cognitive Turn* (London: Routledge, 2006).

therefore, in order to follow the play at all, cannot help creating a mental model of the mind of, for example, Artemis or Apollo, even if such a divine mind is a novel creation; consequently, they cannot see the god on stage without immediately forming a series of expectations about perspective, self-interest and potential future actions. Gods are both human and extra-human.[25] Though stark divides are often posited between gods and mortals, ancient evidence is not always so black and white. For example, at *Eumenides* 61–3 the Pythia refers to the god Apollo in distinctly human terms, as ἰατρόμαντις, τερασκόπος, καθάρσιος.[26] A natural consequence of anthropomorphism is that gods, though their motives may be ultimately unknowable, can be understood to act in familiarly mortal ways, even when, as in the case of Apollo, acting like a *mantis* would seem to dethrone him from his obvious place in the hierarchy.[27] Though precedents for epiphany, both literary and 'real', reveal much about the seriousness of Euripidean gods and are the clear model for the actions of the gods, this is a fertile rather than a constraining scaffolding.[28] Just as we see in mortal predictions the selection and perhaps even distortion of cult details in context and in character, so too we should be attuned to such differences among divine speakers as well.

Euripidean aetiologies vary greatly according to character and reflect the immediate self-interest of each character. In *Hippolytus*, for example, Artemis' promise of cult honours for Hippolytus is pointedly cast in the language of reciprocity (1419, 1423, ἀντὶ τῶνδε τῶν κακῶν). This is a common form of ritual logic, but also particularly fitting for Artemis, the goddess who on the Athenian stage regularly

25 J. Gould, *Myth, Ritual, Memory, and Exchange: Essays in Greek Literature and Culture* (Oxford: Oxford University Press, 2001), pp. 203–34, noted also in R. Buxton, 'Metamorphoses of gods into animals and humans', in J. Bremmer and A. Erskine (eds), *The Gods of Ancient Greece: Identities and Transformations* (Edinburgh: Edinburgh University Press, 2010), pp. 81–91, at p. 90.
26 Elsewhere in tragedy: *Hecuba* 1267, *Iphigenia among the Taurians* 711 and 1128, *Bacchae* 298, Euripides fr. 1110. Outside of tragedy: Plato, *Phdr.* 244c, *Laws* 686a, *Euth.* 3c, *Hom. Hym. Hermes* 533–8, Archilochus fr. 298 W.
27 On anthropomorphism, see A. Henrichs, 'What is a Greek god?', in Bremmer and Erskine, *Gods of Ancient Greece*, pp. 19–39, at pp. 32–5.
28 On the divine side of such scenes, see esp. C. Sourvinou-Inwood, *Tragedy and Athenian Religion* (Lanham: Lexington, 2003), pp. 459–511. She effectively critiques the view of tragic gods as artificial as expressed in J. D. Mikalson, *Honor Thy Gods: Popular Religion in Greek Tragedy* (Chapel Hill: University of North Carolina Press, 1991). In addition to the evidence she provides, I would emphasise the less spectacular though probably individually important acts of divine visitation attested by dedicatory inscriptions such as those collected in G. Renberg, '"Commanded by the gods": An epigraphical study of dreams and visions in Greek and Roman religious life' (diss., Duke University, 2003).

demands retribution.[29] Artemis receives similar treatment in *Iphigenia among the Taurians* from Athena, who marks Artemis' cult as reciprocal in a way that is distinct from the other predictions and injunction in that extensive speech (1459, ἄποιν'). By contrast, in *Andromache*, Thetis appears to Peleus when he is in the position in which we find Thetis in the *Iliad*, that of mourning parent (1231). Her predictions and commands to Peleus are shaped by her role as mourning mother. She commands that Neoptolemus, her grandson, be buried and she directs Andromache's fate towards the survival of the Trojan line, but this is in large part subsidiary to her aim that her line with Peleus should not perish (1249–52). The bulk of her speech is then concerned with detailed instructions to Peleus for his immortalisation, setting the stage for him to wait by the sea for her, recalling perhaps the *Iliad* scene where she and the Nereids mourn for Patroclus. When she leaves Peleus with the command that he is to cease his grieving, the declaration of burial and even of the continuation of the Trojan and Greek families falls into place, not as independent data scattershot from the storehouse of aetiological possibilities, but rather as a carefully constructed and characterised set of concerns about familial continuity, which makes her point to Peleus that he can in fact, stop grieving and continue on to his happy immortality with her. There is an immediate rhetorical purpose, but also one which is circumscribed by the character of Thetis, appropriate to Thetis and to a certain extent egocentric to Thetis. As one last illustration, in Euripides' latest play with a fully preserved aetiological end, Apollo appears at the end of *Orestes* and gives, in the space of fifty lines, a rapid-fire succession of predictions and commands, including the possible worship of Helen along with her brothers the Dioscuri and the naming of a town after Orestes. The contrast with Artemis and Thetis highlights Apollo's distinctive mode of speech. He explains what has happened and what will happen with a density of prediction and awareness appropriate to the prophetic god and unparalleled elsewhere. Indeed, this is precisely what Orestes remarks on after Apollo's speech: ὦ Λοξία μαντεῖε, σῶν θεσπισμάτων / οὐ ψευδόμαντις ἦσθ' ἄρ', ἀλλ' ἐτήτυμος (1666–7). Where Orestes thought he heard an avenging spirit (1669, ἀλαστόρων), he hears instead prophecy. These are the two faces of Apollo, and Orestes is rightly relieved to be speaking to the prophetic rather than the punishing incarnation. As a speech with an aetiological dimension, Apollo's means of prediction are a stylised exaggeration of his role

---

29 Besides the Iphigenia stories that were the subject of plays by all major tragedians, Artemis would also have played some role in a number of lost plays (Aeschylus' *Callisto*, Euripides' and Sophocles' *Meleager* plays).

and distinct from that of Artemis or Thetis. Differing subjects and
modes of explanation are, for both playwrights, an important tool of
characterisation.

As characters speak differently, their distinctive interests and perspectives on the future shape the kind of information they provide
and, consequently, any history of foundation extracted from tragedy
comes packaged with the bias of the characters voicing it. So,
for example, in *Andromache*, Thetis describes the future tomb of
Neoptolemus at Delphi as 'a reproach (ὄνειδος) to the Delphians, so
that his grave may proclaim (ἀπαγγέλληι) that he was violently slain
by the hand of Orestes' (1241–3). Scullion, in a carefully argued note,
claims that the verb ἀπαγγέλληι is nowhere else used metaphorically
and can only imply that there was an inscription at Delphi to this
effect.[30] Denying Euripides a novel use of metaphor is dangerous
ground, but the more pressing problem is that neither Scullion nor
Seaford (who rightly makes the case against Scullion's use of this
point as evidence for Euripidean invention of cult) gives Thetis any
role in the interpretation of this speech.[31] But Thetis is no distanced
observer. That the tomb was marked is sufficient for it to be, in the
eyes of Neoptolemus' grandmother, thought of as an inscription
which will proclaim his violent death. In Pindar, Neoptolemus' tomb
is the observer of the procession and judge of the sacrifice (*Nem.*
7.47, 'overseer'). Rutherford suggests that Neoptolemus had a role
in Delphic *theoxenia*, acting as arbiter of the division of meat and
thus reversing through cult his actions as disrupter of sacrifice in the
myth.[32] What Thetis says in *Andromache* conjures an image of this cult
in terms which highlight the injustice done to Neoptolemus through
analogy with the general script of action for the cult. The censure
which the tomb shouts out mimics the scenario wherein Neoptolemus
corrects the different sort of violent slaughter, that is, sacrifice, which
the Delphians perform. This might explain some of the forced metaphorical reach in the tomb that reports without implying an inscription, but it also highlights the way that such judgement depends on
Thetis' particular hopes for the future cult and its potential interpretation, one which is not disinterested or without a particular perspective.

There is not space here to treat other cases at length, though
I would submit, in general, that debates over the veracity of cult
information in tragic aetiology are a false problem, and that this

---

30 Scullion, 'Tradition and invention', p. 219 n. 6.
31 Seaford, 'Aitiologies of cult in Euripides', pp. 222–3.
32 I. Rutherford, *Pindar's Paeans* (Oxford: Oxford University Press, 2001), pp.
     314–15, with *Paean* 6.103–20 and *Nem.* 7.38–47.

information can be understood best as the rhetorically selective and biased reports of characters.[33] So, for example, recent inscriptional evidence records purifications to the Hyacinthides, where in the *Erecththeus* fr. 370 Athena paints the future cult worship of the Hyacinthides with a markedly militaristic brush.[34] Artemis in *Hippolytus* overemphasises the continuing nature of Hippolytus' worship and casts the cult in terms which are jarringly Artemisian, specifically interpreting an act of dedication as a mourning rite for premature death. In *Iphigenia among the Taurians* the apparent disparity between the tragic account of Iphigenia receiving dedications of clothes for women who die in childbirth and the more regular procedure of dedicating offerings for success in childbirth reflects the way that Athena has selectively tweaked the terms of her promise of future cult, in keeping with the kind of premature death which is Artemis' domain. She makes the cult more appealing and more applicable through interpretation, not invention or reflection, of the general shape of the practice. There is no simple calculus of cult information against cult reality such that we can compute Euripidean aetiology as either true reflection of public knowledge or invention of non-existent cults to be interpreted in those terms. What Euripides does is far more interesting and in no case, I would submit, is a prediction without bias.

In closing, we can reconsider a case which has long been viewed as aberrant aetiology. In *Iphigenia among the Taurians*, during the recognition scene between Orestes and his long-lost, thought-to-be-sacrificed sister Iphigenia, Orestes tells how he ended up being so far afield in the first place (939–86). We hear the surprising new detail that not all the Furies were satisfied after the trial at Athens and that some continued to pursue Orestes until, in despair, he demanded of Apollo that Apollo help. The god instructed Orestes to take the Taurians' statue of Artemis to Athens. Orestes dwells at some length on his reception at Athens and – what concerns us here – seems aware of the practice instituted in the wake of his stay there. His story is, for the audience, a particularly vivid recounting of how a signature practice of the second day of the Anthesteria festival came to be. In order to avoid excluding the guest but at the same time avoid pollution from having this guest share in the communal wine, the Athenian king (usually Pandion in later accounts) makes everyone drink from their

---

33 In addition to the discussions of Scullion and of Seaford cited above, see W. Allan, *The Children of Heracles* (Warminster: Aris & Phillips, 2001), pp. 215–19

34 Agora I 7577 Face B 16 (Gawlinski 2007): [ν] ν ν ν ℎυακιν[θίσι] / [ᵃᵐᵒᵘⁿᵗ] καθαρμ[όν] ('for the Hyacinthides, a purification').

own pitcher of wine, the *chous*.[35] Commentators struggle to explain this passage as a variant on the kinds of divine ending speeches which scholars have assumed to be normative for Euripidean aetiologising. So, on the grounds that the 'unsettling background' of Orestes' side of the story 'would be out of place at the end of the play', the most recent commentator concludes that this 'excursus' was 'not unnecessary' and was 'perceived by the audience as a celebration of the Athenian community's cohesion and its successful negotiation of ritual/religious challenges'.[36] So too Cropp follows Wolff's interpretation that it is 'advertising to Eur.'s audience the importance of such ritual institutions and their dependence on careful negotiation between humans and the divine'.[37] The terms here are probably familiar, viewing aetiology in terms of the collective, civic, positive ideology of Athens which, when placed in its supposedly natural position at the end of the play, would bridge unstable past and stabilising present. Such views mistake the aetiologising voice of Orestes for a sound-bite from the playwright.

As a function of character, Orestes imitates his patron Apollo, and, distinct from other mortal speakers, is especially self-aware and a reader of signs. For example, in *Eumenides*, Orestes had promised to protect Athens after his death; that is, he predicted his own future hero cult (762–74). In the *Oresteia*, he was pointedly tested as an 'expounder' rival to Apollo (*Cho.* 118, 552, *Eum.* 595, 609). Both aetiological retrospection and prediction are the mark of kings in relation to their own lands. For example, Pelasgus in Aeschylus' *Suppliants* speaks of the origin of the name of the land Apia and, much like Orestes, uses this origin story in order to lay out two possible outcomes for his auditors (260–70). Through his origin story he conveys to the Danaids that if they are hostile snakes, they will be destroyed, as Apis killed the snakes that were infesting the land long ago; if they are natives returning to the land, then they will be protected, as Apis did for the people through that same act of violent killing. In Euripides' *Suppliants*, it is striking that Theseus is in fact the one to institute cults; Athena appears at the end to confirm them. So too, it is against this role of king as expert on his lands' foundations that we should situate Theseus' role in *Heracles*, where he offers Heracles

35 For other accounts, see R. Hamilton, *Choes and Anthesteria: Athenian Iconography and Ritual* (Ann Arbor: University of Michigan Press, 1992).
36 P. Kyriakou, *A Commentary on Euripides' Iphigenia in Tauris* (Berlin: de Gruyter, 2006), pp. 311–12.
37 M. Cropp, *Euripides, Iphigenia in Tauris* (Warminster: Aris & Phillips, 2000), p. 231, with C. Wolff, 'Euripides' *Iphigenia among the Taurians*: Aetiology, ritual, and myth', *ClAnt* 11 (1992), pp. 308–34, at pp. 325–9.

sanctuaries in the land, and in Sophocles' *Oedipus at Colonus*, where Theseus is the only one who knows the place of Oedipus' disappearance. In *Iphigenia among the Taurians*, then, Orestes declares, by the form of his aetiological retrospection, that he is royalty of Athens. Like Pelasgus, he makes a point of using explanations not to ruminate on the past but to project a possible outcome. The frame of expectations in the first part of the speech sets up the surprise twist in the last part. He begins by glossing the Areopagus court as the one that Zeus established for Ares, implying a happy resolution, and then he explains how the Athenians successfully managed his pollution at the Anthesteria. This looks like a favourable pattern. But in the last part of his speech, where he describes the Areopagus trial, the schema of resolution in continuing practice is not fulfilled, as not all the Furies are successfully transmuted to *Semnai Theai* and Orestes must again run to Apollo in Fury-driven madness. His new task, to steal Artemis' cult statue, is the one that must be undertaken with Iphigenia's help, and he closes his speech by appealing to her to help him. By setting up his request with successful outcomes elsewhere (though obviously not definitive solutions for his plight), Orestes frames what he is asking in terms of its likelihood to succeed in some way. That is, aetiology is not really about explanation at all but is rather servant to persuasion and to Orestes' immediate self-interest.

This passage, too often considered deviant, is perhaps the most difficult case of Euripidean aetiology to explain if we start from assuming that the *deus ex machina* type of ending is conventional or that it is Euripides who is the explainer of greatest moment. The problem is not with the passage, but with these starting points. Were we to interpret the Choes passage as a reflection of Euripides' voice, it might seem that Euripides is simply flattering his audience with Orestes' gratuitous Athens shot. But there is a point to Orestes knowing more than others do and there is a point to making him use that knowledge to try to convince others to help him. If we are looking for a model through which to glimpse the scenario of ancient explanation of subsequent practice which would be, in turn, most analogous to Euripides' role as explainer, then this is, perhaps, the closest we get to a conventional retrospective scenario of explaining foundations. It is, notably, history with an immediate, prospective aim which shapes the account in selective and biased terms. Like Toelken and his Navajo myths, if we parse this as 'aetiological', as a narrative meant to explicate past and present, then we have missed the point.

To return briefly to seers and prediction, mantic activities required claims to knowledge of both the past and the future and, further, regularly involved explication for future foundations and, consequently,

knowledge of past foundations.[38] So, for example, titles of works by
known seers are less obviously how-to manuals for divination than
histories of past prophecies by famous seers.[39] Striking is Aristotle's
notice that Epimenides of Crete (the legendary figure who probably
did not call himself a *mantis* but shared many of their attributes) 'used
to divine, not the future, but only things that were past but unclear'
(*Rhet.* 3.17.10). Aristotle's larger point is that deliberative speaking,
because it is about the future, is more difficult than forensic speech,
which is about the past. Epimenides provides evidence that 'even
manteis' know the past and, though it is not a direct quotation, one
has the sense that what Epimenides was advertising was not a novel
ability but rather a pithy framing of what prophetic personnel regularly did. Outside of the developing genre of historiography, then, we
might well suspect that accounts of origins were often delivered not as
retrospection but rather as admonition or in the service of paradigms
for predictions and immediate actions.[40] In this sense, when Euripides
stages a history of cult through voices of prophecy or, in those rarer
cases, retrospection targeting the future, he reveals something of the
reality of discourse about origins in the fifth century.

The long fondness for historiographic claims to explain, going
back at least to Herodotus' *historie* of *aitia*, has conditioned modern
readers to approach tragic explanation of the past with a particular bias. Explanation is key to modern definitions of the historian's
project, perhaps most strikingly in forays into 'virtual' or counterfac-
tual history which claim historical value by exposing the underlying
mechanics of explanation.[41] Closer to home, in an insightful study of
fifth-century commemorative genres in Athens, Deborah Boedeker
distinguishes the memorialising modes of literary and visual arts,
tragedy included, from the practice of historiography by separating
the discontinuous past of art from the continuous past articulated in
historiographers, which 'presents a series of events in a fixed sequence
– logical rather than analogical – where this event follows that, and

38 Flower, *Seer in Ancient Greece*, p. 78.
39 Flower, *Seer in Ancient Greece*, p. 52.
40 The exact relationship between more explicit accounts of religious history,
    which we might expect to include the sort of information often found in
    Euripidean aetiological prediction, and the practices of seers remains obscure.
    Philochorus, a few generations post-Euripides, was a seer and an 'exegete', but it
    is unclear both what status exegetes may have had in Euripides' day and whether
    this combination of prophet and ritual 'expounder' was shared by others. On
    post-classical religious history, see most recently J. Dillery, 'Greek sacred history',
    American Journal of Philology 126/4 (2005), pp. 505–26.
41 N. Ferguson, *Virtual History: Alternatives and Counterfactuals* (New York:
    Basic Books, 1999).

therefore somehow comes from that'.[42] Historiography thus 'sets up a *post hoc ergo propter hoc* view of events' and the authorial voice matters: 'Active authorial judgments stand in contrast to the more silent genres of monumental painting or sculpture, for example, which only show and do not tell, and even to tragedy, where only characters and chorus have voices, not the dramatist.'[43] This is indeed the difference, but we should not lament the absence of the author's voice in Euripidean aetiologies. The fact that the characters have distinctive voices is precisely the point.

42 D. Boedeker, 'Presenting the past in fifth-century Athens', in D. Boedeker and K. A. Raaflaub (eds), *Democracy, Empire, and the Arts in Fifth-Century Athens* (Cambridge, MA: Harvard University Press, 1998), pp. 185–202, at p. 199.
43 Boedeker, 'Presenting the past', p. 202.

9

OLD COMEDY AND POPULAR HISTORY

Jeffrey Henderson

Since antiquity fifth-century topical comedies have been combed for information useful *for* historians, but no one has systematically asked whether their authors can be viewed *as* historians. That topical comedians of any era look much more to current than to past events is only to be expected. But the fifth-century comedians were also poets, and they did occasionally share with most other poets an interest in the less recent past. What past interested them, and what were their sources? Did they simply reflect mythic and popular recollection? Or were their accounts historiographic, utilising factual research, seeking to inform or correct the record and proposing true accounts? If their portrayal of the past was critical, was it framed by the same consistent cultural and political biases now clearly established for their portrayal of contemporary events?[1] Did the nature of their forays into the remoter past change over time? These are questions that deserve more extensive and systematic study, but meanwhile I offer some preliminary analyses, drawing examples mainly from four plays by Aristophanes: *Acharnians* (Lenaea 425) and *Peace* (Dionysia 421) on the run-up to war, *Knights* (Lenaea 424) and *Lysistrata* (Lenaea 411). Each example illustrates a distinctive appeal to the past as an element of the comic poet's response to current issues.

But first we must ask whether the comic perspective on the past was informed by historians. The chronology is close. Topically engaged ('political') comedy was a by-form practised by a subset of poets during what we might call the demagogic era of Athenian history:[2]

---

1 In a nutshell, comic poets criticised democratic culture and politics as shaped by Pericles and his 'demagogic' successors and maintained a Cimonian view of foreign affairs; for an overview see J. Henderson, *Aristophanes Acharnians. Knights* (Cambridge, MA, and London: Harvard University Press, 1998), pp. 12–23.
2 Many, perhaps most, fifth-century comedies were domestic, mythological or otherwise unengaged with public issues, which is probably why so little information about them is preserved.

the 430s to the end of the Peloponnesian War and its aftermath in the 390s. This was also the era of intellectual advances that included the development of historiography proper, as distinct from earlier semi- or proto-historiographic accounts.[3] Athens apparently had had no coherent, authoritative or even chronological narrative of its past (aside from bare archon lists and the like) until Thucydides began tracking the Peloponnesian War and its remote causes in the late 430s and Hecataeus and Herodotus began systematically vetting a welter of mythic, poetic and popular accounts of the more distant past, along critical lines exemplified in such programmatic statements as these:[4]

τάδε γράφω, ὥς μοι δοκεῖ ἀληθέα εἶναι· οἱ γὰρ Ἑλλήνων λόγοι πολλοί τε καὶ γελοῖοι, ὡς ἐμοὶ φαίνονται, εἰσίν. (Hecataeus of Miletus, *FGrHist* 1 F 1a)

I write what I consider true, for Greek accounts are in my view both numerous and laughable.

τὰς ἀκοὰς τῶν προγεγενημένων, καὶ ἢν ἐπιχώρια σφίσιν ᾖ, ὁμοίως ἀβασανίστως παρ᾽ ἀλλήλων δέχονται . . . ὄντα ἀνεξέλεγκτα καὶ τὰ πολλὰ ὑπὸ χρόνου αὐτῶν ἀπίστως ἐπὶ τὸ μυθῶδες ἐκνενικηκότα. (Thucydides 1.20.1)

People accept from one another hearsay accounts of the past, even their own local past, all equally without examination . . . [poets and chroniclers treat subjects] that are beyond the reach of testing and that for the most part have won their way through to the realm of myth so as to be incredible.

Aristophanes for one was clearly engaged with the intellectual currents of his time, so much so that he was teased for it by his older rival Cratinus.[5] But was he aware of the new historiography in particular,

---

3 These are summarily described by Dionysius of Halicarnassus, *Thuc.* 5, as for the most part collections of public traditions, written records, myths and legends presented more or less as the writers had found them; cf. D. Toye, 'Dionysius of Halicarnassus on the first Greek historians', *AJP* 116 (1995), pp. 279–302.

4 All translations in this chapter are my own.

5 Fr. 342 (play unknown): τίς δὲ σύ; κομψός τις ἔροιτο θεατής. ὑπολεπτολόγος, γνωμιδιώτης, εὐριπιδαριστοφανίζων ('"And who are you?" a hip spectator might ask, a subtle word-mincer, a conceit-chaser, a Euripidaristophaniser'); for discussion see E. Bakola, *Cratinus and the Art of Comedy* (Oxford: Oxford University Press, 2010), pp. 24–9. Aristophanes himself often boasts of the intellectual sophistication of his plays, e.g. in the parabasis of *Clouds*, cf. *Wasps* 1043–50.

that is, of formal investigation of the past as distinct from, or as a corrective to, popular models based on the hearsay or mythic past? Evidently not: historiography proper is not among the academic subjects on offer in *Clouds*, nor do Aristophanes or other fifth-century comic poets seem elsewhere even to have noticed, let alone emulated or satirised, historiography or any of its practitioners.

There *is* of course one passage in *Acharnians* that is still generally thought to echo or parody the opening of Herodotus' *Histories*:

καὶ ταῦτα μὲν δὴ σμικρὰ κἀπιχώρια·
πόρνην δὲ Σιμαίθαν ἰόντες Μεγαράδε
νεανίαι 'κκλέπτουσι μεθυσοκότταβοι·
κᾆθ' οἱ Μεγαρῆς ὀδύναις πεφυσιγγωμένοι
ἀντεξέκλεψαν Ἀσπασίας πόρνα δύο·
κἀντεῦθεν ἀρχὴ τοῦ πολέμου κατερράγη
Ἕλλησι πᾶσιν ἐκ τριῶν λαικαστριῶν. (523–9)

Now granted, this was trivial and strictly local. But then some tipsy, cottabus-playing youths went to Megara and kidnapped the whore Simaetha. And then the Megarians, garlic-stung by their distress, in retaliation stole a couple of Aspasia's whores, and from that the onset of war broke forth upon all Greeks: from three sluts!

Here the play's hero, Dicaeopolis, traces the origins of the Peloponnesian War to reciprocal abductions of women, a motif attested elsewhere only in Herodotus, who attributes a similar story about the Persian Wars to Persian sources and then questions it.[6] If Dicaeopolis is alluding to Herodotus, then Aristophanes, and presumably his audience too, knew about historiography and its critical treatment of such (presumably popular) stories as these mutual abductions. But beyond this shared motif, there is no other likely point of contact, here or elsewhere, between Aristophanes and Herodotus. It has been claimed that transitional μὲν δή is distinctively Herodotean, but in fact this usage appears elsewhere in Aristophanes (also in Euripides) and is anyway not so salient as to signal a borrowing, let alone a parody; and all comic references elsewhere to details also found in Herodotus are either traceable to tragedy (especially Aeschylus' *Persians*) or attribut-

---

6 For B. Bravo and M. Węcowski, 'The hedgehog and the fox: Form and meaning in the prologue of Herodotus', *JHS* 124 (2004), pp. 143–64, Herodotus offers the reciprocal abductions only to ridicule, indeed to parody, the sort of uncritical explanation of the origins of great wars then common in Greek poets and prose-writers.

able to travellers' reports of the sort dramatised and ridiculed in the prologue of *Acharnians*.

Ridicule of such reports does suggest the possibility that in the reciprocal abductions 'we should see not so much Aristophanes parodying Herodotus, but rather Herodotus and Aristophanes as *doing the same thing* here. Both are "parodying" popular mentality – provided . . . we do not take "parody" too crudely as a sheer deflating technique, but rather as a provision of a model to build on and refer to.'[7] This does not require us to assume that Aristophanes and his audience appreciated the historiographical distinction between 'popular mentality' and a more credible 'model', only that the comic example of popular mentality be recognisable as such; nor can the parody be of the 'sheer deflating' type, for Dicaeopolis, who in the prologue had ridiculed incredible tales in order to illustrate the mendacity of foreign ambassadors and the gullibility of the Athenian assembly, would hardly have offered in his own account of the war's motivations an explanation designed to sound ridiculous or implausible.

The parodic element in Dicaeopolis' reciprocal abductions is more complex. At this point he is disguised as Euripides' cripple-hero Telephus, from whose speech to the Greeks he has borrowed his own speech to the Acharnians (and beyond them, the audience). His most striking argument is not his self-defence but his defence of the Spartans, so it is reasonable to assume that in Euripides' play Telephus had similarly defended the Trojans; indeed if Telephus had defended only himself and his fellow Mysians, he would have been much less appealing as a model for Dicaeopolis. A defence of the Trojans would have cited Greek misdeeds to match Trojan misdeeds, principally the abduction of Helen. This gives us the tit-for-tat motif also found in Herodotus but probably not reciprocal abductions: that was not part of Trojan War mythology, and if Euripides had invented the variant or adopted it from some unattested earlier account, the absence of testimonia for it, and in such a famous play, is surprising.

But if not from *Telephus* and not from Herodotus, then where did Aristophanes get the idea of reciprocal abductions? Probably not from a mythic exemplar at all, but from recent history. The clue is that Dicaeopolis *names* the whore, Simaetha, and the audience was presumably expected to know something about her.[8] No doubt there

---

7 C. Pelling, *Literary Texts and the Greek Historian* (London and New York: Routledge, 2000), p. 155.

8 So D. M. MacDowell, *Aristophanes and Athens* (Oxford: Oxford University Press, 1999), pp. 61–7; T. Braun, 'The choice of dead politicians in Eupolis' *Demoi*: Themistocles' exile, hero-cult and delayed rehabilitation; Pericles and the origins of the Peloponnesian War', in D. Harvey and J. Wilkins (eds), *The Rivals of*

really had been an episode involving fights over whores between young Athenians and Megarians, fights that had been among, or could be comically placed on a par with, the many reciprocal complaints mentioned by Thucydides as leading to war.[9] If so, Aristophanes' innovation was to update the role of Helen in the run-up to the Trojan War (parodic) by including a recent episode involving Aspasia and privileged young men associated with Pericles[10] that could be connected with the run-up to the Peloponnesian War (topical). Plutarch (*Pericles* 31–2) and Diodorus (12.39 = Ephorus *FGrH* 70 F 196) cite other such attacks on Pericles and (by proxy) on his friends shortly before the outbreak of the war or just after;[11] from among these Aristophanes would have chosen this particular incident because of its suitability for integration into the *Telephus* myth, not because the incident had any more currency as a *casus belli* than other such incidents seized on by Pericles' opponents in order to discredit his policies.

Indeed four years later Aristophanes would again trace the origin of the war to Pericles' exploitation of the Megarian issue as a mask for personal motives, but this time the alleged motive was to distract attention from a scandal involving his friend Pheidias that implicated himself (*Peace* 605–27).[12] Lines 615–18 both reveal Aristophanes' reason for connecting this particular scandal with the disappearance of the goddess Peace (represented in the play as a large statue) and signal its novelty (but not fictionality) in connection with the run-up to war:

(footnote 8 *continued*)
Aristophanes: Studies in Athenian Old Comedy (London and Swansea: Classical Press of Wales, 2000), pp. 213–14; A. H. Sommerstein, *Aristophanes Wealth* (Warminster: Aris & Phillips, 2001), p. 233.

9   Th. 1.67.4 and 1.139.2: 'Among others who came forward with various complaints of their own were the Megarians, who pointed to a great many disagreements . . . But the Athenians neither accepted the other demands nor annulled the decree, accusing the Megarians of cultivating sacred and unowned land and of receiving runaway slaves.'

10 The scholia state (without citing a source) that Simaetha was a lover of Alcibiades.

11 In connection with Pericles' trial in 430 (Th. 2.65.3–4); Thucydides does not record the charge but Plato, *Gorgias* 516a, says that it was embezzlement of public funds (κλοπή). As Bakola, *Cratinus*, pp. 216–17, 309–10, points out, the indictment could well have been brought many months before the actual trial, when the debate about Megara was still under way.

12 Pheidias was convicted of embezzling gold and/or ivory from the chryselephantine statue of Athena, which he had created for the Parthenon as an element of Pericles' controversial building programme, and also of religious impropriety for depicting Pericles fighting an Amazon on the goddess' shield.

(Trygaeus) Well, by Apollo, no one ever told me that, nor had I heard how Pheidias was connected to (προσήκοι) the goddess.
(Chorus Leader) Nor I, until just now. So that's why her face is so lovely, being related to (συγγενής) him![13] There's lots we don't know about.

Clearly Aristophanes did not feel bound to the earlier Simaetha allegation as an official explanation of Pericles' motivation. It is simply that the Simaetha story would have been less effective for his purposes in *Peace*: 'in such a context Pericles' self-*protection* might figure more naturally than any self-*indulgence* in a private quarrel of Aspasia, and the Pheidias allegation is exactly what we need'.[14] Unlike historians, comic poets felt no need to adopt a consistent version of events.

But did the comic poets also feel no need to make their version of events plausible (however satirically pitched)? The scandal involving Pheidias is real enough, but was it among Pericles' other troubles just before the outbreak of war? Despite long-acknowledged uncertainties, the date of the scandal is generally thought to be 438/7, on the basis of reconstructed secondary accounts of Philochorus (*FGrHist* 328 F 121), including the scholia to *Peace* (605α and β). Events of 438/7 would be too early to be plausibly connected with the onset of the war, at least for a proper historian. If that date is sound, Aristophanes was either unconcerned about the chronology or, since it was recent enough for the audience to recall, he actually *intended* the connection to sound implausible, though (as in the case of Simaetha for Dicaeopolis) that would undermine the force of Trygaeus' case against Pericles. But there are no strong reasons for privileging a dubious reconstruction of Philochorus over the testimony of the comic poets, followed by Plutarch and Diodorus, who place this and other such scandals just before the outbreak of the war.[15] The earlier dating in fact rests on an emendation of the *Peace*-scholia as transmitted, which explicitly date the Pheidias prosecution to 432/1.[16]

---

13 Playing on the double sense of προσήκειν 'connected/related to'; the phrase 'Pheidias connected to Peace' became proverbial (Suda φ 246).
14 Pelling, *Literary Texts*, p. 286 n. 38.
15 As recently argued by Bakola, *Cratinus*, pp. 213–20, in connection with Cratinus' *Ploutoi*, which in the aftermath of Pericles' trial (the play is generally dated to 429) seems to have 'dramatized a fictional trial where Hagnon and perhaps other friends of Pericles were tried for their handling of public money' (p. 218).
16 Altering 'in the archonship of Pythodorus' (432/1) to 'in the archonship of Theodorus' (438/7) to make the date of Pheidias' indictment and trial coincide with the accepted (but itself uncertain) date of the dedication of the Athena Parthenos statue, which the scholia also mention. But the scholia, which seem to

Herodotus began his *Histories* with the reciprocal-abductions story as a provisional explanation, to exemplify a myth-oriented and therefore popular model of thinking about the past before quickly confronting it with the historian's more critical model(s), which are rooted in knowable time beginning with Croesus of Lydia. Aristophanes does something similar for his own comic purposes: Dicaeopolis' reciprocal abductions root what might otherwise be merely a 'deflating' parody of *Telephus* in reality and thus give the parodic arguments of his Telephus persona more topical point. The reciprocal abductions in themselves and *qua* parody may come off as incidents too trivial and indeed too characteristic of 'the popular mentality' to enlist as true motivations for a great war (so Thucydides), but persuasive points can of course be made in a parodic and/or satirical context, and that the abductions were too trivial to justify a war is exactly Dicaeopolis' point;[17] indeed much the same point had probably been made in *Telephus*.[18]

Unlike Herodotus, however, Dicaeopolis embraces the popular understanding: for him, as for most of the audience, such motivations really had been determinative factors in bringing about the present war, much as in the realm of myth the abduction of Helen had brought about the Trojan War; in both cases, leaders took the people to war for selfish personal reasons. The same applies to the similar attacks in *Peace* and other comedies. Only later would Thucydides articulate an ἀληθεστάτη πρόφασις through a kind of historiographic analysis unfamiliar to most Athenians at the time, including Aristophanes. Thus Plutarch (*Pericles* 30.4) was not wrong to quote our lines as representing actual Megarian complaints and to use other passages from contemporary comedies as evidence of popular knowledge and understanding in the run-up to war.[19]

(footnote 16 *continued*)
conflate and somewhat jumble different sources, do not state that the dedication and the trial were contemporaneous, only that the trial took place 'after' the statue had been completed; the indictment could of course have been lodged at any time thereafter. For detailed analysis see Bakola, *Cratinus*, pp. 305–12.

17 'The absurdity of these accounts of the war in no way proves that Ar. did not intend or expect them to be taken seriously as arguments against the justice and expediency of beginning or continuing it' (Sommerstein, *Knights*, p. 233).

18 Cf. fr. 722, where Agamemnon apparently declines to risk his life simply to help Menelaus recover Helen.

19 S. Hornblower, *A Commentary on Thucydides. Volume I: Books I–III* (Oxford: Clarendon Press, 1991), p. 111, argues that Thucydides took practically no account of the popular tradition connecting personal scandals with the Megarian decree(s) because 'he found the personal aspect of the vulgar story distasteful, perhaps; Pericles' mistress Aspasia was supposedly behind it, and it would be out of character for Th. to give prominence to this Herodotean female angle'.

Much of the persuasive power of Aristophanes' parody, or rather recycling, of *Telephus* lies precisely in the mode of mythical thinking that still informed popular history in this period: epic and tragedy had no problem with a face that launched a thousand ships, and neither did their audiences. Comedy could operate within this mode as well and at the same time still represent the real world, at least at the time of *Acharnians*. *Acharnians*, for all its pioneering brilliance in paratragedy, was in fact unexceptional in using heroic myth as the primary lens for viewing the past, including the recent past.

As is amply noted by Plutarch and evident in plays like Cratinus' *Dionysalexander*, *Nemesis* and *Ploutoi* and Hermippus' *Moirai*, the comic poets had long been attacking Pericles in this mode, in mythological plots that assimilated Pericles to Zeus, and Aspasia variously to Hera, Helen, Omphale and Deianeira, and that thus portrayed the motivations for the Samian War and then the Peloponnesian War as selfish and personal.[20] In viewing even the recent past through the lens of heroic myth drawn from epic, choral lyric and tragedy – the historical models most familiar and congenial to their audiences – the comic poets sought both to clarify and to enhance the power of their engagement with topical issues.[21] What they were doing in the comic mode was not so different from the mythological lensing employed by Aeschylus in *Persians* and *Eumenides*, and no doubt Euripides in *Telephus*, which was why Dicaeopolis thought the play so suitable for recycling.

And not only poets: in this period myth was also the mode in which Athenian public monuments depicted the past, portraying no historical figures or events other, or more recent, than the tyrannicides and the Persian Wars, which were cast in the timeless and heroic mode that enshrined memory of ancestral deeds.[22] Political, deliberative and diplomatic speeches would occasionally, for practical purposes in a dispute, have appealed to the more recent past in non-poetic/mythologised fashion, but beyond commonly agreed facts, such as an inscribed record or agreement,[23] these appeals were selective,

---

20 Cf. the papyrus hypothesis to Cratinus' *Dionysalexander* (I 44–8) κωμωιδεῖται δ᾽ ἐν τῶι δράματι Περικλῆς μάλα πιθανῶς δι᾽ ἐμφάσεως ὡς ἐπαγηοχὼς τοῖς Ἀθηναίοις τὸν πόλεμον ('in the play Pericles is very convincingly ridiculed by innuendo as having brought the war on the Athenians').

21 It is noteworthy that neither tragic nor comic dramatists took much interest in Attic myths and legends, given their thin coverage by the panhellenic poetic tradition; cf. A. M. Bowie, 'Myth and ritual in the rivals of Aristophanes', in Harvey and Wilkins, *Rivals of Aristophanes*, p. 321.

22 Recall that the insertion of a figure resembling Pericles in a public depiction of the Amazonomachy could be considered an actionable offence: n. 12, above.

23 But note that inscribed decrees were not necessarily permanent records: they could be altered, cancelled or effaced if they were deemed incompatible with

self-serving and contestable, not grounded in a universally agreed (historical) account or constrained by disinterested methods of research. It is unclear whether the annual funeral oration (*epitaphios logos*), a non-agonistic event, regularly referred to the more recent past: our only fifth-century example, Thucydides' version of Pericles' oration of 431, does not. It could be that 'by avoiding comment on such [historical] exploits . . . Pericles shows knowledge of the practice of including them in the funeral oration',[24] but it is at least equally likely that this was not the practice; it is uncommon even in our later examples.

As reflections of popular history – history without ἱστορία – the comic accounts can thus provide a control to set beside the accounts of historians like Herodotus, who problematises mythical/popular explanations, and Thucydides, who ignores them. Although Thucydides duly registers the arguments over the Megarian decree and over Pericles' culpability for starting the war, he prefers to trace and emphasise large national patterns going back several generations that more or less inevitably led to war, and he is completely silent about Aspasia, Pheidias and other private scandals. He is thus out of sync, or better, out of sympathy, with the emphases of comedy and the popular opinion it reflects: at the time most people thought that the war had been triggered by immediate issues like the Megarian Decree and by the self-interest and intransigence of the Olympian Pericles, and for the comic poets all this could be portrayed as a recapitulation of traditional myths for an audience accustomed to thinking this way. Clearly Herodotus and Thucydides had not yet taught people more accurate, critical and disinterested ways to know the past.

Yet by the mid-420s popular history was beginning to develop its own modes of critical inquiry under the twin stimuli of sophistic reality-testing of myth and new techniques of argument in oratory; both developments are reflected and absorbed by tragedy, particularly Euripidean tragedy, and by comedy. A similar change began to affect public monuments such as the temple of Athena Nike, whose construction was resumed at about this time and whose friezes, apparently for the first time, blended historical with myth-historical depictions.

(footnote 23 *continued*)
current interests, for example Th. 5.11 (when constituting Brasidas as their founder after his death in 422, the Amphipolitans destroyed all record of the previous founder, Hagnon); 5.56 (the footnote to the peace treaty of 421 inserted by the Athenians in winter 419/8 and criticised in 411 in *Lysistrata* 513); *IG* i² 43 (378/7), the decree moved by Aristoteles for the second Athenian league, prescribing that the Athenian council be empowered to destroy any stelai in Athens that member cities might consider objectionable thereafter.

24 V. Frangeskou, 'Tradition and originality in some Attic funeral orations', *CW* 92 (1999), pp. 315–36, at p. 320 n. 23.

In the arena of myth and on the role of poets as the chief authorities for the past, Aristophanes responded defensively. In *Clouds* the sophists, along with the orators and litigants who embraced their methods, are denounced for a critical treatment of myths that allows them to be literalised and misapplied, and Euripides is denounced for trivialising and sensationalising myths. In Aristophanes' view, these innovations served to deprive mythology of its larger-than-life dignity and its normative and inspiring functions, leaving humanity to its own, inevitably low and mutable, moral devices. Two passages from *Clouds* (produced at the Dionysia of 423, incompletely revised c. 417) will serve to exemplify these claims against the sophists on the one hand and Euripides on the other:

(Wrong Logos) Now then, I'll proceed to the necessities of nature. Say you slip up, fall in love, engage in a little adultery, and then get caught: you're done for because you're unable to argue. But if you follow me, go ahead and indulge your nature, romp, laugh, think nothing shameful. If you happen to get caught *in flagrante*, tell him this: that you've done nothing wrong. Then pass the buck to Zeus, on the grounds that even he is worsted by lust for women, so how can you, a mere mortal, be stronger than a god? (1075–92)

(Strepsiades of his son, fresh from sophistic training) Then I asked him if he would at least take a myrtle sprig and sing me something from the works of Aeschylus. And he right away said, 'In my opinion, Aeschylus is chief among poets – chiefly full of noise, incoherent, a windbag, a maker of lofty locutions.' Can you imagine how that jolted my heart? But I bit back my anger and said, 'All right then, recite something from these modern poets, that brainy stuff, whatever it is.' And he right away tossed off some speech by Euripides about how a brother, god save me, used to screw his sister by the same mother! (1364–72)

By the time of *Frogs* (Lenaea 405), Aristophanes still assumes that poets are society's teachers and that the mythical past is the touchstone for evaluating human events, but now he concedes that not everything to be found in mythology is benign, and he anticipates Plato by enjoining poets to adopt a critical and self-censoring function, concealing what is bad for society and for individuals, and revealing only what is good:

(Euripides) And what harm, you bastard, did my Stheneboeas do to the community?

(Aeschylus) You motivated respectable women, the spouses of respectable men, to take hemlock in their shame over your Bellerophons.

(Euripides) But the story I told about Phaedra was already established, wasn't it?

(Aeschylus) Of course it was. But the poet has a special duty to conceal what's wicked, not stage it or teach it. For children the teacher is the one who instructs, but grownups have the poet. It's very important that we tell them things that are good. (1049–55)

To changes in the forensic arena, where the post-mythological past was most in evidence, Aristophanes was more adaptive: here, after all, was an arena in which he chose to involve himself. In *Knights* (Lenaea 424) he inaugurated the genre of demagogue-comedy in order to satirise the changed complexion of forensic competition and to enter the fray on its own terms. *Knights* was the first comedy devoted entirely to the ridicule of a single politician, Cleon, and apparently the first to abandon mythological allegory as the vehicle for sustained (as distinct from incidental, one-liner) political satire. To an extent this adaptation was forced: the Olympian and mythic caricatures of Pericles did not suit the new politicians who emerged after his death in 429; for down-to-earth *novi homines* like Cleon and for young, sophistically trained orators like Alcibiades, new caricatures were needed.[25] In Cleon's case, the winning caricature was furnished by Cleon himself: all Aristophanes needed to do was exaggerate Cleon's own qualities, in particular his novel argumentative and rhetorical style.

Knights makes clear that in the sharply competitive political environment of the 420s, appeals to historical events were becoming more prominent in oratory. An example of Aristophanes' take on this development is the exchange in *Knights* 810–19, responding to Cleon's self-comparison with Themistocles:

(Paphlagon) Isn't it really awful that you presume to say such things and to slander me before the Athenians and Demos, after my many fine services – many more, by Demeter, than Themistocles ever did for the city?

---

25 For details and analysis see J. Henderson, 'Demos, demagogue, tyrant in Attic Old Comedy', in K. Morgan (ed.), *Popular Tyranny: Sovereignty and its Discontents in Classical Greece* (Austin: University of Texas Press, 2003), pp. 155–79.

(Sausage Seller) 'City of Argos, hearken to his words!'[26] Are you matching yourself with Themistocles? He found our city's cup half-full and filled it the rest of the way, and he baked the Piraeus as dessert for her lunch, and added new seafood dishes to her menu while taking away none of the old; whereas you've tried to turn the Athenians into tiny-townies by building partitions (διατειχίζων)[27] and chanting oracles. Themistocles' match! And he's exiled from the country, while you wipe your fingers on 'peerless Achilles' baguettes!

Past heroes are no longer beyond compare, but this particular self-comparison can be discredited by citing historical facts that did not need to be elaborated for the spectators. Clearly Themistocles had been in the news, and not only in political speeches. In *Acharnians* there are many evocations of Aeschylus' *Persians*, our only extant (and apparently the last) topical tragedy, among them the assimilation of the final lament of Dicaeopolis/Telephus' rival Lamachus to that of Aeschylus' Xerxes, and they suggest that *Persians* had recently been revived,[28] and with it a reminder of Themistocles' heroic role, and credit for the victory, at Salamis.

Positive memories of Themistocles may have been connected with Euripides' *Telephus* as well, and this would explain the otherwise mysterious quotation of a line from that play in our passage from *Knights*: 'City of Argos, hearken to his words!' This quotation would make sense if Euripides had played up the similarities between Telephus and Themistocles, who in exile had gone to the court of the Molossian king Admetus, and on the advice of Admetus' wife had held their son at an altar as a suppliant, a story that even Thucydides saw fit to mention (1.136–7). It could well be that Aeschylus had already drawn a comparison between Themistocles and Telephus in his own *Telephus*, or even invented the hostage motif itself on the model of Themistocles.[29]

---

26 From Euripides' *Telephus*.
27 'Building partitions' (which are otherwise unattested) seems (with the scholia) to refer to proposed ('you tried') physical structures rather than being metaphorical for political divisions; if they were defensive it may be that after the Pylos victory, when the Spartans abandoned their investment of Attica, they were no longer considered necessary.
28 For detailed discussion see C. Brockmann, *Aristophanes und die Freiheit der Komödie* (Munich and Leipzig: Saur, 2003), pp. 42–141. Familiarity with Aeschylus' works would also be enhanced if, as seems likely from Plato, *Rep.* 376c–398b, they had already become school texts in the fifth century.
29 That the hostage scene featured in Aeschylus' play is stated by the scholiast on *Acharnians* 332, and the iconographic record suggests that it was indeed introduced into the Telephus myth c. the 460s (E. Csapo, 'Hikesia in the *Telephus*

In any event, a connection of Themistocles with Telephus would further deepen the resonance of Dicaeopolis' mythic persona, adding another legendary patriot unjustly condemned, and this resonance would need only brief signalling in the *Knights* passage. The passage differs in not being conducted through the medium of myth but rather in the light of knowable history and citable facts, and the contrast made by the Sausage Seller between Themistocles' continuing exile and Cleon's undeserved privileges in the Prytaneum suggests current debate about Themistocles' rehabilitation, which was indeed to occur after the war, when he was reinterred in a splendid tomb in Piraeus.[30]

It would seem that from the 420s onward, references in oratory and comedy to historical events as such followed a path that began to intersect with the path being taken at the same time by the first historians. In this regard *Lysistrata* of 411 is interesting in that it tries systematically to correct popular misconceptions about the past, indeed about Athens' entire democratic past, from the fall of the tyrants to the Persian invasions to the subsequent tensions with Sparta to the current war. On the one side are the heroine's chief antagonists, the Chorus of Old Men, fervid patriots and Spartan-haters who champion the current popular view of the democratic past as a justification for continued war, appealing not only to personal memory but also to official depictions of civic mythology. They proclaim themselves veterans of the occupation of Leipsydrium against the forces of the tyrant Hippias in 513; of the expulsion of Cleomenes and his Spartan allies in 508/7, which effectively ended the tyranny; of Marathon in 490; of Salamis in 480; of the campaigns of Myronides in the 470s to the 460s; and of the generalship of Phormio in the early years of the present war – a history that in actuality would make them about a hundred and thirty years old.[31] The Old Men see the women's peace initiative as an antidemocratic conspiracy to undo the accomplishments enshrined in this history: the women would conspire with the Spartans and restore the tyranny of Hippias, and their occupation of the Acropolis recalls

(footnote 29 *continued*)
of Aeschylus', *QUCC* 63 (1990), pp. 41–52; cf. C. Preiser, *Euripides: Telephos* (*Spudasmata* 78; Zurich and New York: Olms, 2001), pp. 51–9).

30 In this regard the absence of Themistocles among the resurrected politicians in Eupolis' *Demes* is probably significant; cf. I. C. Storey, *Eupolis: Poet of Old Comedy* (Oxford: Oxford University Press, 2003), pp. 132–3.

31 We can imagine Thucydides' response to such claims! All the same, these Old Men may well echo their actual counterparts: A. H. Sommerstein, *Aristophanes Lysistrata* (Warminster: Aris & Phillips, 1990), pp. 168–9, notes that *Lysistrata* 'is the last Aristophanic play in which the chorus have recollections of the period 514–480, and in *Eccl.* (304) the (pretended) old men's memories of their youth are of the days of Myronides (i.e. in the 450s)'.

barbarian invaders. And so the Old Men compare themselves to Harmodius and Aristogeiton, assuming the very posture of the bronze statues of the young tyrannicides that stood in the Agora (631–5), and they compare the women to Artemisia at Salamis and to the invading Amazons battled by Theseus, as depicted in Micon's paintings in the Peisianacteum (672–9).

After Lysistrata has made both the Athenians and the Spartans her captive audience and proceeds to broker a peace negotiation, she systematically corrects the Old Men's recollections in order to discredit the historical case for continuing the war. Her own credentials for speaking about the past, like the Old Men's, are based on personal recollection and tradition:

ἐγὼ γυνὴ μέν εἰμι, νοῦς δ'ἔνεστί μοι.
αὐτὴ δ'ἐμαυτῆς οὐ κακῶς γνώμης ἔχω,
τοὺς δ' ἐκ πατρός τε καὶ γεραιτέρων λόγους
πολλοὺς ἀκούσασ' οὐ μεμούσωμαι κακῶς. (1124–7)

It's true I'm a woman, but still I've got a mind: I'm pretty intelligent in my own right, and because I've listened many a time to the conversations of my father and other elders I'm pretty well educated too.

Here Lysistrata echoes but significantly alters a speech by the heroine of Euripides' *Wise Melanippe*, who had claimed knowledge from her *mother*, the priestess Hippo (fr. 484); Lysistrata, who has temporarily usurped male authority and is challenging male recollections, needs the authority and recollections of men. The historical facts that Lysistrata goes on to relate are, as in deliberative oratory, no mere history lesson, or mere corrections for the record, but selectively chosen to support her main argument: that Athens and Sparta are old and natural allies who have no good reasons for fighting one another but instead, as in the good old days, should jointly lead Greece in a spirit of panhellenic unity against the barbarians. There is nothing outrageous or ludicrous about this argument: since 431 it had been familiar to the spectators from actual debates about the war, and it would continue to be urged by orators in similar situations well into the fourth century.[32]

At the same time, and again as in oratory, Lysistrata's version of

32 For example, Thucydides 4.20.4 (424), 5.29.3 (421, cf. Aristophanes *Peace* 107–8, 406ff, 1082), Andocides 3.21, Isocrates *Panegyricus passim*, Xenophon, *Hellenica* 6.5.33ff, Demosthenes 9.30–1.

historical facts is tendentious, for example her evidence of mutual benefactions:

> Next, Spartans, I'm going to turn to you. Don't you remember when Pericleidas the Spartan came here once and sat at the altars as a suppliant of the Athenians, pale in his scarlet uniform, begging for troops? That time when Messenia was up in arms against you and the god was shaking you with an earthquake? And Cimon went with four thousand infantrymen and rescued all Sparta? After being treated that way by the Athenians, you're now out to ravage the country that's treated you well? (1137–46)

> And do you think I'm going to let you Athenians off? Don't you remember how the Spartans in turn, when you were dressed in slaves' rags, came with their spears and wiped out many Thessalian fighters, many friends and allies of Hippias? That day when they were the only ones helping you to drive him out? And how they liberated you, and replaced your slaves' rags with a warm cloak, as suits a free people? (1149–56)

It is true that Cimon had joined an allied expedition to help Sparta put down the serf rebellion in 462, but to say that Cimon had 'rescued all Sparta' is a stretch: the allied action did not end the rebellion, and the Athenians did little or no actual fighting, the Spartans having suspected them of being rebel sympathisers and sent them home 'alone among the allies', an insult that got Cimon ostracised, broke the Athenian–Spartan alliance, and led in a few years to war between Athens and the Peloponnesian League. Did Aristophanes expect the audience to be taken in by Lysistrata's edited account? Or did he expect them to laugh knowingly? The spectators could not have been aware of the later, fuller accounts written by Herodotus and Thucydides, so their sources would have been the same as Lysistrata's: fathers and other elders recollecting political debates.[33] But it is telling that just ten years earlier, by the terms of the Peace of Nicias of 421 (Th. 5.23), Athens had sworn to send Sparta as many troops as possible in case of future rebellions; so apparently Lysistrata was not the only one prepared to downplay Cimon's dismissal.

---

33 Even a century later an orator could appeal to family stories to enhance the authority of a historical fact, e.g. Aeschines, *On the Embassy* 77–8: οὐ γὰρ παρὰ τῶν ἀλλοτρίων ἀλλὰ παρὰ τοῦ πάντων οἰκειοτάτου ταῦτα ἐπυθανόμην . . . ὥστε οἰκεῖά μοι καὶ συνήθη τὰ τῆς πόλεως ἀτυχήματα εἶναι τοῖς ὠσὶν ἀκούειν ('for I learned of these events not from outsiders but from my very closest relative . . . and so the city's misfortunes are family stories that I am accustomed to hearing').

Similarly tendentious is Lysistrata's proffered Spartan benefaction: how the Spartans drove out the tyrant Hippias and his allies and 'liberated' the Athenians from virtual slavery. Again, slavery is a stretch, and again Lysistrata omits the sequel: a Spartan army under King Cleomenes came back three years later to stifle the nascent democracy by supporting the archon Isagoras against Cleisthenes' popular faction, who won a resounding victory and thus cleared the way for democracy. Earlier in the play (271–80) the Old Men of the chorus had boasted in detail, and with gross exaggeration,[34] about their victory in this very action, so Lysistrata's omission of it here amounts to trumping the expulsion of Cleomenes with the far more important removal of Hippias, which also trumps the Old Men's earlier equation of the Spartans with tyranny. Again, this was evidently a live issue in 411 and later: Thucydides was to comment that at this time 'the Athenians knew that it was not they and Harmodius who had put an end to the tyranny but the Spartans' (6.53.3), while Herodotus, the Atthidographers, and the orators would play down the role of the Spartans and stress that it was the Alcmaeonids who led the exiled democrats and who sought Delphic help in pressuring the Spartans to come to their aid.

The amount of historical recollection and debate in *Lysistrata* attests to the growing importance, in public deliberation, of facts about the past and their interpretation; a topical comic poet could not afford to neglect such facts in grinding his own axes. Not quite yet do we have to reckon with the influence of historians, who claimed to establish facts and chronologies accurately and disinterestedly, and to distinguish them from mere myth and hearsay, from 'the conversations of my father and other elders'. But to judge from many of the facts served up by later orators, and even by historians, we must wonder whether the availability of historiography would have made much of a difference to Aristophanes and his audiences.

---

34 See Sommerstein, *Aristophanes Lysistrata*, p. 168.

10

ATTIC HEROES AND THE CONSTRUCTION OF THE ATHENIAN PAST IN THE FIFTH CENTURY

H. A. Shapiro

The Athenians of the classical period were masters of reinvention. Beginning in the wake of the Persian Wars, if not earlier, they continually re-created the early history of their city to make it more appropriate to the imperial power and cultural hegemony that rapidly evolved. Many individuals were involved in the project of inventing Athens' past, including mythographers, tragedians, visual artists and even statesmen like Kimon, when he 'discovered' the bones of Theseus on the island of Skiros and, with great fanfare, brought the hero home to Athens in 476/5.[1]

As an archaeologist, I focus in this chapter on the role of the visual arts in creating Athens' early history, and especially on the crucial figures of Theseus and his family. But first, a few preliminary remarks on the role of public monuments in Athens in the early years of the democracy: monuments not just as architectural or art-historical works, but as forms of commemoration, as places of memory, as one of the most conspicuous forms of making 'history without historians'.

I begin with a few sentences from Tonio Hölscher, who for some forty years has been perhaps our most thoughtful student of the connections among history, memory, and the visual arts in both Greece and Rome. He writes,

Monuments are designed and erected as signs of power and superiority. As such, they are effective factors of public life: not secondary reflections but primary objects and symbols of political actions and concepts. Monuments have their place in public space . . . They inevitably address the community and, precisely

I am most grateful to John Marincola for the invitation to participate in the Leventis Conference.

1 Plut. *Theseus* 36.1–2; *Kimon* 8.5–6.

because of their public nature, challenge it, provoking consent or contradiction; they do not allow indifference because recognition automatically means acceptance.[2]

In the Athenian context, the monument has additional historical value because it is almost invariably accompanied by an inscribed text. Take, for example, the first victory monument set up by the new democracy in 506, a mere two years after Kleisthenes' reforms had been put in place in 508.[3] Commemorating the defeat, on a single day, of Boeotian and Chalkidian forces, the monument on the Akropolis consisted of a bronze four-horse chariot and the chains of the prisoners of war whose ransom paid for the monument. All this was recorded in an inscribed epigram on the base (two elegiac couplets), a fragment of which still survives. A new base, with a revised version of the epigram, was made probably in the 450s, when the original monument, damaged or destroyed by the Persians in 480, was replaced.[4] Herodotos saw this replacement copy and recorded it in his *Histories* (5.77) – a nice instance of the monument serving as primary source material for the literary historian.

Or consider the statue group of the tyrant-slayers Harmodios and Aristogeiton.[5] Whether this monument was set up in the Agora relatively soon after the deed, about 510, or – as I would prefer to believe – some two decades later, shortly after the victory at Marathon,[6] it also

2 T. Hölscher, 'Images and political identity: The case of Athens', in D. Boedeker and K. Raaflaub (eds), *Democracy, Empire and the Arts in Fifth-Century Athens* (Cambridge, MA: Harvard University Press, 1998), pp. 153–83, esp. p. 156.

3 A. E. Raubitschek, *Dedications from the Athenian Akropolis* (Cambridge, MA: Harvard University Press, 1949), pp. 168, 173; J. M. Hurwit, *The Athenian Akropolis* (Cambridge: Cambridge University Press, 1999), p. 25, fig. 24, 144; Hölscher, 'Images and political identity', pp. 163–4.

4 R. Meiggs and D. Lewis, *A Selection of Greek Historical Inscriptions to the End of the Fifth Century BC* (Oxford: Clarendon Press, 1998), pp. 28–9. See O. Dally, 'Zwischen serieller Ausfertigung und "Kopie": Zur Bedeutung der Wiederholung von Inschriften im östlichen Mittelmeerraum zwischen dem 6. Jahrhundert v. Chr. Und der römischen Kaiserzeit', in K. Junker and A. Stähli (eds), *Original und Kopie* (Wiesbaden: Richert, 2008), pp. 227–41, esp. pp. 231–3, and P. Funke, 'Wendezeit und Zeitenwende: Athens Aufbruch zur Demokratie', in D. Papenfuss and V. M. Strocka (eds), *Gab es das griechische Wunder?* (Mainz: Phillip von Zabern, 2001), pp. 1–20, esp. pp. 12–13, who argues that the replacement base and monument should have been made very soon after the victory over the Persians, in order to highlight the success of the young democracy, and not, as is usually assumed, in the 450s.

5 On the statue group see most recently S. Kansteiner, *Text und Skulptur: Berühmte Bildhauer und Bronzegiesser der Antike in Wort und Bild* (Berlin: de Gruyter, 2007), pp. 8–14, with earlier references.

6 For the early date: M. W. Taylor, *The Tyrant Slayers* (New York: Arno Press, 1981), pp. 34–7; for post Marathon: H. A. Shapiro, 'Religion and politics in democratic Athens', in W. D. E. Coulson, F. J. Frost, O. Palagia, and H. A. Shapiro (eds), *The*

carried an inscribed epigram (partially preserved) giving the historical context.[7] This is not a funerary monument, nor a votive offering (like the bronze *quadriga* on the Akropolis), but an entirely new class of object: the political monument.[8]

As we would expect, the victories over the Persians in 490 and again in 480/79 led to an ever greater outpouring of monuments, from statues to whole buildings,[9] but I would like to focus here on one monument in particular. In one of the mopping-up operations as the Persians withdrew from Greece, after 479, Kimon cleared out an enemy stronghold at Eion, on the river Strymon in Thrace (Thuc. 1.98.1), and he was permitted to commemorate this victory with a set of three herms in the Athenian Agora (Plut. *Kimon* 7). A red-figure vase made shortly thereafter seems to echo Kimon's monument (Figs 10.1–2).[10] The grinning faces of the herms and their exaggerated *phalloi* have seemed to some observers inconsistent with a public victory monument. But, in the light of the notorious Eurymedon *oino-choe*, which portrays Kimon's great victory in Asia Minor just a few years later as a kind of sexual assault,[11] we may wonder if the painter of the three-herms *pelike*, in rendering the herms as he did, did not also find a cheeky sexual humour in his reflection on Kimon's monument.[12] Indeed, this would be in keeping with the offbeat sense of sexual humour to be found elsewhere in the work of the Pan Painter, starting

(footnote 6 *continued*)
Archaeology of Athens and Attica under the Democracy (Oxford: Oxbow Books, 1994), pp. 123–9, esp. p. 124, following A. E. Raubitschek, 'Two monuments erected after the victory at Marathon', *AJA* 44 (1940), pp. 53–9, esp. pp. 58–9, n. 2; and several scholars of the early twentieth century cited by Raubitschek.

7 See S. Brunnsaker, *The Tyrant-Slayers of Kritios and Nesiotes* (Lund: Hakan Ohlssons Boktrycheri, 1955), pp. 84–95.

8 As stressed by Hölscher, 'Images and political identity', pp. 158–60.

9 W. Gauer, *Weihgeschenke aus den Perserkriegen* (Berlin: Wasmuth, 1968), and, most recently, M. Meyer, 'Bild und Vorbild: Zu Sinn und Zweck von Siegesmonumenten Athens in klassischer Zeit', *ÖJh* 74 (2005), pp. 277–312.

10 Louvre Cp 10793; J. de la Genière, 'Une pélikè inédite du Peintre de Pan au Musée du Louvre', *REA* 62 (1960), pp. 249–53; R. Osborne, 'The erection and mutilation of the *hermai*', *PCPS* 211 (1985; n.s. 31), pp. 47–73, esp. pp. 61–3, pl. 3.

11 Hamburg, Museum für Kunst und Gewerbe 1981.173; K. Schauenburg, 'ΕΥΡΥΜΕΔΟΝ ΕΙΜΙ', *AthMitt* 90 (1975), pp. 97–121; D. Wannagat, '"Eurymedon eimi": Zeichen von ethischer, sozialer und physischer Differenz in der Vasenmalerei des 5. Jahrhunderts v. Chr.', in R. von den Hoff and S. Schmidt (eds), *Konstruktionen von Wirklichkeit* (Stuttgart: Steiner, 2002), pp. 51–71, with earlier references.

12 For very different interpretations of the scene on the *pelike* see Osborne, 'Erection and mutilation of the *hermai*', pp. 61–3, and C. W. Clairmont, *Patrios Nomos* (Oxford: British Archaeological Reports, 1983), pp. 151–3, the latter arguing that it is a kind of ancient 'political cartoon', satirising Kimon and his followers. I do agree there is a self-conscious humour about it, but not in Clairmont's sense.

Figure 10.1   Three herms. Attic red-figure *pelike*, Louvre Cp 10793. C. 470.

with his well-known name-vase, a bell-*krater* in Boston, with a randy, ithyphallic Pan chasing a startled young goatherd through a landscape marked by a rustic wooden herm whose oversized *phallos* echoes that of the god.[13] Could this scene be a similarly subversive riff on the patriotic story of Pan stopping the Athenian runner Pheidippides just before the battle of Marathon to offer his assistance to the Athenians, if only they will adopt his worship (Herodotos 6.105)?

There is none of this overt humour on the reverse of the Louvre vase (Fig. 10.2), which shows a young woman steadying an offering

13 Boston, Museum of Fine Arts 10.185 *ARV²* 550, 1; de la Genière, 'Une pélikè inédite', pl. 12, 1. De la Genière also illustrates a third vase by the Pan Painter (pl. 12, 2), in Laon, with a youth standing between two strikingly ithyphalic herms. Cf. also below, n. 18.

Figure 10.2   Kanephoros and youth with *hydria*. Side B of the *pelike* in
Fig. 10.1.

basket, or *kanoun*, on her head, while a youth prepares to lift a bronze
hydria. But once again, the scene may take on an additional nuance
when viewed in the context of the painter's other work. A *pelike* of
similar shape, now in Newcastle, also features a *kanephoros*, wearing
a long festival mantle, and steadying the basket on her head with
both hands.[14] Here the painter's wry humour stems from the older
woman behind her, most probably her mother, desperately reaching

14 Newcastle University, Shefton Collection 203; N. Kaltsas and A. Shapiro,
   Worshiping Women: Ritual and Reality in Classical Athens (New York: Onassis
   Cultural Center, 2008), pp. 218–19, no. 95 [S. A. Waite].

out both hands. She may be worried about the *kanoun* falling or perhaps fussing over the fancy robe cascading down her daughter's back like a wedding dress. In either case, the motif of the young girl who has been selected for a great honour, along with her loving but irritating mother, lends the vignette an added charm. The *kanephoros* on the Louvre *pelike* (Fig. 10.2) is much more modest, wearing only a *chiton* and with her hair cropped short. But we may wonder if she and the youth wouldn't make a good couple, as we are told that festivals were rare occasions when Athenian girls could be seen in public and admired by the opposite sex. Some have assumed that these two bearers of ritual implements are moving towards the herms on the other side of the vase, in order to engage in some cult activity in front of them.[15] Alternatively, since the female *kanephoros* and the male *hydriaphoros* are well attested for large processions, such as the Panathenaia as depicted on the Parthenon frieze,[16] we might suppose that the three Kimonian herms serve here as a topographical marker of the entrance to the Agora from the northwest, through which the Panathenaic procession passed on its way to the Akropolis.

The precise original location of the Eion herms is not known, but at some point they stood in the Stoa of the Herms, on the north side of the Agora, and may have been moved there in the course of the fifth century, as Evelyn Harrison has suggested.[17] Aeschines certainly saw them there in the middle of the *fourth* century and also records the three epigrams (3.184–5), in a version that diverges from Plutarch's in only a few words. The arrangement of the herms is likewise unknown, but a kind of conversational grouping, as suggested by the Louvre *pelike* (Fig. 10.1), seems likely.[18]

The choice of herms bearing inscribed verses for this victory monument is surely significant, since it could not help but call to mind the famous herms of Hipparchos, set up around Attika by the younger

15 So, e.g., de la Genière, 'Une pélikè inédite, pp. 249, 253.
16 See J. Neils, *The Parthenon Frieze* (Cambridge: Cambridge University Press, 2001), pp. 157–8 (*kanephoroi*), 146–50 (*hydriaphoroi*), with discussion of the Louvre *pelike* on p. 149.
17 E. B. Harrison, *Archaic and Archaistic Sculpture* (Agora XI; Princeton: American School of Classical Studies at Athens Harrison, 1965), p. 111. See R. E. Wycherley, *Literary and Epigraphical Testimonia* (Agora III; Princeton: American School of Classical Studies at Athens, 1957), nos. 296–313, for all the testimonia pertaining to the Eion herms.
18 We may contrast another *pelike* by the same painter that also shows three herms, but disposed entirely differently (and probably not referring to a specific monument), with two side by side on one side of the vase and the third alone on the other side, approached by a youth bringing an offering of a pig: Berlin 1962.62; *ARV*² 1659, 91bis; B. Rückert, *Die Herme im öffentlichen und privaten Leben der Griechen* (Regensberg: Roderer, 1998), p. 200, fig. 10.11.

tyrant in the years before his assassination in 514 and carrying simple inscribed maxims.[19] Kimon might well have chosen herms deliberately, in order to proclaim that these stylised images of the god Hermes no longer bore the taint of tyranny, but could serve equally well as instruments of the democracy.[20]

The two shorter epigrams, each a pair of elegiac couplets, employ elevated epic diction to describe in general terms the hardships of the men who fought at Eion and the example they have set for future generations of Athenians. The second epigram in particular seems to echo the spirit of the young Athenian democracy when it speaks of the *euergesia* (benefaction) of the Athenian commanders and their dedication to *xsunois pragmasi* (the common good).[21]

The third and longest epigram (three couplets) also uses epic diction, but in a very different vein (Plut. *Kimon* 7.5; tr. author):

ἔκ ποτε τῆσδε πόληος ἅμ' Ἀτρείδησι Μενεσθεὺς
  ἡγεῖτο ζάθεον Τρωϊκὸν ἐς πεδίον:
ὅν ποθ' Ὅμηρος ἔφη Δαναῶν πύκα θωρηκτάων
  κοσμητῆρα μάχης ἔξοχον ὄντα μολεῖν.
οὕτως οὐδὲν ἀεικὲς Ἀθηναίοισι καλεῖσθαι κοσμηταῖς
  πολέμου τ' ἀμφὶ καὶ ἠνορέης.

Once from this city Menestheus, together with the Sons of
  Atreus,
Led his men to the divine Trojan plain;

---

19 [Plato] *Hipparchos* 228B–229D; on the herms of Hipparchos see Rückert, *Die Herme im öffentlichen*, pp. 57–67; Osborne, 'Erection and mutilation of the *hermai*', pp. 47–51; H. A. Shapiro, 'Autochthony and the visual arts in fifth-century Athens', in Boedeker and Raaflaub, *Democracy, Empire and the Arts in Fifth-Century Athens*, pp. 125–51, esp. pp. 125–6.

20 Cf. B. D. Meritt, 'Epigrams from the battle of Marathon', in S. Weinberg (ed.), *The Aegean and the Near East: Studies Presented to Hetty Goldman on the Occasion of her Seventy-Fifth Birthday* (Locust Valley, NY: J. J. Augustin, 1956), pp. 268–80, esp. pp. 274–8, who suggested that some of the earliest epigrams celebrating the victory at Marathon had also been carved on herms that stood in the same area as the Eion herms. This would be another argument for the early appropriation of the herm as a 'democratic' monument.

21 The most detailed study of the epigrams and attempt to reconstruct the original poem ('for a poem it was, not a series of three epigrams') is that of F. Jacoby, 'Some Athenian epigrams from the Persian Wars', *Hesperia* 14 (1945), pp. 157–211, esp. pp. 185–211 (quotation on p. 187). Cf. also the comments of A. Blamire, *Plutarch: Life of Kimon* (London: Institute of Classical Studies, University of London, 1989), pp. 112–14, and Harrison, *Archaic and Archaistic Sculpture*, pp. 116–17. The authenticity of the epigrams as recorded by Aeschines is defended by R. B. Kebric, *The Paintings in the Cnidian Lesche at Delphi and their Historical Context* (Leiden: Brill, 1983), pp. 43–4.

Menestheus, who Homer said was an outstanding marshaller of
  battle (*kosmeter*)
Among the well-armoured Achaeans who came to Troy.
Thus there is nothing unseemly for the Athenians to be called
  Marshallers (*kosmetais*), both of war and of manly prowess.

These verses, dated securely just three years after the end of Xerxes'
invasion, are surely among the earliest expressions of the parallel
between the Trojan and Persian Wars, as Greek victories over an
eastern barbarian, a motif to which the Athenians would return over
and over in the rhetoric, literature and art of the fifth century.[22] The
Trojan War was part of the early history of every Greek polis, but
its sudden topicality in the 470s posed a problem for the Athenians,
whose new power and prestige were out of all proportion to their very
modest role in the Homeric epics.

The protagonist of the Eion poem is Menestheus, who led the
Athenian contingent at Troy (*Iliad* 2.552), and, as such, he is given
more prominence in the *Iliad* than any other Athenian hero. Yet
Menestheus' appearances in the epic are few, and he has no great *aris-
teia*. Still, he was virtually all the Athenians of the fifth century had
to work with in asserting their own contribution to the Greek victory
at Troy, and they seem determined – as in this epigram – to make the
most of him.

Menestheus, who had earlier been one of the suitors for the hand
of Helen,[23] brought fifty Athenian ships to Troy, according to the
Catalogue in *Iliad* 2 (556). As a hero, he is celebrated in the epic less as
a doer of great deeds than as a good organiser of chariots and armed
warriors – *kosmesai hippous te kai aneras aspidodotas* (2.554) – in this,
second only to Nestor. There is a deliberate echo of Homer's language
in the Eion epigram, describing Menestheus as the *kosmetera maches
exochon* (line 4). Following his lead, the Athenians of the present
day pride themselves on being the great *kosmetai* of men. The word
is given special importance in the epigram as a line-beginning both

22 A. Erskine, *Troy between Greece and Rome* (Oxford: Oxford University Press,
   2001), pp. 61–92; D. Castriota, *Myth, Ethos, and Actuality: Official Art in Fifth-
   Century b.c. Athens* (Madison: University of Wisconsin Press, 1992), pp. 102–9.
   An even earlier expression of this parallel would be Simonides' recently discovered
   elegy on the battle of Plataea, assuming it was written directly after the battle in
   479: D. Boedeker and D. Sider, *The New Simonides: Contexts of Praise and Desire*
   (Oxford: Oxford University Press, 2001).
23 E. Cingano, 'A catalogue within a catalogue: Helen's suitors in the Hesiodic
   Catalogue of Women (FF 196–204 M-W)', in R. Hunter (ed.), *The Hesiodic
   Catalogue of Women: Constructions and Reconstructions* (Cambridge: Cambridge
   University Press, 2005), pp. 118–52.

Figure 10.3   Departure of Greek heroes for Troy. Attic black-figure
kantharos, Berlin, Antikenmuseum F 1737. C. 550.

times it occurs. Only a few years earlier, in 481, Herodotus reports, an
Athenian envoy to Gelon of Syracuse had asserted that Athens would
never relinquish command of the allied Greek fleet and cited Homer's
praise of Menestheus' skill in marshalling the men to back up this
claim (7.161). The Athenian speaker does not even need to mention
Menestheus by name, only the telltale phrase *ariston diakosmesai
straton*. Though Kimon was surely constrained from putting his own
name on the herms by the Athenian democracy,[24] he seems to appropriate for himself the role of a 'new Menestheus', marshalling the
forces of Athens and its allies to contain the (now much diminished)

24 This is the implication of Plutarch's remark, 'Although Kimon's name is nowhere
    mentioned [in the epigrams], his fellow men took it to be a surpassing honour'
    (*Kimon* 8.1). Cf. Aischines 3.183, who says none of the generals of the Eion
    campaign was allowed to have his name on the dedication, and Blamire, *Plutarch:
    Life of Kimon*, pp. 112–14.

Persian threat and drive the enemy back to Asia. He would soon marshal those same forces to a new purpose, Athens' hegemony in the Aegean, in the decade that followed.

Across the whole of the archaic period that separates Homer from Kimon, we have only a single surviving visual reference to Menestheus, on an unusual black-figure vase of the mid-sixth century (Fig. 10.3).[25] The scene shows Menelaos in *his* role as marshaller of heroes for the expedition to Troy. The focus, however, is on Achilles with his mother Thetis, giving him some last-minute advice, and his companion Patroklos. Bringing up the rear are Odysseus (here written as Olytteus) and, lastly, Menestheus. His inclusion seems to be a bit of local pride on the part of the Athenian painter, who even calls attention to it with the colloquial *hodi*: 'Here he is! This is him!'

The epic tradition associates Menestheus closely with Athens' nearest allies, the heroes from Salamis. In one episode of the *Iliad*, Menestheus, threatened by the Lycian forces of Glaukos and Sarpedon, sends for help from Ajax and his half-brother Teucer (12.319–412). In the Catalogue of Ships, the contingent from Salamis, twelve ships led by Ajax, follows immediately after the Athenian (*Iliad* 2.557–8) – a juxtaposition that the Athenians used as early as the time of Solon to support their claim to the island.[26] By the time of Kimon, Salamis had become fully incorporated into the Athenian state, Ajax one of the Eponymous Heroes, and his son Eurysakes the possessor of a hero shrine in the centre of Athens.[27]

The biggest problem for the Athenians of the fifth century was that their national hero *par excellence*, Theseus, had not been at Troy. He belonged to an earlier generation of heroes, the one that fought the centaurs at the wedding of Perithoös.[28] Instead, his family was represented only by his mother Aithra, who had ended up in Troy as one of Helen's handmaidens (*Iliad* 3.144), and by his two sons, Akamas and Demophon (one of them, Akamas, now also an Eponymous Hero, along with Theseus' father Aegeus), who figure only in the last days of the Trojan War.[29] Around the time of Marathon and just before,

25 *Kantharos*, Berlin F 1737; E. Simon and M. Hirmer, *Die griechischen Vasen* (Munich: Hirmer, 1976), pp. 80–1, pl. 65.
26 Taylor, *Tyrant Slayers*, pp. 21–2.
27 See U. Kron, 'Zur Schale des Kodros Malers in Basel: Eine *interpretatio attica*', in M. Schmidt (ed.), *Kanon: Festschrift Ernst Berger, Antike Kunst* 15 (1988), pp. 291–304, esp. p. 298 on Ajax and Eurysakes.
28 *LIMC* VII 922, s.v. Theseus [J. Neils] for the sources, and S. Mills, *Theseus, Tragedy and the Athenian Empire* (Oxford: Oxford University Press, 1997), pp. 6–13.
29 See E. Cingano, 'Teseo e i Teseidi tra Troia e Atene', in P. Angeli Bernardini (ed.), *L'epos minore, le tradizioni locali e la poesia arcaica* (Rome: Fabrizio Serra Editore, 2007), pp. 91–102, for a detailed study of the sons of Theseus at Troy.

the vase-painters offer evidence that Akamas and Demophon needed to be rescued from the obscurity of their absence from Homer's *Iliad* (they may have arrived in Troy only after the events narrated in the poem), with at least two heroic deeds at Troy.[30] One is the rescue of their grandmother Aithra. This scene is introduced into Attic red-figure as early as the 490s and becomes especially popular about 460, perhaps under the influence of Polygnotos' great *Iliupersis* at Delphi, where the episode was included.[31]

   The second is their capture of the Palladion, the holy cult image of Athena in Troy, which they will bring back to Athens.[32] The earliest allusion to this episode is on a remarkable cup by Makron in the Hermitage (Figs 10.4–6).[33] A vicious fight has broken out between Odysseus and Diomedes, each claiming to hold the 'true' Palladion (Fig. 10.4). Akamas and Demophon are among the heroes who try to mediate (all figures are labelled by inscriptions). The council of unnamed heroes on the other side (Fig. 10.5) will award the statue to Demophon, who will have it brought back to Athens and set up in a sanctuary that will be known as 'Zeus at the Palladion'.[34] Although Theseus' sons at first seem to disappear into the crowd, the painter has cleverly made sure we register their presence by putting their father and grandmother in the tondo of the cup (Fig. 10.6): the young Theseus setting out from Troizen and brandishing the sword that is

30 A third, less heroic instance of Akamas' involvement in the sack of Troy is hinted at by a vase of c. 490, the Brygos Painter's well-known cup Louvre G 152; *ARV*² 369, 1; L. Giuliani, *Bild und Mythos* (Munich: Beck, 2003), pp. 215–18, fig. 44. In a panoramic depiction of the *Ilioupersis* (death of Priam, Andromache defending herself with a pestle), a warrior labelled Akamas is shown leading Polyxena by the hand. Given the context, we may assume Polyxena is being led to her death, sacrificed to appease the ghost of Achilles. Euripides, *Hecuba* 123–5, knows of the involvement of the sons of Theseus in the sacrifice of Polyxena.

31 M. D. Stansbury-O'Donnell, 'Polygnotos's *Iliupersis*: A new reconstruction', *AJA* 93 (1989), pp. 203–15, esp. pp. 207–8, fig. 3. Cf. Kebric, *Paintings in the Cnidian Lesche*, pp. 16–31, who argues strongly for the pro-Athenian, pro-Kimonian flavour of Polygnotos' painting at Delphi, no less so than in the second version of the same subject that he executed in the Stoa Poikile in Athens. For depictions of the rescue of Aithra see *LIMC* I 426–7, s.v. Aithra I [U. Kron]. Attempts to recognise the scene on black-figure vases of the sixth century (e.g. Kron p. 426, nos. 59–65) remain speculative: see M. Mangold, *Kassandra in Athen* (Berlin: Dietrich Reimer, 2000), p. 104.

32 *LIMC* I 436; 442, s.v. Akamas et Demophon [U. Kron]; M. A. Tiverios, 'Peri Palladiou: Oti duo klepseian Diomedes kai Odysseus', in Schmidt, *Kanon*, pp. 324–30.

33 St Petersburg B 649; *ARV*² 460, 13; N. Kunisch, *Makron* (Mainz: Phillip von Zabern, 1997), pp. 134–5, pl. 113. Cf. the discussion of U. Kron, *Die zehn attischen Phylenheroen* (*AthMitt* 5; Berlin: Gebr. Mann, 1976), pp. 150–1, and Kron, in *LIMC* I 442, who points out that the episode recorded on this cup is not attested in any literary source before the fourth century.

34 See Kron, *Die zehn attischen Phylenheroen*, p. 150, for the sources.

Figure 10.4   Odysseus and Diomedes competing for the Trojan Palladion, with Akamas, Demophon and Agamemnon. Attic red-figure cup, St Petersburg, Hermitage B 649. C. 480.

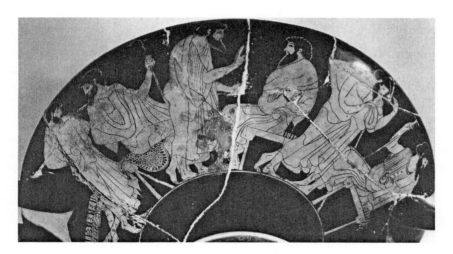

Figure 10.5   Greek heroes at Troy deliberating on the Palladion. Side B of the cup in Fig. 10.4.

one of the *gnorismata*, the tokens of his paternity.[35] Thus three generations of Athens' leading family are portrayed on a single drinking cup, made soon after 480, when much of the Athenian populace was

35 On this much-discussed scene, see Kunisch, *Makron*, p. 134, with earlier references. I have discussed it again most recently in H. A. Shapiro, 'Mother and son: Theseus's farewell to Aithra', in C. Weiss and E. Simon (eds), *Folia in Memoriam Ruth Lindner Collecta* (Dettelbach: J. H. Roll, 2010), pp. 89–94.

Figure 10.6   Farewell of Theseus and Aithra. Interior of the cup in
Fig. 10.3.

evacuated ahead of the Persian invasion and found refuge in Theseus'
native town of Troizen.[36]

Several of these associations converged in a remarkable monument more than a half-century later. In the years about 420, the
sculptor Strongylion made a bronze group depicting Greek warriors
emerging from the Trojan Horse, dedicated by one Chairedemos
on the Athenian Akropolis, just west of the Parthenon.[37] The four
heroes shown, according to Pausanias, were Menestheus, Teucer the
Salaminian, and the two sons of Theseus, Akamas and Demophon.
A remarkable vase fragment a generation later echoes the monument

36 Plutarch, *Themistokles* 10; cf. the Themistokles decree, line 8: Meiggs and Lewis,
   Greek Historical Inscriptions, p. 48.
37 Pausanias 1.23.8; Raubitschek, *Dedications*, pp. 208–9, no. 176; Hurwit, *Athenian
   Akropolis*, p. 229; F. W. Hamdorf, 'Zur Weihung des Chairedemos auf der
   Akropolis von Athen', in N. Kontoleon (ed.), *Stele: Tomos eis mnemen Nikolaou
   Kontoleontos* (Athens: Friends of Nikolaos Kontoleon, 1980), pp. 80–1. The
   monument seems to be referred to in both Aristophanes' *Birds* (1128) and
   Euripides' *Trojan Women* (13–14), produced in 414 and 415, respectively. The date
   c. 420 for the monument is partly an assumption that it will have been a recent
   addition to the Akropolis landscape when the two playwrights mention it.

in its topographical setting.[38] Though Kimon's epigram on the Eion herm had named only Menestheus, it now seems clear that he wanted to evoke the whole Athenian and Salaminian contingents at Troy, including the family of Theseus.

But how are we to reconcile all these patriotic traditions with the very different story, best known from Plutarch's *Life of Theseus* 34–5, of Menestheus as the evil usurper who seized power in Athens while Theseus and Perithoös were off in Hades; welcomed the Dioskouroi when they invaded Attika to recover their sister Helen after Theseus had abducted her from Sparta; and then, on Theseus' return to Athens, drove the hapless hero into exile and a treacherous death at the hands of King Lykomedes of Skyros? Though several other authors also report the story, all are of at least imperial date.[39] The several Attic tragedies that deal with Theseus' kingship never hint at the usurpation of Menestheus. *Hippolytos* has Theseus in exile at Troizen, but under very different circumstances.[40] The likelihood should, I believe, be considered that the connected narrative that we find in Plutarch, and especially the villainous role of Menestheus, post-date the fifth century. As a moralising biographer, Plutarch had to have Theseus come to a bad end on account of his reckless behaviour in late middle age, abducting the under-age Helen and going on the ill-advised adventure to the Underworld with Perithoös. There is no evidence whatever for a negative treatment of Menestheus in either the art or literature of the fifth century, starting with the Eion epigram and including the Trojan Horse of Strongylion and the patriotic cup by the Kodros Painter of c. 430, to which we shall turn next. Though no hero cult of Menestheus is yet attested in Athens or Attika, this is surely just an accident of preservation, as Erika Simon has recently written.[41] Pausanias saw the spot at the old harbour of Phaleron whence Menestheus and the fifty ships set sail for Troy (1.1.2), another link with Theseus, who left from the same harbour for Crete in the previous generation (Plut. *Theseus* 17.6; Pausanias 1.1.2).

The well-known cup in Bologna that gives his name to Beazley's

38 Würzburg H 4695; *CVA* (Würzburg 2), 55, pl. 39, 3.
39 Diodoros 4.63; Apollodoros epit. I 23; Sch. Lykophron 513; Hyginus 79; Servius on *Aeneid* 2.61; 6.21; 6.121. Of fifth-century authors, only Herodotos (9.73) makes a negative comment on Theseus' *hubris* in kidnapping Helen (see M. A. Flower and J. Marincola, *Herodotus Histories Book IX* (Cambridge: Cambridge University Press, 2002), pp. 237–8), but he makes no mention of Menestheus in this context.
40 On Theseus' role in tragedy see Mills, *Theseus, Tragedy and the Athenian Empire*, esp. pp. 186–221, on the *Hippolytos*; and D. Mendelsohn, *Gender and the City in Euripides' Political Plays* (Oxford: Oxford University Press, 2002), pp. 152–79.
41 *LIMC* VI 474, s.v. Menestheus.

Figure 10.7   Greek heroes leaving for Troy in the presence of Athena. Attic
red-figure cup, Bologna, Museo Civico PU 303.

Figure 10.8   Theseus and Phorbas setting out for war. Side B of the cup in
Fig. 10.7.

Kodros Painter represents an extraordinary interweaving of past and
present on the eve of the Peloponnesian War (Figs 10.7–9).[42] Only
one of the ten figures on the exterior is a divinity recognisable without
inscription – Athena in the middle of side A (Fig. 10.7) – but we are
fortunate that all are labelled. Ahead of Athena are the bearded Lykos

---

42 Bologna PU 303; *ARV*² 1268, 1; most fully discussed by C. Sourvinou-Inwood,
    'The cup Bologna PU 273: A reading', *Métis* 5 (1990), pp. 137–53, with earlier
    references, and, most recently, A. Avramidou, *The Codrus Painter: Iconography
    and Reception of Athenian Vases in the Age of Pericles* (Madison: University of
    Wisconsin Press, 2011), pp. 31–3.

Figure 10.9   Kodros and Ainetos. Interior of the cup in Fig. 10.7.

and a youthful, armed Ajax. The goddess looks back towards another youth, Menestheus, and a woman named Melite. The composition on side B is roughly similar (Fig. 10.8), with the central figure now Medea, holding up a helmet. The older/younger pair to the left of her is Aegeus and Theseus, father and son, while a bearded and armed warrior, Phorbas, strides up from the right, and Aithra stands quietly behind.

The theme of this cup is clear – 'mobilising for war' – with interesting parallels between the two sides. Side A shows the departure of the Athenian contingent at Troy, led, appropriately, by Menestheus. Ajax has by now long since been fully co-opted as an Athenian hero. The point is driven home by placing the vigorous Athena between these two heroes. She seems to be hurrying Menestheus along, perhaps reminding him to change out of his traveller's garb and into his armour. Melite is a further reminder of Ajax's integration into the Athenian polis, since the hero shrine of his son Eurysakes, which doubled as the tribal shrine of Aiantis, was located in the deme Melite, in central Athens.[43] Lykos is perhaps less connected to the figures on

43 Kron, *Die zehn attischen Phylenheroen*, pp. 138, 172.

this side of the vase than to his brother Aegeus, standing in the same position on the other side (Fig. 10.8).

That side refers most probably to warfare closer to home, the defence of Athens from the Amazon invasion, led by Theseus and Phorbas.[44] The latter is several times shown as Theseus' chief comrade on Amazonomachy vases of this period,[45] and he had even accompanied Theseus before that, in the taking of Antiope, which proved to be the *casus belli* for the invasion of the Amazons.[46] Theseus is surrounded by no fewer than three members of his family – father, mother and stepmother Medea. Uta Kron is surely right in pointing out that Medea is present here as an Attic heroine, rather than in her dubious role as wicked stepmother.[47] Though, according to the conventions of Attic vase-painting, Athena should only be shown on one side of the cup, her expansive (and symbolic) presence clearly extends to both scenes. Medea could almost be mistaken for Athena at first glance, since she holds up a helmet in the same manner as the goddess frequently does.[48] The overall message of the cup can be stated succinctly: Athenian heroes stand ready to fight for their city, whether abroad or at home. We are also invited to draw a parallel between two eastern enemies, the Amazons and the Trojans. Both were at various times evoked as stand-ins for the Persians, most conspicuously in the sculptural programme of the Parthenon.[49]

Since the ceramic date of the Bologna cup coincides almost exactly with the outbreak of the Peloponnesian War, much has been made of its propaganda value as a heroic model for the Athenians of 431.[50] Though this may be true in a general sense, what is more striking to me is the absence of any overt reference in the exterior pictures to the struggle against Sparta and its Peloponnesian allies. Rather, the paradigmatic scenes on the Kodros Painter's cup stand in the same relation to Athenian military engagements of the day as the public

44 So also Kron, *Die zehn attischen Phylenheroen*, p.138, following Carl Robert.
45 E.g. the *dinos* London 1899.7–21.5; *ARV*² 1052, 29; S. B. Matheson, *Polygnotos and Vase-Painting in Classical Athens* (Madison: University of Wisconsin Press, 1995), p. 452, PGU 34, 165, pl. 143. This vase also includes Akamas, a unique instance of father and son fighting side by side. Euripides, *Suppliants* 680, refers to Phorbas as a fighting companion of Theseus.
46 On the cup attributed to Euphronios, London E 41; *ARV*² 58, 51 (at that time attributed to Oltos); *Euphronios der Maler*. Exhibition catalogue (Berlin: Antikenmuseum, 1991), pp. 190–2.
47 Kron, *Die zehn attischen Phylenheroen*, p. 137.
48 For the motif see N. Kunisch, 'Zur helmhaltenden Athena', *AthMitt* 89 (1974), pp. 85–104.
49 Castriota, *Myth, Ethos, and Actuality*, pp. 134–74.
50 See especially Sourvinou-Inwood, 'Cup Bologna PU 273' for this approach, though she sees both Medea and Menestheus here as sinister figures, which I do not believe.

funeral orations (*epitaphioi logoi*) stood to the battles (including those of the Peloponnesian War) that they memorialised. In these speeches, the Amazonomachy is one of a catalogue of mythological *exempla* for the bravery and the superiority of Athens. Nicole Loraux famously showed how the Athenians 'invented' their past through the medium of these speeches,[51] and I would argue that vase-painting was able to do something similar. The Trojan War, however, so prominent on the vases, is pointedly omitted from the *epitaphioi logoi*, for reasons Loraux has explored.[52]

Even before the introduction of the *epitaphios logos*, a catalogue of the glorious deeds of the Athenians appears in the speech delivered by an Athenian before the battle of Plataia and recorded by Herodotos (9.27). Of the four deeds from the distant past (Marathon is the fifth and most recent), two are those referred to on the Kodros Painter's cup: the defeat of the Amazon invasion and the Athenian contribution at Troy (vaguely described as 'second to none'). The other two are the recovery of the bodies of the defeated Seven against Thebes and their burial at Eleusis, which took place in the kingship of Theseus (Euripides, *Suppliants*), and the friendly reception of Hyllos and the Herakleidai and the defeat of their evil cousin Eurytheus, which took place in the reign of Theseus' son Demophon (Euripides, *Herakleidai*).[53] In our context, it is of particular interest that what links all five episodes in this catalogue (including Marathon, where Theseus appeared in an epiphany) is the participation of Theseus or his sons, or both.

The allusion to contemporary events missing from the exterior of the cup may well be found in the tondo (Fig. 10.9). The warrior is Kodros, the Athenian king whose name became synonymous with heroic self-sacrifice on behalf of the city during an early invasion of Athens by a Peloponnesian army.[54] His companion in the tondo

51 N. Loraux, *L'invention d'Athènes* (Paris: Mouton, 1981), pp. 133–56; W. Kierdorf, *Erlebnis und Darstellung der Perserkriege* (Göttingen: Vandenhoek & Rupprecht, 1966), pp. 84–95.

52 Loraux, *L'invention d'Athènes*, pp. 69–72, arguing that the orators did not want the greatness of the wars of the fifth century to be overshadowed by memories of Troy.

53 See Flower and Marincola, *Herodotus Histories Book IX*, pp. 152–3, on the relationship of the Athenian's speech in Herodotos to the *epitaphioi logoi*, and L. H. Jeffery, 'The battle of Oinoe in the Stoa Poikile: A problem in Greek art and history', *BSA* 60 (1965), pp. 41–57, esp. p. 51, who suggests that all four subjects in the Stoa Poikile were drawn from this catalogue and that Herodotos could have had the paintings in mind when he composed the Athenian's speech.

54 For the sources see Kron, *Die zehn attischen Phylenheroen*, pp. 196, 221–7; *LIMC* VI, 86–7, s.v. Kodros [E. Simon]; N. Robertson, 'Melanthus, Codrus, Neleus, Caucon: Ritual myth as Athenian history', *GRBS* 29 (1988), pp. 201–61, esp. pp. 224–30, on the late invention of the myth of Kodros.

Figure 10.10   Grave stele of a warrior with his father. Athens, National
Archaeological Museum 731. C. 350.

has the enigmatic name Ainetos. Whoever this mysterious figure is – obscure hero or personification ('the praiseworthy one')[55] – he has very much the look of a mature Athenian of his day, in the typical citizen *himation*, who could be the father of this warrior. The image anticipates marble grave stelai of a few decades later, on which a father gazes solemnly at the brave son who has fallen in his prime (Fig. 10.10).[56] It is as if, while the warriors on the cup's exterior are just setting out for war, this one is already dead, but memorialised for his sacrifice.

I end with another remarkable cup by the same painter, which illustrates how Athenian mythmaking, genealogical manoeuvres and the fabrication of the city's heroic past were all alive and operating in the fifth century. Two late sources, Plutarch and Athenaeus, report that Theseus was actually the father of Ajax, by a woman whose name is variously given as Periboia (in Plutarch), Meliboia (in Athenaeus) and Eriboia or Epiboia in other sources.[57] Not that Ajax's Homeric father, Telamon, has been forgotten, merely pushed aside in favour of a 'true' father more pertinent to Athenian interests. We might well have dismissed this story as a late variant (like the story of Menestheus the usurper) if not for this cup of about 435 BCE that came to light some thirty years ago and is now in the Basel Antikenmuseum (Figs 10.11–13).[58] The loss of several key inscriptions prevents a full appreciation of the scenes, but the general sense is clear.

Ajax is the baby wrapped in swaddling clothes, whose mother, Eriboia (her name is inscribed), has borne him out of wedlock (Fig. 10.11). She shyly presents the baby to her husband Telamon. That he will accept the child and raise it as his own may be inferred not only from our knowledge of the story, but from the presence of Apollo on the other side of the cup (Fig. 10.12), the god who sanctions such familial accommodations. The baby's true father, Theseus, appears in the cup's tondo as a young warrior, standing quietly with a woman whose name could be Argeia (Fig. 10.13).[59]

These are the main outlines of the iconographical programme

55 See Sourvinou-Inwood, 'Cup Bologna PU 273', pp. 139–40.
56 Stele from Salamis, Athens NM 731; C. W. Clairmont, *Classical Attic Tombstones* (Kilchberg: Akanthus, 1993), vol. II, p. 805, no. 2.930 (with plate).
57 For the sources see *RE* 11 (1907), 438, s.v. Eriboia [Tümpel].
58 Inv. BS 432; first illustrated in *AntK* 11 (1968), pl. 19, and discussed by E. Berger, 'Zur Deutung einer neuen Schale des Kodrosmalers', *Antike Kunst*, 11 (1968), pp. 125–36; *CVA* (Basel 2), pp. 48–50, pl. 26, 4; 30; 31, 1–3.
59 The inscription is poorly preserved, and despite several attempts has not been read satisfactorily: see Berger, 'Zur Deutung einer neuen Schale des Kodrosmalers', p. 130; Kron, 'Zur Schale des Kodros Malers in Basel', p. 304; *CVA* (Basel 2), 48 [V. Slehoferova].

Figure 10.11   Eriboia presenting the baby Ajax to Telamon. Attic red-figure cup, Basle, Antikenmuseum + Sammlung Ludwig BS 432.

Figure 10.12   Apollo and others. Side B of the cup in Fig. 10.11.

of the cup, as reconstructed by Ernst Berger and modified by Uta Kron.[60] For the role of Apollo's oracle in the life of Theseus, we may be reminded of the same painter's well-known Berlin cup with Aegeus consulting the Pythia (here labelled, significantly, as Themis) in the tondo.[61] It was this encounter that sent Aegeus, who was in search of a remedy for his childlessness, off to Troizen and into the arms of the

60 Berger, 'Zur Deutung einer neuen Schale des Kodrosmalers'; Kron, 'Zur Schale des Kodros Malers in Basel'. For a different interpretation, Avramidou, *Codrus Painter*, pp. 40–2.
61 Berlin, Antikenmuseum F 2538; *ARV*² 1269, 5; K. Schefold and F. Jung, *Die Urkönige: Perseus, Bellerophon, Herakles und Theseus* (Munich: Hirmer, 1988), p. 234, fig. 282; Avramidou, *Codrus Painter*, pp. 39–40.

Figure 10.13   Theseus and a woman (Argeia?). Interior of the cup in
Fig. 10.11.

young Aithra. The missing inscriptions on the Basle cup prevent us
from understanding some details of the story told here, such as who
the crucial figure is who is consulting Apollo and why the unidentified
couple behind him are joined in an intimate handclasp. Since Apollo is
also the god who authorises the founding of colonies, I wonder if these
two youths could be Akamas and Demophon, who were said to be the
oikists of numerous colonies in Asia Minor, Thrace and Cyprus.[62]

The story of Theseus fathering Ajax may have been hinted at as
far back as the early sixth century, when Kleitias placed Epiboia
alongside Theseus on the François Vase, as the Athenian youths and
maidens disembark on Crete.[63] In Bacchylides 17, Eriboia is the girl
Theseus protects from the unwanted advances of the Cretan Minos
(line 14), perhaps with a subtle implication that the young prince may

62 See *LIMC* I 435–6, s.v. Akamas et Demophon [U. Kron]. The two heroes seem
    to be depicted in their role as *oikists* on a slightly earlier vase, the *pelike* now in
    Kyoto, Greek and Roman Museum; E. Simon, *The Kurashiki Ninagawa Museum*
    (Mainz: Philipp von Zabern, 1982), pp. 94–9, no. 40.
63 Florence 4209; ABV 76, 1; see Simon and Hirmer, *Die griechischen Vasen*, pp.
    73–4 and fig. 2 (printed reversed), for a detail of the Theseus frieze and discussion
    of Epiboia.

fancy her for himself.[64] But the full story must have been either quite recently invented or little known when the Kodros Painter unfolded it in the unique images on the Basle cup. Sophokles' *Ajax*, probably produced in the 440s, makes no mention of it (or of Theseus, for that matter, in any context).[65] We may also recall that one of the most spectacular renditions of Theseus' youthful deeds fills the inside and the outside of a cup, now in the British Museum, by none other than our same artist, the Kodros Painter.[66]

This painter was a particular devoté of Athenian heroes and early genealogies. His rendering of the birth of Erichthonios, for example, on another cup in Berlin, is one of the finest and most complex we have.[67] Among the various 'witnesses' to the birth are not only Erechtheus, the king this divine child will grow up to be, but also Theseus' father Aegeus, thus creating a link from Theseus reaching all the way back to the first Athenian king, Kekrops the autochton, depicted on the front of the cup.[68] In this way, the semblance of a continuous and uninterrupted dynasty of early kings is created where none is ever recorded by the mythographers.

This is an astonishing, and perhaps unique, situation, in which a single vase-painter perfectly captures the Athenian *Zeitgeist* of a critical decade, that of the 430s. Athens was busily writing and rewriting its early history, not in the pages of historians like Thucydides, who largely ignores mythical figures like Erechtheus, Theseus or Kodros, but in many other media, from genealogical poetry and tragedy to big sculptural monuments on the Akropolis and elegant drinking cups passed around at the symposia of the aristocracy, who continued to party like it was 475, even as the storm-clouds of war gathered on the horizon.

---

64 G. Ieranò, 'Il filo di Eriboia (Bacchilide 17)', in A. Bagordo and B. Zimmermann (eds), *Bakchylides: 100 Jahre nach seiner Wiederentdeckung* (Munich: Beck, 2000), pp. 183–92, has suggested that the poem hints at a forthcoming wedding of Theseus and Eriboia. G. Danek, 'Heroic and athletic contests in Bacchylides 17', *WSt* 121 (2008), pp. 71–83, esp. p. 75, n. 19, records a suggestion of H. Maehler that Bacchylides chose the name Eriboia more or less randomly from a traditional list of the Athenian maidens, but the repeated references to her in the fifth century, as on the new cup in Basle, indicate that the choice was quite deliberate.

65 In the play, Ajax refers to Eriboia as his mother (569), but only Telamon is named as his father. Pindar, *Isthmian* 6.45, also refers to Ajax as the son of Eriboia by Telamon.

66 London E 84; *ARV²* 1269, 3; Taylor, *Tyrant Slayers*, pls. 20–1; Avramidou, *Codrus Painter*, pp. 37–8.

67 Berlin F 2537 *ARV²* 1268, 2; most recently, Kaltsas and Shapiro, *Worshiping Women*, pp. 178–9, cat. 75 [A. Avramidou] and Avramidou, *Codrus Painter*, pp. 33–6.

68 I have discussed more fully the imagery of this cup in Shapiro, 'Autochthony and the visual arts', pp. 136–7.

11

FAMILY TIME: TEMPORALITY, GENDER AND MATERIALITY IN ANCIENT GREECE

Lin Foxhall

INTRODUCTION: THE GREEKS AND THEIR PASTS

The collective pasts of the Greeks are those most familiar to us from narrative historical accounts, rhetoric, inscriptions and other kinds of written sources traditionally used to piece together historical events. However, it has long been recognised that as in many societies in the ancient and medieval worlds, literacy and writing did not dominate all aspects of memory and record-keeping in Greek communities.[1] As a result, the written pasts of polities and communities were complemented by other kinds of temporal information operating at a different level, often residing in families, though it was not always written down. In some cases memory of these alternative temporalities became embedded in material objects. Especially in the case of elite families, where the collective past might intersect with family history, such family stories sometimes made it to the written record, and a link to a place or an object might reinforce the memory. However, in other cases it is clear that material objects themselves marked relationships and carried memories at a level below the radar of what we usually think of as history. This information is not, of course, 'historical' in any traditional sense of the word, but it must have been critical for how Greeks understood themselves and their relationships in time.

This chapter will address the ways in which material culture offers us a view of Greek familial pasts both in dialogue with and outside the written record. In particular I will focus on the ways in which these alternative pasts were gendered, that is, how the relationship of women to both the familial and the collectively remembered past and future differed from that of men. I shall start with the notion of materiality, to explore how objects become entangled with people in the

---

1 R. Thomas, *Oral Tradition and Written Record in Classical Athens* (Cambridge: Cambridge University Press, 1989), pp. 15–30, 95.

first place, and how they might take on temporal significance. In the following section I investigate ancient Greek notions of kinship and their impact on constructions of family and memory. Finally I consider relationships between women in classical antiquity as they were played out through that most quintessentially feminine of activities, textile manufacture, and how we can see vestiges of these relationships marked on the weaving tools themselves.

MATERIALITY

Materiality is a broad notion widely and variously used by archaeologists and anthropologists to encompass how things become woven into the fabric of human social life and relationships, blurring the distinction between subject and object. There is considerable debate in the scholarly literature about precisely what it does or doesn't mean. 'Things' need not be simply concrete items or artefacts, but can also include other kinds of less obviously concrete things such as images, the internet, musical works and even institutions; basically anything which can be objectified. However, the varied and interesting literature representing current debates on materiality in anthropology and archaeology scholarship concentrates heavily on major monuments and 'notable' or 'special' objects,[2] and much of both the archaeological and anthropological research has focused on 'art' in one form or another. Analysis has primarily centred on the social and political relations of materiality, in archaeology often specifically on the links between monumentality and memory.[3] The things with which I will be most concerned in this chapter are concrete artefacts generally of the most mundane kind.

Technologies therefore also play a key mediating role in dialectic between person and thing, and thus the blurring of subject and object. Technology is sometimes seen as a performance, acting out a relationship with the material world.[4] Certainly numerous ethnographic studies have explored how people, especially children, learn skills and crafts, by watching, imitating, participating and practising with skilled workers as part of a social group. And as a person practises a skill, the task becomes more and more familiar and embodied so that the task

2 L. Meskell, 'Objects in the mirror appear closer than they are', in D. Miller (ed.), *Materiality* (Durham, NC, and London: Duke University Press, 2005), pp. 72–87; C. Tilley, *The Materiality of Stone* (Oxford: Berg, 2004).
3 E.g., N. J. Saunders, 'Crucifix, cavalry and cross: Materiality and spirituality in Great War landscapes', *World Archaeology* 35 (2003), pp. 7–21.
4 L. Douney and M. Naji, 'Editorial', *Journal of Material Culture* 14 (2009), pp. 411–32.

(or at least elements of it) can be done 'without thinking': driving a car is a good example in the modern world.[5]

Material objects are created by people, but they can also take on a life of their own,[6] to become subjects, and much as they are 'objects' in a dynamic dialectical relationship. Objects may thus become part of our 'wallpaper' because they become so embedded in our lives and daily activities that we stop noticing them.[7] Objects once created can transcend time and space. So, for example, a road or a building, once built, channels traffic and plays a role in shaping the use of space beyond the lifetime of the people who built them (and to some extent the specific intentions of those people).

> It is not just that objects can be agents; it is that practices and their relationships create the appearance of both subjects and objects through the dialectics of objectification, and we need to be able to document how people internalize and then externalize the normative. In short we need to show how the things that people make, make people.[8]

Objects themselves become agents in human social interactions. They do not simply serve as a reflection of human social engagement or a signifier of something else,[9] projected on them by human social interactions,[10] as they have a life beyond the reach of the social relationships and the temporal historical setting which produced them in the first place.[11] As such, they also simultaneously accrue additional strata of entanglement in human relations over time.

Human groups, like objects, have life cycles and life histories. The relationship between person (or people) and object develops over time with use, so the life history of an object is much more than its itinerary of passing from hand to hand, since the traditions of producing objects, and of representation, develop a life of their own as a set of

5 M. Naji, 'Gender and materiality in the making: The manufacture of Sirwan femininities through weaving in southern Morocco', *Journal of Material Culture* 14 (2009), pp. 47–73.

6 D. Miller, 'Materiality: An introduction', in Miller, *Materiality*, pp. 1–50, at p. 11; B. Latour, *Pandora's Hope: An Essay on the Reality of Science Studies* (Cambridge, MA: Harvard University Press, 1999).

7 Miller, 'Materiality', p. 5.

8 Miller, 'Materiality', p. 38.

9 W. Keane, 'Signs are not the garb of meaning: On the social analysis of material things', in Miller, *Materiality*, pp. 182–205.

10 S. Küchler, 'Materiality and cognition: The changing face of things', in Miller, *Materiality*, pp. 206–30, at p. 209.

11 C. Pinney , 'Things happen: Or, from which moment does that object come?', in Miller, *Materiality*, pp. 256–72.

loosely agreed conventions which transcend any particular historical moment to some extent.[12] The key here is the focus on the *entangled relationship* as the analytical entity, not on the agency of either person or thing, subject or object.

Objects can attract and evoke stories of the human relationships engaged in their formation, use and movement. Sometimes indicators of these stories become visibly 'marked' on the object itself, either through deliberate marking or via wear, breakage or repair. Of course, the relationships of materiality can be positive or negative, strong or weak, or anywhere in between. The acquisition of skills, which may entail the embodiment of knowledge over many years, may easily become entangled with personal relationships and thus serve as a focus for embodying and remembering those relationships.

Sentiments can transcend time. Objects sometimes constitute and represent relationships between people set in time, recalling and strengthening ties of affection. However, I would argue that such embedded objects have the power to create ties even in the absence of actual face-to-face relationships. This can enable them to become 'historical' markers in the absence of texts, measuring layers of relationships (sometimes generations) rather than, literally, the passing of years. Such objects need not be monumental, but as noted above, those which are not have been less often studied, especially in the classical world. In the words of Colin Renfrew:

> It is in the repertoire of artefacts of daily use that those memories and experiences reside which determine the true nature of a society. The material culture through which those experiences are undergone, through which that engagement is effected, embodies the fundamental and mainstream memories of that society.[13]

FAMILY AND MEMORY

It must be said at the start that ancient Greek structures of kinship were not particularly conducive to the long-term preservation of memories, which seldom extended beyond three generations.[14] Relatedness was reckoned bilaterally, through both the male and

---

12 Pinney, 'Things happen', pp. 265–8.
13 C. Renfrew, 'Towards a theory of material engagement', in E. de Marrais, C. Renfrew and C. Gosden (eds), *Rethinking Materiality* (Cambridge: Macdonald Institute, 2004), p. 30.
14 Thomas, *Oral Tradition*, pp. 124–9

female lines, similarly to present-day European kinship systems. In Athens, descent, at least in the short term, was critical for holding citizen status. This principle had been formally established with the reforms of Kleisthenes late in the sixth century BCE, and was strengthened by Perikles' 'law about bastards' in 451 BCE, limiting citizenship to those whose father and mother were both of citizen status. The difficulty with bilateral kinship is that after two or three generations relationships multiply profusely and often become complicated, so that it is hard to keep track of all of them. (Indeed, how many people in the modern western world know their second or third cousins personally, or even who they are?) A good example is the limit placed on relatedness in Athenian law. Responsibilities and privileges concerning succession and inheritance were confined to the *angchisteia*, defined by Demosthenes (47.73) as 'those related up to the children of cousins', though in practice the use of the concept of *angchisteia* might have been somewhat more flexible.[15] Even with this limitation, relatedness was regularly contested, as demonstrated by the large number of legal disputes over inheritance and citizenship in the corpus of Attic oratory, where proving or disproving kinship connections becomes critical. The difficulty and uncertainty of establishing kinship appear from another perspective in Plato's *Politicus* (257d), where Sokrates claims to be related to two young men, one because he and Sokrates looked alike and the other because they share a name so they must be related (names, of course, often ran in families).

Children of cousins, obviously, share the same great-grandfather, presuming a temporal line of four generations. However, it is interesting that this vertical, temporal link is not how Demosthenes expresses the principle of the *angchisteia*. Instead, he focuses on the contemporary horizontal link, almost certainly much more important in the everyday discourse of social, political, legal and economic relationships, in so far as these can be disentangled. In other words, he presumed that relatedness was normally reckoned via the minimum temporal depth: if you knew that your father and someone else's father were cousins, then you would know that the two of you were related. However, even if you could in theory work it out, you did not necessarily know or think about your common great-grandfather, since for most quotidian purposes that relationship was not relevant.

In Athens and elsewhere in the Greek world, extensive family trees with long lines of ancestors documented were rare, except for

---

15 S. C. Todd, *The Shape of Athenian Law* (Oxford: Clarendon Press, 1993), pp. 217–18.

a few elite families,[16] or royal families, such as the two lineages of
the Spartan kings. Most Greek 'genealogies' begin to include legendary or mythical figures after about three or four generations,
and there is often a gap between the 'real people' and the legendary
heroes.[17] However, there still existed contexts and situations when
real or perceived multi-generational links were important. Family-
like organisations, groups which claimed to be based on kinship links
(and genuinely were to a limited extent), but where it is obvious that
not all the members were actually related to each other, were always
agnatic, founded upon actual and supposed links of men to men. This
practice, of focusing on a single line of relatedness, simplifies the links
and limits the number of relationships that need to be remembered.
Regularly these agnatic groups played important roles in both political and social organisation, and the memory of relatedness over time.

An important and well-studied example is the phratries of classical
Athens.[18] Men's citizenship in classical Athens is normally defined
by modern scholars, following the Aristotelian *Ath. Pol.* (42.1), as
enrolment in a deme. At one level this is correct, but skims over the
fact that virtually all Athenian citizens, rich and poor, appear to
belong to phratries. (The exceptions appear to be a few cases of group
grants of citizenship, for example the Plataeans granted Athenian
citizenship in 427 BCE.[19]) When citizenship was challenged, or in other
circumstances where a man had to prove his parentage, for example
in disputes over inheritance, it was normally the group memory of
the phratry, particularly the oral testimony of members present at
ceremonies marking key life stages such as marriage, the birth of a
child or the introduction of a son, which was cited as definitive proof
of his claims.[20] The deme was an institution of the Athenian state,
directly linked to membership in one of the ten tribes, and thereby
to office holding, military service and other central state duties, as
well as having local political functions of its own. The number of
demes changed somewhat over time but seems to have been relatively

16 Thomas, *Oral Tradition*, pp. 105–6, 123–31; J. K. Davies, *Athenian Propertied
   Families, 600–300 BC* (Oxford: Clarendon Press, 1971); S. C. Humphreys, *The
   Family, Women and Death* (London: Routledge and Kegan Paul, 1983), pp.
   108–11.
17 Thomas, *Oral Tradition*, pp. 157, 190.
18 S. D. Lambert, *The Phratries of Attica*, 2nd edn (Ann Arbor: University of
   Michigan Press, 1998).
19 Lambert, *Phratries*, pp. 50–3.
20 A. C. Scafuro, 'Witnessing and false witnessing: Proving citizenship and kin
   identity in fourth century Athens', in A. L. Boegehold and A. C. Scafuro (eds),
   Athenian Identity and Civic Ideology (Baltimore and London: Johns Hopkins
   University Press, 1994), pp. 156–98; Lambert, *Phratries*, pp. 34–40.

static).[21] In contrast, phratries had no bureaucratic role or other 'official' function in the Athenian state, although they conducted their own business using standard democratic procedures,[22] and do not seem to have been regulated by the state to any significant extent, despite their critical role in political memory.

Agnatic connections were also used to maintain, or present the illusion of, time-depth in Greek families. A family that could be 'shown' to extend over time enhanced its claims to be part of a political elite.[23] Rarely were such claims made overtly on the basis of female lines of descent, or even female links. This is not to say maternal relatives or kinship links through female lines were not important, but that their importance lay in the everyday practice and habits of kinship.[24] The 'outlines' of a lineage emboldened and set in a wider time frame were generally drawn along male lines. Some of the 'family stories' recounted by Herodotos about Athenian families still prominent in his own time provide good examples of these sorts of claims. In 6.103–4, in the narrative leading up to the battle of Marathon, Herodotos pauses to explain the history of the general Miltiades' family, the Philaidai:

> The Athenian troops were commanded by ten generals, of whom the tenth was Miltiades. Miltiades' father, Kimon the son of Stesagoras, had been banished from Athens by Peisistratos son of Hippocrates. While in exile he had the good fortune to win the chariot race at Olympia, thereby gaining the same distinction as his brother by the same mother Miltiades. At the next games he won the prize again with the same team of mares, but this time waived his victory in favour of Peisistratos, and for allowing the latter to be proclaimed the winner was given leave to return to Athens. At a later Olympic festival he won a third time, still with the same four mares. Soon after, Peisistratos having died, he was murdered by Peisistratos' sons, who sent men to waylay him one night near the Council House. He was buried outside Athens, beyond what is called the Sunk Road, and opposite his grave were buried the mares which had won the chariot race three times. This triple victory has once before been achieved by a single team, that of Euagoras the Lakonian, but there are no other instances of it. At the time of Kimon's death, Stesagoras, the elder of his two

21 Lambert, *Phratries*, p. 111.
22 Lambert, *Phratries*, pp. 105–6.
23 Thomas, *Oral Tradition*, p. 98.
24 L. Foxhall, 'The running sands of time: Archaeology and short-term timescales', *World Archaeology* 31.3 (2000), pp. 484–98; and see below.

sons, was living in the Chersonnese with Miltiades his uncle, and the younger son, who was called Miltiades after the founder of the settlement in the Chersonnese, was with his father in Athens. It was this Miltiades who was now an Athenian general.

Herodotos post-dated Miltiades the general by at least two generations, and of course Miltiades' father and grandfather were even more remote in time. The information he presented sounds very much like the sort of information a family would remember,[25] and it seems a reasonable guess that Herodotos' informant was a contemporary descendant of Kimon and Miltiades.[26]

Thomas suggests that the genealogy in Herodotos was likely to have been widely known because of the older Miltiades' position as the founder of a colony, and that Herodotos may even have got his information directly from the Chersonnese.[27] However, the story in this passage is strongly Athenocentric and focuses on a local Athenian monument. The focus on a family tomb might suggest that the information was remembered at least in part because of its link to a known grave. It would certainly have been in the interests of the later fifth-century members of this family to ensure that the story attached to this particular grave was widely disseminated. It seems plausible that someone in the family not only talked to Herodotos, but even encouraged him to include this and other generally complimentary stories (Hdt. 6.34–41, 109, 132–6, 140) about the family in the *Histories*. There are some possible candidates for descendants of the Philaidai contemporary with Herodotos documented in other historical sources: (1) Thettalos son of Kimon son of Miltiades the general was one of the prosecutors of Alkibiades for impiety in 415 BC (Plut. *Alc.* 19.3, 22.4); and (2) Oulios son of Kimon son of Miltiades the general, or Oulios' son Aristokrates. Kleito, the wife of Aristokrates, made a dedication to Athena late in the fifth century BCE.[28] It is generally accepted that parts of the *Histories* were read aloud publicly or semi-publicly, although we know nothing about the venues or the occasions.[29] However, in the context of fifth-century Athens, a certain amount of private sponsorship in the form of offering hospitality

25 Thomas, *Oral Tradition*, pp. 111, 127–8.
26 See Thomas, *Oral Tradition*, pp. 171–2; Davies, *Athenian Propertied Families*, p. 307.
27 Thomas, *Oral Tradition*, pp. 171–2.
28 Davies, *Athenian Propertied Families*, p. 307.
29 R. Thomas, *Herodotus in Context: Ethnography, Science and the Art of Persuasion* (Cambridge: Cambridge University Press, 2000), pp. 20, 257–60; W. Johnson, 'Oral performance and the composition of Herodotus' *Histories*', *GRBS* 35 (1994), pp. 229–54.

and performance venues (even without overt payment) in return for encouragement to highlight the activities of particular families in his monumental work might not seem out of place.[30] If this were the case, it is easy to see why Herodotos might not explicitly cite 'family tradition' as his source.[31]

In Herodotos' account, all of the persons mentioned are male, though it is clear that the family line contained an important female link: Kimon the son of Stesagoras and his half-brother Miltiades shared the same mother, not the same father, yet she is not identified, even by circumlocution, as 'daughter of X'. Indeed, it seems that her name and origins were by Herodotos' time entirely unknown. Clearly the relationships between her two sets of children were close, for Militades the general was named after his father's half-brother Miltiades the tyrant in the Chersonnese. In fact, the younger Miltiades eventually succeeded his uncle as tyrant in the Chersonnese. The important point for the argument here is that ancestry stretching back beyond two or three generations survived only as links in a chain of men – the only family members to be remembered as individuals.[32]

Interestingly, a literary genealogy of this same family which overlaps but does not agree with Herodotos also survives, preserved in a fragment of Pherekydes, an Athenian writing in the first half of the fifth century. On a larger scale, it is clear that Greek communities had a long tradition of using genealogies to justify 'ethnic' and territorial claims.[33] It may be the case that the construction of this genealogy was inspired and affected by political concerns of the family in the fifth century.[34]

Philaios, son of Ajax. Lived in Athens. Philaios begat Daiklos, and he begat Epilykos, and he begat Akestor, and he begat Agenor, and he begat Oulios, and he begat Polykles, and he

30 Apart from the Peisistratids, always portrayed as villains, the three Athenian families which Herodotos discusses in detail are the Philaidai, the Gephyrai (the descendants of Harmodios and Aristogeiton, the tyrant-slayers), and the Alkmeonidai (Thomas, *Oral Tradition*, pp. 144–54). All of these families had living descendants in Athens over the period when Herodotos was active there (Davies, *Athenian Propertied Families*, pp. 472–7, 379–83, 304–8). In the case of the Alkmeonidai he makes reference to contemporary or near-contemporary family members, Pericles (Hdt. 6.131) and Alcibiades' father Kleinias (Hdt. 8.17).

31 Cf. Hdt. 5.57.1, where he gives the Gephryais' own account of their origins and his preferred alternative; Thomas, *Oral Tradition*, p. 98.

32 See Thomas, *Oral Tradition*, pp. 161–73, and Davies, *Athenian Propertied Families*, pp. 298–307.

33 J. M. Hall, *Ethnic Identity in Greek Antiquity* (Cambridge: Cambridge University Press, 1997), pp. 77–99.

34 Thomas, *Oral Tradition*, pp. 164–5.

begat Autophon, and he begat Philaios, and he begat Agamestor, and he begat Teisander, and he begat Miltiades, and he begat Hippokleides who was archon when the Panathenaic festival was established, and he begat Miltiades who founded the colony of the Chersonnese.[35]

Pherekydes' genealogy is strikingly artificial in terms of the realities of Athenian kinship. It begins with the legendary hero Ajax. It is preserved as a single line of men with no information about women (or even siblings), and in that sense is clearly not 'real', apart from any issues about its accuracy. This does, however, suggest that women were not felt to have the same kind of place in long-term memory as men, despite the fact that Greek sources regularly imply that women, especially old women, were important conveyors of traditional tales and information.[36] The information on which it was based is also likely to have originated with the family,[37] some one of whom perhaps commissioned him to write it. Although attempts have been made to explain the discrepancies with Herodotos, or to reconcile them, it may be that families themselves did not necessarily agree about their past, and different individuals or parts of a family understood it differently. The complexities of bilateral kinship and the concomitant lack of time-depth leave considerable room for such disputes.

WOMEN'S RELATIONSHIPS IN THE ANCIENT GREEK WORLD

In contrast, women's relationships in the ancient Greek world are in effect 'prehistoric', relatively untouched by writing despite the abundance of written sources. Generally what we know about women is their relationships to men, and even on tombstones they are often commemorated as the wife or daughter of some man. When we occasionally hear about relationships between women in the written record, it is rarely in their own words. We know that women regularly did things together in groups, and genre scenes in Attic vase-painting showing women together at the fountain house, preparing for weddings or weaving and preparing wool suggest that such activities were commonplace. Sometimes such activities might be elevated to the ritual sphere: women working together to produce the *peplos*

35 *FGrHist* 3 F 2. Translation as in Thomas, *Oral Tradition*, p. 162.
36 Thomas, *Oral Tradition*, p. 109 and n. 44.
37 Thomas, *Oral Tradition*, p. 163.

for the statue of the goddess presented in the Greater Panathenaia must simply have been doing on a grander, civic scale what groups of women regularly did all over the city every day.

Sisters, mothers and daughters were regularly physically separated by marriage, but that did not mean that the emotional ties embedded in these relationships ceased to be meaningful or important. Moreover, women, on moving to new homes on marriage, would have developed new ties and relationships which over time became emotionally meaningful. Although in texts women are most often defined in connection with men, there are hints that affective relationships between women were important. This is particularly clear in the case of closely related women, where ties remained powerful even when they lived in separate households. However, there are examples presented in the literary sources of affective links between women who were unrelated and/or of different statuses. A good example of the bonds between related women is the story in Herodotos (1.61) of the daughter of Megakles married to Peisistratos as part of a political alliance. When Peisistratos refused to have sex with her 'properly', her father heard about his inappropriate treatment of the girl because she had talked to her mother. Whether the story is true (and probably it is not) does not matter; what is important for my purposes is that the account presumes the normality of an intimate relationship maintained between a young bride and her mother. In Antiphon 1, the citizen wife of the household is alleged to have colluded with the family's (unrelated) lodger, a prostitute 'kept' by a family friend in the house, in the murder of her husband. Women's rituals were also celebrated in groups with family and friends. In Lysias 1.20, the adulterous wife of the speaker, Euphiletos, is reported as attending the local Thesmophoria with the mother of her illicit lover. In Menander's *Samia* 21–46, the Adoneia is depicted as being celebrated by the women of neighbouring households together, despite the fact that one is a 'respectable' citizen wife and the other is a *hetaira*.

Some of the most touching accounts we have of women's relationships involve separation and reunification of mothers and daughters. The *Homeric Hymn to Demeter* highlights the emotional reunification of Demeter and Persephone in setting out the aetiological myth behind the ritual of the Thesmophoria, a festival where women usually separated by marriage might be reunited for a brief period in the year.

[386] And when Demeter saw them, she rushed forth as does a Maenad down some thick-wooded mountain, while Persephone on the other side, when she saw her mother's sweet eyes, left the

chariot and horses, and leaped down to run to her, and falling upon her neck, embraced her.

So did they then, with hearts at one, [435] greatly cheer each the other's soul and spirit with many an embrace: their hearts had relief from their griefs while each took and gave back joyousness.

Then bright-coiffed Hecate came near to them, and often did she embrace the daughter of holy Demeter: [440] and from that time the lady Hecate was minister and companion to Persephone. (*HH Demeter* 386–440)

Sappho speaks in similarly affectionate terms about her daughter:

I have a beautiful child who looks like golden flowers, my darling Kleis, for whom I would not take all Lydia or lovely . . . (Sappho fr. 132)

. . . for my mother (once said that) in her youth, if someone had her locks bound in a purple headband, that was indeed a great adornment; but for the girl who has hair that is yellower than a torch (it is better to decorate it) with wreaths of flowers in bloom. Recently . . . a decorated headband from Sardis . . . (Ionian?) cities . . .

But for you, Kleis, I have no way of obtaining a decorated headband; but . . . the Mytilenean . . . to have . . . if . . . decorated . . . (the city has?) these memorials of the exile of the sons of Kleanax, for these (of ours?) . . . wasted away dreadfully . . .(Sappho fr. 98a & b)

Limited as they are, these texts show much more than social relationships founded on obligation or tradition. For women, many of their relationships with other women were close and an important source of strength in a world where their capacity for autonomous action was often constrained, and their movement was sometimes subject to the control of the men in their lives.

LEARNING WOOL-WORKING IN ANCIENT GREECE

There are few activities or artefacts in any society which can be said to be 'gendered', but in the archaic and classical Greek world, the act of manufacturing textiles and the equipment for making them were closely associated with women, both in practical terms and symboli-cally.[38] When a baby was born into an Athenian household, the door was draped in olive branches for a boy, but in spun wool for a girl, a sign of how she would spend much of the rest of her life (Heschyius s.v. *stephanon ekferein*). When textiles and loom weights were dedi-cated as votives in sanctuaries, in the cases where we know the name of the donors, they are always female. In Athenian vase-painting this association between women and weaving is prolifically depicted.[39] It appears also in texts: Xenophon portrays Ischomachos' wife as coming to him 'knowing only how to receive wool and produce a cloak, and having seen how the textile-making tasks are given to the slaves' (Xen. *Oec.* 7.6). What is interesting in this representation is the underlying premise that a girl in her early to mid-teens would have already learned some (but not all) of these critical skills growing up at home.

It is clear from many well-documented ethnographic and histori-cal traditions that becoming a skilled textile worker takes many years and much practice. Anna Portisch studied textile production among Kazakh women in western Mongolia.[40] Textiles are made at home for domestic use and are particularly important components of the wealth exchanged on marriage. Girls start learning to make textiles as children gradually and informally from their mothers and other female relatives.[41] Although men occasionally help out with specific textile-related tasks, overall responsibility is in the hands of women.[42]

Children (boys and girls) encounter these textiles practically from birth. They follow parents, siblings and other relatives, imitate what they are doing and try to 'help'. Children become partly responsible for looking after the sheep whose wool is used for textiles from the age of about 7 or 8. Not until they are large and strong enough at the age of about 12 or 13 do girls begin to help with the preparation of wool for felt.[43] This task is done as a group, with each individual adjusting their movements and their rhythm to synchronise with each other, sometimes to the accompaniment of songs and speech. By 14 or 15 girls learn to help with spinning, starting by producing 'roves'

38 S. Lewis, *The Athenian Woman: An Iconographic Handbook* (London and New York: Routledge, 2002), p. 62.
39 S. Bundrick, 'The fabric of the city: Imaging textile production in classical Athens', *Hesperia* 77 (2008), pp. 283–334.
40 A. Portisch, 'Techniques as a window onto learning: Kazakh women's domestic textile production in western Mongolia', *Journal of Material Culture* 14 (2009), pp. 471–93.
41 Portisch, 'Techniques as a window', pp. 473, 475.
42 Portisch, 'Techniques as a window', p. 476.
43 Portisch, 'Techniques as a window', p. 477.

of fluffed-out wool ready for spinning and by winding the spun wool, before they practise spinning on their own. In addition they also begin to help with sewing and quilting. Even when they marry, girls continue to work under the direction of a mother-in-law.[44]

> Girls' developing of craft knowledge thus integrates several types of understandings rooted in the practices of others and their own participation in these. Through a combination of watching, practising and mimicking others' actions, and incorporating occasional direct instructions, they become proficient in craft production. There is an oscillation between watching and mimicking, watching and practising, and these elements are equally important in the learning process . . . One cannot learn simply by watching, yet without the social environment in which co-learners and elders engage in these specific tasks, it is very hard to form an understanding of the steps through which a finalized *syrmaq* is completed.[45]

Among the Berber carpet-weaving families of the Sirwa Mountains in Morocco, studied by Myriem Naji, the loom is set up as a semi-permanent fixture in the house. Babies and toddlers play around it when they are very small, but gradually boys begin to distance themselves physically and psychologically from the loom.[46] Little girls, however, begin to learn the 'right' ways to sit and to hold the body straight, so that by the time they reach adolescence and begin to participate fully in weaving they have 'embodied' (i.e. learned them so thoroughly that they have become automatic) all of the 'correct' positions and movements, and can blend in with the movements and gestures of the other weavers so that the work progresses smoothly and no one is injured.[47] Even though the finished products are destined for sale, women working together develop close and emotionally charged relationships with each other as well as with the loom and other tools, so that 'embodied engagement with materiality in the making constructs gendered subjects through performance or bodily modification'.[48] In the course of the complex and coordinated movements essential for creating a carpet on the loom, 'weavers share and construct motor representations that allow them to work together

---

44 Portisch, 'Techniques as a window', p. 475.
45 Portisch, 'Techniques as a window', p. 478.
46 Naji, 'Gender and materiality', pp. 52–3.
47 Naji, 'Gender and materiality', pp. 54–5.
48 Naji, 'Gender and materiality', p. 48.

smoothly often with little verbal communication'.[49] The repetition of movements and continual practice in which these weavers engage thus teach the body to perform the right movements automatically (like driving a car, or learning to play a musical instrument); in other words, technology becomes the embodiment of technique. Simultaneously, the practice of working with wool and the associated tools physically marks and shapes the body, e.g. leaving calluses on the fingers, stiff joints and muscles well developed for specific tasks associated with weaving.[50] However, the act of weaving, especially the most skilled and complex elements, is also intensely pleasurable.[51] Weaving also epitomises the moral qualities valued in women: steadfastness, patience and self-control.[52]

In both of these ethnographic examples, girls learn the techniques of textile-working through a range of social interactions with others with whom they are emotionally connected, as well as through repeated physical engagement with materials and tools. Sociality, emotional attachments, physical bodily movement and the engagement with objects and materials all become deeply entangled in this learning process. In general terms, these ethnographically documented learning scenarios are unlikely to be a million miles away from the kind of learning girls must have practised in the ancient world.

What is particularly interesting is the relatively late age at which girls begin to play a significant role in textile production and the social network constructed around it. Many of the tasks associated with weaving needed considerable physical strength as well as coordination. In particular, beating the weft to make it tight is a difficult job on a modern loom where the weaver beats either downward or towards herself (depending on the kind of loom).[53] On an ancient warp-weighted loom, it was necessary for the weaver to beat upwards, necessitating far more physical strength, as well as sufficient height. Working the shuttle and pulling the heddle rods backwards and forwards similarly demanded a long reach as well as strength. The physical demands of weaving on warp-weighted looms are well documented by Marta Hoffmann's study of Norwegian and Lapp weavers still working on these looms in the 1950s. Indeed at the start of weaving, weavers had to stand on a bench to reach the work.[54]

49 Naji, 'Gender and materiality', p. 55.
50 Naji, 'Gender and materiality', p. 62.
51 Naji, 'Gender and materiality', pp. 68–9.
52 Naji, 'Gender and materiality', p. 69.
53 Naji, 'Gender and materiality', p. 62.
54 M. Hoffmann, *The Warp-Weighted Loom* (Oslo: Norwegian Research Council for the Sciences and Humanities, 1974; 1st pub. 1964), pp. 43–4.

Before the age of about 11 or 12, most girls would not have been large
or strong enough to do these jobs. In this light it is significant that
young children do not appear in weaving and textile manufacturing
scenes as participants. Babies and small children are, however, regularly depicted on Athenian and other Greek vases and terracottas with
women in groups or working, for example when women are grinding
grain. The one representation which is sometimes thought to show a
child in a scene of textile-working, a votive plaque from the Acropolis
(Acropolis Museum 2525), in fact almost certainly shows grain grinding, from its similarity with other grain-grinding scenes (e.g. Berlin
Staatliche Museen 1966.21). Indeed, it is possible that toddlers and
young children were discouraged from playing too close to the loom
lest they damage the weaving, the loom assembly or themselves.[55]

Very small girls probably played with bits of wool and thread
dropped by women in the course of their work, and thereby developed
a feel for textiles, while at the same time they watched and imitated the
movements and actions of women at work, listening to their conversations and learning their songs. It seems likely that girls first started to
help by engaging with others in cleaning and sorting wool, preparing
fibres for spinning, as well as participating in various tasks associated
with finishing and storing textiles and clothing. It seems probable
that learning to spin on a drop spindle was the next step, and perhaps
also learning to weave bands and fillets on a fixed-heddle loom (these
bands were also used as the starting point of the warp threads to be
fixed on the loom), before helping with actual weaving on the loom
when they were big enough.

If Greek (or at least Athenian) women regularly married as young
as we conventionally believe, at around 14 years old, then it seems
likely that a girl would have begun her training in textile manufacture in her natal home with her mother and other female relatives,
perhaps around 12 or so, but that this training must have continued
in the company of her mother-in-law and the female relatives of her
husband once she was married. In the wedding scenes depicted on
Athenian vases, the bride often holds a distaff,[56] not only a convenient
icon of her feminine industry, but possibly also indicating the level of
achievement in wool-working she has reached before marriage (spinning, but not full-scale proficiency in weaving). Ferrari has argued
that on Attic vases the common motif, with its many variations, of
the woman spinning or in the presence of wool-working equipment
is intended to suggest the beauty, sexiness, glamour and modesty

55 Naji, 'Gender and materiality', p. 52.
56 Lewis, *Athenian Woman*, p. 62.

of young girls displaying the ideals of femininity.[57] Interestingly in these representations the girls are not weaving, but spinning or carrying out other preparatory processes. The tasks of weaving and textile manufacture under the direction of a mother-in-law and other senior women in her husband's family must have provided one of the primary contexts for a young bride to become integrated within this new household by working as part of the group, and thus to develop a whole new set of emotional ties. In this context, Ischomachos' statement about the extent of his young wife's knowledge and skills is quite interesting: she would have *seen* textile-making tasks distributed to the slaves, but probably not have done it herself, and she could produce a very basic garment, a cloak (*himation*). And, although Xenophon depicts Ischomachos as 'training' his wife, the reality in most families is likely to have been that the training of girls and young women (free and slave) was undertaken by older women.

It should not be surprising, therefore, that the tools of weaving and textile production recovered through archaeology can reveal something of the complex affective networks of female relationships which the texts barely touch upon. These are objects which were once embedded in the everyday tasks and relationships of virtually all women in the ancient Greek world. In a society where women's identity was constrained in many arenas, and most women had little property and few possessions that they could truly call their own, it is easy to see how the tools which defined their work and their femininity, and with which they produced wealth, came to be valued, even though they were not valuable as wealth in their own right. Indeed these were the tools through which close relationships between women, working together in intimate groups, were constructed. In the next section of this chapter I will explore how we can see these relationships on the ground, through the loom weights themselves.

NETWORKS OF WOMEN IN THE METAPONTO COUNTRYSIDE

The *chora* of Metaponto, the rural territory associated with the ancient city, has been the subject of a longstanding programme of intensive survey and excavation by Joseph Carter of the Institute of Classical Archaeology, University of Texas at Austin. This prosperous countryside was located south of the 'heel' of Italy, on the Adriatic coast, in close proximity to indigenous Italic settlements inland.

---

57 G. Ferrari, *Figures of Speech: Men and Maidens in Ancient Greece* (Chicago and London: University of Chicago Press, 2002), pp. 35–60.

The loom weights from the well-documented survey assemblage[58] along with the material from the excavated farmhouses provides us with information about the networks of women resident in this Greek rural landscape. About 400 loom weights were also deposited as votives in the Pantanello sanctuary. It is clear too, but beyond the scope of this chapter, that we can trace relationships and links between women from Greek and from indigenous Italic communities in the region.[59] Most of the loom weights found in the *chora* of Metaponto appear to have been used (not necessarily all in the same way), as indicated by wear marks around the holes, and wear and chips where they knocked other loom weights when hung on the loom.

The taphonomy of loom weights itself suggests that they were valued. Even in excavated assemblages it is unusual to find 'full sets' of loom weights: a Greek loom would normally have needed at least 60–70 loom weights, sometimes more. Even at Olynthos, where the city was abandoned in something of a rush because of the invasion of Philip in 348 BCE, women seems to have taken most of their loom weights with them, and relatively few 'complete sets' were recovered.[60] In the survey data from the *chora* of Metaponto, relatively few sites had more than one loom weight, suggesting that for the most part they were removed when the houses were abandoned (Table 11.1).

Table 11.1 Metaponto survey data (numbers of loom weights per site)

Number of loom weights	Number of sites
1	57 (70%)
2 or more:	24 (30%)
2	18
3	4
5	1
6	1

58 L. Foxhall, 'The loom weights', in J. C. Carter and A. Prieto (eds), *The Chora of Metaponto 3: The Archaeological Survey Bradano to Bassento vol. 2* (Austin: University of Texas Press, 2011), pp. 539–54.

59 A. Quercia and L. Foxhall, 'Temporality, materiality and women's networks: The production and manufacture of loom weights in the Greek and indigenous communities of southern Italy', in K. Rebay-Salisbury, L. Foxhall and A. Brysbaert (eds), *Material Crossovers: Knowledge Networks and the Movement of Technological Knowledge between Craft Traditions* (London: Routledge, forthcoming).

60 N. Cahill, *Household and City Organization at Olynthus* (New Haven: Yale University Press, 2002), pp. 51–2: D. M. Robinson, *The Hellenic House: Olynthus VIII* (Baltimore: Johns Hopkins University Press, 1938), pp. 88–9, 90, 96, 128, 136, 209.

Throughout the Greek world (and beyond) many, though by no means all, loom weights are marked, and a great many of these marks appear to indicate personal possession and perhaps family identity. The marks most commonly known are stamps from signet rings (either stamp seals made from gems or simply engraved into the metal of the ring itself). A particularly large proportion of the loom weights recovered in the Metaponto assemblages were stamped in this way, indicating households with women sufficiently wealthy to own such jewellery.

For the most part these gems and seals have normally been studied as 'art' rather than for their significance as *personal* seals. 'If gems and rings were worn by women it would probably be for their value as jewellery rather than for their use as signets.'[61] However, we know from other sources that such signet rings were commonly used for personal identification in classical antiquity, somewhat as we use PIN numbers today. And, as with PIN numbers, no two stamp seals were identical. There seems to be no obvious reason why they would not be used in this way by women as well as by men. Indeed, loom weights could be marked in many other ways, including inscribed letters, names and other graffiti, fingerprints, and impressions of other objects such as seeds, earrings, dress pins (fibulae), pendants, tweezers and gaming pieces (*astragaloi*, the knuckle bones of sheep) (Figs 11.1a and 11.1b). The use of jewellery other than signet rings and cosmetic paraphernalia, feminine personal items, strongly supports the idea that the marking of loom weights, at least in most parts of the Greek world, was entangled with personal and family identities. This takes on particular significance with objects specifically used by women working together in groups, and in situations where a woman's working group might change due to circumstances largely beyond her control, e.g. on marriage, divorce or the death of a husband.

Concrete examples show how we can track links between women via the loom weights they left behind. Figures 11.2a and b show two loom weights (221–L2 and 358–L1) with identical 'footprint' stamps. Stamps in this form are extremely unusual in the Greek world, although a number of variant footprints are found at Metaponto, suggesting that this is something of a local habit or fashion. The closest parallels for the Metaponto 'footprint' stamps are generally found in areas with a significant Phoenician or Punic presence such as Cyprus and Sardinia. Though we cannot be certain, it is thus possible that the footprint at Metaponto retained some kind of 'ethnic' or group

61 J. Boardman, *Greek Gems and Finger Rings*, 2nd edn (London: Thames and Hudson, 2001), p. 236.

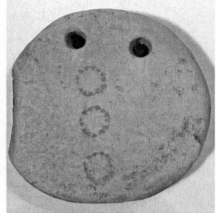

Figure 11.1a and b   Pantanello, Metaponto: loom weights impressed with
(a) a fibula (dress pin) and (b) earrings.

connection with 'Phoenicians', whether imagined or real. More interesting in the case of the specific examples considered here is that the
two loom weights were found at contemporary sites about 3 km apart,
on opposite sides of the Venella valley (Figs 11.2a and b). The simplest
explanation would be that the women in these two households were
related, perhaps taking loom weights from their natal home with them
on marriage. This is not an isolated example: in several other cases in
the Metaponto survey assemblage, loom weights with identical stamps
appear on different sites. However, there are not so many identical
stamps as to suggest that they were a manufacturer's mark rather than
a personal identifier. In cases where loom weights were professionally
made and decorated by the manufacturer (as in the case of mould-
made relief-decorated examples), the distribution pattern is different.

Another example of a loom weight which seems to have travelled
through time as well as space was found in the excavation of the
Fattoria Fabrizio farmhouse (Fig. 11.4). It was recovered inside
the house as part of a domestic deposit from use-life of the house in
the late fourth century BCE. However, the inscription on this pyrami-
dal loom weight, 'IN', dates it to around 500 BCE or not much after
at the latest: the cursive, wiggly iota was not in use after this time.
Indeed, in most Metapontine inscriptions of the archaic period the
wiggly iota was angular, not cursive; the latter is more typical of cities
further south such as Rhegion. So, this loom weight was certainly an
heirloom when it was in use at the time the house was abandoned,
and it is possible that it was brought to the house by a woman from a
different city.

Figure 11.2a and b Metaponto survey: loom weights 221-L2 and 358-L1, with identical footprint stamps found at contemporary sites about 3 km apart, on opposite sides of the Venella valley.

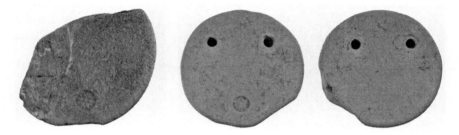

Figure 11.3a and b Metaponto survey: two loom weights with identical rosette stamps.

'Heritage' stamps are found regularly throughout the Greek world,[62] and appear also in the Metaponto assemblage. The three identical stamps on 531–L1, 531–L2 and 532–L1 (Fig. 11.1b) come from two adjacent sites, one slightly later than the other. As in the case of the identical footprint stamps discussed above, this suggests that the women in these two houses were related, perhaps sisters, or more likely mother and daughter or grandmother and granddaughter (Fig. 11.3a and b). However, the rosette stamps on these late fourth/early third-century loom weights (the oscillum/disc type was not in use until well into the fourth century BCE) have their closest parallels in seals of the late seventh/sixth century BCE. The simplest explanation would be that the stamp itself had been passed down the family through the female line.

This may also be the case with the extraordinary stamp on 309–L6 (Fig. 11.5). This loom weight was found with five other plain disc weights typical of the fourth/third century which are very close in

62 G. M. A. Richter, *Engraved Gems of the Greeks, Etruscans and Romans, 1: A History of Greek Art in Miniature* (London: Phaidon, 1968), p. 143; G. R. Davidson, D. Thompson and H. Thompson, *Small Objects from the Pnyx I* (*Hesperia* Suppl. 7; Princeton: American School of Classical Studies in Athens, 1943), p. 84 no. 56, Corinth XII 152.

Figure 11.4   Fattoria Fabrizio farmhouse: inscribed late archaic loom
weight found in late fourth century BCE use context.

weight and seem to belong together. This one, however, is somewhat
lighter, and may be slightly earlier in type, perhaps earlier in the fourth
century: it looks as if this one had been joined with another 'set'.
However, both the shape of the stamp and the motif, a deity holding
two horses in a kind of *potnia theron* ('mistress of the animals') pose,
suggest a sixth-century date for the stamp. The closest parallels I have
been able to find for the motif come from the lead figurines in the sanctuary of Artemis Orthia in Sparta.[63]

The archaeological record in conjunction with what we know about
women's working practices and lives suggests profound engagements
with other women through the practice of textile manufacture. It
seems clear that the tools themselves become a deeply embedded part
of these networks of women and literally come to show the marks of
their relationships. The very concreteness of the loom weights and
other tools which women used together in working groups may have
served as a solid evocation of emotional attachment across time and
space, in a world where women sometimes had little control over their

63 R. M. Dawkins, *The Sanctuary of Artemis Orthia at Sparta* (*JHS* Suppl. 5;
   London: British School at Athens, 1929), p. 266.

Figure 11.5   Metaponto survey: 309-L6, heritage stamp on fourth-century
BCE loom weight.

own movements. Such objects almost certainly attracted stories connecting them with other people and places, past and present. In texts
we sometimes see joyful reunions between mothers and daughters; in
the loom weights we may more often be seeing separations invisible in
the texts, perhaps mitigated by the continued importance of emotional
and familial ties embedded in the relationship of person and object.
Even if we do not know their precise content, here we see evidence for
the existence of stories about women and their families which were
never written down.

CONCLUSION

In this chapter I have pulled out and followed widely disparate threads
of evidence, which intertwine to show us Greek pasts below the radar
of conventional historical texts. These pasts appear to be founded
largely on familial relationships, real or perceived. However, both the
conceptualisations of 'family' and the kinds of stories and memories
transmitted vary along the lines of status, and even more, of gender.
The stories of elite men are, not surprisingly, those most likely to
penetrate the written record of the literate, collective past. The extent
to which women were regularly 'written out' of such memories, even
when they provided crucial links between men, is significant. Regularly
familial memories are lodged in material objects, which may thus serve
as foci of for their transmission, but the kinds of objects, as well as the

kinds of memories they evoke, may vary considerably. Such objects may be monumental, but even humble and non-monumental objects preserved alternative pasts, mostly now beyond our reach. However, the wider value of comparing these alternative pasts is to expose one aspect of the complex and dynamic relationships between gender, space and time as practised in ancient Greek societies.

12

COMMON KNOWLEDGE AND THE CONTESTATION OF HISTORY IN SOME FOURTH-CENTURY ATHENIAN TRIALS

Jon Hesk

Given the frequency with which they refer to past events, the Athenian orators offer us an obvious opportunity for considering the role of 'history' in the key public institutions and discourses of Athenian democracy. Some scholars have traced tendencies and developments with respect to the events and personalities which the orators allude to or pass over. Such patterns across the whole corpus offer us a sense both of the individual political or forensic agendas of certain orators and of broader currents of late fifth- and fourth-century policy and ideology.[1] Surveys of the entire corpus also offer us a sense of the extent of the orators' historical knowledge (and arguably that of the *dēmos*).[2] Others have focused on the ways in which the orators are clearly selecting, concealing or distorting the past in order to serve their individual rhetorical purposes.[3] The use of history (and discussion of the difficulty of using history in fresh and appropriate ways) is particularly central to Isocrates' vision of rhetoric, statesmanship and panhellenism.[4] And speeches commemorating Athens' war dead

---

1 See S. Perlman, 'The historical example, its use and importance as political propaganda in the Attic orators', *SH* 7 (1961), pp. 150–66; M. Nouhaud, *L'utilisation de l'histoire par les orateurs attiques* (Paris: Les Belles Lettres, 1982); J. Ober, *Mass and Elite in Democratic Athens: Rhetoric, Ideology and the Power of the People* (Princeton: Princeton University Press, 1989), pp. 319–22. On references to Solon as a nostalgic strategy to criticise present behaviours and policies, see M. Hansen, 'Solonian democracy in fourth-century Athens', *C & M* 40 (1989), pp. 71–99.

2 See L. Pearson, 'Historical allusions in the Attic orators', *CPh* 36 (1941), pp. 209–29; R. D. Milns, 'Historical paradigms in Demosthenes' public speeches', *Electronic Antiquity* 2.5 (1995).

3 E.g. I. Worthington, 'History and oratorical exploitation', in Worthington (ed.), *Persuasion: Greek Rhetoric in Action* (London: Routledge, 1994), pp. 109–29.

4 E.g. Isoc. *Pangyr.* 7–10 and *Panath.* 149–50 with the discussion of J. Marincola, *Authority and Tradition in Ancient Historiography* (Cambridge: Cambridge University Press, 1997), pp. 276–9. See also the discussion and bibliography of M. Fox and N. Livingstone, 'Rhetoric and historiography', in

(the *epitaphioi logoi*) did their powerful ideological work by constructing a stable and yet adaptable version of Athenian history as 'a long continuum that relies on the re-enactment of great deeds by each generation'.[5] Several recent studies focus on those speeches of Demosthenes, Aeschines and Lycurgus which were delivered in politically charged cases in the aftermath of Chaeronea. These speeches from 'Lycurgan Athens' contrast present depravities in political procedure and personal conduct with a heavily idealised past of constitutional order, political decorum and great military achievements. They do this to shape the jury's outlook on the case at hand. But they are also emblematic of 'an intense preoccupation with, engagement and focus on the city's own past' in Lycurgan Athens.[6] This 'past-connectivity' was a response to a sense of decline in comparison with the Solonian and fifth-century glory days. And it drove all manner of fresh political, religious and cultural initiatives as Lycurgus and other prominent politicians sought to restore the city's strength, confidence and self-image to line up with that idealised past.[7]

This chapter attempts to contribute further to our understanding of appeals to the past which appear in speeches from high-profile public trials between 345 and 330. But I will focus on a particular reading of the significance of these appeals which is put forward in an admirable, fascinating and provocative recent book by Josiah Ober entitled *Democracy and Knowledge: Innovation and Learning in Classical Athens*. The overarching claim of this book is that democratic Athens was a successful state because it was able to overcome barriers to collective action through the efficient aggregation and application of knowledge. And while I am sympathetic to its innovative exploration of Athens as an 'epistemic' or 'deliberative' democracy, my

(footnote 4 *continued*)
I. Worthington (ed.), *A Companion to Greek Rhetoric* (Malden, MA, and Oxford: Blackwell, 2007), pp. 542–60, at pp. 551–3.

5 J. Grethlein, *The Greeks and Their Past: Poetry, Oratory and History in the Fifth Century BCE* (Cambridge: Cambridge University Press, 2010), p. 123. See also the classic account of N. Loraux, *The Invention of Athens: The Funeral Oration in the Classical City* (Cambridge, MA: Harvard University Press, 1986).

6 S. Lambert, 'Some political shifts in Lykourgan Athens', in V. Azoulay and P. Ismard (eds), *Clisthène et Lycurgue d'Athènes: Autour du politique dans la cité classique* (Paris: Publications de la Sorbonne, 2011), pp. 175–90, at p. 187.

7 See e.g. H. Yunis, 'Politics as literature: Demosthenes and the burden of the Athenian past', *Arion* 8 (2000), pp. 97–118; F. Hobden, 'Imagining past and present: A rhetorical strategy in Aeschines 3, *Against Ctesiphon*', *CQ* 57.2 (2007), pp. 490–501; Lambert, 'Some political shifts'; V. Azoulay, 'Lycurgue d'Athènes et le passé de la cité: Entre neutralisation et instrumentalisation', *Cahiers des Études Anciennes* 46 (2009), pp. 149–80; Azoulay, 'Les métamorphoses du *koinon* athénien: Autour du *Contre Léocrate* de Lycurgue', in Azoulay and Ismard, *Clisthène et Lycurgue d'Athènes*, pp. 191–217.

arguments do not aim either to support or to deny this big claim.[8] Instead, I will argue that Ober has mischaracterised the relationship between the orators' use of historical examples in the Athenian courts and the body of 'common knowledge' which he sees as crucial to the ongoing stability and effectiveness of the democracy. My point is that Athenians' decision-making was informed by a much more contested, sophisticated, sceptical and highly self-conscious rhetorical discourse about the political and legal applications of historical 'knowledge' than Ober's analysis admits.

We must begin with a detailed account of Ober's position. He rightly points out that 'where the law offered no clear guidance or the facts of the case were obscure, Athenian juries were required by their oath to seek the most just outcome'.[9] In situations like this, juries relied on a body of common knowledge to inform their verdict. Ober also argues that 'references to past events by litigants added to the repertoire of Athenian common knowledge'.[10] In many cases, then, common knowledge about (for example) Athens' glorious role in the Persian Wars or its past treatment of anti-democratic traitors, the exemplary conduct of famous politicians or unnamed 'ancestors', and especially the past decisions of juries and assemblies on relevant issues must have played a crucial role in informing Athenian juries' deliberations.

But Ober's main point is that this knowledge about the past, along with a commitment to democratic values, was crucial for establishing and maintaining reasonably *predictable* alignments of attitude, judgement and decision-making on the part of citizen jurors and Assembly-goers.[11] Without this element of predictability, neither the elite citizens nor the mass of Athens' citizenry would have been able to plan their lives and sustain a social equilibrium between them. Building this sort of common knowledge in public institutions also addressed the 'carry through' problem faced by people who share goals, but who will not individually act to achieve them unless each believes that others will act likewise. The common knowledge of

---

8 See J. Ober, *Democracy and Knowledge: Innovation and Learning in Classical Athens* (Princeton: Princeton University Press, 2008), pp. 1–38. 'Epistemic' democracy: C. List and R. E. Goodin, 'Epistemic democracy: Generalizing the Condorcet jury theorem', *Journal of Political Philosophy* 9 (2001), pp. 277–306; E. Anderson, 'The epistemology of democracy', *Episteme: Journal of Social Epistemology* 3 (2006), pp. 8–22. 'Deliberative' democracy: J. Elster (ed.), *Deliberative Democracy* (Cambridge and New York: Cambridge University Press, 1998).

9 Ober, *Democracy and Knowledge*, p. 191. See also A. M. Lanni, *Law and Justice in the Courts of Classical Athens* (Cambridge: Cambridge University Press, 2006).

10 Ober, *Democracy and Knowledge*, p. 192.

11 Ober, *Democracy and Knowledge*, pp. 168–83.

Athens' past actions and achievements which was publicised in legal speeches especially promoted awareness of the city's shared goals and its citizens' shared commitment to achieving those goals. But Ober also stresses the importance of rituals, public monuments and Attica's rich array of inward-facing public buildings as crucial for the creation of common knowledge and the awareness of shared commitments that such knowledge fosters.[12]

Lycurgus' speech *Against Leocrates* of 331/30 BCE is Ober's case study for demonstrating that legal speeches could draw on the past in their attempt to align and coordinate citizens' attitudes and collective commitments in other public domains. Leocrates was an Athenian blacksmith-turned-trader whom Lycurgus prosecuted on charges of treasonously leaving Athens when he ought to have remained to help defend the city following the defeat at Chaeronea in 338. He had remained absent from the city until 332. According to Lycurgus, the defeat had prompted the Assembly to pass emergency measures which allowed the city's generals to assign anyone still resident in Athens to undertake guard duty (Lyc. 1.16). The legislation may also have extended the definition of treason to include 'fleeing from risk on behalf of one's country'.[13] Although Lycurgus argues that Leocrates' sailing to Rhodes constituted an act of treason (*prodosia*), he is not able to show that Leocrates left the city after the legislation came into force. As Ober points out, this was a key weakness in his case. But it is also possible that Lycurgus was stretching the definition of *prodosia* to cover sins of omission and non-participation when the law really only provided for active acts of treachery, such as giving strategic information to an enemy or deserting to the other side. It is fairly clear that Lycurgus was using an impeachment procedure (*eisangelia*) against individuals who were not the normal targets of impeachment and in relation to offences which were not normally covered by that procedure.[14] By the time of the trial Lycurgus was becoming a powerful figure in Athens through his control of the public finances and his prominent opposition to Macedon.[15] We know that he had

---

12 Ober, *Democracy and Knowledge*, pp. 190–210.
13 See D. M. Macdowell, *The Law in Classical Athens* (Ithaca, NY: Cornell University Press, 1978), pp. 178–9, 185, citing a fragment of Theophrastus' *Laws* (= Pollux 8.52; *Lexicon Cantabrigiense* s.v. *eisangelia*).
14 Azoulay, 'Métamorphoses du *koinon* athénien', pp. 197–204.
15 S. C. Humphreys, 'Lycurgus of Butadae: An Athenian aristocrat', in J. W. Eadie and J. Ober (eds), *The Craft of the Ancient Historian: Essays in Honor of Chester G. Starr* (Lanham, MD: University Press of America, 1985), pp. 199–252; B. Hintzen-Bohlen, *Die Kulturpolitik des Eubulos und des Lykurg: Die Denkmäler- und Bauprojekte in Athen zwischen 355 und 322 v. Chr.* (Berlin: Akademie, 1997); P. Ismard and V. Azoulay, 'Clisthène et Lycurgue d'Athènes: Le politique à l'épreuve

already successfully prosecuted the general Lysicles for the failure of Chaeronea.[16] We do not know the nature of the charge but it is likely to have involved allegations of betraying Athens to the enemy. He also seems to have successfully prosecuted a member of the Areopagus council called Autolycus for sending his family out of Athens amidst the panic of Chaeronea.[17] In the light of all this, it is interesting that Lycurgus' prosecution was unsuccessful: in a speech delivered later the same year, Aeschines tells us that Leocrates was acquitted by a single vote (3.252). Why did Leocrates' prosecution fail when similar ones had clearly succeeded and Lycurgus himself was in the ascendancy?

Ober argues that the speech concentrates on what he calls two 'commitment equilibria' which depend on aligning the jury with common knowledge.[18] The first of these equilibria is the commitment of the citizenry to undertake sacrifices necessary to maintain polis security, as evidenced by their actions in the aftermath of Athens' military defeat at Chaeronea in 338. The idea here is that Lycurgus characterises the security of the polis in this period as what political theorists call 'a common pool resource'. As a valued possession which is collectively owned by the citizenry, polis security is vulnerable to what theorists call 'a tragedy of the commons'. If self-interested individuals take more from the pool than they give back, the polis becomes insecure. As Lycurgus explicitly says, 'if everyone acted like Leocrates our city would be a wasteland' (1.60). The second equilibrium is the citizens' commitment to enforcing legal sanctions against individuals whose behaviour threatens the first equilibrium.

Lycurgus deliberately shows that these two equilibria are linked: each citizen's commitment to saving the state must be credible to Athenians and outsiders alike. And both internal and external audiences must also believe that Athens really is prepared to take sanctions against those who deviate from such a commitment to contribute to polis security through their acts of desertion and treachery. Because the claim that Leocrates *had* actually broken any law of treason was questionable, Lycurgus' strategy in his speech was to seek what Ober calls 'a cascade of following' based on these two equilibria. The orator effectively stresses that a conviction of Leocrates by a massive majority would signal that polis security was a commonly held Athenian

---

de l'événement', in Azoulay and Ismard, *Clisthène et Lycurgue d'Athènes*, pp. 5–13.

16 See the testimonia and fragments of *Against Lysicles* collected in N. C. Conomis, *Lycurgus: Oratio in Leocratem* (Leipzig: Teubner, 1970), pp. 112–13.

17 See Lyc. 1.53 and testimonia and fragments of *Against Autolycus* collected in Conomis, *Lycurgus*, pp. 96–7.

18 Ober, *Democracy and Knowledge*, pp. 180–94.

preference, and that the legal sanctions which sustained this shared goal were based on rational coordination of shared interests (e.g. 63–7, 141–9). This way the jury would reaffirm and republicise both the credibility of the citizens' shared commitment to sacrifice themselves for polis security and their commitment to criminalise and punish anyone deviating from a willingness to stand and fight. If the jury acquitted Leocrates, on the other hand, it would thereby imply that Leocrates' choosing to leave the city was rational and comprehensible. This would, in turn, signal that Athenian citizens were not credibly committed to collective self-sacrificial action to save the polis. An acquittal would in itself undermine citizens' and outsiders' belief that Athenians were united in their preparedness to fight for the city.

For Ober, the fact of Leocrates' acquittal shows that Lycurgus' strategy was trumped by a third equilibrium. This was the jurors' oath-bound commitment to judge on the basis of the law where the law was clear and to judge in accordance with justice where the law was silent. The jurors' discretion to judge cases in accordance with emotion, equity and the litigants' reputations was considerable. But elite citizens needed to know that juries would limit the scope of their discretion through a commitment to the law and justice. This is where the social equilibrium which underpins Athenian democracy comes into play: if juries dominated by non-elite citizens demonstrated no commitment to the law as a limit on their discretion, then elite litigants would be faced with an unpredictable justice system. This would substantially threaten their continued investment in the democracy's institutions. The jury narrowly acquitted Lycurgus because they decided that Leocrates had not broken any law *and* because they saw that a guilty verdict would damage the courts' reputation for fairness more than an acquittal would disrupt citizens' shared commitment to polis security. For Ober, 'both the *content* of Lycurgus' speech and the *outcome* of the trial underline the delicate balance between competing social goods of enhanced coordination and the preservation of a social equilibrium that was predicated upon a credible commitment to legal rules'.[19]

Now Lycurgus uses 'an unusual and excessive number of historical examples and quotations from the poets'.[20] Unsurprisingly, he narrates and praises the Athenians who died at Chaeronea to defend

---

19 Ober, *Democracy and Knowledge*, p. 185. See also (with a different emphasis) the important discussion of L. Rubinstein, 'Arguments from precedent in Attic oratory', in E. Carawan (ed.), *Oxford Readings in the Attic Orators* (Oxford: Oxford University Press, 2007), pp. 359–71.
20 D. S. Allen, 'Changing the authoritative voice: Lycurgus' *Against Leocrates*', *Classical Antiquity* 19 (2000), pp. 5–33, at p. 10.

Greek freedom (46–9). But he links their fine conduct to the statues of generals, tyrant-slayers and athletes from earlier times which can be seen throughout the city: the valour shown at Chaeronea is explained by the fact that 'alone of the Greeks' the Athenians know how to honour good men (50). But just as Athens fosters more great deeds by honouring them, it must also punish the crimes of men like Leocrates (51–2).

After some anticipation of Leocrates' arguments, Lycurgus launches into a passage of historical and poetic *paradeigmata* that extends for 64 of the speech's 150 sections. We have the following examples: the Athenians' role in ensuring victory at Salamis and the city's glorious hegemonic aftermath (68–74); the ephebic oath and the role of oaths in preserving democracy (75–9); the brave oath sworn by the Greeks at Plataea and the particular glory which that victory conferred on Athens (80–2); the story of how King Codrus sacrificed himself for Athens during a war (83–8); the story of how the Delphic oracle enabled the execution of the Athenian politician Callistratus (92–3); the fable of how the gods rewarded a young Sicilian man for not deserting his father, involving the 'Place of the Pious' (95–7); Praxithea's sacrifice of her daughter via a fifty-five-line quotation from Euripides' *Erectheus* (98–101); quotations from the *Iliad* and Tyrtaeus which exemplify the importance of military duty, including an account of the latter's historical contribution to Spartan discipline and hoplite ideology (102–8); the Simonidean text of the monument to the Athenians at Marathon and of the monument to the Spartans at Thermopylae, accompanied by narrative of their achievements (108–10); four narratives of exemplary and consistent punishments meted out to Athens' traitors in the fifth century (111–23); the stele set up in the aftermath of 404/3 which recorded the immunity granted to those who thwart tyrannical subversion of the democracy (124–6);[21] the Spartans' treatment of their king Pausanias and their law against cowardice (128–9); and quotations from two anonymous poets (92, 132). All the way through this *tour de force* we have Leocrates' conduct condemned by contrast or analogy (e.g. 74, 82, 89, 97, 110). And it is made clear that Leocrates must be convicted if the jury themselves are to be faithful to the values, pledges, conduct and sacrifices of their ancestors, all of which have ensured Athens' glory and the survival of its democracy (e.g. 74, 82, 89, 123, 127).

---

21 Lycurgus seems to have misattributed the motion of Demophantus in 411 to the aftermath of the Thirty: I. Worthington, C. R. Cooper and E. M. Harris, *Dinarchus, Hyperides, and Lycurgus* (Austin: University of Texas Press, 2001), p. 195.

There is nothing quite like this extended passage of positive and negative exemplars elsewhere in the extant corpus of oratory.[22] And before we consider Ober's incorporation of it into his argument it is worth stressing that there are actually several entirely compatible explanations for it. Danielle Allen convincingly characterises Lycurgus' historical and poetic paradigms as a symptom of his radical departure from conceptions of punishment and politics which Athenians usually accepted.[23] Instead of invoking his own personal stake in Leocrates' case or referring to his own anger at his conduct in order to stoke the jury's ire (as was normal), Lycurgus presents himself as a dispassionate prosecutor and projects an 'authoritative voice' which wards off the traditional view that lack of personal involvement with the defendant betokens sycophancy. Lycurgus is stressing that it is in the interests of the entire state and future generations of citizens that Leocrates be made an example of. The historical and poetic examples which embody the Athenians' collective courage and both Athens' and Sparta's willingness to deal severely with traitors reinforce these points. Lycurgus does ask the jury to display anger at Leocrates for what he has done (e.g. 16, 25, 26, 57). But he points out that the jury's ancestors consistently punished traitors with death because of 'truth' (*alētheia*) rather than 'anger' (*orgē*) and because it was in their nature (*phusis*) to 'make war' on treacherous deeds (116).

Vincent Azoulay's analysis of Lycurgus' extensive use of examples from the past usefully complements that of Allen.[24] For Azoulay, Lycurgus is partly using this speech to project his status as a senior statesman of experience and knowledge. He adopts the posture of a supreme educator. Some of his poetic and historical examples even seem designed to draw attention to his own political role and his specific initiatives. But Azoulay also shows that the speech's vast array of historical examples are piled on top of each other as part of a deliberate rhetorical tactic of repetition and accumulation. As Lycurgus says himself, the fact that Athens *repeatedly* and consistently punished traitors with death authenticates his argument (116). The accumulation of examples also implies that Leocrates is being prosecuted as much by history itself as by Lycurgus. Having quoted the epigrams for those

---

22 It is undoubtedly significant that the nearest parallels are the passages of quotation found in Aeschines' *Against Ctesiphon* and Demosthenes' *On the Crown*, which were pitted against each other only a few months after the trial of Leocrates. Although many speeches before 331/30 use historical examples and a few use quotations from classical and archaic poetry, these three speeches must represent something of a shift in tone and tactics. See Hobden, 'Imagining past and present'; Lambert, 'Some political shifts', pp. 187–90, for some explanations.

23 Allen, 'Changing the authoritative voice'.

24 Azoulay, 'Lycurgue d'Athènes et le passé de la cité'.

who fell at Marathon and Thermopylae, Lycurgus says these lines offer 'praise and glory for our city which will always be remembered' (ἔπαινος καὶ τῇ πόλει δόξα ἀείμνηστος, 110). By contrast, Leocrates has 'deliberately disgraced the glory the city has built up through all time' (ἑκὼν τὴν ἐξ ἅπαντος τοῦ αἰῶνος συνηθροισμένην τῇ πόλει δόξαν κατῄσχυνεν, 110).

Ober focuses on one of Lycurgus' stories about fifth-century Athens' exemplary punishment of traitors. Hipparchus, a prominent Athenian of the early fifth century, fled the city rather than face trial for treason (117–19). We are told that the Athenians sentenced him to death in his absence. Then, 'as they did not secure his person to answer for the crime, they took down his statue from the Acropolis and, melting it down, made a stele of it, on which they decreed that the names of wrongdoers and traitors would be inscribed. Hipparchus himself has his name recorded on this stele and other traitors too' (117). Lycurgus next directs the clerk of the court to read the decree which authorised the taking down of Hipparchus' statue and tells him also to read the stele's inscription and list of traitors (118). Lycurgus then draws the lessons from this historical example: first, Athenians then were not over-lenient as they are today. By obliterating his memorial, they did all they could to punish and humiliate Hipparchus in his absence. Second, 'the simple fact of melting down the bronze statue was not enough for them; they wished to leave behind to their successors a lasting example (*paradeigma*) of their attitude to traitors' (119). For Ober, this is excellent evidence of the way in which public action commitments (in this case the punishment of traitors) are made credible through mechanisms of publicity and common knowledge:

In Lycurgus' account it is a concern with creating and sustaining common knowledge regarding credible commitment to sanction that is the thread that ties together the choices of two chrono-logically distinct speakers in the public interest: the anonymous prosecutor of Hipparchus in the early fifth century BC, and Lycurgus himself some 150 years later. The same concern ties together the Assembly's act of authorizing a private monument to be replaced by a public one, and the monument itself. Finally common knowledge ties together various Athenian audiences, across time and space. The jurors listening to Lycurgus in the Athenian courtroom in 330 BC, their ancestors sitting in the Assembly place a century and a half earlier, and the many visitors to the Acropolis who had noticed the stele in the years in between were imaginatively brought together, through Lycurgus' words, into a unified community of knowing. That imagined community shared knowledge about the iniquity of treason and the Athenian commitment to punishing traitors.[25]

This is a brilliant analysis of the rhetorical dynamics that lie behind both Lycurgus' appeal to history and the ideological rhetoric implicit in permanent public inscriptions and monuments. And we could adapt the basic points of this argument to cover many of the other historical and poetic examples in Lycurgus' speech. It should now be clear how well Lycurgus' use of history fits with Ober's overall thesis.

But Ober does not ask what Leocrates and his supporters said in his defence when faced with this and other powerful appeals to the past. Even though we do not have any speeches for the defence, we can make some informed guesses from hints in Lycurgus' speech and by looking at strategies in other extant speeches. Ober's explanation as to why Lycurgus' tactics failed suggests that the defendant must have stressed that he had not broken any actual law in force at the time. This is certainly corroborated by Lycurgus' anticipations of the defence's arguments. They clearly argued that Leocrates' motive for sailing to Rhodes was trade rather than desertion (55). He neither intended to harm Athens nor was liable under the law of treason. After all, he did not desert any official duty related to defence of the city that had been assigned to him (55–9, 68). The defence may well have stressed that Lycurgus was very much stretching the definition of treason laid out in the law on *eisangelia*. But Leocrates' camp also seem to have resorted to examples from history. For Lycurgus tells us that the other side have used the Athenians' abandonment of Attica in 480 as a precedent for the defendant's departure from Athens after Chaeronea (68–9, tr. Harris):

> I get very angry, gentlemen, whenever I hear one of his associates say that it is not treason if someone leaves the city. For example, your ancestors once left the city when they were fighting against Xerxes and crossed over to Salamis. This man is so foolish and holds you in such complete contempt that he thinks it right to compare the most glorious deeds with the most shameful. Where is the valour of these men not well known? What man is so grudging or so completely lacking in ambition that he would not pray to have taken great part in these deeds? They did not desert the city but only moved from one place to another as part of their brilliant plan to confront the danger that faced them.

25 Ober, *Democracy and Knowledge*, pp. 188–9.

Lycurgus goes on to detail Athens' decisive role in engineering and winning the battle of Salamis and asks: 'was this in any way similar to the man who fled his country for a four-day voyage to Rhodes? Would any of these men of old have perhaps tolerated such a crime?' (70). The answer, of course, is that they would have stoned a deserter like Leocrates to death (71).

It has been argued that Leocrates and his friends cannot really have made an analogy between his trip to Rhodes and the Athenians' mass evacuation to Salamis in 480.[26] But I think it is only hard for us to imagine how Leocrates and his team could have spun the Salamis episode in his favour because Lycurgus does such a good job of making the analogy seem absurd and offensive. We can readily conceive of an argument from Leocrates' side which used the evacuation as a means of characterising Lycurgus' search for traitors and deserters as an excessive and absurdly zealous witch hunt. The argument would have run like this: *if Lycurgus pursues me after seven years have passed, when I am an unimportant merchant who held no public offices in respect of defending the city at the time, and just because I went on a business trip with my family, then he would doubtless even impugn the motives of the Athenians who abandoned Attica after Thermopylae.*[27] By imagining Lycurgus prosecuting the Athenian evacuees of 480, the defence would thereby disrupt his construction of an 'imagined community of knowing' through which the jury are encouraged to punish Leocrates as the latest in a long line of notorious traitors. For if Leocrates is no more a traitor than those of the jury's ancestors who escaped the Mede to fight another day, then Lycurgus' prosecution of him becomes an abuse of law and procedure the jury's ancestors would abhor.

It is likely that Leocrates also characterised some of Lycurgus' lessons from history as irrelevant to the case. An analogous argument can be found in Demosthenes' *On the Crown* (18.209):

ἔπειτ', ὦ κατάρατε καὶ γραμματοκύφων, σὺ μὲν τῆς παρὰ τουτωνὶ τιμῆς καὶ φιλανθρωπίας ἔμ' ἀποστερῆσαι βουλόμενος τρόπαια καὶ μάχας καὶ παλαί' ἔργ' ἔλεγες, ὧν τίνος προσεδεῖθ' ὁ παρὼν ἀγὼν οὑτοσί;

---

26 S. Usher, *Greek Oratory: Tradition and Originality* (Oxford: Oxford University Press, 1999), p. 327.
27 Lycurgus himself anticipates that Leocrates' supporters will argue that one man alone cannot cause the destruction of an entire city by his failure to participate in its defence (63). What the defence probably added was that Leocrates was being unfairly victimised.

After that, you accursed and hunchbacked clerk [i.e. Aeschines],
in your desire to deprive me of respect and affection of my fellow
countrymen, you spoke of prizes and battles and deeds of old.
Which of them is pertinent to the case at issue right now?[28]

Demosthenes is here referring to Aeschines' use of Athens' glorious
ancestral past to represent Demosthenes as unworthy of an honorific crown by comparison (Aesch. 3.181–7). As we will see later,
Aeschines' arguments from history look very pertinent to the issue of
Demosthenes' crowning. And Demosthenes' remarks here actually
follow a section of argument in which he himself deploys many of the
same historical events and personages which Aeschines had mentioned
to show that they are in alignment with his own policy of confronting
Macedon and the heroic failure that was Chaeronea (18.202–8). He
is clear that he deserved to be crowned for this policy. Why? Because
Athens' past showed that it was 'neither traditional, nor tolerable, nor
natural' for Athenians to accept subjugation (203).[29]

It made sense for Leocrates and his fellow speakers to attack the
relevance of Lycurgus' use of history in a similar fashion. And while
they may not have associated their powerful opponent's fondness for
historical *paradeigmata* with a past as a lowly 'clerk' in the way that
Demosthenes does, it is telling that Lycurgus' speech anticipates a
claim from Leocrates that he is a private citizen (*idiōtēs*) who has been
entrapped by a *rhetōr* and a clever sycophant (31). Despite Lycurgus'
framing of his *paradeigmata* and quotations as common knowledge,
the sheer extent of them could be represented as the sort of abuse of
expertise and learning which was typical of politicians of his stature.

What is the implication of all this for Ober's arguments? Well, in
one respect, they are unaffected by the point that litigants could use
historical precedent to claim unjust victimisation via an abuse of
law and procedure. Ober does not claim that an appeal to maintain
a 'credible commitment to legal rules' as a limit to a jury's discretion is incompatible with discussion of historical analogies. And he
is clear that the agonistic framework of the courts helped juries to
resist attempts by powerful orators to use common knowledge in
order to create 'cascades of following' in ways which flouted justice
or corrupted difficult decision-making with 'groupthink'.[30] But my

28 My translation here draws on those of S. Usher, *Demosthenes: On the Crown
(De corona)* (Warminster: Aris & Phillips, 1993), and H. Yunis, *Demosthenes: On
the Crown* (Cambridge: Cambridge University Press, 2001), p. 207.
29 For an excellent discussion of the novel and tragic dimensions of Demosthenes'
strategy in this speech, see Yunis, 'Politics as literature'.
30 Ober, *Democracy and Knowledge*, p. 181.

point is rather different. I am observing that the same item of history could be used by one side as common knowledge in order to appeal to 'credible commitment to legal rules', but then could be reinterpreted to constitute common knowledge regarding 'credible commitment to sanction', or common knowledge regarding 'credible commitment to polis security'. This meant that however much a jury knew about Athens' past treatment of traitors or its ancestors' collective actions, it still had to weigh litigants' conflicting interpretations of those events' applicability to the case at hand. And those conflicts *included* explicit or implicit disputes about whether and in what way the jury was in a position to exercise its discretion or how far its verdict was subject to more specific and demonstrable legal constraints. The common knowledge of history which the orators undoubtedly contributed to the *dēmos'* deliberations cannot in itself have helped a jury to arrive at the right balance between 'the competing social goods of enhanced coordination and the social equilibrium that was predicated on a credible commitment to legal rules'. This is because the conflicting appeals to the past which came from both sides in a case simply offered further evidence that both of these social goods needed to be taken account of. These appeals can have done little to help with the question of which verdict would maintain the right balance between those goods in a particular case.

However, a framework in which the exemplarity and relevance of history were publicly and routinely contested must have fostered a measure of critical distance and caution in juries. This critical awareness of the manipulative potential and 'rhetoricity' of historical *paradeigmata* may constitute a fuller and more accurate characterisation of the useful 'historical knowledge' which Athenian jury-members gained from litigants and applied to future cases over time.

One prosecution speech and my own hypothetical reconstruction of the defence are not enough to give a full sense of the sort of sceptical and critical distance on historical exemplarity which I am talking about. But there are two speeches by Demosthenes and three by Aeschines which offer us a unique chance to see how historical examples were used and critiqued by both sides across three trials.[31]

---

31 It is possible that these speeches may have been revised and lengthened for publication. They may thereby develop their critiques of the other side in more extended and pronounced ways. See I. Worthington, 'Greek oratory, revision of speeches and the problem of historical reliability', *C & M* 42 (1991), pp. 55–74 and Worthington, 'History and oratorical exploitation'. Evidence in the texts for revision prior to publication after these three trials is limited to one or two specific cases. See E. M. Harris, *Aeschines and Athenian Politics* (Oxford and New York: Oxford University Press, 1995), pp. 10–15.

These speeches are Aeschines' *Against Timarchus* (Aeschines' prosecution of Timarchus in 345); Demosthenes' *On the False Embassy* and
Aeschines' *On the Embassy* (Demosthenes' prosecution of Aeschines
for ambassadorial misconduct in 343); and Aeschines' *Against
Ctesiphon* and Demosthenes' *On the Crown* (Aeschines' prosecution
of Ctesiphon over his proposal to award a crown to Demosthenes in
330). We do not have Demosthenes' defence speech from the trial of
his friend Timarchus, but Aeschines' speech is commented upon by
Demosthenes in *On the False Embassy*. Space permits me to offer only
a few brief and highly selective illustrations.

We have seen how Demosthenes slammed Aeschines for the alleged
irrelevance of his references to 'prizes and battles and deeds of old' in
On the Crown (18.209). Demosthenes is talking about a very powerful section of Aeschines' prosecution speech (Aesch. 3.181–90). In
order to argue that Demosthenes is unworthy of the honorific crown
which Ctesiphon proposed, Aeschines contrasts Demosthenes' alleged
lipotaxia (desertion) with the victories of Themistocles and Militiades
during the Persian Wars (3.181). He also invokes the democratic forces
from Phyle and Aristeides 'the Just'. Aeschines even calls Demosthenes
'this beast' (*touto thērion*), saying that it is not right to name him on
the same day as these heroes of the ancestral city (181–2). Aeschines
goes on to point out that no written order was made to crown these
ancestral figures for their efforts. Instead they were honoured by
gaining a place in the immortal memory of all Athenians 'to this day'
(182). Then he gives the jury a tour of the Stoa of the Herms, the Stoa
Poikile and the Metroön, in order to examine inscriptions and paintings created in celebration of key moments in Athens' history: battles
against the Persians at Eion and at Marathon, fighting on the plains
of Troy, and the victory of the democrats from Phyle over the Thirty
and their Spartan allies (3.183–7, 190). At each monument, Aeschines
'performs a reading' of the buildings, their inscriptions and images, to
show that in the old days the Athenians honoured the collective valour
over and above the achievements of individual leaders.[32] His point is
that this old habit better served Athens than the present-day practice
of crowning individual benefactors and undeserving scoundrels like
Demosthenes. As Fiona Hobden shows, Aeschines' tactics here are
skilful, creative (without being idiosyncratic) and striking; and while
they play fast and loose with the symbolism of the inscriptions and
paintings he interprets, they are very pertinent to the case at hand.[33]

---

32 Hobden, 'Imagining past and present', p. 495.
33 Hobden, 'Imagining past and present', pp. 494–8. Hobden draws convincing
   parallels with Dem. 23.196–201, delivered in 352 BCE, and sees Aesch. 3.183–90

As we have seen, Demosthenes dismisses these appeals to the past as irrelevant. But he clearly knew that mere dismissal might not be enough. So, in the closing sections of the speech, and while he is defending his conduct since Chaeronea, he adopts a different approach (18.314, tr. Usher):

> You recall the good men of former times (εἶτα τῶν πρότερον γεγενημένων ἀγαθῶν ἀνδρῶν μέμνησαι): and you are right to do so. However, Athenians, it is not right for him to take advantage of the regard you feel for the dead by examining me, who live among you, and comparing me with them.

Demosthenes continues with a conventional argument: men are envied while alive but even their enemies stop hating them once they are dead.[34] It is only just and fair for Demosthenes to be judged and viewed in comparison with his contemporaries, not his predecessors. Furthermore, it is wrong that the huge services which these ancestors rendered should be cited as a means of engendering ingratitude and abuse towards those who act with good will (*eunoia*) these days (316). As Usher points out, this attack on the negative use of historical models has affinities with Aristotle's and Anaxamines' discussions of the proper use of history in deliberative and epideictic oratory.[35] But Demosthenes' next point is less conventional (317–8, tr. Usher):

> Moreover, if I must say as much, my policies and principles, when examined, will be seen as similar and to have the same objectives as those of the men who were praised in the past, while yours resemble those of their detractors (ἡ δὲ σὴ ταῖς τῶν τοὺς τοιούτους τότε συκοφαντούντων). For it is clear that in their time there were men who carped at the living and praised those of past ages, the same malicious practice (βάσκανον πρᾶγμα) as you are following. So you say that I am in no way like them? Are you like them, Aeschines? Is your brother? Is any of our contemporary politicians (τῶν νῦν ῥητόρων)? None, I say. To say no more, my fine

as a considerable elaboration of an existing forensic technique found especially in Demosthenes and Lycurgus, namely 'the advancement of an argument through the physicality of the city' (p. 498). The question of the legality of Ctesiphon's proposal to crown Demosthenes and (hence) the respective merits of each side's cases and tactics is vexed. See e.g. E. M. Harris, 'Law and oratory', in Worthington, *Persuasion*, pp. 130–52, at pp. 143–4; Yunis, *Demosthenes*, pp. 174–83.

34 For the topos, see Thuc. 2.45.1
35 Usher, *Demosthenes*, p. 275. See Arist. *Rhet.* 2.22.5–6, Anax. *Rhet. ad Alex.* 8.

fellow, compare the living with the living, with his peers as in every other sphere – poets, dancers, athletes.

Demosthenes now brings in the example of an Athenian boxer called Philammon who had clearly won the Olympic games in recent years. Demosthenes points out that Philammon did not leave Olympia without a crown because he was not as strong as Glaucus of Carustus (a legendary sixth-century boxer who won victories in all four pan-hellenic games). He was crowned and proclaimed victor because he defeated those who entered the ring against him (319). Demosthenes then draws a lesson which subtly draws on this analogy to athletic contests: when 'loyalty to the state was the focus of public competition open to all' – and here he is referring to the Elatea assembly and its aftermath – Demosthenes was proved to be the clear winner (320). All he asks is that he be compared with contemporary rivals in such contests rather than be pitted against great men from the previous century.

These arguments from Demosthenes exhibit a great degree of critical distance and self-consciousness concerning the force and applicability of historical paradigms. He effectively historicises Aeschines' use of historical examples as an age-old tactic of liars and sycophants. Aeschines is just doing what malicious orators have always done. Even the likes of Miltiades and Themistocles were subjected to the βάσκανον πρᾶγμα of denigrating present conduct by comparing it with that of dead ancestors.[36] Of course Demosthenes himself uses the very tactic he is here criticising in his other speeches.[37] But he does not commit that hypocrisy in this speech. The closest he comes is to stress that Aeschines is no different from Demosthenes in not measuring up to the great leaders of the early fifth century.

This critical historicisation of Aeschines' use of history resonates beyond the immediate concern to sway the jury in this case. For it presents the use of commonly known models from the past to belittle politicians of the present as a *mere* topos designed to secure an unjust verdict on its victims.[38] What Demosthenes does here, in other words, is to enhance scepticism, suspicion and vigilance in his audience concerning the way in which historical common knowledge is presented

---

36 βάσκανος has negative connotations to do with sorcery, envy and (especially) sycophancy: J. Hesk, *Deception and Democracy in Classical Athens* (Cambridge: Cambridge University Press, 2000), p. 213 n. 33; Yunis, *Demosthenes*, p. 173.

37 E.g. Dem. 21.143–50; 23.196–203.

38 On similar debunkings of other topoi and their significance for thinking about rhetorical creativity, see J. Hesk, "'Despisers of the commonplace": Meta-topoi and para-topoi in Attic oratory', *Rhetorica* 25.4 (2007), pp. 361–84.

and applied in all future occasions in which they find themselves listening to arguments of the sort which Aeschines has put forward.

This is not to imply that juries might not also learn to be wary of Demosthenes' own 'historicising' arguments. Aeschines' prosecution speech in this trial actually anticipates these arguments, including his reference to Philammon and Glaucus (3.189). Aeschines says that boxers are measured against each other whereas those who ask for a crown from the city are measured against 'virtue itself' (πρὸς αὐτὴν τὴν ἀρετήν). Demosthenes can't expect to be crowned just because he can demonstrate that he is 'a better citizen than Pataecion'. (Pataecion is unknown to us but he was obviously a good and well-known negative example of a contemporary scoundrel.) The precision of this 'anticipation' makes it possible that Aeschines added it to his great passage on the glorious men and deeds of fifth-century history when he came to revise the speech for publication. Even so, it offers an Athenian readership another layer of critical distance and scepticism as they are shown how a historicising critique of historical exemplarity can itself be challenged by asserting that there are absolute values which are transhistorical. The likes of Themistocles and Miltiades embody virtues and standards of conduct which do not change.

So we have a back-and-forth process, whereby the applicability of alignment strategies based on commonly known examples is disrupted through a certain critical distance and self-consciousness about the use and abuse of historical argumentation. Juries would also have learned from an analogous process in a famous exchange between Demosthenes and Aeschines which actually cuts across two different trials. In *Against Timarchus*, Aeschines had contrasted the defendant's drunken and flailing performance as an orator with the modest, self-contained stances of bygone orators such as Solon, Pericles, Themistocles and Aristides (1.25–6). His evidence is the hand-in-cloak pose of Solon's statue in the agora on Salamis. In *On the False Embassy*, Demosthenes recalls this argument and makes the point that the locals informed him that the statue is merely fifty years old (19.251). Neither the sculptor nor even his grandfather was alive in Solon's day. Demosthenes thereby questions the assumption that the statue accurately memorialises Solon's characteristic oratorical demeanour and makes fun of the fact that Aeschines imitated that *schēma* to the jury (252). The implication is that Aeschines had succeeded in duping the jury with bogus historical evidence.

The statue reminded the jury of the values and laws which Timarchus was trampling on: it was a *sōphrosunēs paradeigma* ('a model of self-restraint', 19.251). Aeschines was using this visible monument to get the jury to vote in accordance with the sorts of collective commitment to right behaviour which the statue embodied. But Demosthenes uses the historical method of dating the evidence to show that Aeschines' alignment strategy was achieved at the cost of historical truth. He thereby contributes to his audience's general wariness about the legitimacy of such alignment strategies by subjecting them to historical method: date an artefact to see if the claims made about its significance are true. Demosthenes then realigns the exemplarity of Solon in his own favour (252–3):

> his mimicry did not include what, politically, would have been much more profitable than an attitude – a view of Solon's spirit and purpose, so widely different from his own. When Salamis had revolted, and the Athenian people had forbidden under penalty of death any proposal for its recovery, Solon, accepting the risk of death, composed and recited an elegiac poem, and so retrieved that country for Athens and removed a standing dishonour. Aeschines, on the other hand, gave away and sold Amphipolis, a city which the king of Persia and all Greece recognised as yours, speaking in support of the resolution moved by Philocrates.

Solon's Salamis elegy had a much better claim to being good historical evidence for Solon's virtues than the statue. And so, Demosthenes rams home the contrast between patriotic Solon and treacherous Aeschines. A jury may not have seen how they were being played by Demosthenes here but, once again, they were at least offered an example of how to test and critique an orator's historical claims through a form of historicising scepticism and suspicion about the evidence presented.

My final example of the way in which the orators contest the force and applicability of well-known historical paradigms comes from Aeschines' speech *On the Embassy*. It offers us a rare, if undoubtedly partial, representation of the way in which the significance of historical precedent was contested in the policy debates of the Assembly during the fourth century. Demosthenes' charge of ambassadorial misconduct against Aeschines partly rested on the claim that Aeschines had changed his tune during Assembly debates over whether to accept a peace agreement with Macedon. In response, Aeschines describes his own contribution to an Assembly debate as to whether to accept Philocrates' proposal of a peace (2.74–8). We hear how the opponents of peace attempted to compare their support for continuing hostilities to the victory at Salamis and how they urged the citizens to look to the Propylaea of the Acropolis and 'the tombs and trophies of our ancestors' (2.74). But Aeschines got up and pointed out that the Athenians should 'imitate our ancestors' wisdom (*euboulia*) but avoid their errors and ill-timed ambition' (*akairos phlionikia*, 75). He called on them to emulate Plataea, Salamis, Marathon, Artemisium and the heroic campaign of Tolmides. But he also enumerated fifth-century acts of folly which should be avoided: the Sicilian expedition and (especially) the corrupt Cleophon's refusal to accept peace on favourable terms with Sparta after Cyzicus and Arginousae (76). He then detailed the resulting folly (*aboulia*) of the Thirty Tyrants and their atrocities (77). Aeschines then links the historical lesson he delivered to the Assembly to the personal testimony and experience of his own family (77–8, tr. Carey):

> And I learned of these events not from outsiders but from my closest relative of all. Our father Atrometus, the man you insult though you do not know him and never saw the man he was in his youth – despite the fact, Demosthenes, that you're descended from Scythian nomads on your mother's side – went into exile under the Thirty and participated in the restoration of democracy. And our mother's brother, our uncle Cleobulus son of Glaucus of Acharnae, served with Demaenetus of the Buzygae when he defeated the Spartan admiral Chilon at sea. So the city's misfortunes are well-known family stories I have heard often.

Aeschines' point here is that he dared to speak of Athens' past failures and foolishness as well as its glories. He challenged a blind military hawkishness grounded in an idealised image of Athens' fifth-century adventures with a more critical and pragmatic stance in which Athens' history included terrible mistakes and their disastrous consequences. And that stance, he claims, was the product not of public knowledge or external influences but of the very personal and intimate first-hand knowledge and experience which he gained from his father and his family.

Obviously, this is meant to tug at the jury's heartstrings and represent Aeschines as an adviser of some acumen and daring, whose learning is homespun rather than bookish. He also shows that his application of historical judgement to the question of Philocrates' peace is ultimately derived from his own family's rootedness in the struggles of the city's past. Atrometus and Cleoboulus have fought on the side of the democrats and against the Spartans respectively. Their involvement in history underscores Aeschines' legitimacy in all senses and provides a contrast with Demosthenes' alleged Scythian blood. But Aeschines' description of the Assembly debate also shows us that the *dēmos* never had one settled or dominant set of historical paradigms which shaped and coordinated their actions and attitudes. Aeschines stressed the foolishness and the consequent suffering of his audience's ancestors as much as or more than their bravery and wisdom in order to make his point. Alignment strategies were questioned and countered with different selections and innovative framings of the past. Aeschines' rhetoric here also shows that it was sometimes important and effective to couch commonly known events in terms of the very personal, private and painful 'knowledge' of individuals and families.

Now, I stress that none of this deals a fatal blow to Ober's arguments about the crucial role that the creation and dispersal of common knowledge played in successfully aligning citizens in relation to public action problems. Ober sees innovation, new learning and critique as the lifeblood of the Athenian democracy's special success.[39] And he never claims that common knowledge was perfectly achieved or always correctly applied in Athens' legal or deliberative spheres. So, he could easily say that Demosthenes' and Aeschines' antagonistic and creative self-consciousness about historical examples are grist to his mill.

But Ober's emphasis on 'common knowledge' about the past as a resource for informing verdicts and deliberations which would be predictable and maintain certain commitments does not do full justice to the way in which historical examples are contested in Athenian oratory. We have seen that these orations from 345–330 BCE also encouraged juries to be aware that the making of knowledge is never a disinterested or neutral business; that it is one thing to know the past, but quite another to apply that knowledge fairly or usefully. For in Athens, the past is never presented to the present for its own sake. In that sense it was an awareness of the rhetoricity of the making of knowledge about the past in certain settings which was as useful as the making of the knowledge itself. That awareness means that we have to balance Ober's stress on the importance of public knowledge of the past as a means of aligning citizens with a concomitant emphasis on the law-courts' fostering of a critical and suspicious awareness that one is always being made subject to alignment.

---

39 Ober, *Democracy and Knowledge*, pp. 105, 122–3, 180–1.

13

PLATO AND THE STABILITY OF HISTORY

Kathryn A. Morgan

It is a difficult task to isolate a Platonic theory of history, and equally problematic to specify the function he thought historical discourse should perform. Plato surely knew the works of Herodotus and Thucydides, and also the more popular forms of historical discourse, as his masterly pastiche of the funeral oration in the *Menexenus* shows.[1] Like Thucydides, he never explicitly defines the genre we call 'history', preferring to speak of 'inquiry into ancient matters' or 'the truth about ancient matters'. When he talks about the authors of *suggramata*, technical treatises, he can envision works on law and government, medicine or rhetoric, but not (apparently) historical compositions. As we shall see, historical narrative in Plato strays into territory closely associated with myth, and part of the task of this chapter is to investigate the implications of this overlap. I shall be focusing my attention on a group of narratives from dialogues that are generally regarded as late and that allow us a good view of the sweep of the past: the *Statesman*, the *Timaeus* and *Critias*, and Book 3 of the *Laws*. All of them present a cosmic history marked by cataclysm and destruction, although each has a slightly different

The author wishes to express her thanks to Claudia Rapp, Andrea Nightingale, Alex Purves and Mario Telò.

1 R. Weil, *L''archéologie' de Platon* (Paris: C. Klincksieck, 1959), pp. 26, 45. For an example of Plato's intertextual relationship with Herodotus see the discussion of Plato's Solon in Egypt below. For Thucydides and Plato see S. Hornblower, *Thucydides* (Baltimore: Johns Hopkins University Press, 1987), pp. 112–25. For a recent discussion of the *Menexenus* (and connections with the funeral oration) see S. D. Collins and D. Stauffer, 'The challenge of Plato's *Menexenus*', *Review of Politics* 61 (1999), pp. 85–115; F. Pownall, *Lessons from the Past: The Moral Use of History in Fourth-Century Prose* (Ann Arbor: University of Michigan Press, 2004), pp. 38–64. On the whole I align myself with Loraux's view of the oration in the *Menexenus* as an ironic manipulation of generic commonplaces (N. Loraux, *The Invention of Athens*, tr. A. Sheridan (Cambridge, MA: Harvard University Press, 1986), pp. 176, 189, 264–70; first published as *L'invention d'Athènes: Histoire de l'oraison funèbre dans la 'cité classique'* (Paris: Mouton, 1981)).

flavour. Surveying these narratives will allow us to concentrate on some distinctive features of Plato's approach to the past: the way that the past and the investigation of it are cut off from the present, and the circumstances under which the past may be allowed to inform our current projects. After sketching the content of these cosmic histories, I shall look briefly at an influential paradigm for interpreting Plato's 'theory of history' before suggesting a change in focus: rather than asking whether Plato thought history conformed to a pattern, we should examine how he historicises the historiographic impulse and the role and usefulness he assigns to historical knowledge. In this connection it will prove significant that Plato constructs a universe where long-term accurate historical knowledge turns out to be both impossible and possibly irrelevant.

HISTORIES OF CATACLYSM

Issues of historical time and narrative are not prominent in Plato's early and middle dialogues. This is in keeping with their ethical focus; discussion centres on understanding the soul and its various virtues. The temporal perspective under which we are to view the soul is a long one, since the soul is immortal and will be reborn (*Resp.* 498c–d) and individual lifetimes are trivial in comparison with all of time (*Resp.* 608c–d). In some of the later dialogues, however, we see a greater interest in (truly universal) history and in the process by which historical narratives are constructed. The context of these accounts is cosmic history (analogous to the *longue durée* in which we must place the soul), and leaves room for the consideration (in *Statesman* and *Timaeus*) of the activity of a creator deity. These accounts all spring from the postulation of cosmic upheaval and deploy a particular historiographic strategy: that of the rationalisation of myth.

Let us start with the *Statesman*. Here (268d–269c) an Eleatic Stranger tells the younger Socrates that they must use a 'great myth' in their search for the definition of a king – particularly appropriate since young Socrates is only just beyond childhood.[2] In this instance the myths in question are, first, the story of Atreus and the reversal of the course of the sun and other heavenly bodies in the sky; second, that of the Age of Cronus; and third, autochthony.

---

2 For the connection between myth and childhood, see L. P. Brisson, *Plato the Myth Maker*, ed. and tr. G. Naddaf (Chicago: University of Chicago Press, 1998), pp. 62, 82–3; K. A. Morgan, *Myth and Philosophy from the Presocratics to Plato* (Cambridge: Cambridge University Press, 2000), pp. 175–7, 251–2.

All of these arise from the same event, and in addition to these countless others even more amazing than these, but because of the length of time some of them have faded from memory, while others are spoken of separately, scattered each from the other. No one has told the event that causes all of them, but it must now be told. For telling it will be fitting for our demonstration of the king.

The truth in question is that the world goes through phases in its rotation, in which God alternately helps the rotation and then lets go, so that the direction of rotation is reversed. Whenever a reversal occurs, there is great destruction (269c–271a). Autochthony belongs to a period of divine control under the rule of Cronus (271a–d), whereas sexual reproduction belongs to the current age and those like it (273e–274a). When god gives up control of the world, a gradual decline into chaos occurs because of the predominance of the bodily factor, and this, in the end, causes god to take control once more.[3] The 'history' in this scenario is fairly minimal and schematic, brought in to set up political analysis. It does, however, make use of the familiar historiographic trope of the fading of memory through time, and also the discovery of an underlying cause that explains a number of different phenomena. It also uses transformations of myth as basis for a new analysis. Like Hecataeus and Acusilaus with their rationalising narratives, the Stranger looks for a historical truth that lies behind mythological accounts.[4]

In the *Timaeus*, the focus shifts further (though not so very far) towards historical narrative as we would understand it and towards the processes by which such narratives are developed and transmitted. The action of both *Timaeus* and *Critias* is set in motion by Socrates' desire to see the ideal polis in action and performing something worthy of it (*Ti.* 19b–c). This desire will be fulfilled by the narration in summary (and partly also in full) of the story of the ancient struggle between the empire of Atlantis and Athens many thousands of years before. No one in Athens knows this story, apart from its narrator Critias and his family (and now his audience in the dialogue). How

3 This scenario of alternating revolutions is fraught with interpretative difficulties. Is our current age one controlled by deity or not? Is the 'Age of Cronus' in the myth opposed to the 'Age of Zeus' in terms of its revolution? Consideration of these problems is beyond the scope of this chapter, but G. R Carone, 'Reversing the myth of the *Politicus*', *CQ* 54 (2004), pp. 88–108, works through the issues in detail (with a review of the scholarship).

4 For Hecataeus and Acusilaus, see C. Fornara, *The Nature of History in Greece and Rome* (Berkeley: University of California Press, 1983), pp. 4–6; Morgan, *Myth and Philosophy*, pp. 65–6.

then has it been preserved? Because Solon once, we are told, brought the tale back from his travels in Egypt, where he had had an interesting encounter with an Egyptian priest. Of particular interest for us is the priest's assessment of Greek historical knowledge. He tells Solon, who is attempting to draw him out about the past, that the Greeks are intellectual children:

> 'You are all young,' he said, 'in your souls, for you have in them no ancient report from antique hearsay, nor any learning grey with age. The reason for this is the following: there have been and will be many destructions of mankind for many reasons, the greatest through fire and water, but other lesser ones because of countless different causes. The story that is told even by you – that Phaethon, the child of the Sun, once yoked his father's chariot, but because he was unable to drive along his father's route he burned some parts of the earth and was himself destroyed by a thunderbolt – this has the form of a myth, but the truth is a deviation of the heavenly bodies as they moved around the earth, and the destruction of the surface of the earth over a long period of time.' (*Ti.* 22b–d)

Once again Greek myths are presented as reflections of an underlying historical reality to which the Greeks themselves are oblivious. Greek ignorance means that they are unaware of the amazing story of ancient Athens and Atlantis, both cities founded by gods, where the former approximated the excellences of the ideal state of the *Republic* and the latter declined from ancient virtue into greed and imperialism.

In our third exhibit, *Laws* Book 3, the interlocutors, led by an Athenian Stranger, are trying to investigate the first beginning of a state, as part of their inquiry into laws and lawgivers, along with the development of virtue and vice.

> – I think [that we can study the development of vice and virtue in a city] starting from the expanse of time and our inexperience of it and the changes that take place in it.
> – What do you mean?
> – Well, do you think that you ever could learn the amount of time that has occurred in the period cities have existed and men have formed governments in them?
> – Not at all easily.
> – But it would be immense and impossible to grapple with?
> – Absolutely.

– So then, isn't it the case that countless cities in countless lands have come into existence among us during this time, and according to the same calculation of extent no fewer have been destroyed. And these cities have been governed with all forms of government at various times in every location. Sometimes they have become greater after being small and sometimes smaller after being great, and worse after being better and better after being worse. (*Leg.* 676a–c)

The immensity of historical time is an obstacle to detailed knowledge.[5] An interesting corollary is that almost any conceivable form of government has existed at some point. The task, therefore, is to discover the cause of change and in turn the basic form of a city. Yet the notion of the historical past as a kind of archive in which all possible political combinations and thus historical trajectories are stored challenges the significance of any one historical narrative. Any history one tells will be merely an example of a more general type. We shall see later how the account of the *Laws*, despite its claims to do justice to particular Greek histories, is in fact in thrall to a model of paradigmatic history. For the moment, however, we must return to the rationalisation of myth, which makes its appearance at *Leg.* 677a. Here the Stranger asks Clinias the Cretan:

– Do you think that ancient tales have a certain truth?
– What sort of tales?
– That there have been many destructions of mankind due to inundations and sicknesses and many other things, in which only a small part of mankind is left.
– Everyone thinks that something like this is credible.

Here in the *Laws* the Athenian Stranger's interlocutor finds nothing strange in the rationalising assumption that there is truth behind myths of disaster; it is so obvious as almost not to need comment. This is certainly not the case when the theory of cyclic destructions of mankind is presented in the *Timaeus* and the *Statesman*, where the Eleatic Stranger and the Egyptian priest are telling their respective audiences something they did not know before. The *Laws*, then, generates an atmosphere of consensus rather than revelation, and it is no accident that this occurs in a dialogue where the movement from

---

5 The adjectives *apleton* and *amēchanon* here ('immense' and 'impossible to grapple with') lend a heroic note, as though the investigator is wrestling with a monstrous beast.

past to present to future is most smoothly effected – a point to which we shall return.

In the *Timaeus*, *Statesman* and *Laws*, the problem with historical knowledge is not just the normal difficulty of finding out what happened long ago, but that cosmic obstacles are set in the way of investigation. If most of humanity is periodically wiped out by fires, floods and/or cosmic reversals, we have to deal not just with the problems of memory or partisanship, but also with cultural trauma as civilisation is periodically forced to begin anew. As we shall see, the cultures of each cycle have no understanding of the cycle that has preceded their own, or even of the fact (and its implications) that history is cyclic. Their viewpoint must, therefore, be chronologically parochial. The immensity of time envisaged by Plato's speakers is exponentially greater than that which causes problems for Herodotus and Thucydides, both of whom face the problem that knowledge is lost with the passage of time.[6] The great stretch of history in question in Plato's dialogues is not confined to the ages analysed by the Greek historians, but stretches back even further. To be sure, within our cycle our familiar historians may well have produced interesting accounts (which would, in turn, have to be judged by Platonic political and ethical standards), but the schema we have been sketching recontextualises them and thus changes their meaning, by projecting a future point after which both their knowledge and their methodology will be lost. The only cultural memory that survives the cycles is one of cosmic trauma and the past, as a result, becomes mythologised. Like early historicising rationalisers, Plato's authoritative speakers can strip away the mythological veil and reveal the more mundane truth underneath. There is, however, a difference. Investigators such as Hecataeus would rationalise myth by stripping away the marvellous to leave the merely credible (thus Heracles did not descend to the Underworld and defeat the hound of hell, but killed a particularly poisonous snake nicknamed the 'hound of Hades', *FGrHist* 1 F27). Plato's rationalisations work in the opposite direction, revealing a truth more terrifying and marvellous than we had expected: not Phaethon falling from his chariot, but the end of life as we know it. When the Eleatic Stranger in the *Statesman* mentions the myths of Atreus and Phaethon, he takes care to inform his audience that there are 'countless others even more amazing than these'.

The universe is, then, more surprising than we think. Plato's relentless focus on the big (cosmic) picture makes the work of the historians

---

6 Hdt. 1.1, Thuc. 1.1.3: 'What happened before [this war] and even earlier was impossible to discover because of the amount of time (σαφῶς μὲν εὑρεῖν διὰ χρόνου πλῆθος ἀδύνατα ἦν).' Cf. Weil, *L''archéologie' de Platon*, p. 17.

and historicising rationalisers of myth seem small by comparison. One way of understanding the contrast is to view it as reflecting the difference between cosmology (with its universal interests) and historiography (with its focus on *res gestae*). This is indeed a germane distinction, but what is most interesting for present purposes is that the kind of cosmos we inhabit (one characterised by catastrophe and discontinuity) dictates the nature of historiography and its connection with the discourse of myth.[7] The imposition of periodic catastrophe means that historical and mythological investigation must address issues of radical discontinuity. Moreover, because catastrophe creates cultural discontinuity and trauma, mythologising becomes an inescapable aspect of the investigation of the past, rather than (as it is for Thucydides) a poetic or sentimental tendency that can be overcome by the rigorous application of stringent methodological standards. The destruction of culture at the time of catastrophe would also entail the destruction of any historiographic standards. Popular myths about floods and conflagration are all that is left and access to long-term history is thus through rationalisation of myth, so that mythical patterns take a privileged and foundational role.

A PATTERN OF DECADENCE?

The recurrence of patterns of cataclysm has tempted some to read 'decadence' as Plato's governing notion of history. In 1951, R. G. Bury presented a succinct summary of this approach. We have seen already how in the *Statesman* the world slowly decays when god removes his hand from the tiller of the cosmos. This is caused by the bodily element in the cosmos, which gradually causes the world to move towards its original disharmony until it is in danger of destruction (at which point god again takes over) (273a–e). In the *Republic* the idealised polis is subject to decline: 'since everything that is born is subject to destruction, not even a constitution like this will endure for all time, but it will be dissolved' (8.546a). After this introduction, we are presented with the gradual degeneration of the city into tyranny. So too in the *Timaeus/Critias* we observe Atlantis sinking (so to speak) into vice and defeat because of the fading of the divine element in its kings and the concomitant growth of greed. Finally Book 3 of the *Laws* narrates the deterioration of the Dorian states (except for Sparta), as well as that of Athens and Persia (the representatives of pure democratic and monarchic constitutions).[8] If we add to this

---

7 A point also made in passing by Weil, *L''archéologie' de Platon*, pp. 13–14.
8 R. G. Bury, 'Plato and history', *CQ* 44 (1951), pp. 86–93, at pp. 86–9.

picture a nostalgic portrayal of the Age of Cronus in *Laws* Book 4 (713b–e), we have a temptingly simple picture of the pessimistic philosopher. In this approach, human greed and corruption, stemming from the bodily nature of the cosmos, dictate historical degeneration, on both the cosmic and the historic level. For Bury and other adherents of this approach, human nature gives shape to history: 'Ultimately all the phenomena, all the secondary causes of History are to be traced back to one and the same primary Cause, the Soul. That is the lesson which Plato would teach the historian: it is the core of his Philosophy of History.'[9] In a similar vein Raymond Weil argued that the pseudo-history of the *Timaeus*, a history that had all the virtues of myth, allowed Plato to define historical causality specifically as the rhythms of the world and the quality of souls. These two were interlinked: 'It is only through the mediation of passions that material causes operate.'[10] Thus cataclysms and heavenly declinations would be material causes that express psychic disturbances. We would be dealing with the operations of an en-souled cosmos where the pathetic fallacy of projecting human passions onto nature is no fallacy.

This line of interpretation, especially in its crude form, is overstated. It seems unlikely that the schematic presentation of psychic and civic decline into tyranny that we meet in the *Republic* is meant to reflect actual processes. This is surely one instance where we may fruitfully deploy Frutiger's notion that diachronic presentation in Plato can sometimes be a heuristic device for untangling a complex synchronic reality.[11] Andrea Nightingale has shown that Plato's scenario, particularly as we meet it in *Laws* Book 3, is much more complex than a simple tale of decline. In some ways humans progress over time while in others they lose valuable qualities; technology can be a blessing or a curse.[12] Neither progress nor decline is simple, and a narrative of increasing social complexity can be given either a positive or a nega-

---

9 Bury, 'Plato and history', p. 89.
10 Weil, *L''archéologie' de Platon*, p. 32. Weil allows that decadence is not inevitable, since god may intervene, but it seems clear that decline is the natural course in the absence of divine control. He concludes that Plato never harmonises accounts of progress and decadence.
11 P. Frutiger, *Les mythes de Platon* (Paris: F. Alcon, 1930), pp. 190–1.
12 A. Nightingale, 'Historiography and cosmology in Plato's *Laws*', *Ancient Philosophy* 19 (1999), pp. 299–326, at pp. 306–11. J. de Romilly, *The Rise and Fall of States According to Greek Authors* (Ann Arbor: University of Michigan Press, 1977), pp. 1–12, mounts a more general argument that imposing patterns of decadence on Greek authors (including Plato) is misguided. G. Naddaf, 'The Atlantis myth: An introduction to Plato's later philosophy of history', *Phoenix* 48 (1994), pp. 189–209, at pp. 200–3, 208, while arguing against Vidal-Naquet's version of the decadence thesis, also pushes for a reading of the *Laws* as expressing a 'wholly realizable solution' (p. 208) to problems of political deterioration.

tive cast. In the accounts of both *Timaeus/Critias* and *Laws* it is clear that the march of time brings improvement as well as decline; only the *Statesman* envisages a scenario of progressive and inevitable degeneration. This latter vision is connected to the role played by divinity. If the mythical part of the dialogue presents the world being wound up and running down like a spinning top under divine agency and its lack, then the social and political progression of humanity is connected to the issue of divine guidance. When the world is left to its own devices, it, and we, decline.[13]

We should guard against the notion that recurrent cataclysm comes as a kind of divine punishment for corruption. In the *Statesman*, the return of god to the helm, while it causes cataclysm, is in fact an amelioration of the situation. In *Timaeus*, Solon's Egyptian priest tells us that destruction comes whenever civilisation is advanced and at moderately regular intervals (except, of course, in the case of Egypt):

> each time your civilisation and that of others have just been equipped with letters and everything else cities need, then once again after the usual number of years a deluge comes sweeping down upon them from the skies like a plague and leaves only those who are illiterate and uncultured, so that once again you become young, as it were, and start from the beginning, knowing nothing of what happened here or in your own country in ancient times. (23a–b)

To be sure, the repeated floods talked about by the Egyptian priests are seen in terms of the gods purifying the earth with water (*Ti.* 22d), but when the cataclysm overwhelms corrupt Atlantis (in Critias' summary account), there is no indication that this is a punishment – for if it were it would be a punishment also for the virtuous Athenians whose exploits are celebrated in the myth.[14]

It is thus too reductive an interpretation of complex material to

---

13 Yet even here, the comments made by the Eleatic Stranger about the Age of Cronus make us doubt whether many ethical or intellectual advances were made when mankind was managed directly by god. At *Plt.* 272b–d he remarks that if humans in that age did not use their leisure for inquiry and philosophical discussion, their state would be inferior to our own. As J. Dillon, 'Plato and the golden age', *Hermathena* 153 (1992), pp. 21–36, at pp. 28–30, points out, it is by no means certain from the text that their leisure was so employed. For an optimistic reading of human progress in the *Statesman* myth, see Carone, 'Reversing the myth', esp. pp. 106–7.

14 See S. Broadie (2001), 'Theodicy and pseudo-history in the *Timaeus*', *OSAP* 21 (2001), pp. 1–28, at pp. 2–6, for an illuminating examination of how issues of theodicy are *not* connected with cataclysm in the *Timaeus* account.

read Platonic accounts of cataclysm as expressing a material reflection of the operation of the soul in history or as indications of some belief Plato may have held about the way the universe really works. It is doubtless true to say that the problematics of the human soul are central to any Platonic notion of history, but it is equally true to say that Thucydides thinks that human nature is the primary driver of historical change. The interest is in how this notion cashes out and what difference it makes in the kind of history that each of them envisions. Plato's pseudo-histories are not going to tell us anything about what really happened or even about what Plato thought really happened. It may be fruitful to sideline issues of divine governance and cosmic order in favour of a focus on cultural knowledge and on the operation of constructing history. Periodic destructions may (or may not) be a matter of divine purgation, but they are pre-eminently a fact of nature with particular cultural effects. We should note the convenience of the cyclic destruction scenario for these dialogues whose interests are so largely political. Each period of destruction creates an almost blank slate that can render more accessible, for theoretical purposes, the development of society and the identification of forces at work for change. The scenario functions as a heuristic device rather than emphasising a picture of history as decadence.

A BLANK SLATE

The creation of a cultural blank slate allows Plato's speakers to explore the role of historical knowledge within a developing society. This is most explicit in *Timaeus/Critias*, where the concern with the construction of historical models is central. It is here that, as we have seen, Greek methodological ignorance is foregrounded: Greeks are intellectual children because their historical sensibility does not take cyclic destruction into account (*Ti.* 22b–c). Greek ignorance of the rationalised truth thus comes as a revelation (in contrast to the *Laws*, where the principle of rationalisation is accepted as commonplace). According to the Egyptian priest the Greeks have no ancient knowledge. The periodic destruction of mankind in most areas means that only those who are without letters and without culture are left. As soon as cities anywhere start to acquire the attributes of civilised life, the destruction comes again. At the beginning of the *Critias*, Critias explains how only the names of historical actors survive in oral tradition:

[Hephaestus and Athena put good men in Attica] whose names have been preserved, but whose deeds have disappeared due to the destructions of their successors and the expanse of time. For the race that remained on each occasion, as was said previously, was left behind in the mountains and without writing, a race that had heard only the names of those who had been powerful in the land and few things connected with their deeds. So they were happy to give their names to their offspring, since they did not know the excellence and the laws of those who came before, unless it was shadowy traditions about them. This was because they and their children existed in want of the necessities of life for many generations, and they directed their attention to the necessities they lacked. They therefore directed their discourse also to those things and neglected those that had taken place previously and long ago. For mythology and inquiry into ancient matters arrive in cities along with leisure, when they see that people are provided with the necessities of life, but not before that (μυθολογία γὰρ ἀναζήτησίς τε τῶν παλαιῶν μετὰ σχολῆς ἅμ' ἐπὶ τὰς πόλεις ἔρχεσθον, ὅταν ἴδητόν τισιν ἤδη τοῦ βίου τἀναγκαῖα κατεσκευασμένα, πρὶν δὲ οὔ). In this way the names of the ancients were preserved without their deeds. (*Crit.* 109d–110a)

Similarly in the primitive city of the *Laws* specialist cultural knowledge is lost for thousands of years. The survivors are unsophisticated, with no expertise in politics or anything else. Musical culture is quite recent: within the last two or three thousand years, that is, 'yesterday or the day before'. Indeed, the Athenian comments 'if these advances [made in previous cycles] had survived through all of time embellished to the point that they are now, how would anything new ever be discovered?' (*Leg.* 677b–d). We find, moreover, that in the first stages of renewal before the return of cities, humans were naive (εὐήθεις, 679c). When they heard something called good or bad they thought they were hearing the truth and believed it, 'for nobody was clever enough to suspect a lie, as they do now' (679d). This had its advantages. People were more just, more courageous, more truthful, more pious. Yet it takes only a moment's reflection to see that this absence of a critical attitude would be fatal to the development of an analytic historical sensibility. As Thucydides says, 'men accept from each other the traditions of their predecessors, even if they concern their own countries, with a uniform lack of scrutiny . . . for the majority make no effort in the investigation of the truth and they turn rather to what is ready at hand' (1.20).

In the wake of cataclysms, then, the human race loses not only agriculture and metallurgy, but a cultural and, above all, a historical sensibility. The absence of a critical mindset in the early civilisation of the *Laws* and the *Timaeus/Critias* is clear. In the *Critias* passage cited above, mythology and historical inquiry are paired as cultural products of the leisured city. We can gloss them as the reporting of cultural hearsay and the attempt to investigate that hearsay more closely. History is thus marked as an advanced cultural product while simultaneously being set in a cosmic framework that renders its project intellectually troubling, since it is difficult to see how much real progress will ever be made given that destruction follows relatively closely on the heels of literacy. The cosmos guarantees a trajectory of steady socialisation and increasing complexity, a narrative that might well be thought to be one of progress, only to send the human race back to the drawing board. Ethical simplicity and its advantages come at the expense of intellectual sophistication, and we should note that philosophy as it is configured in Platonic dialogues is also a product of leisure culture.[15] No one who is obsessed with achieving a subsistence level of existence will show an interest in either philosophy or history. Both will be elite activities.

It is also instructive to look at the issue of Greek historical naivety from the standpoint of its Herodotean predecessor. As has long been recognised, Plato's portrayal of Solon and the Egyptians in the *Timaeus* looks back to a scene in Herodotus (and indirectly Hecataeus) where Herodotus tells of his visit to Egypt (2.142–3).[16] Herodotus narrates how the Egyptians count 341 uninterrupted generations from the first to the last king of Egypt (for a total of 11,340 years). They tell also how the sun twice changed its direction during their history (twice rising from where it currently sets and vice versa), but added that this did not affect Egypt at all: there was no change in the way people died or in the way they were affected by disease. He juxtaposes this encounter with a vignette of the experiences of his predecessor, Hecataeus, who had made the same trip and tried to trace his own genealogy back sixteen generations to a god. The priests, says Herodotus, cast doubt on these calculations and proposed alternative genealogies (showing to their own satisfaction that no man had been born of a god within 345 generations). The next three chapters in Book 2 cast a sceptical eye upon Greek versus Egyptian religious traditions and lead to Herodotus' conclusion on the subject of Pan and Dionysus that 'they [the Greeks] trace their genealogy from the time they first learned of them' (2.146).

Plato   has   developed   this   material   on   Greek   genealogical

---

15 Morgan, *Myth and Philosophy*, pp. 176–7.
16 Weil, *L''archéologie' de Platon*, p. 15; C. Gill, 'Plato's Atlantis story and the birth of fiction', *Ph&Lit* 3 (1979), pp. 64–78, at p. 75.

inadequacy. Herodotus' narrative has several goals: to establish the Egyptians as historical experts whose authority is based on precise record-keeping, to undermine the notion that any living Greek could be a descendant of a god, and to suggest that the Greeks are working with a drastically foreshortened timescale. In Plato this last point is thematised and made even more explicit. In Herodotus, the Greeks just have it wrong; in Plato we learn that 'You Greeks are always children – there is no old Greek . . . You are all young in your souls, for you have in them no ancient report from antique hearsay, nor any learning grey with age' (22b). Inaccuracy and pretension are replaced by chronic intellectual disability. The cycle of catastrophe means that Greeks are perpetually psychic children. Besides developing the motif of Greek immaturity, Plato also deepens the significance of the solar reversals mentioned by the Egyptians. These anticipate both the reversals of the *Statesman* and the deviations of the heavenly bodies in the *Timaeus*, although these latter do not affect Egypt (22c–e). Both Herodotus' history and the *Timaeus* present the immunity of Egypt, but in Plato's account it is clear, as it is not in Herodotus, that the rest of the world is subject to disasters, and that these very disasters are the root cause of Greek historical disability. Plato expands and merges the disparate elements of Herodotus' account into one unified picture, and in so doing he one-ups the historiographic trope (Greeks in the face of superior historical authority) that the historian had formulated.[17]

The development of historical investigation, even in its most basic mythological form, is marked by cultural belatedness. The cosmic structure of cataclysm guarantees that this must always be the case. Yet, as noted above, the structure is also extremely useful as a heuristic convenience. This impression is reinforced in the passage of the *Laws* referred to above, where the Stranger dismisses the possibility of carry-over from cycle to cycle. If too much knowledge survived from a previous cycle, how could we isolate and investigate new discoveries? How could the conversation of *Laws* 3 achieve its goal of discovering the principle of change in history? Starting civilisation repeatedly with a modified blank slate is an opportune device for those with 'scientific' interests in state formation and performance.[18] A similar impulse

17 In making Solon, rather than Herodotus or Hecataeus, his Egyptian traveller, Plato is reinforcing a preference stated earlier, that philosopher-statesmen are superior to poets and sophists when it comes to narrating the distinguished exploits of cities.

18 It is no accident that the cyclic structure discussed here matches in some respects the fate of the individual soul in dialogues (such as *Phaedrus*, *Republic* and *Timaeus*) where individual souls undergo multiple incarnations but start each one with some memory, perhaps a dim one, of the real nature of the universe that they experience while disincarnate. They access this realm through recollection,

towards the creation of a blank slate is harnessed in the *Republic* to ethical and political ends. The famous Noble Lie (*Resp.* 414b–415d), taken in conjunction with other passages about philosophic rule, is a perfect example of the need to start from scratch and wipe out the past. In Book 3, the Lie itself envisages an ideal situation where all of the citizens can be brought to believe that their own vision of their past was a dream, and that they have, on the contrary, just been born from the earth already assigned to certain metallic social and intellectual classes. In Book 6, Socrates suggests that philosopher kings will take the city and the characters of its citizens as if they were a drawing tablet and then draw the outlines of the just city. First, however, they will have to clean the tablet, and this is not easy (501a). So it is that in Book 7 the founders of the ideal city once entrusted with rule will banish everyone over the age of ten and then bring up the children in virtue (540d–541a). If we adjust for the different interests of this dialogue, we can see that the founders here are anticipating the kind of cultural erasure achieved by cataclysms in the later dialogues, the difference being that knowledgeable representatives of the philosophical way of life survive the social trauma. In the *Republic*, social and ethical engineering replaces the construction of history we will see in the later dialogues.

MYTH AND HISTORY

I ended the first part of this chapter with the assertion that Platonic cataclysms exist precisely for the sake of rendering historical inquiry a matter of mythologising, so that the collocation that has been of such interest to scholars, that of history and myth, is guaranteed by cosmic structure. There is a general consensus that *mythologia* and history are closely related in Plato.[19] In this and the following section we shall examine this relationship in more depth, first taking as our starting point Socrates' theorising of it in the *Republic*, and then proceeding to the problematic transition from myth to history (a moment that

(footnote 18 *continued*)
a form of memory. These recollective memories thus correspond to the vague traditions (perhaps only names) that, as has been noted above, the survivors of cataclysms bring with them into their new world and then pass on.
19 See in particular C. Gill, 'The genre of the Atlantis story', *CPh* 72 (1977), pp. 287–304; C. J. Rowe, 'Myth, history and dialectic in Plato's *Republic* and *Timaeus-Critias*', in R. Buxton (ed.), *From Myth to Reason? Studies in the Development of Greek Thought* (Oxford: Oxford University Press, 1999), pp. 263–78. Cf. M. Detienne, *The Writing of Orpheus: Greek Myth in Cultural Context*, tr. J. Lloyd (Baltimore: Johns Hopkins University Press, 2002), pp. 146–9 (first published as *L'écriture d'Orphée* (Paris: Gallimard, 1989)).

had exercised both Herodotus and Thucydides) in *Laws* and *Timaeus/Critias*.

One of the core passages for the mingling of myth and history in Plato is *Republic* 2.382c–d. The context is the famous discussion on the censorship of poetry considered untrue and harmful. After a discussion of the iniquity of *real* falsehood, namely falsehood in the soul, Socrates passes on to the question of falsehood in words. This can sometimes be useful and thus does not deserve our hatred. We could use it against enemies, or as a medicine for a friend, or 'in the mythical tales we were just now speaking about, because we do not know what the truth is about ancient matters, we make them useful by likening falsehood to truth' (καὶ ἐν αἷς νυνδὴ ἐλέγομεν ταῖς μυθολογίαις, διὰ τὸ μὴ εἰδέναι ὅπῃ τἀληθὲς ἔχει περὶ τῶν παλαιῶν, ἀφομοιοῦντες τῷ ἀληθεῖ τὸ ψεῦδος ὅτι μάλιστα, οὕτω χρήσιμον ποιοῦμεν). The main focus of the passage as a whole is a critique of poets who represent the gods as liars: no god would need to make up stories about the past because he did not know (διὰ τὸ μὴ εἰδέναι τὰ παλαιὰ ἀφομοιῶν ἂν ψεύδοιτο), Socrates goes on to say, and so there is no lying poet in god (2.382d). It is significant, however, that Socrates dismisses, almost in passing, the possibility of knowing anything about ancient matters. This does not, of course, preclude that one might have accurate knowledge about the more recent past, but it does remind us, for example, of Thucydides' frank avowal of the difficulty of accurate knowledge about what happened before the Peloponnesian War (τὰ γὰρ πρὸ αὐτῶν καὶ τὰ ἔτι παλαίτερα σαφῶς μὲν εὑρεῖν διὰ χρόνου πλῆθος ἀδύνατα ἦν, 1.1.3), a difficulty he solves by making inferences about the past based on what he sees in the present.[20]

Socrates' comment locates inquiry about the past firmly in the realm of poetic endeavour; historical reconstruction is a matter of informed inference, ideally governed by principles of moral utility. The comment is also a pointed reworking of the announcement of the Muses in Hesiod's *Theogony*, 'we know how to speak many false things like genuine things, but also how to proclaim true things, when we wish' (ἴδμεν ψεύδεα πολλὰ λέγειν ἐτύμοισιν ὁμοῖα, / ἴδμεν δ' εὖτ' ἐθέλωμεν ἀληθέα γηρύσασθαι, *Theog.* 27–8).[21] Plato makes Socrates

20 Cf. J. Morrison, 'Preface to Thucydides: Rereading the Corcyrean conflict (1.24–55)', *ClAnt* 18 (1999), pp. 94–131, at pp. 101–2.
21 E. Belfiore, 'Lies unlike the truth: Plato on Hesiod, *Theogony* 27', *TAPA* 115 (1985), pp. 47–57, considers *Republic* 2 to be an exploration of Hesiod's claims about the Muses, concluding that Socrates' statements at 382d are focused on matters (gods, heroes and the Underworld) about which no facts can be ascertained. See also L. H. Pratt, *Lying and Poetry from Homer to Pindar: Falsehood and Deception in Archaic Greek Poetics* (Michigan: University of Michigan Press, 1993), pp. 147–8,

cleave this declaration down the middle: poets may well liken the false to the true, because they do not know anything (and the ignorance of mortals is of course an epic commonplace), but no god would do so. In Hesiod we are dealing with a statement of perceived theological fact; in Thucydides and Plato with a methodology of extrapolation (note that the 'likeness' word is adjectival in Hesiod (ὁμοῖα) but verbal in Plato (ἀφομοιοῦντες/ἀφομοιῶν)).[22] Socrates theorises the extrapolation of the false from the true, although the precise valence of 'false' here is difficult to specify. One solution is to deploy the problematic category of fiction. If falsehood, *pseudos*, is taken to mean 'fiction', then we would have a statement that we create fiction by extrapolating from the truth.[23] The use of *pseudos* would put the focus squarely on fabrication, with Socrates' prescription that the object of the exercise should be utility. Or one might interpret *pseudos* as what is unverifiable. Either solution downgrades the importance of historical inquiry.[24] For Socrates, ancient history can only ever be used for ethical and paradigmatic purposes; it is in principle unknowable. Only after systematic extrapolation has taken place can the material be 'useful'.

Historical narration is thus always interested and often creative ('poetic'). Socrates' general statement in the *Republic* connecting narratives of the past with mythology and falsehood should be associated with the cycles of cataclysm in other dialogues. All reflect a desire that reconstruction of ancient history shall start from first principles. In the *Republic* the starting place is the lying and immoral tales of poets about the past, which are themselves examples of reconstruction and extrapolation and must also undergo transformation in order to make

(footnote 21 *continued*)
who, with Gill, 'Plato's Atlantis story', pp. 66–70, understands the distinction as one 'between factual truth and representative truth'.

22 For further considerations on extrapolation in Thucydides, see J. Morrison, 'Memory, time, and writing: Oral and literary aspects of Thucydides' *History*', in C. J. Mackie (ed.), *Oral Performance and its Context* (Leiden: Brill, 2004), pp. 95–116, at pp. 98–100.

23 Gill, 'Plato's Atlantis story', p. 76, argues that in the Atlantis myth of the *Timaeus and Critias*, Plato is playing the 'game of fiction . . . presenting the false as true', although he later disavowed the utility of fiction as an analytic category in Plato (C. Gill, 'Plato on falsehood – not fiction', in C. Gill and T. P. Wiseman (eds), *Lies and Fiction in the Ancient World* (Exeter: Exeter University Press, 1993), pp. 38–87, at pp. 46, 51, and *passim*).

24 For Brisson, *Plato the Myth Maker*, pp. 91–102, the discourse of *mythos* in Plato is in principle unfalsifiable because its referent is inaccessible to the intellect or belongs to a distant past of which an author has no experience. Faced with our problematic passage in *Republic* 2, he explains the connection of myth with false discourse by positing a change in perspective whereby standards of truth and falsity have changed, now confirming to the higher discourse of the philosopher (pp. 105–9).

them useful.[25] In *Statesman*, *Timaeus* and *Laws* the cosmos itself guarantees the truth of Socrates' assertion in the *Republic* that we cannot really know about the distant past. Adam remarks tartly in his commentary on the *Republic* that 'Plato seems to have supposed that ancient history and mythology could be manufactured to order',[26] and this seems to be largely justified. The ethical and political usefulness of any given narrative is primary.

Saying that that Plato produces a mythologised history thus means both that myth and history are intertwined for him at the level of methodology, and that when he refers to historical or quasi-historical events he uses them to make a moral or political point.[27] The Atlantis myth is an obvious and acknowledged example of this. I have argued elsewhere that Plato's presentation of the myth in *Timaeus/Critias* foregrounds the transformation of history into myth and vice versa. On the one hand, the war between Athens and Atlantis is a moralised transposition and amalgamation of the Persian and Peloponnesian Wars, together with Athenian ambitions for regaining empire in the fourth century at the time of the Social War. This is history mythologised to make the moral clearer: land power (good) against sea power (bad), the temptations of empire (bad), lawfulness and austerity against opulence and greed.[28] Yet the narrative also models explicitly and outrageously the transferral of the idealised and mythologised state of the *Republic* into the world of history. The interlocutors in the dialogue assert and accept that these events really happened. Critias remembers the story of Athens and Atlantis that Solon told his grandfather Critias, and proposes to use it to satisfy Socrates' desire for an account that will set into narrative motion the ideal citizens of a state like that which we see outlined in the *Republic*. Socrates is delighted: the deed of the ancient Athenians is 'not merely spoken of, but actually happened' (οὐ λεγόμενον μέν, ὡς δὲ πραχθὲν ὄντως, 21a). The ideal state

---

25 The *Republic*'s 'Noble Lie' is itself an example of this utilitarian employment of mythical/historical narrative, as Gill, 'Plato on falsehood', pp. 52–4, points out, rightly connecting it with *Resp.* 382c–d.

26 J. Adam, *The Republic of Plato*, 2 vols (Cambridge: Cambridge University Press, 1902), vol. 1, p. 123.

27 Not that moralising history is unique to Plato. Indeed, whatever we think of the moral didacticism (implicit or explicit) of Herodotus and Thucydides, fourth-century historians contemporary with and subsequent to Plato were certainly obtrusive in their treatment of the past as a moral paradigm (see Pownall, *Lessons from the Past*).

28 K. A. Morgan, 'Designer history. Plato's Atlantis story and fourth-century ideology', *JHS* 118 (1998), pp. 101–18. See also the important studies of P. Vidal-Naquet, 'Athènes et l'Atlantide: Structure et signification d'un mythe platonicien', *REG* 77 (1964), pp. 420–44, and L. P. Brisson, 'De la philosophie politique à l'épopée: Le "Critias" de Platon', *RMM* 75 (1970), pp. 402–38.

that was described 'as if in myth' (ὡς ἐν μύθῳ) will now be transferred to the realm of truth (ἐπὶ τἀληθές) (26c–d). The tale, he adds, has the great advantage of 'not being an invented *mythos* but a true *logos*' (μὴ πλασθέντα μῦθον ἀλλ' ἀληθινὸν λόγον, 26e). We move from an account that was mythologised according to a set of principles to something that actually happened and is true (except, of course, that it is not).

In the case of Atlantis, the transition from myth to history is a conceptual one and showcases the similarity of the two types of narrative, as well as the differences. Yet it is clear that Plato's treatment of the story is intended to evoke historiography. The specifics of the communication of the story from Solon to Critias' grandfather to Critias himself have been constructed to demonstrate the mechanics of oral (or mostly oral) transmission.[29] As Gill has remarked, the circumstantial details of the narrative itself are elaborated beyond what one might expect from an account whose only purpose is to illustrate a moral.[30] It is, therefore, an attractive suggestion that in the later part of his writing career Plato's interest in history and prehistory increased.[31] The final section of this chapter will explore the limits of this interest. If it is true that Plato became authentically interested in generalising from historical realia, this might pose a challenge to my contention that he creates a universe where history is impossible. We shall see that, despite claims to the contrary, the survey of Greek history in Book 3 of the *Laws* is no real exception to the practice of mythologised history.

MOVING FROM MYTH TO HISTORY IN THE *LAWS*

If the story of Atlantis in the *Timaeus* shows Plato 'playing the game of being a historian',[32] then his survey of respective pasts of the Dorian kingdoms of the Peloponnese, of Athens and of Persia in *Laws* Book 3 has been accorded even greater significance. The purpose of the interlocutors in this part of the discussion is to analyse the cities of the past in order to be able to see what causes civic change historically, and although the interlocutors are clearly envisioning an exercise in abstraction, the approach here is meant to be inductive (676c).[33] Book 3 was called by Weil Plato's 'archaeology' and is seen

---

29 And have been so studied: Brisson, *Plato the Myth Maker*, pp. 25–39.
30 Gill, 'Plato's Atlantis story', p. 74.
31 Gill, 'Genre of the Atlantis story', pp. 294, 299; cf. Gill, 'Plato's Atlantis story', pp. 75–6.
32 Gill, 'Plato's Atlantis story', p. 75.
33 Gill, 'Genre of the Atlantis story', p. 301: 'the interest in . . . surveying historical events to formulate descriptive generalizations'.

by him as marking a change in Plato's approach to historical material. Weil acknowledges that Plato's fabrications of history are designed to make a point, but also suggests that history becomes more and more important for Plato until, in the *Laws*, we leave the realm of legend and are presented with a systematic history of events.[34] Here too there is a commingling of myth and history, as stories of cyclic cataclysm give way to events known from other sources,[35] but what Plato is doing is serious history. Even champions like Weil, however, concede that the historical sketch in *Laws* 3 is schematic, reductive and partly imaginary. Quite apart from the discontinuities of civilisation dealt with in the first part of this chapter, the part of the narrative that focuses on Greece in (what we call) the historical period is hugely superficial; nobody would ever consult *Laws* 3 to find out what actually happened. It is, again, moralising history: the account of the foundation of the three Dorian kingdoms of Argos, Messenia and Lacedaemonia, where early hopes for law-abiding and virtuous monarchies are dashed, is followed by the juxtaposition of Athens and Persia as the two foundational types of government: democracy and monarchy. Both start out well but end badly: the Athenians lose their habit of obedience to the laws and the Persian monarchs are overcome by arrogance and ambition. If we ask where 'history' resides in this account, we must reply that we recognise the narratives because we already know them from elsewhere. We would not use them as a basis for historical reconstruction.

What, then, are we to make of the marked transition made by the Athenian Stranger from the time of myth to a time within the intellectual grasp of the present? This move is, of course, made both by Herodotus and Thucydides. Herodotus (1.5) contrasts the stories of Io, Helen and others with the man whom he himself knows first to have committed aggression towards the Greeks. Thucydides (1.1), in turn, is unwilling to trust hearsay even about the events immediately preceding the Peloponnesian War, not to mention the stories about remote antiquity. Where does the Stranger draw the line? His narrative had started, as we have seen, with the certainty that civilisations are periodically destroyed. He follows this with his reconstruction of early societies and urbanisation, starting at the point where all specialist knowledge was lost for tens of thousands of years. There was no city or legislation, no war or *stasis*, since people were lonely and therefore sociable: simple good men, living probably under a kind of patriarchal royalty. Slowly larger communities developed, as did

---

34 Weil, *L''archéologie' de Platon*, pp. 32–3.
35 Weil, *L''archéologie' de Platon*, pp. 43–6.

legislation, followed by the emergence of aristocracies and monarchies. Finally came cities, and, to cut a long story short, the Trojan
War and the return of the Dorians to the Peloponnese. This is the
point at which the Stranger chooses to sum up what has preceded and
make a new beginning: 'We looked at a first and second and third city,
succeeding each other, we think, in their foundations in the immense
stretches of time, but now this our fourth city or if you wish, race, has
arrived, founded in the past and still now founded' (683a–b).

This is an important transition. At 682e the Stranger had referred
to the Lacedaemonian traditions of the return of the Dorians:
'everything that happened next [after the Dorians reassembled],
you Lacedaemonians recount in your traditions (μυθολογεῖτε).' The
moment of the foundation of Lacedaemon, however, marks the end
of a digression that began in Book 1: 'We have arrived back again, as
if by divine dispensation, at the very place from which we digressed
in our discussion about laws, and our discourse gets a good hold, for
it has come to the actual foundation of Lacedaemon' (682e–683a). It
also gives the Stranger the opportunity to make his new beginning
now that he has arrived at a city 'founded in the past and still now
founded'. The next step is to ask his interlocutors to project themselves into the time when the three Dorian cities were founded in the
Peloponnese:

> Let us transport ourselves in our minds to that time (γενώμεθα δὴ
> ταῖς διανοίαις ἐν τῷ τότε χρόνῳ) when Lacedaemon and Argos and
> Messene and those areas subject to them had come pretty much
> under the control of your forefathers, Megillus. As for what fol-
> lowed, they resolved, as the myth/tradition says (ὥς γε λέγεται τὸ
> τοῦ μύθου), to divide the host into three parts and settle the three
> cities of Argos, Messene, and Lacedaemon. (683c–d)

The foundation of Lacedaemon is where the interlocutors can get a
good grip, where mythological traditions transform themselves into
knowable and useful material so that the discussion can engage with
the central issue of constitutions. It is, Weil remarks, the point where
the history of the three Dorian states really starts.[36]

It is also the moment where the Stranger obtrusively marks the
convergence of history and theory. After naming the three original
kings of the Dorian kingdoms, he declares that everyone swore at
that time to come to the aid of the kings if anyone tried to undermine
them. He then returns to an axiom he says they established earlier in

36 Weil, *L'archéologie' de Platon*, p. 44.

the conversation: 'By Zeus, is any kingdom or rule ever dissolved by any force other than itself? Or shall we now forget that when we came across these arguments a little previously we made this hypothesis?' (683e).[37] They now have the chance to see this axiom in action:

> So now we shall confirm this point, for we have arrived at the same conclusion having come across deeds that happened, as it seems (ἔργοις γενομένοις, ὡς ἔοικεν), so that we shall not search for the same conclusion in the matter of something empty (οὐ περὶ κενόν τι), but in the matter of something that happened and is true (περὶ γεγονός τε καὶ ἔχον ἀλήθειαν). (683e–684a)

The Stranger then proceeds to reconstruct a series of foundational oaths and laws, together with measures for land distribution (measures that worked particularly well because there was no reason to object to the land allotments and there were as yet no long-terms debts – a blank slate again) (684d–e). In the sections that follow the interlocutors speculate on the causes for the decline and corruption of two of the three foundations (Argos and Messene) and the preservation of Lacedaemon.

This sequence of narrative and argument is noteworthy. The moment of foundation is presented as decisive for the nature of the tradition (one that now relies on events that took place) and it also sets up the opportunity for confirmation of *a priori* assumptions (in this instance the hypothesis that governments fall only through their own faults). The collocation is not an innocent one. At the point where we embark on the analysis of a period that is clearly meant to be less conjectural and mythical than what has come before, the Stranger introduces a principle of history (governments fall through their own faults) that will govern our interpretation of the historical period (the examination of the events that really happened, we note, is supposed to *confirm* this principle). The lesson is repeated again at 688d and its universal application to past, present, and future is underlined: '[that the three Dorian kings fell not through cowardice or military ignorance but through vice and folly] that these things happened like this in the past, and happen now too in similar cases and will happen like this in the future, I shall try to discover by going through the narrative and reveal to you, my friends, to the best of my ability'. Yet we are also supposed to be reassured, somehow, by the assurance that we are

---

37 It is troubling, of course, that this axiom has not been previously stated in the course of the *Laws*; cf. E. B. England (ed.), *The Laws of Plato*, 2 vols (Manchester: Manchester University Press, 1921), vol. 1, pp. 360–1 ad 683e5.

now dealing with fact rather than abstract discussion.[38] What guarantees the authenticity of the procedure, it seems, is that the major player in the scenario, Lacedaemon, is still in existence.

When we examine the reconstruction of the failures of the Dorian cities produced by the Stranger, we see that it is, indeed, an exercise in historical imagination designed to produce useful conclusions. Thus it is 'pretty clear' that the purpose of their alliance was protection against enemies (685b–c). It is likely (εἰκός) that the founders expected their constitutional arrangements to last (to which Megillus responds 'Of course it's likely') (686a). The decline of Argos and Messene must have started when the kings became arrogant and eager for luxury, as 'most instances' suggest (τὸ μὲν εἰκὸς καὶ τὸ πολύ, 691a). It is, moreover, possible to 'guess most reasonably' (μετριώτατα τοπάσαι) what happened in the past (691d). The entire sequence is a conjectural reconstruction.[39] This is, of course, no sin in itself. Historians always work with and manipulate what is plausible in order to create their vision of the past, and the criterion of likelihood was an obvious and favoured option when dealing with events in the heroic past.[40] Yet when we juxtapose this narrative of Dorian decline and (partial) preservation with the statements of the Athenian Stranger considered above (on the happy arrival at the territory of hard facts), it is hard not to feel discomfort. In spite of the rhetoric of change from myth to what actually happened, the material on one side of the divide is just as conjectural as that on the other. The methodology is continuous.

Why then does Plato make his Stranger choose the foundation of Sparta as the transition to the realm of the verifiable, the *spatium historicum*? This issue is all the more pressing because both Herodotus and Thucydides had made their historical space commence much later, with Croesus and the fifth century respectively. Plato, by contrast, pushes back many centuries before them. He may not have been the first to draw the line where he did. Ephorus (later in the fourth century) began his universal history with the return of the Heracleidae (that is, the arrival of the Dorians), and was probably acting upon precedent. As Fornara remarks, 'It cannot be coincidence that Hellanicus of Lesbos, a strong influence on Ephorus, had terminated his many mythographical works precisely at this point.'[41] Yet even if Plato does make historical time begin where Hellanicus ended the ages of myth, we still need to explain why he used Hellanicus as his model here.

---

38 If this is what *kenon* means (cf. England, *Laws*, p. 361 ad 683e9).
39 Weil, *L'archéologie' de Platon*, p. 44.
40 Fornara, *Nature of History*, p. 8.
41 Fornara, *Nature of History*, p. 9.

This must partly be because of the dialogue's interest in constitutions and constitutional change. In order to be able to verify any political hypothesis, his investigators had to have enough time to work with to be able to see a process of change. He has also placed his transitional point far enough back for the momentum of his reconstruction to carry him through the subsequent histories of Athens and Persia.

Most important, however, is that the point of transition is a point of continuity. The historical sketch had started with the observation that many cities had come into existence and perished in the great length of time; the foundation of Lacedaemon, however, marks the stage where the past reaches through into the present, a point of stability (at least in the case of Sparta). The city (or 'race') was 'founded in the past and [is] still now founded' (683a),[42] and its history proves congruent with previously suggested political truths. As we saw in the previous section, this technique is familiar from the Atlantis narrative of the *Timaeus*, which was motivated by Socrates' desire to see ideal citizens in action. Socrates was curious about Critias' proposed narrative: 'But what kind of deed done by this city was this one that Critias narrated according to what Solon heard, a deed that was not merely spoken of but really happened?' (οὐ λεγόμενον μέν, ὡς δὲ πραχθὲν ὄντως, 21a), and was pleased that a state described described 'as if in myth' would now be transferred to the realm of truth (ἐπὶ τἀληθές) (26c–d). He makes much of the fact that the details of the Atlantis story match precisely the abstract entity that had been hypothesised by previous discussion, and that it is *absolutely true*. The *Laws* presents just the same movement from an account that was mythologised according to a set of principles to something that actually happened. Yet in neither dialogue are we (most of us) in any danger of believing this – no more than we believe the Athenian Stranger's account of the degeneration of Athens and Persia later in Book 3. The stories of historical Athens, Sparta, Argos, Messene and Persia are very much like those of Atlantis. We are offered a demonstration of the congruence between history and theory. In the case of Atlantis, the Egyptian priests who preserve the story act as guarantors of historiographical continuity even as the Greeks themselves are catastrophically cut off from their past. In the *Laws* it is the continuity of Sparta that guarantees congruence.[43]

---

42 The Stranger's qualification 'or, if you wish, race' is curious and deserves further attention, transporting us, as it does, to a quasi-Hesiodic world of successive races. The Dorians self-represented as an ethnic group, but it is striking that the fourth city receives ethnic qualification when no prior one did.

43 Athens, the heroine of the Atlantis story, could not hope to be a paradigm of continuity in the *Laws* because it was a paradigm case of democracy. This entailed

As this chapter draws to a close it is worth pausing over Weil's question, one he posed even as he conceded that the narrative of *Laws* 3 was largely imaginary: do we not need to explain Plato's systematic recourse to a history that was relatively well known?[44] Yes we do. I remarked earlier that the rationalising approach to myths of cataclysm was taken for granted only in the *Laws*, as opposed to *Timaeus and Statesman* where it came as a revelation. In the *Laws* there is a smoothness of intellectual texture: everyone agrees to the rationalising approach, everyone agrees that the history of Messene and Argos is one of pleonectic kingship gone mad. In spite of cataclysm, everyone can see a continuous historical development from the return of the Dorians to the present. This perception of continuity between past and present makes the historical narrative of the *Laws* rhetorically effective in context. As opposed to the procedure in *Statesman* and *Timaeus*, historical lessons are applied to contemporary and quasi-contemporary societies, although in carefully controlled circumstances. We do not find a real desire to investigate recent and not-so-recent history, but to find exemplification in it of more general conclusions about the operation of constitutions. A crucial aspect of the Stranger's reconstruction of the past is to model strategies of historical investigation and their reception, and the complexities of his rhetoric surrounding the foundation of Lacedaemon must be seen in the context of this project. What is it we learn about the uses of history (and particularly in the context of a discussion about state-building)? That an investigator and his audience derive the greatest intellectual profit when they can see a continuum and make connections between past and present, but also when they feel they can distinguish the point at which theory or mythology becomes fact and truth. The issue is intellectual control over the material, and as we have seen, the move to say, 'this is material that I control' is made by both Herodotus and Thucydides. The identical impulse to control and validate the past is modelled by Plato's characters even when the material on the one side of the divide between myth and history is nearly as mythical or theoretical as that on the other. It is the gesture that is important.

Plato uses the familiar outlines of archaic and classical history in the *Laws* because the familiarity lends verisimilitude to his ethical and political trajectories and because he has realised that 'designer history' is most effective when connected to, rather than cut off from, a present

---

(footnote 43 *continued*)
eliding the Peisistratid tyranny that came before it, so that Athens enters the scene at 698b as possessing an 'ancient constitution'.
44 Weil, *L''archéologie' de Platon*, p. 33 n. 4.

reality. Like any orator, Plato uses history to make his point and has no qualms about making any adjustments that are necessary to ensure a good fit.[45] He is, of course, painting a broader canvas than the history of any particular city; the scale is cosmic. Invention and schematisation do not surprise; what is more surprising (in the case of the *Laws*) is *a priori* invention in a context that purports to be an inductive investigation into the principles and results of state-formation. It is even more startling and paradoxical to combine this with a cosmic structure designed to block long-term historical sensibility and encourage *a priori* reconstruction.

At the end of the eschatological myth of the *Phaedo*, Socrates says: 'It is inappropriate for a sensible man to insist that these matters are exactly as I have narrated them. Nevertheless, that either these things or things like them are the case . . . this, it seems to me, is a fitting suggestion' (114d). One might, with some modification, take this as emblematic of Plato's historical reconstructions also. He has no desire to become bogged down in details or in the explanation of matters he deems unimportant. He carves the past of the cosmos into predictable chunks. He parades rationalisation as an interpretative tool because it is a practice that allows one to pick and choose as genuine the pieces of the past that are conducive to one's purposes. But like Socrates in the *Phaedrus* when faced with the rationalising possibility that the rape of the Athenian princess Oreithyia by the wind god Boreas was merely a case of a young girl getting blown off a rock by accident, he refuses to get drawn in too far. If he were to play that game, he would be obliged to spend his time explaining centaurs and Gorgons and other mythical monsters (*Phdr.* 229b–e). He has bigger fish to fry. Not for Plato Thucydides' *talaiporia*.[46] He is perhaps more interested in how the many turn to ready-made models, since he would have dismissed with contempt the notion that a history of fifth-century Greece could be a possession for all time.

Narratives of cataclysm thus have an important methodological and heuristic part to play in Plato's manipulation of the past.

45 Cf. the comments of R. Fowler ('Herodotos and his contemporaries', *JHS* 116 (1996), pp. 62–87, at p. 82) on Herodotus: 'If he massages his data to produce typical patterns, it is because, to him, that is the structure of truth and reality. Future historians of historiography will identify ways of thinking that have affected our explanations of historical events, and with a similar lack of generosity accuse us of lying, or at any rate, of writing nothing better than historical fiction.' Plato, however, works at a considerably higher level of generality.

46 Thuc. 1.20.2–1.21.1, also quoted above: 'the majority make no effort in the investigation of the truth and they turn rather to what is ready at hand' (οὕτως ἀταλαίπωρος τοῖς πολλοῖς ἡ ζήτησις τῆς ἀληθείας, καὶ ἐπὶ τὰ ἑτοῖμα μᾶλλον τρέπονται).

Although Plato has adopted many of the historiographical gestures we find in Herodotus and Thucydides, he surrounds them with a cosmic machinery that produces a different interpretative universe. While these fifth-century historians construct a historical space and methodology that enable them to exercise exact control over the recent past and present (respectively), and to predict that the result of their work will be an account that prevents great deeds from being obliterated or helps them last forever, Plato makes his characters theorise the slow growth of historical sensibility but dooms accounts so produced to future destruction. This approach has its irritations, but at the same time it allows an interestingly experimental approach to the development of historical thinking, one that repeatedly presents an intellectual blank slate and its concomitant opportunities. It lets Plato meditate on the uses of history and the emotional and political value of deploying a past that is or is not cut off from the present. Finally, it permits him to present a valuably complicated picture of the relationship between inquiry into the past and the difficult category of 'myth'. Plato presents a world of historically parochial and belated Greeks with a problematically foreshortened vision of the past. This is, of course, an ethically driven vision, but it is a vision in line with a larger philosophical project in which we are all encouraged to look beyond local interests and see the soul in a more universal context.

14

INSCRIBING THE PAST IN FOURTH-CENTURY ATHENS

S. D. Lambert

THE PAST IN THE HISTORY OF FOURTH-CENTURY ATHENS

The past might feature rather prominently in the narrative that a modern historian would construct of the history of Athens in the fourth century BC. From an external perspective, that of Athens' role and status in the Greek world, the dominant feature before 338 was arguably the Second Athenian League – a deliberate attempt to resurrect Athens' fifth-century maritime empire, to make the past present. After 359 the main story was the astonishing growth of the power of Macedon under Philip II and Alexander, of Athens' vigorous attempts to resist, culminating in a decisive defeat at Chaironeia in 338 and a subsequent process of adaptation to a new world order in which the city's political status was radically reduced. I have argued elsewhere that an intense engagement and preoccupation with the city's past, particularly, but not only, the glory days of the fifth century, runs as a golden thread through a number of the key developments in the city's policy-making through this traumatic later phase.[1] For example, an impetus to connect with the past through the myth and ritual of religious practice contributed to a surge in the attention being directed by the city to its religious life in the Lykourgan period, to its sacrifices, festivals and theatre. The last of these highlights that this was a phenomenon that operated at more than one level: the events played out on the tragic stage connected the audience with a heroic and mythical past; but the political focus on the theatre as cultural institution – the building works, the statues of Aeschylus, Sophocles and Euripides, and so on – also served to

---

1 S. D. Lambert, 'Some political shifts in Lykourgan Athens', in V. Azoulay and P. Ismard (eds), *Clisthène et Lycurgue d'Athènes: Autour du politique dans la cité classique* (Paris: Publications de la Sorbonne, 2011), pp. 175–90.

connect the city with a period of its own history that was acquiring heroic and mythical qualities: the glory days of the fifth century. The city was seeking to emphasise and enhance its role and status as leading centre of Greek culture, a role that was rooted in the fifth century, at a time when its political power and military status were ebbing away. In a longer perspective, one which arguably runs to the present day, this second phase was much more important than the first: it marked the secular transition of Athens from a city whose external identity resided primarily in its contemporary political and military power, to one whose external identity resided primarily in its cultural heritage and prestige; a city, in other words, defined more by its past than its present.

From an internal perspective too the past loomed over Athens' fourth-century present. The prevailing democratic system and culture, in fourth-century Athenian minds, were those created by the political heroes of the past – Solon, Cleisthenes, Pericles – and inherited in their main features from the fifth century. What was new was that, outside the philosophical schools, this system and culture were no longer contentious, and that was in part because the traumatic experience of the regime of the Thirty, the narrow and brutal oligarchy imposed on Athens by the Spartans at the end of the Peloponnesian War, had made everyone a democrat. But as the growth in Macedonian power had a traumatic effect on Athens' external identity, so it transformed the city's internal political land-scape. Following the failure of Athens' rebellion against Macedon after the death of Alexander in 323, Antipater had the leaders of the resistance executed, abolished the ancestral democracy and replaced it with an oligarchy in which possession of wealth was a prerequisite for political participation. The long-term effect, however, was not to uproot and destroy democracy as an aspect of Athens' distinc-tive identity, but to embed it as part of the city's 'heritage' from the past, to be self-consciously reactivated and reintroduced, with greater or lesser cynicism and artificiality, on several occasions over the following century, usually at the instigation or at least with the co-operation of a dominant external power.

INSCRIPTIONS AS SOURCES FOR STUDY OF DEVELOPING ATTITUDES TO THE PAST

So, my thesis is that the past played an important role in fourth-cen-tury Athenian history and that the development of collective Athenian attitudes to it is accordingly an interesting and worthwhile topic of investigation. One can of course pursue it in many media, including monuments and physical artefacts of many kinds, as well as written sources.[2] I propose in this chapter to pursue it in a medium which is both a physical artefact and a written text: inscriptions, specifically inscribed laws and decrees. They are a type of written evidence which has some advantages, for example over the works of historians and philosophers, which reflect individual authorial or elite perspectives. Inscribed laws and decrees, I would contend, reveal much more clearly the collective attitudes of the citizens. Admittedly they were proposed by individual politicians; but they were also agreed by a majority of the citizens present and voting. And those citizens not only voted them into law, they also gave them a special significance (by no means accorded to all) by having them inscribed and set up as monuments – mostly on the Acropolis, the sacred space at the heart of the city. They are a deliberate and significant expression of the collective Athenian mind.[3]

The importance of inscriptions as a source for developing attitudes to the past is also apparent from the way that they impinge on other contemporary written sources. Beginning probably in the context of the revision and reinscribing of Athenian law in the last decade of the fifth century, a culture developed of searching out, discovering and indeed inventing 'documents' of the past, many of them inscriptions. It is a culture which develops and intensifies over the course of the fourth century, reaching a climax in Lykourgos' *Against Leokrates*. This speech contains a remarkable catalogue of examples from 'history', several of them 'documented' by inscriptions, designed to impress on the jury the importance of patriotic behaviour, with the objective of convicting a man accused of fleeing Attica in the aftermath of the battle of Chaironeia. We can also observe this development in the epigraphical record. Two of the documents referred to by Lykourgos are the 'ancestral oath of the ephebes' and the 'oath which the Greeks swore before the battle of Plataia'; and we also have inscribed versions

---

2 For a recent survey of appeals to the past in the fourth century, mostly in the orators, see P. J. Rhodes, 'Appeals to the past in classical Athens', in G. Herman (ed.), *Stability and Crisis in the Athenian Democracy: Proceedings of a Conference in Jerusalem, 2009, in memory of A. Fuks* (Stuttgart: Steiner, 2011), pp. 13–30.

3 The weight of this significance is illustrated by the first six inscriptions listed in the Appendix, which all restore the title of *proxenos* to men whose awards are said to have been annulled by or under the Thirty; in no. 2 the proxeny actually *is* the stele. The city expresses its collective will by erecting inscriptions which express it or pulling down earlier inscriptions which contradict it; e.g. in the Prospectus of the Second Athenian League (no. 10), any stelai at Athens unfavourable to any city that joins will be torn down. See also no. 11, no. 16.

of these two supposed 'documents', set up in the temple of Ares in Acharnai at around the same period.[4]

This phenomenon is eloquent witness to an increasing intensity of interest in the past as the fourth century progressed; and to a focus on inscriptions, authentic or otherwise, as sources of knowledge of the past; but the inscriptions I am going to discuss do not belong to this category of discovered or invented 'documents' of the past. They are all genuine contemporary laws and decrees, proposed by individual politicians and passed by the collective of Athenian citizens sitting in plenary as the Assembly or in committee, as the Council or as *nomothetai*. Over 750 such inscriptions survive from the fourth century. Most of them belong to one of three categories: inter-state treaties, religious regulations and, easily the most numerous, honorific decrees.

Honorific decrees are not only the most numerous category, they are also the most liable to include explicit references to the past, because the honours are invariably justified in terms of past actions. Sometimes these are simply the past actions of the honorand, but quite frequently they include the actions of his ancestors. The highest honour Athens normally bestowed on foreigners was the Athenian citizenship, by definition a hereditary status, and other honours were also often hereditary, including the most common awarded in inscribed decrees, the proxeny, which formally bestowed on the honorand the duty of representing Athenian interests in his home city. This hereditary tendency meant that honorific decrees supplied a natural peg on which to hang references to the past, and this retrospective aspect can be expressed in the physical arrangements for inscribing them: it is not uncommon for the text of a decree to refer to an earlier one in the same location honouring an ancestor, and for the later decree to specify that it be inscribed on or next to the earlier one.

I made a start on this topic elsewhere, where my focus was specifically on the Lykourgan period.[5] This chapter reports the results of a survey I have now carried out of all the c. 550 inscribed Athenian laws and decrees of 403–321. The Appendix lists the thirty-three which I

---

4 P. J. Rhodes and Robin Osborne, *Greek Historical Inscriptions 404–323 BC* (Oxford: Oxford University Press, 2007; 1st pub. 2003), no. 88. On the discovery, invention and fabrication of inscriptions of the past at this period see especially J. K. Davies, 'Documents and "documents" in fourth century historiography', in P. Carlier (ed.), *Le IVe siècle av. J.-C.: Approches historiographiques* (Nancy: de Boccard, 1996), pp. 29–39; also C. Habicht, 'Falsche Urkunden zur Geschichte Athens im Zeitalter der Perserkriege', *Hermes* 89 (1961), pp. 1–35.

5 S. D. Lambert, 'Connecting with the past in Lykourgan Athens: An epigraphical perspective', in H.-J. Gehrke, N. Luraghi and L. Foxhall (eds), *Intentional History: Spinning Time in Ancient Greece* (Stuttgart: Steiner, 2010), pp. 225–38.

have identified as of interest. I have *not* strictly listed every reference to the past in every inscription – that would include every justification clause for every honorific decree and would not have yielded very interesting results. What I have done is to identify those which contain references not only to the immediate past circumstances of the decree, but to a more distant past, or which are otherwise interesting or significant. I have covered systematically only the period to 321, a restriction driven by practical limitations on what can realistically be covered in a single chapter, but I have included as the last item on the list one rather significant and illuminating case from the last decade of the century.

DEVELOPING ATTITUDES TO THE PAST IN INSCRIBED FOURTH-CENTURY LAWS AND DECREES

We may establish immediately that, before about 350, there is virtually no specific or explicit reference to any past event beyond the immediate context or rationale for the decree.

No. 7 nicely illustrates the potential for references to the past that the hereditary nature of honours created. It honours Sthorys of Thasos for his services as a seer at the battle of Knidos in 394, awarding him the Athenian citizenship. The wording of the decree makes clear that the service at Knidos was the culmination of a series of good deeds not only by himself but also by his ancestors, who were Athenian *proxenoi*, and it is specified explicitly that the new decree is to be set up next to previous decrees that honoured him, but nothing specific is said about his previous services or those of his ancestors. The focus is on the immediate context.

The main – practically the only – exception to this general silence about the past is references to the Thirty. The first six inscriptions on the list are all renewals of proxenies stated to have been destroyed by the Thirty.[6] This is consonant with other indications of the power of the memory of the Thirty in the early years of the fourth century, and of the tendency for people to define themselves and to be defined by others with reference to their relations to that regime.[7]

---

6 Whether no. 18 should be added to this list is unclear, as the circumstances in which this proxeny stele had 'disappeared' are not made explicit.

7 See for example A. Wolpert, *Remembering Defeat: Civil War and Civic Memory in Ancient Athens* (Baltimore: Johns Hopkins University Press, 2002), in relation to the orators; J. L. Shear, 'Cultural change, space and the politics of commemoration', in R. Osborne (ed.), *Debating the Athenian Cultural Revolution* (Cambridge: Cambridge University Press, 2007), pp. 91–115, on the significance of the regime in the development of the monumental topography of the Agora; P. J. Rhodes, 'Stability in the Athenian democracy after 403 BC', in B. Linke, M. Meier

In a remarkable number of the extant speeches of Lysias of the 390s and 380s the speaker is concerned to attack or defend actions and attitudes in relation to the Thirty; and it is an impression also conveyed by the rest of the epigraphical record. The most notable set of inscriptions from the decade following the restoration of democracy in 403 is a group specifically honouring the heroes of the restoration.[8] One of them (*SEG* 48.45) includes an epigram celebrating the collective efforts of those patriots who risked their lives by opposing the Thirty, or rather 'those who had sought to rule with unjust laws', and the extent to which these inscriptions entered popular consciousness is shown by Aeschines, who in 330, and intent on contrasting these heroes of democracy with the cowards of Chaironeia, cites this very epigram from this very inscription (Aeschin. 3.187–90).

These proxeny renewals show that in the 390s and 380s Athenians were defining not only their relations with each other in terms of attitudes to the Thirty, but also their relations with foreigners. Interestingly in at least two of the six it is (unusually) the honorands themselves who pay for the reinscription of the proxenies; it is as if they have something to prove to a new democracy still preoccupied with defining people by their attitudes to the hated regime. It may also be relevant here that, as Julia Shear has emphasised, although the Thirty were Athenians, they were not only installed with Spartan support, they were articulated in commemorative terms as if they were foreign, external enemies of the city – enemies from whom foreigners wishing to cultivate Athenian good will would, it seems, need to be careful to distance themselves.

The enduring importance of the memory of the Thirty in the first half of the fourth century is confirmed by the decrees for Eukles and Philokles, no. 17 on the list, inscribed at the same time on the same stone at some date in the decade or so before 356. Philokles has just been appointed herald of the Council and people in succession to his father, Eukles, and has had not only the decree recording his own appointment inscribed, but also the earlier decree, dating a generation earlier, which had originally appointed his father. The earlier decree justifies Eukles' appointment on the grounds of services performed by him in relation to the restoration of the democracy in 403, and the later decree includes a reference to the earlier appointment and its rationale

---

(footnote 7 *continued*)
and M. Strothmann (eds), *Zwischen Monarchie und Republik: Gesellschaftliche Stabilisierungsleistungen und politische Transformationspotentiale in den antiken Stadtstaaten* (Stuttgart: Steiner, 2010), pp. 13–30, on the contribution made by the memory of the Thirty to the stability of the fourth-century democracy.
8 Well discussed by Shear, 'Cultural change'.

in wording which echoes the earlier one. Your or your father's participation in the restoration of the democracy was something that was patently still guaranteed to make you popular in Athens a generation after the events. Interestingly, there are (uncertain) indications that Eukles may originally have been a foreigner who was awarded the citizenship for his services; and interestingly too, like the restored proxenies, it seems that the decrees were inscribed at the honorand's own initiative and expense. This is not so much the city making a statement about the democratic credentials of Philokles and his family as Philokles making a statement about his family's own democratic credentials.[9]

Before 350 the only other specific references to a past that is at all distant from the immediate context occurs in decrees concerning relations between states, and the reference is invariably to the King's Peace, made in 386 (and subsequently renewed), or to events in the Greek world that have taken place since the King's Peace. In no. 9, of 384/3, Athens is very anxious to put across the message that its alliance with Chios is not intended in any way to threaten or undermine the King's Peace made two years earlier, and the decree refers explicitly to that Peace, and in quite a wordy fashion. In no. 10, the Prospectus of the Second Athenian League in 378/7, eight years after the Peace, the Athenians state explicitly that one of the purposes of the new League is 'so that the peace and friendship sworn by the Greeks and the King in accordance with the agreements may be in force and endure'; and the collective weight and significance of these inscribed words is confirmed by the fact that, at some subsequent point in the history of the League, they were deliberately erased from the stone. Ten years later, after the Spartan defeat at Leuktra had shaken up the balance of power, pushing Athens into alliance with Sparta against Thebes and raising questions in people's minds about the continuing relevance of the Second Athenian League, the King's Peace is still being referred to as the setter of the diplomatic framework. When envoys from Dionysios of Syracuse come to Athens in 369/8 (no. 13) they are praised not only because they are good men with regard to the people of Athens and the allies, but because they 'come in support of the King's Peace, which was made by the Athenians and the Spartans and the other Greeks'; and when, in the same year, envoys from Mytilene come to Athens inquiring about the future of the Second Athenian League (no. 14), Athens carefully spells out in its reply that

9 The monuments erected on public initiative in the immediate aftermath of the Thirty had, as far as Athenians were concerned, carefully emphasised collective resistance to the Thirty, not the actions of specific individuals.

it had led the league against Sparta 'when the Spartans were campaigning against the Greeks, contrary to the oaths and the agreement [= King's Peace]'.

After 386 Greek cities were operating quite consciously and deliberately within the diplomatic framework of the King's Peace: it set the parameters of Athenian inter-state relations just as the United Nations Charter, the North Atlantic Treaty and the European Union treaties set the parameters of the inter-state relations of western European states in the modern world; and it was natural for international actions to be justified with reference to it – especially perhaps international actions that might otherwise be vulnerable to criticism.

There are some apparent allusions to practices common in Athens' fifth-century empire in decrees relating to the Second League: e.g. in the prohibition on Athenians owning property in member states in the Prospectus (no. 10) and in the provision in no. 12, of 373/2, that the Parians should send offerings to the City Dionysia and the Panathenaia; but the fifth-century empire is never explicitly mentioned.

After c. 350 we begin to get more explicit references to a more distant past in honorific decrees. As we have seen, in earlier decrees there are vague references to the services of ancestors. After mid-century these begin to become more specific.

The path-breaker is no. 19, of 347/6, honouring Spartokos and Pairisades, brothers who had recently succeeded their father, Leukon, as rulers of the Bosporan kingdom, a crucial source of supply of Athenian grain. The decree not only names the honorands' father, but also their grandfather, Satyros, who had ruled the kingdom between 433/2 and 389/8 – more than forty years previously. A number of factors are relevant here: the references to this ruling family in Demosthenes 20, *Against Leptines*, show that their crucial role in Athens' food supply gave their names currency in the Assembly and law-courts. Moreover the effect of this decree is to confirm for the new rulers honours, including the Athenian citizenship, which had originally been granted to Satyros and Leukon; and the text of the new inscription provides explicitly that it is to be inscribed (in fact in Piraeus) on a stele and set up 'near the one of Satyros and Leukon'. Not very many state decrees were set up in the Piraeus and it sounds as if the 'stele of Satyros and Leukon' was something of a Piraeus landmark. One wonders whether it might also be relevant that the proposer of this decree with its quiet historical allusions was Androtion the historian of Attica.[10]

---

10 It is not coincidental in relation to the topic of this chapter that another historian of Attica, Phanodemos, was to be one of the most prominent Athenians in the epigraphical record of the Lykourgan period (e.g. proposer of no. 27).

This is the earliest fourth-century inscription to mention by name a foreigner whose services to Athens extended back beyond what one may perhaps characterise as the psychological hurdle of the regime of the Thirty and into the Peloponnesian War period, and it does so very unobtrusively. The defeat by Philip at Chaironeia nine years after Androtion's decree and its profound consequences in terms of the reduction of Athens' status and power – including the loss of the Second Athenian League – intensified the backward-looking tendency in the collective Athenian mind: the past – in particular the glory days of the fifth century – were a better time than the present and held powerful lessons for present conduct. This is illustrated very well by two inscriptions which go much further than any earlier inscribed decree, not only in that they allude in a more detailed way to events located in a more distant past, but also in that there is a clear agenda and purpose in terms of the politics of the present. The inscriptions are no. 21, a decree providing for the repair of a statue of Athena Nike originally dedicated from the spoils of Athenian victories in western Greece in the 420s, and no. 22, honouring two brothers, Phormio and Karphinas of Akarnania. I shall deal with these decrees quite briefly here.[11]

I have included a full translation of no. 21 in the Appendix. It sets out in detail the precise circumstances in which the statue was originally dedicated, mentioning specific campaigns that can be verified from Thucydides. This Nike was probably in bronze, but the measure is of a piece with one of Lykourgos' proud achievements: the restoration of the golden Nikai on the Acropolis which had been melted down for coin towards the end of the Peloponnesian War.[12] One of the elements of restoration was apparently the 'raising' of the statue (probably by increasing the height of its base). This is not only a textbook case of the use of a religious vehicle or cover to express collective national aspiration at a time when explicit expression of such aspirations was difficult – raising Victory at a time of defeat; it is also characteristic of the Lykourgan period that it does so in a way that reaches back to the past for inspiration and example, and not just to a vague, generalised past, but to a specific, 'documented' episode.

No. 22 is a more subtle case, and the past-connective agenda is less explicit, but in essence it is doing much the same thing.

11 I have previously discussed the decrees in Lambert, 'Connecting with the past', and returned to them in Lambert, 'Some political shifts'. On no. 22 see also J. K. Davies, 'Hegesippos of Sounion: An underrated politician', in S. D. Lambert (ed.), *Sociable Man: Essays in Greek Social History in Honour of Nick Fisher* (Swansea: Classical Press of Wales, 2011), pp. 11–24.

12 [Plut.] *Lives of Ten Orators* 852b, cf. Paus. 1.29.16.

The two brothers being honoured in this case were leaders of a small Akarnanian contingent that had fought with the Athenians at Chaironeia and they are now being welcomed as exiles, in effect activating the honorary Athenian citizenship that had originally been awarded to their grandfather. One of the pair is named Phormio and the grandfather who had originally been granted Athenian citizenship was also Phormio. This elder Phormio was undoubtedly named for the Athenian general Phormio who campaigned successfully in western Greece during the Archidamian War – precisely the same area and period as the one alluded to by the decree about the statue of Athena Nike. And again the text of the decree refers explicitly to the earlier decree which had awarded the elder Phormio the citizenship (which must have been passed in c. 400) and which, the decree states, was 'inscribed on the Acropolis'. The past-connective agenda here is confirmed by the identity of the proposer, the forceful anti-Macedonian politician Hegesippos of Sounion, probable author of [Demosthenes] 7, and known by the nickname 'Topknot' (*Krobylos*) for the archaic fashion in which he wore his hair. As John Davies has emphasised,[13] this should not be seen as a mere sartorial affectation, but as an eloquent symbol of a political agenda. Hairstyles, like religious statues, could be potent signifiers.

My survey has yielded just one other significant case of a historical reference in the decrees of the Lykourgan period. Again it occurs in an honorific decree and again it relates to ancestors of the honorand. It is no. 30, of 327/6, which honours a member of a famous Rhodian family of mercenary commanders, which had married into the Persian aristocracy, and one of whose members, Barsine, bore a son, Herakles, to Alexander the Great. The identity of the honorand is uncertain, but the wording of lines 29–34, in which Mentor is described as 'the father of Thymondas', suggests that it may have been this Thymondas, who is best known for commanding the Greek mercenaries for Darius against Alexander at Issos in 333. Thymondas' father was well remembered for his favourable treatment of Greek mercenaries in Egypt in the 340s, some of whom one can perhaps imagine among the Athenians who voted for this decree; but the decree also mentions two other ancestors of the honorand: Pharnabazos, satrap of Daskylion 413–387, who had co-operated with Athens in the 390s when Sparta was fighting Persia; and his son Artabazos, who had co-operated with Athenian general Chares in the 350s, when Artabazos was in revolt from the Persian king.

There does not seem here to be a deliberate attempt to connect with

13 Davies, 'Hegesippos of Sounion'.

the fifth-century glory days: the historical points of reference all seem to be post-403. The context is military and one might perhaps construct this as, in a way, the linear descendant of those passages in Homer in which two heroes on the battlefield stand and recite their ancestry and discover their family connections. But still we have the specificity – the named ancestors – which, as we have seen, is absent from decrees of the earlier part of the century. There was a clear fashion for connecting with specific past events and people in the post-Chaironeia world, and this decree should be seen as part of that trend. One might suspect that there is also intended to be a reassuring comfort-value in these particular references. In the real world, following first Chaironeia and now Alexander's conquest of the east, Athens had in ten years been reduced from big fish in the Greek pond to political minnow in the vast new eastern Mediterranean world created and dominated by the Macedonians. But Pharnabazos and Artabazos were big names to conjure with: they were indeed classic names of powerful Persian satraps, borne not only by the two specific individuals referred to here, but by a succession of Persians stretching back for as long as Greeks had had to do with Persians. The world may have changed very fast, but this decree surely projected a nostalgic reassurance – in truth perhaps an illusion – that actually it had stayed the same: there was still a Pharna- or an Arta- – or at least a descendant of one – out there; the Persian Empire had, in a sense, not disappeared after all; and Athens could still deal with its potentates on equal terms. The parallels between this decree and the one honouring the Akarnanians are rather striking, and there is perhaps another connection: Hegesippos, proposer of that decree, is best known as a virulent anti-Macedonian. The proposer of our decree is unfortunately unknown, but it is unlikely to be irrelevant that Thymondas was best known for leading the Greek mercenaries against Alexander at Issos. If connecting-with-the-past implied an aspiration to restore the Athens of its glory days, that also had implications for current attitudes and policies towards the Macedonians, a subject which divided Athenians after Chaironeia no less than it had before.

Though I do not have the space in this chapter to extend my systematic survey of historical references in Athenian laws and decrees beyond 321, I have included, as no. 33, what is, I think, the most striking example of past-referencing in the inscribed decrees of the final decades of the century. It is a decree of 307/6, proposed by the leading politician Stratokles shortly after the ousting of Demetrios of Phaleron and the so-called restoration of democracy under the aegis of Antigonos and Demetrios Poliorketes. It honours posthumously the politician Lykourgos, who had died in 325. Athens had

started regularly honouring its own citizens with inscribed decrees
in the 340s, but there is not one such decree among items 1–32 in the
Appendix. That is because they do not mention past events, ancestors and such-like: such subject matter was part of the culture of
relations with outsiders, not of relations between the equal citizens
of a democracy. In contrast no. 33, the earliest extant decree awarding the so-called 'highest honours' to an Athenian (including a statue
and *sitesis* in the *prytaneion*), does refer to the honorand's ancestors,
Lykomedes (his great-grandfather) and Lykourgos (his grandfather), commemorating their public burial in the Kerameikos and
their manly virtue (*andragathia*). This is significant in a 'democratic'
context, because we are told that Lykourgos' grandfather was killed
by the Thirty,[14] though, interestingly, this is not explicitly asserted in
the text of the decree itself; and because the family belonged to the
distinguished *genos* Eteoboutadai, though this too is not explicitly
asserted, a perhaps more readily understandable reticence.[15] This
decree, however, is past-connective in the more radical sense that it
is wholly about a dead man, a figure of the past, and makes a series
of striking statements about him and his achievements, asserting a
heroic role for him not only on the domestic Athenian scene, but as
a major figure in the wider world. The decree panders to Athenian
aspirations to freedom and autonomy and to be a big player on the
international stage, all of it to an extent a mirage in the world of 307/6;
and there is also an element of mirage in the assertions made about
Lykourgos. Consistently with the other post-Chaironeia decrees we
have been considering, there is a strongly anti-Macedonian flavour
about this past-connective decree; but there is little sign that, in reality,
Lykourgos had pursued the openly confrontational approach to
Alexander that the decree implies. There are no statements of defiance
in his extant speech or in his inscribed laws and decrees; his opposition to Alexander was more subdued and implicit.[16] But the most

---

14 [Plut.] *Lives of Ten Orators* 841a–b.
15 Contrast the *pinax* set up by Lykourgos' son, Habron, in the Erechtheum,
   and illustrating the succession of priests of Poseidon Erechtheus in the *genos*
   (including himself) back to Boutes and Erechtheus the son of Earth and
   Hephaistos ([Plut.] *Lives of Ten Orators* 843e–f, cf. J. Blok and S. D. Lambert,
   'The appointment of priests in Attic *gene*', *ZPE* 169 (2009), pp. 109–14).
   Reticence about *genos* membership is a marked feature of Athenian decrees
   honouring Athenians, even those who honoured priests who were appointed
   from *gene* (cf. S. D. Lambert, 'The social construction of priests and priestesses
   in Athenian honorific decrees from the fourth century BC to the Augustan
   period', in M. Horster and A. Klöckner (eds), *Civic Priests* (Berlin: de Gruyter,
   2012), pp. 67–134).
16 On the extent to which this decree distorted historical reality see the
   recent papers of P. Brun, 'Lycurgue d' Athènes: Un législateur?', in P. Sineux

significant point for our purposes is that it was Lykourgos who, more than anyone, was responsible for the backward-looking culture of Athens in the post-Chaironeia era; he who established authoritative texts of Aeschylus, Sophocles and Euripides and had their statues erected in the theatre; and his speech against Leokrates that marks the high-water mark for the practice of adducing documented, historical examples to inform the present. Lykourgos the great citer of historical examples has now himself become one big historical example, a role he was to continue to perform in Hellenistic Athens.[17] Stratokles' decree honouring Lykourgos is the clearest possible sign that Athens would, for the future, be living off its past.

APPENDIX:

REFERENCES TO THE PAST IN INSCRIBED ATHENIAN LAWS AND DECREES, 403–321 BC

Abbreviations:

Ag. 16: A. G. Woodhead, *The Athenian Agora. Vol. XVI: Inscriptions. The Decrees* (Princeton: American School of Classical Studies at Athens, 1997).

Davies (2011): J. K. Davies, 'Hegesippos of Sounion: An underrated politician', in S. D. Lambert (ed.), *Sociable Man: Essays in Greek Social History in Honour of Nick Fisher* (Swansea: Classical Print of Wales, 2011).

Lambert (2004): S. D. Lambert, 'Athenian state laws and decrees, 352/1–322/1: I Decrees honouring Athenians', *ZPE* 150 (2004), pp. 85–120 = Lambert, *Inscribed Athenian Laws and Decrees 352/1–322/1 BC: Epigraphical Essays* (Leiden and Boston: Brill, 2012), pp. 3–47.

Lambert (2005): S. D. Lambert, 'Athenian state laws and decrees, 352/1–322/1: II Religious regulations', *ZPE* 154 (2005), pp. 125–59 = Lambert, *Inscribed Athenian Laws and Decrees 352/1–322/1 BC*, pp. 48–92.

Lambert (2006–7): S. D. Lambert, 'Athenian state laws and decrees, 352/1–322/1: III Decrees honouring foreigners. A. Citizenship, proxeny and euergesy'. *ZPE* 158 (2006), pp. 115–58, and 'B. Other awards', *ZPE* 159 (2007), pp. 101–54 = Lambert, *Inscribed Athenian Laws and Decrees 352/1–322/1 BC*, pp. 93–183.

Lambert (2007): S. D. Lambert, 'Athenian state laws and decrees, 352/1–322/1:

(ed.), *Le législateur et la loi dans l'antiquité: Hommage à F. Ruzé* (Caen: Presses Universitaires de Caen, 2005), pp. 187–200; P. J. Rhodes, '"Lycurgan" Athens', in A. Tamis, C. J. Mackie and S. Byrne (eds), *Philathenaios: Studies in Honour of Michael J. Osborne* (Athens: Greek Epigraphical Society, 2010), pp. 81–90; and M. Faraguna, '"Lykourgan" Athens?', in Azoulay and Ismard, *Clisthène et Lycurgue d'Athènes*, pp. 67–88.

17 As emphasised most recently by Eric Perrin (E. Perrin-Saminadayar, *Éducation, culture et société à Athènes: Les acteurs de la vie culturelle athénienne (229–88). Un tout petit monde* (Paris: de Boccard, 2007)).

IV Treaties and other texts', *ZPE* 161 (2007), pp. 67–100 = Lambert, *Inscribed Athenian Laws and Decrees 352/1–322/1 BC*, pp. 184–218.

Lambert (2010): S. D. Lambert, 'Connecting with the past in Lykourgan Athens: An epigraphical perspective', in H.-J. Gehrke, N. Luraghi and L. Foxhall (eds), *Intentional History: Spinning Time in Ancient Greece* (Stuttgart: Steiner, 2010), pp. 225–38.

Moreno (2007): A. Moreno, *Feeding the Democracy: The Athenian Grain Supply in the Fifth and Fourth Centuries BC* (Oxford: Oxford University Press, 2007).

Nat.: M. Osborne, *Naturalization in Athens* (Brussels: Koninklijke Academie voor Wetenschappen, Letteren en Schone Kunsten van België, 1981–3).

RO: P. J. Rhodes and Robin Osborne, *Greek Historical Inscriptions 404–323 BC* (Oxford: Oxford University Press, 2007; 1st pub. 2003).

Scafuro (2009): A. C. Scafuro, 'The crowning of Amphiaraos', in L. Mitchell and L. Rubinstein (eds), *Greek History and Epigraphy: Essays in Honour of P. J. Rhodes* (Swansea: Classical Press of Wales, 2009), pp. 59–86.

Whitehead (2008): D. Whitehead, 'Athenians in Sicily in the fourth century BC', in C. Cooper (ed.), *Epigraphy and the Greek Historian* (Toronto: University of Toronto Press, 2008), pp. 57–67.

1. *IG* II² 6; *SEG* 29.83
Date: After 403
Description: Restoration of proxeny for Eurypylos and four brothers [from Thasos?]
Proposer: Monippides (not otherwise known)
Text: . . . since the stele on which was their proxeny was destroyed under the Thirty, the secretary of the Council shall inscribe the stele at the expense of Eurypylos . . .

2. *IG* II² 52
Date: After 403
Description: Restoration of proxeny for grandson of Xanthippos
Proposer: –
Text: . . . since his [grandfather?] Xanthippos was *proxenos* and the Thirty destroyed the proxeny, the secretary of the Council shall inscribe them as *proxenoi* and benefactors of the Athenians . . .
Comment: The original stele for Xanthippos may be *IG* I³ 177.

3. Ag. 16.39
Date: After 403
Description: Restoration of proxeny
Proposer: –
Text: . . . the secretary of the Council shall inscribe the decree on a stone stele on the acropolis, since the stele set up for them previously was destroyed under the Thirty . . .

4. *IG* II² 9; *SEG* 14.35; 32.41
Date: After 403
Description: Restoration of proxeny
Proposer: –
Text: . . . since the stele set up for them previously was destroyed under the Thirty, the secretary of the Council shall inscribe . . .
Comment: The original decree (of 410/9?) was perhaps inscribed below this decree.

5. *IG* II² 66c; *SEG* 14.40; 15.83
Date: After 403
Description: Restoration of proxeny for a Kaphyan
Proposer: –
Text: . . . from Kaphyai [*in Arcadia*] and . . . since the stele was destroyed under the Thirty . . .

6. Ag. 16.37
Date: After 403
Description: Restoration of proxeny for family from Ialysos [Rhodes]
Proposer: –
Text: . . . since their [father?] was *proxenos* and benefactor and the stele was destroyed under the Thirty, the secretary of the Council shall inscribe him and his brothers *proxenoi* and benefactors at the expense of . . .

7. Ag. 16.36; Nat. D8
Date: 394/3
Description: Citizenship grant to the *mantis* Sthorys of Thasos, for services at sea-battle (= Knidos)
Proposer: –
Text: . . . since his ancestors were *proxenoi* and benefactors . . . since Sthorys has continued his previous enthusiasm for the Athenians . . . he is a good man . . . and his ancestors previously . . . inscribe this decree at the expense of Sthorys on a stele where the previous decrees for him have been inscribed . . .
Comment: Sthorys is mentioned c. 389 in decree honouring Thasians, *IG* II² 24.14–15.

8. *IG* II² 31; Nat. PT 31
Date: 386/5
Description: Decree honouring Hebryzelmis, king of Odrysian Thrace

Proposer: –
Text: . . . he shall have everything granted to his ancestors [*? citizenship*] . . .

9. *IG* II² 34; RO 20
Date: 384/3
Description: Alliance with Chios
Proposer: –
Text: . . . the common discussions which took place among the Greeks, have been mindful to preserve, like the Athenians, the peace and friendship and the oaths and the existing agreement which the king and the Athenians and the Spartans and the other Greeks swore [= King's Peace, 386] . . . there shall remain in force the peace and the oaths and the agreement . . . make the Chians allies on a basis of freedom and autonomy, not contravening any of the things written on the stelai about the Peace . . .

10. *IG* II² 43; RO 22
Date: 378/7
Description: Prospectus of the Second Athenian League
Proposer: Aristoteles (minor politician)
Text: . . . so that the Spartans shall allow the Greeks to be free and autonomous, and to live at peace occupying their own territory in security [[and so that the peace and friendship sworn by the Greeks and the King in accordance with the agreements may be in force and endure]] . . . for those who make alliance with Athenians and the allies, the people shall renounce whatever Athenian possessions there happen to be, private or public, in the territory of those who make the alliance . . . for whichever of the cities making the alliance there happen to be unfavourable stelai in Athens, the Council . . . shall be empowered to destroy them . . .

11. Ag. 16.46
Date: 375?
Description: Alliance with Kephallenia
Proposer: –
Text: . . . *anti-Athenian laws in Kephallenia to be destroyed and erased* . . .

12. RO 29
Date: 373/2
Description: Decree relating to Paros
Proposer: –

Text: . . . in accordance with tradition (*kata ta patria*) and (the Parians shall) send for the Panathenaia a cow and panoply and for the Dionysia a cow and phallus as a commemoration (*mnemeion*) since they happen to be colonists of the Athenian people . . .

13. *IG* II² 103; Nat. D 10; RO 33
Date: 369/8
Description: Decree relating to Dionysios of Syracuse
Proposer: Pandios (minor politician)
Text: . . . praise Dionysios the archon of Sicily, and the sons of Dionysios, Dionysios and Hermokritos, because they are good men with regard to the people of Athens and the allies, and come in support of the King's Peace, which was made by the Athenians and the Spartans and the other Greeks . . .

14. *IG* II² 107; RO 31
Date: 369/8
Description: Decree relating to Mytilene
Proposer: Kallistratos (politician)
Text: . . . reply to the envoys who have come that the Athenians fought the war for the freedom of the Greeks and when the Spartans were campaigning against the Greeks, contrary to the oaths and the agreement [= King's Peace], they themselves went in support, and they called on the other allies to go and render the support due to the Athenians, abiding by the oaths, against those contravening the treaty . . .
Comment: Context is that Mytilenean envoys have come to Athens with questions about future of the Second Athenian League following Sparta's defeat at the battle of Leuktra.

15. *IG* II² 216 + 261 = *SEG* 14.47
Date: 365/4?
Description: Decree about *paradosis* (formal handover by treasurers to their successors) of sacred objects on Acropolis
Proposer: –
Comment: Decree refers to archonship of Kalleas (377/6) in context of *paradosis* of the statue (*agalma*) and processional vessels (*pompeia*) and everything else on the Acropolis from one year's treasurers of Athena to the next. Also refers to a decree proposed by Androtion which dealt with these matters.

16. *IG* II² 111; RO 39
Date: 363/2
Description: Decree concerning Ioulis on Keos

Proposer: Aristophon (general who had imposed settlement on Ioulis after revolt)
Comment: Text contains extensive detail about background to decree: Chabrias had settled the island after initial revolt; then there had been a counter-revolution by men who had thrown over the stelai (i.e. those recording the settlement imposed by Chabrias), killed members of pro-Athenian party etc.

17. *IG* II² 145; Nat. T20; Ag. 16.52
Date: 1. 402–399 **2.** before 356/5
Description: 1. Decree of 402–399 appointing Eukles herald of the Council and people – inscribed on same stele as no. 2 and at same time
2. Decree of before 356/5 appointing his son Philokles to same post
Proposers: 1. Eurippides (politician)
2. Melanopos (politician)
Text: 1. . . . since Eukles was a good man concerning the Athenian people and the return (*kathodos* – i.e. in 403/2) and the freedom of the Athenian people, he shall be herald . . .
2. . . . since Eukles the father of Philokles was a good man concerning the Athenian people and the return and the freedom of the Athenian people . . . and since he seems to be suitable and orderly . . . *he shall be herald like his father* . . .
Comment: This succession of heralds continued in the same family to 140/39.

18. *IG* II² 172; *SEG* 32.67
Date: Shortly before 350
Description: Decree honouring Democharis of N-
Proposer: Kratinos (minor politician?)
Text: Since Democharis son of Nymphaios of N- is renewing the proxeny which he shows was granted to his ancestors, be it decreed by the Council, since his stele has disappeared (ἠφάνισται αὐτῶ[ι ἡ στήλη]) . . . [*proposal*] . . . to praise Democharis son of Nymphaios because he is a good man concerning the Athenian people, both himself and his ancestors . . .

19. *IG* II² 212; RO 64; Lambert (2006–7) no. 3; Moreno (2007) 260–79
Date: 347/6
Description: Decree honouring Spartokos and Pairisades sons of Leukon, rulers of Bosporan kingdom (shortly after they succeeded their father)
Proposer: Androtion of Gargettos (historian of Attica, *FGrHist* 324)

Text: *Decree maintains reciprocal relations between Athens and the ruling dynasty of the Bosporan kingdom. Mentions Satyros (ruler 433/2–389/8, grandfather of honorands) and Leukon (ruler 389/8–349/8, father). Stele to be set up near stele of Satyros and Leukon (in Piraeus).*
Comment: Dem. 20 *Against Leptines* confirms relations with this dynasty were crucial for Athenian grain supply.

20. *IG* II² 283; Lambert (2006–7) no. 85; Lambert (2007) 83–4; Whitehead (2008)
Date: c. 337?
Description: Decree honouring Ph- of Salamis
Proposer: –
Text: Honorand had brought grain cheaply from Egypt, ransomed citizens from Sicily and sent them home at his own expense, and donated a talent for the *phylake* (protection of the city).
Comment: The donation for the *phylake* is perhaps a reference to the *epidosis* following the battle of Chaironeia in 338. The context in which citizens had been ransomed from Sicily is obscure (cf. Whitehead).

21. *IG* II² 403; Lambert (2005) no. 3; Lambert (2010) 226–8, 232
Date: 340–330
Description: Decree on repair of statue of Athena Nike
Proposer: – of Lakiadai (unidentifiable)
Text: . . . concerning the statement of those who were appointed by the people about the repair of the statue of Athena Nike **which the Athenians dedicated from the Ambrakiots and the (10) army at Olpai and those who stood against the Corcyraean people and from the Anaktorians,** that the Council shall decide: that the – shall bring them before the people [-] at the next Assembly (15) and put the matter on the agenda, and submit the opinion of the Council to the people, that it seems good to the Council both concerning the sacrifice to the goddess that the priestess of Athena should perform the propitiatory sacrifice on behalf of the people, since the exegete (20) requires it . . . the money . . . that – of the people shall give . . . since the statue-maker . . . made . . . higher . . . (25) . . . of the Athenians the . . . (30) [to praise] the statue-maker, – of Boeotia because . . . of the city . . . [just as?] in the . . .
Comment: The statue was originally dedicated from spoils of victorious campaigns in western Greece during the Archidamian War (420s) (Thuc. 3.85, 106–12, 114; 4.2–3, 46, 49).
The wording was perhaps taken from that on the original statue base. For this type of wording cf. *IG* I³ 522 (inscribed shield dedicated in Agora c. 425):

Ἀθηναῖοι   The Athenians [dedicated this]
ἀπὸ Λακεδ-   from the Laked-
αιμ[ο]νίων   aimonians
ἐκ [Πύ]λο   from Pylos

22. *IG* II² 237; RO 77; Lambert (2006–7) no. 5; Lambert (2010) 234–5; Davies (2011)
Date: 338/7
Description: Decree honouring Phormio and Karphinas and other Akarnanian exiles
Proposer: Hegesippos of Sounion (leading anti-Macedonian politician, probable author of [Demosthenes] 7, known as 'Topknot' (*Krobylos*) for the archaic fashion in which he wore his hair
Text: . . . since Phormio and Karphinas are ancestral friends of the Athenian people and preserve the good will towards the Athenian people which their forefathers handed on to them . . . since the Athenian people made Phormio the grandfather of Phormio and Karphinas an Athenian, and his descendants, and the decree which did this was inscribed on the Acropolis . . .
Comment: The honorands had fought with the Athenians against Philip of Macedon at Chaironeia.

23. *SEG* 12.87; Ag. 16.73; RO 79; Lambert (2007) no. 14
Date: 337/6
Description: Law permitting the killing of anyone attempting to overthrow democracy and set up a tyranny
Proposer: Eukrates of Piraeus (executed when Macedonians abolished the Athenian democracy in 322/1)
Comment: This law seems to re-enact earlier anti-tyranny laws (e.g. law attributed to Solon by *Ath. Pol.* 8.4) and adds a prohibition on sessions of Areopagos during a revolution. However, there is no explicit reference to earlier laws.

24. *SEG* 16.55; Lambert (2005) no. 8
Date: Shortly after 338/7?
Description: Makes arrangements for a festival (*to celebrate Peace of Corinth?*)
Proposer: –
Comment: Refers to 'the stele about the Peace', i.e. the Peace of Corinth with Philip II, 338/7.

25. *IG* II² 373 + 242; Lambert (2006–7) no. 34
Date: 337/6 and 322/1

Description: Decrees honouring Euenor of Akarnania (a doctor)
Proposer: Diophantos of Myrrhinous (politician)
Comment: The later decree is inscribed in a different hand but on the same stone as earlier one. Euenor was later awarded citizenship, *IG* II² 374.

26. *IG* II² 337; RO 91; Lambert (2005) no. 4
Date: 333/2
Description: Decree granting Kitians from Cyprus right of ownership of a plot of land to build a temple of Aphrodite
Proposer: Lykourgos of Boutadai (leading politician)
Text: . . . about what is decided to have been the lawful (35) supplication of the Kitian merchants who are asking the people for right of ownership of a plot of land on which to found a sanctuary of Aphrodite, that the people shall decide to give the merchants (40) of the Kitians the right to own a plot of land on which to found the sanctuary of Aphrodite, **as the Egyptians have founded the sanctuary of Isis.**
Comment: The reference is probably to a recent foundation of a temple of Isis and not to a measure of Lykourgos' fifth-century BCE ancestor, nicknamed 'the Egyptian' (Aristophanes, *Birds* 1296, *PCG* Kratinos F32, Pherekrates F11).

27. *IG* II² VII 4252; Lambert (2004) 107; Scafuro (2009)
Date: 332/1
Description: Decree honouring the god Amphiaraos
Proposer: Phanodemos of Thymaitadai (historian of Attica, *FGrHist* 325)
Text: . . . since he takes good care of those Athenians and others who come to the sanctuary . . .
Comment: This wording is normally used for (human) foreign honorands who have been hospitable to Athenian visitors.

28. *IG* II² 351 + 624; RO 94; Lambert (2006–7) no. 42
Date: 330/29
Description: Decree honouring Eudemos of Plataia for contributions to building of Panathenaic stadium and theatre
Proposer: Lykourgos of Boutadai (leading politician)
Text: . . . previously offered to the people a donation of 4,000 drachmas 'towards the war', had it been needed . . .
Comment: The reference is perhaps to the failed revolt against Macedon led by king Agis of Sparta in 331.

29. *IG* II² 399; Lambert (2006–7) no. 56
Date: 328/7?
Description: Decree honouring Eurylochos of Kydonia
Proposer: Demades of Paiania (leading politician)
Comment: Names [father] as earlier benefactor.

30. *IG* II² 356; RO 98; Lambert (2006–7) no. 103
Date: 327/6
Description: Honorific decree; honorand's name not preserved (Thymondas?)[18]
Proposer: –
Text: . . . previously his ancestors Pharnabazos and Artabazos continued to benefit the Athenian people and were useful to the people in the wars and Mentor the father of Thymondas rescued the Greeks who were campaigning in Egypt, when Egypt was taken by the Persians [in 343/2] . . .
Comment: Pharnabazos: Persian satrap of Daskylion 413–387. Had co-operated with Athens against Sparta in 390s (see RO no. 9, no. 10 and no. 12, with notes)
Artabazos: co-operated with Athenian general Chares in 350s (Diod. 16.22.1).
Mentor: mercenary commander for Persians in Egypt, winning over Greek mercenaries fighting for Egypt, 343/2; fled with Darius after Gaugamela, 331; went over to Alexander, with most of his sons, 330; satrap of Bactria, 329; governor of rock of Arimazes, 327 (Diod. 16.42–51 etc.)
Thymondas: commanded Greek mercenaries for Darius against Alexander the Great at Issos, 333 (Arr. *Anab.* 2.13.2, Curt. 3.3.1 etc.)

31. *IG* II² 360; RO 95; Lambert (2006–7) no. 43
Date: 325/4
Description: Decree honouring Herakleides of Salamis
Proposer: Demosthenes of Lamptrai (minor politician)
Text: . . . the secretary . . . shall inscribe this decree and the other praises which there have been for him on stone stele and stand it on the Acropolis
Comment: The decree of 325/4 is duly followed on the stone by four earlier decrees honouring Herakleides, dating back to 330/29,

---

18 The usual identification of the honorand as an (otherwise unattested) Memnon should be rejected. The traces once visible in l. 11, and taken by Kirchner in *IG* II² to be from that name, were probably from the name of the proposer of the decree. See *IG* II³.

which had not been inscribed at the time they were passed and had apparently been retrieved by the secretary from the state archive.

32. *IG* II² 365; Lambert (2006–7) no. 107
Date: 323/2
Description: Decree honouring Lapyris of Kleonai
Proposer: Epiteles of Pergase (minor politician)
Text: . . . the secretary of the Council shall inscribe this decree on the stele on the Acropolis on which is inscribed the proxeny for Echenbrotos of Kleonai the ancestor of Lapyris.
Comment: The earlier stele referred to is extant (*IG* II² 63), inscribed in 402–377, and this decree is inscribed not on it, but on a separate stone.

33. *IG* II² 457 (= [Plut.] *Lives of Ten Orators* 852)
Date: 307/6
Description: Decree honouring Lykourgos of Boutadai (who had died in 325)
Proposer: Stratokles of Diomeia (leading politician)
Text: . . . and Lykourgos' ancestors, Lykomedes and Lykourgos, both while living were honoured by the people, and on their deaths the people granted them public burial in the Kerameikos on account of their manly virtue . . . [Lykourgos] built the arsenal and the theatre of Dionysos and the Panathenaic stadium and repaired the gymnasium at the Lyceum and adorned the whole city with many other buildings, and when the Greeks were beset by fears and great dangers when Alexander overpowered Thebes [in 335] and conquered the whole of Asia and the other parts of the inhabited world, he continued implacably to oppose him on behalf of the people and showed himself unimpeachable on behalf of the fatherland and the salvation of all the Greeks throughout his life, striving for the freedom and autonomy of the city by every means . . . etc.

15

THE POLITICS OF THE PAST: REMEMBERING REVOLUTION AT ATHENS

Julia L. Shear

One day in Athens, in the archonship of Pytharatos, Laches, the son of Demochares, of Leukonoe made a request of the *boule* and the *demos*: he asked them to grant his father Demochares highest honours for his services to the city, not least because

> he was exiled on behalf of the democracy and he took no part in the oligarchy and he did not hold any office after the *demos* had been overthrown; he alone of the Athenians who took part in civic life in his generation did not plot to change the fatherland to another form of *politeia* other than democracy; and he made both the legal judgements and the laws and the courts and property safe for all Athenians through his civic actions and he never did anything against the democracy either by word or by deed.[1]

In response to this request, the Athenians did, indeed, grant Demochares, the nephew of Demosthenes, these honours, as we know from the *Life* of Demosthenes in the *Lives of the Ten Orators*.[2] So the Athenians appropriately rewarded one of their great patriots in 271/0 BCE.

At first sight, we might take these honours, and the request in which they are preserved, as evidence for the city's highest honours and another manifestation of the culture of praise and reward in Hellenistic Athens.[3] To do so, however, is to ignore the very strong

---

1 [Plut.] *Mor.* 851D–F. Pytharatos' archonship is dated to 271/0: B. D. Meritt, 'Athenian archons 347/46–48/47 B.C.', *Historia* 26 (1977), pp. 161–91, at p. 174; A. G. Woodhead, *Agora Vol. XVI: Inscriptions: The Decrees* (Princeton: American School of Classical Studies at Athens, 1997), p. 268.
2 [Plut.] *Mor.* 847D–E.
3 E.g. P. Gauthier, *Les cités grecques et leurs bienfaiteurs (IVe–Ier siècle avant J.-C.): Contribution à l'histoire des institutions* (*BCH* Supplement 12; Athens: École Française d'Athènes, 1985), pp. 77–92; I. Kralli, 'Athens and her leading citizens in the early Hellenistic period (338–261 B.C.): The evidence of the decrees

politics of this particular document and the ways in which it (re-) constructs the Athenians' collective memories of the revolution from Demetrios Poliorketes in 286 BCE, a date for which I have argued elsewhere.[4] Modern scholars regularly understand these events as the liberation of Athens from external foreign rule.[5] Our ancient sources, however, show that the revolution was preceded by periods of tyranny and oligarchy; consequently, the revolution entailed not only regaining freedom from foreign domination, but also overthrowing oligarchy and re-establishing democracy. The Athenians needed to ask how they were to restore the *demos*' rule and how they were to negotiate their memories of the divisive period which preceded the revolution. As we shall see, the Athenians successfully remade Athens

awarding highest honours', *Archaiognosia* 10 (1999–2000), pp. 133–61. They have also recently been discussed in connection with intentional history; N. Luraghi, 'The *demos* as narrator: Public honours and the construction of the future and the past', in L. Foxhall, H.-J. Gehrke, and N. Luraghi (eds), *Intentional History: Spinning Time in Ancient Greece* (Stuttgart: Steiner, 2010), pp. 247–63.

4 J. L. Shear, 'Demetrios Poliorketes, Kallias of Sphettos, and the Panathenaia', in G. Reger, F. X. Ryan and T. F. Winters (eds), *Studies in Greek Epigraphy and History in Honor of Stephen V. Tracy* (Bordeaux: Ausonius Éditions, 2010), pp. 135–52; so also T. L. Shear, Jr., *Kallias of Sphettos and the Revolt of Athens in 286 B.C.* (*Hesperia* Supplement 17; Princeton: American School of Classical Studies at Athens, 1978), pp. 60–73. The scholarly *opinio communis* follows Habicht and Osborne in placing the revolution one year earlier in 287; C. Habicht, *Untersuchungen zur politischen Geschichte Athens im 3 Jahrhundert v. Chr.* (*Vestigia* 30; Munich: Beck, 1979), pp. 45–67; M. J. Osborne, 'Kallias, Phaidros and the revolt of Athens in 287 B.C.', *ZPE* 35 (1979), pp. 181–94; C. Habicht, *Athens from Alexander to Antony* (Cambridge, MA: Harvard University Press, 1997), pp. 95–7. Proponents of this view need to explain the cancellation of the Panathenaia of 286.

5 E.g. E. Will, 'The formation of the Hellenistic kingdoms', in F. W. Walbank, A. E. Astin, M. W. Frederiksen and R. M. Ogilvie (eds), *The Cambridge Ancient History. Vol. VII.1: The Hellenistic World*, 2nd edn (Cambridge: Cambridge University Press, 1984), pp. 101–17, at p. 108; N. G. L. Hammond and F. W. Walbank, *A History of Macedonia. Vol. III: 336–167 B.C.* (Oxford: Oxford University Press, 1988), pp. 230–1; Habicht, *Athens from Alexander to Antony*, pp. 91, 95–7; G. Shipley, *The Greek World after Alexander, 323–30 B.C.* (London: Routledge, 2000), pp. 123–4; G. J. Oliver, *War, Food, and Politics in Early Hellenistic Athens* (Oxford: Oxford University Press, 2007), pp. 121–3; R. M. Errington, *A History of the Hellenistic World, 323–30 B.C.* (Malden, MA: Blackwell, 2008), p. 56. Shear, Jr. and Green discuss the internal situation; Shear, Jr., *Kallias of Sphettos*, pp. 61–73; P. Green, *Alexander to Actium: The Historical Evolution of the Hellenistic Age* (Berkeley: University of California Press, 1990), pp. 123–8. In contrast, discussions of the overthrow of the Thirty focus on Athenians, not Spartans; e.g. P. Krentz, *The Thirty at Athens* (Ithaca, NY: Cornell University Press, 1982), pp. 69–101; M. Ostwald, *From Popular Sovereignty to the Sovereignty of Law: Law, Society and Politics in Fifth-Century Athens* (Berkeley: University of California Press, 1986), pp. 475–96; D. M. Lewis, 'Sparta as victor', in D. M. Lewis, J. Boardman, S. Hornblower and M. Ostwald (eds), *The Cambridge Ancient History. Vol. VI: The Fourth Century B.C.*, 2nd edn (Cambridge: Cambridge University Press, 1994), pp. 24–44, at pp. 32–7.

as democratic and they remembered the difficult events of the preceding years as the restoration of democracy and as external war. In so doing, the Athenians were guided by their collective responses to the earlier oligarchies and revolutions at the end of the fifth century and they modelled their actions on those of their ancestors. In the early third century, the city's past showed Athenians how to respond to the present and how to remember the difficult events which they had experienced.

DEMETRIOS AND THE ATHENIANS

In 307, Demetrios sailed into the Peiraieus and proclaimed the liberation of Athens, the expulsion of Kassandros' garrison, and the restoration of the laws and the ancestral constitution.[6] His actions led directly to the departure of Demetrios of Phaleron, who had been appointed ten years earlier by Kassandros to govern the city.[7] Demetrios needed to maintain his control of Athens, but his proclamation precluded the appointment of a governor; instead, he needed to act indirectly and to rely on Athenians who supported his regime. Our evidence suggests that he used this strategy both between 307 and 301 and after he regained the city in 295. Maintaining his rule over Athens was Demetrios' primary consideration and the details of the city's political system seem not to have concerned him, hence the democracy and oligarchy which the Athenians experienced. *Stasis* and tyranny accompanied the city's repudiation of Demetrios after the battle of Ipsos in 301 and civil strife also occurred before the revolution.

Demetrios' announcement in 307 indicated that democracy once again controlled Athens,[8] but this decision also constrained him. Governors and garrisons were incompatible with the rule of the *demos* and Demetrios needed the support of important Athenians. Among his important supporters was Stratokles of Diomeia, who proposed extensive and unprecedented honours for Demetrios and his father Antigonos, as well as at least two subsequent measures desired by Demetrios.[9] He was evidently a very active politician: twenty-four decrees moved by him before 301 are extant and eleven of them

---

6 Plut. *Demetr.* 8.4–7; cf. Diod. 20.45.1–2, 46.1.
7 Plut. *Demetr.* 9.3; Diod. 20.45.4–5.
8 On Athenian democracy at this time, see A. J. Bayliss, 'Athens under Macedonian domination: Athenian politics and politicians from the Lamian War to the Chremonidean War', PhD thesis, Macquarie University, 2002, pp. 101–4.
9 Plut. *Demetr.* 10.4–11.1, 24.6–11, 26.1–4; Diod. 20.46.2.

honoured Antigonid officials.[10] Stratokles was not the only Athenian working for Demetrios and men such as [Ka]laidas, Philostratos, and an anonymous man from Thria who also moved decrees honouring his associates must have supported him on other occasions.[11] They were not able, however, to keep the city loyal to Demetrios and Antigonos after their defeat at the battle of Ipsos in 301, when the Athenians refused to receive Demetrios back in the city.[12]

Subsequently, in 300, Lachares, a commander of mercenary troops, made himself tyrant after disputes among the generals.[13] The dissension was severe: our ancient sources describe the situation as *stasis* and they report fighting between Lachares and the hoplite general Charias, as well as the involvement of soldiers from Peiraieus.[14] Lachares' actions were encouraged by Kassandros, and Lysimachos was also supporting the Athenians at this time;[15] this regime was certainly not well disposed to Demetrios. He, in turn, moved against the city. His attack led first to the capture of Eleusis and Rhamnous and then to the surrender of the city after a naval blockade and severe famine.[16]

After the overthrow of Lachares in 295, Demetrios controlled the forts at Eleusis and Rhamnous, while, on the proposal of Dromokleides, the Athenians gave him the Peiraieus and Mounichia and he installed a garrison on the Mouseion.[17] As in 307, he does not seem to have installed a governor, and the rule of the *demos* was reinstated: a new *boule* and new generals were elected and the rest

---

10 W. B. Dinsmoor, *The Archons of Athens in the Hellenistic Age* (Cambridge, MA: Harvard University Press, 1931), pp. 13–14, with C. Habicht, 'Athenisches Ehrendekret vom Jahre des Koroibos (306/5) für einen königlichen Offizier', *AJAH* 2 (1977), pp. 37–9, at p. 39 n. 15, and *SEG* XXXVI 164; Habicht, *Athens from Alexander to Antony*, p. 71; Bayliss, 'Athens under Macedonian domination', p. 225 n. 2. Antigonid officials: listed by I. Kralli, 'Athens and the Hellenistic kings (338–261 B.C.): The language of the decrees', *CQ* 50 (2000), pp. 113–52 at pp. 130–1.

11 *IG* II² 498; *SEG* XXXVI 165; M. J. Osborne, *Naturalization in Athens Vol. II* (Brussels: AWLSK, 1981), D51. On the importance of such links, see Kralli, 'Athens and the Hellenistic kings', pp. 122–3; Bayliss, 'Athens under Macedonian domination', p. 231.

12 Plut. *Demetr*. 30.4.

13 *P.Oxy*. 2082 frs. 1–2 = *FGrHist* 257a F1–2, with P. J. Thonemann, 'Charias on the Acropolis', *ZPE* 144 (2003), pp. 123–4; Habicht, *Athens from Alexander to Antony*, pp. 82–3. For the date, cf. Men. *Imbrioi* test. 1 (*PCG*) = *P.Oxy*. 1235.105–12. For Lachares as tyrant, see Plut. *Demetrios* 33.1, 8; Paus. 1.25.7.

14 *Stasis*: *P.Oxy*. 2082 fr. 1; Plut. *Demetr*. 33.1; fighting: *P.Oxy*. 2082 fr. 2; Peiraieus soldiers: *P.Oxy*. 2082 fr. 2; A. J. Bayliss, 'Curse-tablets as evidence: Identifying the elusive "Peiraikoi soldiers"', *ZPE* 144 (2003), pp. 125–40, at pp. 138–9. Paus. 1.29.10 may point to further unrest.

15 Paus. 1.25.7; *IG* II² 657.9–16.

16 Plut. *Demetr*. 33.1–34.1.

17 Plut. *Demetr*. 34.6–7.

of the official year was divided into twelve prytanies;[18] democratic
rule is further attested in the Elaphebolion of 294.[19] These circumstances will again have forced Demetrios to work through his supporters in Athens. Among these men were certainly Dromokleides
and Stratokles.[20] Dromokleides' proposal had given the king control
of the Peiraieus, and he proposed at least one other measure in
the king's favour.[21] Further honours were proposed by supporters who are now nameless.[22] Gorgos' decree for Demetrios' official
Herodoros should also identify the author as well-disposed towards
the king.[23]

The city did not remain under democratic rule: Olympiodoros was
archon in both 294/3 and 293/2, an unprecedented situation, and, from
294/3 to 292/1, the secretary of the Council was replaced by a registrar
(*anagrapheus*), the same situation which had existed during the oligarchy in 321–318.[24] This evidence indicates that the city was again
ruled by a few, and inscriptions for Athenians active in the revolution
from Demetrios refer to the overthrow of democracy and a period of
oligarchy.[25] In addition to Dromokleides, Stratokles also supported
this regime and its close links to Demetrios, as his honorary decree
for Philippides of Paiania, the *basileus* in 293/2, shows.[26] Other office-
holders, like Phaidros of Sphettos, who held multiple generalships,
should also have been supporters.[27] Some men, such as Philippides
of Paiania, may have become involved in order to provide the best
course for the city, as Hagnon and Sophokles did in 411; others, like
Olympiodoros, who led the Athenians against the Mouseion in 286,[28]
may subsequently have become disillusioned or they may have been
keeping their options open, much as Theramenes did in the late fifth
century. Demetrios' acquiescence to the return of the oligarchic exiles

18 *IG* II² 644; 645; 682.21–4; Habicht, *Athens from Alexander to Antony*, pp. 88–9;
    Woodhead, *Agora Vol. XVI*, p. 237; M. J. Osborne, 'The archonship of Nikias
    Hysteros and the secretary cycles in the third century B.C.', *ZPE* 58 (1985),
    pp. 275–95 at pp. 275–82; Bayliss, 'Athens under Macedonian domination', pp.
    106–7; cf. Plut. *Demetr.* 34.5.
19 *IG* II² 646.1–3, 22–3.
20 Stratokles: *SEG* XLV 101.
21 Plut. *Demetr.* 13.1–3.
22 Plut. *Demetr.* 12.1–2.
23 *IG* II² 646.
24 Habicht, *Athens from Alexander to Antony*, pp. 90–1; S. V. Tracy, *Athens
    and Macedon: Attic Letter-Cutters of 300 to 229 B.C.* (Berkeley: University of
    California Press, 2003), pp. 12–13; Woodhead, *Agora Vol. XVI*, pp. 240–1; Meritt,
    'Athenian archons', p. 172; Shear, Jr., *Kallias of Sphettos*, pp. 53–5.
25 [Plut.] *Mor.* 851F; *SEG* XXVIII 60.80–3.
26 *SEG* XLV 101.
27 *IG* II² 682.24–47.
28 Paus. 1.26.1; Habicht, *Athens from Alexander to Antony*, pp. 95–6.

in 292/1 indicates his lack of concern for the nature of the regime, and the exiles will have had good reason to support him further.[29] In the absence of a governor, the king had to rely on these oligarchic Athenians.[30]

Not all Athenians supported the oligarchy, and the city was evidently divided. Phaidros' honorary decree states that, in 288/7, 'when difficult times (καιρῶν δυσκόλων) encompassed the city, Phaidros preserved the peace in the countryside . . . and he was responsible for bringing in the corn and other crops from the countryside'.[31] The phrase 'difficult times' suggests unrest within the city, as well as in the countryside,[32] and division over the correct course of action. That Phaidros fought on behalf of the 'common safety' (κοινῆς σωτηρίας) rather than the safety of the *demos* or polis, like men honoured after the revolution, reinforces this impression of strife between Athenians.[33] The stress in Phaidros' decree that the laws of the city were still in force at the end of his term as general suggests that the internal situation was still under control.[34] As general in the following year, Phaidros is described as continuing to do 'everything according to both the laws and the decrees of the *boule* and the *demos*'.[35] This phrase justifying his behaviour implies that not everyone saw his actions as appropriate and in the best interests of the city. *Stasis*, accordingly, accompanied the revolution and Athenians were divided, as they had been in the 290s when Lachares was tyrant. In 286, the Athenians needed both to re-establish democracy and to free themselves from Macedonian rule.

---

29 Return of exiles: Dion. Hal. *Dein.* 2–3, 9; Philoch. *FGrHist* 328 F67, 167; [Plut.] *Mor.* 850D; Habicht, *Athens from Alexander to Antony*, pp. 90–1.

30 No evidence supports Habicht's contention that Olympiodoros served as Demetrios' 'commissar or representative'; Habicht, *Athens from Alexander to Antony*, pp. 90–1.

31 *IG* II² 682.30–6; Shear, Jr., *Kallias of Sphettos*, p. 69. I remain unconvinced that the 'corn and other crops' are the same as the 'corn' brought in by Kallias, as suggested by Habicht and Osborne; *SEG* XXVIII 60.23–7; Habicht, *Untersuchungen zur politischen Geschichte*, pp. 52–4; Osborne, 'Kallias, Phaidros', pp. 185–6.

32 Shear, Jr., *Kallias of Sphettos*, p. 69.

33 *IG* II² 682.32–3. Safety of the *demos*: *IG* II² 650.18–19; *SEG* XXVIII 60.30–2; safety of the polis: *IG* II² 654.20–1; 657.32–3; cf. *IG* II² 666.9–14; 667.1–2.

34 *IG* II² 682.38–40; Shear, Jr., *Kallias of Sphettos*, p. 69. Hence the lack of evidence for intervention by the Macedonian soldiers; contrast *SEG* XXVIII 60.12–16, which describes the revolution itself.

35 *IG* II² 682.45–7.

DEMOCRACY AFTER DEMETRIOS

Since the revolution from Demetrios also involved *stasis* and the overthrow of oligarchy, re-establishing democracy in Athens was not simply a matter of freeing the city from Macedonian control or even choosing new councillors and magistrates. Instead, the rule of the *demos* needed to be shown as a viable and functioning system which would not be overthrown again. To this end, the Athenians used a number of strategies. Honorary decrees provided a particularly useful medium because they were products of the democracy and they monumentalised its processes. The contents of the documents rewarding citizens further focused on the rule of the *demos* and emphasised its importance. They also helped to delineate how the good Athenian should behave when democracy was threatened.

In re-establishing democracy, decrees and other honours were particularly suitable because they had to be proposed, discussed and approved by the *boule* and the *demos* before the texts could be inscribed and the honours awarded. Subsequently, the inscriptions and bronze statues served to commemorate the activities of the democracy and also the process of their creation, a significant dynamic which sets them apart from most other memorials.[36] Reading the decrees served to reperform the earlier actions in the Assembly, and it created and maintained memories of these actions. In this permanent form, they showed the *demos* perpetually in the process of ruling the city. These dynamics were not new at this time: they had been used to very good effect after the oligarchies of 411 and 404/3, as I have discussed elsewhere.[37] The increase in the number of inscriptions after the democrats regained control of the city[38] suggests that third-century Athenians were conscious of these dynamics. The documents include honours for various individuals, both Athenians and foreigners, who helped the *demos* to regain control, and there are indirect indications that not all the decrees which were passed are preserved. The honorary documents for non-Athenians may be quite specific about their actions, such as the decree for Zenon, or they may be couched in rather more general terms, as, for example, the decree

---

36 Monuments usually ignore the processes which brought them into being; J. E. Young, *The Texture of Memory: Holocaust Memorials and Meaning* (New Haven, CT: Yale University Press, 1993), p. 14; J. L. Shear, *Polis and Revolution: Responding to Oligarchy in Classical Athens* (Cambridge: Cambridge University Press, 2011), p. 8. Exceptional nature of inscriptions: Shear, *Polis and Revolution*, pp. 8–9, 105–6.

37 Shear, *Polis and Revolution*, pp. 96–106, 159–65, 247–57.

38 Woodhead, *Agora Vol. XVI*, p. 245.

for Artemidoros of Perinthos.[39] Unlike the decrees for citizens, they do not focus particularly on democracy.

In contrast, the rule of the *demos* is an important focus both of the request for the highest honours for Demochares and of the honorary decree for Kallias of Sphettos. In the document about Demochares' rewards, this importance is flagged up immediately by the form of the text: it requests the *boule* and *demos* to grant the highest honours.[40] They should so honour Demochares 'because he was a benefactor and a good adviser to the *demos* of the Athenians and he benefited the *demos* as follows'.[41] This phrase stresses that his activities took place in the democratic city, and it brings out the importance of the rule of the *demos* because actions in relation to other entities are not considered. The emphasis on the Athenian people continues in the description of Demochares' services to the city. His early activities led to his banishment by 'the men who overthrew the *demos*'.[42] His recall by the *demos* in the archonship of Diokles in 286/5 inaugurates a second phase of his career. These first two sections emphasise that Demochares was politically active only under democracy, and they demonstrate the power of the people which recalled a man exiled on its behalf. The final section of the request focuses further on Demochares' relationship to the *demos*. Here, we are told specifically that Demochares was exiled on behalf of the democracy, that he had no part in the oligarchy, and that he held no office after the *demos* was overthrown. Nor did he plot to change the democratic *politeia*. By his actions, Demochares also made the laws and the courts and their judgements safe for 'all Athenians'. The laws and the courts are integral parts of the democracy and apply to everyone resident in the city, but they must be carried out by the actions of the individual citizens. We are presented with a particular picture of the honorand: a man active only on behalf of democracy, which is important enough for him to go into exile on its behalf.

This text also sets up patterns of behaviour, both positive and negative. The good Athenian is easily identified. He is a democrat who works on behalf of the *demos* and makes safe characteristic aspects of its rule for everyone. He defends the democracy both by word and by deed and he is willing to go into exile on its behalf. The actions of the bad Athenian are also delineated: he is an oligarch who plots against democracy and holds office after the *demos* has been overthrown. Both by word and by deed, he harms democracy and he does not care

39 Zenon: *IG* II² 650; Artemidoros: *IG* II² 663; Woodhead, *Agora Vol. XVI*, 172.
    Since I place the revolution in 286, I associate these inscriptions with those events.
40 See above, n. 1.
41 [Plut.] *Mor.* 851D.
42 [Plut.] *Mor.* 851E.

about 'all the Athenians'. This imagery is extremely uncompromising, particularly in the aftermath of a revolution which involved not only fighting against Macedonians, but also *stasis* within the city. In the aftermath of the events, this identity will not have been comforting to anyone who was not an ardent democrat during the revolution, and it leaves little room for integrating these men back into 'all the Athenians'. The focus here on the good Athenian as democrat also reinforces the importance of democracy in this document.

The emphasis on the rule of the *demos* and of a man's actions on its behalf are also important dynamics in the long honorary decree for Kallias of Sphettos, who played an important role in the revolution (Fig. 15.1).[43] The design of the decree immediately brings out the importance of the people: *demos* is the very first word of the text and the phrase 'it was decreed by the *boule* and the *demos*' is set off in its own line.[44] There can be no question about the authority behind this document. While Kallias' name is appropriately the second word in the decree proper, it is immediately followed by the phrase 'when the revolution of the *demos* took place against those occupying the city', and the next twenty-nine lines describe in detail Kallias' actions on behalf of the *demos*.[45] This word appears repeatedly in this section of the inscription and there can be no doubt about its importance. These lines also make the relationship between Kallias and the people clear: 'Kallias fought on behalf of the *demos* and, attacking with his soldiers, although he was wounded, he did not at any moment shrink from any danger on behalf of the safety (σωτηρίας) of the *demos*'.[46] At the time of the peace process, Kallias, at the request of the generals and the *boule*, 'served as an envoy on behalf of the *demos*'.[47] While the sections which follow in lines 43–78 concern Kallias' services to the city in the years after the revolution, the final clauses about his career come back to the events in 286. Here, we learn that Kallias did something on behalf of the *patris* when the *demos* had been overthrown, and he allowed his property to be confiscated under the oligarchy 'so as no[t] to do [anything a]gainst either the laws or the democ[rac]y of all the Athenians'.[48] Again, the focus is on the *demos* and its rule and, as in Demochares' request, the laws are an important part of this system. Kallias' actions here match those of Demochares and are described in exactly the same terms.

43 *SEG* XXVIII 60.
44 *SEG* XXVIII 60.1, 10.
45 *SEG* XXVIII 60.11–13.
46 *SEG* XXVIII 60.28–32.
47 *SEG* XXVIII 60.36–8.
48 *SEG* XXVIII 60.78–83.

Figure 15.1   SEG XXVIII 60: the decree in honour of Kallias of Sphettos.

In Kallias' decree, we are also presented with another image of the good Athenian. Again, he is a democrat who works on behalf of the *demos* both in peace and, especially, in war, when he fights for the people and for their *soteria*. When a democrat's property is confiscated by an oligarchy, he himself is in exile and so, once again, the good Athenian goes into exile on behalf of democracy. In exile, he cannot hold office and so he cannot support a regime other than the rule of the people. The image presented here fits well with the good Athenian in Demochares' request, but it also extends the imagery by stressing the importance of fighting on behalf of the *demos*. Only in this way can a man be a good Athenian, and this definition leaves no room for citizens who previously supported the oligarchy and were not active on behalf of the safety of the *demos*. Presented in a decree, this image also emphasises the importance of the rule of the *demos*, a dynamic visible elsewhere in this document, as well as in the request for Demochares. Inscribing the text further served to display the power of the *demos* and its control of the city, while it also provided readers with an opportunity to reperform the assembly's earlier actions. Set up in the city, the inscription emphasised that Athens was once again democratic.

THE *DEMOS* AND THE MODEL OF THE PAST

Both Kallias' decree and Demochares' request emphasise the importance of the *demos* and its rule, and together they present a very uncompromising picture of the good Athenian. These strategies, however, were not used for the first time to respond to the events of 286. Instead, the proposers were drawing on imagery developed at the end of the fifth century to respond to the oligarchies of 411 and 404/3. Of the earlier documents invoked, the decree of Demophantos with its focus on democracy proved to be an especially potent reference point. For third-century Athenians, the interconnections with the past reinforced the dynamics of their own documents and made the memory politics explicit. The associations also served to refine the images of the honorands as good Athenians and of the *demos* itself.

The decree and oath of Demophantos particularly focus on the importance of democracy, and this emphasis is repeatedly visible in the inscribed documents connected with these responses to oligarchy.[49] In 410/9, this decree, too, presented an uncompromising view

---

49 Decree of Demophantos: Andok. 1.96–8; J. L. Shear, 'The oath of Demophantos and the politics of Athenian identity', in A. H. Sommerstein and J. Fletcher (eds), *Horkos: The Oath in Greek Society* (Exeter: Bristol Phoenix Press, 2007), pp.

of what it meant to be Athenian: a democrat who kills tyrants and oligarchs on behalf of the city and, if necessary, dies for Athens. This image is similar to what we have seen in Demochares' request and especially in Kallias' honorary decree. As in the third century, in 410/9, Demophantos left no room for anyone who had previously supported oligarchy. The interrelationship between the request for Demochares and Demophantos' decree does not stop at this point. The request stresses that Demochares never held office after the *demos* was overthrown and never plotted against the democracy; he also never did anything against the democracy 'either by word or by deed'. Demophantos' decree specifies how Athenians should act 'if anyone overthrows the democracy at Athens or holds office after the democracy has been overthrown'.[50] In addition, the oath requires the good Athenian to kill such a man 'both by word and by deed and by vote and by my own hand'.[51] In writing his request, Laches clearly modelled part of his description on the clauses of Demophantos' decree. Here, the past provides a way of dealing with a difficult present, and it particularly makes clear how the good Athenian should act when the democracy has been threatened. The relationship between the two texts also has further implications for the memory politics of the earlier document. In 271/0, Demophantos' decree was evidently still visible in the city, presumably in front of the Old Bouleuterion where Lykourgos placed it in 330 (Fig. 15.2).[52] Laches knew that it was connected with the overthrow of democracy and *stasis*, events very similar to those which had enveloped the city in the early third century. Invoking this earlier text also (re-)created for listeners and subsequent readers memories of the events which it commemorated.[53]

The invocation of Demophantos' decree was not limited to the request for Demochares, and it served as a reference point for two other decrees awarding the highest honours. The document rewarding Philippides of Kephale states that he, too, 'never [d]i[d] anything agains[t the d]emocracy [e]ith[er by word or] by deed'.[54] Since some of his most important benefactions involve the city's relationship with

148–60, at pp. 150–3; Shear, *Polis and Revolution*, pp. 96–9. Responses to fifth-century oligarchies: Shear, *Polis and Revolution*, pp. 96–106, 247–57.

50 Andok. 1.96.
51 Andok. 1.97.
52 Lykourg. *Leok*. 124–5.
53 For an example of these dynamics, see Lykourg. *Leok*. 126–7; Shear, *Polis and Revolution*, pp. 159–63.
54 *IG* II² 657.48–50, with Gauthier's restoration of [πέπραχ]ε[ν] in line 49; P. Gauthier, 'Notes sur trois décrets honorants des citoyens bienfaiteurs', *RP* 56 (1982), pp. 215–31, at p. 222 n. 28. This phrase occurs nowhere else in the corpus of Attic inscriptions.

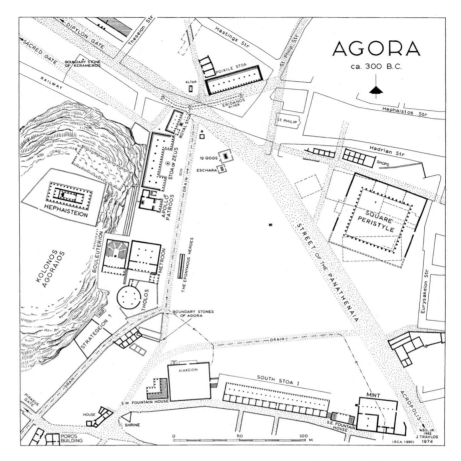

Figure 15.2 Plan of the Agora in c. 300 BCE. Earlier, in the fifth century, the structure of the Metroon was the city's (Old) Bouleuterion.

Lysimachos, this phrase connects Philippides with the revolution, in which he was otherwise not involved.[55] Similarly, Kallias' decree stresses that he never did anything against the laws or the democracy of all the Athenians.[56] Although the phrase 'by word or by deed' does not appear here, the reference to actions against the democracy invokes Demophantos' decree, as does the emphasis on 'all the Athenians', who are twice described as swearing Demophantos' oath.

---

55 His connection with the revolution is further suggested by lines 31–2, which record that 'when the *demos* had recovered its freedom, he continued doing and saying what was advantageous for the safety of the city'. This passage constructs Philippides as an Athenian active on behalf of the safety of the city, an image which we have already seen in connection with Kallias.

56 *SEG* XXVIII 60.81–3.

In both instances, these references emphasise the two honorands' status as good democratic Athenians who were in exile when the rule of the *demos* was overthrown and so could not hold office under another regime. In the case of Philippides' document, the reference to Demophantos' decree shows that, already in 283/2, the restored democrats were associating their revolution from Demetrios with the events at the end of the fifth century.[57]

While Demophantos' decree describes political regimes other than democracy, it does not use the term 'oligarchy'.[58] In contrast, both the request for Demochares and Kallias' decree explicitly use this term,[59] and they set up an opposition between oligarchy and democracy. This strategy finds its parallel in the responses to the Thirty. For example, Theozotides' decree rewarding the sons of dead democrats sets up an explicit contrast between democracy, which the dead men aided, and oligarchy, under which they died.[60] In the documents recording the sales of the property of the Thirty and their supporters, the oligarchs, whose property is being sold, are juxtaposed with the *demos*, which is doing the selling.[61] The epigram from the decree honouring the living Athenians who brought back the *demos* juxtaposes their actions with their opponents': 'they first began to depose those ruling the city with unjust statutes (θεσμοῖς) and hazarded their lives'.[62] Although the word used here is *thesmos*, the emphasis on laws, both good and bad, recalls the claims that Demochares made the laws safe and that Kallias never acted against the laws. Athenian laws had been the focus of much attention both after 411 and after 404/3 when they were collected and reorganised.[63] Memories of those events may lie behind the

---

57 Euthios' archonship in 283/2: Meritt, 'Athenian archons', p. 173; Woodhead, *Agora Vol. XVI*, pp. 256–7.
58 Shear, 'The oath of Demophantos', p. 150; Shear, *Polis and Revolution*, pp. 75, 98–9, 111, 162–3.
59 [Plut.] *Mor.* 851F; *SEG* XXVIII 60.81.
60 *SEG* XXVIII 46, especially lines 4–6; Shear, *Polis and Revolution*, pp. 248, 250, 259–60.
61 *SEG* XXXII 161; Shear, *Polis and Revolution*, pp. 249–50, 260.
62 *SEG* XXVIII 45.73–6, with Aischin. 3.190.
63 The bibliography on this project is extensive; see e.g. S. Dow, 'The Athenian calendar of sacrifices: The chronology of Nikomakhos' second term', *Historia* 9 (1960), pp. 270–93; Ostwald, *From Popular Sovereignty*, pp. 407–11, 414–18, 511–24; N. Robertson, 'The laws of Athens, 410–399 bc: The evidence for review and publication', *JHS* 110 (1990), pp. 43–75; P. J. Rhodes, 'The Athenian code of laws, 410–399 bc', *JHS* 111 (1991), pp. 87–100; S. C. Todd, 'Lysias against Nikomakhos: The fate of the expert in Athenian law', in L. Foxhall and A. D. E. Lewis (eds), *Greek Law in its Political Setting: Justification and Justice* (Oxford: Oxford University Press, 1996), pp. 101–31; J. Sickinger, *Public Records and Archives in Classical Athens* (Chapel Hill: University of North Carolina Press, 1999), pp. 93–105; S. D. Lambert, 'The sacrificial calendar of Athens', *ABSA*

third-century references. More recent history, however, may also have been involved because (some of) the city's laws had been (re)published in 304/3.[64]

The request for Demochares and the decree for Kallias make it clear that the honorands were in exile after the democracy was overthrown, and the image of the good Athenian is that of a man exiled for democracy, as we have already seen. The focus is on the individual, but the imagery implies, too, that good Athenians were in exile in the period leading up to the revolution, a strategy also visible in the decree for Philippides. In this way, the texts again recall the events at the end of the fifth century when the *demos* itself was remembered as being exiled and the return from Phyle was figured as the restoration of the *demos* from exile.[65] In the early third century, these parallels construct the events of 286 as the restoration of democracy. In the case of Demochares, the text specifies that 'he was recalled (κατῆλθεν) by the *demos* in the archonship of Diokles', and it employs a form of the verb κατέρχομαι. In the fifth- and fourth-century texts, this verb is regularly employed to describe the return from Phyle, and its use in the request for Demochares makes the connections with the earlier event explicit. The correspondences between the situation at the end of the fifth century and the revolution from Demetrios, however, are not exact because, in the third century, only individual Athenians were actually in exile and the *demos* could not properly be said to have been banished from the city. These differences bring out for us how the third-century Athenians have taken an aspect of the response to the Thirty and then adapted it to suit their own experiences and their own needs in responding to the revolution against Demetrios.

These earlier responses are invoked yet again in the request for Demochares and the decree for Kallias through bronze statues of the honorands which are to be set up in the Agora.[66] In Kallias' case, the

(footnote 63 *continued*)
97 (2002), pp. 353–99; M. Gagarin, *Writing Greek Law* (Cambridge: Cambridge University Press, 2008), pp. 182–8; Shear, *Polis and Revolution*, pp. 72–96, 229–30, 232, 238–47.

64 *IG* II² 487.4–10; Habicht, *Athens from Alexander to Antony*, p. 70; W. S. Ferguson, *Hellenistic Athens: An Historical Essay* (London: Macmillan, 1911), pp. 103–4; Gagarin, *Writing Greek Law*, pp. 228–9.

65 E.g. Lys. 12.57–8; 13.47; 14.33; 24.25; 25.18, 20–2; 26.2; fr. 165.34–8 (Carey); Isok. 16.12–14; Aischin. 3.187; cf. Lys. 2.61; A. Wolpert, *Remembering Defeat: Civil War and Civic Memory in Ancient Athens* (Baltimore: Johns Hopkins University Press, 2002), pp. 91–5; S. Forsdyke, *Exile, Ostracism, and Democracy: The Politics of Expulsion in Ancient Greece* (Princeton: Princeton University Press, 2005), pp. 260–4.

66 [Plut.] *Mor.* 851D; *SEG* XXVIII 60.95–6. At some later date, the statue for Demochares was transferred to the Prytaneion; [Plut.] *Mor.* 847D, E.

publication clause specifies that the inscription is to be erected next to the statue.[67] We know that the honours for Demochares were awarded as requested, and it seems very likely that the resulting honorary decree was also set up next to the statue in the Agora. This location brought these commemorative monuments physically into a space which the responses to the fifth-century oligarchies had turned into the space of the citizen.[68] The inscribed monuments which the third-century texts invoke were all located here, so that the new inscriptions and statues were visually juxtaposed with their models. The physical presence of the earlier inscriptions will have further emphasised the connections between the responses to the revolution against Demetrios and to the events in the late fifth century. With its focus on democracy and the citizen, this setting reinforced the stress on the *demos* and its rule which we saw in the two third-century texts. The statues of Kallias and Demochares will have presented the two men as good democrats and exemplars for their fellow citizens. In this way, they repeated some of the dynamics, although probably not the physical appearance, of the figures of Konon and Euagoras which were erected in front of the Stoa of Zeus Eleutherios to commemorate their victory at Knidos in 394/3 (Fig. 15.2), and which marked the end of the transformation of the Agora in the late fifth and early fourth centuries.[69] In the case of Demochares' figure, its appearance will have had further ramifications for the image of the honorand. According to the *Life* of Demosthenes, it showed Demochares wearing a *himation* and a sword, the costume which he wore to address the *demos* when Antipatros was demanding the surrender of the orators.[70] While the *himation* emphasised the honorand's actions as a statesman, the sword was decidedly martial. It linked him to the various military memorials in the Agora, particularly the Stoa Poikile and those in and around the Stoa of Zeus (fig. 15.2).[71] In this setting, the sword suggested that Demochares had contributed to the revolution against Demetrios in a military capacity, and it linked his actions with those of the earlier Athenians whose martial deeds were commemorated in various monuments in the square.

For Kallias' statue, the combination of the figure, the inscribed text and the setting in the Agora must have been particularly potent. The

67 *SEG* XXVIII 60.104–7.
68 J. L. Shear, 'Cultural change, space, and the politics of commemoration in Athens', in R. Osborne (ed.), *Debating the Athenian Cultural Revolution: Art, Literature, Philosophy and Politics 430–380 B.C.* (Cambridge: Cambridge University Press, 2007), pp. 91–115; Shear, *Polis and Revolution*, pp. 112–22, 132–3, 263–85.
69 Isok. 9.56–7; Dem. 20.69–70; Paus. 1.3.2–3; Shear, 'Cultural change', pp. 107–9, 113–15; Shear, *Polis and Revolution*, pp. 274–81, 284.
70 [Plut.] *Mor.* 847D.
71 Military monuments: Shear, 'Cultural change', pp. 105–6, 111–12.

text configures him not only as a democrat but also as a man active on behalf of the safety of the *demos*, and his actions make him into a saviour of the people. This construction borrowed another strategy from the early fourth-century monuments for Konon and Euagoras, which, though their location in front of the Stoa of Zeus Soter, presented the honorands as saviours of Athens.[72] Juxtaposed with the early fourth-century figures and inscriptions, Kallias' statue and decree will have stressed that he had followed the model of the earlier men and behaved like a good democratic Athenian. These parallels may have been further reinforced by the setting of the monument: the decree was found reused over the Great Drain in front of the Stoa Basileios and, together with the figure, it may have been erected not far away (Fig. 15.2).[73] Such a location would have placed it near both the Stoa of Zeus and the statues of Konon and Euagoras, so that the relationships were clearly visible. In the third century, the juxtaposition of Demochares' and Kallias' figures and the inscriptions will have made the memory politics both explicit and visible. At this time, responding to the overthrow of the *demos* followed the patterns of remembrance established over one hundred year earlier. These memories showed the Athenians how the rule of the *demos* could be displayed and how the image of the good citizen should be re-created. In this way, the Athenians were able to come to terms with the difficult present.

REMEMBERING *STASIS*?

Both the request for Demochares and the decree for Kallias focus appropriately on the actions of the honorands. This strategy, however, created gaps into which memories could fall and so be forgotten. Although both texts refer to the overthrow of the *demos*, they are very coy about who exactly did this terrible deed and what happened in the city. The stress on 'all the Athenians' in both documents implies disunity and the accompanying *stasis*. This term, however, is distinctly avoided, and only the cognate *epanastasis* is used once in Kallias' decree to describe the actions of the *demos* against those occupying the city.[74] Civil strife cannot be remembered as such because it involves citizens pitted against each other.[75] In the aftermath of the revolution, the Athenians faced the problem of how to remember these events. The solution was to turn them into external war in much the same way

---

72 Shear, 'Cultural change', pp. 107–8, 110; Shear, *Polis and Revolution*, pp. 277–8.
73 Shear, Jr., *Kallias of Sphettos*, pp. 1–2 with n. 1.
74 *SEG* XXVIII 60.12.
75 Shear, *Polis and Revolution*, p. 295; cf. N. Loraux, *The Divided City: On Memory and Forgetting in Ancient Athens* (New York: Zone Books, 2002), p. 101.

that the events of 404/3 were made into victory over external enemies, hence modern scholars' narratives of liberation from a foreign king.

Demochares' request tells us very little about his opponents: they are simply the men who overthrew the *demos*. In part, this decision must have been dictated by his lack of participation in the revolution itself. In contrast, Kallias' decree describes exactly these events. Here, too, the description of the opponents is circumscribed. They appear initially as the men who were occupying the city and the soldiers expelled from the *asty*.[76] We hear also of hostile forces in the fort on the Mouseion Hill and in the Peiraieus, while Demetrios and his army appear several times.[77] The effect is to obscure any participation by Athenians and to shift the focus on to external enemies: the Macedonians and Demetrios. This strategy appears even more clearly in the honorary decree granting a certain Strombichos citizenship in return for his services to the city in the Chremonidean War.[78] The text reports that, 'when the *demos* took up arms on behalf of its freedom', Strombichos, a Macedonian officer, was persuaded to change sides and he joined in besieging the Mouseion with the *demos*. He acted for the freedom of the people and he was jointly responsible for the deliverance (*soteria*) of the city. In 266/5, some twenty years after the events in 286, internal dissent does not appear in the text; instead, the focus is on the military forces and the attack on the Mouseion.

The decrees for both Strombichos and Kallias combine their military actions with their focus on the *soteria* of the city or *demos*. In Kallias' case, no military dangers deterred him from actions on behalf of the safety of the *demos*.[79] Linking *soteria* with military action locates the safety of the *demos*/city in relation to external enemies, and it reinforces the construction of the revolution as war against Macedonians rather than civil strife between Athenians. This same strategy appears in the honorary decree for Zenon, a commander of undecked warships for Ptolemy I. In addition to helping to secure the city's corn supply, he is also described as 'joining in the f[ighting] (συναγωνιζό[μενος]) [for the] safety [of the *dem*]*os*'.[80] As with our other examples, this phrase directs attention to enemies outside the

---

76 *SEG* XXVIII 60.12–14.
77 Hostile forces: *SEG* XXVIII 60.14–16; Demetrios: *SEG* XXVIII 60.16–18, 27–8, 36.
78 *IG* II² 666.1–17 and 667.1–6 = Osborne, *Naturalization Vol. I*, D78. Date (archonship of Nikias of Otryne): Meritt, 'Athenian archons', p. 174.
79 See above, n. 46.
80 *IG* II² 650.14–17. The inscription's state of preservation precludes certainty about Zenon's actions; for suggestions, see Shear, Jr., *Kallias of Sphettos*, pp. 20–1; Habicht, *Untersuchungen zur politischen Geschichte*, pp. 48–50; Osborne, 'Kallias, Phaidros', pp. 189–90; Oliver, *War, Food, and Politics*, p. 123 n. 67.

boundaries of the city and it obscures any discord within it. In this context, the term *soteria* can refer to the events of the revolution, but without raising the spectre of *stasis*.[81] Instead, it directs attention towards the city's external enemies so that the fighting is configured as regular military action.

Remembering the revolution as war against Macedonians rather than civil strife between citizens was not limited to these inscriptions. Pausanias reports that the Athenians killed in the assault on the fort on the Mouseion Hill were buried with the other war-dead in the *Demosion Sema*.[82] This decision emphasised that these men had died fighting external enemies, not Athenians, and the rituals of their burial will have stressed exactly this point: they were no different from the men buried in the other, earlier graves, some of which Pausanias described. This connection was reinforced by the Athenians' decision to dedicate the shield of Leokritos to Zeus Eleutherios.[83] These honours were appropriate because Leokritos died in the fighting after being the first man to scale the wall and to enter the fort on the Mouseion. As a dedication, the shield will have been displayed in the god's stoa in the northwest corner of the Agora, where military victory against external enemies was particularly celebrated.[84] Subsequently, when Pausanias came to describe the assault, he also remembered it as Athenians fighting against Macedonians and no other enemies.[85] In these ways, accordingly, the Athenians collectively (re)constructed the events as military action against external enemies, and they forgot the internal divisions which had also occurred. Conspicuously ignoring civil strife allowed it to be reconstructed as fighting against non-Athenians and stressed that the Athenians were forgetting. Since the burial of the dead will have occurred soon after the hostilities had ended, the Athenians' construction of this response to revolution must have begun almost immediately. These decisions then continued to shape how the events would be remembered for at least the next twenty years.

By adopting these memory politics, the Athenians again followed the model set by the responses to the Thirty at the end of the fifth century. The men killed fighting against that oligarchy had

---

81 Compare Osborne, *Naturalization in Athens, Vol. II* (Brussels: AWLSK, 1982), p. 158. The revolution is also alluded to by the phrase 'when the *demos* recovers the *asty*/its freedom', but it serves to obscure, rather than emphasise, the military events; *IG* II² 654.17–18; 657.31.
82 Paus. 1.29.13.
83 Paus. 1.26.1–2.
84 Shear, 'Cultural change', pp. 111–12.
85 Paus. 1.26.1–3.

also been buried in the *Demosion Sema*.[86] Through the agency of
Theozotides' decree, their sons were assimilated to the war-orphans:
they were brought up at state expense and, when they reached
manhood, they were presented with the war-orphans in the theatre.[87]
A trophy, that quintessential military monument, was erected and the
Lakedaimonians killed in the fighting were buried near the Dipylon
Gate and not far from the *Demosion Sema*.[88] In the epigraphical texts,
the term *stasis* is avoided and the Thirty tend to disappear from view.[89]
In this way, the fifth-century Athenians turned *stasis* into external war
with the Spartans, and they collectively and conspicuously allowed
civil strife to slip into the gaps of memory and so be forgotten. For
their third-century descendants, borrowing these strategies allowed
them to obscure the part played by their fellow citizens and their
support of the Macedonians. Focusing on the Macedonians provided
the divided Athenians with a common enemy responsible for their
problems; concentrating on *stasis*, however, would have perpetuated
their disunity. Celebrating this victory, therefore, created an occasion
in which all Athenians could participate together, and it allowed them
to begin the process of healing their divisions.

THIRD-CENTURY STRATEGIES

In the aftermath of the revolution of 286, the Athenians had to restore
democracy and to decide how to remember the difficult events which
had occurred. In so doing, they looked back to the ways in which their
ancestors had collectively responded to the oligarchies in the late fifth
century, and here they discovered a series of helpful documents and
strategies: the decree and oath of Demophantos, the stress on democracy and the display of its actions, restoration from exile, remembering
the events as external war and forgetting *stasis*. As their ancestors had
done, so they, too, used the Agora, which had been remade in the late
fifth and early fourth centuries into the space of the democratic citizen.
The parallels with the fifth-century strategies also emphasised that the
restoration of democracy in 286 had been achieved by citizens, rather
than an outside power, as it had been in 307. While the Athenians were
clearly using the past in order to deal with the present, they did not

---

86 Lys. 2.64; N. Loraux, *The Invention of Athens: The Funeral Oration in the Classical
    City* (Cambridge, MA: Harvard University Press, 1986), pp. 35–6, 200; Shear,
    Polis and Revolution, p. 292.
87 *SEG* XXVIII 46; Shear, *Polis and Revolution*, pp. 291–4.
88 Lys. 2.63; S. C. Todd, *A Commentary on Lysias, Speeches 1–11* (Oxford: Oxford
    University Press, 2007), pp. 262–3; Shear, *Polis and Revolution*, pp. 298–9.
89 Shear, *Polis and Revolution*, pp. 294–301.

adopt all the strategies from the fifth century. Instead, they took over only those features which were relevant to their own situation, and they had to acknowledge both the continuing Macedonian control of the Peiraieus and their dependency on aid from foreign kings. Simply reverting to the strategies of the late fifth and early fourth centuries would not solve the problems facing the city after 286.

The revolution from Demetrios brought freedom only to the city itself because the Peiraieus and the fortresses in Attica remained in Macedonian hands. In 285/4, the decree in honour of the Paionian king Audoleon records his promise of future support and his assistance 'towards the recovery of the Peiraieus and the freedom of the city'.[90] In 283/2, Philippides' honours report that, after the revolution, he requested money and corn from Lysimachos 'so that the *demos* remains free and the Peiraieus and the forts might be recovered as quickly as possible'.[91] In the following year, Euthios is given permission to seek further benefits 'when the Peiraieus and the *asty* are reunited'.[92] Despite at least one failed attempt to recapture the seaport, it remained under Macedonian control and was not reunited with the city.[93] Of the forts, Eleusis was back in Athenian control by 284/3, when Philippides as *agonothetes* first put on extra games for Demeter and Kore 'as a memorial of the [freedom] of the *demos*'.[94] By the start of the Chremonidean War, Athens had also regained control of Rhamnous, but the circumstances and date remain unknown; other installations remained in Macedonian hands.[95] Particularly in the

---

90 *IG* II² 654.30–5 = Osborne, *Naturalization Vol. I*, D76; Diotimos' archonship in 285/4: Meritt, 'Athenian archons', p. 173; Woodhead, *Agora Vol. XVI*, p. 255.

91 *IG* II² 657.31–6; cf. Woodhead, *Agora Vol. XVI*, 176.5–6.

92 Woodhead, *Agora Vol. XVI*, 181.28–31.

93 Habicht, *Athens from Alexander to Antony*, pp. 124–5; Woodhead, *Agora Vol. XVI*, p. 252; Habicht, *Untersuchungen zur politischen Geschichte*, pp. 95–107; Osborne, 'Kallias, Phaidros', pp. 192–4; Oliver, *War, Food, and Politics*, pp. 55–63; *contra*: G. Reger, 'Athens and Tenos in the early Hellenistic age', *CQ* 42 (1992), pp. 365–83, at pp. 368–79; Shear, Jr., *Kallias of Sphettos*, pp. 29, 79; P. Gauthier, 'La réunification d'Athènes en 281 et les deux archontes Nicias', *REG* 92 (1979), pp. 348–99; failed attempt: Paus. 1.29.10; Polyainos 5.17.1; Habicht, *Athens from Alexander to Antony*, pp. 124–5; Shear, Jr., *Kallias of Sphettos*, pp. 82–3; Oliver, *War, Food, and Politics*, pp. 58–60.

94 *IG* II² 657.43–45; Shear, Jr., *Kallias of Sphettos*, p. 84; A. Bielman, *Retour à la liberté: Libération et sauvetage des prisonniers en Grèce ancienne. Recueil d'inscriptions honorant des sauveteurs et analyse critique* (*Études epigraphiques* 1; Athens: École Française d'Athènes, 1994), p. 78; cf. Habicht, *Athens from Alexander to Antony*, p. 129; Oliver, *War, Food, and Politics*, pp. 125–6; *contra*: K. Clinton, 'Macedonians at Eleusis in the early third century', in O. Palagia and S. V. Tracy (eds), *The Macedonians in Athens, 322–229 B.C.: Proceedings of an International Conference held at the University of Athens, May 24–26, 2001* (Oxford: Oxbow, 2003), pp. 76–81, at pp. 77–8.

95 *I.Rhamnous* 3.5–7; Habicht, *Athens from Alexander to Antony*, pp. 129, 130.

immediate aftermath of the revolution, the continuing Macedonian presence in the Peiraieus and other forts will have reinforced the construction of the events of 286 as military action against external enemies. It also gave the Athenians a common foe against which they could all agree to direct their attention together. Expelling the remaining Macedonian forces, consequently, brought the divided citizens together, and this shared purpose served to begin healing the fractures caused by the revolution. The references in the decrees will have reinforced these dynamics and they repeatedly reminded the Athenians of their united resolve in removing the Macedonian garrisons.

The aid requested from Audoleon and Lysimachos in order to recover the Peiraieus emphasises the Athenians' continuing dependency on the good will of various kings. Indeed, Kallias' decree demonstrates that the support of Ptolemy I was crucial for the success of the revolution. Similarly, the request for Demochares records his embassies to both Lysimachos and Ptolemy, and these two kings' names appear in other inscriptions honouring individuals who either participated or supported the Athenians in the revolution.[96] In the decrees, the effect is to shift the focus away from the city of Athens and to situate the events in the larger international sphere. Such decisions reflect the changed realities of third-century Athens, but the strategies also contrast with the documents generated by the Athenians after the revolutions in the late fifth century. That material is focused on Athenians and the city, while leading powers from elsewhere in the Greek world are not invoked or otherwise made visible. In the third century, it proved impossible for the Athenians to escape the political realities of the day, particularly their dependence on foreign kings and their lack of control of the Peiraieus and the other forts.

The references to the kings and the Athenians' lack of control of the Peiraieus make the third-century documents significantly unlike the texts connected with the late fifth-century revolutions. For us, this contrast brings out an important difference between the responses: while the third-century Athenians faced some of the same issues and adopted many strategies from the fifth century, they were not blindly repeating what their ancestors had already done. Instead, they took the appropriate approaches and adapted them to suit the particular circumstances which they now faced. In some cases, the current situation allowed the Athenians to make very close connections with the fifth-century responses to revolution, as we see with some aspects of the request for Demochares and the decree for Kallias, but those same

---

96 Demochares: [Plut.] *Mor.* 851E; other references: e.g. *IG* II² 650.10; 663.3–4, 17; cf. Woodhead, *Agora Vol. XVI*, 172.7. Audoleon's name appears in *IG* II² 655.

documents also do not hesitate to mention foreign kings well disposed towards the city, an element which has no parallel in the fifth century. Copying all aspects of the earlier responses would not solve the city's problems; instead, the Athenians had to pick and choose the appropriate strategies from their ancestors' earlier actions. Not all aspects of the past were now relevant and some of them had to be ignored and so forgotten.

That the third-century responses to the revolution are the result of conscious choice is brought out by a final document which also recalls the events: the honorary decree for Phaidros of Sphettos which was passed soon after the end of the Chremonidean War.[97] Some twenty-three lines of this lengthy inscription concern the years between 288/7 and 286/5, but they present a very different picture (Fig. 15.3).[98] Despite extensive subsequent erasures, there are no traces of exile or of fighting on behalf of the *demos*, as there are in the other texts. Since the erasures were made in 200 BCE when references to Macedonian kings were removed from Athenian documents,[99] their content must have concerned Demetrios rather than any of the other kings. The text emphasises keeping the peace, counselling the *demos* and following the laws and decrees of the *boule* and *demos*, but it carefully does not indicate the nature of the regime.[100] Perusal of earlier sections of the decree also shows that Phaidros was general when Lachares was tyrant,[101] and he certainly held office under the subsequent oligarchic regime. This text presents a very different image both of the revolution and of the honorand from those of the other documents. Unlike our other honorands, Phaidros was not rewarded after the revolution and, indeed, his career seems to have languished. When the city was once again under close Macedonian control in the 250s, Phaidros could finally get his highest honours, but doing so required the creation of a very different memory of the revolution against Demetrios. Both the strategies of the 280s and 270s and the influence of fifth-century

---

97 M. J. Osborne, 'The archons of *IG* II² 1273', in A. P. Matthaiou and G. E. Malouchou (eds), *Ἀττικαί ἐπιγραφαί: Πρακτικά συμποσίου εἰς μνήμην Adolf Wilhelm (1864–1950)* (Athens: Greek Epigraphical Society, 2004), pp. 199–211, at pp. 207–10, and A. Henry, 'Lyandros of Anaphlystos and the decree for Phaidros of Sphettos', *Chiron* 22 (1992), pp. 25–33, both with further references; cf. e.g. Habicht, *Athens from Alexander to Antony*, p. 155; Luraghi, 'The *demos* as narrator', p. 255.

98 *IG* II² 682.30–52; cf. Luraghi, 'The *demos* as narrator', p. 255.

99 Livy 31.44.4–9; H. I. Flower, *The Art of Forgetting: Disgrace and Oblivion in Roman Political Culture* (Chapel Hill: University of North Carolina, 2006), pp. 34–40 with further references.

100 *IG* II² 682.33–4, 36–7, 39, 46–7.

101 *IG* II² 682.21–4.

Figure 15.3   IG II² 682: the decree in honour of Phaidros of Sphettos (EM
10546).

responses were now inappropriate: memories of the past once again
had to be (re)constructed in relation to current realities.

As Phaidros' decree shows, the revolution against Demetrios continued to be remembered collectively some thirty or so years after
it took place, and the *demos* was still honouring supporters like
Strombichos in familiar ways as late as 266/5. The burial of the dead
in the *Demosion Sema*, however, indicates that the initial decision

about the Athenians' response to the events must have been taken almost immediately and, by 283/2, the fifth-century responses were being specifically invoked. In this way, the responses to the revolution will also have helped to re-establish the democracy and to reunite the fractured Athenians. This long period of public response in the third century contrasts with the collective response to the Thirty, which happened much more quickly: the statues set up in 394/3 for Konon and Euagoras seem to mark its conclusion.

That the third-century Athenians looked back to the past testifies to the still powerful memories of the earlier oligarchies more than one hundred years after the events. Their politics of remembrance were evidently more complicated than we might have imagined from fourth-century texts such as Lysias 2, Plato's *Menexenos* and Aischines' speech against Ktesiphon, which all present the events as external war fought against the Spartans and forget *stasis*.[102] Third-century Athenians certainly knew this strategy and they clearly drew on it, but they also remembered the connections between the fifth-century responses and oligarchy and civil strife. This association, which was largely ignored in the collective public sphere, will have been reinforced both by narrative histories and by the legal speeches, the memories and responses of individual men. The actions of the third-century Athenians also bring out the importance of the past and the ways in which it can serve as a model for the present. As Phaidros' decree demonstrates, however, memories of earlier events were not infinitely malleable.[103] As a finite resource,[104] the past could not be used indiscriminately in the present, and not all Athenians could be presented as ardent democrats and revolutionaries against Macedonian kings.

---

102 Shear, *Polis and Revolution*, pp. 303–6.
103 Malleability of memory: Young, *The Texture of Memory*, pp. x, 2; J. Fentress and C. Wickham, *Social Memory* (Oxford: Blackwell, 1992), p. 29; S. E. Alcock, *Archaeologies of the Greek Past: Landscape, Monuments and Memories* (Cambridge: Cambridge University Press, 2002), p. 17: G. Cubitt, *History and Memory* (Manchester: Manchester University Press, 2007), pp. 158–9, 202–3, 214.
104 A. Appadurai, 'The past as a scarce resource', *Man* 16 (1981), pp. 201–19.

16

'REMEMBERING THE ANCIENT WAY OF LIFE': PRIMITIVISM IN GREEK SACRIFICIAL RITUAL

Emily Kearns

Before there were 'historians', there was 'sacred history' – at least, there was in many societies. Indeed, one might almost say that for such cultures the primary way of apprehending the past was through its narrative and depiction in the central texts of the various religious traditions. The lives of Abraham and Moses, of Rama and Krishna, and so on, defined not only a group's sense of its identity, but also its view of the stages through which it and the world had passed. Ancient Greece, however, is notoriously lacking in sacred texts; many myths existed not in continuous, more or less canonical redactions, but in fragmented local forms, while on the other hand Homer and the epic tradition have only an oblique connection with the religious systems of the Greek cities. If we are to look for a link between Greek religion and views of the past, we must look elsewhere. And while some views of Greek religion in the last half-century or so have been unhelpfully reductive (to render the concept 'religion' meaningful in a Greek context it would be better to think of the more inclusive 'things to do with the gods' than merely of 'ritual'), it remains true that ritual practice bulks very large, and should probably be regarded as occupying the central position in the Greek religious complex. Yet it is apparent that religious ritual cannot of itself say anything about the past. That can only be done by texts which touch on religious matters, or alternatively by our own interpretations of the fragmentary information we possess on the subject of religious ritual. The pitfalls in the second case are obvious, although it is a method almost universally used in the study of Greek religion. The other possibility may bring us closer to contemporary standpoints, but we are still dependent on the often idiosyncratic views of probably untypical individuals.

These are serious limitations, but for the post-classical period at least there is an abundance of material to suggest that links between cult practice and past ages were part of the framework of ordinary thought, so that the relationship between *ideas* about religion and ideas about the past is certainly a legitimate subject for investigation. It seems most unlikely that this connection should have appeared *ex nihilo* in the Hellenistic period, and as we shall see there is some direct evidence for its existence earlier. But before we examine the material (or part of it) in detail, it may be helpful to consider why the link between ritual and the past should exist, and how it might be expressed within Greek culture.

If ritual is in the strict sense meaningless, as maintained notably by Frits Staal, it does not at all follow that it remains meaningless in the perception of those who practise or observe it.[1] Indeed, if we wish to assume that the formation of the ritual itself is always primary (a proposition which is something of an act of faith), one might say that here is a vacuum waiting to be filled. Even simple sorts of statement about ritual – that it must be done this way because the deity likes it so, or because it is ancestral custom, or, simplest of all, because this is the right way to do it – create meaning and set the ritual in a context.[2] And it is a documentable fact that Greek statements about ritual are frequently more complex than this. Nick Lowe once proposed 'a thought-experiment: suppose one were actually able to ask the Hierophant, the chief priest of the Eleusinian mysteries, as one initiate to another, what the secret ritual of revelation actually meant. It is hard to imagine he would simply answer, "Oh, it doesn't mean anything really; it's just something you *do*."'[3] Of course, the Mysteries are a particularly high-profile case, and further, whatever meaning the hierophant might have proposed, even though it was the hierophant

1 F. Staal, 'The meaninglessness of ritual', *Numen* 26 (1979), pp. 2–22; Staal, *Rules Without Meaning: Ritual, Mantras and the Human Sciences* (Frankfurt: Peter Lang, 1989). With different overall aims and interests, Maurice Bloch reaches an allied and perhaps even more radical conclusion: 'Religion is the last place to find anything "explained" because . . . religious communication [that is, for Bloch, ritual] rules out the very tools of explanation' (M. Bloch, 'Symbols, song, dance and features of articulation: Is religion an extreme form of traditional authority?', *European Journal of Sociology* [= *Archives Européennes de Sociologie*] 15 [1974], pp. 55–81, at p.71). Staal admits (in the *Numen* article, p. 3) that 'such absorption [in the correct performance of ritual], by itself, does not show that a ritual cannot have symbolic meaning'.

2 Cf. Staal, 'Meaninglessness of ritual', p. 3, listing possible reasons given by brahmins for performing rituals: 'we do it because our ancestors did it; because we are eligible to do it; because it is good for society; because it is good; because it is our duty; because it is said to lead to immortality; because it leads to immortality'. He claims that symbolic explanations are given only seldom and in relation to minor specifics. My own experience of listening to Tamil brahmins has been that they are usually very keen to explain the symbolic significance of their actions to participants and spectators in the ritual.

3 N. J. Lowe, 'Thesmophoria and Haloa: Myth, physics and mysteries', in S. Blundell and M. Williamson (eds), *The Sacred and the Feminine in Ancient Greece* (London and New York: Routledge, 1998), pp. 149–73, esp. p. 162.

who proposed it, would not have quite the same status of unalterable truth that the ritual itself possessed. It might be supplemented by other explanations, or even with time superseded entirely; the point is that explanations tend to be supplied. Plato, in a well-known passage from *Meno*, attests the existence of priestly personnel who 'have taken the trouble to be able to give an account of the practices they engage in'.[4] His immediate context relates to ideas with an 'Orphic' or similar flavour, concerning the immortality of the soul; his words suggest that at least some priests and priestesses might be expected to supply other types of explanation as well.

In general, religious ritual has two features, or apparent features, which might seem to make it particularly prone to the need for an explanation. First, there is a degree of fixity, which often makes it appear that the sequence of actions can never change, and must therefore date back to time immemorial. And it is of course true that although in practice ritual may alter either suddenly or gradually, it cannot simply be changed at will. Second, the actions prescribed in ritual seem frequently strange, even counterintuitive. Sometimes the strangeness is due to some divergence from the norm in a particular case, and sometimes it is the norm itself which might seem poorly calculated to please the divine and to cement divine–human relations. The Greek context supplies many examples of local and particular rituals details of which struck observers (and no doubt practitioners) as odd, and it is clear also that the normal distribution of the sacrificial meat, in which the divine recipients are allotted a scanty portion of less attractive meat than that received by their worshippers, was a practice arousing some curiosity.[5]

In Greece as elsewhere, for some participants the default explanation would no doubt suffice: it is so because it is so, or in a more nuanced way, because it is in accordance with ancestral practice – κατὰ τὰ πάτρια. But going beyond this, it seems that there are perhaps three main types of explanation for ritual. The first relates specific cultic features to the intended recipient (god or hero) – thus the prescription of a dark-coloured sacrificial victim might be related to the fact that the deity thus honoured is connected with the earth or the Underworld.[6]

4 Plato, *Meno* 81a: οἱ μὲν λέγοντες εἰσι τῶν ἱερέων τε καὶ τῶν ἱερειῶν ὅσοις μεμέληκε περὶ ὧν μεταχειρίζονται λόγον οἵοις τ'εἶναι διδόναι.

5 This is suggested for an early date by Hesiod's strange story of the attempt by Prometheus to deceive Zeus, resulting in the latter's deliberate choice of the more attractive looking, but actually less edible, portion: *Theogony* 535–61. New Comedy is more explicit, e.g. Menander, *Dyskolos* 447–53, com. adesp. fr. 142.

6 This phenomenon has often been seen as part of a systematic distinction between 'Olympian' and 'chthonian', both in deities and in the forms of sacrifice

Second, there are explanations which invoke the purpose of the ritual. Thus, for instance, the fact that at the sacrifice for the Seasons, probably at one of the midsummer festivals in Athens, the gods' portions and the entrails are not roasted or grilled but boiled like the rest of the meat is explained by Philochoros as due to a wish to be spared excessive heat and drought.[7] But it is the third type of explanation which concerns us now: that which maintains that the current form of the ritual derives from a past time when this form was the one logically to be expected; the present is explained by the circumstances of the past. Broadly speaking, of course, the perceived connection of ritual with the past is fundamental, simply because ritual is understood as having been handed down from past times.[8] But we are concerned here with those cases where the past relates in a more particular and individual way to the present. There are many types of past-related explanations for ritual, all of which could broadly be labelled 'aetiological', but we can make a further distinction between aetiologies in the usual sense, in which it is a very specific set of circumstances invoked to account for the ritual form, and explanations which rely on a more general idea of conditions in the past. Aetiologies in the more usual sense are extremely well documented in a range of genres. They may either be self-standing stories, like (for instance) that of a certain Embaros pretending to sacrifice his daughter while actually sacrificing a goat, which gives an *aition* for the cult of Artemis Mounichia at Peiraieus, or they may tap into the structure of panhellenic mythology, evoking well-known figures like Odysseus, Orestes or Iphigeneia; but either way they depend on the narrative of a particular event situated in

---

(footnote 6 *continued*)
offered to them, but this hypothesis is now more controversial. See R. Schlesier, 'Olympian versus chthonian religion', *Scripta Classica Israelica* 11 (1991–2), pp. 38–51, challenging the assumption; S. Scullion, 'Olympian and chthonian', *Class. Ant.* 13 (1994), pp. 75–119, attempting to reinstate it partially; R. Hägg and B. Alroth (eds), *Greek Sacrificial Ritual Olympian and Chthonian* (Stockholm: Paul Astroms, 2005); G. Ekroth, *The Sacrificial Rituals of Greek Hero-Cults in the Archaic to the Early Hellenistic Periods* (*Kernos* suppl. 12, Liège: Centre International d'Étude de la Religion Grecque Antique, 2002). However, the simple observation that dark victims are *sometimes* offered to 'earthy' deities is incontestable, e.g. *Il.* 3.103–4, *IG* II² 1358 (Tetrapolis calendar, Attica, fourth century BCE), LSCG 96.25 (Mykonos, third/second century BCE).
7 *FGrHist* 328 F 173; see R. Parker, *Polytheism and Society at Athens* (Oxford: Oxford University Press, 2005), p. 204.
8 See the formulation of Barbara Kowalzig, *Singing for the Gods: Performances of Myth and Ritual in Classical Greece* (Oxford: Oxford University Press, 2007), p. 53: 'All rituals carry with them if not elements of a real past, certainly of a perceived one.'

mythological time.[9] The other form, if perhaps from our point of view equally speculative, refers to supposed lifestyle differences between now and the remote past, and is less reliant on mythological elements. It is clear that this latter sort of connection can very easily be modified, so that instead of the explanation itself forming a bridge between two givens, the ritual and the view of the past, ritual practices become actual evidence for the life of earlier ages. In particular the modalities of sacrifices are taken to give information about ancient diets, the main subject of this chapter.

This process can be seen in quite a developed form in a passage from Book 6 of the *Laws*, where Plato is using a theory which suits his argument, but which would probably also be recognised by his audience:

> We see that even now among many peoples the custom of sacrificing each other remains, and we hear of the opposite among others, when they[10] would neither venture to taste ox flesh nor did they sacrifice animals to the Gods, but rather flour mixtures, and grains moistened with honey, and other pure offerings of that kind. They abstained from flesh as something it was not right to eat or with which to pollute the altars of the Gods, but those of us then living led what is called an Orphic life, keeping to everything that is without a soul, and conversely abstaining from everything that possesses one.[11]

The contextual argument is that as diet and customs have changed over time, so they can also change in the future. In other words, Plato's primary interest here is actually not the reconstruction of human history, but the use of what he at least presents as widely accepted methodology and theories in the service of a quite different argument. 'What you say is widely reported and easy to credit', says the speaker's interlocutor Kleinias in Bury's translation.[12] The

---

9 Embaros: Bekk. Anecd. 1.445.1–13, Eustath. *Il.* 2.732 (331.25). Odysseus: e.g. Paus. 8.14.5–6. Orestes: Paus. 8.34.1–3, as well as in Athens (Aesch. *Eumenides,* Eur. *IT* 947–60). Iphigeneia: Phanodemus, *FGrH* 325 F 14, schol. Ar. *Lys.* 645. On aetiology in general see Kowalzig, *Singing for the Gods,* pp. 24–32.

10 Following Schanz's ἐτόλμων μέν for MSS ἐτολμῶμεν.

11 Plato, *Laws* 782c–d: τὸ δὲ μὴν θύειν ἀνθρώπους ἀλλήλους ἔτι καὶ νῦν παραμένον ὁρῶμεν πολλοῖς· καὶ τοὐναντίον ἀκούομεν ἐν ἄλλοις, ὅτε οὐδὲ βοὸς ἐτόλμων μὲν γεύεσθαι, θύματά τε οὐκ ἦν τοῖς θεοῖσι ζῷα, πέλανοι δὲ καὶ μέλιτι καρποὶ δεδευμένοι καὶ τοιαῦτα ἄλλα ἁγνὰ θύματα, σαρκῶν δ' ἀπείχοντο ὡς οὐχ ὅσιον ὂν ἐσθίειν οὐδὲ τοὺς τῶν θεῶν βωμοὺς αἵματι μιαίνειν, ἀλλὰ Ὀρφικοί τινες λεγόμενοι βίοι ἐγίγνοντο ἡμῶν τοῖς τότε, ἀψύχων μὲν ἐχόμενοι πάντων, ἐμψύχων δὲ τοὐναντίον πάντων ἀπεχόμενοι.

12 *Laws* 782d: καὶ σφόδρα λεγόμενά τ' εἴρηκας καὶ πιστεύεσθαι πιθανά.

method explains certain customs now current or allegedly current by taking them to be survivals of practices which were once far more widespread. It is evident that sacrifices which diverge from the norm in opposite directions – human sacrifices on the one hand, bloodless offerings on the other – have become bound up with two opposing pictures of the lifestyle of primitive mankind; early humans were either cannibals or vegetarians, or perhaps both at different times. Plato invokes the supposed customs of certain non-Greeks as evidence for a once quite normal habit of cannibalism (ἀλληλοφαγία, 'each-other eating', in Greek); but he may also have in mind the tradition of human sacrifice in the worship of Lykaian Zeus in Arcadia,[13] and numerous Greek cults for which the *aition* involved a human sacrifice changed or averted. On the other side of the equation, Plato seems to recount the conclusions reached by others[14] with regard to a past time; other primitive people neither consumed animate beings themselves nor offered them to the Gods; the mention of a 'so-called Orphic lifestyle' indicates that whatever source Plato is following here must have made a similar connection between practices current among a relatively small group of contemporary people, seen as diverging from the norm, and what was supposed once to have been the prevailing custom. The 'Orphic life', in other words, just as much as the barbarian human sacrifices, testifies to the state of primitive humanity. Sacrifice is able to function in this way because while it is at the heart of most religious ritual, its human dimension relates closely to what people eat, which itself is taken as an indicator of what people are, in particular of their degree of civilisation. Plato's words, as we have seen, suggest that there is nothing very novel about the type of argument used. It is noticeable that he does not refer to specific instances suggestive of human sacrifice, or to particular cults in which only bloodless offerings are acceptable, but rather attempts to provide the strongest possible evidence for differently based past diets by adducing contexts in which human sacrifice is normal, and the avoidance of bloodshed a rule universally applied. This leads him to areas outside the usual experience of Greek sacrifice, but it is apparent that a link could also be made between past conditions and certain peculiarities in the rituals of numerous individual Greek cults.

Cult complexes such as those of the two Artemises of eastern Attica (Brauronia and Tauropolos) or Artemis Orthia in Sparta, which link an element of ritual, perhaps the shedding of blood, with a tradition of the commutation of human sacrifice to this vestigial form, have

13 Which he mentions in *Rep.* 8.565d.
14 Note ἀκούομεν contrasting with ὁρῶμεν.

often an *aition* – 'real' or 'invented' – of mythological type, whether this relates to a well-known figure like Iphigeneia or whether it forms a purely local myth.[15] And the *aition* is usually clear that the original human sacrifice happened either in non-Greek lands, or, more often, as a terrible last resort demanded in extreme circumstances.

It is nonetheless the case that each cult – and even more strongly, for those with a knowledge of different local traditions, several cults together – indicates quite clearly that, exceptional circumstances or no, human sacrifice is no longer performed. There is then some overlap here between the mythological *aition* and the more general reference to past conditions, as story and cult taken together create the category of a past age in which such sacrifices could happen and demarcate it from the present time, in which they cannot. For the opposite kind of divergence from the norm, a similar point could be made about the *aition* of the Bouphonia rite, performed for Zeus Polieus in Athens. In this strange ritual, oxen are led past a table on which are placed cereal offerings, and the first to taste those offerings is sacrificed, in a somewhat unusual way; the killing is then presented as culpable slaughter, the sacrificed ox is stuffed as though still alive and the sacrificial knife is found guilty and cast into the sea. In the past, much has been made

---

15 Artemis at Brauron: two myths refer to the shedding of blood, one in sacrifice, Suda s.v. ἄρκτος ἢ Βραυρωνίοις, Phanodemus *FGrH* 325 F 14; the ritual details are uncertain. Tauropolos at Halai, Eur. *IT* 1458–61; on these see H. Lloyd-Jones, 'Artemis and Iphigeneia', *JHS* 103 (1983), pp. 87–102. A. Orthia: Paus. 3.16.7–11. On the wider diffusion of this type of Artemis, see F. Graf, 'Das Götterbild aus dem Taurerland', *AW* 10.4 (1979), pp. 33–41, and in general, P. Bonnechere, *Le sacrifice humain en Grèce ancienne* (Liège: Centre International d'Étude de la Religion Grecque Antique, 1994), esp. pp. 26–62; D. D. Hughes, *Human Sacrifice in Ancient Greece* (London and New York: Routledge, 1991), pp. 71–138. Euripides in particular has been suspected, perhaps rightly, of inventing *aitia*, but for our purposes it does not make much difference whether the *aition* was a 'traditional' one, developing gradually from a local basis, or whether it came into existence as the creation of a historian or tragedian; 'literary' *aitia* have a tendency to gain wider acceptance. More radical is the view that the tragedians, again particularly Euripides, invented cult practice, including the supposed rites of Artemis Tauropolos at Halai: see F. M. Dunn, *Tragedy's End: Closure and Innovation in Euripidean Drama* (New York and Oxford: Oxford University Press 1996), esp. pp. 62–3; S. Scullion, 'Tradition and invention in Euripidean aitiology', in M. Cropp, K. Lee and D. Sansone (eds), *Euripides and Tragic Theatre in the Late Fifth Century* (Champaign, IL: Stipes, 2000 = *ICS* 24–5 [1999–2000]), pp. 217–33; for a more balanced view, Romano in this volume. I cannot, however, accept the point that Menander, *Epitr.* 415–17, disproves Euripides' version of the Tauropolia by showing the real character of the festival, since festivals (for instance the Anthesteria) may exhibit quite diverse 'characters' at different points and for different participants. More generally, I believe that even if Euripides was inventing details, they must at least have been details which would make sense to his audience because they belonged to a familiar type.

to hang on this cult complex and its accompanying myth.[16] More recently we have become accustomed to regard such an atypical rite with caution, and it is certainly not my intention to use the Bouphonia to make any general points about sacrifice; I merely observe that while the story explaining this bizarre cult practice certainly relates one specific event to one specific cult, it also contains in its narrative frame the tradition of a past time in which the sacrifice and therefore the consumption of the ploughing ox, perhaps of all animals, was not the norm; it is clear in the story that the cakes or grains which were placed on the altar and which the unfortunate ox ate were the sacrificial currency of the 'pre-modern' age, and also that that age came to an end when the oracle ratified the killing of the ox and commanded its annual repetition. At least by the fourth century, then, and demonstrably earlier in the case of the 'end of human sacrifice' motif, the rituals of certain cults could be taken as referring to the sacrificial and perhaps dietary norms of past ages (although myth generally shrinks from introducing cannibalism into Greek sacrificial contexts[17]) and to the moment when that norm was changed, to create the customs of the present day.

Let us now look a little more closely at the view that early humanity abstained from sacrificing and eating meat, and the possible correlatives of such a time in cult. Probably the earliest extant author to describe a vegetarian past clearly is Empedocles. Of course he is *parti pris* for vegetarianism anyway, and when looking at the present age he represents normal animal sacrifice as exactly equivalent to cannibalism, because of the transmigration of souls.[18] His past also differs from the way the past is normally conceived, being strongly conditioned by a cyclical view of the universe. The age when Love was dominant will inevitably one day come round again, so in a sense the events of the past, or at least past states, are not *absolutely* past. Still,

---

16 Beginning with Theophrastus, who is quarried *in extenso* by Porphyry, *De abstinentia* 2 (the Bouphonia at 2.10, 29–30); in recent times by Karl Meuli ('Griechische Opferbräuche', in O. Gigon, K. Meuli, W. Theiler, F. Wehrli and B. Wyss (eds), *Phyllobolia für Peter von der Mühll* (Basle: Benno Schwabe, 1946), pp. 185–288) and then Walter Burkert (*Homo Necans: The Anthropology of Ancient Greek Sacrificial Ritual and Myth*, Eng. tr. (Berkeley and Los Angeles: University of California Press, 1983; German orig. 1972), esp. pp. 136–43).

17 It is possible that myths such as those of Tantalos and Thyestes, which present the cooking of children's butchered bodies in a cauldron and their subsequent consumption, may relate to the boiling of sacrificial and other meat together for the feast at a sacrifice, but their narratives do not incorporate sacrifice as such.

18 Empedocles fr. 137 D–K (128 Inwood).

from the perspective of contemporaries at the present stage of the
Empedoclean world-cycle, the transition towards the rule of Strife, the
stage of the rule of Love corresponds more or less exactly with that
mythical, pre-modern and often pre-heroic stage of human existence
(in the vaguer and more generally prevalent conception) when things
were done differently, so it is this area of the past that Empedocles
populates with his worshippers of Kypris:

> For them there was no god Ares, no Battle-din; there was no
> king Zeus, or Kronos, or Poseidon, but Kypris was queen [some
> words missing]. Her they would worship with pious images,
> painted animals, and variously scented perfumes, and sacrifices of
> unmixed myrrh and smoky/fragrant frankincense, pouring to the
> ground libations of golden honey. The altar was not drenched with
> the unmixed blood of bulls, but this was the greatest abomination
> among mankind, to excise the life and to eat the goodly limbs.[19]

Empedocles does not say where he draws this picture from, but it is
evident that it cannot be a simple fantasy; the offerings made as standard in his past ages bear a strong resemblance to the bloodless offerings of his own time. There is a heavy and rather exotic emphasis on
perfumes and incense, it is true, but incense was certainly an obvious
offering to the Gods as much in bloodless as in bloody sacrifice.
Libations of honey rather than wine are mentioned, I suggest, at least
partly because wineless libations commonly accompanied bloodless
sacrifice; if bloodless sacrifice is therefore the more ancient form, so
too must be wineless libations.[20] The 'painted animals' may seem less
familiar, but I think could be an idea inspired by the custom of making
cakes and similar vegetal offerings in the shape of the animals which
would not on that occasion be sacrificed. Cakes, often shaped in this

---

19 Empedocles fr. 128 D–K (122 Inwood):

> οὐδέ τις ἦν κείνοισιν Ἄρης θεὸς οὐδὲ Κυδοιμός
> οὐδὲ Ζεὺς βασιλεὺς οὐδὲ Κρόνος οὐδὲ Ποσειδῶν,
> ἀλλὰ Κύπρις βασίλεια.
> τὴν οἵ γ' εὐσεβέεσσιν ἀγάλμασιν ἱλάσκοντο
> γραπτοῖς τε ζώιοισι μύροισί τε δαιδαλεόδμοις
> σμύρνης τ' ἀκρήτου θυσίαις λιβάνου τε θυώδους,
> ξανθῶν [v.l. ξουθῶν] τε σπονδὰς μελιτῶν ῥίπτοντες ἐς οὖδας·
> ταύρων δ' ἀκρήτοισι φόνοις οὐ δεύετο βωμός,
> ἀλλὰ μύσος τοῦτ' ἔσκεν ἐν ἀνθρώποισι μέγιστον,
> θυμὸν ἀπορραίσαντας ἐνέδμεναι ἠέα γυῖα.

20 Although wineless libations could also be employed with animal sacrifice. On
these libations, see A. Henrichs, 'The "sobriety" of Oedipus: Sophocles *OC* 100
misunderstood', *HSCP* 87 (1983), pp. 87–100.

way, were a staple of bloodless sacrifice, and an understanding of the phrase along these lines seems to be implied in the tradition found in Diogenes Laertius and Athenaeus, that Empedocles offered to Zeus at Olympia a model ox made either from barley meal and honey – normal components of what we call sacrificial 'cakes' – or of myrrh and frankincense, a variant surely inspired by the prominence of incense in this passage of Empedocles' poem.[21] Empedocles then uses the familiar currency of a particular type of offering in his own day, that of Plato's 'so-called Orphic lifestyle', and no doubt his own – to that extent there may be some truth in the story of his Olympian offering, even if the philosopher has been confused with an athlete of the same name – to extrapolate to a generalised style of offerings in past times. But because in the contemporary world 'bloodless offerings' could equate to 'inexpensive, minor offerings' as well as to 'pure offerings' he has made his materials into something more rich and strange, in particular giving a special emphasis to the perfumes and incense as costly, high-grade ingredients in the ensemble, a pure equivalent to the costly ox. This could be seen as a kind of 'soft' primitivism; the life of these past humans was happy, innocent and pious, but it was certainly not devoid of material good things, even those now considered luxuries.

More usually, it seems, the bloodless sacrifices of bygone days were seen in terms of ancient simplicity. Perhaps a basically linear view of history is more conducive to the concept of the growth of complexity in human culture and society than is the cyclical structure of Empedocles, and the comparison with the present day was surely also influential: as we have seen, the bloodless offerings of contemporary times generally appeared more basic, less showy and sophisticated than animal sacrifice (though to be sure there were many gradations within animal sacrifice itself). A likely fifth-century example of this association is to be found in a fragment of the early comic poet Chionides (though Athenaeus, who preserves it for us, is in some doubt as to the play's authorship). In Athenaeus' paraphrase 'the Athenians, when setting a meal before the Dioskouroi at the prytaneion, placed on the table cheese, barley pastries, ripe olives and leeks, creating a reminder of the ancient way of life'.[22] Only the list of foodstuffs can be a direct quotation from the text, and even that, for metrical reasons, cannot be quite

---

21 D.L. 8.53 (from Favorinus); Athen. 1.3e; the tradition gives a chapter title to Detienne's discussion of Pythagorean dietary prescriptions (M. Detienne, *Les jardins d'Adonis* (Paris: Gallimard, 1972), pp. 71–114; revised edn (Paris: Gallimard, 2002), pp. 58–90).

22 Chionides fr. 7 K–A, Athen. 4.137e: ὁ δὲ τοὺς εἰς Χιωνίδην ἀναφερομένους Πτωχοὺς ποιήσας τοὺς Ἀθηναίους φησίν, ὅταν τοῖς Διοσκούροις ἐν πρυτανείῳ ἄριστον

right as it stands, but the context must still be indicative. What is being described is a cult meal, a theoxeny for the Dioskouroi, intriguingly reminiscent of that promised to them in a fragment of Bacchylides, in which they will receive sweet wine, song and a friendly disposition, and, one imagines, similarly simple food, rather than slaughtered bulls served in surroundings of gold and purple.[23] This simplicity may then be something to do with the Dioskouroi themselves – it certainly is unlikely that all theoxeny meals were characterised by simple fare – but there is surely no reason why the explanation given by Athenaeus, that it recalls the Athenians' ancient way of life, should not have been part of the original context. The comic poets are well aware of a tradition of ancient times when food was somehow different; usually in comedy this means more abundance, more variety and no hassle in preparing it, since this picture is more suited to the general preoccupations of comedy,[24] but in a play entitled *Beggars* (Πτωχοί) one can see that a different picture might seem appropriate. But since there is nothing intrinsically funny in the idea that the meal for the Dioskouroi, or Anakes to give them their Attic title, was consciously reminiscent of 'ancient times' it is likely that the dramatist was invoking an idea already known to his audience, the humour perhaps lying in the application of the point which is now lost to us.

But what exactly was understood by this 'ancient way of life'? How ancient is ancient? The word ἀρχαῖος is capable of several different applications, not only the etymological 'primeval', and of course we cannot even be sure of the exact words used by Chionides in linking the meal with a former way of life. But let us recall that the divine recipients of the feast were associated with Attica in mythology, which according to Herodotus related that Kastor and Polydeukes had come there in pursuit of Theseus, who had abducted their sister Helen. So far, relations were perhaps not very promising, but Xenophon knows of their initiation at Eleusis, suggesting that he also knew something like the tradition of their adoption by the local hero Aphidnos for this purpose, and hence their integration into the polis.[25] It would make a good deal of sense then if the festival meal was thought to allude to this event, recapitulating an original meal at the *prytaneion* (which

προτιθῶνται, ἐπὶ τῶν τραπεζῶν τιθέναι τυρὸν καὶ φυστὴν δρυπεπεῖς τ'ἐλάας καὶ πράσα, ὑπόμνησιν ποιουμένους τῆς ἀρχαίας ἀγωγῆς.

23 Bacchylides fr. 21 Maehler. On ritual theoxenies, see M. Jameson, 'Theoxenia', in R. Hägg (ed.), *Ancient Greek Cult Practice from the Epigraphical Evidence* (Stockholm: Paul Aströms, 1994), pp. 35–57.

24 See J. Wilkins, *The Boastful Chef: The Discourse of Food in Ancient Greek Comedy* (Oxford: Oxford University Press, 2000), pp. 110–23. The point is noted already in Athenaeus, who collects these passages at 6.267e–70a.

25 Herodotus 9.73, perhaps from the *Theseid*; Xen. *Hell.* 6.3.6; Plut. *Thes.* 33.2.

according to Pausanias was near to their sanctuary)[26] in which the Anakes were received into citizenship, in which case the 'ancient lifestyle' would be that of Attica in the heroic age. Not primitive times, then, when people might be either cannibals or vegetarians; although the meal is in fact a vegetarian one, it seems very unlikely that anyone joining up the dots would have supposed that Theseus and the Dioskouroi abstained from meat. The point is the simplicity of the meal, not its exclusion of a doubtful material. And a further point would surely be that this was somehow the characteristic, the 'real' food of Attica; the 'recollection made' could not have been a neutral matter of supposed historical fact, but a celebration of the kind of food that made Attica great. A similar idea may have been behind the so-called *kopis* feasts in Sparta, which Athenaeus treats in an adjoining section. These were held in connection with various festivals, and the 'ancient simplicity' motif is suggested by the fact that the diners reclined on rough mattresses or beds of straw (*stibades*) in specially constructed tents or bothies. The *kopis* was certainly not vegetarian, but the only animals sacrificed were goats, and each diner was given a meal of set form and ingredients – meat products, a special cake, cheese and *tragemata* or 'nibbles' of beans and figs. Again, though all Spartan meals seemed notoriously simple, poor even, to other Greeks, this may have been thought to indicate the kinds of food available at an early stage of culinary development – no boiling of pea soup, for instance – but looked at from another perspective could also have celebrated the institution of civilised eating; the cooking of domesticated animals, the use of their milk, and above all perhaps a system of eating based on agriculture – cereals, fruits and vegetables.

Whether or not this idea belongs in the Spartan *kopis*, it is certainly a theme which grows in popularity with authors seeking to explain the origins of civilisation. Various advances were canvassed as the crucial one which put an end to a primeval 'wild', often cannibalistic, diet; most often, and most convincingly, the cultivation of cereals, but also the discovery of honey and of figs (as we shall see shortly). That the idea certainly became a familiar one is shown by a fragment of the comic dramatist Athenion, who makes one of his characters expound in great and parodic detail how the art of cooking meat is actually what put an end to cannibalism and enabled the birth of civilisation.[27] But the roots of the idea are certainly well established in the fourth

---

26 Paus. 1.18.1–3; on the topography, see G. C. R. Schmalz, 'The Athenian *prytaneion* discovered?', *Hesperia* 75 (2006), pp. 33–81.
27 Athenion, fr. 1 K–A. This author has been dated to the fourth or third centuries, but may be as late as the first.

century, when Isocrates, speaking of Eleusis, points out that the establishment of agriculture through Demeter's gift to the Eleusinians and hence the Athenians 'distinguished our life from that of the animals'; indeed the idea is probably implicit already in the fifth-century Athenian claim to first fruits for Eleusis from the rest of Greece.[28] So it is not surprising to find that this nexus of ideas, too, appears among the explanations of various cult practices: such-and-such a ritual commemorates the introduction of such-and-such a food, the first time it was eaten, or the beginning of a civilised diet in general. The testimonia are often late, but the habit of thought is probably a good deal earlier. We might think also of the well-established pattern of the hero worshipped alongside a god and commemorated as the first recipient of the god's instruction who disseminated the new technique among humanity in general, such as Triptolemos at Eleusis or the various and often less fortunate Dionysiac heroes; it is surely likely that in many of these cases aspects of the related cult complex were understood to refer to the introduction of that new technique, most often something concerning diet.[29]

A more general example lies to hand in the case of the Haloa, one of the women's festivals in Athens. Here the scholia to Lucian, it has long been recognised, in the midst of a confusing and perhaps confused jumble of information, contain snippets which suggest a knowledgeable ultimate source.[30] The idea seems to be that the foods set out at the women's feast, containing 'all foods from land and sea except those forbidden in the Mysteries', represent 'civilised nourishment', αἱ ἥμεροι τροφαί. At any rate, this is what the archons represent to the foreigners present, extending the point made by Isocrates; in this festival celebrating the Two Goddesses, Dionysos and perhaps Poseidon, it is not only agriculture in the narrow sense of the cultivation of cereal crops, but all components of the civilised diet which are claimed to have had their origins in Attica and thence been disseminated to the rest of the world. The festival is full of peculiar features, and this angle can hardly exhaust the 'meanings' that were available to contemporary actors and observers; from the wording of the scholion, it might seem as though it were a particularly public and male meaning attached to a group of rituals which possibly had quite other

---

28 Isoc. *Panegyricus* 28; *IG* I³ 78 (= *I.Eleusis* 28), with Clinton, *I.Eleusis* II 5–7.
29 On institutor heroes, see A. Kleingünther, Πρῶτος εὑρετής (Leipzig: Dieterich, 1933); A. Brelich, *Gli eroi greci* (Rome: Angelo Brelich, 1969), pp. 166–84.
30 Schol. Lucian, *Dial. Mer.* 7.4. On the Haloa, see A. Brumfield, *The Attic Cults of Demeter* (New York: Beaufort Books, 1981), pp. 104–31; Parker, *Polytheism and Society*, pp. 199–201; and Lowe, 'Thesmophoria and Haloa'.

significances to the women who were the primary celebrants. But from our point of view, what is important is that a prominent feature of the festival is thus linked with a crucial moment in the past. The ritual here represents and commemorates not simply a vague, indefinite primitive past, whether that is presented for our approval (the 'ancient simplicity' form) or horrified repulsion (the 'human sacrifice' type and its congeners), but the actual moment of transition from a wild and unattractive past to the civilised present.

This kind of representation of the 'early diet' theme is quite a common one, as the mythological pattern of the benefactor god and/or the institutor hero is also widely diffused, but in its individual instances it is usually attached to particular cults. Most often, perhaps, these are connected with Demeter or Dionysos, but this is not invariable. My final example appears in a ritual centred on Athena, and as with the Haloa, the information derives from a late source, or rather sources.[31] It is impossible to be quite sure that the connection is old, but as we have seen the thought patterns it represents are certainly found in the classical period. Hesychius and Photius gloss ἡγητηρία as a string of figs carried in the procession at the Plynteria, a summer observance when the statue of Athena was washed and her temple closed, and further explain the name as due to the supposed fact that the fig was the first component of ἥμερος τροφή to be experienced, the 'leader' into a civilised life. A much more likely *prima facie* reason for the name would seem to be simply that the fig string 'led' the procession, but recherché explanations are by no means always unattractive to those participating in a ritual,[32]and the mythical tradition surrounding the festival also speaks of very early times, specifically of Athena's first priestess Aglauros, daughter of the Athenian culture-hero Kekrops, and the institution of the customs we know now. Christiane Sourvinou-Inwood has in fact suggested that 'primordiality' is a key part of the meaning of the Plynteria festival mix,[33] but I think it is important to note once more the difference from a simple then-and-now antithesis; as at the Haloa, it is the moment of change which is highlighted, and the change is seen as a positive thing, but here the focus is sharper; the implied history would narrate that

31 Hesychius s.v. ἡγητηρία (παλάθη σύκων, ἣν ἐν τῇ πομπῇ τῶν Πλυντηρίων φέρουσιν· ὅτι ἡμέρου τροφῆς πρώτης ταύτης ἐγεύσαντο). Cf. Photius s.v. ἡγητηρία. Less clear, but deriving from the same tradition, is Athen. 3.74d.
32 Indeed both explanations could have been current together, or it could have been thought that the leading of the procession was symbolic of the fig's role in history.
33 C. Sourvinou-Inwood, *Athenian Myths and Festivals: Aglauros, Erechtheus, Plynteria, Panathenaia, Dionysia* (Oxford: Oxford University Press, 2011), pp. 140–1, 151–8.

other changes took place after mankind discovered, or was shown, how to cultivate and eat figs, but that this was the key development which made possible what followed. Thus it would seem that even within the ritual complex of the same polis different, complementary and supplementary narratives were entirely possible.

The material for such narratives, as we have seen, could be drawn not only from the familiar rituals of one's own city, but from other Greek communities and beyond the Greek world as well. Differing styles of ritual, united only by their puzzling features, which invited the question 'why do we do this?', produced different pictures of the past. Some could be linked with specific incidents in the mythological-heroic past, while others suggested more general pictures of a past contrasting with the way we do things now. In one version, the past was a time of wildness and savagery typified by the demand for human sacrifice and perhaps, by a further step of association, by cannibalism. In another, the past evoked was a gentler world in which even animal sacrifice had yet to be instituted, when life was simpler and therefore perhaps better. A third view concentrated on the process of civilisation or else the single moment when the change to a civilised diet and lifestyle began. In essence, these are separate, unitary pictures of the past, and yet it is easy to see how they can be put together and made into a continuous narrative; the wild version of the past is susceptible to the taming and civilising process which in a cult context is usually ascribed to the intervention of a god or a hero or both, resulting in a diet and lifestyle dominated by agriculture, a state now in this combined narrative no longer primordial, but still ancient, belonging to the very beginning of the civilised life, so that if desired the narrative can still incorporate the motif of over-complexity and moral decline dating from this point. If we look again at the Plato passage (above, p. 305), it is evident that one possible interpretation could be based along these lines: the discoveries of agriculture put an end to cannibalism and enabled people to live on food that is 'lifeless', ἄψυχον, although this second type of diet survives now only among small groups.

Of course, when the Greeks thought along these lines they were not restricted to the 'evidence' of cult. A basis for ideas about the remote past was available to all Greeks, even if they did not accept the full picture, in the poems of Hesiod and, for the heroic age, Homer and the Epic Cycle. This allowed and encouraged people to think not only about the mythological past, but also about still more remote times when life was even more different from now than it was in the heroic age; and most Greek cities had their traditions of an original culture-hero who instituted the components of present-day civilised life. This was the framework, sometimes heavily modified, into which the data quarried from cult were typically placed, and the evidence of Plato (above) strongly suggests that by his time the process was well under way, with differing views of the past widely available. But the process does not stop there: once it is accepted that the detail of ritual gives out clues to the past, ritual itself is approached and experienced in the light of this connection. The line which might at first seem to begin with the ritual experience and proceed to the explanation in terms of the past is completed as a circle. In fact, it is a chicken-and-egg question, and the process must have worked in both directions. Explanations come together to create a narrative past, which feeds into the understanding of cult, which stimulates more questions and more explanations . . . If religious ritual itself does not (at least in ancient Greece) incorporate a narrative of the past, it nonetheless has clearly a para-narrative which attempts to answer some of the most fundamental questions about the history of humanity.

17

THE GREAT KINGS OF THE FOURTH CENTURY AND THE GREEK MEMORY OF THE PERSIAN PAST

Lloyd Llewellyn-Jones

The Persians and their vast empire exerted a remarkable hold over the Greek imagination. Greek art from the late archaic period and throughout the classical age contains an abundance of images of the Otherness of the Persians, showing them as pampered despots and effeminised defeated soldiery. Greek literature too overflows with references to all kinds of diverse Persian exotica: Persian-sounding (but fake) names, references to tribute, to *proskynesis*, law, impalement, the King's Eye, good roads, eunuchs, gardens, harems, drinking and gold. Christopher Tuplin presents a useful composite picture of the Persians as seen in Greek literature:

> They . . . possess a large empire . . . whose only (other) physical, floral or faunal characteristics are extremes of heat and cold, mountains, citrus fruit, camels, horses, peacocks, cocks, (perhaps) lions for hunting, *paradeisoi*, road systems measured in *parasangs* and travelled by escorted ambassadors and official messengers . . . There is great wealth . . . Persians are liable to pride, hauteur, and inaccessibility . . . They enjoy a luxurious life-style (exemplified by clothing, textiles, food and drink, tableware, means of transport, fans and fly-whisks, furniture) in a positively organized, regimented fashion: but the queens are sexually virtuous and sometimes energetically warlike . . . Their policy is defined by a tyrannical ideology and systems of deferential behaviour and hierarchical control which deny equality . . . [They] value mere power and are inimical to the principal of Law – except that there have been 'good' Persian kings to whom some of this does not apply. Eunuchs will be encountered; and impalement or crucifixion is employed as a punishment.[1]

---

1 C. J. Tuplin, *Achaemenid Studies* (Stuttgart: Steiner, 1996), p. 164.

Such representations helped to mould classical Greek self-identity.[2] It is interesting to note that, from the late archaic period to the age of Alexander the Great, each successive generation of Greeks had its own particular way of reconfirming, as needed, national identity against the ever-changing yet ever-present external Persian threat. The infamous cultural construction of the Persian barbarian has been best explored in its fifth-century context, but in this chapter I will concentrate on less familiar images of the Great Kings and their Persian subjects in fourth-century Greek sources, chiefly through the material evidence contained in vase-painting and relief sculpture. This chapter will question how the Greeks of the fourth century related to their historical interaction with the Persians during the Great Wars of the previous century and will attempt to explore how the Graeco-Persian past was filtered into a contemporary understanding too. In particular, this chapter will explore a series of representations of the Great King and his court created in the period c. 380–330 BCE, images which harked back to an earlier historical age while simultaneously making an adroit comment about the contemporary political scene.

Over recent decades, the work of Achaemenid scholarship has proved that the Persia of Darius III on the eve of its conquest by the Macedonians was far from the moribund state depicted by Plato, Isocrates and the troublesome Epilogue of Xenophon's *Cyropaedia*.[3] Nevertheless, it must be conceded that things were not always going well for the Persian Empire throughout the fourth century: it was often beset with revolts. The reign of Darius II in particular was conspicuous for frequent revolts, led partly by satraps who had acquired a power base in regions where their families had ruled for generations. Ctesias mentioned a revolt by Darius' full brother Arsites, assisted by Artyphios, son of the satrap Megabyzus, who had mounted a revolt during Artaxerxes I's reign (Ctesias F15 § 52). The revolt of the satrap Pissouthnes at Sardis was crushed by Tissaphernes, probably in 422 BCE (Ctesias F15 § 53), who bribed Pissouthnes' Greek mercenary troops to abandon their commander. The Paphlagonian eunuch Artoxares, who had once helped Darius to become king, also attempted a coup at an uncertain date (Ctesias F15 § 54). In addition, the novella-like tale of the insubordination of Teritouchmes, married to a daughter of Darius II, may well mask a more serious threat to the throne (Ctesias F15 § 55–6). There is evidence of trouble in Egypt

2 The theme propounded by E. Hall, *Inventing the Barbarian: Greek Self-Definition through Tragedy* (Oxford: Clarendon Press, 1989).
3 Arguments for the flourishing of the empire under the later Achaemenids and into the reign of Darius III are neatly synthesised by P. Briant, *Darius dans l'ombre d'Alexandre* (Paris: Fayard, 2003).

in 410 BCE, prelude to a successful revolt in 404 BCE while, in the heart of the empire, the crushing of a Median revolt (Xenophon, *Hellenica* 1.11.19) was followed by a campaign against the Cadusii. The end of Darius' reign witnessed a major attempted *coup d'état* (that of Prince Cyrus the Younger) in 401 BCE, which heralded decades of trouble into the new century: a revolt by Evagoras of Cypriot Salamis between 391 and 380 BCE, by the Phoenicians c. 380 BCE and, most alarmingly, in the western satrapies in the 360s and 350s BCE (led by prominent rebels such as Datames of Cappadocia, Ariobarzanes of Phrygia and Autophradates of Lycia). Moreover, Egypt's secession from the empire between 405 and 343 BCE was a major blow to the finances and morale of the Persian Great Kings. And throughout all of this time (certainly from the period of Tissaphernes' sojourn in Asia Minor, which signalled the start of intensified Persian interference in Greek affairs during the Peloponnesian War), major players were the Greek city-states and, subsequently, the growing strength of Macedon.[4]

The Greeks remained a familiar part of the Persian world-view as much as the Persians remained central to the Greeks', but how much of the historical process of the Persian Empire did the Greeks understand? Outside of the authors of *Persica*, did the Greeks reflect upon the issue of Persian history? Clearly the Epilogue of the *Cyropaedia* (8.1–27) suggests so, with it overarching desire to depict Persian history as a gradual, if inevitable, slide into moral depravity, achieved through the narrative technique of looking back to Persia's brief golden age, the reign of Cyrus the Great, and comparing it with the moral and political bankruptcy of a contemporary Persia. 'I maintain,' says the author (*possibly* Xenophon, but probably not),[5] 'that the Persians of the present day . . . are less reverent towards the gods, less dutiful to their kin, less upright in their treatment of men, and

4 Interestingly, Artaxerxes III's chief objective was to consolidate royal authority and to terminate the revolts which threatened to break up the empire. Wars against the rebel Cadusii (Justin 10.3.2), a major campaign (c. 356–352 BCE) against rebellious western satraps, and the reconquest of Egypt were carried through with vigour and aggression. Details of the various campaigns are unclear, but, clearly, considerable success was achieved. For a narrative overview see P. Briant, *From Cyrus to Alexander: A History of the Persian Empire* (Winona Lake: Eisenbrauns, 2002), pp. 681–90, and M. A. Dandamaev, *A Political History of the Achaemenid Empire* (Leiden: Brill, 1989), pp. 306–13. See also C. J. Starr, 'Greeks and Persians in the fourth century BC: Part I', *Iranica Antiqua* 11 (1975), pp. 39–99, and Starr, 'Greeks and Persians in the fourth century BC: Part II', *Iranica Antiqua* 12 (1977), pp. 49–116.

5 See, for example, comments by S. W. Hirsch, *The Friendship of Barbarians: Xenophon and the Persian Empire* (Hanover and London: University Press of New England, 1985), p. 142.

less brave in warfare than they were of old' (8.27). This, though, is far removed from pure history.

What do our non-historical sources have to say about the process of Persian history? This chapter aims to explore that question by examining some texts outside of the Greek historiographic corpus – namely philosophy, legal speeches and poetry – but, more intriguingly, I will attempt to answer the question by analysing some key iconographic evidence and read the evidence for a Greek understanding of the Persian past through the prism of material culture.

I begin with a lively, colourful relief scene on a squat *lekythos* of c. 380 BCE, signed by the Athenian artist Xenophantos, but found at Dubrux near Kirch in the Crimea (Fig. 17.1); it is the earliest of three works to be explored in this chapter.[6] Its shoulder shows conventionalised mythological Gigantomachy and Centauromachy scenes, but the body of the vase depicts Persians hunting in a royal *paradeisos*.[7] The body of the vase is loosely divided into two registers, both linked by a tall date palm, gilt tripods and acanthus columns.[8] At the base of the vase a charioteer named Abrokomas delivers a death blow to a wild boar while above him, mounted on a white horse, a youthful-looking Darius spears a wounded deer. To the left of Darius is a group of Persians: the bearded Cyrus, holding an axe, moves towards his hunting dog, which jumps up eagerly to greet him but is prevented from doing so by an unnamed page. To the left of Darius three Persians finish off another boar: the bearded Eurylaos aims his spear at it, Klytios (almost erased from the vase)

---

6 St Petersburg, State Hermitage Museum P 1837.2. For details see L. Stephani, 'Erklärung einiger Vasengemälde der Kaiserlichen Ermitage, Tafel IV', *CRPétersb.* (1866), pp. 139–47; M. Tiverios, 'Die von Xenophantos Athenaios signierte große *Lekythos* aus Pantikapaion: Alte Funde neu betracht', in J. H. Oakley, W. D. E. Coulston and O.Palagia (eds), *Athenian Potters and Painters* (Oxford: Oxford University Press, 1997), pp. 269–84; M. C. Miller, 'Art, myth and reality: Xenophantos' *lekythos* re-examined', in E. Csapo and M. C. Miller (eds), *Poetry, Theory, Praxis: The Social Life of Myth, Word and Image in Ancient Greece* (Oxford: Oxford University Press, 2003), pp. 19–47; B. Cohen (ed.), *The Colours of Clay: Special Techniques in Athenian Vases* (Los Angeles: J. Paul Getty Museum, 2006), pp. 141–2. See also J. Boardman *Persia and the West*. London: Thames & Hudson, 2000), pp. 213–16 and H.A. Shapiro, 'The invention of Persia in classical Athens', in M. Eliav-Feldon, B. Isaac and J. Ziegler (eds), *The Origins of Racism in the West* (Cambridge: Cambridge University Press, 2009), pp. 57–87, esp. pp. 83–4.

7 The theme is taken up by Xenophantos on other occasions too. In fact, the vase belongs to a group of six similar *lekythoi*, each of which depicts a hunt (of boar, lion or deer), and all of which have been attributed to a single workshop. See Miller 'Art, myth and reality', p. 32 with fig. 2.9.

8 The decoration is sumptuous: eight of the thirteen hunters and all of the game are mould-made relief figures painted and partially gilded.

Figure 17.1   Line drawing of the Xenophantos *lekythos*. St Petersburg,
State Hermitage Museum P 1837.2.

thrusts his spear into its neck, and an unnamed youth awkwardly
delivers a back-thrust with his javelin. In the lower register, two
hunters of two mythical beasts, a griffin and a horned lion-griffin, are
named as Artamis and Seisames.

In this lively if somewhat chaotic scene, the worlds of fantasy and
reality converge. To achieve this Xenophantos employs some *bona fide*
Achaemenid imagery within the picture,[9] but toys with its use. Many
of the details of the hunting scene are derived from real Persian practices, which were well known to the Greeks of the fourth century, who
seem to have developed something of a passion for stories of royal

9 Miller, 'Art, myth and reality', pp. 23–39. I suggest that the griffin in the scene
   takes its inspiration from the Achaemenid-style Homa-bird found on column
   capitals at Persepolis and elsewhere.

hunts in the great *paradeisoi* of the empire.[10] The mythologisation of the Persian hunt occurs in the fifth century too, but Margaret Miller reads the Xenophantos *lekythos* as a definitive turning point in the mythologicalisation and marginalisation process of the Persian image, in which they ultimately morph into the eastern combatants of griffins in the Arimasps myth.[11]

What can be done, though, with the names of the hunting Persians? They are, of course, credible Achaemenid names in their (Latinised) Greek forms: Darius and Cyrus are the names *par excellence* of the kings and princes of the Achaemenid royal house,[12] while we find that an Abrokomas was a satrap of Syria at the end of the fifth century under Artaxerxes I, who thereafter sent him to Phoenicia, perhaps in preparation for an Egyptian campaign (Xenophon, *Anabasis* 1.3.20; Isocrates 4.140; Diodorus 14.20.5); Artamis might be cognate with the city of Adramyttion (in the satrapy of Hellespontine Phrygia), while Seisames 'the Mysian' is listed as one of the Persian dead in Aeschylus' *Persai* (322).[13] Herodotus, however, tells the story of Seisames who was killed by Cambysses (5.25), and of another Seisames who commanded troops in Xerxes' expedition (7.66), while Sekunda has suggested that Seisames might have been the name of an early fifth-century satrap of Mysia.[14] Whatever the reality, there is little doubt that Seisames is a well-attested Persian name.[15] Of course the decidedly Hellenic names Eurylaos, a name shared with one of the Epigoni, who was also an Argonaut and who led the Argives at Troy (Pausanias 2.20.5; Apollodorus 1.9.13, 3.7.2; Homer, *Iliad* 2.565), and Klytios, the name of one of the brothers of King Priam of Troy (Homer, *Iliad* 3.146), are

---

10 Tuplin, *Achaemenid Studies*, pp. 80–131; J. Barringer, *The Hunt in Ancient Greece* (Baltimore: Johns Hopkins University Press, 2001), pp. 183–92. For Near Eastern hunting practices see W. Helck, *Jagd und Wild im alten Vorderasien* (Hamburg and Berlin: Parey, 1968), and T. T. Allsen, *The Royal Hunt in Eurasian History* (Philadelphia: University of Pennsylvania Press, 2006).

11 Miller, 'Art, myth and reality', pp. 39–44.

12 Two Cyruses and two Dariuses were well known in Greece by the early fourth century: Cyrus the Great, the founder of the empire, and Cyrus the Younger, best known for his rebellion against his brother Artaxerxes II; Darius I, best known for his invasion of Greece in the 490s BCE; and Darius II, the father of Artaxerxes II (see below). However, there were several crown princes bearing the name Darius too. See Ctesias F13 § 24, 33, F14 § 34.

13 See E. Hall, *Aeschylus: Persians* (Warminster: Aris & Phillips, 1997), p. 112, and A. F. Garvie, *Aeschylus: Persae* (Oxford: Oxford University Press, 2009), p. 169.

14 N. Sekunda, 'Itabelis and the satrapy of Mysia', *AJAH* 14 (1998), pp. 73–102, esp. p. 93.

15 R. Schmitt, 'Die Iranier-Namen bei Aischylos', *SBWien* 337 (1979), pp. 56–7, no. 4.1.12; see also J. M. Balcer, *A Prospographical Study of the Ancient Persians Royal and Noble c. 550–450 BC* (Lampeter: Edward Mellen, 1993).

out of place here, although Michalis Tiverios suggests that they are Greeks in Persian service and therefore depicted wearing Persian court livery.[16] In fact, Tiverios argues that the *lekythos* depicts a specific royal hunt in the western part of the empire late in the fifth century BCE: the location is the *paradeisos* at Kelainai, where Apollo defeated Marysas and where Cyrus the Younger had both a palace and a *paradeisos* (Xenophon, *Anabasis* 1.2.7)[17] – this would explain Artamis and Seisames hunting mythical beasts[18] – and the participants in this real, historical hunt, says Tiverios, are Abrokomas, the satrap of Syria, Cyrus, the brother of Atraxerxes II (before his rebellion), and Darius, Artaxerxes' crown prince. This hunt would therefore have taken place a few years before Cyrus's death (at Cunaxa) in 401 BCE.

Historically, this cannot work: crown prince Darius must have been a babe in arms at the time of his uncle Cyrus' rebellion and death, so it is impossible to read this scene as an exact event in time (besides which, given that the scene is painted on a *lekythos*, there is probably a funerary resonance to this scene too, which removes it from the real). Instead we have in this lively scene a blurring of history whereby several *bona fide* historical personages become conflated into standardised 'royal Persians', a theme which we will explore in greater depth below. While it is impossible to dismiss the idea that the viewer of this fourth-century image may well have read into the vase the events of Cyrus the Younger's revolt (for the rebellion was, after all, a keenly felt and talked-about event in the Greek-speaking world), it is more likely that the names 'Cyrus' and 'Darius' would have either reminded the viewer of the earliest kings of the Persian past, those who first pulled Greece into the powerful Persian orbit, or else would simply have called to mind a generic image of 'royal Persia'.

Certainly an actual moment in Achaemenid history cannot be looked for in the Xenophantos *lekythos*, but does that mean that the Greeks had no interest in recalling the Persian past, or, for that matter,

16 Tiverios, 'Die von Xenophantos', p. 278. Certainly the hunters are easily recognisable as Persians and wear long-sleeved tunics over trousers; some also wear the *kandys*, a coat with hanging sleeves. They wear the *kidaris* on their heads. The appearance of the hunters on the Xenophantos *lekythos* is carefully constructed, which, together with their Persian names, leaves little doubt that they are supposed to represent Persian courtiers.
17 See further Hdt. 7.26.3.
18 See Miller, 'Art, myth and reality', although see further arguments by H. M. Franks, 'Hunting the *eschata*: An imagined Persian Empire on the *lekythos* of Xenophantos', *Hesperia* 78 (2009), pp. 455–80, esp. p. 480, who suggests that the *lekythos* 'illustrates Persian territorial aspirations, which extend to the very limits and most extreme places of the world, and which, as the product of hubristic ambition, must ultimately go unfulfilled'.

their own important intervention in the flow of Persian history? Were the Greeks content to settle for a nebulous 'once upon a time' quality in their involvement with the Persian past?

On one level, that question can be answered with an affirmative, reflected in a tendency in fourth-century literary sources, as in the Xenophantos *lekythos*, to create a standardised 'Great King' – a depersonalised description allowing for an open identification of any (or all) Persian kings as a single entity.[19] Isocrates, for instance, routinely equates Xerxes with Artaxerxes II (5.42; 12.157–8), while Lysias (2.27) attributes the battle of Marathon to the campaigns of Xerxes. Aeschines (3.132) too creates a confluence of Xerxes with an unnamed king of the fourth century:

> Is not the king of the Persians, he who channelled Athos, he who bridged the Hellespont, he who demanded earth and water of the Greeks, he who dared to write in his letters that he was lord of all mankind from the rising sun to its setting – is he not now struggling, not just for the lordship over others, but for his very life?

Here Aeschines' composite Great King straddles the historical narrative: he has shown his hubristic desire to conquer free Greece (à la Xerxes) and now must face up to the reality of Macedonian invasion (à la Darius III).

Fourth-century oratory and philosophy frequently utilise materials which at first glance might be thought of as an attempt at Persian history, but upon inspection are seen to be 'pretty unspecific and cast little special light upon Athenian knowledge of Persia and the Persians'.[20] It is a fact that, by and large, with the exception of the (often anonymous) Great King, hardly any Persians are named in the Greek philosophical and legal sources at all.[21] Interestingly, if rarely, however, when the need is paramount, authors can be startlingly specific in referring to monarchs and their historical deeds and contexts. For instance, Isocrates (5.99–100) takes pains to compare and contrast carefully the characters and policies of Artaxerxes II and Artaxerxes III so as to

---

19 On the issue of the depersonalisation of individuals in modern synchronic historiography see comments by T. Petit, 'Symchronie et diachronie chez les historiens de l'Empire achéménide', *Topoi* 3 (1993), pp. 39–71, esp. pp. 60–4.
20 Tuplin, *Achaemenid Studies*, p. 154.
21 Exceptions are: Amestris (Plato, *Alcibiades* 123c); Datis (Demosthenes 59.94), Mardonius (Demosthenes 24.129); Tissaphernes (Isocrates 16.18) and Cyrus the Younger (who is, anyway, very much a special case; see Demosthenes 15.24; Isocrates 4.145, 5.90, 9.58).

demonstrate the latter's military weakness and the ease by which he might be overpowered by a unified Greek taskforce:

> In order for you to know the temper and power of each, it is proper for me to also speak to you about the two kings, the one against whom I am advising you to take up arms, and the other one against whom Clearchus made war. In the first place, the father [Artaxerxes II] of the present king once defeated our city[22] and later the city of the Lacedaemonians, while this king [Artaxerxes III] has never crushed any of the armies which have been ravaging his territories. Secondly [Artaxerxes II] took the whole of Asia from the Greeks by the terms of the Treaty [of Antalcidas], while [Artaxerxes III] is so far from exercising his power over others that he is not even in control of the cities which have surrendered to him.

In a similar vein, but taking a much broader historical narrative sweep, in Book 3 of the *Laws*, written around 360 BCE, Plato reserves a relatively long exposition for Persian society (II, 639c–698a), dedicated by and large to a description of, and explanation for, its decadence and degeneracy. To couch his argument, Plato calls upon a potted version of Persian history and, with a somewhat cavalier attitude, retells the story of the political development of Persia from the days of Cyrus the Great to those of Xerxes:

> ATHENIAN: So how are we to explain the disaster under Cambyses, and the almost total recovery under Darius? To help our reconstruction of events, shall we have a go at guessing?
> CLEINIAS: Yes, certainly this topic we've embarked on will help our investigation.
> ATHENIAN: My guess about Cyrus, then, is that although, doubtless, he was a great commander and a loyal patriot, he never, even superficially, considered the problem of decent education. As for running his household, I'd say he never paid any attention to that at all!
> CLEINIAS: And how should we interpret that kind of statement?
> ATHENIAN: I mean, he probably spent his life after adolescence on campaign and handed over his children to the women to

---

22 A mistake: Isocrates is possibly thinking more generally about the Athenian defeat in the Peloponnesian War in which Sparta received Persian assistance; Artaxerxes II acceded to the throne in 405 BCE, the year of the battle of Aegospotami, the last major battle of the war.

bring up. These women reared them from their formative years as though they were already 'Heaven's Chosen-Ones', and fawned over them accordingly. They wouldn't allow anyone to scold their god-sent darlings in anything, and they forced everyone to rhapsodise about whatever the child said or did. You can imagine the type of person they produced.

CLEINIAS: A great education it must have been, to judge from what you say!

ATHENIAN: It was a womanish education, conducted by the royal harem. The teachers of the children had recently come into considerable wealth, but they were left all alone, without men, because the army was preoccupied in the field.

CLEINIAS: That makes sense.

ATHENIAN: The children's father . . . just didn't notice that women and eunuchs had given his sons the education of a Mede [i.e. of great luxury] and that it had been debased by their so-called 'heaven-sent' status. That is why Cyrus' children turned out as children naturally do when their teachers have never corrected them. So when, on the death of Cyrus, they succeeded to their inheritance they were living in a riot of unrestrained luxury . . . [But] Darius was no royal prince, and his upbringing had not encouraged him to self-indulgence . . . But Darius was succeeded by Xerxes, whose education reverted to the old royal practice of pampering . . . So Xerxes, being a product of this kind of tutoring, naturally had a career that resembled that of the misfortunate Cambyses, and ever since hardly any king of the Persians had been truly 'great' except in title and magnificence. I hold that the reason for this is not just bad luck, but the shocking life that children of despots and fantastically wealthy parents almost always lead.

Here, then, Plato argues that under Cyrus, Persia had witnessed an age when freedom of speech, liberty, community and co-operation reigned, only to be quashed by the oppressive regime of his successor Cambyses. Under the lawgiver-king Darius, Persia experienced a renaissance of thought (and deed), which once again gave way to the megalomaniac autocracy of Xerxes; from thereon in, says Plato, in a passage informed more by Greek prejudice than historical fact, 'the Persians have failed to halt on the downward slope of decadence (*truphē*)' (697c).[23]

---

23 The contrast between the fate of the two pairs of kings (Cyrus–Darius/Cambyses–Xerxes) is equally unreal. The pairing occurs elsewhere in Plato: *Epistle* 332AB,

It would appear from Plato's *Laws* that the dynastic squabbling of the sons of Cyrus II and the eventual seizure of the throne by Darius was a pivotal moment in Achaemenid history well known to the Greeks – versions of the story are delivered by Aeschylus (*Persai* 773–80),[24] Herodotus (3.1–87)[25] and Ctesias (F13 § 11–18)[26] (and there were no doubt others too)[27] – and it is also known that the history of Cyrus the Great (and the legends that sprang up around his life) always enjoyed great renown in the Greek-speaking world.[28] Plato's explanation of the political development of Achaemenid history fits in neatly with the general Greek discourse; he regards the entire thrust of Persian history as being determined by the relationships of the royal family and the duty of the kings to educate their successors in the ideals of freedom. Persian degeneracy was inevitable, he propounds, since even at the beginning of the process of creating an empire, Cyrus' campaigns away from the political heartland meant that his sons were reared by the women and eunuchs of the court and, with the exception of Darius, who was not a king's son and therefore not exposed to dangerous harem tutorage, all subsequent Persian monarchs have been degenerate by definition of their womanly education.

Plato uses the chronological development of Persian history to

320D; *Phaedrus* 258C. Antisthenes apparently wrote two dialogues on the pairing of Cyrus and Darius.

24 See comments by H. D. Broadhead, *The Persae of Aeschylus* (Cambridge: Cambridge University Press, 1960), pp. 278–82; Hall, *Aeschylus: Persians*, pp. 161–3; Garvie, *Aeschylus: Persae*, pp. 300–5.

25 See comments in D. Asheri, A. Lloyd and A. Corcella, ed. O. Murray and A. Moreno, *A Commentary on Herodotus Books I–IV* (Oxford: Oxford University Press, 2007), pp. 397–478.

26 See D. Lenfant, *Ctésias de Cinde: La Perse, L'Inde, autre fragments* (Paris: Les Belles Lettres, 2004), pp. 118–21; L. Llewellyn-Jones and J. Robson, *Ctesias' History of Persia: Tales of the Orient* (London: Routledge, 2010), pp. 179–80.

27 The first author of a *Persica* proper was Dionysus of Miletus, who seems to have attempted an outline of Persian history from the end of the reign of Cambyses II (522 BCE) to the end of the reign of Darius the Great (486 BCE); see R. Drews, *The Greek Accounts of Eastern History* (Cambridge, MA: Harvard University Press, 1973), p. 36; D. Lenfant, 'Greek historians of Persia', in J. Marincola (ed.), *A Companion to Greek and Roman Historiography* (Oxford: Wiley-Blackwell, 2007), vol. I, pp. 201–9, esp. p. 201. The *Persica* of Charon of Lampsacus, who seems to have written a concise narrative (in only two books) of Persian history from its legendary origins to the time of Themistocles' meeting with Artaxerxes I, must have covered Darius I's appropriation of the throne. It is also clear that Hellanicus of Lesbos covered the events of early Achaemenid history, including the murder of Cambyses' successor and the accession of Darius the Great. As a contemporary of Herodotus, it is possible that Hellanicus' *Persica* worked as a parallel (if more concise) redaction of the better-known *Histories*. See Drews, *Greek Accounts*, pp. 23–4; Lenfant, 'Greek historians of Persia', p. 202; Llewellyn-Jones and Robson, *Ctesias*, pp. 48–9.

28 See especially Briant, *From Cyrus to Alexander*, pp. 14–16.

support his stance; he lists, in the correct order, the main players in Persia's slide into degeneracy: Cyrus, Cambyses, Darius, Xerxes – the 'gang of four' who for the Greeks fundamentally defined the Persian experience. Interestingly, while Plato clearly knows about Artaxerxes I, the Great King of his own day (see, for instance, *Alcibiades* 121b, 123c–123d), he writes him out of the *Laws*. The ostracism of Artaxerxes from the text is deliberate and serves Plato's purpose: to show that the enfeebled kings of the present day are nameless entities of little political or military clout compared with the Great Kings of an earlier, more noble age.

Indeed, a similar tack is taken in many of the great orations of the early fourth century. Isocrates' *Panathenaikos* of 380 BCE, for example, has been seen as the defining moment in the negative stereotyping of the barbarised Persian;[29] his agenda is to belittle and deride the Persia of his day and he does so by once again marginalising all mention of its current rulers. The spirit of Xerxes looms comparatively large in the *Panathenaikos* (12.49ff, 161, 189) but the name of Artaxerxes II is conspicuous by its absence.[30] Even in his *Evagoras* of around 370 BCE there is no mention of this king, or of his predecessor Darius II, who was so frequently at loggerheads with the Cypriot ruler (see Ctesias F30).[31] In praising Evagoras' exploits, Isocrates is content to say, with one breath, that he was so superior a person that 'when the kings of that time beheld him they were terrified for their power' (9.23), while with another that Evagoras equalled the elder Cyrus in greatness. He expands (9.37):

Of those who lived later, perhaps indeed of all, the one hero who was most admired by the greatest number was Cyrus, who deprived the Medes of their kingdom and gained it for the Persians. But while Cyrus with a Persian army conquered the Medes, a deed which many a Greek or a barbarian could easily

29 B. Isaac, *The Invention of Racism in Classical Antiquity* (Princeton: Princeton University Press, 2004), pp. 285–6. See further L. Mitchell, *Panhellenism and the Barbarian in Archaic and Classical Greece* (Swansea: Classical Press of Wales, 2007), pp. 171–2. On fourth-century oratory and its relationship to the Persian past see also J. Marincola, 'The Persian Wars in fourth-century oratory and historiography', in E. Bridges, E. Hall and P. J. Rhodes (eds), *Cultural Responses to the Persian Wars: Antiquity to the Third Millennium* (Oxford: Oxford University Press, 2007), pp. 105–25.
30 He is present in abstracted form, often merged together with Xerxes, at 12.104, 106. He is simply 'the King' at 12.162, without a name.
31 On Evagoras see further G. S. Shrimpton, *Theopompus the Historian* (Montreal and Kingston: McGill-Queen's University Press, 1991), pp. 7–10, 91–2, 93, 103; M. A. Flower, *Theopompus of Chios History and Rhetoric in the Fourth Century BC* (Oxford: Oxford University Press, 1994), pp. 163–96.

do, Evagoras manifestly accomplished the greater part of the deeds which have been done through strength of his own mind and body. Again, while it is not at all certain from the expedition of Cyrus that he would have endured the dangers of Evagoras, yet it is obvious to all from the deeds of Evagoras that the latter would have readily attempted the exploits of Cyrus. In addition, while piety and justice characterised every act of Evagoras, some of the successes of Cyrus were gained impiously: for the former destroyed his enemies, but Cyrus slew his mother's father. Consequently if any should wish to judge, not of the greatness of their successes, but of the essential merit of each, they would justly award greater praise to Evagoras than even to Cyrus.

Judging from the works of the orators and philosophers, it can be argued that the Greeks of the fourth century were capable of pinpointing a precise moment in Persian history, at least as far as they understood the Persian historical process, if only to reflect upon their own Hellenic past and present. Frustratingly, it is at this point in the fourth century that our literary sources all but disappear, and to investigate further the Greek perception of Persian history we must inevitably turn to the iconographic evidence, like Xenophantos' hunting *lekythos*, for support. The *lekythos* seems to be consistent with the way in which we can generally read fourth-century attitudes to both the Persia of the contemporary world and that of the past, but the idea might be more clearly delineated with an image painted onto a vase of a slightly later date: the famous name-vase of the Darius Painter, an Apulian volute-*krater*, dating to around 330 BCE (Fig. 17.2), was almost certainly created during the reign of Alexander the Great, sometime between his accession to the Macedonian throne and his destruction of Persepolis.[32]

While the vase is the product of a Greek workshop in southern Italy, that need not devalue its usefulness as a reflection on Greek rhetoric about the Persian Empire and its past: for here is a multifaceted allegory of the Persian Wars of the early fifth century from a

32 Apulian volute-*krater* by the Darius Painter; Naples, Museo Archeologico Nazionale 81947 (H 3253). On the dating of the vase and general interpretations of its iconography see M. Schmidt, *Der Dareiosmaler und sein Umkreis: Untersuchen zur Spätapulischen Vasenmalerei* (Munich: Aschendorff, 1960); M. Daumas, 'Aristophane et les Perses', *REA* 89 (1985), pp. 289–305; A. H. Sommerstein, *Aeschylean Tragedy* (Bari: Levante, 1996), p. 69; O. Taplin, *Pots and Plays: Interactions between Tragedy and Greek Vase Painting of the Fourth Century BC* (Los Angeles: J. Paul Getty Museum, 2007), pp. 235–7, with a fine colour plate 92; Hall, *Inventing the Barbarian*, p. 84; Hall, *Aeschylus: Persians*, p. 8; Garvie, *Aeschylus: Persae*, p. xvi; Shapiro, 'Invention of Persia', pp. 84–5.

Figure 17.2 Line drawing of the 'Darius Vase'; Apulian volute-*krater* by the Darius Painter. Naples, Museo Archeologico Nazionale 81947 (H 3253).

late fourth-century perspective, although scholars read the meaning of vase in multivalent ways. Some see it as a theatrical scene and read the vase as a representation of the theatre space itself: the chorus in the orchestra, the protagonists on the *skene*, and the gods on the roof-space, waiting to descend *ex machina*.[33] Many of the Persians on the vase wear Greek theatre costume – sleeved and elaborately patterned robes and headdresses; but it is hard to verify if these are theatre costumes *per se*: throughout the fifth century the Greek representation of Persians and other orientals blurred the reality of dress with the costume of the stage, so that it is impossible to tweak out accurately the pure imaginary from the deliberately theatrical.

It has been suggested that the figures on the vase may have been inspired by a now-lost drama, or restaging of a drama, perhaps Phrynichos' *Persai*.[34] It is certainly true that the memory of the Persian Wars did not die out from the Greek tragic tradition and we know of several fourth-century and third-century tragedies with subjects set

33 A. D. Trendall and T. B. L. Webster, *Illustrations of Greek Drama* (London: Phaidon, 1971), no. III.5.6.
34 Trendall and Webster, *Illustrations*, p. 112. See further Hall, *Inventing the Barbarian*, pp. 63–4.

in the Graeco-Persian past,[35] although regrettably little of them has survived: Theodectas' *Mausolus* (72 *TgrF* T 6–7) and Moschion's *Themistocles* (97 *TgrF* F 1) are cases in point, and Moschion's play certainly included a vivid description of a battle, echoing Aeschylus' surviving *Persai*. Another *Themistocles* can be attributed to the Hellenistic playwright Philicus, and there was even a satyr play called *Persai* dating to the second century BCE. It would seem, then, that the Persian War narrative (and the role of Themistocles in particular) underwent what might be seen as a canonisation process in tragic theatre, as well as in oratory and historiography during the fourth century.

Contemporary lyric poetry also took the Persian Wars as a theme. Apart from Simonides' lyric poem on Salamis (fr. 536), by the late fifth century BCE Choerilus of Samos' epic *Persica* was dealing in hexameter with Xerxes' invasion, although its complete scope remains unclear.[36] Dated to around 410/9 BCE is the remarkable *Persai* of Timotheus of Miletus, a flamboyant Mozartian-like concert aria for a solo voice in which the performer imitated a host of Persian barbarians, from the pidgin-Greek-speaking soldiery (slowly drowning) to the lofty lamentations of Xerxes himself.[37] As Horden notes, 'the fourth century was . . . clearly a fruitful time . . . for Athenian interest in the [Persian] Wars', and he suggests that the upsurge in poetic activity centred on the Wars can be explained by 'the political difficulties experienced by Athens in their resistance to Macedon'.[38] Certainly, Timotheus' *Persai*, the ultimate jingoistic, triumphalist, popular classic (and thus much beloved of the philhellene Plutarch),[39] abounds with terminology and imagery drawn from the longstanding Greek creation of the barbarian 'other'; the same resonances are found too in Euripides' comi-tragedy *Orestes* of 408 BCE.[40]

That the Darius Vase continues the Saidian orientalising trend in its depiction of the luxury-loving barbarian is perhaps not surprising,

35 E. Hall, 'Aeschylus' *Persians* and images of Islam', in Bridges et al., *Cultural Responses to the Persian Wars*, pp. 167–99, esp. pp. 170–3.
36 *POxy.* 1399. See J. G. Winter, *Life and Letters in the Papyri* (Ann Arbor: University of Michigan Press, 1933), p. 199.
37 J. H. Horden, *The Fragments of Timotheus of Miletus* (Oxford: Oxford University Press, 2002), pp. 121–248; E. Hall, *The Theatrical Cast of Athens: Interactions between Greek Drama and Society* (Oxford: Oxford University Press, 2006), pp. 270–87.
38 Horden, *Fragments of Timotheus*, p. 123.
39 Plutarch cites Timotheus on several occasions: see D. A. Campbell, *Greek Lyric V: The New School of Poetry and Anonymous Songs and Hymns* (Cambridge, MA: Harvard University Press, 1993), pp. 91–3.
40 See M. Wright, *Euripides: Orestes* (London: Duckworth, 2008).

and Hall has suggested that it is in fact evidence for a splendid (but unknown) fourth-century play about the Persian invasion. She argues that a fragment of a tragedy (tr. fr. adesp. 685) which includes the disjointed words and bitty sentences, 'O race of Persians . . . of a wretched father . . . King . . . I will lament' is a dirge for Darius (or some other Great King), and can be related directly to the Apulian vase.[41] Certainly, a theatre setting for the vase scene is plausible, but it would be short-sighted to limit it to only that context, and, of course, we must in no way think of it as a photographic record of a particular staging of some lost fourth-century tragic *Persai*.

The Apulian volute-*krater* is richly decorated: three separate registers provide some kind of narrative, but how can they be contextualised? In the centre of the middle band, dominating the scene, is the enthroned, named and imperious figure of the Great King Darius; a messenger stands on a podium to his side (i.e. in front of the king; the artist is rendering three dimensions in a two-dimensional medium). The messenger is Greek, judging from his *pilos* and travelling cloak – the traditional get-up of the tragic messenger (although there is a possibility, of course, that he is a Persian messenger newly returned from Greece; his Greek clothing is not a cause for concern if he is a Persian, because several of Darius' councillors wear Greek robes – *himatia* – too). Whatever his origin, the messenger holds up the fingers of his right hand as he makes a pronouncement. The round podium on which he stands bears the inscription *PERSAI*, which *might* refer to the title of the play or, more generically (and more probably), to the location of the scene – the royal court in the city of the Persians.

The Great King is flanked by an armed bodyguard, holding a spear and a scimitar, and is attended by a group of bearded councillors, three of whom wear oriental costume; two of the courtiers are of an advanced age, and appear to be perturbed and in the thick of a debate, judging from the animated gesticulation, and the body language they adopt: several councillors lean into the scene, intent on listening. For his part, the Great King looks majestically aloof and calm.

Set in between two incense burners, the lowest register shows a royal treasurer seated at a low table (this cannot be another representation of Darius; the figure, in a Greek *himation* and short beard, is far too prosaic for that of a Great King). He is a royal treasurer (a representative of the Great King), counting pebbles and arranging them into correct columns as he tallies up on his wax tablet the value of the goods pouring in from the empire in the form of tribute,

---

41 Hall, *Aeschylus: Persians*, p. 8.

brought to court by well-dressed satraps who appear before him: there is a sack of money (?) about to be placed on the table and some gold or silver dishes being proffered too. This will all help provide funding for the war effort against Greece. The three empty-handed satraps perform an elaborate obeisance; their gift-giving has already taken place.

Taken together, these two scenes suggest a specific (if highly imaginative) moment in the year 490 BCE, just predating Marathon, when the Persians set themselves on the course for war.[42] But the outcome of the war is preordained: the top register leads the viewer into the divine plane, and in an almost Homeric assemblage of gods, paralleling the Persian war council below, the viewer meets with sceptre-bearing Zeus (directly placed above the sceptre-bearing Darius) accompanied by a winged Nike – the Greek victory to come – and the divine twins Apollo and Artemis (on whose festival the battle of Marathon was fought). Standing next to Zeus is the elegantly dressed, but somewhat timorous, figure of Hellas, for, as Alan Shapiro notes, the scene is 'an accurate reflection of the mood of Greece on the eve of Marathon'.[43] But Hellas has nothing to fear: she is protected by the armed Athene, who places a supporting hand on her shoulder. Seated at an altar with a herm is the figure of imperial (sceptre-bearing) Asia, plucking at her veil; Asia is certainly queenly, accustomed to command, while, in comparison, Hellas looks younger, lacking in confidence. Of the two, Asia has more to dread, for standing in front of her, in a hunting costume and with snakes in her hair, is the Fury-like figure of Apatē (Deception or Deceit).[44] She holds two flaming torches, and it has been argued that she is about to declare war by throwing them between the combatants,[45] but there is little to support this; instead perhaps we see here the flames of deceitful ambition. Jon Hesk has noted that this 'depiction of the divine and daimonic machinery behind the Persian Wars'[46] revolves around the juxtaposition of Athene and Apatē and implies a divinely inspired cunning which enabled the Athenians to snatch victory from the jaws of defeat. But there can be other interpretations: Apatē is attempting to lure Asia away from the safety of the altar; or the Persians are self-deceived or are attempting to deceive

42 See Shapiro, 'Invention of Persia', p. 84.
43 Shapiro, 'Invention of Persia', p. 86.
44 Apatē is closely associated with Atē (Blindness, Recklessness) – a word favoured by Homer and Aeschylus. The Darius Painter might therefore be depicting the Persian Wars as a perversion of divine order. On this idea see further Shapiro, 'Invention of Persia', p. 86.
45 Trendall and Webster, *Illustrations*, p. 112.
46 J. Hesk, *Deception and Democracy in Classical Athens* (Cambridge: Cambridge University Press, 2000), pp. 7–11, 107–8, 146–51.

the Greeks about their greatness, expressed through the grandeur and grovelling of Darius' theatrical court: all smoke and mirrors, but little substance.

Shapiro sensibly suggests that the Darius Vase presents a depiction of the clash of civilisations, played out through the female personifications of Asia and Hellas, first encountered, during Atossa's dream, in Aeschylus' *Persai* of 472 BCE: 'Two beautifully dressed women appeared . . . , one decked out in Persian robes, the other in Doric dress . . . and they were faultlessly lovely . . . a conflict between the two arose' (181ff). A similar image was still being employed in the Hellenistic period, for, according to a poem by Moschus (2.8.15), Europa herself once dreamed that two women, one an Asiatic barbarian and the other a civilised Greek, struggled over possession of Europe, while a third-century engraved marble slab known as the Arbela Relief (in the Palazzo Chigi, Rome) depicts a shield embossed with a scene of the battle of Gaugamela. On it, a crowned Europa and an identically crowned Asia appear as twins holding between them the shield depicting the mêlée; the only identifiable differences between the twin figures are Europa's few extra inches of height and Asia's sandaled feet – a memory, perhaps, of proverbial eastern softness.[47]

The scene on the Darius vase, with its 'delusional air of unreality', is a radical departure from the traditions of vase-painting: 'no other artist has attempted . . . to envisage a specific moment in the history of the confrontation between Persia and Greece',[48] Shapiro suggests, although, as he concedes, in the lost arts of wall-painting there were specific moments in history recorded in vivid coloured frescos: the Athenian Stoa Poikile, a kind of victory monument to the Persian Wars, famously housed a vast fresco by Polygnotos of Thasos depicting the battle of Marathon, which can be dated to around 460 BCE. To all intents and purposes this seems to have been a documentary-like depiction of the events of the battle, albeit interwoven with mythological narratives and figures of the gods and heroes who

---

47 In the autumn of 331 BCE, Darius III used Arbela as his base before he marched to Gaugamela, where he was defeated by Alexander and his forces. An inscription above the relief, referring to Alexander, reads: 'I am a relative of Heracles and Zeus, son of Philip and Olympias'; another, beneath the relief, says: 'Kings and their peoples, as many as the Ocean allots the lands of the earth, cowered before my spear.' See *IG* XIV.126. See also M. Fuhrmann, *Philoxenus von Eretria* (Göttingen: Göttingen University Press, 1933), pl. 3.

48 See Shapiro, 'Invention of Persia', p. 86. For the Stoa Poikile see T. L. Shear, 'The Athenian Agora: Excavations of 1980–1982', *Hesperia* 53 (1984), pp. 5–19; for the Marathon paintings see M. D. Stansbury-O'Donnell, 'The painting programme of the Stoa Poikile', in J. M. Barringer and J. M. Hurwit (eds), *Periklean Athens and its Legacy* (Austin: University of Texas Press, 2005), pp. 73–87.

steered the outcome of the event – as is suggested on the Darius Vase too.[49]

The scene on the vase is conceived of in an entirely Greek style and depicts the Persians in a way that conforms wholly to their views of Achaemenid hierarchy. The Great King sits above his subjects' heads, although a meaningful interaction between sovereign and councillors is suggested – an image drawn from Herodotus' constitutional debate of Book 3 of the *Histories*, and other such Greek conceptions of the Great King in council. Yet the vase-painter steers us towards believing that we are observing life at a historically verifiable Persian court, at an exact moment in time. The middle register is, of course, a formal audience scene, while the lower register allows us to look at the workings of the imperial bureaucracy inside the palaces' treasuries.

The Greeks were fascinated by the affairs of the royal and satrapal courts of the Persian Empire, and they correctly envisage the Great King's palace as an impenetrable fortress, not just of stone and wood, but of ceremony and etiquette: as Aristotle puts it, '[The king] himself, so it is said, established himself at Susa or Ecbatana, invisible to all, dwelling in a wonderful palace; many gateways one after another, and porches many *stades* apart from one another, were secured by bronze doors' (Aristotle, *Mund.* 398a).

From the offset, the Greek imagination attempted to peer into the halls and chambers of the palaces of the Great King: Aeschylus' *Persai* takes us into the heart of the court at Susa, and even presents Xerxes' much-honoured Mother and her opulent trappings to the hungry gaze of the Athenian audience. Herodotus takes us into the council chambers, banqueting halls and even harem quarters of the royal palaces, and by the early fourth century the Great King's court became the *locus classicus* of the popular *Persica* of Ctesias, Dinon and Heracleides, so much so that I think we can classify them properly as court histories.[50] I have little doubt that these populist histories, and Ctesias' novelistic work in particular, had a profound effect upon the representations of Persian life we see in fourth-century Greek iconography, where we are truly encouraged to enter into the world of '*le roi imaginaire*'.

Tales of defiant Greeks, like Herodotus' Bulis and Sperchis (*Histories* 7.136), appearing in audience before the Great King must have been popular, since the theme has a long history,[51] and

---

49 See Shapiro, 'Invention of Persia', p. 84. He notes that 'the fate of nations is in the hands of the gods; the Justice of Zeus protects the Hellenes'.
50 Llewellyn-Jones and Robson, *Ctesias*, pp. 66–8.
51 Compare Aelian *VH* 1.29, who recounts Ismenias' ruse of dropping a ring in front of the Great King so that he might be thought to be performing *proskynesis* as he stooped to pick it up.

probably drew on a folk-tale motif whereby Greek *sophrosyne* was
seen to triumph over Persian servility. The theme is still active as
late as Philostratus' third-century CE *Imagines*, which is imbedded
in generic Greek stories of the Great King's court.[52] His *ekphrasis*
of Themistocles' famous audience with Artaxerxes I in Babylon
(*Imag.* 2.31) draws upon a single historical event briefly outlined by
Thucydides (1.138) and elaborated on by Plutarch (*Them.* 29.5–6)
and Nepos (*Them.* 9.5).[53] Philostratus creates the picture of the
sophisticated Greek, noble in his confinement within the gilded cage
that is the Persian court, lecturing the Great King and his eunuchs,
who are posed before him in a kind of theatrical tableau 'iridescent
in gaudy costumes against an opulent palace setting'.[54] Undeniably,
Philostratus' description has some remarkable parallels with the
theatre-like scene painted on the Darius Vase; it begins with a description of the physical features of the court itself and then examines the
scene which unfolds therein:

> A Greek among foreigners, a real man among the unmanly,
> louche, and luxury-loving; he is an Athenian to judge from his
> short rough cloak (*tribōn*). I think he pronounces some wise
> saying to them, trying to correct them. [Here are] Medes and the
> centre of Babylon . . . and the king on a throne decorated with
> ornamented peacocks. The painter does not ask to be praised for
> his fine depiction of the [royal] headdress (*tiara*) and the tasselled
> robe (*kalasiris*) and the sleeved tunic (*kandis*), nor the monstrous
> shapes of colourfully woven animals which are [typically] foreign
> . . . but he should be praised for . . . the faces of the eunuchs. The
> court is also gold . . .we breathe in incense and myrrh, with which
> the foreigners pollute the freedom of the air; one spear-bearer is
> conferring with another about the Greek, in awe of him as his
> great achievements begin to be realised.

Next, Philostratus speculates on the events of that famous audience:

> For I believe that Themistocles the son of Neocles has come from
> Athens to Babylon after the immortal victory at Salamis because
> he has no idea where in Greece he might be safe, and that he is

52 On Philostratus see G. Anderson, *Philostratus: Biography and Belles Lettres in the
    Third Century AD* (London: Croom Helm, 1986), and E. Bowie and J. Elsner (eds),
    Philostratus (Cambridge: Cambridge University Press, 2009).
53 See J. L. Marr, *Plutarch: Lives. Themistocles* (Warminster: Aris & Phillips,
    1998), pp. 152–3.
54 Hall, *Theatrical Cast*, p. 185.

discussing with the king how indebted Xerxes was to him while he was commander of the Greek forces. His Median surroundings do not intimidate him, he is as confident as if standing on the rostrum; and his language is not his native one, but Themistocles speaks like a Mede, which he took the trouble to learn there. If you doubt this, look at his audience, how their eyes indicate that they understand him, and look at Themistocles, whose head tilts like one speaking, but his eyes show his hesitance, because what he is speaking is newly learned.

While Philostratus purports to be describing a real wall-painting,[55] it does not mean to say that he faithfully draws on an actual scene of Themistocles standing before the king, but when comparing his vivid description to the elaborately painted Darius Vase, it can be ascertained how certain Greek conventions in thinking about the Great King's court had become truisms.

The painted image of Darius might be made in a style recognisable to a Greek audience, and was no doubt pandering to their sense of superiority over the effeminate barbarians, but nevertheless, I would suggest that alongside the gorgeous robes and elaborate thrones depicted on the vase, there is a trace of the historically verifiable in the scene which affords it a certain credibility in trying to depict a 'real-life' moment in historical time.

Undoubtedly there are *bona fide* Achaemenid motifs located on the vase: the salaaming postures of the satraps in the lower register of the vase correspond neatly with figures found in a similar position on the base of a monumental Egyptian-style statue of Darius I from Susa;[56] likewise the representation of the spear-bearer behind Darius' throne (looking very much at ease with his ankles crossed and a scimitar casually slung over his shoulder)[57] is, to all intents

---

55 Anderson, *Philostratus*, p. 264, suggests that Philostratus might have derived his description of Themistocles before the Great King from an original showing Herakles at the court of Omphale, or Achilles among the women; the theme, he suggests, is much the same: 'the hero among women'. The Hellene in an oriental court is a standard sophic theme from the time Philostratus visits the audience with Artaxerxes in his *Life of Apollonius of Tyana* 29. See further Anderson, *Philostratus*, p. 268.

56 J. Perrot, *Le palais de Darius à Suse : Une résidence royale sur la route de Persépolis à Babylone* (Paris: Presses Universitaires Paris Sorbonne, 2010), pp. 256–99. See also L. Llewellyn-Jones, 'The first Persian Empire 550–330 BC', in T. Harrison (ed), *The Great Empires of the Ancient World* (London: Thames & Hudson, 2009), pp. 97–121, esp. p. 100; M. C. Root, *The King and Kingship in Achaemenid Art* (Leiden: Brill, 1979), pl. XI, fig. 11.

57 For a clear close-up photograph of this detail see Llewellyn-Jones, 'First Persian Empire', p. 109.

and purposes, fashioned on bodyguards regularly depicted (but depicted upright and standing to attention) on Achaemenid brick-reliefs from Susa, or relief sculpture from Persepolis.[58] The famous Bisitun inscription of Darius I, with its accompanying relief, shows the king accompanied by two weapon-bearers (perhaps Gobryas and Intaphernes) and a spear-bearer bringing up the rear.[59] The Darius Vase's Achaemenid-style motifs appear to have been lifted directly from authentic Persian iconographic sources, suggesting that Greeks artists could be surprisingly *au fait* with centralised royal Persian imagery.[60] Indeed, the overall feel of the audience scene on the Darius Vase is fashioned after a Persian image specifically authorised by the Persian monarchy, but one which must have been a familiar motif to Greek viewers too (in Asia Minor at least): I refer, of course, to the royal audience scene.

Originating in monumental relief panels at the Achaemenid palaces (certainly at Persepolis – see Fig. 17.3 – but probably at Susa and Babylon too, as well as in the satrapal palaces dotted throughout the empire), the intricate iconographical composition was deliberately disseminated throughout the empire in the form of seals, gemstones and other types of inlaid jewellery, or in painted leather panels, or woven textiles, such as those reported to have decorated Alexander's funeral catafalque (Diodorus 18.26.6).[61] It must have remained a well-known device throughout the lifespan of the Achaemenid dynasty because an unexpected detail taken from the glorious 'Alexander Sarcophagus' from Sidon, designed and executed sometime between 325 and 311

58 For the brickwork representations see Perrot, *Palais de Darius*, pp. 323, 335. For the Persepolis reliefs see, for instance, H. Kokh, *Persepolis and its Surroundings* (Tehran: Yassavoli, 2006), pp. 60, 70–1.

59 Root, *King and Kingship*, p. 186, pl. VI fig. 6.

60 This theme is very well explored by M. Millar, *Athens and Persia in the Fifth Century BC: A Study in Cultural Receptivity* (Cambridge: Cambridge University Press, 1997), esp. pp. 56ff. On the cultural and artistic interaction between Greece and Persia, especially in Asia Minor, see E. R. M. Dusinberre, *Aspects of Empire in Achaemenid Sardis* (Cambridge: Cambridge University Press, 2003); L. Llewellyn-Jones, 'The big and beautiful women of Asia: Ethnic conceptions of ideal beauty in Achaemenid-period seals and gemstones', in S. Hales and T. Hodos (eds), *Material Culture and Social Identities in the Ancient World* (Cambridge: Cambridge University Press, 2010), pp. 171–200; C. H. Roosevelt, *The Archaeology of Lydia, from Gyges to Alexander* (Cambridge: Cambridge University Press, 2009). For a fuller picture of the cultural interaction see S. M. R. Darbandi and A. Zournatzi (eds), *Ancient Greece and Ancient Iran: Cross-Cultural Encounters* (Athens: National Hellenic Research Foundation, 2008).

61 On the dissemination of the imperial image see especially L. Allen, '*Le roi imaginaire*: An audience with the Achaemenid king', in O. Hekster and R. Fowler (eds), *Imaginary Kings: Royal Images in the Ancient Near East, Greece and Rome* (Munich: Steiner, 2005), pp. 39–62. See also Root, *King and Kingship*.

Figure 17.3   Reconstruction of the audience scene, originally from the
northern Apadana staircase at Persepolis and later moved to the Treasury.

BCE, depicts – inside a Persian soldier's shield – an exact reproduction
of the standard imperial audience scene.[62]

Of course, the motif was open to interpretation according to locale.
The west face of the tomb of the Lycian governor Payava (c. 360
BCE), for instance, shows him as part of a local delegation in audience
before the seated satrap Autophradates. The scene's composition
and its component details, such as the style of the satrap's throne, are
comfortably adapted from Achaemenid court scenes.[63] Predating the
Payavan relief by some twenty years is a well-known slab from the
frieze on the base of the Nereid Monument, also from Lycia. It shows
an embassy of Greek-looking elders approaching the seated figure of
Erbinna, the last of the powerful independent rulers of Xanthos, who,
enthroned like a satrap, is depicted in Persian court style, his head
shaded by a parasol, and his feet raised off the ground on a footstool; a
youthful bodyguard in Greek dress stands behind the throne holding a

62 L. Allen, '*Roi imaginaire*', p. 61, fig. 9.
63 See I. Jenkins, *Greek Architecture and its Sculpture* (London: British Museum
    Press, 2006), pp. 179–84; C. Brunz-Özgan, *Lykische Grabreliefs des 5. und 4.
    Jarhunderts v. Chr.* (Istanbuler Mitteilungen Beiheft 3; Tübingen: Wasmuth,
    1987).

Greek shield. The subject perhaps records a real-life episode in which Erbinna received an embassy from a captured city (indeed, the siege of a city is shown elsewhere in the same frieze), but certainly draws on the conventions of the official Achaemenid audience scene.[64]

The Darius Vase therefore has parallels in a long-established and well-disseminated Achaemenid iconographic motif for depicting individuals in audience before the Great King. This all contributes to the verisimilitude of envisioning an exact time and place for the vase's scene, centring as it does on Darius' interview with the messenger. Or does it? While I concur with Shapiro's assessment that the Darius Painter makes a bold step towards depicting an exact moment in historical time, I want to take the argument a step further to suggest that the artist is actually, and skilfully, giving us a multi-layered approach to history. Past and present are merged in this scene; we can view the vase's temporal location, like its triple registers, on (at least) three levels. The vase does indeed show the moment when the threat of east–west conflict borders on reality; this is also the moment when Darius' ambitions for the conquest of Greece get the better of him. But a question remains: which Darius is this meant to be? The vase's annotations, especially the names 'Darius', 'Hellas' and 'Deceit', support a story involving Darius the Great, but the situation, like the theatrical, orientalised costumes of the king and his courtiers, allows for a more generic and transferable reading of the scene. By the time the Darius Vase was created, there had been three Great Kings named Darius, each of them notorious among the Greeks in his own right: Darius I (522–486 BCE), the monarch who initiated the Great Wars of the past; Darius II (423–405 BCE), who contributed with such vigour to the prolonging of the Peloponnesian War; and Darius III (336–330 BCE), who according to some accounts (Diodorus 17.1–3, 8–10; Justin 10.3.2–5) was a valiant warrior and had tirelessly met Alexander in the field, until his death – at around the time this vase was crafted.[65] With three Great Kings bearing the name Darius, I suggest that three simultaneous readings are possible, as, in effect, one reads the complete history of Persian involvement with the Greeks through this one vase. Ultimately, of course, each Darius was ruined by a form of deceit, be it bad council or ambitious, and deceitful, courtiers or blood-kin.

Of these three kings, it is the Greek memory of Darius II, perhaps the

---

64 Jenkins, *Greek Architecture*, pp. 186–202. The seated figure might be interpreted as the Lydian satrap himself, but the likeliest solution to the figure's identity is to name him as Erbinna himself, the ruler who commissioned the monument and who was interred in its burial chamber.

65 On the conflict between the reality and later reputation of Darius III see Briant, *Darius dans l'ombre d'Alexandre*.

least familiar in our present trio of monarchs, that I wish to examine further here. Known to us best, perhaps, from the mentions he warrants in the works of Thucydides (8.5.4–6, 80.1–2), Xenophon (*Hel.* 1.4.1–7; 5.8–9; *Anab.* 1.1–1) and Ctesias (F 15 § 48–52), Darius II, the sixth Achaemenid King of Kings, came to the throne late in 423 BCE, having already been satrap of Hyrcania. His father was Artaxerxes I; his mother, according to Ctesias, was a Babylonian concubine, Cosmartidene (F 15 § 47); Greek authors therefore wrongly considered him a bastard (and nicknamed him *nothos*), perhaps not fully understanding the institution of royal concubinage.[66] The Athenians were familiar with Darius II from the outset of his reign, and they appear to have begun negotiations with the king almost immediately upon his accession to the throne. Margaret Miller has explored the comparatively rich evidence for Athenian embassies to the Persian court early in the reign of Darius, and she stresses the fact that in this period many Athenians of upper rank had visited his court.[67] This might well help explain the new red-figure vogue for scenes of the Great King enjoying the pleasures of the court: his female fan-bearers, his gorgeously attired courtiers, and his dancers and musicians (a topos scene of oriental hedonism similarly expounded on the stage by Euripides in his *Orestes* of 408 BCE).[68]

Athenian–Persian relations soured quickly when in 413 BCE the Athenians interfered in Persian affairs by supporting the rebel Amorges against the throne. From thereon in, Darius' reign, as we have had occasion to note, became conspicuous for frequent revolts, led partly by satraps but more threateningly by his own blood-kin. His two eldest sons, Artaxerxes and Cyrus (the Younger), both aimed for the throne. Deciding to keep Artaxerxes close to him at court, Darius sent the younger son, Cyrus, to Ionia to coordinate Persian efforts as Darius began to create a more cohesive Greek policy. Angered by the Athenian championship of Amorges, he decisively sided with the Spartans. Consequently, Cyrus began to pump Persian gold into the Spartan war effort as new warships were constructed and troops were

66 For the Greek idea of illegitimacy see D. Ogden, *Greek Bastardy* (Oxford: Clarendon Press, 1996); for Persian concubinage see the discussion in L. Llewellyn-Jones, "'Help me Aphrodite!' Representing the royal women of Persia in Oliver Stone's *Alexander*', in F. Greenland and P. Cartledge (eds), *Responses to Alexander* (Madison: Wisconsin University Press, 2009), pp. 150–97, esp. 264–6.

67 M. Miller, *Athens and Persia in the Fifth Century B.C.: A Study in Cultural Receptivity* (Cambridge: Cambridge University Press, 1997), pp. 27, 89, 111.

68 See in particular a red-figure bell-*krater*, c. 400, Vienna Kuntshistorisches Museum 158; *ARV(2)* 1409, 1; Shapiro, 'Invention of Persia', p. 79, fig. 3.18, with p. 81, fig. 3.20, for a Persian dancer performing the 'oklasma' (Athens, National Archaeological Museum 12683, c. 400 BCE).

levied. On the back of this, the Persians restated their old claim on the sovereignty of the cities of western Asia Minor, and Cyrus bought the services of Greek mercenaries, many of whom were garrisoned in the Persian-controlled cities of Ionia. In the autumn of 405 BCE, just as the Spartan grip on Athens was tightening, Darius II became ill and summoned Cyrus to rejoin the court at Babylon.[69]

Interestingly, coinage issued at this troublesome time demonstrates how the image of the Great King penetrated the Greek psyche. An Attic tetradrachm, for example, was used by the Persian authorities to pay Greek mercenaries; the reverse shows the bearded and crowned head of a Great King, in all probability Darius II, at the foot of Athene's owl.[70] Another Attic tetradrachm, however, shows a clean-shaven crowned head stamped on Athene's cheek – this, it is argued, is an image Cyrus the Younger himself, stamped on a coin issued by the prince for recruiting his Greek forces in Asia Minor.[71]

It is against this background that Aristophanes produced his comedy *Frogs* in 405 BCE. Alan Sommerstein persuasively suggests that we can read into the play something of the Athenian reaction to Darius II's Greek policy and his Spartan partisanship.[72] In 405, only two things might possibly have saved a battered, bruised and hungry Athens: a negotiated peace with the Spartan enemy and their Persian allies, or the death of the Great King, which would, at the very least, plunge the empire into chaos and, best of all, probably halt (if only temporarily) the Persian funding of the Peloponnesian fleet. It is little wonder then that in *Frogs* Dionysus gleefully recalls enjoying best in Aeschylus' old tragedy, *Persai*, the scene where the chorus listened to the dead Darius and lamented and mourned the loss of their king (1026–9):

AESCHYLUS: I produced *The Persians*, and taught [the audience] always to be keen to defeat their enemies, thereby gilding an already splendid achievement.
DIONYSUS: I for one enjoyed the bit when <they listened to> the dead Darius, and right away the chorus clapped their hands together, like this, going 'iaow-oy!'

69 See Llewellyn-Jones and Robson, *Ctesias*, pp. 9–11.
70 A. Kuhrt, *The Persian Empire: A Corpus of Sources from the Achaemenid Period* (London: Routledge, 2010), p. 355.
71 W. Weiser, 'Die Eulen von Kyros dem Jüngeren: Zu den ersten Münzporträts lebender Menschen', *ZEP* 76 (1989), pp. 267–96.
72 A. Sommerstein, *Aristophanes: Frogs* (Warminster: Aris & Phillips, 1996), pp. 246–7.

Here, clearly, Darius I deliberately becomes conflated with Darius II, and the mention of a 'dead Darius' gives the audience of *Frogs* something to be hopeful about. At the end of 405 or early in 404 BCE Athenian hopes were indeed met with the death of Darius II at Babylon.

It is clear then that the Greeks had a good idea about the character and policies of Darius II; he was very much part of their political reality. That the Greek memory of Darius was kept alive *after* his death can be confirmed too by a badly weathered stone base from Olympia, dating to 330 BCE (contemporaneous, therefore, with the Darius Vase), which once held a statue of the celebrated Thessalian pankratiast Poulydamas, possibly by none other than the master sculptor Lysippos, although this is much debated.[73] Poulydamas had triumphed at Olympia in 408 BCE and an accompanying inscription, Pausanias tells us, listed some of his feats of strength: he could hold a bull by its hind legs, so that it could not tear itself loose; when the bull finally managed to get free, it leftits hooves in Poulydamas' hands. According to another story, Poulydamas could stop a chariot with galloping horses by holding the wagon from behind with just one hand. More than all these feats, though, he was famous for wrestling, Herakles-like, a lion to its death: 'On Mount Olympus Poulydamas conquered a lion, a huge and dangerous beast, without the help of any weapon. To this venture he was brought by the ambition to equal the works of Herakles, because Herakles also, as the legend goes, conquered the lion in Nemea.'[74] The base represents his victory over the lion, and shows both Poulydamas wrestling the beast and the immediate aftermath. Most interesting, though, is a long horizontal relief (Fig. 17.4) scene depicting a moment in Poulydamas' life which won him most renown, since the relief was commissioned and carved some eighty years after the event. Poulydamas is shown performing a remarkable feat of strength – he is lifting a man (a royal bodyguard in fact) over his head in the presence of none other than the Great King Darius II himself. Pausanias (6.5.7) provides the details of the story and sets it within its Persian historical context:

73 For a discussion of the base and debates surrounding it see A. Kosmopoulou, *The Iconography of Sculptured Statue Bases in the Archaic and Classical Periods* (Madison: University of Wisconsin Press, 2002), pp. 156–64.
74 Pausanias 6.5.7. Pausanias goes on to say that Poulydamas' last story concerns the end of his life. One day the athlete was in a mountain cave with his friends when the roof started to fall in on them, and the friends ran out of the cave. Poulydamas stayed inside, thinking he was strong enough to support the roof. He was, however, crushed by the mountain. After his death, he was honoured at Olympia as a hero with healing powers.

Figure 17.4   Poulydamas statue base by Lysippos, c. 330 BCE; front relief.
Olympia Museum 45.

Artaxerxes' bastard son, Darius, who led the Persian people and took the throne from his legitimate son, Sogdius, when he became king sent a messenger to Poulydamas, because he knew of his wonderful deeds, and persuaded him, with promises of gifts, to come to Susa for Darius to see him. At Susa, Poulydamas challenged three of those Persians who were called Immortals, and fought alone against three of them together and killed them. Some of the deeds I have mentioned are on the pedestal at Olympia, and others are explained in the inscription.

The scene on the relief depicts the Great King sitting on his throne wearing the long-sleeved oriental robe, but with a Greek-style *himation* slung over it, where it falls in folds on his lap; the long flaps of his tiara headdress fall forward down to his chest.[75] The king's left hand holds a sceptre (originally crafted as a metal fixture and now lost), which was once picked out in paint.[76]

Poulydamas stands in front of the monarch, lifting the flailing and kicking body of the Immortal well above his head, as the soldier struggles to break free. To the right of the group stand four female figures – a queen and concubines, possibly. These court ladies are certainly conjured from the Greek imagination and are dressed in Greek *chitōnes* and *himatia*, much in the style of the depictions of

75 On the tiara see C. Tuplin, 'Treacherous hearts and upright tiaras: The Achaemenid king's head-dress', in C. Tuplin (ed.), *Persian Responses: Political and Cultural Interaction with(in) the Achaemenid Empire* (Swansea: Classical Press of Wales, 2007), pp. 67–97.

76 His upraised right hand somewhat breaks with artistic convention and perhaps is meant to show Darius surprised and overawed by the strength of the Greek athlete.

Hellas and Asia on the Darius Vase. The female at the front of the group is shown in a standard Greek way as she raises a section of her robe in a veiling gesture.[77] The presence of the royal women dovetails neatly with standard Athenian images of the Great King created from the latter part of the fifth century onwards;[78] superficially these are imagined scenes of court life or the royal harem where the focus, says Shapiro, is on the male as a 'truly Persian peacock'.[79] It is worth noting, however, that a series of seals and gemstones from Persian-occupied Asia Minor, no doubt commissioned by and for satrapal and local princely courts, also show the image of nobles with their women, although in these Anatolian scenes both parties are always depicted in Achaemenid dress.[80]

While we have in the Poulydamas relief a stop-frame moment in real time, an event that historically took place at Darius II's court at Susa at some point between 410 and 405 BCE, I think that it is possible to read the scene in another context entirely, reflecting the date in which the base was commissioned and crafted, that is to say, around the time of Alexander's conclusive triumph over Darius III at Gaugamela. It is possible to read the relief scene as a moment in the past (some eighty years earlier) projected into the present. The relief is not only a flagrant inversion of the normal regularity of the imperial Achaemenid audience scene, but a metaphor for the overthrow of the Persian Empire itself. This is endorsed by the depiction of Poulydamas' wrestling a lion. Undeniably Heraklean in its inspiration, the scene has simultaneous Achaemenid undertones which cannot be ignored. In Achaemenid royal ideology the lion symbolises strength, while the image of the slaughtering of a lion by a hero-king, regularly seen in Persian monumental and glyptic art, is used to underline the Great King's power over his empire and the forces of chaos that threaten it.[81] It is possible to see the same ideology incorporated into the Poulydamas scene, but here combined with the victory over the Persian military represented by the defeated Immortal. Darius II, in effect, becomes conflated with his namesake, Darius III, who witnesses, first-hand, the shock and awe of the overthrow of his realm by a Greek force that turned out to be even greater than its reputation had heralded. For

77 On the veiling gesture see L. Llewellyn-Jones, *Aphrodite's Tortoise: The Veiled Woman of Ancient Greece* (Swansea: Classical Press of Wales, 2003), pp. 98–120.

78 See Shapiro, 'Invention of Persia', p. 76 n. 59, for a list of 'Persian domestic or court scenes' on red-figure *lekythoi*.

79 Shapiro, 'Invention of Persia', p. 76.

80 There is probably a rich interplay for this motif operating between Anatolia and the Greek mainland. See Llewellyn-Jones, 'Big and beautiful women of Asia'.

81 Root, *King and Kingship*, pp. 81, 82, 88, 98, 110, 232, 236.

his part, Poulydamas is simultaneously his historical self, the mythical Heracles, the personified Greece and, perhaps, an Alexander too.

It would appear that the Greeks of the late classical period understood the workings of Persian history; the Greek historians, in particular those working within the genre of *Persica*, ensured that they had access to a chronological outline of Persian history, at least as far as they saw it. The Greeks, we have seen, could use the Persian past with great precision (or an attempt at precision at least): Aeschylus had already demonstrated that in his bid to chronicle Median and Persian royal genealogy in his *Persai* (lines 765–81) of 472 BCE.[82] Nevertheless, the Greeks were equally capable of overwriting Persian history and willing to do so, skewing the historical process for their rhetorical, cultural or theoretical needs, omitting and ostracising persons and events from the picture. But the Greeks could also reflect on the workings of the historical process, allowing past events to be paralleled by the present. Literary sources were clearly revelling in this practice: the Cyrus the Great of Xenophon's *Cyropaedia* is, of course, the Cyrus the Younger of the *Anabasis*; we are familiar with that. We are less familiar perhaps with the way in which fourth-century iconography utilises the cultural *indica* of Persian civilisation to create a picture of a 'real' historical Persia whilst simultaneously adjusting the focus of the scene so that we shift backwards and forwards in a moment of time. When we accept that the process of history can be filtered through non-historical texts and images, we must acknowledge that the Greeks were capable of, and enjoyed, creating a sophisticated interplay with the Persian past.

82 Garvie, *Aeschylus: Persae*, pp. 274–5, 300–5.

18

COMMENTARY

Simon Goldhill, Suzanne Saïd and Christopher Pelling

I

All societies tell or write versions of the past. Any such version of the past could have a claim to be called history. The subtitle *History without Historians*, however, invites us to consider an opposition between the history told by historians and the history told by other writers or tellers of stories of the past (and that is how the authors of this volume take it). This opposition is integrally and significantly implicated with the self-definition of history by historians (and by historians I mean for the moment the self-defining set of historiographers starting for most of us, as for most ancient Greeks and Romans, with Herodotus and Thucydides). There are multiple models of how the past is conceived not just within the historiographical tradition but also within a single author as multi-layered as Herodotus.[1] Nonetheless, there are some assumptions without which it would be hard for any writer to affiliate himself to the historiographical tradition: history needs to be critical, critical of other versions of the past, of how the past is to be understood and what its implications for today are; history needs to postulate a coherent and explanatory narrative; history is committed to telling a story of the past which is true (though we could leave open how such truth is determined, for all that accurate representation of the past is likely to be involved).

If we take such an account of historiography and of the subtitle of the collection, it seems to me that the consequences are likely to be as

---

1 See esp. R. Thomas, *Herodotus in Context: Ethnography, Science and the Art of Persuasion* (Cambridge: Cambridge University Press, 2000); also D. Lateiner, *The Historical Method of Herodotus* (Toronto and London: University of Toronto Press, 1989); J. Gould, *Herodotus* (London, 1989); J. Marincola, *Authority and Tradition in Ancient Historiography* (Cambridge: Cambridge University Press, 1997). This short piece could be very heavily annotated, but that would not be in the spirit of the invitation to write it.

follows: we will find multiple versions of the past extant in the ancient world from before and after the invention of historiographers' history; these will include Homer, the Stoa Poikile's images, Greek tragedy, plenty of oratory including the funeral orations, Plato's accounts of Socrates, and many other prose and verse texts from throughout the Graeco-Roman world. In each case, especially those I have cited by name, it would be easy to show that they are not history by the historiographer's self-defining categories (though each has in contemporary scholarship become part of the arsenal of those writing ancient history today). We could thereby dismiss them as bad history (a naive move few would explicitly adopt); or we could postulate a different type of writing about time, the past and its relation to the present – against which Herodotus and Thucydides set themselves – which also makes historiography the yardstick but is a far more subtle version of the easy dismissal. We could even see these other versions of the past as eventually competitive with historiography (as some would claim Plato in *Laws* 3 is). But it seems to me that one danger of taking this approach is that we may be committing ourselves to a Whiggish narrative of the development of the writing of history (triumphing in the nineteenth century's familiar lauding of Thucydides as the paradigm and founder of the critical history which is a dominant genre of the nineteenth century and its so-called 'historical self-consciousness'). Such a definition of the canon of the genre of historiography (with the usual games about marginal inclusion and exclusion) distorts what might be at stake in postulating a historical self-awareness in ancient culture. At its most extreme, such an approach threatens to conclude that although there are multiple views of the past circulating in ancient culture, there is no 'real history' except that written by historians: history is the product of a self-defining club, then and now. There is no history without historians, without what historians say is to count as history. Myth, entertainment, poetry, art, records, inscriptions . . . but no *history*.

A counter-case would start with Homer. Homer provides Greek culture with a view of the past; it knows it is a view of the past ('Ten men of today . . .'); and it knows that epic itself is constructing a memorial of the past for the present and discusses such construction within its performance.[2] You can visit Homer's Troy with Alexander or with Caesar or with Lucan. Pindar's myths link present and past in a significant and causal manner, and offer correctives to impious

---

2 See esp. A. Ford, *Homer: The Poetry of the Past* (Ithaca, NY: Cornell University Press, 1992); J. Grethlein, *The Greeks and Their Past: Poetry, Oratory, History in the Fifth Century BC* (Cambridge: Cambridge University Press, 2010).

versions of the past, and although his poetry may have been written for a sung celebration of victory, you can read Pindar inscribed on a temple; tragedy is a machine for rewriting the myths of the past as stories for the modern polis, and the texts are kept, we are told, as state archives; the funeral orations offer the more recent past as exemplary and normative models; so too do the monumentalising art and epigraphic habits of the fifth-century culture of the polis, which has its own political agendas and strategies of representation. Cities need to construct genealogical arguments as part of the diplomacy of interaction at the political level. From Isocrates through to Lucian ('How to write history'), from the Second Sophistic's well-known obsession with a classical past to oratory's skills in telling a past narrative, there are self-conscious techniques for telling the past, self-aware constructions of different narratives of the past. Every budding orator – which means pretty well every educated Greek – was encouraged to imagine himself into the role of figures from the past, and to declaim accordingly.

This view would remind us that historians in the sense of self-defined historiographers are a particular and peculiar breed. Aristotle, whose every step can be defined as *historia*, whether it is an inquiry into the nature of animals, the development of the Athenian constitution or the history of the genre of tragedy, demonstrates the fluidity of the categories of intellectual inquiry marked out by *historia*. Following this line of argument, every text or object that purports to represent the past is history, and the historiographers are only one rather extreme position in a broad range of accounts of the past. Indeed, one could argue that the historiographers were not only extreme but even rather marginal to the discursive authority of ancient culture in the fifth century and far beyond. The category of 'history' as a genre, unlike rhetoric or philosophy or medicine or tragedy, is rather late in achieving anything like firm lineaments. (What is the Greek for historian, after all? *Sungrapheus* has nothing like the purchase of *rhetor*, *philosophos*, *sophistes*, *iatros*, *tragodopoios*; *historikos* is rare until later periods.) This approach concludes that all versions of the past, written, oral, visual, are history, and that therefore the idea of 'history without historians' has little explanatory purchase: most history is not written, painted, inscribed or told by self-defining historians, and although the later canon will make Herodotus and Thucydides the fathers of history, this retrospective narrative has little value for how the past is conceived or narrated in ancient Greek culture. At its most extreme: any representation of the past is a history, anyone who produces a history is a historian: there can be no history without historians.

These two approaches towards disambiguating the subtitle '*History without Historians* leave us therefore in two dead ends, for all that the travelling towards them can be revelatory: either history is really only what historians write, or every representation of the past is really a history (and some small section gets formed as a self-serving but scarcely determinative canon of historiography).

I would like therefore to re-pose the question of how a historical self-consciousness in the ancient world might be conceptualised: what is historical discourse in the classical polis?

The nineteenth century provides a model it is hard to escape from, but which I think is deeply distorting for the ancient world. For the nineteenth century (to oversimplify grotesquely), critical history is a master discourse, not only providing best-sellers for the swelling reading classes, but also developing a world-view of nationhood, the individual self and the placement of the self within time.[3] It also provides a dominant paradigm of scholarship at one level, and an expectation of popular culture at the other – from George Grote to Walter Scott, as it were. We are its heirs, not just in our commitment to the so-called good old days of Merrie England, but also in our conceptualisations of progress, of the burden of the past, of our duty to the past in heritage, our notions of modernity as a way of thinking about the here and now. This Romantic sense of history is, I would claim, barely visible in the ancient world, and perhaps nowhere in the classical city. (The best case for similarity, I would suggest, might be Pausanias, whose narrative is imbued with a sense of a lost past, a decaying landscape, scarred by the development of empire, and a material world of the past whose stories speak in fragments to the contemporary world – and, perhaps above all, with the sense that the *pepaideumenos*, the subject of the *periegesis*, needs this sense of history to find himself within the landscape of Greece.) It is customary to describe the fifth-century BCE in particular as an age of rapid cultural

---

3 See esp. R. Koselleck, *Futures Past: On the Semantics for Historical Time*, tr. K. Tribe (Cambridge, MA: Harvard University Press, 1985); Koselleck, *The Practice of Conceptual History: Timing History, Spacing Concepts*, tr. T. Pressner et al. (Stanford: Stanford University Press, 2002) – with whom my argument here is most pertinently in dialogue; also J. Burrow, *A Liberal Descent: Victorian Historians and the English Past* (Cambridge: Cambridge University Press, 1981); P. Bowler, *The Invention of Progress: The Victorians and Their Past* (Oxford: Oxford University Press, 1989); P. Fritzsche, *Stranded in the Present: Modern Time and the Melancholy of History* (Cambridge, MA: Harvard University Press, 2004); B. Mellman, *The Culture of History: English Uses of the Past 1800–1953* (Oxford: Oxford University Press, 2006). I have had my go at this in S. Goldhill, *Victorian Culture and Classical Antiquity: Art, Opera, Fiction, and the Proclamation of Modernity* (Princeton: Princeton University Press, 2011).

transformation, and, with that, one might expect there to have developed a strong sense of historical self-consciousness, a strong recognition of change and hence an awareness of the difference between the past and present as a question to be explained. As if – to continue the misleading nineteenth-century parallel – the Persian Wars were the French Revolution of the Greek world, the event which changes everyone's sense of time and historical self-awareness. This turns out to be only partly the case. So if we ask how a sense of history defines a sense of self, what parameters can we give for the classical polis? Let us begin with some propositions that I hope are uncontentious.

Genealogy matters for individuals and for cities. Quality is defined in part by descent and it brings normative expectations.

Memorialisation of the past for the future is central to social ambition, political commitment, private and civic celebration. It marks the discourse and landscape of the city.

So the exempla of the past become the models for the present: the Persian Wars can be recognised and dismissed as an encouragement to virtue and manliness by Plutarch because of their long and continuing tradition of use. Homer's heroes speak to the classical polis.

Corollary to this is the recognition of distance: the past can be nobler or more backward, more glorious or more squalid, than today; a model to be lived up to or a model to be spurned.

There is some recognition, therefore, with whatever ironies – in Aristophanes, say, or Plato – that the good old days have disappeared in modern manners and attitudes. There is, in other words, some limited awareness of 'the age in which we live'. As the age of heroes has passed, so the age of noble simplicity that our forefathers knew has passed. New music exists.

But these propositions need a further framework. The structures for ancient education remain poetry, rhetoric and philosophy. Each of these *technai* is in an important sense *anti-historical*. As Aristotle's no doubt tendentious argument has it, poetry is more philosophical than history because of its commitment to *to eikos* – generalisation, likelihood – rather than history's interest in the mere sequence of events. 'Wie es eigentlich gewesen' is explicitly dismissed as a valid basis for argument in the rhetorical handbooks: *to eikos* is the key to *to pithanon*. Exempla also have a timeless quality. The orator who imagines himself into the role of Alexander is not exploring the past as a foreign country, nor is he open to correction in historiographical terms: there is no issue of sources or accuracy, but of plausibility. Self-definition – again, to speak in the very broadest of terms – is organised around polarities that do not include modernity as a framework: Socrates is pleased to have been born a Greek, a male, a human;

someone else might have added Athenian, educated, rich, handsome, healthy and so forth. Would 'in this age' have ever have been a crucial term? By the Roman imperial period, it was possible, even necessary, for at least most elite Romans to distinguish between the Republic and the empire, and then between dynasties. But even in the empire there is little equivalent in Greek writing of the same period (as even Aelius Aristides' *Roman Orations* or Plutarch's attempt to explain the fortune of the Romans shows). Similarly, despite Thucydides' *Archaeology*, which postulates progress from the past to what now obtains, and despite Protagoras' myth of the coming of *dike* in Plato's *Protagoras*, a sense of progress stretching into the future is not generally part of the self-definition of Athenian technology or politics (unlike the politics and technology of the nineteenth century).[4] How the world might change has a very limited range of expectation. Although a story of the past can explain how things are as they are, man's continuing and present placement in time is not a pressing question.

So if we read through Hellenistic literature from the New Comedy of Menander, through Callimachus, Theocritus and Apollonius, we find little sense of an acute sense of placement within time – a sense of a fundamental self-definition through history as constructed by historiographers, although there are flashes of influence of historiographical texts in Apollonius in particular. Contrast this with Virgil, whose intertextual reconstruction of Theocritus in the *Eclogues* is distinguished precisely by its introduction of a political history, just as the *Aeneid*, although it takes Apollonius as a model for Book IV in particular, is quite different from Homer or Apollonius in its sense of epic as a foundation of historical self-awareness. *Aeneid* VI's vision of the Underworld contrasts tellingly with *Odyssey* XI exactly in its historical consciousness.

What strikes me as particularly interesting (especially in contrast to the Victorian paradigm) is that while the *historia* of Herodotus and Thucydides can and should be seen as part of the contest of discourses that make up the fifth-century polis, and while a tradition of historiography subsequently develops as a genre, nonetheless there is precious little influence of historiography in what we have been calling

---

4 Classic accounts in J. B. Bury, *The Idea of Progress: An Inquiry into its Origin and Growth* (London: Macmillan, 1920), and E. R. Dodds, *The Ancient Concept of Progress and Other Essays on Greek Literature and Belief* (Oxford: Clarendon Press, 1973); see also S. Blundell, *The Origins of Civilization in Greek and Roman Thought* (London and Dover, NH: Croom Helm, 1986); T. Cole, *Democritus and the Sources of Greek Anthropology* (Cleveland: Case Western Reserve Press, 1967; repr. Atlanta: Scholars Press, 1990), and esp. G. Lloyd, *The Revolutions of Wisdom* (Berkeley, Los Angeles and London: University of California Press, 1987).

historical consciousness outside the more narrowly circumscribed historiographical tradition in Greek writing (until Pausanias and perhaps some other writing of the Second Sophistic: texts, that is, from deep within the Roman Empire). There are, of course, exceptional and contentious cases, such as Plato's *Laws* 3 or Lycurgus' *Against Leocrates*. Rather, it is rhetoric (and in some circles philosophy) that has a far more insidious and powerful effect. It is the tradition and training of rhetoric that continue to dominate the elite representation of the past in Greek culture. So however we construct history without historians, we can't have history without rhetoric.

Simon Goldhill

II

One hundred years after the fundamental article of Felix Jacoby on the development and growth of Greek historiography, the Leventis conference organised by John Marincola in 2009 aimed at indirectly illuminating its status by looking at 'the vast variety of engagement with the past that is everywhere visible in Greek culture' (Marincola, p. 13) and confronting that with the founding fathers of history, Herodotus and Thucydides. The various chapters in this volume focus on 'hot' (Assmann) or 'intentional' (Gehrke) 'memory' embedded in various literary genres : archaic epic (Grethlein on Homer and Currie on Hesiod, early lyric (Boedeker and Bowie), Pindar (Pavlou), tragedy (Scodel and Romano), Old Comedy (Henderson), orators (Hesk) and Plato (Morgan), visual arts of the fifth (Shapiro) and fourth (Llewellyn-Jones) centuries, inscriptions of the fourth (Lambert) and third (Shear) centuries BCE. There are also two attempts to deal with more unusual sites of memory: Kearns focus on the modalities of sacrifices which 'are taken to give information about ancient diets' (p. 305) and Foxhall uses the marked loom weights found in the *chora* of Metaponto to show us 'Greek pasts below the radar of conventional historical texts' (p. 183) and reconstruct a female past founded largely on familial relationships. One is much tempted to ask for more and to regret the absence of chapters devoted to later texts.

    Such a collection invites us not only, after Strasburger and Bowie, to enlarge our view of the ancestors of Greek historiography and better contextualise historiography as a genre. It may also help us to reconsider our conception of historical method (or methods), question the opposition between the most ancient past – what we usually call myth – and the recent one, and partly blur the boundaries between historiography and other literary genres by pointing out the poetry of Herodotus' histories, the Herodotean co-existence of various *logoi* on the past in Hesiod's *Works and Days* (Currie) or the use of familiar historical tropes in Plato's discourse on the past (Morgan). Last but not least, this juxtaposition of various chapters often leads to suggestive and unexpected connections. I would like here to focus on the chapters devoted to literary texts and attempt to evaluate their contribution to these questions.

Without questioning Homer's status as the first ἱστορικός (Plutarch, *Essay on the life and poetry of Homer* 74) because of his topic (the *Iliad* purports to be a true narrative guaranteed by divine eyewitnesses) and his mimetic presentation of events and characters (including the use of direct speeches), as well demonstrated by Strasburger, Grethlein focuses on the Homeric (mostly Iliadic) view of the past, a past inhabited by heroes whose superiority to the men of today (οἷοι νῦν βροτοί εἰσ': 4×) is taken for granted and separated from the present of the poet and his audience by an unbridgeable gulf (all the allusions to 'men of the future' or 'posterity' are never found in the narrative but only in speeches). Besides this past, there is also a 'plupast' (Grethlein), that is, the previous past embedded in the narratives of the wrath of Achilles and the return of Odysseus. This past is relatively recent. It usually stretches back only one or two generations, excepting some genealogies which extend to eight (Aeneas), six (Glaucos) or four (Diomedes and Theoclymenes) generations. But it is always portrayed as a faraway time (the wrath of Meleager is 'an action of old and not a new thing', *Il.* 9.527–8) and its men are usually 'far better' (*Il.* 1.260) than the heroes of the poem: only Nestor, who belongs to former generations, is able to lift his cup and no Achaean, with the exception of Achilles, can wield the spear of Peleus. This superiority, which is only contested twice in the *Iliad* (4.404–6 and 15.641–3), 'provides exempla with special authority' (p. 19). As opposed to the epic past, which left no trace whatsoever in the present of the audience (the wall built by the Achaeans was totally erased by Apollon and Poseidon in *Il.* 12.13–33), this plupast, mostly known through speeches echoing the tradition, has left some material traces in the epic present: objects (in the *Iliad* the sceptre of Agamemnon, the club of Ereuthalion, the helmet of Merion, the corselet of Meges, the bowl of silver which is the prize of the foot race, or in the *Odyssey* the bow of Odysseus), walls and unidentified stones. Graves are also the visible sign of the *kleos* of the warrior or his victorious adversary.

The Hesiodic past of the *Works and Days* is in some ways identical with the Homeric one: its reality is guaranteed by the Muses and it is cut from and contrasted to the present in the myth of Prometheus and Pandora, as well as in the myth of the races, which portrays five discrete and successive races – a complex text subtly read by Currie. On the other hand, the confrontation between Herodotus' *Histories* and the *Works and Days* also enables us to perceive some similarities in purpose and method. In purpose, with the construction of a past that illuminates the present from an ethical standpoint. In method, with the implicit criticism of other accounts of the past (since the Muses are not only able to tell the truth if they wish, but also to tell lies similar to the truth), the concern to establish some coherence between the discrepant Greek and Near Eastern accounts in the myth of the races, and the inclusion of incompatible accounts of the past, such as the myth and Prometheus and Pandora and the myth of the races, even if one may be reluctant to push further the analogy and explain their agreement on certain key points as a way of highlighting what is meant to stand as historical fact and a prefiguration of Herodotus' method, as did Currie.

As opposed to Homeric poems, in archaic lyric the present and the poet come to the fore and one may point out some similarities with Herodotus. Boedeker reminds us that Stesichorus, in his *Palinode*, exposed, before Herodotus' new version of the Helen story and Thucydides' *Archaeology*, the lack of reliability of the Homeric song, and Ibycus (fr. 151 PMGF) openly criticised the accuracy of the Homeric Catalogue of Ships and chooses to celebrate the beauty of three young heroes neglected or ignored by Homer in order to praise the contemporary Polycrates better. Alcaeus, before Herodotus, explicitly echoed 'what is said' (ὡς λόγος, fr. 42 V v.1) and 'does not take responsibility for the tale's veracity' (p. 70). With Sappho, 'the present illuminates the past as much as the past does the present' (p. 76). In a sequel to his influential papers demonstrating how several elegiac poets, who narrated at some length both the early and the more recent past of their cities, were 'ancestors of Herodotus', Bowie turns to the accounts of the most ancient past (that is, 'myth') given by two melic poets originating from western Greece, Stesichorus of Himera and Ibycus of Rhegium, and opposes their various ways of reconstructing it. In order to emphasise his own Greekness, Stesichorus often chose to tell some traditional Greek myths as well as stories set in mainland Greece that bear no relation to the main body of mythology. But he also told myths located in his native city (Daphnis), whereas Ibycus relocated in Sicily well-known myths such as the abduction of Ganymede or probably referred to the foundation of his own city.

Pindar's *Epinicians* are mostly concentrated on the present and the praise of contemporary victorious athletes. But, as pointed out by Pavlou, they give much place to a past which spans from myth to contemporary history. In contrast to Homer and Hesiod, Pindar replaced the Muses with tradition as the main source of information and did not hesitate to criticise former accounts of the past openly. He also broke with the linearity of the epic narrative and its presentation of a 'past . . . "walled off" or cast as superior to the present', for his 'primary concern was . . . to draw analogies between past and present' (pp. 105, 101) and to stress the continuity of the family, from its mythical ancestors to the victor.

The two papers on tragedy (Scodel and Romano) both emphasise in their own way the complexity of the tragic past where anachronism is not the exception but the rule, to quote B. Knox. Scodel points out obvious discrepancies in the portrait of the past by different characters according to their self-interest in the *Troades* (Helen and Hecuba) and in Sophocles' *Electra* (Clytemnestra and Electra). She establishes a convincing parallel between these tragic characters and Herodotean figures who present versions of the past that make their own nations appear guiltless. In the *Troades,* she draws attention to a rational rewriting of Helen's story by Hecuba, who treats Aphrodite as a metaphor for Helen's attraction to Paris, as did Gorgias in his *Helen*, without denying, as the sophist did, Helen's responsibility. In the *Orestes*, Scodel also interprets Tyndareus' claims that Orestes should have followed a law established by the ancestors long ago by prosecuting his mother and throwing her out of his house (494–5, 500–3, 512–15) as 'a deliberate transfer of a contemporary kind of argument about the past to a remote past', specially appealing at a time when 'democrats and oligarchs both claimed ancestral support' (pp. 119–20). On the other hand Romano, who questions any interpretation of Euripidean aetiologies of the prophetic form as a direct exchange between playwright and audience, chooses to locate his human seers (Polymestor in *Hecuba* and Eurystheus in the *Heraclidae*) in the contemporary Athenian landscape of divination. In *Iphigeneia in Tauris* he dismisses Orestes' report of the foundation of Athenian Choes as a kind of historical explanation and interprets it as a self-serving argument. He refuses any authoritative value to the predictions of divine speakers such as Artemis, Thetis and Apollo, since they only reflect their character. Yet his conclusion suggest a convincing parallel between these biased and subjective aetiologies and the historical discourse about foundations, which was also self-serving.

The chapters of Henderson on Old Comedy and Hesk on fourth-century oratory provide us a glimpse of a 'popular' or, better, 'civic' past that contrasts with the allegedly scientific historiography. Henderson attempts to define the Aristophanic past and its sources by looking at four plays, *Acharnians, Peace, Knights* and *Lysistrata,* performed between 425 and 411. Obviously this past, known only by hearsay (Trygaeus in the *Peace* and Lysistrata) or personal memories (the chorus of old men in *Lysistrata*), has nothing to do with the one reconstructed by the historians. Accordingly, Henderson excludes any influence of Herodotus' prologue on *Ach.* 523–9, which traces the origin of the Peloponnesian War to reciprocal abduction of women. His comparison between Thucydides' explanation and the comic presentation of the causes of the war by Dicaeopolis in *Acharnians* and Hermes in *Peace*, both contrasting a trivial beginning with its disastrous consequences, only allows us to measure the gap between a critical historian, who looks for 'the true though unavowed' cause of the war and minimises the importance of the Megarian decree and 'some other grounds of complaint' (1.67.4) put forward by the Megarians, and a comic poet relying on the popular view privileging Pericles and the Megarian decree. Aristophanes also exposes a tendentious reading of the mythical or historical past: in *Clouds* (1075–92) he criticises the use of mythological precedents by the Euripidean characters, and condemns in *Frogs* (1049–55) the negative examples he set by staging women committing adultery. Elsewhere his target is the tendentious use of the Athenian past by orators. In *Knights* the appeal to the great figures of Athenian past by contemporary politicians, such as Creon's self-comparison with Themistocles, is deemed totally inapt. In *Lysistrata* he exposes the official depiction of Athenian civic historical myths, such as that of the tyrant-slayers Harmodius and Aristogiton, by the chorus of old men, as well as the carefully edited version of the good old days where Athens and Sparta were helping each other given by Lysistrata, and in *Ecclesiazusae* he makes fun of the opposition between an idealised fifth-century past, the time of Myronides, imbued with a deep commitment to the city, and a present characterised by individual selfishness. The chapter by Hesk on 'Common Knowledge and the Contestation of History in Some Fourth-Century Athenian Trials' also looks at the uses of a popular and civic past and strongly criticises Ober's recent contention that 'a shared repertoire of common knowledge along with a commitment to democratic values meant that . . . jurors would often align in more or less predictable ways'.[5] Hesk convincingly demonstrates that Athenian decision-making was informed by a much more sceptical attitude. Through a reading of the few cases where we happen to have the arguments used by both sides (Aeschines' *Against Timarchus* and its criticism later on by Demosthenes, *On the Embassy*; Aeschines' and

5 J. Ober, *Democracy and Knowledge: Innovation and Learning in Classical Athens* (Princeton: Princeton University Press, 2008), p. 191.

Demosthenes' speeches *On the Embassy*; Aeschines' *Against Ctesiphon* and Demosthenes' *On the Crown*) and a reconstruction from one speech (Lycurgus' *Against Leocrates*) of the historical arguments used by the other, he points out passages that question the relevance and applicability of some historical exempla, appeal to another set of historical precedents, reinterpret in an opposite way the same item of history and debunk a rosy portrait of Athenian past. He also demonstrates the influence of contemporary critical historiography on Demosthenes, who in 19.251 questions 'bogus historical evidence' (Solon's statue supposedly portraying Solon's oratorical demeanour is merely fifty years old) and 'realigns the exemplarity of Solon in his own favour' by relying on a good historical evidence, Solon's Salamis elegy (pp. 223, 224).

Morgan's chapter on the late dialogues of Plato (*Statesman*, *Timaeus*, *Critias* and *Laws* 3) invites us not only to confront the historical and philosophical views of the past but also to look at the influence of historiography on Plato's 'history'. In the *Statesman* Plato starts from existing myths, the ancient stories, known from tradition and hearsay about Atreus and Thyestes, the rule of Cronus, the men born from the earth and the fall of Phaethon. But he is not content to adapt them to his demonstration, as he does for the Prometheus myth in the *Protagoras* or the *Gorgias*; he makes use of familiar historiographical tropes such as the fading of memory with time and the search beyond the mythical form for the 'truth', that is, the unique underlying cause that explains all these scattered phenomena, a rationalisation of myth which is, I think, closer to Thucydides than to Hecataeus and Acusilaus, the two mythographers cited by Morgan. Indeed, this search for the most ancient past is not for Plato, as it is for the historian, an end in itself, but a fitting contribution towards his goal: the exposition of the king. After reading the chapter by Currie, one is also struck by some similarities: like Hesiod's myth of the races, it is not a simple story of decline. It is 'a heuristic device for untangling a complex synchronic reality' (p. 234) which has, to echo Currie, a 'fundamental ethical dimension' (p. 64). In the *Timaeus/Critias* Plato's historicisation of the myth goes even further. Plato's narrative of the struggle between ancient Athens and Atlantis is a grandiose rewriting of the Persian Wars, presenting the ideal city of the *Republic* in the guise of the ancient Athens and substituting for the Persians a hubristic empire mirroring both the insolence of Xerxes and the greed of imperial Athens).[6] And the history of its transmission from the

---

6 P. Vidal-Naquet, *The Atlantis Story: A Short History of Plato's Myth* (Exeter: Exeter University Press, 2007).

Egyptian priest who told it to Solon to its actual narrator, Critias, obviously echoes both Herodotus' introduction of the true story of Helen (2.116) and his narrative of his own visit to Egypt (2.142–3). In *Laws* 3, the survey of the respective pasts of the Dorian kingdoms of the Peloponnese, of Athens and of Persia, which begins with the most ancient past, but truly starts with the return of the Heraclidae and the foundation of Lacedaemon (the termination of Hellanicus' mythographical works and the beginning of Ephorus' *Universal History*), is also a piece of 'moralising history' (p. 245): the interpretation of the events is governed by *a priori* assumption (governments fall through their own faults) in order to demonstrate 'the congruence between history and theory' (p. 249).

So even if one contests, as does Simon Goldhill, the primacy unduly given to critical historiography, one has to acknowledge the interest of its confrontation with other views of the past.

Suzanne Saïd

III

The past mattered. It mattered already to Homer's heroes, harking back to those earlier days when mortals were better and stronger (Grethlein); it mattered to Homer's hearers and then his readers, dwelling on that world when gods mingled more readily and visibly on earth. It may have mattered to Epimenides, with his purification of Athens (Marincola). It mattered to Pindar's athletes, linked poetically with their ancestors (Pavlou). It mattered to Sappho as she mused first on Helen and then on Anactoria, and the two musings meshed (Boedeker). It certainly matters in the plots of tragedy, where events from the back-story hang heavily over play after play. It was *how* it mattered that was difficult to track, and needed to be contested rhetorically. Enough was at stake for it to be worthwhile for tragic characters to have their own heavily charged narratives of earlier happenings, especially of their personal pasts (Scodel); for a 'memory politics' to develop (Shear); and for fourth-century orators to produce their own slanted version of how they, or their domestic or foreign enemies, fitted into the long narrative of Athenian history (Hesk), where warfare may have changed but the required resilience and commitment had not. Importance, contestation, rhetoric: the three go together. And, whatever view we form of the debt of other genres to historiography or the differences between them, those three are constants in historiography too. Herodotus' programmatic homing-in on the *aitiē* of the great war (proem) becomes, at least initially, a discussion of who was to blame, 'the Persian word-experts say that Phoenicians were *aitioi* for the rift' (1.1.1): historiographic techniques of attaching or deflecting blame, and crafting the narrative story to suit, have something in common with the rhetorical deftness so clear in Antiphon's *Tetralogies*, even if the infrastructure of the argument is not usually laid so bare as it is by Polybius in his attack on Fabius Pictor (3.8) – *eikos* arguments, *ad hominem* questioning and so on. And, in historians as in orators, silences can be as telling as words. Xenophon's reader is not allowed to know about the Second Athenian Confederacy, and we can trace skilfully combative silences in Thucydides too: this was *not* Pericles' war, not a matter of Megarian decrees; you needed to look further back, to the 470s and to the first forty rather than the last ten of those crucial fifty years. And all this was worth doing because a lot was at stake. Understanding what was important about the present meant delving into the past, and in ways where it could be anticipated that people would disagree. Cases needed to be made.

So in one way no 'bridge between past and present' (Romano, p. 130) needed building; it was already there, and it was the *sort of* bridge, and where it led, that needed to be argued. Awareness of the links did not, of course, mean blindness to the ways in which the past had changed, whether in decline – not necessarily simple or linear decline, as Hesiod (Currie) and Plato (Morgan) show – or in technical progress or power structures or moral values. It is true, too, that the aetiological explanations of tragedy are often counterintuitive or problematic, and that some of tragedy's prophecies imply future narratives that are themselves contestable (Romano again), just as the characters' own past narratives are sometimes incompatible with one another. But need it follow that talk of that 'bridge between past and present' is inappropriate for such aetiological passages? One could equally argue that the emotional engagement of particular speakers with such partisan narratives, well brought out by Romano, implies an even closer bridge: the present mattered to the past, just as the past still matters to the present. If some of the aetiological suggestions seem rum or off-key, then that is no surprise. They can seem rum or off-key to characters in the play as well, morally if not factually, as they do to Electra, Orestes, and the chorus at Eur. *El.* 1292ff; one suspects too that Hippolytus might have found cold comfort in Artemis' promise of a marital hair-cutting custom at *Hipp.* 1423–30, marking the moment when girls give up the virginity that was his pride. Relating the mythical past to the present may be as unstraightforward for the tragic audience as relating their own pasts to the dramatic present is for the characters within the plays themselves; the aetiological passages may well be selective as well as partisan, with their unsettling elements and their half-truths; but the relation can still be there, and the texture of explanation can be right even if one knows that the particular details may not be. It points to the right place to look.

But surely – one might say – incompatible versions of the past cannot all be *true*? Surely historiography has more of a commitment to truth, to ironing out inconsistencies in one's conceptual scheme of how the past came about? This raises the point addressed by Currie, as he reflects on the various versions of the past in *Works and Days* and the complications in putting them altogether into a coherent scheme: how far does this imply 'a discourse with truth-values' (p. 57)? That recalls the fundamental question posed by Paul Veyne – not so much as it is put in his book's title, *Did the Greeks Believe in Their Myths?*,[7] but rather, did they believe in their myths in a different way from the way they believed in the truth or falsity of more everyday matters? It is doubtless right to think that, say, the 'myth' of the origin of justice in Plato's *Protagoras* or the 'social contract' theory set out in *Republic* 2 are not to be taken as a literally accurate reconstruction of past events. Morgan shows in this volume how 'diachronic presentation in Plato can sometimes be a heuristic device for untangling a complex synchronic reality' (p. 234, citing Frutiger). Cynthia Farrar also had good things to say about this in her *Origins of Democratic Thinking*, particularly (again) in connection with Plato's Protagoras.[8] Something similar may be true of Hesiod's myth of the ages (Currie), though there we will be dealing not so much with 'a complex synchronic reality' as with a simplified model of diachronic development, one which produces a fable-version which reflects but drastically reduces the complexities of real history. Such a picture may indicate the deep structure embedded in the messiness of historical reality, it may be what that historical progress amounted to; it acknowledges that a sophisticated cultural feature is a consequence of development over time and helps you to understand that development, and it is historical in that it shows a sense of the importance of history; but it does not imply that everything really happened in quite so toy-town a way. It may capture a truth, but does so in an idiom that invites belief in a different way, more symbolic than literal.

---

7 P. Veyne, *Did the Greeks Believe in Their Myths? An Essay on Constitutive Imagination* (Chicago: University of Chicago Press, 1988); tr. by P. Wissing of French original, *Les Grecs ont-ils cru à leurs mythes? Essai sur l'imagination constituante* (Paris: Éditions de Seuil, 1983).

8 C. Farrar, *The Origins of Democratic Thinking* (Cambridge: Cambridge University Press, 1988), esp. p. 88: 'Protagoras' story is not a naturalistic account of the rise of human society. Protagoras was interested not in how the world came to be, but in how it was' – and his speech in Plato's dialogue too is to be seen similarly as expressing 'insights into man's present condition, not his origins'.

Still, we run a risk of being too simple about historiography if we simply contrast that 'mythical' mindset with that of the historians, or indeed if we think about that historiographic 'commitment to truth' as if it always presents itself in exactly the same register. On the Roman side, David Levene has argued that Livy similarly combines in his own narrative versions which not merely *are* incompatible but were recognised by the author, and would be recognised by his readers, as such; as Levene notes, analogies can be found in Plutarch's *Lives*, though those cases are possibly less extreme.[9] There would be attractions as well as difficulties in reading that approach back into classical Greek, and sidestepping rather than confronting such old chestnuts as the reconcilability of Herodotus' two Spartan king lists, for instance, or the disentangling of various problems of pre-Marathon chronology. But whether or not we follow Levene and his implications, stories such as Herodotus' version of Deioces (1.96–101) should give us pause. Deioces was the Median king who made it clear that the society needed him to impose just solutions, and then entrenched his position by cultivating a mysterious and charismatic inaccessibility. Is it unreasonable to take that as a similar fable to those of Hesiod or Plato, one that captures an element of truth but one that the reader should not interpret literally? And dealing in 'truth' in this emblematic register at some points need not preclude a shaping of truth-questions in a sharper, yes-or-no fashion at others: was it the Alcmaeonids who held up the shield in 490 (6.121–4)? Did the Corinthians fight well or badly at Salamis (8.94)? Or, to go much earlier, did or did not Helen go to Troy (2.120)? The Constitutions Debate at 3.80–2 may combine both registers. Herodotus insists that this really took place, and does so on two different occasions (3.80.1, 6.43.2). That is a claim that we should not wave away, as he himself stresses its paradoxical quality – *Persians* considering democracy, and doing so *in open debate*: this is quite enough to make it understandable why a Greek audience should have found speeches (*logoi*) of that sort incredible (*apistoi*) (3.80.1). But need it follow that the debate happened quite like this, with the arguments formulated in the terms that Herodotus gives? Readers whose expectations were shaped by epic may have been more sophisticated

---

9 D. S. Levene, *Livy on the Hannibalic War* (Oxford: Oxford University Press, 2010), pp. 317–92, e.g. pp. 382, 385: 'Part of Livy's anomalous presentation of causation . . . concerns not merely connections that would appear loose or indeed counterintuitive to the modern reader, but things which he himself indicates do not represent reality . . . [I]n Livy we have an historian who presents narrative sequences which are avowedly impossible in the terms in which he sets them up . . . simply because that allows him to create a narrative which makes sense of his wider moral and political themes.' Levene goes on to point out the Plutarch analogy at pp. 385–6.

than that, and been content to explore the world of what-might-have-been, what-was-really-at-stake, as well as that of what-really-was.

That may bring some aspects – not by any means all – of historiographic 'truth' closer to ideas we might normally associate with myth; but, like other genres, historiography can also borrow from myth in subtler ways. Henderson's contrast of Herodotus and Aristophanes' *Acharnians* is here thought-provoking. When Dicaeopolis gives his tongue-in-cheek version of the outbreak of the war, many have thought that Aristophanes is 'parodying' Herodotus' opening chapters in the sense of making fun of them; Henderson and I agree that this is not the right way of looking at it, and that it is better to see Aristophanes as adapting a traditional pattern, one also reflected in Euripides' *Telephus*, to accommodate recent events – 'recycling' rather than parody, as Henderson puts it, and viewing through a mythical 'lens' (p. 151).[10] But is Aristophanes here totally different from Herodotus? Both authors can be seen as 'building on' that sort of mythical pattern, Aristophanes for comic purposes and Herodotus to deepen the level of historical interpretation: if Aristophanes' Dicaeopolis thought that 'such motivations really had been determinative factors in bringing about the present war' (Henderson, p. 150), perhaps Herodotus would not have disagreed too strongly when it came to explaining his own war, even if he would want to interpret 'such motivations' in a way that went beyond sexual abductions. For at least that narrative pattern of 'and then . . . and then . . .', with each side retaliating and responding to the other, does capture something important about the reciprocal way in which Herodotus sees recent history as playing out: that was brought out clearly by John Gould.[11] Still, in Herodotus' narrative this is soon overlaid and complicated by other ways of explaining it as well, in particular a drive to expansion and imperialism; indeed, already in 1.1–4 it is more than a matter of retaliation, as Paris' abduction of Helen is driven not by a quest for revenge but by a conviction that he is likely to get away with it.[12] Elsewhere too we may see historians not rejecting mythical patterns, but rather exploring how real-world events have mapped on to those patterns and furnished updated counterparts: Cleisthenes of Sicyon's banquet (Hdt. 6.126–31) can be seen as a recent version

---

10 Henderson assumes there was some genuine recent 'episode involving fights over whores between young Athenians and Megarians': that is the point where we part company (C. B. R. Pelling, *Literary Texts and the Greek Historian* (London and New York: Routledge, 2000), pp. 153–4).

11 Gould, *Herodotus*.

12 T. Rood, 'Herodotus' proem: Space, time, and the origin of international relations', Ἀριάδνη 16 (2010), pp. 43–74, at pp. 56–8.

of the suitor-contests of the *Odyssey* and, more especially, Pelops' wooing of Hippodameia, with Cleisthenes' clash with Hippocleides a less murderous equivalent of prospective father-in-law and son-in-law; Thucydides' version of the Sicilian adventure may be a complex and godless and unsettling version of the traditional nexus *atē–hubris–nemesis*;[13] the Liberation of the Cadmeia in 378 reruns the Seven Against Thebes in contemporary terms (Xen. *Hell.* 5.4.1–12).[14] None of those counterparts is exact or one-to-one, but in each case historians borrow and 'build on' a mythical model, and reflection on that model can help their readers to reflect on both the continuities and the differences of history.

So historiography is a capacious way of writing. There are moods and contexts in which historians can distinguish what they do from 'the mythical', as Thucydides does in waving τὸ μυθῶδες away from his own writing (1.22.4), or indeed as Herodotus does in doubting the presence of Helen at Troy. There are also moods and contexts where historians approximate much more closely to the ways in which other writers and genres handle traditional material. In historiography too we see the combination of generalisation and homing-in on particular moments (Llewellyn-Jones), as particular case studies are made to support a broader patterning that in its turns adds credibility to the inflection given to the case studies (Kearns); the alertness to partisan bias (Romano) in weighing variant versions, and the likelihood that evaluation of a character will guide our readiness to believe his or her story (Scodel); the importance of family traditions in moulding and preserving memory (Foxhall); an awareness of the fragility of historical knowledge (Morgan), so that there are times when one accepts that knowledge may have disappeared, 'wiped out through the passing of time' (Hdt. proem), so that the distant past may only be recovered 'sufficiently, given how long ago it happened' (Thuc. 1.21.1, cf. 1.1.3 and Morgan, p. 232); an acknowledgement of particular variations which may reflect local manipulation for ideological reasons (Shapiro), but may also point to the multifaceted quality of human experience itself, just as – to take the most extreme case – Helen herself remains as ambiguous and variegated as she ever was, and as capable of inspiring differing responses (Boedeker). The past may rhyme with the present but not in ways that correspond exactly (Shear), and that is why inspirational lessons may be learned (Lambert) but with some

---

13 F. M. Cornford, *Thucydides Mythistoricus* (London: Arnold, 1907), pp. 201–20, esp. p. 220: 'What need of further comment? Tychê, Elpis, Apatê, Eros, Phthonos, Nemesis, Atê – all these have crossed the stage, and the play is done.'

14 U. Schmitzer, 'Sieben Thebaner gegen Thebes: Bemerkungen zur Darstellungsform in Xenophon, *Hell.* 5.4.1–12', *WJa* 22 (1998), pp. 123–39.

freedom of choice and the present 'not entirely in its grip' (Pavlou, p. 104). Learning the right lessons could require a timely silence too: if historians' audiences needed to be steered away from thinking of the Second Athenian Confederacy or from blaming Pericles, so also the Athenian public needed to be protected from memories of civic strife (Shear). Any *lieu de mémoire* is also a *lieu d'oubli*, as memorials selectively prescribe what still matters and bury what does not. So, if – and it is a big 'if' – it is legitimate to think of a 'genre' of historiography before the fourth century, there is interchange and overlap with other genres as well as divergence. Differences of course remain, but the way Aristotle puts it is very precise: poetry deals *more* with the general and what-might-happen, history *more* with the specific and what-Alcibiades-did-and-suffered (1451a26–b11) – but it is not a complete contrast, but a matter of degree.

If, then, the mythical past offers a matrix for thought experiment (Scodel), that is partly because it allows moral issues to be addressed with a smaller encumbrance of circumstantial detail than they carry in real life, then encourages the reapplication of that thinking to make sense of the more confusing everyday world. Once again, historiography is not dissimilar, even though its distinctive feature is that it does engage with that mass of real-life circumstance. The historians themselves are also extrapolating and suggesting recurrent patterns to make sense of what-Alcibiades-did-and-suffered, and helping readers to disentangle the telling facts from the purely contingent to see how this might be a case study for broader truths about, say, Athens or democracy or individualism or rhetorical flair. And Thucydides at least could hope that the historical text itself could point readers in the same direction, suggesting that they – we – use the shape of past events to distinguish the recurrent patterns in our contemporary experience, those things that 'happened and will happen again in the same or similar form, the human condition being what it is' (1.22.4). The writers do part of the thought-experimental work; in some genres and authors they do more and in some they do less. But the rest is up to the audiences, both the immediate and the long-term, both them and us.

Christopher Pelling

INDEX LOCORUM

I. LITERARY SOURCES

II. EPIGRAPHICAL SOURCES

III. PAPYRI

IV. NON-CLASSICAL SOURCES

INDEX